Windows 95:
A Developer's Guide

Jeffrey Richter

Jonathan Locke

M&T BOOKS

M&T Books
A Division of MIS:Press, Inc.
A Subsidiary of Henry Holt and Company, Inc.
115 West 18th Street
New York, New York 10011

Limits of Liability and Disclaimer of Warranty

Library of Congress Cataloging-in-Publication Data

Richter, Jeffrey.
    Windows 95 : a developer's guide / Jeffrey Richter, Jonathan
  Locke.
      p.   cm.
    ISBN 1-55851-418-X
    1. Operating systems (Computers) 2. Microsoft Windows 95.
  I. Locke, Jonathan. II. Title
  QA76.76.O63R5454 1995
  005.265--dc20   95-24178
                                        CIP

DEDICATION

To Lucy "LuLu" Gooding, for exposing me to the exciting things which life has to offer.

—J "Boog-Ums" R

C O N T E N T S

Acknowledgments xi

Introduction xvii

Chapter One:
Win32 Applications: From Start to Finish 1

A Win32 Application 2
Bringing Windows into the Picture 4
A Window Class's Window Procedure 5
Maintaining a Window Procedure 9
   Message Crackers 9
   Message Maps 11
Preparing to Register a Window Class 13
Registering a Window Class 16
   What RegisterClassEx Does 18
Window Class Attributes 20
The Scope of Window Classes 25
   Module Local Window Classes 25
   Process Global Window Classes 27
   System Global Window Classes 28
Unregistering a Window Class 29
Creating Windows 30
   Process and Thread Identification 33
A Window's Attributes 35
Window Styles 39
Window Properties 43
Window Messages 45
   Class-Defined Integer Messages 46
   Application-Specific Integer Messages 48
   System-Global String Messages 49

How the Window/Application Lives and Dies 49
System Shutdown 55
The Voyeur Application 59
   Voyeur's Initialization 62
   Peering into Windows 62
   Selecting a Window 67
   After Selecting a Window 69
   Drawing a Frame Around the Window 70
   Setting the Class and Window Information 73
   Appending the Style Information 75

Chapter Two: Anatomy of a Dialog Box 93

Dialog Boxes Are Windows 93
Designing the Appearance of a Dialog Box 94
Creating the Parent and Child Windows 101
The Dialog Box Class Window Procedure 105
Adding Keyboard Navigation
   to a Modeless Dialog Box 109
What Makes a Modal Dialog Box Modal? 111
   Dynamic Modal Dialog Boxes 113
Dialog Boxes as Your Main Window 114
Dialog Box Tab Order 120
   The Tabstop Application 123

Chapter Three: Dialog Box Techniques 133

Expanding/Shrinking Dialog Box Technique 133
   The Dialog Expand Application 135
   Designing the Dialog Box 136
   The ExpandBox Function 137
Modalless Dialog Box Technique 146
   The Modalless Dialog Box Application 148
Dynamic Dialog Box Technique 162
   The Dynamic Dialog Box Application 163
   Building the Dialog Box Template 166
   Managing the Dialog Box
      Templates Memory Block 168
The Layout Dialog Box Technique 188

Using Layout 190
The Implementation of Layout 194
The DlgSize Application 196
Other Applications of Layout 198

Chapter Four: Custom Controls 225

Rules of Thumb for Designing Custom Controls 226
The Anatomy of a Custom Control 227
   Window Styles 227
   Custom Window Messages 228
   Parent Notification 228
   Implementing Your Custom Control 232
Designing the Legend Programmer's Interface 233
   Writing Some Legendary Code 236
Designing the Bargraph Control 247
   Designing the Bargraph Programmer's Interface 247
   Implementing the Code for Bargraph 251
The Custom Control Application 267

Chapter Five:
Window Subclassing and Superclassing 305

How Window Subclassing Works 305
   Creating New Window Messages
     for the Subclassed Window 312
   Associating Additional Data
     with a Subclassed Window 314
   The NoDigits Application 314
How Window Superclassing Works 323
The Arcade Application 329
   The AniBtn Window Class 334
   The Window Superclassing Library 339

Chapter Six: Hooks 363

Local and Remote Hooks 363
Installing Hooks 365
Uninstalling a Hook 369

Hook Chains 370
The Fourteen Types of Windows Hooks 371
    1. WH_CALLWNDPROC 372
    2. WH_CALLWNDPROCRET 372
    3. WH_GETMESSAGE 372
    4. WH_KEYBOARD 376
    5. WH_MOUSE 376
    6. WH_HARDWARE 376
    7. WH_MSGFILTER 380
    8. WH_SYSMSGFILTER 380
    9. WH_JOURNALRECORD 384
    10. WH_JOURNALPLAYBACK 384
    11. WH_SHELL 392
    12. WH_CBT 395
    13. WH_FOREGROUNDIDLE 400
    14. WH_DEBUG 401
The KeyCount Application 402
The AppLog Application 421
The Echo Application
  (a Macro Recorder) 432
  The Echo Application Code 434
  The Recorder Code 436
The Capture Application 453
  Local Input States 454
  Journal Record Hooks
    and Local Input State Processing 457

Chapter Seven:
Dragging and Dropping Files 465

Becoming a Dropfile Target 467
  How It Works 468
The Touch Application 471
Becoming a Dropfile Source Application 479
  Dropfile Source Application 482
Other Uses for Drag-and-Drop 501

Chapter Eight: Processing Keystrokes 503

The Keyboard and Scan Codes 503
Keyboard Drivers and Virtual-Key Codes 504
From Driver to System Input Queue 505
The Key State Arrays 506
The Keystroke Messages 511
The System Key Difference 516
Simulating Keystrokes
    to Other Application Windows 518
    Why Sending or Posting
        Keyboard Messages Is a Bad Idea 519
    What About Calling keybd_event? 521
    Using Ye Olde Journal Playback Hook 522
The SKDemo Application 522
    The SendKeys Function 541
    SendKeys 547

Chapter Nine: Version Control 551

The VerShow Application 566

Appendix A: The Win95ADG.h Header File 585

Build Options 585
    Warning Level 4 585
    Defining Versions 586
    STRICT Type Checking 586
    Unicode 587
    CPU Portability Macros 587
Useful Macros 587
    The adgARRAY_SIZE Macro 587
    The adgINRANGE Macro 588
    The adgASSERT and adgVERIFY Macros 588
    The adgHANDLE_DLGMSG Macro 588
    Window Extra Byte Macros 589
    The adgMB Macro 590

The adgINITSTRUCT Macro 590

The adgSETDLGICONS Macro 591

The adgWARNIFUNICODEUNDERWIN95

    Macro 591

The WM_CAPTURECHANGED

    Message Cracker Macros 592

Appendix B: The MsgCrack Utility 599

Index 603

ACKNOWLEDGMENTS

Although our names appear by themselves on the cover of this book, many people have contributed in some form or another to this book's creation. We would like to take this opportunity to thank all those who helped out.

Our Tremendous Technical Editor

More than any other single person, we are indebted to our technical editor, Jeff Cooperstein. It is through Jeff's careful proofreading and detailed testing that we caught many important mistakes and omissions. Without Jeff's input, this book would have been a lesser work. In addition to his work as a technical editor, Jeff also went beyond the call of duty and wrote a good deal of code for this book's setup program. We thank him for all his help.

Our Trusty Technical Proofreaders

We would like to thank our technical proofreaders Laura Butler, Brian Raiter, Paul McKee and Tom Hussey. Without their efforts, reading and re-reading our text, many errors, small and large, would have gone unnoticed and many improvements would not have been made. Thank you all!

In addition to those who proofread for us, there were a number of key people who answered questions for us and provided advice. We would like to Jeff Bogdan, Laura Butler, John Colleran, Bob Day, Eric Flo, Chris Guzak, Ian James, Scott Ludwig, Mike Schmidt and Sanford Staab.

Our Multimedia and Graphic Design Gurus

We would like to thank Joy Silver for producing a wonderful set of icons for the various applications in this book (I think we should point out that the Voyeur icon was not drawn by Joy—it was drawn long ago and has remained the same for sentimental reasons).

We would also like to thank the folks at Alki Software and Raster Ranch for producing the introduction and credits AVI files. In particular we are grateful for the help of Peter Rinearson, Mitch Craig, Tom Hussey and Wis Rinearson.

Thanks also go to Aaron Daar of Workshop 4 for engineering the AVI files on our multimedia CD-ROM, for giving us general multimedia advice and for laying out and burning the final CD-ROM disc for us.

Special Thanks

We would like to thank the following people for helping us assemble the NTPerl distribution on the CD-ROM: Sunil Shah, Robert Brown, Larry Wall, Clark Williams and Dean Troyer. Without them, our MsgCrack Perl script (see Appendix B) would not exist.

Thanks also to Steve Hammack for digging up statistics on Windows 1.0 for use in Chapter 6, to Harriet Landrum and Steve Koscho for giving us a copy of Asymetrix 3D/FX and to Rene Fuller for providing German and French foreign language translations for the VerShow application in Chapter 9.

Jeff's Personal Acknowledgments

I would like to thank Lucy Gooding for her love, understanding, and emotional support. Lucy helped me come to terms with the logistics of doing this book. I mostly appreciate the times when she tried to take me away from it all; even if only for a little while. We'll be swinging on the dance floor now!

This book would not be the book it is without the additional input from Jonathan Locke. I rarely find someone that I feel has the right mix of responsibility, technical knowledge, tenacity, approachability, common sense, business acumen, etc. After working with Jonathan for about a year, I knew that he had the right mix and recruited him to help reduce my work load in producing this book. Jonathan's largest contributions can be found in the Custom Control chapter, the Hooks chapter, the Layout section of the Dialog Box Techniques chapter, and in Appendix B. But Jonathan's influence can be found throughout all of the chapters. We worked very closely together doing research, discussing what the applications should do and fine-tuning the sentences of each chapter's text. It was Jonathan's idea to add video files to the CD-ROM. It has definitely been a pleasure working with him and exchanging ideas. He has become a good friend and concert partner (although I think he got sick and tired of hearing me hum *The Talking Drum*).

Jim Harkins is one of my best friends who always helps me rationalize my thoughts about difficult decisions. He is my resident networking expert and ensures that TJ-Net stays up and running at all times. Most importantly, Jim has been invaluable during the writing of this book by video taping all my favorite TV shows. We frequently have deep discussions about episodes of the Rockford Files and Charlie's Angels.

Scott Ludwig and Valerie Horvath are my closest friends. My only wish is that I didn't travel so much so that I could spend more time with them. When we do get time together, we spend most of our quality time surfing the Net exploring color images and computer news articles. In between searches, Val keeps me occupied by feeding me white chocolate—Yum, it's so good!

Susan Ramee and I have been through so very much through the years. We have seen each other's highs and lows and have been supporting each other's hopes and desires for years.

To Donna Murray for her love, support, and friendship over the years. I admire you for always pursuing your dreams.

My mom and dad, Arlene and Sylvan, who bought me my first computer (a TRS-80 Model 1[1]). They were afraid that I would use the computer for a week and then toss it in the closet next to the chemistry lab and Goodyear blimp. I hope you know that I love you both very much and could never have accomplished all I have without your love and support over all these years.

---

[1]I still run some of the old TRS-80 software from time to time. But now, I run it using a TRS-80 16-bit MS-DOS emulator software package. And, I run this package in Windows NT's Windows-on-Windows subsystem layer on my DEC Alpha. The computer industry sure has come a long way!

Jonathan's Personal Acknowledgments

I would like to thank my family, friends, mentors and co-workers for all their support and help over the years. Each and every one of these people has left their mark on my life, and in some unfathomable way, on this book.

My earliest computer buddies, Tim Boudreau and Gene Masse, for their inspiration and encouragement. We had a lot of fun and learned a great deal from our in-depth explorations of our TRS-80 microcomputers.

Especially big thanks to all the folks at The Evergreen State College. I met some of my best friends there. I met James McGuire in registration line on my first day and my good friend Aaron Daar (who helped us with the multimedia CD-ROM for this book) the following year in the same registration line. But most of my friends I met in and around the Evergreen Computer Center. There isn't space enough to mention everyone, but I would like to mention a few of those who inspired and supported me most: Mike Hamrick, Brian Raiter, Mike McQueen (MMQ), Bruce Moreland, Mark Lewin, Tim Fleehart, George Shaw, Steve Hammack, Dwight Moody, Dan Fain, Corwin Bell, Andy Hamlin, Don Coffin, Richard Sauer, William Jones, Ryan Finholm, Sheri Hinshaw, John Cooper and Scott "Scooter" Hungerford. But most of all, my roommate and good friend Robert Brown served as my mentor through thick and thin. He helped me with everything from algorithms, to 'C', to EMACS. Robert introduced me to hacker culture and gradually helped me to understand what programmers refer to as "The Right Thing".

I would also like to thank my faculty at Evergreen. Some of my best friends at Evergreen were faculty members. I especially remember Peter Randlette, Judy Bayard and Will Humphreys as wonderful people. They didn't just teach me. They inspired me.

I have made many new friends in the Seattle area doing consulting work for software companies. My first Windows programming job led me to BioSonics, a small engineering company in North Seattle. My supervisor there, Tyler Brooks, turned out to be a good friend as well as a good boss. It took a lot of vision in those days to see Windows as the future—but Tyler did—and his vision rubbed off on me. I can't possibly list everyone who has helped me since then, but I can at least list their respective companies. I give many thanks to all the folks at Alki Software Corporation, Asymetrix Corp., BioSonics, Clinical Kinematics, Intermec, Pacific Scientific, Rockwell, SynApps Software, Sealevel Software and, of course, Microsoft.

Thanks to Brad Hayes, my fitness trainer, for the experience and encouragement that has kept me healthy and sane throughout a year of working full time while writing this book.

Most of all, I would like to give special thanks to Jeff Richter for providing me with the (character building!) opportunity of writing this book with him. It was a lot of fun working with him over the past year. He is quite possibly the hardest working person I have ever met and I have the utmost respect for him as a programmer, a speaker, a writer and a friend.

INTRODUCTION

Although it has been a truly staggering amount of work, we have really enjoyed writing this book. We have both been writing programs for Windows 95 since early in 1994, and seeing the whole thing come to fruition has been very suspenseful and exciting. In writing this book, we have essentially found ourselves watching over the shoulders of the Windows 95 team, sharing in their triumphs and their tragedies. We feel lucky to have had this perspective because relatively few people get the opportunity to watch a new operating system being built from front row seats—one day at a time. When Windows 95 hits the shelves and proves itself to be the unparalleled success we are certain it will be, it will be all too easy to forget the long and difficult road that led to Windows 95. But we will not soon forget because we, in writing this book, have traveled that road too; and the rewards of our journey have been many. We would like to offer our congratulations to our traveling companions on the Windows 95 team for writing an operating system that will change the world.

Think of this book as a set of short stories told to you by Jeff and Jon. Each chapter tells of one of our exciting adventures traveling through the towns along the Windows 95 highway. We have run through the fields[2], scaled the walls[3], dodged the bullets[4], and jumped over the pitfalls[5] just to share our experiences with you. We are a little worse for wear but are here to relay our experiences to you so that you can avoid many of the difficulties that we overcame. It is our sincere hope that this book will make you a better Win32 software developer.

---

[2]A euphemism for the seemingly endless search for someone able to explain exactly how WM_QUEUESYNC works in cooperation with journal hooks.

[3]A euphemism for Jeff's treacherous climb over the wall that separates the Windows 95 and Windows NT teams to ensure that the DIALOGEX template worked on both platforms.

[4]A euphemism for Jonathan's difficult search for non-existent hook codes and parameters such as MSGF_NEXTWINDOW and HSHELL_TASKMAN's wParam.

[5]A euphemism for everything else we ran into.

Prerequisites

This book addresses many of the more advanced features of Win32 programming. As an intermediate/advanced book, it assumes that you already have some experience writing Windows applications. In particular, you should know how to build Win32 applications and dynamic-link libraries. You should also have experience with the following:

- Registering window classes
- Creating your own window procedures
- Creating modal and modeless dialog boxes
- Communicating with child windows/controls

The topics presented in this book build on your existing knowledge in order to give you the true story of how both Windows 95 and Windows NT work. There are many procedures that we, as Win32 developers, simply take for granted everyday. Various chapters explore these areas in great depth and illustrate exactly what goes on "under the hood."

About the Applications

The purpose of the applications is to demonstrate, with real code, concepts that are important when writing rock-solid Win32 applications. Each chapter in this book presents a foundational set of Win32 programming concepts. The accompanying applications help to make these concepts concrete (you know, rock-solid). Each application has a narrative relating some of the trials and tribulations we encountered while developing the code. You will find many useful tips by reading these descriptions. The comments and the source code itself will provide you with even greater understanding.

Copyrights

The copyright notices attached to each sample application are not intended to prevent you from using the applications or any part of the application code. In fact, if it suits your purpose (or can be modified to suit your purpose), we would very much like you to use the code we have written. The intent of the copyright notices is simply to claim exclusive rights to republish the material in future books and articles. However, any software you produce that uses code from this book (or is derived from code in this book) must contain the following notice in its About box:

```
Portions Copyright (c) 1995 by Jeffrey Richter.
```

Use of the C Language

When it came time to decide on a language for the applications in this book, we were torn between C and C++. For large projects, we generally use C++, but the fact of the matter is that most Windows programmers are not using C++ yet, and we didn't want to alienate our largest potential audience. So every application in this book is written in C code.

Message Cracker Macros

If you are not writing your Win32 application using C++ and a Windows class library (such as Microsoft's Foundation Classes), we highly recommend that you use the message cracker macros defined in the WindowsX.H header file. These macros make your programs easier to write, read, and maintain. For more information on message crackers and their uses, see the "Programming Techniques" book included with the Win32 SDK.

Unrelated Code

We wanted to remove any code from the applications that was not directly related to the techniques we wanted to demonstrate. Unfortunately, this rather idealistic goal is not achievable when writing Windows applications. Still we have done our best to reduce irrelevant code wherever possible. For example, unlike most Windows programming books which repeat the code for registering a window class along with every application in the book, the user interface for most of the applications in this book is a modal dialog box created by simply calling the *DialogBox* function. As a result, most of the applications in this book do not initialize a WNDCLASSEX structure or call the *RegisterClassEx* function.

STRICT Compliance

All of the applications have been compiled with the STRICT identifier defined, which catches many common coding errors. For example, the passing of an incorrect handle type to a function is caught during compilation instead of at runtime. For more information about using the STRICT identifier, refer to the Programming Techniques documentation included with the Win32 SDK.

Error Checking

Error checking should be a big part of any software project. Unfortunately, proper error handling can greatly increase the size and complexity of a software project. In order to make the applications in this book more understandable and less cluttered, we have not put a great deal of error-checking code into them. If you incorporate any of our code fragments in your own production code, we strongly encourage you to examine our code closely and add any appropriate error checking.

Bug Free

We would love to say that all of the applications are bug free. But, as with all software, it's only bug free until someone finds a bug! We have, of course, given our code numerous walk-throughs with the hope of catching everything. But if you do find a bug, we would appreciate your reporting it to us via Jeff's Internet address: v-jeffrr@microsoft.com.

Platforms

The bulk of our research and development for this book has been on machines with Intel CPUs. We have also recompiled and tested all the sample programs on MIPS machines and on DEC Alpha AXP machines, using the compilers and linkers that come with Visual C++ 2.x.

Compilers

Some of the applications make use of Microsoft-specific compiler extensions. It will be necessary to make minor modifications to the source code in order to compile the sample applications using a compiler produced by another vendor.

Many of the applications take advantage of Win32 features that have been added to Windows 95 since Visual C++ version 2.0 shipped. So, simply using the header files and library files that ship with Visual C++ 2.0 will not be enough to compile all of the applications. You will also need to use the header and library files that ship with the Win32 SDK. Visual C++ 2.2 and later include the proper files making the Win32 SDK unnecessary.

Unicode

This book was written with Unicode in mind. All the applications can be compiled as either native Unicode or ANSI applications. For details on recompiling the applications for Unicode, refer to Appendix A.

Perl

The MsgCrack.BAT batch file (see Appendix B) included with this book is not actually a batch file at all. It is a Perl script. To run this script, a Win32 port of Perl (which runs on Windows 95 and Windows NT) has been included on the CD-ROM disc that comes with this book in the NTPerl sub-directory of the MsgCrack.0B directory.

The following descriptive paragraph is extracted from the Perl documentation:

> "*Perl—Practical Extraction and Report Language... Perl is an interpreted language optimized for scanning arbitrary text files, extracting information from those text files, and printing reports based on that information. It's also a good language for many system management tasks. The language is intended to be practical (easy to use, efficient, complete) rather than beautiful (tiny, elegant, minimal). It combines (in the author's opinion, anyway) some of the best features of C, sed, awk, and sh, so people familiar with those languages should have little difficulty with it...*"

When it comes to tasks like the one performed by MsgCrack.BAT, Perl has a big advantage over most other programming languages. We would like to encourage you to take a closer look at Perl because you may find that it comes in handy as well. But keep in mind that it is a free product, and as such it is unsupported.

Installing the Applications

The companion CD-ROM disc contains the source code for all the applications presented in this book. In addition, EXE and DLL files for the x86, MIPS and Alpha AXP are included. Because none of the files on the disc are compressed, you can simply insert the disc and load the source code files; you can also run the applications directly from the disc.

On the CD-ROM disc, the root directory contains the installation software and the Win95ADG.H header file discussed in Appendix A. The root directory also contains several subdirectories. Among these directories are x86.BIN, MIPS.BIN and Alpha.BIN, each of which contains the EXE and DLL files for their respective CPU platform. If you are running Windows NT on a platform other than x86, MIPS or Alpha, you can still access the source code files, but you will not be able to execute any of the applications without building them yourself. This means you will need to install the source code files on your hard disk. The section "Installing the Applications on Unsupported CPU Platforms" later in this introduction discusses how to perform this installation.

The remaining subdirectories contain the source code files for the applications. Each application is in its very own subdirectory. The eight-letter name of each subdirectory is the name of the application, and the subdirectory's extension indicates the chapter in the book where the application is presented. For example, the subdirectory DlgSize.03 identifies the Dialog Size application presented in Chapter 3.

If you are interested only in examining the source code or running the applications, you do not have to copy anything to your hard disk. However, if you want to modify, compile, or debug the applications, you will need to copy the files to your hard disk. The next two sections explain how to access the application files depending on whether you are running Windows 95 or Windows NT 3.51.

The Auto-play Welcome Application

When you insert a CD-ROM disc into your CD-ROM drive, Windows 95 detects the disc and can automatically execute a program contained on that disc. The CD-ROM disc supplied with this book has been prepared to take advantage of this feature. When you insert the disc, the Welcome application provides the following options:

Introduction	Plays an introductory video for the book.
Video Demos	Plays application demonstration videos narrated by the authors which describe the functionality and important features of the applications presented throughout the book.
Setup	Installs the application source code (and optionally the executable files) on your hard disk.
Explorer	Allows you to execute the applications directly from the CD-ROM disc using the Windows explorer.
Credits	Plays a credits video.
Training	Plays a shameless self-promotional video for Jeff's Win32 programming seminars

Installing the Applications on Unsupported CPU Platforms

If you need to install the applications on an unsupported CPU platform (one other than x86, MIPS or Alpha), you will not be able to run the Setup GUI program on the CD-ROM disc because there will not be a Setup executable available that will run on your CPU. So, in order to install the application files on your hard disk, you will need to run the INSTALL.BAT batch file contained in the root directory of the CD-ROM disc.

To run the INSTALL.BAT file, you must specify a location where the files should be installed. For example, the following line assumes that the disc is in drive D and that you want to install the source code files to the Win95ADG directory on drive C (this directory will be created if it doesn't exist):

```
C:\>D:\INSTALL C:\Win95ADG
```

The INSTALL batch file will copy the source files to your hard drive. The sample programs are installed so that each sample resides in its own subdirectory. The eight-letter name of each subdirectory contains the name of the sample program, and the subdirectory's extension indicates the chapter in the book where the program is presented. For example, the subdirectory Clock.02 identifies the Clock sample application that is presented in Chapter 2.

CHAPTER ONE

Win32 Applications: From Start to Finish

It seems so simple: the user wants to run an application. First, the user invokes an application by navigating the Windows Taskbar. Then, after starting the application, the user sees a window on the screen. Everything that the application has to offer to the user is somehow obtainable by performing various actions on this window. When the user no longer wishes to interact with the application, the user selects the window's Close box and poof—the application goes away.

From the user's perspective, the window *is* the application. To the programmer, the application and the window are two very distinct concepts that should never be confused. In fact, there are many useful applications that do not create windows at all. Understanding the differences between the application and the window early in your Win32 programming career is an important key to writing good software. When I first started writing Windows applications, I did not fully understand this difference, and I fell subject to various difficult-to-find bugs.

The purpose of this chapter is to explain the concepts of Win32 processes, window classes, and window instances. I will then show how Windows expects all these concepts to interact with each other.

A Win32 Application

When you write a Win32 application, you will typically use a programming language such as C or C++. You then compile your source code modules and link the OBJ files with any libraries (LIB files) you might need, and this produces your application's EXE file. This EXE file sits dormant on the hard drive until the user invokes it (usually via the Taskbar).

When the system invokes an EXE file, the system creates a process. A process is a 4-GB virtual address space—no more, no less. Initially, this address space is empty. Then, the system starts to populate it by putting code and data into it. First, the system finds the application's EXE file on the disk and loads the entire contents of the EXE file into the process's address space. Then, the system locates any dynamic-link libraries (DLLs) that are required by the EXE file and loads the entire contents of these DLL files into the process's address space.[1]

After the address space is populated with all the code and data for the application's EXE file and all the required DLL files, the system creates the process's primary thread. A thread is an abstract concept, which can be difficult to grasp at first for the new Win32 programmer. Threads are maintained by the operating system and are charged with only one responsibility: execute code. When a new process is created, the system also creates a new thread (called the process's primary thread). The system initializes this thread by telling it the address in the process's address space where code should begin executing. Usually, the primary thread is told to begin executing with the C-Runtime's startup code.

---

[1]The system doesn't actually load the entire EXE file into RAM; it uses a much more efficient means of manipulating memory. Basically, this means that we, as developers, can write our code believing that all the code and data contained in the EXE, and the code and data contained in every DLL needed by the EXE (and other DLLs), are actually loaded into the address space. In reality, the system swaps 4-KB blocks (called pages) between the hard disk and RAM as needed. This swapping occurs transparently to us, so we can ignore this detail for the purposes of this discussion.

The C-Runtime's startup code is responsible for initializing the components of the C-Runtime system so that any calls you may make to functions such as malloc or signal will work correctly. After the C-Runtime's startup code has initialized, your code can begin to execute. The C-Runtime startup code assumes that your application code is contained in a function called WinMain, which must have the following prototype:

```
int WINAPI WinMain (HINSTANCE hinstExe, HINSTANCE hinstExePrev,
   LPSTR lpszCmdLine, int nCmdShow);
```

The C-Runtime startup code calls your WinMain function, passing it the preceding four parameters. From our perspective, this is where the application begins running. Inside the WinMain function is where all the application's magic takes place. If your WinMain function looks like this:

```
int WINAPI WinMain (HINSTANCE hinstExe, HINSTANCE hinstExePrev,
   LPSTR lpszCmdLine, int nCmdShow) {

   return(0);
}
```

then you have no magic to perform, and no windows are presented to the user. Instead, your WinMain function exits as soon as it starts. When WinMain returns, the process's primary thread returns to the C-Runtime's startup code. The startup code now performs any cleanup for the C-Runtime system. Then, the C-Runtime's startup code calls the Win32 ExitProcess function, which causes the process's primary thread to terminate. This means that no more code will execute and that the process's 4 GB address space of code and data will be completely destroyed.

The process has completed its life-cycle. Of course, all this takes place in a matter of seconds (at most). There are no windows created, so no windows are ever presented to the user. This is an incredibly useless application!

Before leaving this section, I want to point out that a process is a single instance of a running application. For example, you may write an application whose code is contained in an EXE file called MyApp.EXE. If the user invokes this EXE file seven times, then the system will create seven processes. Each process has its very own 4 GB address space, and the code and data for the EXE file image and all required DLLs are loaded into each process's address space.[2]

Also, the system assigns a 32-bit value to each process running in the system. This value is called the process's ID. The Win32 API contains only a few functions that accept a process ID as a parameter. In order for threads in one process to be able to manipulate another process, you will be required to obtain the ID for the process you wish to manipulate. In addition, the system assigns a unique ID to each thread.

Bringing Windows into the Picture

To users, the windows that appear on the computer's monitor are the most important aspect of any application. It is via an application's windows that the user communicates with the program and instructs the program as to which actions are to be performed.

To the Win32 software developer, the window on the screen is also quite important, but not as important as the window class. The window class defines a window's appearance and describes how the window should behave (usually in response to a user's keystrokes and mouse movements). A window is merely an instance of a window class. When developers write Win32 applications, they spend much of their time developing and fine-tuning a window's class but very little time writing code to create windows.

---

[2]Again, the system uses memory much more efficiently than suggested here. For example, the system will not actually have seven copies of the EXE and DLL files loaded into memory. However, the system deals with the code and data sharing transparently to us, so we can ignore this detail for the purposes of this discussion.

As far as the operating system goes, the window class must be explicitly defined before any windows can be created. The process of defining a class is called registering the class. Registering a class does not create any windows. However, once the class is defined, any number of windows of the class can be created. Usually, an application will register a single window class with the system. However, a single application may register several window classes. You would register several classes if you wanted to create windows that have different appearances or different behaviors.

A Window Class's Window Procedure

Without a doubt, the most important part of any Windows application is the window class's window procedure. You will spend countless hours developing and fine-tuning the behavior of window procedures throughout your Windows career. A window class's window procedure describes how instances of the window class should appear and behave. Whenever the user requests that an action be performed, the window procedure is notified of the user's request, and it is the window procedure that is responsible for performing the desired actions.

A window procedure is simple in its design. Every window procedure must have the following prototype:

```
LRESULT WINAPI WndProc (HWND hwnd, UINT uMsg, WPARAM wParam, LPARAM lParam);
```

However, the name of the function does not have to be called WndProc (as shown here); the name can be any name that you desire. For example, if you register several window classes in your application, you will have to assign each of their window procedures different names.

Whenever an action is requested of an instance of a window class, the system calls the window class's window procedure. The first parameter, hwnd, is the handle of the window that has the requested action. Remember that you can create several windows of a single window class. Since the single window procedure is called to handle actions for all instances of a single window class, the window procedure is passed the handle of the specific window to which the action is related.[3]

The second parameter, uMsg, identifies the type of action that has been requested of the window. Microsoft defines many of "standard" actions in the **WinUser.H** header file. Each action is defined as a numerical value that uniquely identifies the action. Table 1.1 shows some of the standard actions.

Table 1.1 *Some standard window messages.*

Identifier in Windows header file	Numeric value	Description
WM_PAINT	0x0000000F	The window needs to re-paint its client area.
WM_CLOSE	0x00000010	The user is requesting to close the window.
WM_CHAR	0x00000102	The user has pressed a character on the keyboard.
WM_MOUSEMOVE	0x00000200	The user has moved the mouse over the window's client area.
WM_LBUTTONDOWN	0x00000201	The user has clicked the mouse's primary button over the window's client area.

Table 1.1 shows only five of the standard actions defined. In actuality, there are several hundred actions that a window procedure could choose to handle. However, do not let this large number intimidate you. Usually, a window procedure handles a few dozen window messages and ignores the rest. For example, the following code fragment shows the typical structuring of a window class's window procedure.

---

[3]For you C++ programmers out there, this is the window class equivalent of a C++ class member function's hidden *this* parameter.

```
LRESULT WINAPI WndProc (HWND hwnd, UINT uMsg, WPARAM wParam, LPARAM lParam) {

   LRESULT lResult = 0;    // Assume zero return

   switch (uMsg) {
      case WM_PAINT:
         // Paint the window's client area.
         ...
         break;

      case WM_CHAR:
         // Add a character to a buffer.
         ...
         break;

      default:
         // For all messages not explicitly handled,
         // do default processing.
         lResult = DefWindowProc(hwnd, uMsg, wParam, lParam);
         break;
   }

   return(lResult);
}
```

As you can see, this window procedure explicitly looks for only two
(of the hundreds of possible) messages: WM_PAINT and WM_CHAR.
Any window message not explicitly handled is passed to the Win32
DefWindowProc function. This function is part of the operating sys-
tem, and if you could see the source code for it, you would see a large
switch statement much like the one shown in the preceding
WndProc function. However, the switch statement inside the
DefWindowProc function explicitly handles many more messages.

For example, the DefWindowProc function checks for the
WM_NCPAINT window message. When it receives it, it paints all
the non-client components of the window (like the caption, borders,
and menu bar). DefWindowProc also handles the WM_SYSCOM-
MAND message so that any menu option selected from the window's system menu is executed correctly. DefWindowProc explicitly
handles many window messages, but not all. Any window message
that is not handled by your window procedure and DefWindowProc
is simply ignored, and no action is taken in response to it.

The only thing left to discuss is the window procedure's last
two parameters, wParam and lParam. These two parameters are

7

both 32-bit values. Their actual meaning depends on the message indicated in the uMsg parameter. For example, when a window procedure receives a WM_MOUSEMOVE message, the wParam parameter indicates which mouse buttons are pressed down and whether the user is holding the Control or Shift key on the keyboard. The lParam parameter indicates the location of the mouse cursor on the screen with respect to the window's client area. If the window procedure receives a WM_CHAR message instead, the wParam parameter indicates the value of the character generated by the user, and the lParam parameter contains a set of flags. If the window procedure receives a WM_PAINT message, the wParam and lParam parameters are meaningless and should not be referenced while processing this message.

You can get very creative when designing your window procedure. When your window procedure receives a window message, you can do one of the following:

- Pass the message to DefWindowProc. This has the effect described in the Microsoft Win32 Programmer's Reference. Any message not recognized by DefWindowProc is ignored, and zero is returned.

- Process the message. This is usually accomplished by including a case statement or a message cracker (from **WindowsX.H**) for the message in your window procedure. Any operation can be performed and a value appropriate for the message should be returned.

- Process the message and call DefWindowProc (in either order). This is usually accomplished by including a case statement for the message in your window procedure. However, the code for the case includes an explicit call to DefWindowProc. This executes the operations defined by DefWindowProc as well as any additional actions you may desire. A value appropriate for the message should be returned; this is usually the value returned by DefWindowProc, but it does not have to be.

- Ignore the message by performing no action when the window procedure receives this message. An appropriate value for the message should still be returned (usually zero).

Maintaining a Window Procedure

As you look at the switch statement presented earlier, imagine what it would look like after you added support for a few dozen more messages—the switch statement would get extremely long. In fact, I personally have seen switch statements that are several thousand lines long. Do not adopt this programming practice because it makes your class's window procedure very difficult to maintain, modify, read, and understand! Over the years, programmers have developed several techniques to help maintain window procedures. Of all these techniques, two of them stand out: message crackers and message maps. Both of these techniques share a common rule: each window message should be handled by its very own function. In other words, if you want your window procedure to process the WM_SIZE and WM_CHAR messages, you will create two functions. Usually, these functions would be called something like OnSize and OnChar, respectively.

Message Crackers

Message crackers are mostly used by C programmers and are simply a set of #define macros contained in the **WindowsX.H** header file. You should include this header file immediately after including the **Windows.H** header file. All the window procedures presented throughout this book take advantage of the message cracker macros.[4]

Here is an example of how to write a message cracker function to process the WM_SIZE message.

```
void WndClassName_OnSize (HWND hwnd, UINT state, int cx, int cy) {
    .
    .
    .
}
```

The prototype for this function can be found inside the **WindowsX.H** file by searching for "WM_SIZE". Here are a few things to notice about this function:

---

[4]For a more complete discussion of message crackers, see Appendix A of *Advanced Windows*, Microsoft Press, 1995.

- The prototype in **WindowsX.H** indicates that this function doesn't return anything (using void). This means that the operating system doesn't care what the return value from a WM_SIZE message is.

- The name of the function begins with the prefix "WndClass Name_" because our application could register several window classes. Each of these classes may handle the WM_SIZE message in different ways and therefore, the C language requires that each OnSize function have a different prefix in order to associate the function with the correct window class.

- The first parameter to all message cracker functions is the handle of the window that the message applies to. Remember that several windows can be created from a single window class. The preceding function describes the behavior for all windows of this class when they receive a WM_SIZE message. This parameter is frequently used inside the function in order to perform other actions on the window.

- The remaining parameters are not wParam and lParam. This is a major benefit! As I mentioned earlier, the meaning of the wParam and lParam parameters varies depending on the message. If you were not using message crackers and were instead using a big switch statement, you would have to decipher these two parameters yourself—a step that is quite error-prone. However, when you use message crackers, the macros automatically translate the wParam and lParam parameters for you before passing them to your message function. By the way, this translation, called cracking, explains how the message crackers got their name.

What is not shown here is how the WndClassName_OnSize function is called. When using message crackers, you still must create and maintain a window procedure. This procedure looks like this:

```
LRESULT WINAPI WndClassName_WndProc (HWND hwnd, UINT uMsg,
    WPARAM wParam, LPARAM lParam) {

    switch (uMsg) {
        HANDLE_MSG(hwnd, WM_SIZE,      WndClassName_OnSize);
        HANDLE_MSG(hwnd, WM_MOUSEMOVE, WndClassName_OnMouseMove);
    }
    return(DefWindowProc(hwnd, uMsg, wParam, lParam));

}
```

Of course, the function is a window class procedure, and it must use the function prototype that Windows expects of all window class procedures. However, you'll notice that we use the HANDLE_MSG macro (also defined in **WindowsX.H**) instead of case statements inside the switch statement. This macro takes three parameters: the hwnd identifying the window, the defined value indicating the message you wish to handle (WM_SIZE, for example), and the name of the function that is to be called to handle the message (WndClassName_OnSize, for example).

The HANDLE_MSG macro also includes a return statement that returns the value from the message cracker function. In the case of a message cracker function that returns void, 0 (zero) is returned. When using the message crackers, the most common mistake made by programmers is that they forget to add the appropriate HANDLE_MSG line to the window procedure's switch statement; I have often forgotten to do this myself. I write the message cracker function for the message I want to handle, but because there isn't an entry in the switch statement, my function never gets called. Always remember to add your message cracker functions to your window procedure.

Message Maps

Message maps are usually used by C++ programmers who are using a Windows class library such as Microsoft's Foundation Class (MFC) Library. When using Microsoft's Visual C++ compiler, you can easily add processing to a class's window procedure using the Class Wizard dialog box (see Figure 1.1).

From this dialog box, select the window class at the top and then the desired window message from the Messages listbox. To add the function to your window class procedure, simply select the Add Function button. This causes Visual C++ to add a message map function to your source code file. For a WM_SIZE message, the function will look like this:

```
void CAboutDlg::OnSize(UINT nType, int cx, int cy)
{
    CDialog::OnSize(nType, cx, cy);

    // TODO: Add your message handler code here.

}
```

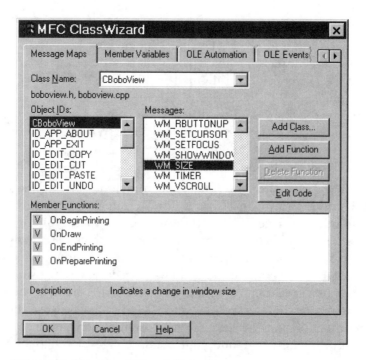

Figure 1.1 *The Class Wizard dialog box.*

This function looks almost identical to the message cracker function shown in the previous section. Here is a brief list of the differences:

- The name of the function is always OnSize, regardless of which window class it belongs to. This is possible when using MFC because MFC creates a C++ class for each window class. The message handler functions, such as OnSize, are accessible within the scope of the C++ class (CAboutDlg in this example).

- None of the MFC message map functions have a window handle as a parameter because the window can be identified using the implied *this* parameter to all these functions. By default, any window manipulation functions that you call within a message map function will refer to the same window that received the WM_SIZE message. This makes your code much more readable and manageable.

- Like the message cracker functions, message maps crack a message's wParam and lParam parameters and pass them as typed parameters to the message map function.

- Because the MFC framework allows you to use C++ inheritance to modify the behavior of existing window classes, the Class Wizard adds a call to the base class's message map function. In the preceding example, the Class Wizard added the explicit call to CDialog::OnSize because the CAboutDlg class is derived from the CDialog class.

What is not shown here is how the MFC framework calls the CAboutDlg::OnSize function. This process is more involved than the message cracker method, which simply adds a HANDLE_MSG line to the window procedure. In MFC, the CAboutDlg::OnSize message function must first be added to the class's definition inside a header file, and an entry must be added to the class's message map table contained inside the implementation (CPP) file. Fortunately, the Class Wizard does this additional work for you automatically.[5]

I will not be discussing Microsoft's Foundation Class Library any further in this book. However, I thought it would be useful to give you a small taste of some of the benefits offered by Microsoft's Foundation Class Library and Visual C++. For the remainder of the book, we will use the message cracker macros contained in the **WindowsX.H** header file.

Preparing to Register a Window Class

When your application is invoked, your application code must initialize a WNDCLASSEX structure and call the RegisterClassEx function before you can create any window instances of the window class. A WNDCLASSEX structure follows:

```
typedef struct _WNDCLASSEX {
    UINT        cbSize;
    UINT        style;
```

---

[5]For more information on MFC and window procedures, see the Visual C++ documentation.

```
    WNDPROC      lpfnWndProc;
    int          cbClsExtra;
    int          cbWndExtra;
    HINSTANCE    hInstance;
    HICON        hIcon;
    HCURSOR      hCursor;
    HBRUSH       hbrBackground;
    LPCTSTR      lpszMenuName;
    LPCTSTR      lpszClassName;
    HICON        hIconSm;
} WNDCLASSEX;
```

All the members in this structure identify attributes of a window class. Table 1.2 briefly describes each of these members.

Table 1.2 *The WNSCLASSEX structure's data members.*

Member	Description
cbSize	Indicates the size of the WNDCLASSEX structure. You should always initialize this to sizeof (WND-CLASSEX).
style	Indicates the styles of the window class. All class style identifiers start with the letters CS_ (such as CS_VREDRAW). Do not get class styles confused with window instance styles (discussed later), which start with the letters WS_.
lpfnWndProc	Indicates the memory address (within the process's 4-GB address space) of the window class's window procedure (discussed in the previous section).
cbClsExtra	Tells the system how many additional bytes to reserve when registering the window class. See the "Window Class Attributes" section later in this chapter.
cbWndExtra	Tells the system how many additional bytes to reserve when creating a window of this window class. See the "A Window's Attributes" section later in this chapter.

Member	Description
hInstance	Indicates the EXE or DLL that is registering the window class. For an EXE, you should set this member to the first parameter passed to the application's WinMain function. If a DLL is registering a window class, you should initialize this member to the first parameter passed to the DLL's DllMain function. See "The Scope of Window Classes" section later in this chapter for more information.
hIcon	Indicates the handle of the icon that represents the window. This icon usually contains a 32×32 pixel image and a 16×16 pixel image.
hCursor	Indicates the handle of the cursor the system should display when the mouse is over the window's client area.
hbrBackground	Indicates the handle of a brush the system should use to fill the background of the window's client area.
lpszMenuName	Indicates the zero-terminated string that specifies the menu template resource that all instances of this window class should use.
lpszClassName	Indicates the zero-terminated string that specifies the name you wish to give to the window class.
hIconSm	Indicates the handle of the small icon that represents the window. This icon is displayed on the system's Taskbar and at the top-left of a window's caption bar. This member is usually set to NULL, causing the system to look for a 16×16 icon in the icon identified by the hIcon member. If the icon identified by hIcon does not have a 16×16 pixel counterpart, the system shrinks the 32×32 pixel icon. You would initialize the hIconSm member only if you want a small icon that is totally different than the icon identified by the hIcon member.

The most important member of the WNDCLASSEX structure is lpszClassName. This member indicates the name of the window class. Whenever you register a window class, you must specify a name for the class by setting the lpszClassName member to point to a zero-terminated string. You will have to use this name to create one or more windows of the window class using the CreateWindowEx function (discussed later). When you call CreateWindowEx, you pass it the name of the window class that you wish to create an instance of. The function compares the class name parameter with each of the registered window class names. If a matching registered class can be found, an instance of the class is created and a handle identifying the window instance is returned. If the specified class name cannot be found among the registered window class names, CreateWindowEx returns a window handle of NULL, indicating failure.

Registering a Window Class

After you have initialized the WNDCLASSEX structure, you must register the window class so that the operating system is made aware of it. This is done by calling the RegisterClassEx function:

```
ATOM RegisterClassEx(CONST WNDCLASSEX *pwc);
```

Usually, an application initializes a WNDCLASSEX structure and calls RegisterClassEx soon after the application's WinMain function begins executing. The RegisterClassEx function returns an atom number that identifies the window class name (specified in the lpszClassName member). If the window class could not be registered, RegisterClassEx returns an atom value of INVALID_ATOM (which is defined as 0).

The following code shows all the steps necessary to register a window class.

```
LRESULT WINAPI MyWndClass_WndProc (HWND hwnd, UINT uMsg,
   WPARAM wParam, LPARAM lParam) {

   // This is the window class's window procedure
   // discussed in the previous section.
   .
   .
   .
}
```

```
int WINAPI WinMain (HINSTANCE hinstExe, HINSTANCE hinstExePrev,
   LPSTR lpszCmdLine, int nCmdShow) {

   WNDCLASSEX wc;
   ATOM atomClassName;

   // Initialize all members in the structure to 0 (zero).
   // NOTE: Other sample source code presented throughout this book
   // will use the adgINITSTRUCT macro (discussed in Appendix A) to
   // initialize a data structure for use.
   ZeroMemory(&wc, sizeof(wc));

   // Set the size of the WNDCLASSEX structure.
   wc.cbSize = sizeof(wc);

   // Give the window class a name.
   wc.lpszClassName = "My Window Class Name";

   // Tell the system the address of this class's window procedure.
   wc.lpfnWndProc = MyWndClass_WndProc;

   // Tell the system that the EXE file is registering the window class.
   wc.hInstance = hinstExe;   // First parameter to WinMain.

   // NOTE: All other members can remain zero but are usually
   // initialized as shown later.

   // Allow the window to receive mouse double-click messages.
   wc.style = CS_DBLCLK;

   // This window class requires no additional class information.
   wc.cbClsExtra = 0;

   // Window instances created of this class require no additional information.
   wc.cbWndExtra = 0;

   // Tell the system which icon should be displayed when the system
   // needs to show a large icon to represent windows of this class.
   // IDI_APP identifies an icon in the EXE file's resource section.
   wc.hIcon = LoadIcon(hinstExe, IDI_APP);

   // Tell the system which cursor should be displayed when the mouse
   // is positioned over a window's client area.  IDC_ARROW identifies
   // a standard arrow cursor offered by the system.
   wc.hCursor = LoadCursor(NULL, IDC_ARROW);

   // Windows of this class should have their background painted using the
   // color selected by the user in the Desktop.Properties dialog box.
   wc.hbrBackground = (HBRUSH) (COLOR_WINDOW + 1);

   // Tell the system what menu template should be used when creating a
   // menu for each window instance of this class.
   // IDM_APP identifies a menu template in the EXE file's resource section.
   wc.lpszMenuName = MAKEINTRESOURCE(IDM_APP);

   // Tell the system which icon should be displayed when the system
```

17

```
// needs to show a small icon to represent windows of this class.
// The IDI_APP icon contains a 16 x 16 and a 32 x 32 pixel image.
wc.hIconSm = wc.hIcon;

// Register the window class with the operating system.
atomClassName = RegisterClassEx(&wc);

if (atomClassName == INVALID_ATOM) {

   // The window class could not be registered.  Call GetLastError
   // to determine why. Usually it's because a class with the same
   // name has already been registered.
} else {

   // The window class was successfully registered. Windows can now
   // be created from this class.
}

// The remainder of the application's code goes here.
.
.
.

}
```

Only after a window class has been registered can an application create one or more windows based on the window class by calling the CreateWindowEx function (discussed later in this chapter).

What RegisterClassEx Does

When you call RegisterClassEx, it performs the following sequence of events:

1. Checks the class name to see if a class with the same name, registered by the same EXE or DLL file, already exists. If so, RegisterClassEx returns INVALID_ATOM.

2. If the class style CS_GLOBALCLASS is specified, checks the class name to see if a class with the same name is registered by any EXE or DLL in the process's address space. If so, RegisterClassEx returns INVALID_ATOM. For more information about the CS_GLOBALCLASS style, see "The Scope of Window Classes" section later in this chapter.

3. Allocates a block of memory to store information about the class. The block is large enough to hold all the information in the WNDCLASSEX structure plus the number of bytes that were specified in the cbClsExtra member.

4. Copies the contents of the WNDCLASSEX structure into the memory block and initializes the extra bytes to zero. These additional bytes are reserved for your class's window procedure to use; the operating system does not use them at all. The information stored in the extra bytes is shared and available to every window based on the registered class. The management of these extra bytes is left entirely up to the programmer.

5. Allocates memory to store the name of the class's menu. The lpszMenuName field is changed to point to this memory block.

6. Adds the class name to the system's local atom table[6] and saves the atom in the window class's memory block. This atom can later be retrieved by calling GetClassWord using the GCW_ATOM identifier (discussed in more detail later).

7. Returns the atom obtained in the previous step from the RegisterClassEx function. Once the atom is known, it can be used in functions where the class name is a parameter. For example, to create an instance of a window that has just been registered, you could do the following:

```
// Create and initialize the members in the wc structure.
WNDCLASSEX wc;
   .
   .
   .
// Register the window class with the operating system.
ATOM atomClassName = RegisterClassEx(&WndClass);

if (atomClassName != INVALID_ATOM) {

   // Create a window instance based on the window class.
   HWND hwnd = CreateWindowEx(0, MAKEINTATOM(atomClassName), NULL,
      WS_CHILD, ...);
}
   .
   .
   .
```

---

[6]In Windows, there is a global atom table that is shared by all processes, and each process also has its own local atom table. The system's local atom table is a local atom table that is owned by the system. This means that a process can't access this atom table using the documented local or global atom functions.

Window Class Attributes

The Win32 API contains functions that allow you to retrieve and modify the information about a registered window class. These functions are described in this section.

GetClassInfoEx can be used to fill a WNDCLASSEX structure with information about a previously registered class:

```
BOOL GetClassInfoEx(HINSTANCE hinst, LPCSTR lpszClassName, PWNDCLASSEX pwc);
```

The first parameter to the function, hinst, identifies the EXE or DLL that registered the window class. This value should be NULL if you desire the information for any of the Windows system global classes (discussed later). The second parameter, lpszClassName, is either the address of a zero-terminated string containing the name of the class that you are interested in or the atom for a class name (passed by using the MAKEINTATOM macro). The last parameter, pwc, is the address of a WNDCLASSEX structure that is to be filled with the attributes of the window class. You should initialize the cbSize member to sizeof(WNDCLASSEX) prior to calling GetClassInfoEx.

You should be aware of four things when using GetClassInfoEx:

- When you register a window class, the system does not save the class name with the internally allocated window class data structure; it saves only the atom value. So, before GetClassInfoEx returns, it sets WNDCLASSEX's lpszClassName member to the value you pass as the second parameter to GetClassInfoEx. There is no documented function for getting a class's string name from an atom. The GetAtomName and GlobalGetAtomName functions will not work because class atoms are not local to the calling process and are not global to the system; they are local to the system.[7]

---

[7]In footnote 6, I said that the system's local atom table cannot be accessed using the documented local or global atom functions. However, you can use the documented GetClipboardFormatName function to access the system's local atom table:

```
int GetClipboardFormatName(UINT uFormat, LPTSTR lpszFormatName,
    int cchFormatName);
```

This function will return a string for a system-local atom. You can also use this function to convert a registered window message atom value returned by the RegisterWindowMessage function (discussed later in this chapter) to a string value.

- When you register a window class, the system makes an internal copy of the class's menu name. When GetClassInfoEx returns, the lpszMenuName member will contain the address to the internal menu name string. This is a bug in the operating system—you should never have direct access to an operating system string, and you should never write to the memory at this address.

- GetClassInfoEx sets the WNDCLASSEX's hInstance member to the value of the hinst parameter passed to GetClassInfoEx. If you want the actual value, you must call GetClassLong (hwnd, GCL_HMODULE).[8]

- GetClassInfoEx can only retrieve information about window classes that have been registered by the calling process. So, for example, calling GetClassInfoEx in an effort to obtain information about the "NOTEPAD" class will fail because the process calling GetClassInfoEx is not NOTEPAD.

After the WNDCLASSEX structure has been filled, GetClassInfoEx returns the atom value of the class (even though the function is prototyped as returning a BOOL). Needless to say, the GetClassInfoEx function cannot return the contents of the class extra bytes. Win32 does not supply an inverse function to GetClassInfoEx that lets you change all the class information in one call. What differentiates this function from the functions I'm about to discuss is that it does not require a handle to an existing window to access the data.

The GetClassWord, GetClassLong, SetClassWord, and SetClassLong functions allow you to retrieve and change the window class attributes for a registered window class:

```
DWORD   GetClassLong(HWND hwnd, int nIndex);
WORD    GetClassWord(HWND hwnd, int nIndex);
DWORD   SetClassLong(HWND hwnd, int nIndex, LONG dwNewLong);
WORD    SetClassWord(HWND hwnd, int nIndex, WORD wNewWord);
```

---

[8]In 16-bit Windows, an HMODULE and an HINSTANCE identified two different things. In Win32, HMODULEs and HINSTANCEs are the same and can be used interchangeably.

To get or change any of the class attributes, you must supply a handle to an existing window that was created from the class you are interested in and an identifier that specifies the attribute that you are interested in. You must pass this window handle as the first parameter to any of these four functions. The second parameter, nIndex, indicates which attribute you are interested in retrieving or changing. Table 1.3 shows the list of class attributes and the name of the identifier that you should pass as the second parameter to these functions. Each of the identifiers begins with either a GCW_ or a GCL_ prefix. The W or L immediately before the underscore indicates whether the value retrieved is a 16-bit value (a WORD) or a 32-bit value (a LONG).

Table 1.3 *Class attributes and their identifiers.*

Class attribute	Windows.H identifier	Attribute can be changed?
Atom	GCW_ATOM	No
Style	GCL_STYLE	Yes
Window procedure address	GCL_WNDPROC	Yes
Class extra bytes	GCL_CBCLSEXTRA	No
Window extra bytes	GCL_CBWNDEXTRA	Yes
Registrant's HINSTANCE	GCL_HMODULE[9]	No
Icon	GCL_HICON	Yes[10]
Small icon	GCL_HICONSM	Yes
Cursor	GCL_HCURSOR	Yes
Background brush	GCL_HBRBACKGROUND	Yes
Menu name	GCL_MENUNAME	No

[9]In 16-bit windows, there was a difference between an HINSTANCE and an HMODULE. However, in Win32 the distinction has completely vanished— they are the same. To make it easier for developers to port their existing 16-bit Windows code to Win32, Microsoft did not replace the GCL_HMODULE identifier with a new GCL_HINSTANCE identifier. Just know that when you are requesting the HMODULE of a window class you are retrieving its HINSTANCE value.

[10]While you can change the large and small icon for a window class by changing this value, you will not be affecting windows that have already been created of this class. To change the icon associated with an existing window, use the WM_SETICON and WM_GETICON messages.

The last column in Table 1.3 shows whether you can change the class attribute using either the SetClassWord or SetClassLong functions. For example, if you make the following call:

```
SetClassLong(hwnd, GCL_HMODULE, hInstance);
```

the call will act as though you made the following call instead:

```
GetClassLong(hwnd, GCL_HMODULE);
```

That is, SetClassLong will return the current value of the class's HMODULE attribute but the attribute will not be changed.

The most common reason for changing the window class structure is to change window attributes before creating a new window. Unfortunately, the SetClassLong and SetClassWord functions are inconvenient because they require a handle to a window of the desired class in order to make any changes. The Win32 API offers no satisfactory solution to this problem. To change an attribute of ethe window class, you must create a window of the desired class, call SetClassLong or SetClassWord, destroy the window, and create a new window of the same class.

Here is an example of how you could change all edit windows in your process so that the mouse cursor will be an up arrow instead of an I-beam:

```
// Create a window instance of the edit window class.
HWND hwndEdit = CreateWindowEx(0, "edit", "", WS_OVERLAPPED,
   0, 0, 0, 0, NULL, NULL, hInstance, NULL);

// Change the cursor handle to that of the up arrow.
SetClassLong(hwndEdit, GCL_HCURSOR, (LONG) LoadCursor(NULL, IDC_UPARROW));

// Destroy the edit window.
DestroyWindow(hwndEdit);

// From this point on, all edit windows will display an up arrow instead
// of an I-beam mouse cursor when the mouse enters their client area.
```

Because the system always refers to the window class attributes when it's going to display a cursor, the up arrow will appear for edit windows that were created before executing the preceding code as well as those that will be created in the future. Note that, even though the edit window class is a system global class, each process registers its own edit window class. This means that the preceding code fragment changes edit windows for the calling process only—no other process's edit window classes are affected.

When you register a window class, you get to create some additional attributes of your own. You tell the system how many bytes you need for these attributes by setting the cbClsExtra member of the WNDCLASSEX structure before calling RegisterClassEx. The system never touches these bytes directly (except to initialize them to zero when the class is registered). You can get and set any of these extra bytes by calling the GetClassWord, GetClassLong, SetClassWord, or SetClassLong functions and passing an index into the extra bytes for the nIndex parameter. For example, to change the first 4-byte value of the class's extra bytes to the system time, make the following call:

```
SetClassLong(hwnd, 0, GetTickCount());
```

The hwnd parameter must identify a window that has been created of the desired class. The second parameter, 0, indicates the offset into the window class's extra bytes where the long value is to be saved.[11] Note that this is a byte offset, not a long offset. So, if we wanted to save two long values in the class's extra bytes, we would first set the WNDCLASSEX's cbClsExtra value to 8 (2 * sizeof(long)) and then access the second long value by calling SetClassLong as follows:

```
SetClassLong(hwnd, 4, lSomeValue);
```

The third parameter is the new value that we wish to store in the window class's extra bytes. Because working with window and class extra bytes is somewhat clumsy and error-prone, I have developed a set of macros to simplify the job. I present my macros in Appendix A of this book and use the macros throughout all the sample applications.

---

[11]By the way, all the predefined index values, GCW_ATOM, GCL_STYLE, GCL_WNDPROC, GCL_CBCLSEXTRA, GCL_CBWNDEXTRA, GCL_-HMODULE, GCL_HICON, GCL_HICONSM, GCL_HCURSOR, GCL_HBR-BACKGROUND, and GCL_MENUNAME have negative indexes so that they do not conflict with any of your attribute indexes.

The Scope of Window Classes

In a system where different applications are registering window classes and where DLLs are also registering window classes, it becomes extremely important that the system organize all the window classes. For example, in 16-bit Windows, it is possible for one application to register a window class and for a completely different application to create an instance of this window class. There are also times where one application would not be able to register a window class because a completely different application registered a window class with the same name. In a robust operating system, these possibilities should not be allowed—a process should not be allowed to affect or be affected by another process.

The Win32 environment ensures that this does not happen because it requires that every process register all window classes that it expects to create windows of. One application cannot register window classes for another application, and an application cannot create instances of window classes that were registered by another application.

Registered window classes are limited to a single process. Now, within each process, there are three different types of window classes: module local, process global, and system global.

Module Local Window Classes

Module local window classes are registered by code in an EXE or DLL file for its sole use. For example, if an application contains the following code:

```
int WINAPI WinMain (HINSTANCE hinstExe, HINSTANCE hinstExePrev,
    LPSTR lpszCmdLine, int nCmdShow) {

    WNDCLASSEX wc;
    adgINITSTRUCT(wc, TRUE);

    wc.lpszClassName = "Exe-registered WndClass";
    wc.hInstance = hInstance;    // EXE is the registrant.
    // Set wc's remaining members
    .
    .
    .
    // Register the class
    RegisterClassEx(&wc);
    .
    .
    .
    return(0);
}
```

Then, if the following code in a DLL executes:

```
HWND DllCreateAnExeWindow () {

    return(CreateWindowEx(0, "Exe-registered WndClass", ..., g_hinstDll, ...));
}
```

the function DllCreateAnExeWindow will always fail and return
NULL. The reason is because the window class is registered by
the EXE file whose HINSTANCE value is the first parameter to
WinMain. When the DllCreateAnExeWindow function is called,
it is passing the correct window class name, "Exe-registered
WndClass," but it is passing the DLL's HINSTANCE value that
was saved in the global variable g_hinstDll. When you call the
CreateWindowEx function, the system not only compares window
class names but also compares the HINSTANCE value of the window class registrant with the HINSTANCE value of the window
instance creator. Both the class name and the HINSTANCE values
must match, or the system will not create a window of the window
class.

So, you may be asking yourself if there is any way for code in a
DLL to create an instance of a window that was registered by code
in an EXE, or vice versa. The answer is yes; in fact, there are two
ways. The first is simply to make the HINSTANCE values match.
For example, we could rewrite the DllCreateAnExeWindow function as follows:

```
HWND DllCreateAnExeWindow () {

    // Get the EXE's HINSTANCE value
    HINSTANCE hinstExe = GetModuleHandle(NULL);

    return(CreateWindowEx(0, "Exe-registered WndClass", ..., hinstExe, ...));
}
```

Notice that I am calling the GetModuleHandle function and passing NULL to it. This call causes GetModuleHandle to return the
HINSTANCE value of the EXE file in the process's address space.
Now, when CreateWindowEx is called, the EXE file's HINSTANCE
value is passed, and the window is created successfully.

Unfortunately, this solution will not fix the problem where we have code in a DLL that registers a window class and code in an EXE or another DLL that wishes to create an instance of that class. To fix this problem, we would have to obtain the registrant's HINSTANCE value and pass the value around as a parameter so that other EXEs or DLLs could create instances of the window. I'm sure that you must be thinking that this would be terribly inconvenient and that there must be a better way. Well, we're in luck; it's called Process global window classes.

Process Global Window Classes

Process global window classes are registered window classes that are available to the EXE and any DLLs contained in the process's address space. By far, the most common usage of Process global classes is when a DLL contains the window procedures for a set of useful window classes. When the DLL is loaded into the process's address space, its DllMain function is called, and this function calls RegisterClassEx for each of the window classes offered by the DLL. The application (or other DLLs) may now want to call CreateWindowEx to create instances of these window classes.

An excellent example of this method is demonstrated by the new common controls offered by Windows 95 and Windows NT 3.51. Microsoft has created a large set of extremely useful window classes such as up/down controls, tree listboxes, status bars, and toolbars. The window procedures for each of these window classes are contained in a DLL called **ComCtl32.DLL** that ships with the operating system. By default, an application cannot create any instances of these window classes because these classes must be registered for every process that wants to use them. To use these classes, this DLL must be loaded into the process's address space.[12] When it is loaded, the code in the DLL calls RegisterClassEx for every window class in the DLL.

---

[12]An application can do this by calling the LoadLibrary function or by placing a call to the InitCommonControls function contained inside **ComCtl32.DLL**:

```
VOID WINAPI InitCommonControls(VOID);
```

Now, all an application has to do to create an instance of one of these window classes is place a simple call to CreateWindowEx passing the EXE's HINSTANCE value. Why does this work? The code in **ComCtl32.DLL** turns on the CS_GLOBALCLASS class style in each of its class's WNDCLASSEX structures before calling RegisterClassEx. When the system sees that a window class is being registered with the CS_GLOBALCLASS style, the system treats the window class as a process global window class instead of a module local window class. In fact, the existence of this class style is the only difference between a process global window class and a module local window class.

Internally, the CS_GLOBALCLASS style tells the system that the HINSTANCE value of the class registrant and the window creator do not have to match—only the class names have to match. This means that code in the EXE and any code in a DLL will have no problems creating instances of process global window classes like the new common controls.

System Global Window Classes

The operating system registers system global window classes when a process is created. When the user invokes a process, like Notepad, the system creates the process's 4-GB address space, creates the process's primary thread, and automatically registers a set of window classes that are instantly available to the process. The application code needs only to make a simple call to CreateWindowEx in order to create one or more instances of each of these system global window classes.[13]

---

[13]In reality, Windows 95 registers a single set of the system global window classes. Then, if an application makes changes to any of class attributes for these classes, the system detects this change and registers a process global window class on the fly with the same class name. This action is transparent to the programmer. Because few applications modify the attributes of a system global window class, registering a new class is quite unusual; therefore, the system conserves memory by not registering a new set of classes when each process is created but registers new classes only when absolutely necessary.

In Windows NT, the system actually registers a new set of window classes when each process is created.

To use these system global classes, call CreateWindowEx and pass it the class name of the type of window you wish to create. A list of the more common system global window classes that you can use in your applications follows:

```
button, combobox, edit, listbox, mdiclient, scrollbar, static
```

Although these classes are frequently referred to as child controls, they are no different from process global window classes that you register yourself, except that every process running has access to these classes.

The system also registers a number of window classes that are used implicitly by processes. The system automatically creates instances of these window classes as needed. For example, when you call the DialogBox or CreateDialog function, the system creates a window instance of a dialog box class. (See Chapter 2 for more details about this window class.) You will never call CreateWindowEx passing the name of the dialog box class. Instead, the DialogBox and CreateDialog functions call CreateWindowEx on your behalf.

Unregistering a Window Class

Although it is infrequently done, you can unregister a window class by calling the UnregisterClass function:

```
BOOL UnregisterClass(LPCTSTR lpszClassName, HINSTANCE hInstance);
```

This function takes just two parameters: lpszClassName, the name of the class that you wish to unregister (or an atom using the MAKEINTATOM macro), and an hInstance which identifies the EXE or DLL that registered the class in the first place.

UnregisterClass first determines if the class that you are attempting to unregister exists, and if so, it then verifies that there are no window instances of the class in existence. If the class exists and there are no windows of it in existence, then UnregisterClass unregisters the window class. You will no longer be able to create any windows of this window class. If either of the two tests fail, UnregisterClass does not unregister the window class and simply returns FALSE.

Note that a DLL may be loaded into the process's address space, at which point the DLL may register some module local and/or process global window classes. It is now possible that the DLL could be unloaded from the process's address space (usually by an explicit call to the FreeLibrary function). If this happens, there may be windows that have been created or that could be created in the future but the window procedure for these window classes is no longer in the process's address space. Attempting to use windows of these classes will result in an access violation. It would be convenient if the operating system checked to see if a DLL that registered some window classes was being removed and the system could automatically try to unregister the DLL's windows classes. However, this task is difficult for the operating system to perform, and it is up to you to make sure that any DLLs that your windows need remain resident in the process's address space.

Although the system cannot automatically unregister window classes when a DLL is removed from a process's address space, the system does automatically unregister all a process's window classes when the process is terminated. In fact, it is because of this "feature" of the operating system that most programmers never call the UnregisterClass function.

Creating Windows

Once a window class has been registered, you can create one or more instances of the class by calling the CreateWindowEx function, passing the name of the desired window class (or the class name atom using the MAKEINTATOM macro) in the second parameter (lpszClassName):

```
HWND CreateWindowEx(DWORD dwExStyle, LPCTSTR lpszClassName,
    LPCTSTR lpWindowName, DWORD dwStyle,
    int X, int Y, int nWidth, int nHeight,
    HWND hWndParent, HMENU hMenu, HINSTANCE hInstance, LPVOID lpParam);
```

This function sends several messages to the window procedure associated with the window class. Specifically, the CreateWindowEx function sends the messages listed in Table 1.4. While the messages are sent in the order shown, this ordering is not guaranteed; Microsoft may insert additional messages in the future. When writing window procedures, you should always try to make your message-handler functions as atomic as possible. In other words, each message handler shouldn't rely on the processing of other messages.

Table 1.4 *Messages sent by CreateWindowEx.*

Window message	Description
WM_GETMINMAXINFO	This message is sent by CreateWindowEx to help determine the initial size of the window.[14]
	Most window procedures process this message if they need to fine-tune the window's minimum or maximum size.
WM_NCCREATE	This message is sent in order to let Def-WindowProc perform any initialization for the window.
	Most window procedures ignore this message and simply pass it on to DefWindow-Proc.

continued...

---

[14]The fact that this message is sent first is actually a bug in the operating system, but for reasons of backward compatibility, this bug will never be fixed. The system sends the WM_GETMINMAXINFO message to a window procedure whenever the window is being resized. The reason why sending the WM_GETMINMAXINFO message as the first message to a window is a bug is because the window has not been fully initialized yet (by processing the WM_NCCREATE and WM_CREATE messages). So, the first time a window procedure receives the WM_GETMINMAXINFO message it may not have all the information available in order to process this message correctly. Frequently, handling this message must include code that checks to see if the window is fully initialized. If the window is not initialized, the remaining processing of the WM_GETMINMAXINFO message is skipped.

Window message	Description
WM_NCCALCSIZE	This message is sent by CreateWindowEx to calculate the size and position of the window's client area.
	Most window procedures ignore this message and simply pass it on to DefWindowProc.
WM_CREATE	This message is sent to allow the window procedure to perform any one-time initialization for the window.
	Some window procedures process this message to initialize state variables for a window or to create child windows. The window procedure can indicate that the initialization has failed by returning -1 from the processing of this message. If -1 is returned, the window is destroyed and CreateWindowEx returns NULL to its caller.
WM_SIZE	This message is sent to notify the window procedure of the window's initial size. Some window procedures process this message to rearrange the contents of the window's client area.
WM_MOVE	This message is sent to notify the window procedure of the window's initial position. Most window procedures ignore this message and simply pass it on to DefWindowProc.

The following code example demonstrates how to abort window creation if the window's initialization fails:

```
#define GCL_DATA    0
.
.
.
LRESULT lResult = 0;
```

```
    .
    .
    .
case WM_CREATE:
    pData = HeapAlloc(GetProcessHeap(), 0, BUFFERSIZE);
    if (pData == NULL)
        lResult = -1;    // Halt creation of window
    else {
        SetClassLong(hwnd, GCL_DATA, (LONG) pData);
        // lResult initialized to 0, window creation OK.
    }
    break;

case WM_DESTROY:
    // Free block of memory created during WM_CREATE message.
    pData = GetClassLong(hwnd, GCL_DATA);
    if (pData != NULL)
        HeapFree(GetProcessHeap(), 0, pData);
    break;
    .
    .
    .
return(lResult);
```

This code fragment also demonstrates how WM_DESTROY should be used to perform window cleanup. In this example, the memory block allocated by WM_CREATE is freed. It is extremely important to note that the system sends the WM_DESTROY message even if the return value from processing the WM_CREATE message is -1. If the check to determine if pData was NULL in the preceding code fragment was not done, we would be calling HeapFree and passing it an address of NULL. This is obviously something that must not be done.

Process and Thread Identification

Some applications (usually system-level tools) want to manipulate a process that owns a thread that created a specific window. For example, you may want to write an application that allows the user to select a window on the screen and then terminates the process that created the window. Here is an example of code that does this:

```
DWORD dwProcessId;
HANDLE hProcess;

// Find the handle to Calculator's window (as an example).
HWND hwnd = FindWindow(NULL, "Calculator");
GetWindowThreadProcessId(hwnd, &dwProcessId);
```

33

```
hProcess = OpenProcess(PROCESS_TERMINATE, FALSE, dwProcessId);
TerminateProcess(hProcess, 0);
CloseHandle(hProcess);
```

The preceding code obtains a process ID from a window handle and then obtains a handle to a process kernel object from the process ID. First, the GetWindowThreadProcessId function is called:

```
DWORD GetWindowThreadProcessId(HWND hwnd, LPDWORD lpdwProcessId);
```

This function accepts a window handle as its first parameter and returns the ID of the thread that created the window. If you want the ID of the process that owns the thread, you must pass in the address of a DWORD as the lpdwProcessId parameter. If you are not interested in the process ID, you can pass NULL. In the preceding code fragment, we are interested in the process ID and simply ignore the thread ID.

Now, with the process ID, we can open a handle to the process kernel object by calling OpenProcess:

```
HANDLE OpenProcess(DWORD fdwAccess, BOOL fInherit, DWORD IDProcess);
```

With the first parameter, fdwAccess, we tell the system what we intend to do with the process handle. In the preceding code fragment, I passed the PROCESS_TERMINATE identifier because we will be using the handle to terminate the process. When we call OpenProcess, it performs a security check to make sure that we have access to terminate the process. If we do not, OpenProcess will return NULL. Because Windows 95 does not support security like Windows NT, Windows 95 always grants this access. The second parameter, fInherit, indicates whether the handle can be inherited by any new processes spawned by our process. Finally, we pass the process ID obtained by our call to GetWindowThreadProcessId for the third parameter, IDProcess.

Now, with the handle to the process object, we call Terminate-Process:

```
BOOL TerminateProcess(HANDLE hProcess, UINT uExitCode);
```

The hProcess parameter indicates which process we wish to terminate, and the uExitCode parameter indicates the process's exit code. Finally, after terminating the process, we call CloseHandle to close the process kernel object, potentially freeing it from system memory. Without the call to CloseHandle, we would be leaking system memory until our process terminated.

A Window's Attributes

The CreateWindowEx function can create windows only from a registered class. If CreateWindowEx finds a class registered with the same name as the one requested, it allocates a block of memory to store information about the window instance. The block contains some of the information in the window class structure and some of the information that was passed to the CreateWindowEx function. The system extends the size of the block by the number of bytes specified by the cbWndExtra value in the WNDCLASSEX structure and initializes these bytes to zero. Every window instance receives its own set of extra bytes. Like the class extra bytes, these are available solely for the window procedure's own use.

The Win32 API contains functions that allow you to retrieve and modify the information in the window structure after the window has been created. These functions are described in the following paragraphs.

The GetClassName function retrieves the class name that was used to create the window:

```
int GetClassName(HWND hwnd, LPTSTR lpszClassName, int nMaxCount);
```

The first parameter, hwnd, is the handle of the window; the second parameter, lpszClassName, is the address to a buffer that is to be filled with the class name; and the last parameter, nMaxCount, is the maximum length of this buffer. The return value indicates the length of the string in characters.

The GetWindowWord, GetWindowLong, SetWindowWord, and SetWindowLong functions allow you to retrieve and change the attributes of an existing window:

```
DWORD    GetWindowLong(HWND hwnd, int nIndex);
WORD     GetWindowWord(HWND hwnd, int nIndex);
DWORD    SetWindowLong(HWND hwnd, int nIndex, LONG dwNewLong);
WORD     SetWindowWord(HWND hwnd, int nIndex, WORD wNewWord);
```

To get or change any of the window's attributes, you must supply a handle to an existing window and an identifier that specifies the attribute that you are interested in. You must pass this window handle as the first parameter to any of these four functions. The second parameter, nIndex, indicates which attribute you are interested in retrieving or changing. Table 1.5 shows the list of window instance attributes and the names of the identifiers that you should pass as the second parameter to these functions. All the identifiers begin with a GWL_ prefix. The L immediately before the underscore indicates that the value retrieved is a 32-bit value (a LONG).

Note that the SetWindowWord and SetWindowLong functions will work correctly only if the thread calling these functions is owned by the same process that owns the thread that created the window. In other words, one process cannot change the window attributes of a window created by another process, although one process can get the attributes of a window created by another process (see Table 1.5).

Table 1.5 *Window attributes and their identifiers.*

Window attribute	Windows.H identifier	Can attribute be changed?
Window procedure address	GWL_WNDPROC	Yes
Creator's HINSTANCE	GWL_HINSTANCE	Yes
Window's parent window	GWL_HWNDPARENT	Yes
Window's ID/menu	GWL_ID	Yes
Window extended styles	GWL_EXSTYLE	Yes
Style	GWL_STYLE	Yes
User data	GWL_USERDATA	Yes

Unlike the window class attributes, all the window instance attributes are LONG values and must be retrieved or modified using

GetWindowLong or SetWindowLong, respectively. Also, all the window instance attributes can be changed whereas some of the window class attributes were read-only. Most of the window attributes should be self-explanatory, but I'll bring some points to your attention.

First, when a thread in one process queries the window procedure address of a window created by a thread in another process, GetWindowLong always returns 0x00000000 because Microsoft thought that the window procedure address would not be useful to the other process. Of course, it would be useful for a debugging application (like Spy[15]) and the Voyeur sample application shown at the end of this chapter. However, a thread in one process can successfully query a window class's window procedure address even if that class is registered by a thread in another process because Microsoft simply overlooked this situation. They intended to disallow it, but the developers forgot to handle this case.

Second, while the operating system does allow you to change the HINSTANCE value associated with a window instance, you are strongly encouraged not to do this. Microsoft allows it for backward compatibility reasons, but some applications took advantage of this capability to perform some unsightly hacks.

Third, when you call SetWindowLong with GWL_STYLE or GWL_EXSTYLE, the system does not simply change the window's attributes to reflect the new style bits. Instead, the system first sends a WM_STYLECHANGING message to the window procedure. The wParam parameter is set to either GWL_STYLE or GWL_EXSTYLE and the lParam is set to the address of a STYLESTRUCT structure:

```
typedef struct tagSTYLESTRUCT {
   DWORD   styleOld;
   DWORD   styleNew;
} STYLESTRUCT, * LPSTYLESTRUCT;
```

---

[15]The Spy++ application that comes with Visual C++ shows the window procedure address associated with a window, but it uses alternate techniques to obtain this information.

This structure contains the current style flags for the window in the styleOld member and the potential set of new style flags in the styleNew member. The window procedure can validate the flags in the styleNew member and even alter them if it likes. After the WM_STYLECHANGING message has been processed, the system updates the windows flags and sends a WM_STYLECHANGED message to the window procedure (the wParam and lParam parameters are identical to the WM_STYLECHANGING message). The window procedure can do whatever it chooses now that it knows that its styles have changed.[16]

The most common reason for calling SetWindowWord or SetWindowLong is to manipulate data that are associated with a specific window. Here is an example of how you could keep track of how long a window has been in existence:

1. Define an identifier to be used for referencing the window extra bytes:

```
#define GWL_STARTTIME   (0)
```

2. Register the class, making sure that 4 window extra bytes will be reserved for every window of this class:

```
WNDCLASSEX wc;
.
.
.
wc.cbWndExtra = sizeof(LONG);
RegisterClassEx(&wc);
```

3. When the window is created, initialize the window extra bytes to the system time:

```
case WM_CREATE:
   SetWindowLong(hwnd, GWL_STARTTIME, GetTickCount());
   break;
```

---

[16]The WM_STYLECHANGING and WM_STYLECHANGED messages are not sent to a window procedure when a window class's style is changed. For example, the following line does not cause any window messages to be sent:

```
SetClassLong(hwnd, GCL_STYLE, lNewStyle);
```

4. Determine the total time the window has been in existence:

```
DWORD dwSecondsRunning = (GetTickCount() -
    GetWindowLong(hwnd, GWL_STARTTIME)) / 1000;
```

In the preceding example, I needed only 4 extra bytes to store the time. Microsoft expects that it will be common to store one 4-byte value with every window that is created and preallocates a 4-byte block inside every window's internal data structure. You can easily get or set this 4-byte value by calling GetWindowLong or SetWindowLong using the GWL_USERDATA identifier. Like any extra bytes you allocate, the system does not manipulate this value at all except to initialize it to zero when the window is first created.

This 4-byte place holder turns out to be incredibly useful. For example, you might create a dialog box that contains several buttons, listboxes, and/or edit windows. If you determine that you need to associate some data with one of these windows you need some place to put it. Because you did not register these system global window classes, you cannot use any of their extra bytes. However, Microsoft promises that the window procedures for these classes will not touch the 4-byte value at GWL_USERDATA. This means that you can store whatever 32-bit value you want in GWL_USERDATA and be assured that it will not be corrupted by the system.

When you register your own window classes, the window procedure for your class should not use its own GWL_USERDATA value. Leave this value for the code that creates and manipulates instances of your window class. Things will be much easier for users of your class if they too can associate data with instances of your class. Besides, you don't need this 4-byte value; you can set the WND-CLASSEX's cbWndExtra member as you desire, since you are registering the class yourself.

Window Styles

CreateWindowEx's fourth parameter, dwStyle, allows you to specify a set of styles that affects this one instance of this window class (in contrast to class styles that affect all windows based on the window class). The dwStyle parameter is a 32-bit value in which the high 16 bits specify style information that is understood and interpreted by the operating system itself. That is, the operating system has defined a set of styles that have meaning to all windows created, regardless of their window class. Table 1.6 shows these system-defined styles. Notice that each style is prefixed by the letters WS_. This indicates that the identifier is a window style.

Table 1.6 *Window class styles.*

Style category	Identifier	Value
Type	WS_OVERLAPPED	0x00000000L
	WS_POPUP	0x80000000L
	WS_CHILD	0x40000000L
Initial states	WS_MINIMIZE	0x20000000L
	WS_VISIBLE	0x10000000L
	WS_DISABLED	0x08000000L
	WS_MAXIMIZE	0x01000000L
Clipping styles	WS_CLIPSIBLINGS	0x04000000L
	WS_CLIPCHILDREN	0x02000000L
Appearance	WS_CAPTION	0x00C00000L
	WS_BORDER	0x00800000L
	WS_DLGFRAME	0x00400000L
	WS_THICKFRAME	0x00040000L
	WS_HSCROLL	0x00100000L
	WS_VSCROLL	0x00200000L
	WS_SYSMENU	0x00080000L
Capabilities	WS_MINIMIZEBOX	0x00020000L
	WS_MAXIMIZEBOX	0x00010000L
Input focus sequence	WS_GROUP	0x00020000L
	WS_TABSTOP	0x00010000L

Note that the WS_CAPTION style is a combination of WS_BORDER and WS_DLGFRAME. Because a window cannot have both the

WS_BORDER and WS_DLGFRAME styles, the system interprets both bits being on as the WS_CAPTION style.

Also note that the WS_MINIMIZEBOX and WS_MAXIMIZE-BOX styles have identical values to the WS_GROUP and WS_TAB-STOP identifiers. The system treats these bits as WS_GROUP and WS_TABSTOP when the window is a child of a dialog box window to determine the input focus sequence. However, if the window has a caption, the system treats these bits as WS_MINIMIZEBOX and WS_MAXIMIZEBOX.

The operating system itself does not interpret the low 16 bits of the dwStyle parameter. These 16 bits are specific to each window class. The window class procedure determines the meaning of these bits. For the system global window classes (such as listboxes, buttons, and scrollbars), Microsoft defined styles for each of these classes. When you register your own window classes, you can create your own definition for these 16 bits. Table 1.7 shows each of the operating system's global window classes and the prefix with which each class's specific styles begins.

Table 1.7 *Prefixes for the system global window class style indentifiers.*

System global class	Prefix
DIALOG	DS_
BUTTON	BS_
COMBOBOX	CBS_
EDIT	ES_
LISTBOX	LBS_
MDICLIENT	MDIS_
SCROLLBAR	SBS_
STATIC	SS_

DS_ styles are specified on the STYLE line in a dialog-box template. The system knows to use these styles when the DialogBox or CreateDialog function implicitly creates the dialog box window.

When examining the values for these identifiers in the Windows header files, you will notice that many of the values repeat. For example, BS_DEFPUSHBUTTON and SS_CENTER both have a value of 0x00000001. This does not cause a conflict because only the window procedure associated with the corresponding class will see these style bits. Each class will interpret the bits differently.

A window procedure can retrieve style information by using the GetWindowLong function. Once the styles are retrieved, the procedure can AND the style with a particular identifier to see if the style is on or off. This information can then be used to modify the behavior of the window.

Beginning with Windows 3.0, Microsoft added several new styles that can affect a window. These new styles are called extended window styles and are specified in the first parameter to CreateWindowEx, dwExStyle. Like the window style value, the extended window style value is 32 bits long. However, Microsoft has reserved all 32 bits to represent styles interpreted by the operating system. None of the extended style bits can be used for class-specific information. The **WinUser.H** header file defines the valid extended window styles (all extended window styles have the prefix WS_EX_). The list appears in Table 1.8.

Table 1.8 *Window class extended styles.*

Extended style category	Identifier	Value
Appearance	WS_EX_DLGMODALFRAME	0x00000001
	WS_EX_STATICEDGE	0x00020000
	WS_EX_CONTEXTHELP	0x00000400
	WS_EX_TOOLWINDOW	0x00000080
	WS_EX_WINDOWEDGE	0x00000100
	WS_EX_CLIENTEDGE	0x00000200
	WS_EX_APPWINDOW	0x00040000
Communication	WS_EX_TOPMOST	0x00000008
	WS_EX_TRANSPARENT	0x00000020
	WS_EX_NOPARENTNOTIFY	0x00000004
	WS_EX_ACCEPTFILES	0x00000010
	WS_EX_MDICHILD	0x00000040
	WS_EX_CONTROLPARENT	0x00010000

Extended style category	Identifier	Value
Orientation	WS_EX_LEFT	0x00000000
	WS_EX_LTRREADING	0x00000000
	WS_EX_RIGHTSCROLLBAR	0x00000000
	WS_EX_RIGHT	0x00001000
	WS_EX_RTLREADING	0x00002000
	WS_EX_LEFTSCROLLBAR	0x00004000

Window Properties

Window properties give the programmer another way to associate data with windows. Properties are extremely useful if you want to associate data with a window instance for a class that you did not register yourself. If you didn't register the window class yourself, you don't know how many extra bytes were specified in the WNDCLASSEX structure. Although you can retrieve this information by calling GetClassInfoEx or GetClassLong, you can be sure that if extra bytes were allocated, they are being used by the window procedure that operates on this class. Using these extra bytes for your own purpose would surely interfere with the behavior of this window.

Properties allow you to associate data with a window by using a string name instead of modifying the information stored in the internal window structure. Only 32-bit values may be associated with a property. Because the system must associate property string names with a window, properties are slower to use and require more memory than window extra bytes.

The Win32 API supplies five functions to manipulate properties of a window:

■ The SetProp function associates a property with a window:

```
BOOL SetProp(HWND hwnd, LPCTSTR lpString, HANDLE hData);
```

■ The RemoveProp function removes a property associated with a window:

```
HANDLE RemoveProp(HWND hwnd, LPCTSTR lpString);
```

■ The GetProp function retrieves a property associated with a window:

```
HANDLE GetProp(HWND hwnd, LPCTSTR lpString);
```

■ The EnumProps and EnumPropsEx functions retrieve the list of all properties associated with a window:

```
int EnumProps(HWND hwnd, PROPENUMPROC lpEnumFunc);
int EnumPropsEx(HWND hwnd, PROPENUMPROCEX lpEnumFunc, LPARAM lParam);
```

The following example shows how you can acquire some information in a modal dialog box and return that information to the caller:

1. The caller allocates memory for the information that will be retrieved by the modal dialog box:

```
#define MAX_USERS_NAME_LEN    (30)
      .
      .
      .
pData = malloc(MAX_USERS_NAME_LEN + 1);
DialogBoxParam(hinstExe, MAKEINTRESOURCE(IDD_USERNAME), hwnd,
    UserName_DlgProc, (LONG) pData);
// The local memory block will contain the user's name.
      .
      .
      .
```

2. The dialog box procedure associates the memory handle with the dialog box window:

```
case WM_INITDIALOG:
    // The lParam contains the last parameter value passed to
    // DialogBoxParam. This is the handle to the local block of memory.
    SetProp(hwnd, "Memory", (HANDLE) lParam);
    // Perform any other initialization for the dialog box.
      .
      .
      .
```

3. The dialog box will fill the block of memory when the user clicks OK:

```
case IDOK:
   pszName = (PSTR) GetProp(hwnd, "Memory");
   GetDlgItemText(hwnd, ID_USERNAMEEDITBOX,
      (LPSTR) pszName, MAX_USERS_NAME_LEN);
      .
      .
      .
   EndDialog(hwnd, IDOK);
   break;
```

4. When the dialog box is destroyed, the property should be removed. This isn't strictly necessary because the system automatically removes any properties associated with a window when that window is destroyed. However, explicitly removing the property is considered good form.

```
case WM_DESTROY:
   RemoveProp(hwnd, "Memory");
   break;
```

Of course, you can always associate a 4-byte value with a window by using the GetWindowLong and SetWindowLong functions with the GWL_USERDATA identifier. In fact, this method is quicker and easier than using properties. However, if you have several pieces of data that you need to associate with a window, a 4-byte value is not enough room. The best thing to do in this case is to allocate a block of memory large enough to hold a data structure with members for all the data you desire and then store the pointer to this memory block in the GWL_USERDATA value. Because of the 4-byte GWL_USERDATA value, window properties are used infrequently.

Window Messages

Window messages are sent as unsigned 32-bit integer values in the range of 0x00000000 to 0xFFFFFFFF. Microsoft divides this range into four sections and defines each section's meaning (see Table 1.9).

Table 1.9 *Window message sections.*

Message section	Section's meaning
0x00000000 to WM_USER[17] - 1	All standard window messages. This includes all messages that begin with the WM_ prefix. You should never create messages that fall in this range.
WM_USER to WM_APP[18] - 1	Class-specific integer messages.
WM_APP to 0x0000BFFF	Application-specific integer messages used for a single process.
0x0000C000 to 0x0000FFFF	System-global string messages. These are the message numbers returned by the RegisterWindowMessage function.
0x00010000 to 0xFFFFFFFF	Messages reserved by Microsoft for exclusive use by the system.

Class-Defined Integer Messages

When you register your own window class, you can create messages that perform operations specific to that class. Suppose that you created an INFO window class that maintained a block of memory and allowed other windows access to that block. You could create a class-specific message for the INFO window; when it received the message, it would return the address of the block of memory. The list of class-specific messages should be placed in a header file, **Info.H**, for example. This file should be included by all modules that will send messages to INFO windows. **Info.C**, should look like this:

```
#define IM_GETMEMORY   (WM_USER + 0)
```

[17]WM_USER is defined as 0x00000400 in the **WinUser.H** header file.

[18]WM_APP is defined as 0x00008000 in the **WinUser.H** header file.

In the file that contains the window procedure for an INFO window class, **Info.C**, the following code fragment should exist:

```
#include "Info.H"
    .
    .
    .
case IM_GETMEMORY:
    lResult = GetWindowLong(hwnd, GWL_MEMORYHANDLE);
    break;
    .
    .
    .
return(lResult);
```

Class-specific messages should be sent only to windows of the class that defines the messages. Sending a class-specific message to a window of another class will have an unpredictable effect.

The 16-bit Windows header file defines class-specific messages that can be sent to the system global classes. Notice that each message begins with a unique prefix (see Table 1.10).

Table 1.10 *Prefixes for the system global window class message identifiers.*

System global class	Message prefix
DIALOG	DM_
BUTTON	BM_
COMBOBOX	CB_
EDIT	EM_
LISTBOX	LB_
MDICLIENT	(none)
SCROLLBAR	SBM_
STATIC	STM_

When creating the Win32 API, Microsoft decided to change the numeric values of these messages. For example, in 16-bit Windows, the BM_SETCHECK message is defined as (WM_USER + 1). But in Win32, the BM_SETCHECK message is defined as 0x00F1. This means that the message is no longer part of the class-specific message section but has been moved to the standard message section. Microsoft can do this, of course, because they produce the operating system and they also produce the system global window classes.[19]

However, if you look at the new common controls, you'll see that their messages are defined to be in the class-specific message section. For example, the TB_ENABLEBUTTON message, which enables or disables a button on a toolbar window, is defined as (WM_USER + 1). Note that the system will not allow messages in this range to be broadcast to all other windows in the system.

Application-Specific Integer Messages

Integer values in this range are reserved for a specific process. In other words, when a window class is designed, its window procedure should not define any messages that are in this range. This way, an application can define some application-specific messages that it knows will not conflict with any messages expected by any windows. An application might do this if it wanted to use the PostThreadMessage function to post a message to a thread instead of a window:

```
BOOL PostThreadMessage(DWORD idThread, UINT Msg, WPARAM wParam, LPARAM lParam);
```

Also, an application would define an application-specific message if it was going to subclass some of the window that it creates. The application-specific message would be processed by the subclass procedure but would be ignored by the original window procedure. See Chapter 5, "Window Subclassing and Superclassing," for more details.

Note that, like the class-specific integer window messages, the system will not allow application-specific messages to be broadcast to all other windows in the system.

---

[19]Microsoft made the system class messages less than WM_USER for 16-bit to 32-bit thunking. There are 16-bit applications that send messages like EM_GETLINE to non-edit control windows. Since the system doesn't know that these window classes use the same semantics for a EM_GET-LINE message, the system would be unable to thunk the parameters correctly. By making the system control-specific messages less than WM_USER, Win32 ensures you can send these messages to non-system class windows.

System-Global String Messages

You create system-global string messages when you wish to send a message and are unsure of the receiving window's class. When you register a system-global message, you're telling the system that there is a new "standard" message that any window in any application can recognize.

We create a new string message by calling RegisterWindow-Message:

```
UINT RegisterWindowMessage(LPCTSTR lpString);
```

This function accepts a character string and returns a numeric value in the range of 0x0000C000 to 0x0000FFFF. Internally, the RegisterWindowMessage function creates an atom from the system's local atom table just like the RegisterClassEx function. If another call to RegisterWindowMessage is placed from any application with the same character string, the system returns the same numeric value that was returned the first time. Because of this, different windows will be using the same integer value to represent the same string message.

All applications that wish to use these new messages should call RegisterWindowMessage during initialization. Once a window message has been registered, it remains in existence until the system is shut down and restarted. This is because there is no function to unregister a string window message.

How the Window/Application Lives and Dies

Examine the following skeleton of a Win32 application:

```
int WINAPI WinMain (HINSTANCE hinstExe, HINSTANCE hinstExePrev,
    LPSTR lpszCmdLine, int nCmdShow) {

    WNDCLASSEX wc;
    ATOM atomClassName;
    .
    .
    .
    // Initialize the wc structure.
    atomClassName = RegisterClassEx(&wc);
```

```
    // Create a window of the registered class.
    hwnd = CreateWindowEx(0, MAKEINTATOM(atomClassName), ...);

    return(0);
}
```

This code registers a window class and creates an instance of the class. However, the process's primary thread returns from WinMain causing the C-Runtime library to perform any cleanup, and the thread and the process terminate. When a thread terminates, the operating system destroys any windows that were created by the thread (window classes are unregistered when the process terminates).

Because the thread and process terminate immediately after creating the window, the application is almost useless. So, a message loop is introduced into our WinMain function as follows:

```
int WINAPI WinMain (HINSTANCE hinstExe, HINSTANCE hinstExePres,
  LPSTR lpszCmdLine, int nCmdShow) {

    WNDCLSSEX wc;
    ATOM atomClassName;
    MSG msg;
    .
    .
    .
    // Initialize the wc structure.
    atomClassName = RegisterClassEx(&wc);

    // Create a window of the registered class.
    hwnd = CreateWindowEx(0, MAKEINTATOM(atomClassName), ...);

    // A simple message loop
    while (GetMessage(&msg, NULL, 0, 0)) {
       DispatchMessage(&msg);
    }
    // End of the simple message loop

    return(0);
}
```

This message loop consists of a call to the GetMessage function. If GetMessage returns TRUE, the DispatchMessage function is called. When DispatchMessage returns, the while loop continues by calling GetMessage again. Now, let me explain what is really happening here. Once a window is created, it's sole reason for existing is to execute code in response to window messages. There are two ways for a message to get to a window class's window procedure: the message can be sent, or the message can be posted. Messages are sent using the SendMessage function:[20]

```
LRESULT SendMessage(HWND hwnd, UINT uMsg, WPARAM wParam, LPARAM lParam);
```

If the thread making this call is also the thread that created the window, the SendMessage function calls the window procedure directly. The window procedure processes the window message and returns an LRESULT value back to the SendMessage function. The SendMessage function then returns this LRESULT value back to the caller. If the thread calling SendMessage is sending a message to a window created by a different thread, what happens internally is more complicated than what is described here, but the end result (i.e., the LRESULT that is returned) is the same.

Messages are posted to a window using the PostMessage function:

```
BOOL PostMessage(HWND hwnd, UINT uMsg, WPARAM wParam, LPARAM lParam);
```

This function causes a window message to be placed in a queue of window messages. Every thread in the system has its own message queue. So, if a process contains 20 threads, there are also 20 message queues. The PostMessage function determines which thread created the window identified by the hwnd parameter. PostMessage then appends this message to the end of this thread's message queue. This means that if a single thread creates 100 windows, messages posted to any of these 100 windows are appended to this one thread's message queue.

When a thread calls the GetMessage function, the function examines the thread's message queue. If there are no messages in the queue, the system puts the thread to sleep and no longer schedules any CPU time to the thread. When a message appears in the thread's queue, the system wakes up the thread, and GetMessage copies the the message from the queue into the MSG data structure whose address is passed as GetMessage's first parameter. GetMessage removes the message from the thread's queue and returns to the thread's message loop. If GetMessage returns TRUE,

---

[20]Other functions exist for sending window messages such as SendNotify-Message, SendMessageTimeout, and SendMessageCallback. However, to simplify this discussion, I'll just discuss SendMessage.

the code inside the while loop executes. In the preceding code, this is a simple call to DispatchMessage, which is passed the MSG structure that was initialized by the call to GetMessage:

```
LRESULT DispatchMessage(CONST MSG *lpMsg);
```

DispatchMessage acts very much like the SendMessage function: it calls the window class's window procedure directly, passing it the hwnd, uMsg, wParam, and lParam values that are contained inside the MSG data structure. The window procedure returns an LRESULT value back to DispatchMessage, which returns it back to the thread that called DispatchMessage. The message loop shown above doesn't use this LRESULT value. In fact, I have never seen a message loop that uses this LRESULT value for anything.

It is important to note that the GetMessage function pulls messages from the calling thread's message queue only. So, if you create additional threads in your process and these threads call the CreateWindowEx function to create windows, then each of these threads must have their own message loop. It is also important to note that a thread's message loop keeps a thread from terminating. Because the thread doesn't terminate immediately, any windows created by the thread are also not destroyed—they stay in existence waiting to process window messages.

Of course, the thread's message loop will terminate when the GetMessage function returns FALSE. The GetMessage function will return FALSE only when a WM_QUIT message is pulled from the thread's message queue. A WM_QUIT message will never be seen by any window procedure because the message loop will terminate and DispatchMessage will not be called.

And now, we will discuss how a WM_QUIT message ends up in a thread's message queue. Here is the normal sequence of events. First, when the user clicks a window's Close box or chooses the window's system menu's Close option, a WM_CLOSE message is sent to the window's window procedure. This message indicates that a user is requesting that the window be closed. We do not have to honor this request, but we usually do. If the WM_CLOSE message is allowed to pass through to DefWindowProc, DefWindow Proc handles the WM_CLOSE message by calling the Destroy Window function.

Second, the DestroyWindow function tells the operating system that the window is to be destroyed. This is not a request, this is a demand! The operating system will send a WM_DESTROY message to the window class's window procedure.[21] In response to the WM_DESTROY message, the window procedure for an application's main window places a call to PostQuitMessage:

```
BOOL PostQuitMessage(int nExitCode);
```

This function places a WM_QUIT message in the calling thread's message queue[22] and returns immediately so that the window procedure can complete its WM_DESTROY message handling. This call to PostQuitMessage is critical. It is where we, as developers, make the connection between a window's lifetime and a thread's (or process's) lifetime. I have frequently seen programmers forget to put the call to PostQuitMessage in the WM_DESTROY message handling. If PostQuitMessage is not called, the window is destroyed, but the thread does not terminate; therefore, the process itself does not terminate! What we have here is a running process that offers no windows to the user. Since the process offers no user-interface to the user, the user has no idea that the process is still running and using system resources. The only way that a process like this can be terminated is by using the Close Program dialog box, logging off, or shutting down the system.

---

[21]Actually, a single call to DestroyWindow may cause the system to destroy many windows in addition to the window whose handle was passed to DestroyWindow. For example, any windows that are owned by the window being destroyed are also destroyed. In addition, any children, grandchildren, great-grandchildren, and so on are also destroyed. First, the system sends each of these windows a WM_DESTROY message starting with the window passed to DestroyWindow. Then, each of these windows receives a WM_NCDESTROY message. However, the WM_NCDESTROY message is sent from the bottom-up. So, the window passed to DestroyWindow will be the last to receive the WM_NCDESTROY message; all its children will have processed it first.

[22]In reality, a bit is set rather than a message being posted. For more information see *Advanced Windows*, Microsoft Press, 1995.

Let me point out that DefWindowProc does not call PostQuit-Message as a default response to a WM_DESTROY message because an application may create many windows. Usually, only one of these windows is identified as the window that represents the lifetime of the thread (or process). If DefWindowProc called PostQuitMessage by default, the thread would terminate its message loop as soon as the first window (any window) was closed. Imagine a running application where the user opens the File Open dialog box and after selecting the OK button, the whole application closes. This is, of course, ridiculous.

After the WM_QUIT message is queued for the thread, the thread finishes handling the window's WM_DESTROY message. The window handles the WM_NCDESTROY message that is sent to it and then is destroyed. Now, the message loop regains control and, this time, retrieves the WM_QUIT message; GetMessage returns FALSE and the message loop will terminate. Notice that the window is already destroyed at this point. So, when the thread terminates, the system will see that there are no more windows created by this thread still in existence, and the system will not have to destroy any windows forcefully.

When the system forcefully destroys windows (because the creating thread is terminating), the system does not send WM_CLOSE, WM_DESTROY, or WM_NCDESTROY messages to the window procedure. After all, how could it? The thread has terminated and can't execute any more code. So, the window is not notified that it is being destroyed. If the window procedure prompts the user to save any unsaved data while handling a WM_CLOSE message, this code will not execute. In addition, any cleanup that is normally done while handling WM_DESTROY or WM_NCDESTROY messages will also not be executed. It is best for windows to be destroyed by calling the DestroyWindow function rather than relying on the system to force windows to be destroyed because the creating thread has terminated.

System Shutdown

When the user attempts to log off or shut down, the system notifies all running processes of the user's request.[23] The system doesn't actually notify all running processes—the system actually broadcasts a WM_QUERYENDSESSION message to any unowned windows that have the WS_OVERLAPPED window style. Notice the distinction here: if a process creates five unowned, overlapped windows, each window receives a WM_QUERYENDSESSION message. If a process doesn't create any unowned, overlapped windows, that process doesn't receive the WM_QUERYENDSESSION message and therefore is given no notification that the user is logging off or shutting down.

When the system sends the WM_QUERYENDSESSION message, it tells the window that the user wants to end the Windows session and the system asks the window if it minds. The WM_QUERYENDSESSION message is similar to the WM_CLOSE message in that it is a request to end the session. While handling the WM_QUERYENDSESSION message, the window procedure can decide to deny this request, which will stop the Windows session from ending. If you wish to grant the request to end the session, your window procedure must return TRUE; if you wish to deny the request, return FALSE.

---

[23]An application shuts down the system by calling the ExitWindowsEx function:

```
BOOL ExitWindowsEx(UINT uFlags, DWORD dwReserved);
```

This function broadcasts a WM_QUERYENDSESSION to all the overlapped, unowned windows except any windows created by the calling thread. The system assumes that the thread calling ExitWindowsEx knows that the system is shutting down and that it would be difficult for the thread to know when another thread was trying to shut down the system instead.

Normally, a window procedure handles the WM_QUERYEND-SESSION message by checking to see if there are any unsaved data that the user has forgotten to save. For example, if you start WordPad, type some text (without saving it), and then attempt to shutdown Windows, WordPad displays the dialog box shown in Figure 1.2 when it receives the WM_QUERYENDSESSION message:

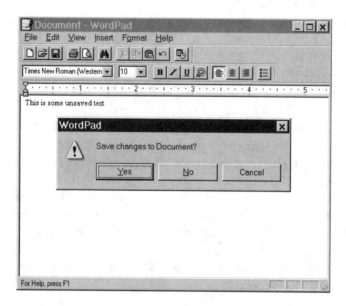

Figure 1.2 *The WordPad dialog box asking user to save unsaved data.*

If the user selects Yes, the file Save As dialog box appears. After the user saves the file, TRUE is returned back to the system so that the system can continue logging off or shutting down. If the user selects No, nothing is presented to the user, and TRUE is returned back to the operating system. However, if the user selects Cancel, FALSE is returned back to the operating system, and the user's Windows session is not ended. If DefWindowProc is allowed to handle the WM_QUERYENDSESSION message, it always returns TRUE back to the system.

After all the windows have responded to the WM_QUERYEND-SESSION message, the system broadcasts a WM_ENDSESSION message to all the windows. For a WM_ENDSESSION message, the wParam parameter is TRUE if the Windows session is actually ending;

it is FALSE if it is not. The documentation for the WM_ENDSESSION message states the following:

> *If the fEndSession parameter is TRUE, the Windows session can end any time after all applications have returned from processing this message. Therefore, an application should perform all tasks required for termination before returning from this message. The application need not call the DestroyWindow or PostQuitMessage function when the session is ending.*

Let's examine the last sentence in more detail. If you do not call the DestroyWindow or PostQuitMessage function, who will? The answer is no one! That's right, your window will not receive the WM_CLOSE, WM_DESTROY, or WM_NCDESTROY messages at all. Instead, after the system has finished sending WM_ENDSESSION messages to all the unowned, overlapped windows, the system will forcefully call the TerminateProcess function for every process running in the Windows session. This means that none of the running processes will terminate cleanly. In my opinion, Microsoft should not be encouraging developers to build applications like this.

Let me demonstrate this point by showing you some odd behavior exhibited by Microsoft's own WordPad. Start WordPad, use the View menu to turn off the window's Toolbar, and click the Close box to terminate WordPad. Now, start WordPad again and see that its window is displayed without the Toolbar. You see that WordPad saves its view settings in the Registry when the user closes the window.

Now, go back to the View menu and turn on the window's Toolbar but do not close the window by clicking on its Close box. Instead, go to the system's Taskbar and log off the system. The system will send a WM_QUERYENDSESSION message followed by a WM_ENDSESSION to WordPad's window. The WordPad process is terminated, and its window is destroyed. Now, log back into the system and invoke WordPad. What do you expect to see in WordPad's window? Should we see its Toolbar?

In my opinion, we should see the Toolbar because it was visible the last time we used WordPad. However, when you run WordPad, you'll see that the Toolbar is not visible because WordPad was terminated when we logged off. This means that its threads did not have the opportunity to update its Registry settings to reflect the current user's settings. WordPad is just one example of an application that behaves this way. Many other applications do not update their settings when the session is terminating. I recommend that you not follow the advice of Microsoft's documentation for the WM_ENDSESSION message but that you destroy your window and terminate your application appropriately. The skeleton code for doing just this follows:

```
BOOL Cls_OnQueryEndSession (HWND hwnd) {

    BOOL fOKToEndSession = TRUE;

    if (g_fIsDataUnsaved) {

        // Present message box
        int n = MessageBox(hwnd, "Do you want to save changes?",
            "Application caption", MB_YESNOCANCEL | MB_ICONWARNING);

        if (n == IDYES) {
            .
            .
            .
            // Present a file save dialog box here
        }

        if (n == IDCANCEL)
            fOKToEndSession = FALSE;
    }

    return(fOKToEndSession);
}


////////////////////////////////////////////////////////////////////////////


void Cls_OnEndSession (HWND hwnd, BOOL fEnding) {

    if (fEnding) {

        // If the session is really ending, explicitly destroy the window.
        DestroyWindow(hwnd);

        // DestroyWindow sends WM_DESTROY and WM_NCDESTROY messages.
    }
}


////////////////////////////////////////////////////////////////////////////


void Cls_OnDestroy (HWND hwnd) {
```

```
    // The main window is being destroyed; signal the message loop to terminate
    // so that the thread and process terminate.
    PostQuitMessage(0);
}


///////////////////////////////////////////////////////////////////////////////


void Cls_OnClose (HWND hwnd) {

    // We handle WM_CLOSE the same way we would handle a logoff or shutdown.
    BOOL fOKToClose = Cls_OnQueryEndSession(hwnd);
    Cls_OnEndSession(hwnd, fOKToClose);
}
```

The preceding set of message cracker functions are demonstrated in the Voyeur application discussed in the next section. You can find them in the **Voyeur.C** source code file.

The Voyeur Application

The Voyeur application (**Voyeur.EXE**), shown in Listings 1.1-1.4, (starting on page 76) demonstrates the following concepts, which are discussed in this chapter:

- How to create a window procedure using the message crackers and to register a window class.
- How to create a single instance of this window.
- How to retrieve information about a window and its class using the various functions discussed throughout this chapter.
- How to terminate an application properly, even if the system is shutting down.

When you invoke the application, the main application window shown in Figure 1.3 appears. Voyeur's client area shows all the information associated with a window on the screen. The user instructs Voyeur to begin peering into windows by clicking the secondary mouse button within its client area, dragging the mouse over a window, and then releasing the mouse button.

Figure 1.3 *The Voyeur starting window.*

Clicking the secondary mouse button puts Voyeur in the background causing other windows to rise to the top. In addition, Voyeur changes the mouse cursor into a pair of eyes that can be positioned anywhere on the screen. When the cursor enters a window, a frame is drawn around the window. After you select a window to examine, Voyeur updates its client area with information about the selected window. Voyeur also forces itself to the top of the screen so that you have a clear view of Voyeur without having to move any windows out of the way.

Figure 1.4 shows Voyeur in action. In this example, Voyeur is displaying the information for the Windows 95 Taskbar. For convenience, Voyeur interprets the class styles, window styles, and extended window styles—displaying each style's text name. The actual hexadecimal value of the styles is also given. Also, the class extra bytes, window extra bytes, and window properties are shown in Figure 1.4.

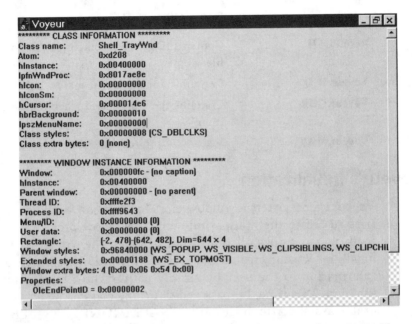

Figure 1.4 *Voyeur displaying information for the Windows 95 Taskbar.*

Table 1.11 describes the files used to create this application.

Table 1.11 *Files used to build the Voyeur Application.*

File	Description
Voyeur.C	Contains WinMain and main window class's window procedure and message cracker functions.
VoyHelp.C	Contains helper functions that retrieve information about a window instance and its class. Puts the resulting string in the edit window.
Voyeur.RC	Contains dialog box template for main application window and its icons.

continued...

File	Description
Resource.H	Contains ID for all resources in the **Voyeur.RC** file
Voyeur.ICO	Contains the icon for the main window.
Voyeur.CUR	Contains the cursor used when mouse capture is on.
Voyeur.MAK	Visual C++ project makefile.

Voyeur's Initialization

Voyeur first registers a window class for its main window and then tries to create the main window. The window procedure for the main window does all its initialization in the Voyeur_OnCreate handling. Voyeur creates the edit child window that will display information to the user by simply calling the CreateWindowEx function. This time, I'll pass "edit" for the class name and use several class-specific styles like ES_READONLY, ES_LEFT, and ES_MULTILINE. Once the edit window has been created, the EM_SETTABSTOPS message is sent to the edit window so that the contents of the edit window looks nicer. It's a good idea to halt Voyeur's main window creation if its edit child window cannot be created. In this case, WinMain would see NULL returned from the CreateWindowEx call and terminate the program.

Notice that I create the edit window with a width and height of 0 (zero) pixels. I can do this because I always resize the edit window when the main application window's window procedure receives a WM_SIZE message (Voyeur_OnSize), which will come shortly after the WM_CREATE message.

Peering into Windows

Voyeur allows you to select a window after you click the secondary mouse button over the main window's client area. Because the edit child window covers Voyeur's entire client area, the main window's window procedure will never receive a WM_RBUTTONDOWN message; the message is sent to the edit window instead. However, the system does send a WM_PARENTNOTIFY message to the main window when the user clicks the mouse button over the edit window. So, the

main window's window procedure traps the WM_PARENTNOTIFY
message instead of the WM_RBUTTONDOWN message.

```
void Voyeur_OnParentNotify (HWND hwnd, UINT msg, HWND hwndChild, int idChild) {

    switch (msg) {

    case WM_RBUTTONDOWN:
        // When the user clicks the secondary mouse button over the edit
        // window, the system notifies the parent window by sending the
        // WM_PARENTNOTIFY message. Once here, we enter "peer" mode.

        // Send Voyeur's window to the back of the window manager's list.
        // This causes any windows that are overlapped by Voyeur to become
        // visible, allowing the user to peer into these windows.
        SetWindowPos(hwnd, HWND_BOTTOM, 0, 0, 0, 0, SWP_NOMOVE | SWP_NOSIZE);

        // Force all mouse messages to come to this window.
        SetCapture(hwnd);

        // Change the mouse cursor to eyes to give the user a visual indication
        // that Voyeur is "peering."
        SetCursor(LoadCursor(GetWindowInstance(hwnd),
        MAKEINTRESOURCE(IDC_EYES)));

        // Set the window handle of the last viewed window to NULL.
        adgSETWINDOWLONG(hwnd, VOYEUR_WNDEXTRABYTES, hwndLastSubject, NULL);
        break;
    }
}
```

First, we check if the reason that we are being notified is because
the user clicked the secondary mouse button. If it is, we then move
our window behind all other windows by calling SetWindowPos,
passing HWND_BOTTOM as the second parameter. This allows any
windows originally covered by Voyeur to appear in front of it. This
feature allows us to access windows that we might not otherwise be
able to pass the mouse cursor over.

Windows maintains a list of all windows in the system. This is
called the window manager's list. In addition to width and height, a
window also has a position that describes how close it is to the
"top" of the screen. This front-to-back position is called the window's z-order, named for the z-axis of a three-dimensional coordinate system. The topmost window on the screen is the one at the
top of the window manager's list. When painting the screen,
Windows uses the z-order to clip display output. This guarantees

that windows closer to the top of the window manager's list will not be painted over by windows closer to the bottom of the list.

When the user clicks on an application's caption bar, Windows forces that window to the top of the window manager's list and activates the application. When this application's window is moved to the top of the window manager's list, all its child windows and owned pop-up windows (including dialog boxes) are also moved to the top of the list. As you can see, windows can change their positions in this list very easily. Programs can use the SetWindowPos function to alter the z-order maintained by the window manager's list.

Starting with Windows 3.1, Microsoft has added a new extended window style, WS_EX_TOPMOST. Any window created with this style is always positioned in front of any windows that do not have this style. This style is most useful for things like keeping the Windows Help engine always visible—when the user switches back to the application, the window containing the help text will remain unobscured. Of course, Windows guarantees that any children and owned pop-ups of a window containing the WS_EX_TOPMOST style are on top of the window even if they, themselves, do not have the WS_EX_TOPMOST style specified.[24]

The only way to change the topmost status of a window is by using the SetWindowPos function. This function can change a window's z-order position and will set or reset the WS_EX_TOPMOST flag in the window's extended styles. You cannot alter a window's topmost status by getting the window's current extended styles with GetWindowLong, toggling the WS_EX_TOPMOST bit and then setting the new styles back with SetWindowLong. Windows simply ignores your request if you attempt to do so.

---

[24]At a Windows 3.1 conference, one of the speakers stated that this new feature will probably be the most misused feature of 3.1—you should use this feature only when it adds value to your application. Another option is to let users decide how they wish to use your application—the Windows Help application has a menu item that allows the user to determine whether or not to make the Help window a topmost window.

The second parameter to SetWindowPos is used to change the z-order of the window. Normally, this parameter indicates the handle of the window behind which this window should be positioned. However, several new identifiers have been defined in **WinUser.H** that can be passed as the second parameter to SetWindowPos to alter a window's position in the z-order and the window's topmost status. The list appears in Table 1.12.

Table 1.12 *SetWindowPos identifiers that change a window's z-order.*

Windows.H identifier	Value	Meaning
HWND_TOP	NULL	If the window is a topmost window, it is positioned above all topmost windows. If the window is a non-topmost window, it is positioned above all non-topmost windows.
HWND_BOTTOM	1	Positions the window at the bottom of the z-order. If the window was a topmost window, it loses its topmost status.
HWND_TOPMOST	–1	Changes the window's status, making it a topmost window.
HWND_NOTOPMOST	–2	Places the window above all non-topmost windows. If the window is a topmost window, it is changed to a non-topmost window.

By using two of the preceding identifiers, we can position Voyeur's window at the top or bottom of the window manager's list. The line

```
SetWindowPos(hwnd, HWND_BOTTOM, 0, 0, 0, 0, SWP_NOMOVE | SWP_NOSIZE);
```

in Voyeur_OnParentNotify causes Voyeur's main window and edit window to be positioned at the bottom of the window manager's list. Any other application's windows originally behind Voyeur will be closer to the top of the screen and will automatically be sent

WM_NCPAINT and WM_PAINT messages causing them to redraw. (The SWP_NOMOVE and SWP_NOSIZE flags cause the position and size parameters to be ignored.)

After Voyeur's window has been positioned behind all other windows, Voyeur_OnParentNotify tells Windows that all mouse messages should be sent to theVoyeur_WndProc function no matter where the mouse is located on the screen. Then we load the "eyes" cursor from the resource section of the program file and make it the mouse cursor. This gives the user a visual indication that Voyeur is in "peer" mode.

Finally, we need to remember the window handle of the window that the mouse most recently passed over. I decided to use the technique described in Appendix A for manipulating window extra bytes. So, I need to create a data structure that has a handle to a window as a member[25] and will set and get these extra byte values using the macros discussed in Appendix A:

```
typedef struct {
    HWND hwndLastSubject;          // Handle for last peered window
} VOYEUR_WNDEXTRABYTES;
.
.
.
adgGETWINDOWLONG(hwnd, VOYEUR_WNDEXTRABYTES, hwndLastSubject);
adgSETWINDOWLONG(hwnd, VOYEUR_WNDEXTRABYTES, hwndLastSubject, NULL);
```

When the parent window receives the WM_PARENTNOTIFY message, I initialize these extra bytes to NULL. This tells Voyeur that the mouse has not yet passed over a window. The hwndLastSubject value contains the handle of the window that Voyeur was just looking at. This value is used in the Voyeur_OnMouseMove and Voyeur_OnRButtonUp functions to show or hide the frame drawn around the window under the mouse cursor.

---

[25]I will not use the GWL_USERDATA for this variable because I am implementing this window class myself. Always remember to leave the GWL_USERDATA bytes for a user of your class. If you are implementing the class yourself, you can always explicitly set aside the necessary number of window extra bytes.

Selecting a Window

By default, no window has mouse capture. This means that the system sends mouse messages to the window that is under the mouse cursor when the message occurs. However, it's possible for a window to "steal" all the mouse messages from other windows by calling the SetCapture function:

```
HWND SetCapture(HWND hwnd);
```

When a thread calls SetCapture, it tells the system that all mouse messages should be directed to the specified window regardless of where the mouse is on the screen and which window is under the mouse cursor. Because the Voyeur_OnParentNotify function calls SetCapture, passing its own window as the parameter to SetCapture, Windows will direct all mouse messages (WM_RBUTTONDOWN, WM_RBUTTONUP, WM_RBUTTONDBLCLK, WM_MOUSEMOVE, and so on) to Voyeur's main window.

Once capture is set, Voyeur's window will receive all WM_MOUSEMOVE messages. Each time it gets one, it must determine which window is under the mouse cursor and update its display to reflect the class and window information for this window. This is done in Voyeur_OnMouseMove.

To determine which window is under the mouse cursor, we need to get the location of the mouse cursor on the screen. We cannot use the values in Voyeur_OnMouseMove's x and y parameters because this coordinate is relative to Voyeur's client area. So, I used the GetMessagePos function:

```
DWORD GetMessagePos(VOID);
```

This function returns the location of the mouse cursor for the message most recently pulled from the thread's message queue. The LOWORD of the return value is the x-coordinate and the HIWORD contains the y-coordinate. These coordinates are always relative to the screen. We can then determine the handle of the window that is under the mouse cursor using the following code:

```
DWORD dwMousePos = GetMessagePos();
POINT ptMouse;
HWND hwndSubject;
 .
 .
 .
// Get the handle of the window under the mouse cursor.
ptMouse.x = LOWORD(dwMousePos);
ptMouse.y = HIWORD(dwMousePos);
hwndSubject = WindowFromPoint(ptMouse);
```

Next, we check to see if the thread that created the window is the same as Voyeur's thread. This prevents the viewing of window and class information for any windows created by Voyeur itself:

```
// If window is created by Voyeur, ignore it.
if (GetWindowThreadProcessId(hwndSubject, NULL) == GetCurrentThreadId())
    return;
```

If the window happens to be the same as our last subject, then the information in the edit window will be the same as before and no further actions need to be taken. Otherwise, we remove the frame around the previous window and draw a frame around our new window. Both actions are done by calling VoyHelp_DrawWindow-Frame.

```
// If our new subject is the same as our last subject, there is no need to
// update our display.
if (hwndLastSubject == hwndSubject)
   return;

// Remove the frame, if any, around the currently selected window.
if (hwndLastSubject != NULL)
    VoyHelp_DrawWindowFrame(hwndLastSubject);

// Draw a frame around our new window.
VoyHelp_DrawWindowFrame(hwndSubject);
```

Finally, VoyHelp_UpdateWindowInfo is called to fill the edit window with information relevant to our new subject window. Also, we save our new subject window handle in the window extra bytes:

```
// Update the window's information. This function is in the VoyHelp.C
// source file.
VoyHelp_UpdateWindowInfo(GetDlgItem(hwnd, IDC_WNDINFO), hwndSubject);

// Save the handle to the most recent subject window.
adgSETWINDOWLONG(hwnd, VOYEUR_WNDEXTRABYTES, hwndLastSubject, hwndSubject);
```

After Selecting a Window

You complete window selection by releasing the secondary mouse button. When Voyeur gets a WM_RBUTTONUP message, the Voyeur_OnRButtonUp function is called. This function is very small—all it does is release mouse capture:

```
void Voyeur_OnRButtonUp (HWND hwnd, int x, int y, UINT keyFlags) {

   // We must have mouse capture or we will never get here because the edit
   // child window always covers our entire client area.

   // Allow other windows to receive mouse messages.
   ReleaseCapture();
}
```

When mouse capture is released, the system sends the window the new WM_ONCAPTURECHANGED message:

```
// I have defined message cracker macros for the WM_CAPTURECHANGED message
// because Microsoft did not do this in the WindowsX.H header file.

/* void Cls_OnCaptureChanged(HWND hwnd, HWND hwndNewCapture) */
#define HANDLE_WM_CAPTURECHANGED(hwnd, wParam, lParam, fn) \
   ((fn)((hwnd), (HWND)(wParam)), 0L)
#define FORWARD_WM_CAPTURECHANGED(hwnd, hwndNewCapture, fn) \
   (void)(fn)((hwnd), WM_CAPTURECHANGED, (WPARAM)(HWND)(hwndNewCapture), 0L)


void Voyeur_OnCaptureChanged (HWND hwnd, HWND hwndNewCapture) {

   HWND hwndLastSubject = (HWND)
   adgGETWINDOWLONG(hwnd, VOYEUR_WNDEXTRABYTES, hwndLastSubject);

   // If we don't "peer" into a window, we don't have to remove its
   // surrounding frame.
   if (hwndLastSubject != NULL)
      VoyHelp_DrawWindowFrame(hwndLastSubject);

   // Force Voyeur to appear on top of all other windows.
   BringWindowToTop(hwnd);
}
```

Unfortunately, Microsoft forgot to add message cracker macros for the WM_CAPTURECHANGED message so I have created them and put them inside the **Voyeur.C** file myself. You can steal these macros for your own application if you need to process this message. The Voyeur_OnCaptureChanged function removes any frame around the most recently passed-over window and releases the mouse capture.[26]

The last line:

```
BringWindowToTop(hwnd);
```

tells Windows to bring Voyeur and its edit window back to the top of the window manager's list. Remember that the Voyeur_OnParent-Notify function called SetWindowPos to position Voyeur's main window to the back of the window manager's list. Instead of calling BringWindowToTop, we could have called

```
SetWindowPos(hwnd, HWND_TOP, 0, 0, 0, 0, SWP_NOMOVE | SWP_NOSIZE);
```

to accomplish the same operation. In fact, this is exactly how Microsoft has implemented the BringWindowToTop function internally.

Recall that the Voyeur_OnParentNotify function called the SetCursor function in order to change the mouse cursor to a pair of eyes. However, the Voyeur_OnRButtonUp function does not call SetCursor to put the mouse cursor back to the normal arrow. Here is why I do not have to explicitly set the mouse cursor shape back to an arrow. If the mouse has not been captured, Windows sends a WM_SETCURSOR message to the window procedure associated with the window under the mouse cursor whenever the mouse moves within the window. The DefWindowProc function automatically changes the mouse cursor back to the cursor selected when the window's class was registered. For this reason, the mouse cursor will not maintain the shape of the eyes once we call the ReleaseCapture function. The system does not send WM_SETCURSOR messages when a window has captured the mouse.

Drawing a Frame Around the Window

Voyeur's VoyHelp_DrawWindowFrame function draws a frame around any window whose handle is passed to it. When called a second time for a given window, this function removes the frame.

---

[26]The WM_CAPTURECHANGED message is not supported on Windows NT 3.51 but will be supported on future versions. For this reason, I manually send a WM_CAPTURECHANGED message to Voyeur's main window inside the Voyeur_OnRButtonUp function.

The main requirement for drawing a frame around a window is that the frame must be visible. This may sound obvious, but in a graphical environment, where a window can be any color or combination of colors, what color do you choose? The best answer is whatever color the window is not. In other words, the frame should be drawn in the inverse color of the screen. This choice guarantees that the frame will be visible and has an added advantage for us. If we draw the frame again in the same location, the screen will be restored to its original colors, which has the effect of removing the frame. So, only one function is needed to draw and remove the window's frame.

The code for VoyHelp_DrawWindowFrame looks like this:

```
// This function draws a frame around a given window. The frame is drawn in
// the inverse screen color, which allows a second call to this function to
// restore the screen display to its original appearance.
void VoyHelp_DrawWindowFrame (HWND hwndSubject) {

    HDC hdc;
    RECT rc;
    HPEN hpen;

    // Retrieve location of window on screen
    GetWindowRect(hwndSubject, &rc);

    // Get a device context that allows us to write anywhere within the window.
    // NOTE: GetDC would allow us to write only in the window's client area.
    hdc = GetWindowDC(hwndSubject);

    // Save the original device context attributes.
    SaveDC(hdc);

    // To guarantee that the frame will be visible, tell Windows to draw the
    // frame using the inverse screen color.
    SetROP2(hdc, R2_NOT);

    // Create a pen that is 3 times the width of a nonsizeable border. The
    // color will not be used to draw the frame, so its value could be
    // anything. PS_INSIDEFRAME tells windows that the entire frame should be
    // enclosed within the window.
    hpen = CreatePen(PS_INSIDEFRAME, 3 * GetSystemMetrics(SM_CXBORDER),
        RGB(0, 0, 0));
    SelectObject(hdc, hpen);

    // We must select a NULL brush so that the contents of the window will not
    // be overwritten.
    SelectObject(hdc, GetStockObject(NULL_BRUSH));

    // Draw the frame. Because the device context is relative to the window,
    // the left-top corner is (0, 0) and the right-bottom corner is (width of
```

```
// window, height of window).
Rectangle(hdc, 0, 0, rc.right - rc.left, rc.bottom - rc.top);

// Restore the original attributes and release the device context.
RestoreDC(hdc, -1);
ReleaseDC(hwndSubject, hdc);

// We can destroy the pen only AFTER we have restored the DC because the DC
// must have valid objects selected into it at all times.
DeleteObject(hpen);
}
```

This function first retrieves the rectangle (in screen coordinates) of the desired window. Next, we obtain a device context for the entire window using the GetWindowDC function. With the device context returned from this function, Windows gives us permission to write anywhere within the area occupied by the window. If we had used the GetDC function, Windows would allow us to only write in the client area of the window.

Before drawing a rectangle around the window, we must prepare the device context by specifying that drawing with the pen should yield the inverse of the screen color. This is done by setting the ROP2 value to R2_NOT. Next, we create a thick pen so that our frame will be seen easily. We specify a pen style of PS_INSIDE-FRAME so that Windows will draw the frame within the window's area. The width of the pen is specified as three times the width of a nonsizeable window border. This means that it should look fine on any monitor with any resolution.

Let's say that you were running Windows with a screen resolution of 10,000 × 10,000 pixels (don't we wish?!). Drawing a 1-pixel-high line across the screen will probably go completely unnoticed. However, Microsoft guarantees that the width of a nonsizeable window border will be visible, regardless of the resolution at which the user is running Windows. So, basing the width of the frame surrounding the window on the nonsizeable window border value guarantees that our frame will be visible.

The last parameter to the CreatePen function specifies the pen's color. Because the ROP2 value is set to R2_NOT, the pen's color won't actually be used when the frame is drawn. For this reason the color may be any value. I arbitrarily selected black.

Because the Rectangle function fills the rectangle with the brush currently selected in the device context, we must select a

NULL_BRUSH. This selection will let us draw a frame without obscuring the remaining contents of the window.

We draw the frame by calling Rectangle. Because the coordinates are relative to the device context, the top-left corner of the rectangle is point (0, 0). The lower-right corner is (width of window, height of window).

The remainder of the function releases the device context and deletes the pen. Note that the order of these lines is important. A device context must have handles to existing objects within it at all times. If we delete the pen before releasing the device context, an error occurs. Once the device context is released, the pen may be deleted.

Setting the Class and Window Information

VoyHelp_SetClassInfo (in **VoyHelp.C**) accepts an address to a string buffer and a handle to the window whose class information is to be appended to the buffer. GetClassName is used to obtain the name of the class of the window. Once we have the class name, the remaining window class information is obtained by calling the GetClassWord and GetClassLong functions. Note that it would have been more convenient to call the GetClassInfoEx function here instead. However we cannot because, as stated earlier in this chapter, the GetClassInfoEx function cannot be used to obtain information about a class registered by a thread in another process.

The remainder of the VoyHelp_SetClassInfo function appends the strings to the end of the string buffer. Because all this information will ultimately be placed into the edit window, the repainting of Voyeur's client area is the responsibility of the edit window. This way, our application never has to worry about processing WM_ PAINT messages.

Appending the "Extra bytes:" information is as simple as calling the VoyHelp_AppendExtraBytes function in **VoyHelp.C**. This function is used for both class extra bytes and window extra bytes. If you are interested in the class extra bytes, pass GCL_CBCLS-EXTRA for the last parameter and pass GCL_CBWNDEXTRA for the window instance's extra bytes. Unfortunately, retrieving the extra byte values is not as straightforward as we might like. The problem is that there is not a GetClassByte function. So, if a class has 3 class extra bytes, calling

```
GetClassWord(hwnd, 2);
```

causes a problem because this function actually will retrieve the value of the third and fourth extra bytes simultaneously. But, because the class doesn't have a fourth extra byte, the system complains when we make this call. Instead, we must do some slightly fancy footwork to make sure that we never request the value of an extra byte that doesn't exist. To solve this problem, we must call GetClassWord repeatedly, incrementing the offset by one each time and appending the value in the LOBYTE or HIBYTE of each returned word to the string. See the source code for the details.

VoyHelp_SetWindowInfo is similar to VoyHelp_SetClassInfo. Most of its information is retrieved by the GetWindowWord and GetWindowLong functions. GetWindowText gets the captions of the window (and its parent, if it exists).[27] The window's thread ID and process ID are obtained by calling GetWindowThreadProcessId, and the window's location and dimensions are determined by calling GetWindowRect.

Appending the window "Extra bytes:" information is as simple as calling the VoyHelp_AppendExtraBytes function, passing GCL_CBWNDEXTRA for the third parameter. When the "Wnd styles:" information is being appended, only the top 16 bits of the value returned by

```
GetWindowLong(hwnd, GWL_STYLE);
```

[27]Here is an interesting note about the GetWindowText function: this function sends a WM_GETTEXT message to the desired window only if that window is created by a thread (any thread) in the calling process. When you call GetWindowText passing the handle to a window created by a thread in another process, the system internally calls that window's DefWindowProc directly in order to get the window's text. This code is executed by the calling thread and not by the thread that created the window. Because GetWindowText works this way, you should avoid intercepting the WM_GETTEXT message in your own window procedures or at least have some default that DefWindowProc can return.

Microsoft implemented GetWindowText like this so that a thread can get a window's text even if the thread that created the window is suspended or hung. For example, the Taskbar must always be able to show a button with the window's caption.

are examined. Remember, that the bottom 16 bits are window-class specific. Voyeur cannot determine the meaning of these bits for the selected window.

Appending the Style Information

Because Voyeur works with three different types of style bits—class styles, window styles, and extended window styles—it's useful to have one function that converts style bits into strings.

VoyHelp_AppendStyleStrings accepts the pointer to a string buffer, a pointer to an array of STYLELIST structures, and a DWORD representing the style bits to be checked. Each STYLELIST structure contains a value for the style and a text string that should appear if that style bit is on. These style arrays are declared as follows:

```
typedef struct {
    DWORD dwID;
    LPTSTR szName;
} STYLELIST;


#ifdef UNICODE
#define TABLEENTRY(Value)    Value, L#Value
#else
#define TABLEENTRY(Value)    Value, #Value
#endif
const STYLELIST g_szClassStyles[] = {
    TABLEENTRY(CS_VREDRAW),
    TABLEENTRY(CS_HREDRAW),
        .
        .
        .
    { 0,    NULL   }
};

const STYLELIST g_szWindowStyles[] = {
    TABLEENTRY(WS_POPUP),
    TABLEENTRY(WS_CHILD),
        .
        .
        .
    { 0, NULL }
};

const STYLELIST g_szExtWindowStyles[] = {
    TABLEENTRY(WS_EX_DLGMODALFRAME),
    TABLEENTRY(WS_EX_NOPARENTNOTIFY),
```

```
        .
        .
        .
    { 0, NULL }
};
```

This method is very general and easily expanded to accommodate styles that future versions of Windows might offer. Unfortunately, it does have some drawbacks. For example, an overlapped window is denoted by having no window style bits on. Voyeur will simply not append a string for this window's style instead of saying "WS_OVER-LAPPED". Styles represented by multiple bits are not displayed. For example, a window created with the WS_CAPTION style will be represented by "WS_BORDER" and "WS_DLGFRAME" in the edit window instead of "WS_CAPTION." Finally, Voyeur cannot determine if bit 17 of the window style's DWORD means WS_TABSTOP or WS_MAXIMIZEBOX. This is also true for bit 18, WS_GROUP or WS_MINIMIZEBOX. For this reason, Voyeur displays both styles when applicable.

Voyeur.ICO

Listing 1.1 *Voyeur.C*

```
/*********************************************************************
Module name: Voyeur.C
Written by: Jeffrey Richter
Notices: Copyright (c) 1995 Jeffrey Richter
Purpose: Displays class and window information for a selected window.
*********************************************************************/


#include "..\Win95ADG.h"        /* See Appendix A for details */
#include <windows.h>
#include <windowsx.h>
#pragma warning(disable: 4001)   /* Single-line comment */
#include <tchar.h>
#include "Resource.h"


///////////////////////////////////////////////////////////////////


// Prototype of function contained in VoyHelp.C source file.
void VoyHelp_DrawWindowFrame (HWND hwndSubject);
void VoyHelp_UpdateWindowInfo (HWND hwndEdit, HWND hwndSubject);
```

```
//////////////////////////////////////////////////////////////////


// The following structure is for the window's extra bytes.
// For more information, see the macros presented in Appendix A.
typedef struct {
   HWND hwndLastSubject;       // Handle for last peered window.
} VOYEUR_WNDEXTRABYTES;



//////////////////////////////////////////////////////////////////



// The ID given to the edit child window.
#define IDC_WNDINFO        1000



//////////////////////////////////////////////////////////////////


BOOL Voyeur_OnCreate (HWND hwnd, LPCREATESTRUCT lpCreateStruct) {

   // Create the edit control that fills the client area.
   HWND hwndEdit = CreateWindowEx(0, __TEXT("EDIT"),
      __TEXT("Click and drag the right mouse button to select a window."),
      WS_CHILD | WS_HSCROLL | WS_VSCROLL | WS_VISIBLE | ES_AUTOHSCROLL |
      ES_AUTOVSCROLL | ES_LEFT | ES_MULTILINE | ES_READONLY,
      0, 0, 0, 0, hwnd, (HMENU) IDC_WNDINFO, GetWindowInstance(hwnd), NULL);

   adgASSERT(IsWindow(hwndEdit));
   if (hwndEdit != NULL) {

      // Set a tab stop at 17 characters in. There are 4 horizontal dialog
      // box units per character.
      UINT uTabStop = 4 * 17;
      Edit_SetTabStops(hwndEdit, 1, &uTabStop);
   }

   // When processing the WM_CREATE message, a return value of -1 indicates
   // that the window could not be created. However, when using message
   // crackers, the return value from the *_OnCreate function should be FALSE
   // to indicate failure and TRUE to indicate success. The message cracker
   // macro translates the cracker function's return value into a return value
   // for the system. In other words, if we return FALSE from this function,
   // the system gets -1, and if we return TRUE from this function, the system
   // gets 0.
   return(hwndEdit != NULL);   // Return TRUE if edit window created.
}


//////////////////////////////////////////////////////////////////
```

77

```
void Voyeur_OnSize (HWND hwnd, UINT state, int cx, int cy) {

   // When the user resizes the main window, we must resize the edit child.
   SetWindowPos(GetDlgItem(hwnd, IDC_WNDINFO), NULL,
      0, 0, cx, cy, SWP_NOZORDER);
}


/////////////////////////////////////////////////////////////////////////////


void Voyeur_OnParentNotify (HWND hwnd, UINT msg, HWND hwndChild, int idChild) {

   switch (msg) {

      case WM_RBUTTONDOWN:

         // When the user clicks the right mouse button over the edit window,
         // the system notifies the parent window by sending the
         // WM_PARENTNOTIFY message. Once here, we enter "peer" mode.

         // Send Voyeur's window to the back of the window manager's list.
         // This causes any windows that Voyeur overlaps to become
         // visible, allowing these windows to be "peered" into.
         SetWindowPos(hwnd, HWND_BOTTOM, 0, 0, 0, 0, SWP_NOMOVE | SWP_NOSIZE);

         // Force all mouse messages to come to this window.
         SetCapture(hwnd);

         // Change the mouse cursor to eyes. This provides a visual indication
         // to the user that Voyeur is "peering."
         SetCursor(LoadCursor(GetWindowInstance(hwnd),
            MAKEINTRESOURCE(IDC_EYES)));

         // Set the window handle of the last viewed window to NULL.
         adgSETWINDOWLONG(hwnd, VOYEUR_WNDEXTRABYTES, hwndLastSubject, NULL);
         break;
   }
}


/////////////////////////////////////////////////////////////////////////////


void Voyeur_OnMouseMove (HWND hwnd, int x, int y, UINT keyFlags) {

   // We must have mouse capture or we would never get here because the edit
   // child window always covers our entire client area.

   // Get the current mouse position in screen coordinates. NOTE: We cannot
   // use the x and y parameters because they are relative to the window's
   // client area.
   DWORD dwMousePos = GetMessagePos();
   POINT ptMouse;
   HWND hwndSubject;
   HWND hwndLastSubject = (HWND)
```

78

```
    adgGETWINDOWLONG(hwnd, VOYEUR_WNDEXTRABYTES, hwndLastSubject);

    // Get the handle of the window under the mouse cursor.
    ptMouse.x = LOWORD(dwMousePos);
    ptMouse.y = HIWORD(dwMousePos);
    hwndSubject = WindowFromPoint(ptMouse);

    // If the window is created by Voyeur, ignore it.
    if (GetWindowThreadProcessId(hwndSubject, NULL) == GetCurrentThreadId())
      return;

    // If our new subject is the same as our last subject, there is no need to
    // update our display.
    if (hwndLastSubject == hwndSubject)
      return;

    // Remove the frame, if any, around the currently selected window.
    if (hwndLastSubject != NULL)
      VoyHelp_DrawWindowFrame(hwndLastSubject);

    // Draw a frame around our new window.
    VoyHelp_DrawWindowFrame(hwndSubject);

    // Update the window's information. This function is in VoyHelp.C.
    VoyHelp_UpdateWindowInfo(GetDlgItem(hwnd, IDC_WNDINFO), hwndSubject);

    // Save the handle to the most recent subject window.
    adgSETWINDOWLONG(hwnd, VOYEUR_WNDEXTRABYTES, hwndLastSubject, hwndSubject);
}


//////////////////////////////////////////////////////////////////////////////


void Voyeur_OnCaptureChanged (HWND hwnd, HWND hwndNewCapture) {

    HWND hwndLastSubject = (HWND)
    adgGETWINDOWLONG(hwnd, VOYEUR_WNDEXTRABYTES, hwndLastSubject);

    // If we don't "peer" into a window, we don't have to remove its
    // surrounding frame.
    if (hwndLastSubject != NULL) {
      VoyHelp_DrawWindowFrame(hwndLastSubject);

      // Force Voyeur to appear on top of all other windows.
      BringWindowToTop(hwnd);
    }

    adgSETWINDOWLONG(hwnd, VOYEUR_WNDEXTRABYTES, hwndLastSubject, NULL);
}


//////////////////////////////////////////////////////////////////////////////
```

```
void Voyeur_OnRButtonUp (HWND hwnd, int x, int y, UINT keyFlags) {

    // We must have mouse capture or we would never get here because the edit
    // child window always covers our entire client area.

    // Allow other windows to receive mouse messages.
    ReleaseCapture();

#ifndef WINDOWSNT_COMPATIBILITY

    // Because Windows NT 3.51 doesn't support the new WM_CAPTURECHANGED
    // message, I must explicitly send this message to Voyeur's main window.
    // Unfortunately, this means that Voyeur's main window will receive this
    // message twice when running under Windows 95. I have taken care to
    // ensure that the code in Voyeur_OnCaptureChanged works with no ill side
    // effects if it is called twice. When future versions of Windows NT
    // support the WM_CAPTURECHANGED message, the following line should be
    // removed.
    FORWARD_WM_CAPTURECHANGED(hwnd, NULL, SendMessage);
#endif
}


/////////////////////////////////////////////////////////////////////////////



BOOL Voyeur_OnQueryEndSession (HWND hwnd) {

    // For demonstration purposes, pretend that there is unsaved data.
    BOOL fIsDataUnsaved = TRUE;
    BOOL fOKToEndSession = TRUE;

    if (fIsDataUnsaved) {

        // Present message box.
        int n = MessageBox(hwnd, __TEXT("Do you want to save changes?"),
           __TEXT("Voyeur - Example technique for proper shutdown"),
           MB_YESNOCANCEL | MB_ICONWARNING);

        if (n == IDYES) {

            // You would present a File Save dialog box here.
        }

        if (n == IDCANCEL)
            fOKToEndSession = FALSE;
    }

    return(fOKToEndSession);
}


/////////////////////////////////////////////////////////////////////////////
```

```
void Voyeur_OnEndSession (HWND hwnd, BOOL fEnding) {

    if (fEnding) {

        // If the session is really ending, explicitly destroy the window.
        DestroyWindow(hwnd);

        // DestroyWindow will send WM_DESTROY and WM_NCDESTROY messages.
    }
}


///////////////////////////////////////////////////////////////////////////


void Voyeur_OnDestroy (HWND hwnd) {

    // The system will automatically destroy the edit child window.

    // The main window is being destroyed; signal the message loop to terminate
    // so that the thread and process terminate.
    PostQuitMessage(0);
}


///////////////////////////////////////////////////////////////////////////


void Voyeur_OnClose (HWND hwnd) {

    // We handle WM_CLOSE the same way we would handle a logoff or shutdown.
    BOOL fOKToClose = Voyeur_OnQueryEndSession(hwnd);
    Voyeur_OnEndSession(hwnd, fOKToClose);
}


///////////////////////////////////////////////////////////////////////////


LRESULT WINAPI Voyeur_WndProc (HWND hwnd, UINT uMsg,
    WPARAM wParam, LPARAM lParam) {

    switch (uMsg) {

        // Standard Windows messages.
        HANDLE_MSG(hwnd, WM_CREATE,         Voyeur_OnCreate);
        HANDLE_MSG(hwnd, WM_SIZE,           Voyeur_OnSize);
        HANDLE_MSG(hwnd, WM_PARENTNOTIFY,   Voyeur_OnParentNotify);
        HANDLE_MSG(hwnd, WM_MOUSEMOVE,      Voyeur_OnMouseMove);
        HANDLE_MSG(hwnd, WM_RBUTTONUP,      Voyeur_OnRButtonUp);
        HANDLE_MSG(hwnd, WM_CAPTURECHANGED, Voyeur_OnCaptureChanged);
        HANDLE_MSG(hwnd, WM_CLOSE,          Voyeur_OnClose);
        HANDLE_MSG(hwnd, WM_DESTROY,        Voyeur_OnDestroy);
```

```
      HANDLE_MSG(hwnd, WM_QUERYENDSESSION, Voyeur_OnQueryEndSession);
      HANDLE_MSG(hwnd, WM_ENDSESSION,      Voyeur_OnEndSession);
   }
   return(DefWindowProc(hwnd, uMsg, wParam, lParam));
}


///////////////////////////////////////////////////////////////////////////

int WINAPI WinMain (HINSTANCE hinstExe, HINSTANCE hinstPrev,
   LPSTR lpszCmdLine, int nCmdShow) {

   WNDCLASSEX wc;
   ATOM atomClassNameVoyeur;
   HWND hwndMain;
   MSG msg;

   adgWARNIFUNICODEUNDERWIN95();

   adgINITSTRUCT(wc, TRUE);
   wc.lpfnWndProc   = Voyeur_WndProc;
   wc.cbWndExtra    = sizeof(VOYEUR_WNDEXTRABYTES);
   wc.hInstance     = hinstExe;
   wc.hIcon         = LoadIcon(hinstExe, MAKEINTRESOURCE(IDI_VOYEUR));
   wc.hCursor       = LoadCursor(NULL, IDC_ARROW);
   wc.lpszClassName = __TEXT("Voyeur");
   wc.hIconSm       = wc.hIcon;

   atomClassNameVoyeur = RegisterClassEx(&wc);
   adgASSERT(atomClassNameVoyeur != INVALID_ATOM);
   if (atomClassNameVoyeur == INVALID_ATOM)
      return(0);

   hwndMain = CreateWindowEx(0, MAKEINTATOM(atomClassNameVoyeur),
      __TEXT("Voyeur"), WS_OVERLAPPEDWINDOW | WS_VISIBLE,
      CW_USEDEFAULT, SW_SHOW,  // NOTE: Win32 doc bug: y is ShowWindow
                               // identifier when x is CW_USEDEFAULT.
      CW_USEDEFAULT, 0,        // The system sets width and height.
      NULL, NULL, hinstExe, NULL);

   adgASSERT(IsWindow(hwndMain));
   if (IsWindow(hwndMain)) {

      // Continue to loop until a WM_QUIT message comes out of the queue.
      while (GetMessage(&msg, NULL, 0, 0)) {

         TranslateMessage(&msg);
         DispatchMessage(&msg);
      }
   }

   UnregisterClass(MAKEINTATOM(atomClassNameVoyeur), hinstExe);
```

```
   // The message box has no owner because the main window
   // has been destroyed.
   adgMB(__TEXT("Voyeur terminated."));

   return(0);
}



//////////////////////////////// End of File ////////////////////////////////
```

Listing 1.2 *VoyHelp.C*

```
/**************************************************************************
Module name: VoyHelp.c
Written by: Jeffrey Richter
Notices: Copyright (c) 1995 Jeffrey Richter
Purpose: Voyeur helper functions.
**************************************************************************/


#include "..\Win95ADG.h"          /* See Appendix A for details */
#include <windows.h>
#include <windowsx.h>
#pragma warning(disable: 4001)    /* Single-line comment */
#include <tchar.h>


/////////////////////////////////////////////////////////////////////////////


// This function draws a frame around a given window. The frame is drawn in
// the inverse screen color, which allows a second call to this function to
// restore the screen display to its original appearance.
void VoyHelp_DrawWindowFrame (HWND hwndSubject) {

  HDC hdc;
  RECT rc;
  HPEN hpen;

  // Retrieve location of window on-screen.
  GetWindowRect(hwndSubject, &rc);

  // Get a device context that allows us to write anywhere within the window.
  // NOTE: GetDC would allow us to write only in the window's client area.
  hdc = GetWindowDC(hwndSubject);

  // Save the original device context attributes.
  SaveDC(hdc);
```

```
   // To guarantee that the frame will be visible, tell Windows to draw the
   // frame using the inverse screen color.
   SetROP2(hdc, R2_NOT);

   // Create a pen that is three times the width of a nonsizeable border. The
   // color will not be used to draw the frame, so its value could be
   // anything. PS_INSIDEFRAME tells windows that the entire frame should be
   // enclosed within the window.
   hpen = CreatePen(PS_INSIDEFRAME, 3 * GetSystemMetrics(SM_CXBORDER),
      RGB(0, 0, 0));
   SelectObject(hdc, hpen);

   // We must select a NULL brush so that the contents of the window will not
   // be overwritten.
   SelectObject(hdc, GetStockObject(NULL_BRUSH));

   // Draw the frame. Because the device context is relative to the window,
   // the top-left corner is (0, 0) and the lower right corner is (width of
   // window, height of window).
   Rectangle(hdc, 0, 0, rc.right - rc.left, rc.bottom - rc.top);

   // Restore the original attributes and release the device context.
   RestoreDC(hdc, -1);
   ReleaseDC(hwndSubject, hdc);

   // We can destroy the pen only AFTER we have restored the DC because the DC
   // must have valid objects selected into it at all times.
   DeleteObject(hpen);
}


//////////////////////////////////////////////////////////////////////////


typedef struct {
   DWORD dwID;
   LPTSTR szName;
} STYLELIST;


//////////////////////////////////////////////////////////////////////////


#ifdef UNICODE
#define TABLEENTRY(Value) Value, L#Value
#else
#define TABLEENTRY(Value) Value, #Value
#endif


//////////////////////////////////////////////////////////////////////////


const STYLELIST g_szClassStyles[] = {
   TABLEENTRY(CS_VREDRAW),
```

```
      TABLEENTRY(CS_HREDRAW),
      TABLEENTRY(CS_KEYCVTWINDOW),
      TABLEENTRY(CS_DBLCLKS),
      TABLEENTRY(CS_OWNDC),
      TABLEENTRY(CS_CLASSDC),
      TABLEENTRY(CS_PARENTDC),
      TABLEENTRY(CS_NOKEYCVT),
      TABLEENTRY(CS_NOCLOSE),
      TABLEENTRY(CS_SAVEBITS),
      TABLEENTRY(CS_BYTEALIGNCLIENT),
      TABLEENTRY(CS_BYTEALIGNWINDOW),
      TABLEENTRY(CS_GLOBALCLASS),
      { 0, NULL }
   };

const STYLELIST g_szWindowStyles[] = {
      TABLEENTRY(WS_POPUP),
      TABLEENTRY(WS_CHILD),
      TABLEENTRY(WS_MINIMIZE),
      TABLEENTRY(WS_VISIBLE),
      TABLEENTRY(WS_DISABLED),
      TABLEENTRY(WS_CLIPSIBLINGS),
      TABLEENTRY(WS_CLIPCHILDREN),
      TABLEENTRY(WS_MAXIMIZE),
      TABLEENTRY(WS_BORDER),
      TABLEENTRY(WS_DLGFRAME),
      TABLEENTRY(WS_VSCROLL),
      TABLEENTRY(WS_HSCROLL),
      TABLEENTRY(WS_SYSMENU),
      TABLEENTRY(WS_THICKFRAME),
      TABLEENTRY(WS_GROUP),
      TABLEENTRY(WS_TABSTOP),
      { 0, NULL }
   };

const STYLELIST g_szExWindowStyles[] = {
      TABLEENTRY(WS_EX_DLGMODALFRAME),
      TABLEENTRY(WS_EX_NOPARENTNOTIFY),
      TABLEENTRY(WS_EX_TOPMOST),
      TABLEENTRY(WS_EX_ACCEPTFILES),
      TABLEENTRY(WS_EX_TRANSPARENT),
      { 0, NULL }
   };


///////////////////////////////////////////////////////////////////////



// This function appends the text names of the styles to a string buffer. It
// is used for the class styles, window styles, and extended window styles.
void VoyHelp_AppendStyleStrings (LPTSTR szBuf, const STYLELIST Styles[],
   DWORD dwStyleFlags) {

   int nStyleIndex, nNumStyles = 0;
```

```
    _tcscat(szBuf, __TEXT(" (")); // Start with an open paren.

    for (nStyleIndex = 0; Styles[nStyleIndex].szName != NULL; nStyleIndex++) {

        // If style bit is set, append style text to the string.
        if (Styles[nStyleIndex].dwID & dwStyleFlags) {

            // If this is not the first style, preface the string with ", ".
            if (nNumStyles++ > 0)
                _tcscat(szBuf, __TEXT(", "));

            _tcscat(szBuf, Styles[nStyleIndex].szName);
        }
    }

    // If no style string was appended, say so.
    if (nNumStyles == 0)
        _tcscat(szBuf, __TEXT("none"));

    _tcscat(szBuf, __TEXT(")\r\n")); // End with a close paren.
}


/////////////////////////////////////////////////////////////////////////////


void VoyHelp_AppendExtraBytes (LPTSTR szBuf, HWND hwndSubject,
    int nExtraBytesID) {

    int nExtraByteNum = 0;
    int nExtraBytes = GetClassLong(hwndSubject, nExtraBytesID);
    BYTE bByte;

    WORD (WINAPI* pfnGetWord)(HWND hwnd, int nOffset) =
        (nExtraBytesID == GCL_CBCLSEXTRA) ? GetClassWord : GetWindowWord;

    wsprintf(_tcschr(szBuf, 0), __TEXT("%s extra bytes:\t%u ("),
        (nExtraBytesID == GCL_CBCLSEXTRA) ? __TEXT("Class") : __TEXT("Window"),
        nExtraBytes);

    // Append the extra byte values to the string.
    for (; nExtraByteNum < nExtraBytes; nExtraByteNum++) {

        if (nExtraByteNum == 0) {

            bByte = LOBYTE(pfnGetWord(hwndSubject, nExtraByteNum));
        } else {

            // Put a leading space after the first extra byte.
            _tcscat(szBuf, __TEXT(" "));

            // This is necessary to stay within the extra bytes.
            bByte = HIBYTE(pfnGetWord(hwndSubject, nExtraByteNum - 1));
        }
        wsprintf(_tcschr(szBuf, 0), __TEXT("0x%02x"), bByte);
    }
```

```
   if (nExtraByteNum == 0) {

      // Put none if there are no extra bytes.
      _tcscat(szBuf, __TEXT("none"));
   }

   _tcscat(szBuf, __TEXT(")\r\n"));
}


/////////////////////////////////////////////////////////////////////////


// This appends the class information about the passed-in window
// (hwndSubject) to the passed-in string.
void VoyHelp_SetClassInfo (LPTSTR szBuf, HWND hwndSubject) {

   TCHAR szClassName[100] = { 0 };

   // Put a heading at the beginning of this section.
   _tcscat(szBuf, __TEXT("********* CLASS INFORMATION *********\r\n"));

   // Get the class name of the window.
   GetClassName(hwndSubject, szClassName, adgARRAY_SIZE(szClassName));

   // NOTE: We must use GetClassWord/Long here instead of GetClassInfoEx
   // because GetClassInfoEx does not work for classes that are registered by
   // another process.
   wsprintf(_tcschr(szBuf, 0),
      __TEXT("Class name:\t%s\r\n")
      __TEXT("Atom:\t0x%04x\r\n")
      __TEXT("hInstance:\t0x%08x\r\n")
      __TEXT("lpfnWndProc:\t0x%08x\r\n")
      __TEXT("hIcon:\t0x%08x\r\n")
      __TEXT("hIconSm:\t0x%08x\r\n")
      __TEXT("hCursor:\t0x%08x\r\n")
      __TEXT("hbrBackground:\t0x%08x\r\n")
      __TEXT("lpszMenuName:\t0x%08x\r\n")
      __TEXT("Class styles:\t0x%08x"),
      szClassName,                                    // Class name
      GetClassWord(hwndSubject, GCW_ATOM),            // Atom
      GetClassLong(hwndSubject, GCL_HMODULE),         // hinst of registerer
      GetClassLong(hwndSubject, GCL_WNDPROC),         // Window procedure
      GetClassLong(hwndSubject, GCL_HICON),           // Handle of icon
      GetClassLong(hwndSubject, GCL_HICONSM),         // Handle of small icon
      GetClassLong(hwndSubject, GCL_HCURSOR),         // Handle of cursor
      GetClassLong(hwndSubject, GCL_HBRBACKGROUND),   // Handle of brush
      GetClassLong(hwndSubject, GCL_MENUNAME),        // Menu name
      GetClassLong(hwndSubject, GCL_STYLE));          // Class-style flags

   VoyHelp_AppendStyleStrings(szBuf, g_szClassStyles,
   GetClassLong(hwndSubject, GCL_STYLE));

   VoyHelp_AppendExtraBytes(szBuf, hwndSubject, GCL_CBCLSEXTRA);

   _tcscat(szBuf, __TEXT("\r\n"));
```

```
}


//////////////////////////////////////////////////////////////////////////


// This function is called by the system when we call EnumPropsEx in the
// following SetWindowInfo function.
BOOL WINAPI VoyHelp_PropEnumProcEx (HWND hwnd, LPTSTR lpszString,
   HANDLE hData, DWORD dwData) {

   LPTSTR szBuf = (LPTSTR) dwData;
   if ((DWORD) lpszString <= 0x0000FFFF) {
      // The property is an atom
      wsprintf(_tcschr(szBuf, 0), __TEXT("    Atom %04x = 0x%08x\r\n"),
         lpszString, hData);
   } else {
      // The property is a string
      wsprintf(_tcschr(szBuf, 0), __TEXT("    %s = 0x%08x\r\n"),
         lpszString, hData);
   }
   return(TRUE);                     // Continue enumerating properties
}


//////////////////////////////////////////////////////////////////////////



// This appends the window instance information about the passed-in window
// (hwndSubject) to the passed-in string.
void VoyHelp_SetWindowInfo (LPTSTR szBuf, HWND hwndSubject) {

   TCHAR szWndText[100], szWndPrntText[100];
   HWND hwndParent = (HWND) GetWindowLong(hwndSubject, GWL_HWNDPARENT);
   DWORD dwProcessID;
   RECT rc;

   // Put a heading at the beginning of this section.
   _tcscat(szBuf,
   __TEXT("********* WINDOW INSTANCE INFORMATION *********\r\n"));

   // Get text of subject window.
   if (GetWindowText(hwndSubject, szWndText, adgARRAY_SIZE(szWndText)) == 0)
      _tcscpy(szWndText, __TEXT("(no caption)"));

   // Get text of subject window's parent window.
   if (IsWindow(hwndParent)) {

      if (GetWindowText(hwndParent, szWndPrntText,
         adgARRAY_SIZE(szWndPrntText)) == 0) {

         _tcscpy(szWndPrntText, __TEXT("(no caption)"));
      }
   } else {
```

```
        _tcscpy(szWndPrntText, __TEXT("(no parent)"));
}

GetWindowRect(hwndSubject, &rc);
GetWindowThreadProcessId(hwndSubject, &dwProcessID);

// NOTE: The WndProc is not shown because Windows always returns NULL when
// a thread in one process queries GWL_WNDPROC for a window created by a
// thread in another process.
wsprintf(_tcschr(szBuf, 0),
    __TEXT("Window:\t0x%08x - %s\r\n")
    __TEXT("hInstance:\t0x%08x\r\n")
    __TEXT("Parent window:\t0x%08x - %s\r\n")
    __TEXT("Thread ID:\t0x%08x\r\n")
    __TEXT("Process ID:\t0x%08x\r\n")
    __TEXT("Menu/ID:\t0x%08x (%d)\r\n")
    __TEXT("User data:\t0x%08x (%d)\r\n")
    __TEXT("Rectangle:\t(%d, %d)-(%d, %d), Dim=%d x %d\r\n")
    __TEXT("Window styles:\t0x%08x"),
    hwndSubject, szWndText,                          // Handle & caption
    GetWindowLong(hwndSubject, GWL_HINSTANCE),       // Creator's hInstance
    hwndParent, szWndPrntText,                       // Parent's handle & caption
    GetWindowThreadProcessId(hwndSubject, NULL),     // Creating thread's ID
    dwProcessID,                                     // Process ID owning thread
    GetWindowLong(hwndSubject, GWL_ID),              // HMENU/ID
    GetWindowLong(hwndSubject, GWL_ID),
    GetWindowLong(hwndSubject, GWL_USERDATA),        // User data
    GetWindowLong(hwndSubject, GWL_USERDATA),
    rc.left, rc.top, rc.right, rc.bottom,            // Rectangle
    rc.right - rc.left, rc.bottom - rc.top,          // Dimensions
    GetWindowLong(hwndSubject, GWL_STYLE));          // Styles

VoyHelp_AppendStyleStrings(szBuf, g_szWindowStyles,
    GetWindowLong(hwndSubject, GWL_STYLE));

wsprintf(_tcschr(szBuf, 0), __TEXT("Extended styles:\t0x%08x "),
    GetWindowLong(hwndSubject, GWL_EXSTYLE));

VoyHelp_AppendStyleStrings(szBuf, g_szExWindowStyles,
    GetWindowLong(hwndSubject, GWL_EXSTYLE));

VoyHelp_AppendExtraBytes(szBuf, hwndSubject, GCL_CBWNDEXTRA);

_tcscat(szBuf, __TEXT("Properties:\r\n"));
if (EnumPropsEx(hwndSubject, VoyHelp_PropEnumProcEx, (LONG) szBuf) == -1) {

    // The window has no properties.
    _tcscat(szBuf, __TEXT("  (none)\r\n"));
}

_tcscat(szBuf, __TEXT("\r\n"));
}
```

```
////////////////////////////////////////////////////////////////////////

void VoyHelp_UpdateWindowInfo (HWND hwndEdit, HWND hwndSubject) {

   TCHAR szBuf[8192] = { 0 };    // A very big string buffer

   // Add the class information to the string.
   VoyHelp_SetClassInfo(szBuf, hwndSubject);

   // Add the window instance information to the string.
   VoyHelp_SetWindowInfo(szBuf, hwndSubject);

   // Update the edit class window with the subject's info.
   SetWindowText(hwndEdit, szBuf);
}


///////////////////////////// End of File //////////////////////////////////
```

Eyes.cur

Listing 1.3 *Voyeur.RC*

```
// Microsoft Visual C++ generated resource script.
//
#include "resource.h"

#define APSTUDIO_READONLY_SYMBOLS
/////////////////////////////////////////////////////////////////////////
//
// Generated from the TEXTINCLUDE 2 resource.
//
#include "windows.h"


/////////////////////////////////////////////////////////////////////////
#undef APSTUDIO_READONLY_SYMBOLS


/////////////////////////////////////////////////////////////////////////
//
// Icon
//

IDI_VOYEUR              ICON    DISCARDABLE    "VOYEUR.ICO"

#ifdef APSTUDIO_INVOKED
/////////////////////////////////////////////////////////////////////////
//
// TEXTINCLUDE
//

1 TEXTINCLUDE DISCARDABLE
BEGIN
    "resource.h\0"
END
```

```
2 TEXTINCLUDE DISCARDABLE
BEGIN
    "#include ""windows.h""\r\n"
    "\0"
END

3 TEXTINCLUDE DISCARDABLE
BEGIN
    "\r\n"
    "\0"
END

/////////////////////////////////////////////////////////////////////////////
#endif    // APSTUDIO_INVOKED


/////////////////////////////////////////////////////////////////////////////
//
// Cursor
//

IDC_EYES                 CURSOR  DISCARDABLE    "EYES.CUR"

#ifndef APSTUDIO_INVOKED
/////////////////////////////////////////////////////////////////////////////
//
// Generated from the TEXTINCLUDE 3 resource.
//


/////////////////////////////////////////////////////////////////////////////
#endif    // not APSTUDIO_INVOKED
```

Listing 1.4 *Resource.H*

```
//{{NO_DEPENDENCIES}}
// Microsoft Visual C++ generated include file.
// Used by Voyeur.RC
//
#define IDI_VOYEUR          102
#define IDC_EYES            103

// Next default values for new objects
//
#ifdef APSTUDIO_INVOKED
#ifndef APSTUDIO_READONLY_SYMBOLS
#define _APS_NEXT_RESOURCE_VALUE    104
#define _APS_NEXT_COMMAND_VALUE     40001
#define _APS_NEXT_CONTROL_VALUE     1000
#define _APS_NEXT_SYMED_VALUE       101
#endif
#endif
```

CHAPTER TWO

Anatomy of a Dialog Box

Dialog boxes are a consistent, convenient way for applications to request information from the user. The dialog editor that comes with Visual C++ makes it easy to design dialog boxes. It relieves the programmer of responsibility f or many tedious details, such as calculating window locations for controls. The dialog editor can also be used by nonprogrammers, allowing much of the application's interface to be designed by other members of a design team.

In this chapter, we discuss the internal workings of dialog boxes. Specifically, we discuss exactly what dialog boxes are, how to create templates for them, and how the system manipulates them. This chapter serves as a prelude to the next chapter, Dialog Box Techniques. In that chapter, we explore how to exploit dialog boxes in order to implement features that are commonly used by many commercial applications.

Dialog Boxes Are Windows

The most important thing to remember about dialog boxes is that they are just windows. There is nothing magical about a dialog box. This window usually contains several child windows (commonly called controls), but the dialog box window doesn't have to have any child windows at all. Because many applications present windows with child windows, Microsoft has added a number of functions to the Win32 API to make dealing with this type of window more convenient. Many developers refer to this collection of functions as the Windows' Dialog Box Manager. To say that there is such a thing as the Dialog Box Manager would make dialog boxes seem to be grander than ordinary windows. Because of this, I prefer to say that there is no such thing as a Dialog Box Manager—just a set of functions to make working with child windows a little easier.

In the next several sections, we will examine many of the Win32 functions that make dealing with windows with child windows (hereinafter referred to as dialog boxes) more convenient. Also note that there are many Win32 functions that have Dlg in their name such as GetDlgItem:

```
HWND GetDlgItem(HWND hDlg, int nID);
```

Because Dlg is in their name, it is implied that these functions work only with dialog boxes—windows created by calling DialogBoxParam or CreateDialogParam, and the like. But, the Dlg in the name is misleading. All this function does is scan the child windows of the parent window, looking for a window whose ID matches the value of the nID parameter. GetDlgItem can be used with any parent-child window relationship, not just dialog boxes. This is true of almost all the Win32 functions that appear to manipulate only dialog boxes. Feel free to use these functions with any windows you desire. Perhaps it would have been better if Microsoft had prototyped the function as follows instead:

```
HWND GetChildWindowFromID(HWND hwndParent, int nIDChild);
```

Designing the Appearance of a Dialog Box

When you select the Run... option from the Start menu, the dialog box shown in Figure 2.1 appears.

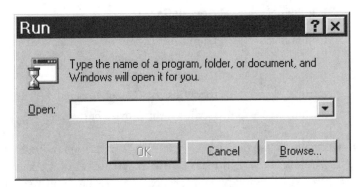

Figure 2.1 *The Run dialog box.*

This parent window (the one that says Run in its caption) contains seven immediate child windows as shown in Figure 2.2. Table 2.1 indicates all the child windows.

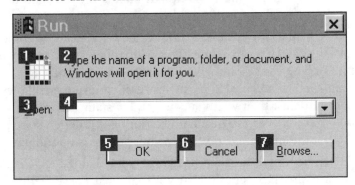

Figure 2.2 *The Run dialog box with its child windows.*

Table 2.1 *The child windows of the Run dialog box*

#	Window class	Description
1	Static	Contains the icon that appears in the top left.
2	Static	Contains the Type the name... text.
3	Static	Contains the Open: text.

Continued...

95

#	Window class	Description
4	ComboBox	Contains the history of executed programs, folders, and documents.
5	Button	Contains the OK button.
6	Button	Contains the Cancel button.
7	Button	Contains the Browse button.

If we were not to use the convenient Win32 functions to help us create such a window, we would have to call CreateWindowEx manually once for the parent window and then call CreateWindowEx seven more times to create each child window. Now, calling CreateWindowEx seven times isn't too bad, especially if we put the call in a loop, but for each call, we have to specify the proper window class, caption, styles, x, y, width, height, and so on. If we had to determine all these values (especially the x, y, width, and height manually), it would take us a very long time to lay out the child windows.

So, to help us lay out these child windows, Visual C++ comes with a tool called a dialog box editor. This editor allows us to select the different window classes and position them on a parent window using drag-and-drop techniques. You can very easily move the child windows around and adjust their width and height. For static and button window classes, you can even assign them text during this design stage and not have to set the appropriate text when your process is up and running.

When you have finished designing your dialog box, Visual C++ writes a dialog box template to your applications RC file. For the dialog box shown in Figure 2.1, the template looks like this:

```
IDD_RUN DIALOG DISCARDABLE  0, 0, 230, 88
STYLE WS_POPUP | WS_VISIBLE | WS_CLIPSIBLINGS | WS_CAPTION | WS_SYSMENU
CAPTION "Run"
FONT 8, "MS Sans Serif"
BEGIN
    ICON            "",IDC_ICON,8,10,18,20
    LTEXT           "Type the name of a program, folder, or document, and
Windows will open it for you.",
                    IDC_STATIC,36,10,186,20
    LTEXT           "&Open:",IDC_STATIC,8,40,20,8
    COMBOBOX        IDC_RUNHISTORY,36,38,186,30,CBS_DROPDOWN |
                    CBS_AUTOHSCROLL | CBS_DISABLENOSCROLL | WS_TABSTOP
    DEFPUSHBUTTON   "OK",IDOK,64,64,50,14
    PUSHBUTTON      "Cancel",IDCANCEL,116,64,52,14
    PUSHBUTTON      "&Browse...",IDC_BROWSE,170,64,50,14
END
```

This template is really a text script and cannot be processed by the Win32 functions. The script must be compiled into a binary form first. This is the responsibility of the resource compiler. The resource compiler parses the text script and produces a binary image. For Windows 95 and Windows NT 3.51, Microsoft has defined a new DIALOGEX dialog box template that is a superset of the old DIALOG template. The new template has the following format:

```
DialogTemplateName DIALOGEX x, y, cx, cy, helpID
STYLE style
EXSTYLE exStyle
FONT height, name, weight, italic
CAPTION captionText
MENU menuName
CLASS className
LANGUAGE languageID
VERSION versionNumber
CHARACTERISTICS characteristicsValue
BEGIN
    CONTROL controlText, id, className, style,
        x, y, cx, cy, exStyle, helpID
        BEGIN
            data-element-1,
            ...
        END
    ...
END
```

For the remainder of this chapter, I will refer to the new DIALOG EX template and the binary data structures that are produced for it. Unfortunately, the resource compiler that ships with Visual C++ 2.x does not understand the new DIALOGEX template. However, the resource compiler that ships with the Win32 SDK can compile the new DIALOGEX template and produces a binary image that consists of a DLGTEMPLATEEX structure, an optional FONTINFOEX structure, and zero or more DLGITEMTEMPLATEEX structures.

The new *EX structures support the following new features:

■ Help IDs can be assigned to the dialog box and any of its children.

■ Extended window styles can be assigned to the dialog box and any of its children.

- Weight and italic settings can be associated with the font.
- Control-specific data can be assigned to the children.

Although the old DLGTEMPLATE and DLGITEMTEMPLATE structures are defined in **WinUser.H**, Microsoft has not defined the old FONTINFO structure or any of the new, extended structures. This can make working with dialog boxes a little inconvenient, but most of the time we do not have to manipulate these data structures ourselves. We will now examine the new extended dialog structures. Lets start with the DLGTEMPLATEEX structure:

```
typedef struct { // dlttex
    WORD    wDlgVer;           // Always 1
    WORD    wSignature;        // Always 0xFFFF
    DWORD   dwHelpID;
    DWORD   dwExStyle;         // Such as WS_EX_TOPMOST
    DWORD   dwStyle;           // Such as WS_CAPTION
    WORD    cDlgItems;
    short   x;                 // In pixels
    short   y;                 // In pixels
    short   cx;                // In dialog box units
    short   cy;                // In dialog box units
    // Zero-terminated Unicode string for the menu name
    // Zero-terminated Unicode string for the class name
    // Zero-terminated Unicode string for the window title
} DLGTEMPLATEEX, *PDLGTEMPLATEEX;
```

This data structure defines the attributes of the parent window. The wSignature member is always 0xFFFF. When parsing a dialog box template's binary image, the system always examines this member first. If the value is 0xFFFF, the system knows that this template is a new DLGTEMPLATEEX structure instead of the old DLGTEMPLATE structure (it is impossible for the old DLGTEM-PLATE structure to have 0xFFFF 2 bytes into the structure). Once the system determines that this is a new DLGTEMPLATEEX structure, the system then checks the wDlgVer member to see which DLGTEMPLATEEX structure it is parsing. Currently, only one type of DLGTEMPLATEEX structure exists so the value of the wDlgVer member will always be 1. However, this design makes it easy for Microsoft to extend the DLGTEMPLATEEX structure in future versions of Windows.

The cdit member indicates the number of child windows that follow in the compiled binary dialog box template. Notice that the menu, class, and title of the window appear as comments in the preceding structure because these values are zero-terminated strings of arbitrary length. When the resource compiler produces the binary image, these strings are appended immediately after the fixed portion of the DLGTEMPLATEEX structure. These strings are always stored in the binary image as Unicode[1] strings—not ANSI strings. This is true even on Windows 95. But that makes sense doesn't it? After all, an Intel Win32 EXE file can be executed on both Windows NT and Windows 95 without recompiling. On Windows 95, the operating system reads these strings and converts them from Unicode to ANSI before creating any windows.

If the style member of the DLGTEMPLATEEX structure has the DS_SETFONT bit turned on, there is a FONTINFOEX structure immediately following the window title. This structure is defined as follows:

```
typedef struct {
    short   nPointSize;
    short   nWeight;      // Such as FW_NORMAL
    short   fItalic;      // TRUE or FALSE
    // Zero-terminated Unicode string for the font name
} FONTINFOEX, *PFONTINFOEX;
```

This structure allows you to select a specific font to be used for the child windows of the dialog box. Now, in addition to all the information needed to describe the parent window, there are zero or more DLGITEMTEMPLATEEX structures used to describe each child window:

```
typedef struct {
    DWORD   dwHelpID;
    DWORD   dwExStyle;    // Such as WS_EX_CONTROLPARENT
    DWORD   dwStyle;      // Such as WS_TABSTOP
```

[1]For more information about Unicode, see the Win32 Programmers Reference and my *Advanced Windows* book.

```
short    x;           // In dialog box units
short    y;           // In dialog box units
short    cx;          // In dialog box units
short    cy;          // In dialog box units
DWORD    id;
// Zero-terminated Unicode string for the class name
// Zero-terminated Unicode string for the control title
WORD     wExtraCount;   // Usually 0
// wExtraCount bytes of raw data
} DLGITEMTEMPLATEEX, *PDLGITEMTEMPLATEEX;
```

This data structure is very similar to the DLGTEMPLATEEX structure. The members describe the attributes for a single child window. Instead of the zero-terminated menu string contained in the DLGTEMPLATEEX structure, the DLGITEMTEMPLATEEX structure has an id member because child windows cannot have menus. In fact, the documentation for CreateWindowEx states that the hMenu parameter is interpreted as an integer ID when creating a child window. The id member represents an integer value that you assign to each child window. This ID makes it easy for you to manipulate child windows.

For example, you may have some code where you want to send an LB_ADDSTRING message to a listbox child window. In order to call SendMessage, you must have the handle of the listbox child window. However, when you are writing your code, you have no idea what the listbox window's handle will be at runtime. Thus, you can assign the listbox window an ID in the dialog box editor. This ID will always be the same; therefore, you can use the SendDlgItemMessage function to send the LB_ADDSTRING message:

```
LRESULT SendDlgItemMessage(HWND hwndParent, int nID, UINT uMsg,
    WPARAM wParam, LPARAM lParam);
```

The first parameter identifies the handle to the parent window, and nID is the integer ID value that you assigned to the child window. When you call SendDlgItemMessage, it scans the children of the parent window until it finds a window whose ID matches the nID parameter. Once a match has been found, the function knows the handle of the child window and calls SendMessage internally. Here is another example of a function that has Dlg in its name (SendDlgItemMessage) but does not have to be used with dialog boxes. You can use the SendDlgItemMessage function to send a message to a child window of a parent regardless of how that parent window was created.

Now, immediately following the id member is some variable length fields. The first two are zero-terminated Unicode strings that identify the child's window class and its title, respectively. Following the window title is the window's creation data information. The creation data consists of two parts: a 2-byte value that indicates the number of bytes in the creation data followed by the actual data itself. The creation data are used very infrequently and I will not go into any more detail here.

After the resource compiler has produced the binary image of the DLGTEMPLATEEX, the optional FONTINFOEX structure, and all the necessary DLGITEMTEMPLATEEX structures, this image is placed into your EXE file. Now, in order to create all these windows, you must call a Win32 function that locates this template in your EXE file and creates the windows. We will discuss these functions in the next section.

Creating the Parent and Child Windows

When we want to create a dialog box, we have to obtain an address to a memory block with the DLGTEMPLATEEX, FONTINFOEX, and DLGITEMTEMPLATEEX structures contained in our EXE file's resources. We usually do this by calling the CreateDialogParam function[2]:

```
HWND CreateDialogParam(HINSTANCE hinst, LPCSTR lpTemplateName,
    HWND hwndOwner, DLGPROC pfnDlgProc, LPARAM lParamInit);
```

---

[2]The CreateDialog function no longer exists in the Win32 API. You may continue to use it, however, because of the following macros defined in the **WinUser.H** header file:

```
#define CreateDialogA(hInstance, lpName, hWndParent, lpDialogFunc) \
    CreateDialogParamA(hInstance, lpName, hWndParent, lpDialogFunc, 0L)

#define CreateDialogW(hInstance, lpName, hWndParent, lpDialogFunc) \
    CreateDialogParamW(hInstance, lpName, hWndParent, lpDialogFunc, 0L)

#ifdef UNICODE
#define CreateDialog CreateDialogW
#else
#define CreateDialog CreateDialogA
#endif // !UNICODE
```

CreateDialogParam is a very short and simple function. If you had Microsoft's source code for this function, you would see that it looks something like this (I have left out error checking for clarity):

```
HWND CreateDialogParam(HINSTANCE hinst, LPCSTR lpTemplateName,
   HWND hwndOwner, DLGPROC pfnDlgProc, LPARAM lParamInit) {

   // Find the dialog box template resource in the EXE file.
   HRSRC hrsrc = FindResource(hinst, lpTemplateName, RT_DIALOG);
   HGLOBAL hglblRes = LoadResource(hinst, hrsrc);

   // Obtain the memory address of the dialog box template.
   PDLGTEMPLATEEX pDlgTemplate = (PDLGTEMPLATEEX) LockResource(hglblRes);

   // Create the parent window and child windows using the
   // template contained in the memory block.
   HWND hwndDlg = CreateDialogIndirectParam(hinst, pDlgTemplate,
      hwndOwner, pfnDlgProc, lParamInit);

   // NOTE: Windows NT does not require that resources be unlocked or freed;
   // however, Windows 95 does have this requirement.  It is always safer to
   // clean up than to leak memory for your process.
   UnlockResource(pDlgTemplate);
   FreeResource(hglblRes);

   // Return the handle of the parent window.
   return(hwndDlg);
}
```

You can easily see from the preceding code that the CreateDialog-IndirectParam function is responsible for doing the bulk of the work involved in creating a dialog box. Let's examine what this function does in more detail. First, here is the prototype for the function:

```
HWND CreateDialogIndirectParam(HINSTANCE hinst, PCDLGTEMPLATEEX pDlgTemplate,
   HWND hwndOwner, DLGPROC pfnDlgProc, LPARAM lParamInit);
```

The second parameter, pDlgTemplate, must point to the first byte of a dialog box template's binary image. CreateDialogIndirect-Param will parse this block of memory by doing the following:

1. Convert any DS_* styles to WS_* styles. For example, the DS_MODALFRAME style becomes WS_EX_DLGMODAL-FRAME, the DS_CONTEXTHELP style becomes WS_EX_

CONTEXTHELP, and the WS_DLGFRAME style becomes WS_EX_WINDOWEDGE.[3]

2. If the DS_FONT style exists, CreateFontIndirect is called to create a logical font from the FONTINFOEX structure given in the block.

3. Width and height values are converted from dialog box units to pixels via the MapDialogRect function.

4. The parent window is created by taking the members in the DLGTEMPLATEEX structure and calling CreateWindowEx. For this parent window, the extended styles, class name, caption, styles, x, y, width, height, and menu information is right in the memory block. For CreateWindowEx's hInstance and hwndParent parameters (yes, parent windows can have owners or parents too), the hinst and hwndOwner values passed to CreateDialogIndirectParam are used.

   Most of the time, we do not explicitly specify a window class name when using Visual C++ to design a dialog box. When no window class name is specified, CreateDialogIndirectParam calls CreateWindowEx, passing the name of a built-in dialog box window class. This dialog box class is a system global window class. But, unlike other system global classes like ListBox or Edit, this class does not have an elegant name. Instead, this class is simply called #32770, which is also the class atom value. Because this is a system global window class, Microsoft has implemented the window procedure for this class inside the **User32.DLL** file. However, Microsoft documents the name of this window procedure as DefDlgProc, and we will discuss it in the next section.

5. If a help ID other than zero is associated with the template, SetWindowContextHelpId is called, passing it the handle of the parent window and the help ID:

   ```
   BOOL SetWindowContextHelpId(HWND hwnd, DWORD dwContextHelpId);
   ```

---

[3]CreateDialogIndirectParam always includes the WS_EX_CONTROLPARENT extended window style when creating the dialog box's main window regardless of whether the DS_CONTROL style is specified.

If the user requests help on the dialog box, the dialog box procedure receives a WM_HELP message where the lParam parameter points to a HELPINFO structure. The dwContextId member of this structure will have the dialog box's context help ID in it.

6. If DS_SETFONT exists, the parent receives a WM_SETFONT message.

At this point, the parent window has been fully created and initialized. CreateDialogIndirectParam now cycles through each of the DLGITEMTEMPLATEEX structures in order to create each child window.

7. Each child window is created by taking the members in the DLGITEMTEMPLATEEX structure and calling CreateWindowEx. For each child window, the extended styles,[4] class name, caption, styles, and ID information is right in the memory block.

   The x, y, width, and height values are first converted from dialog box units to pixels. For CreateWindowEx's hInstance and hwndParent parameters, the hinst value passed to CreateDialogIndirectParam and the handle of the newly created parent window are used, respectively.

8. If the child window cannot be created, CreateDialogIndirectParam destroys the parent window and any children that were created and returns NULL. However, you can override this default behavior by specifying the DS_NOFAILCREATE class-specific style for the parent window. If DS_NOFAILCREATE is specified, CreateDialogIndirectParam continues to create any remaining child windows and returns the handle to the parent window back to the caller.

9. If the child window has a help ID other than zero, SetWindowContextHelpId is called, passing the handle of the child window and the ID value from the data structure.

   If the user requests help on the child window, the dialog box procedure receives a WM_HELP message where the lParam parameter points to a HELPINFO structure. The dwContextId member of this structure will have the child windows context help ID in it.

---

[4]CreateDialogIndirectParam always includes the WS_EX_NOPARENTNOTIFY extended window style when creating the child windows.

10. A WM_SETFONT message is sent to the child window to tell it what font it should use for painting text.

Now, after the parent window and all its child windows have been created, CreateDialogIndirectParam sends a WM_INITDIALOG message to the parent window. The lParam of this message contains the value that you passed for CreateDialogIndirectParam's lParamInit parameter.

At this point, we have not discussed CreateDialogIndirectParam's pfnDlgProc parameter. We will discuss this parameter in the next section.

The Dialog Box Class Window Procedure

As mentioned in the previous section, Windows registers the dialog box system-global window class when each process initializes. The window procedure for this window class is implemented inside **User32.DLL** by Microsoft and is called DefDlgProc:

```
LRESULT DefDlgProc(HWND hwndDlg, UINT uMsg, WPARAM wParam, LPARAM lParam);
```

This function matches the prototype for a standard window procedure because it is one. This window procedure exists in order to make dealing with dialog boxes easier, just like the other dialog box functions.

When we design a dialog box we must also create a dialog box procedure. This procedure must have the following prototype:

```
BOOL DlgProc (HWND hwnd, UINT uMsg, WPARAM wParam, LPARAM lParam);
```

This function looks exactly like a window procedure, but the return value is a BOOL instead of an LRESULT. This distinction is very significant. When Microsoft was designing the dialog box mechanism, they wanted to make things easier for developers. When any window messages come to the parent window, they go to the dialog box class window procedure, DefDlgProc. DefDlgProc then calls our application's dialog box procedure.

To make things easier for us, all our application's dialog box procedure has to do is return TRUE or FALSE indicating whether or not we processed the message. If we process the message (return TRUE), then DefDlgProc will not do any further processing and simply returns to the system. However, if our dialog box procedure does not process the message (returns FALSE), DefDlgProc carries out its default processing for the window message, which will most likely result in a call to the DefWindowProc function.

In theory, this sounds like a nice approach. However, many window messages expect a meaningful return value after they are processed. For example, the WM_CTLCOLOREDIT message requires that a handle to a brush be returned. If our application's dialog box procedure handles the WM_CTLCOLOREDIT message, how do we indicate the desired brush handle *and* that we processed the message? Also, how would a dialog box procedure respond to a WM_QUERYENDSESSION message?

For some of these messages, Microsoft modified the built-in DefDlgProc function to check explicitly for certain messages and to return to the system whatever value is returned from the application's dialog box procedure. But, as the Windows API continued to develop, Microsoft realized that they needed a way for an application's dialog box procedure to indicate that it processed a message and what the result of that message is. So, Microsoft added 4 extra bytes to every dialog box window that is created. This 4-byte value can be examined and altered by calling GetWindowLong and SetWindowLong using the DWL_MSGRESULT identifier. So, an application's dialog box procedure can set a result by calling:

```
SetWindowLong(hwndDlg, DWL_MSGRESULT, lResult);
```

and can also indicate that it processed the message by returning TRUE or FALSE. To make this more convenient, the **WindowsX.H** header file contains a useful macro:

```
#define SetDlgMsgResult(hwnd, msg, result) (( \
        (msg) == WM_CTLCOLORMSGBOX      || \
        (msg) == WM_CTLCOLOREDIT        || \
        (msg) == WM_CTLCOLORLISTBOX     || \
        (msg) == WM_CTLCOLORBTN         || \
        (msg) == WM_CTLCOLORDLG         || \
        (msg) == WM_CTLCOLORSCROLLBAR   || \
        (msg) == WM_CTLCOLORSTATIC      || \
        (msg) == WM_COMPAREITEM         || \
        (msg) == WM_VKEYTOITEM          || \
        (msg) == WM_CHARTOITEM          || \
        (msg) == WM_QUERYDRAGICON       || \
        (msg) == WM_INITDIALOG            \
    ) ? (BOOL)(result)                    \
      : (SetWindowLong((hwnd), DWL_MSGRESULT, (LPARAM)(LRESULT)(result)), TRUE))
```

This macro performs both actions at once. If the message is any of the 12 listed in the macro, the result indicates that the message was processed and is the return value from the application's dialog box procedure. But, for any other message, the result is stored in the window's extra bytes, and a value of TRUE is returned indicating that the message was processed.

In order to help clarify what is really going on here, the following pseudo-code fragment shows the general architecture of the DefDlgProc function:

```
LRESULT DefDlgProc (HWND hwndDlg, UINT uMsg, WPARAM wParam, LPARAM lParam) {

   BOOL fProcessedByApp = FALSE;

   // Assume that the application's dialog box
   // procedure doesn't process the message.
   SetWindowLong(hwndDlg, DWL_MSGRESULT, 0);

   // Get the address of the application's dialog box procedure.
   DLGPROC pfnDlgProc = (DLGPROC) GetWindowLong(hwndDlg, DWL_DLGPROC);
   if (pfnDlgProc != NULL) {

      // Call the application's dialog box procedure.
      fProcessedByApp = pfnDlgProc(hwnd, uMsg, wParam, lParam);
   }

   switch (uMsg) {
      case WM_CTLCOLORMSGBOX:
      case WM_CTLCOLOREDIT:
      case WM_CTLCOLORLISTBOX:
      case WM_CTLCOLORBTN:
      case WM_CTLCOLORDLG:
      case WM_CTLCOLORSCROLLBAR:
      case WM_CTLCOLORSTATIC:
      case WM_COMPAREITEM:
      case WM_VKEYTOITEM:
      case WM_CHARTOITEM:
      case WM_INITDIALOG:
      case WM_QUERYDRAGICON:

         // If uMsg is any of the preceding messages, return whatever
         // the application's dialog box procedure returned.
         // NOTE: Even though fProcessedByApp is declared as a BOOL, it can
         //       contain a 32-bit value.  This is necessary when an
         //       HBRUSH is returned from a WM_CTLCOLOR* message.
         return((LRESULT) fProcessedByApp);
   }

   if (fProcessedByApp) {

      // If the application's dialog box procedure processed the message,
      // return whatever the application's dialog box procedure stored
      // in the dialog window's DWL_MSGRESULT extra byte value.
      return((LRESULT) GetWindowLong(hwndDlg, DWL_MSGRESULT));
```

107

```
    }

    // If we get here, the application's dialog box procedure did not process
    // the message so we should do it using a regular switch statement.
    switch (uMsg) {

        case DM_GETDEFID:
            // Process a DM_GETDEFID message.
            break;

        case DM_SETDEFID:
            // Process a DM_SETDEFID message.
            break;

        case DM_REPOSITION:
            // Process a DM_REPOSITION message.
            break;

        case WM_*:
            // Process various other messages.
            break;

        default:
            lResult = DefWindowProc(hwndDlg, uMsg, wParam, lParam);
            break;
    }
    return(lResult);
}
```

The only thing left out of our discussion is an explanation of how the DWL_DLGPROC extra bytes get initialized with the address of your application's dialog box procedure. Answering this question is quite simple. When you call CreateDialogParamIndirect, you pass it the address to your dialog box procedure in the pfnDlgProc parameter. Just after CreateDialogParamIndirect creates the parent window, it makes the following call:

```
SetWindowLong(hwndParent, DWL_DLGPROC, pfnDlgProc);
```

After this line is executed, DefDlgProc notifies our applications dialog box procedure of all window messages sent to the parent window's window procedure. This means that our dialog box procedure will not be notified of WM_CREATE and WM_NCCREATE messages.

Due to this architecture, there is a common bug that many developers make. The following code fragment comes from a dialog box procedure:

108

```
case WM_SOMEMSG:
   SetDlgMsgResult(hwnd, uMsg, 5);
   SetWindowText(hwnd, "New window text");
   return(TRUE);
```

This code fragment sets the DWL_MSGRESULT window bytes to 5 intending that the result of processing the message will be 5. But then, the code calls the SetWindowText function. This function forces a WM_SETTEXT message to be sent to DefDlgProc. When DefDlgProc is called recursively, it executes this code:

```
// Assume that the application's dialog box
// procedure doesn't process the message.
SetWindowLong(hwndDlg, DWL_MSGRESULT, 0);
```

This, of course, overwrites the 5 with a 0 (zero). After the WM_SET-TEXT message is processed, the call to SetWindowText returns, and TRUE is returned back to DefDlgProc (DefDlgProc will see that zero is the result instead of the intended value, 5). The way to fix this problem is to reorder the code as follows:

```
case WM_SOMEMSG:
   SetWindowText(hwnd, "New window text");
   SetDlgMsgResult(hwnd, uMsg, 5);
   return(TRUE);
```

Adding Keyboard Navigation to a Modeless Dialog Box

The CreateDialogParamIndirect function creates what is commonly referred to as a modeless dialog box. That is, it simply creates a parent window and a bunch of child windows. After all these windows have been created, CreateDialogIndirectParam returns and the code continues executing.

One of the nice features of a dialog box is that you get an enormous amount of keyboard navigation for free. For example, when a dialog box is presented to a user, the user is able to direct the keyboard focus to different controls by pressing the Tab (or Shift+Tab) key. The user can select the default pushbutton by pressing the Enter key or dismiss the dialog box by pressing the Esc key. In addition, the user can use arrow keys and mnemonic keys to change focus among the various child windows. When Windows was originally designed in the early 1980s, it did not have good keyboard support. Because adding keyboard support to Windows was an afterthought, Windows contains many hacks that attempt to graft keyboard support into the system. For keyboard navigation of dialog boxes, the hack comes in the form of a function called IsDialogMessage:

```
BOOL IsDialogMessage(HWND hwndDlg, PMSG lpmsg);
```

This function is usually called from inside your thread's message loop as follows:

```
int WINAPI WinMain (...) {

   MSG msg;

   // Create the dialog box parent window and all its child windows.
   HWND hwndDlg = CreateDialogParam(...);
   .
   .
   .
   while (GetMessage(&msg, NULL, 0, 0)) {

      // After a message is pulled from the queue, IsDialogMessage checks to see
      // if it is a keyboard message destined for the dialog box or any of its
      // children.  If it is a navigational key, IsDialogMessage performs the
      // navigation and returns TRUE.  For anything else, IsDialogMessage
      // returns FALSE, and the message is processed normally.
      if (!IsDialogMessage(hwndDlg, &msg)) {

         TranslateMessage(&msg);
         DispatchMessage(&msg);
      }
   }
   .
   .
   .
   return(0);
}
```

If you do not modify your thread's message loop so that it calls IsDialogMessage, your dialog box will not support keyboard navigation; however the user will still be able to use the mouse.

What Makes a Modal Dialog Box Modal?

The most common type of dialog box is the modal dialog box. A modal dialog box is a dialog box that must be dismissed before the user can continue to interact with the application. The File Open dialog box is an excellent example of a modal dialog box. When the file open dialog box is not visible, the user is free to work with the application's windows by pressing keys or clicking and moving the mouse. But, when the File Open dialog box is visible, the user can no longer type into the application's main window, and if the user clicks the mouse over the main window, the system just beeps. The user must exit the current mode to continue using the application. The user does this by dismissing the modal dialog box.

We create a modal dialog box by calling the DialogBoxParam function[5]:

```
int DialogBoxParam(HINSTANCE hinst, LPCSTR lpTemplateName, HWND hwndOwner,
   DLGPROC pfnDlgProc, LPARAM lParamInit);
```

If you had Microsoft's source code for the DialogBoxPararm function, you would see that it looks something like this (again, I left out error checking for clarity):

```
int DialogBoxParam(HINSTANCE hinst, LPCSTR lpTemplateName,
   HWND hwndOwner, DLGPROC pfnDlgProc, LPARAM lParamInit) {

   if (IsWindow(hwndOwner)) {

      // The owner window should be disabled so that it no longer
      // receives keystrokes or mouse input.

      HWND hwndActive = hwndOwner;
      while (GetWindowStyle(hwndActive) & WS_CHILD) {

         // If the caller passed the handle of a child window,
         // walk up until we find a popup or overlapped window.
         hwndActive = GetParent(hwndActive);
      }

      EnableWindow(hwndActive, FALSE);
   }
```

---

[5]Like the CreateDialog function, the DialogBox function no longer exists in the Win32 API. You may continue to use it however because of similar macros that are defined in the **WinUser.H** header file.

```
// Create the modeless dialog box (parent window and child windows).
HWND hwndDlg = CreateDialogParam(hinst, lpTemplateName,
    hwndOwner, pfnDlgProc, lParamInit);

// The undocumented DWL_ENDDIALOGCALLED extra byte value is
// initialized to FALSE by the system when the window is created.
// See the following pseudo-code for the EndDialog function for more details.
SetWindowWord(hwndDlg, DWL_ENDDIALOGCALLED, FALSE);

// Stay in a message loop until EndDialog is called (the undocumented
// DWL_ENDDIALOGCALLED extra bytes value is set by EndDialog).
// This message loop makes this dialog box modal.
while (!GetWindowWord(hwndDlg, DWL_ENDDIALOGCALLED)) {
    GetMessage(&msg, NULL, 0, 0);

    // If EndDialog has not been called for this window,
    // continue this message loop.
    if (!IsDialogMessage(hwndDlg, &msg)) {
        TranslateMessage(&msg);
        DispatchMessage(&msg);
    }
}

// Loop ended because EndDialog was called.

// Get the value passed to EndDialog (the undocumented
// DWL_DLGRESULT extra bytes value is set by EndDialog).
int nResult = GetWindowLong(hwndDlg, DWL_DLGRESULT);

// Destroy the parent window and all its child windows.
DestroyWindow(hwndDlg);

// Return the value passed to EndDialog back to
// the thread that invoked the modal dialog box.
return(nResult);
}
```

You can easily see from the preceding code that a modal dialog box is really not much more than a modeless dialog box. In fact, there are really just two things that make a modal dialog box modal. The first is that DialogBoxParam disables the owner window. For a File Open dialog box this means that the owner window, usually the main application window, will no longer receive any hardware (keyboard or mouse) messages; it will receive all other messages, however. The second difference is that DialogBoxParam enters into a message loop of its own. Because there is a GetMessage loop inside DialogBoxParam, the DialogBoxParam function will not return immediately to its caller. You'll also notice that the message loop contains a call to IsDialogMessage, which ensures that keyboard navigation works properly for the modal dialog box.

In order for the message loop to terminate, the code in the dialog box procedure must place a call to the EndDialog function:

```
BOOL EndDialog(HWND hwnd, int nResult);
```

This function is passed the handle of the dialog window you wish to terminate and a return value that will be returned from the DialogBoxParam function. The EndDialog function reenables the parent window and sets some undocumented values in the dialog window's extra bytes. The DialogBoxParam function's message loop sees that these extra bytes have changed and terminates its message loop, returning EndDialog's nResult parameter back to DialogBox-Param's caller.

The following pseudo-code shows what the EndDialog function looks like internally:

```
BOOL EndDialog(HWND hwnd, int nResult) {

    HWND hwndOwner = GetParent(hwnd);

    if (IsWindow(hwndOwner))
        EnableWindow(hwndOwner, TRUE);

    // Set the undocumented DWL_ENDDIALOGCALLED and DWL_DLGRESULT extra byte values
    // so that the modal dialog box ends and the desired return value is stored
    // away so that it can be retrieved inside of the DialogBoxParam function.
    SetWindowLong(hwnd, DWL_ENDDIALOGCALLED, TRUE);
    SetWindowLong(hwnd, DWL_DLGRESULT, nResult);

    // Force the message loop inside DialogBoxParam to wake
    // up and see that the dialog box is terminating.
    PostMessage(hwnd, WM_NULL, 0, 0);

    return(TRUE);  // EndDialog was successful
}
```

Dynamic Modal Dialog Boxes

The DialogBoxIndirectParam function can also be used to create a modal dialog box:

```
int DialogBoxIndirectParam(HINSTANCE hinst, PCDLGTEMPLATE hTemplate,
    HWND hwndOwner, DLGPROC pfnDlgProc, LPARAM lParamInit);
```

Where the DialogBoxParam function assumes that the dialog box template is in the EXE file's resources, the DialogBoxIndirectParam function is a lower-level function that requires just a pointer to the dialog box template. This means that the dialog box template does not have to be in a resource; it could be created dynamically in a block of memory. This function will be demonstrated in a the **DlgDyn.03** application presented in Chapter 3.

Dialog Boxes as Your Main Window

The Clock application (**Clock.EXE**), shown in Listings 2.1-2.3, (starting on page 117) demonstrates how to use a dialog box as your application's main window. This technique is my favorite because it can save you an enormous amount of time and trouble. Using this technique, you can write a Windows application without having to register a window class, without calling CreatingWindowEx, and without creating a message loop. I use this technique in almost all the applications presented throughout this book.

Most of the applications in this book present a window when executed. This window serves as the applications user-interface, allowing the user to interact with the application. The easiest way for me to design a user-interface is, of course, to use the Visual C++ dialog box editor. For example, let's say that I wanted to make a small application that simply updates the time. When you run the application, its window looks like Figure 2.3.

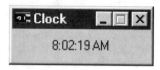

Figure 2.3 *A small clock application.*

Table 2.2 describes the files used to create this application.

Table 2.2 *Files used to build the Clock Application.*

File	Description
Clock.C	Contains WinMain and main window's dialog box and message cracker functions.
Clock.RC	Contains dialog box template for main application window and its icons.
Resource.H	Contains ID for all resources in the **Clock.RC** file
Clock.ICO	Contains the icon for the main window.
Clock.MAK	Visual C++ project makefile.

To create this application, I start a new project in Visual C++ and immediately go to the dialog box editor where I design the look of the window. The dialog box looks like Figure 2.4.

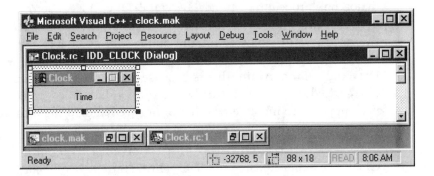

Figure 2.4 *The dialog box for the clock application.*

Then, I have to write some code to make this application work. All I need are five small functions. First, I have to write a dialog box function that looks like this:

```
BOOL WINAPI Clock_DlgProc (HWND hwnd, UINT uMsg, WPARAM wParam, LPARAM lParam) {

   switch (uMsg) {

      // Standard Windows messages.
      adgHANDLE_DLGMSG(hwnd, WM_INITDIALOG, Clock_OnInitDialog);
      adgHANDLE_DLGMSG(hwnd, WM_TIMER,      Clock_OnTimer);
```

115

```
        adgHANDLE_DLGMSG(hwnd, WM_COMMAND,    Clock_OnCommand);
    }
    return(FALSE);    // We didn't process the message.
}
```

This is a standard dialog box procedure. Notice that instead of using the HANDLE_MSG message cracker macro from **WindowsX.H**, I used my own adgHANDLE_DLGMSG macro. This macro is defined in the **Win95ADG.H** header file discussed in Appendix A of this book:

```
// The normal HANDLE_MSG macro in WindowsX.H does not work properly for
// dialog boxes because DlgProcs return a BOOL instead of an LRESULT
// (like WndProcs). This adgHANDLE_DLGMSG macro corrects the problem:
#define adgHANDLE_DLGMSG(hwnd, message, fn)                    \
    case (message): return (SetDlgMsgResult(hwnd, uMsg,       \
        HANDLE_##message((hwnd), (wParam), (lParam), (fn))))
```

Recall that the return value from a dialog box procedure is not the same as the return value from a window procedure. Because of this difference, you should not use the HANDLE_MSG macro inside a dialog box procedure. My adgHANDLE_DLGMSG macro calls the SetDlgMsgResult macro (defined in **WindowsX.H**) in order to set the return value properly for the dialog box procedure. Note that the dialog box procedure returns FALSE at the end and does not call DefWindowProc. Again, this is because the procedure is not a window procedure and the return value from a dialog box procedure is just supposed to indicate whether or not we handled the message.

Then, we have to create three functions to handle the window messages: Clock_OnInitDialog creates a 1-second timer, Clock_OnTimer updates the IDC_TIME static control about once a second, and Clock_OnCommand checks for IDCANCEL. If Clock_OnCommand didn't check for IDCANCEL, the user would not be able to close the dialog box window.

The last function that needs to be written is the WinMain function. Because we are using this dialog-box-as-our-main-window technique, the implementation of the WinMain function is almost trivial. Here it is, in its entirety:

```
int WINAPI WinMain (HINSTANCE hinstExe, HINSTANCE hinstPrev,
    LPSTR lpszCmdLine, int nCmdShow) {

    // Create the application window.
    DialogBox(hinstExe, MAKEINTRESOURCE(IDD_CLOCK), NULL, Clock_DlgProc);

    return(0);
}
```

I can't think of a simpler function than this that does so much work. The single call to DialogBox causes the main window and all of child windows to be created. Then, the thread enters its own message loop that is contained inside the DialogBoxParam function. When the dialog box is closed, the message loop terminates, DialogBoxParam returns, and our application terminates. There is no need for us to register any window classes or create any message loops.

Listing 2.1 *Clock.C*

Clock.ico

```
/**************************************************************************
Module name: Clock.c
Written by: Jeffrey Richter
Notices: Copyright (c) 1995 Jeffrey Richter
Purpose: Demonstrates using a dialog box for an application's main window.
**************************************************************************/


#include "..\Win95ADG.h"          /* See Appendix A for details */
#include <windows.h>
#include <windowsx.h>
#pragma warning(disable: 4001)     /* Single line comment */
#include "resource.h"


///////////////////////////////////////////////////////////////////////


BOOL Clock_OnInitDialog (HWND hwnd, HWND hwndFocus, LPARAM lParam) {

    SetTimer(hwnd, 1, 1000, NULL);              // 1 second intervals

    FORWARD_WM_TIMER(hwnd, 1, SendMessage);     // Force an initial update

    adgSETDLGICONS(hwnd, IDI_CLOCK, IDI_CLOCK);
    return(TRUE);                               // Accept default focus window.
}


///////////////////////////////////////////////////////////////////////


void Clock_OnTimer (HWND hwnd, UINT id) {

    // Show current time
    TCHAR szTime[100];
    GetTimeFormat(LOCALE_USER_DEFAULT, 0, NULL, NULL,
        szTime, adgARRAY_SIZE(szTime));
    SetDlgItemText(hwnd, IDC_TIME, szTime);

}
```

117

```
///////////////////////////////////////////////////////////////////////////


void Clock_OnCommand (HWND hwnd, int id, HWND hwndCtl, UINT codeNotify) {

   switch (id) {
      case IDCANCEL:                  // Allows dialog box to close
         EndDialog(hwnd, id);
         break;
   }
}




///////////////////////////////////////////////////////////////////////////


BOOL WINAPI Clock_DlgProc (HWND hwnd, UINT uMsg,
   WPARAM wParam, LPARAM lParam) {

   switch (uMsg) {

      // Standard Window's messages
      adgHANDLE_DLGMSG(hwnd, WM_INITDIALOG, Clock_OnInitDialog);
      adgHANDLE_DLGMSG(hwnd, WM_TIMER,      Clock_OnTimer);
      adgHANDLE_DLGMSG(hwnd, WM_COMMAND,    Clock_OnCommand);
   }
   return(FALSE);                      // We didn't process the message.
}




///////////////////////////////////////////////////////////////////////////


int WINAPI WinMain (HINSTANCE hinstExe, HINSTANCE hinstPrev,
   LPSTR lpszCmdLine, int nCmdShow) {

   adgWARNIFUNICODEUNDERWIN95();
   adgVERIFY(-1 != DialogBox(hinstExe, MAKEINTRESOURCE(IDD_CLOCK),
      NULL, Clock_DlgProc));

   return(0);
}


//////////////////////////// End of File ///////////////////////////////////
```

Listing 2.2 *Clock.RC*

```
//Microsoft Visual C++ generated resource script.
//
#include "resource.h"

#define APSTUDIO_READONLY_SYMBOLS
```

```
///////////////////////////////////////////////////////////////////////
//
// Generated from the TEXTINCLUDE 2 resource.
//
#include "windows.h"

///////////////////////////////////////////////////////////////////////
#undef APSTUDIO_READONLY_SYMBOLS


#ifdef APSTUDIO_INVOKED
///////////////////////////////////////////////////////////////////////
//
// TEXTINCLUDE
//

1 TEXTINCLUDE DISCARDABLE
BEGIN
    "resource.h\0"
END

2 TEXTINCLUDE DISCARDABLE
BEGIN
    "#include ""windows.h""\r\n"
    "\0"
END

3 TEXTINCLUDE DISCARDABLE
BEGIN
    "\r\n"
    "\0"
END


///////////////////////////////////////////////////////////////////////
#endif    // APSTUDIO_INVOKED


///////////////////////////////////////////////////////////////////////
//
// Dialog
//

IDD_CLOCK DIALOG DISCARDABLE  0x8000, 5, 88, 18
STYLE WS_MINIMIZEBOX | WS_VISIBLE | WS_CAPTION | WS_SYSMENU | 0x800
CAPTION "Clock"
FONT 8, "MS Sans Serif"
BEGIN
    CTEXT           "Time",IDC_TIME,0,4,88,12,SS_NOPREFIX
END


///////////////////////////////////////////////////////////////////////
//
// Icon
//
```

```
IDI_CLOCK                    ICON    DISCARDABLE    "Clock.ico"

#ifndef APSTUDIO_INVOKED
/////////////////////////////////////////////////////////////////////////////
//
// Generated from the TEXTINCLUDE 3 resource.
//


/////////////////////////////////////////////////////////////////////////////
#endif    // not APSTUDIO_INVOKED
```

Listing 2.3 *Resource.H*

```
//{{NO_DEPENDENCIES}}
// Microsoft Visual C++ generated include file.
// Used by Clock.rc
//
#define IDC_TIME               100
#define IDD_CLOCK              101
#define IDI_ICON1              102
#define IDI_CLOCK              102

// Next default values for new objects
//
#ifdef APSTUDIO_INVOKED
#ifndef APSTUDIO_READONLY_SYMBOLS
#define _APS_NEXT_RESOURCE_VALUE     103
#define _APS_NEXT_COMMAND_VALUE      40001
#define _APS_NEXT_CONTROL_VALUE      1000
#define _APS_NEXT_SYMED_VALUE        101
#endif
#endif
```

Dialog Box Tab Order

The techniques shown in this section drive home the concept that a dialog box is not much more than an ordinary window. I will discuss how a dialog box's tab order works and will also show how controls can be added and removed from the dialog box after it has already been created and displayed.

Let's begin by discussing tab ordering. Every time a window is created, the system adds the window to an internal tree of structures. This tree is called the window manger's list. When CreateDialogBoxIndirectParam creates child windows, they are

120

inserted one by one into this tree. For operations that affect child windows, Windows consults the list. If a parent window is hidden, for example, all its child windows are also hidden. If a parent window is destroyed, all its child windows are also destroyed.

If we create a dialog box template that looks like the one shown in Figure 2.5, the resource editor produces a dialog box template that looks like this:

```
IDD_DLGTABS DIALOG DISCARDABLE 0, 0, 248, 106
STYLE WS_MINIMIZEBOX | WS_VISIBLE | WS_CAPTION | WS_SYSMENU
CAPTION "Tabstop Application"
FONT 8, "MS Sans Serif"
BEGIN
    CONTROL         "Checkbox &1",IDC_CHECK1,"Button",BS_AUTOCHECKBOX |
                    WS_TABSTOP,8,8,50,10
    CONTROL         "Checkbox &2",IDC_CHECK2,"Button",BS_AUTOCHECKBOX |
                    WS_TABSTOP,8,20,50,10
    CONTROL         "Checkbox &3",IDC_CHECK3,"Button",BS_AUTOCHECKBOX |
                    WS_TABSTOP,8,32,50,10
    PUSHBUTTON      "&Add dialog control",IDC_ADDDLGCNTL,8,60,64,14
    LTEXT           "Placeholder for control parent dialog box\n\nThis window
is destroyed when the ""Add dialog control"" button is pressed.",
                    IDC_CTRLPRNT,80,8,104,92
    DEFPUSHBUTTON   "OK",IDOK,192,4,50,14
    PUSHBUTTON      "Cancel",IDCANCEL,192,21,50,14
END
```

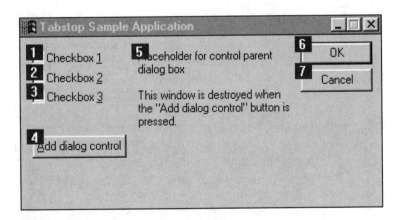

Figure 2.5 *A dialog box template.*

The order of the CONTROL statements in this dialog box is extremely important. CreateDialogIndirectParam calls CreateWindowEx to create each of the child windows in the order shown. This means that the three checkboxes are created first followed by the Add Dialog Control button, the static control, and the OK and Cancel buttons. Because of this ordering, pressing the Tab key will take the user through each of the checkboxes to the Add Dialog Control button. Pressing the Tab key while on the Add Dialog Control button will set focus to the OK button because static windows never get focus. If the Cancel button has focus and the user presses the Tab key again, focus wraps around and is given back to the first check box.

When a control has focus and the user presses the Tab key, the IsDialogMessage function calls the GetNextDlgTabItem function to determine which window should be the new recipient of the keyboard focus:

```
HWND GetNextDlgTabItem(HWND hwndDlg, HWND hwndCtl, BOOL fPrevious);
```

This function searches through the window manager's list looking only at children of the dialog box. More specifically, it begins searching with the window that currently has focus and scans forward through the list looking for the next child window (skipping over any hidden, disabled, or static windows) that has the WS_TAB-STOP style set. If you change the order of the windows in the window manager's list, you change the tabstop order as well.

When IsDialogMessage sees that the user pressed the Tab key, it calls GetNextDlgTabItem like this:

```
SetFocus(GetNextDlgTabItem(hwndDlg, GetFocus(), FALSE));
```

Normally, GetNextDlgTabItem examines only the immediate child windows of the dialog box window. However, this behavior is altered if one or more child windows has the new WS_EX_CON-TROLPARENT extended window style set. As GetNextDlgTabItem examines each child window looking for the WS_TABSTOP style, it also checks for the WS_EX_CONTROLPARENT style. If the WS_EX_CONTROLPARENT style is on, GetNextDlgTabItem continues its search by looking at any child windows of the window that has the WS_EX_CONTROLPARENT style set. These windows are grandchildren of the dialog box itself. If any of these grandchildren have the WS_TABSTOP style, GetNextDlgTabItem has found the window that should have focus and returns its handle.

If none of the grandchildren have the WS_TABSTOP style, GetNextDlgTabItem pops back up a level and continues searching the dialog box's immediate child windows. If any of the grandchild windows also have the WS_EX_CONTROLPARENT style, GetNextDlgTabItem continues its search by going down another level and checks the dialog box's great-grandchildren for the WS_TABSTOP style.

The Tabstop Application

The Tabstop application (**TabStops.EXE**) shown in Listings 2.4-2.6 (starting on page 127) demonstrates how the tabbing order of dialog box controls is determined and how this order can be altered. It also shows how controls can be added and removed from a dialog box after it has been created and displayed. When you invoke the application, it displays the dialog box shown in Figure 2.6.

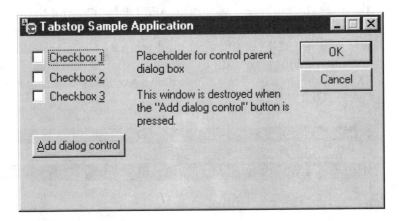

Figure 2.6 *A dialog box with tabbed dialog box controls.*

Using this dialog box, you can easily press the Tab key to move the focus from one control to the next. Verify that the tab order coincides with the order of the CONTROL statements in the dialog box template. Also note that you can use the mnemonic keys to change focus. For example, pressing Alt+A will give focus to the Add Dialog Control button and simulate pressing the button as well.

Notice the text in the middle of the dialog box that reads "Placeholder for control." This text is inside a static control. Static controls do not get focus, and therefore pressing Tab when the focus is on the Add Dialog Control button will give focus to the OK button, skipping over the static control.

Table 2.2 describes the files used to create this application.

Table 2.2 *Files used to build the TabStops application.*

File	Description
TabStops.C	Contains WinMain and the main window's dialog box and message cracker functions.
TabStops.RC	Contains dialog box template for main application window and its icons.
Resource.H	Contains ID for all resources in the RC file.
TabStops.ICO	Contains the icon for the main window.
TabStops.MAK	Visual C++ project makefile.

To affect the tab order, select the Add Dialog Control button. When you do this, the TabStops_OnCommand function receives the WM_COMMAND notification and replaces the placeholder static control window with a mini-dialog box that is contained inside the EXE file's resources. This other dialog box looks like that shown in Figure 2.7.

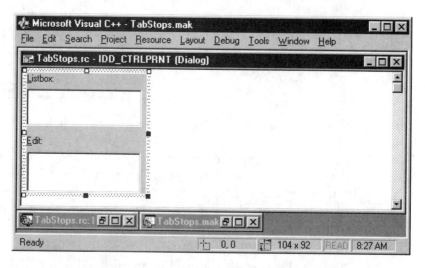

Figure 2.7 *The dialog box child window that replaces the placeholder static control when the user selects the Add Dialog Control button.*

124

Its associated text script looks like this:

```
IDD_CTRLPRNT DIALOG DISCARDABLE 0, 0, 104, 92
STYLE WS_CHILD | WS_VISIBLE
FONT 8, "MS Sans Serif"
BEGIN
    LTEXT           "&Listbox:",IDC_STATIC,0,0,29,8
    LISTBOX         IDC_LIST1,0,12,100,28,LBS_SORT | LBS_NOINTEGRALHEIGHT |
                    WS_VSCROLL | WS_TABSTOP
    LTEXT           "&Edit:",IDC_STATIC,0,48,16,8
    EDITTEXT        IDC_EDIT1,0,60,100,32,ES_MULTILINE | ES_AUTOHSCROLL
END
```

Notice that this dialog box has none of the border styles (WS_BOR-DER, WS_DLGFRAME, etc.) specified and that the WS_CHILD style is specified. After replacing the placeholder static window with this dialog box, the new application's window appears.

What we have done here is replace a single window with another. It just so happens that the new window is a parent window that contains four child windows of its own. But, to do this replacement and have it work properly, we need to alter the position of windows in the window manager's list so that tabbing works correctly. I will now explain how this window replacement is accomplished.

When the user clicks the Add Dialog Control button, the TabStops_OnCommand processes the message. First, it determines the location and dimensions of the placeholder static control window:

```
// Determine the location and size of the existing static child window.
hwndCtlOld = GetDlgItem(hwnd, IDC_CTRLPRNT);
GetWindowRect(hwndCtlOld, &rc);
MapWindowRect(HWND_DESKTOP, hwnd, &rc);  // Macro in windowsx.h
```

Then, the mini-dialog box is created from the dialog box template stored in the EXE file's resource. Notice that the handle of the main dialog box window is passed to CreateDialogParam so that the main dialog box is the parent of this new mini-dialog box.

```
// Create the child dialog box window from the resource's template.
hwndCtlNew = CreateDialogParam(GetWindowInstance(hwnd),
    MAKEINTRESOURCE(IDD_CTRLPRNT), hwnd, NULL, 0);
```

Now, this dialog box needs to be positioned and resized so that it is in the exact same position as the placeholder static window. This is done by calling SetWindowPos:

```
// Position and size the dialog box child window so that it is in the
// exact location as the existing static child window.
// NOTE: The dialog box child is placed immediately after the existing
//       static window so that the controls within it are properly
//       located in the tabbing order.
SetWindowPos(hwndCtlNew, hwndCtlOld, rc.left, rc.top,
   rc.right - rc.left, rc.bottom - rc.top, SWP_SHOWWINDOW);
```

In addition to specifying x and y coordinates, SetWindowPos also allows us to specify a position in the window's z-order. SetWindow-Pos's second parameter indicates a window handle. This window handle identifies the window that should come immediately before the mini-dialog box. In the call to SetWindowPos, the second parameter identifies the placeholder static control. This means that the new mini-dialog box will be inserted into the window manger's list immediately after the static control.

Just positioning the mini-dialog box in the window manager's list is not enough to ensure that tabbing works correctly. In order to allow the child windows of the mini-dialog box to be considered in the tab order, the mini-dialog box must also have the WS_EX_CONTROLPARENT style. I add this style to the mini-dialog box window by executing the following line:

```
// Make sure that the window has the WS_EX_CONTROLPARENT style so
// that IsDialogMessage considers the dialog box's children
// as the user navigates with the keyboard.
ModifyWndStyle(hwndCtlNew, 0, WS_EX_CONTROLPARENT, TRUE);
```

Now that we have created and positioned the mini-dialog box, we no longer need the placeholder static window. So, we destroy it:

```
// Destroy the existing static child window that was used only
// for placement.
DestroyWindow(hwndCtlOld);
```

Finally, since we have added the dialog control, we can disable the Add Dialog Control button and make the OK button the new default pushbutton:

```
// Disable the Add Dialog Control button since we have just
// done this and we do not want to allow it to be done a second time.
EnableWindow(hwndCtl, FALSE);
```

```
// We also must tell the Add Dialog Control button to redraw
```

```
// itself in the not default pushbutton state and to set the
// OK button as the new default pushbutton.
Button_SetState(hwndCtl,
    Button_GetState(hwndCtl) & ~BS_DEFPUSHBUTTON);
SendMessage(hwnd, DM_SETDEFID, IDOK, 0);
```

Disabling the button causes a problem. When the window that has focus is disabled, the window can no longer have focus. The system appropriately takes focus away from the window but does not know which window to give focus to. So, we end up with a situation where no window has focus! If no window has focus, the user can no longer work with the application using the keyboard. To ensure that this application doesn't get into this state, I explicitly set focus to another child (or possibly a grandchild) of the dialog box. I do this by calling SetFocus and GetNextDlgTabItem as follows:

```
// The button that had focus has been disabled so we must explicitly
// set focus to a different window.
SetFocus(GetNextDlgTabItem(hwnd, hwndCtl, FALSE));
```

Listing 2.4 *TabStops.C*

TabStops.ICO

```
/***********************************************************************
Module name: TabStops.c
Written by: Jeffrey Richter
Notices: Copyright (c) 1995 Jeffrey Richter
Purpose: Demonstrates dialog box tab ordering and adding/deleting controls.
***********************************************************************/


#include "..\Win95ADG.h"         /* See Appendix A for details */
#include <Windows.h>
#include <Windowsx.h>
#pragma warning(disable: 4001)   /* Single line comment */
#include "Resource.h"


///////////////////////////////////////////////////////////////////////


void ModifyWndStyle (HWND hwnd, DWORD dwRemove, DWORD dwAdd,
    BOOL fExtendedStyles) {

    int nOffset = fExtendedStyles ? GWL_EXSTYLE : GWL_STYLE;
    SetWindowLong(hwnd, nOffset,
        (GetWindowLong(hwnd, nOffset) & ~dwRemove) | dwAdd);
}
```

```
/////////////////////////////////////////////////////////////////////////////

BOOL TabStops_OnInitDialog (HWND hwnd, HWND hwndFocus, LPARAM lParam) {

   adgSETDLGICONS(hwnd, IDI_TABSTOPS, IDI_TABSTOPS);
   return(TRUE);                       // Accept default focus window.
}


/////////////////////////////////////////////////////////////////////////////

void TabStops_OnCommand (HWND hwnd, int id, HWND hwndCtl, UINT codeNotify) {

   HWND hwndCtlOld, hwndCtlNew;
   RECT rc;

   switch (id) {

      case IDOK:
      case IDCANCEL:                  // Allows dialog box to close
         EndDialog(hwnd, id);
         break;

      case IDC_ADDDLGCNTL:

         // Determine the location and size of the existing static child window.
         hwndCtlOld = GetDlgItem(hwnd, IDC_CTRLPRNT);
         adgASSERT(IsWindow(hwndCtlOld));
         GetWindowRect(hwndCtlOld, &rc);
         MapWindowRect(HWND_DESKTOP, hwnd, &rc);    // Macro in windowsx.h

         // Create the child dialog box window from the resource's template.
         // NOTE: I pass NULL for the dialog box procedure address below
         // because this is a sample application. DefDlgProc will do all the
         // processing itself. Normally, you would pass the address of a
         // dialog box procedure to handle messages for the child dialog.
         hwndCtlNew = CreateDialog(GetWindowInstance(hwnd),
            MAKEINTRESOURCE(IDD_CTRLPRNT), hwnd, NULL);
         adgASSERT(IsWindow(hwndCtlNew));

         // Position and size the dialog box child window so that it is in the
         // exact same location as the existing static child window. NOTE: The
         // dialog box child is placed immediately after the existing static
         // window in the z-order so that the controls within it are properly
         // located in the tabbing order.
         SetWindowPos(hwndCtlNew, hwndCtlOld, rc.left, rc.top,
            rc.right - rc.left, rc.bottom - rc.top, SWP_SHOWWINDOW);

         // Make sure that the window has the WS_EX_CONTROLPARENT style so
         // that IsDialogMessage considers the dialog box's children
         // as the user navigates with the keyboard.
         ModifyWndStyle(hwndCtlNew, 0, WS_EX_CONTROLPARENT, TRUE);
```

```
                  // Destroy the existing static child window that was only used
                  // for placement anyway.
                  DestroyWindow(hwndCtlOld);

                  // Disable the "Add dialog control" button since we have just
                  // done this and we do not allow it to be done a second time.
                  EnableWindow(hwndCtl, FALSE);

                  // We also must tell the "Add dialog control" button to redraw
                  // itself in the not default pushbutton state and to set the
                  // OK button as the new default pushbutton.
                  Button_SetStyle(hwndCtl,
                     GetWindowStyle(hwndCtl) & ~BS_DEFPUSHBUTTON | BS_PUSHBUTTON,
                        TRUE);
                  SendMessage(hwnd, DM_SETDEFID, IDOK, 0);

                  // The button had the focus and has now been disabled so we must
                  // explicitly set focus to a different window.
                  SetFocus(GetNextDlgTabItem(hwnd, hwndCtl, FALSE));
                  break;
          }
}


///////////////////////////////////////////////////////////////////////////////


BOOL WINAPI TabStops_DlgProc (HWND hwnd, UINT uMsg,
   WPARAM wParam, LPARAM lParam) {

   switch (uMsg) {

      // Standard Window's messages
      adgHANDLE_DLGMSG(hwnd, WM_INITDIALOG,  TabStops_OnInitDialog);
      adgHANDLE_DLGMSG(hwnd, WM_COMMAND,     TabStops_OnCommand);
   }
   return(FALSE);                    // We didn't process the message.
}


///////////////////////////////////////////////////////////////////////////////


int WINAPI WinMain (HINSTANCE hinstExe, HINSTANCE hinstPrev,
   LPSTR lpszCmdLine, int nCmdShow) {

   adgWARNIFUNICODEUNDERWIN95();
   adgVERIFY(-1 != DialogBox(hinstExe, MAKEINTRESOURCE(IDD_TABSTOPS),
      NULL, TabStops_DlgProc));

   return(0);
}


//////////////////////////////// End of File //////////////////////////////////
```

Listing 2.5 *TabStops.RC*

```
//Microsoft Visual C++ generated resource script.
//
#include "resource.h"

#define APSTUDIO_READONLY_SYMBOLS
/////////////////////////////////////////////////////////////////////////////
//
// Generated from the TEXTINCLUDE 2 resource.
//
#include "windows.h"

/////////////////////////////////////////////////////////////////////////////
#undef APSTUDIO_READONLY_SYMBOLS


#ifdef APSTUDIO_INVOKED
/////////////////////////////////////////////////////////////////////////////
//
// TEXTINCLUDE
//

1 TEXTINCLUDE DISCARDABLE
BEGIN
    "resource.h\0"
END

2 TEXTINCLUDE DISCARDABLE
BEGIN
    "#include ""windows.h""\r\n"
    "\0"
END

3 TEXTINCLUDE DISCARDABLE
BEGIN
    "\r\n"
    "\0"
END


/////////////////////////////////////////////////////////////////////////////
#endif    // APSTUDIO_INVOKED


/////////////////////////////////////////////////////////////////////////////
//
// Dialog
//

IDD_TABSTOPS DIALOG DISCARDABLE  -32768, 5, 248, 106
STYLE WS_MINIMIZEBOX | WS_VISIBLE | WS_CAPTION | WS_SYSMENU
CAPTION "Tabstops"
FONT 8, "MS Sans Serif"
BEGIN
```

```
    CONTROL         "Checkbox &1",IDC_CHECK1,"Button",BS_AUTOCHECKBOX |
                    WS_TABSTOP,8,8,56,10
    CONTROL         "Checkbox &2",IDC_CHECK2,"Button",BS_AUTOCHECKBOX |
                    WS_TABSTOP,8,20,56,10
    CONTROL         "Checkbox &3",IDC_CHECK3,"Button",BS_AUTOCHECKBOX |
                    WS_TABSTOP,8,32,56,10
    PUSHBUTTON      "&Add dialog control",IDC_ADDDLGCNTL,8,60,64,14
    LTEXT           "Placeholder for control parent dialog box\n\nThis window
is destroyed when the ""Add dialog control"" button is pressed.",
                    IDC_CTRLPRNT,80,8,104,92
    DEFPUSHBUTTON   "OK",IDOK,192,4,50,14
    PUSHBUTTON      "Cancel",IDCANCEL,192,21,50,14
END


IDD_CTRLPRNT DIALOG DISCARDABLE  0, 0, 104, 92
STYLE WS_CHILD | WS_VISIBLE
FONT 8, "MS Sans Serif"
BEGIN
    LTEXT           "&Listbox:",IDC_STATIC,0,0,29,8
    LISTBOX         IDC_LIST1,0,12,100,28,LBS_SORT | LBS_NOINTEGRALHEIGHT |
                    WS_VSCROLL | WS_TABSTOP
    LTEXT           "&Edit:",IDC_STATIC,0,48,16,8
    EDITTEXT        IDC_EDIT1,0,60,100,32,ES_MULTILINE | ES_AUTOHSCROLL
END



/////////////////////////////////////////////////////////////////////////////
//
// Icon
//

IDI_TABSTOPS            ICON    DISCARDABLE     "TabStops.ico"

#ifndef APSTUDIO_INVOKED
/////////////////////////////////////////////////////////////////////////////
//
// Generated from the TEXTINCLUDE 3 resource.
//


/////////////////////////////////////////////////////////////////////////////
#endif    // not APSTUDIO_INVOKED
```

Listing 2.6 *Resource.H*

```
//{{NO_DEPENDENCIES}}
// Microsoft Visual C++ generated include file.
// Used by TabStops.rc
//
#define IDC_STATIC              -1
#define IDC_CTRLPRNT            101
```

```
#define IDD_TABSTOPS                       102
#define IDD_CTRLPRNT                       103
#define IDI_TABSTOPS                       104
#define IDC_CHECK1                         1000
#define IDC_CHECK2                         1001
#define IDC_CHECK3                         1002
#define IDC_LIST1                          1004
#define IDC_EDIT1                          1005
#define IDC_ADDDLGCNTL                     1006

// Next default values for new objects
//
#ifdef APSTUDIO_INVOKED
#ifndef APSTUDIO_READONLY_SYMBOLS
#define _APS_NEXT_RESOURCE_VALUE           106
#define _APS_NEXT_COMMAND_VALUE            40001
#define _APS_NEXT_CONTROL_VALUE            1007
#define _APS_NEXT_SYMED_VALUE              101
#endif
#endif
```

CHAPTER THREE

Dialog Box Techniques

In Chapter 2, I showed what functions are offered by the system in order to make dealing with dialog boxes and windows with child windows easier. This chapter introduces several techniques that make it easier to manipulate dialog boxes in your own applications. Each of the techniques is accompanied by an application that demonstrates the concepts presented in each section.

Expanding/Shrinking Dialog Box Technique

Any new application involves a learning curve for the user. To help a user learn, the application can initially hide some of its functionality. Then, as the user becomes more adept, the program can reveal its advanced features. Many modern applications offer this kind of hand-holding. The expanding/shrinking dialog box is a technique that allows you to hide some of your applications more advanced features. The Windows 95 Choose Profile dialog box (shown in Figure 3.1) is an example of an expanding/shrinking dialog box.

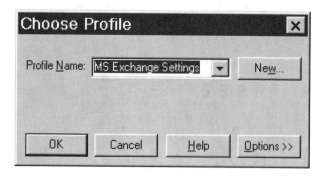

Figure 3.1 *The Windows 95 Choose Profile dialog box.*

This dialog box shows the most common and necessary options to the user. To change some of the more advanced features, the user simply clicks on the Options >> button, and the dialog box expands to show some additional controls as shown in Figure 3.2. This dialog box does not allow the user to shrink the dialog box again (because the Options button is disabled); however, many dialog boxes that offer the expanding option allow the user to shrink the dialog box up again. If you are creating an expanding/shrinking dialog box, you can decide for yourself how you want it to operate.

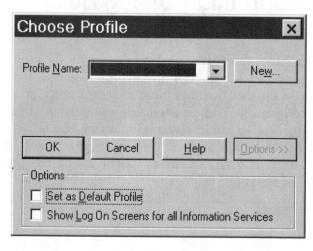

Figure 3.2 *The expanded Choose Profile dialog box.*

The Dialog Expand Application

The Dialog Expand application (**DlgXpnd.EXE**), shown in Listings 3.3-3.5, (starting on page 140) demonstrates how to create an expanding and shrinking dialog box. When you invoke the application, the dialog box shown in Figure 3.3 appears. This is the shrunken view of the dialog box. To view the more complicated options, the user simply clicks the Options button causing the dialog box to expand as shown in Figure 3.4. Now, the user has access to all the controls and can shrink the dialog box back to its initial size by again clicking the Options button.

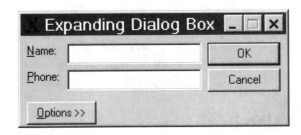

Figure 3.3 *The Dialog Expand application in shrunken state.*

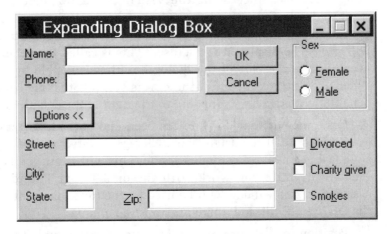

Figure 3.4 *The Dialog Expand application in expanded state.*

Table 3.1 describes the files used to create this application.

Table 3.1 *Files used to build the DlgXpnd application.*

File	Description
DlgXpnd.C	Contains WinMain and the main window's dialog box and message cracker functions.
ExpndBox.C	Contains a library of functions that make it much easier for you to expand/shrink a dialog box. You can use this file in your own applications.
ExpndBox.H	Contains prototypes for the functions contained in the **ExpndBox.C** file. Any source file that uses the library of functions in **ExpandBox.C**, must include this file.
DlgXpnd.RC	Contains dialog box template for main application window and its icons.
Resource.H	Contains ID for all resources in the RC file.
DlgXpnd.ICO	Contains the icon for the main window.
DlgXpnd.MAK	Visual C++ project makefile.

Designing the Dialog Box

The first step to creating an expanding/shrinking dialog box is to design its appearance using the Visual C++ dialog editor. You'll want to design the dialog box so that it shows all the controls. The top-left portion of the dialog box should contain the controls that will always be displayed to the user. This is called the default area because it is the part of the dialog box that is visible by default. When a dialog box expands, it uncovers controls that are below the default area and controls that are to the right of the default area.

Once the entire dialog box has been laid out, add a static window, which I call the default box. Change the style of this window so that it is a black, rectangular frame. This will allow you to easily identify it while you work with the dialog box. The identifier assigned to this window will be used by the functions contained in the **DlgXpnd.C** file and, therefore, must be unique.

Position the default box so that it starts in the top-left corner of the dialog box and contains all the controls that should be visible when the dialog box is in its default state. Figure 3.5 shows the final dialog box with the default box. You can see the right line of the default box just to the right of the OK and Cancel buttons and the bottom line of the default box is just below the Options button.

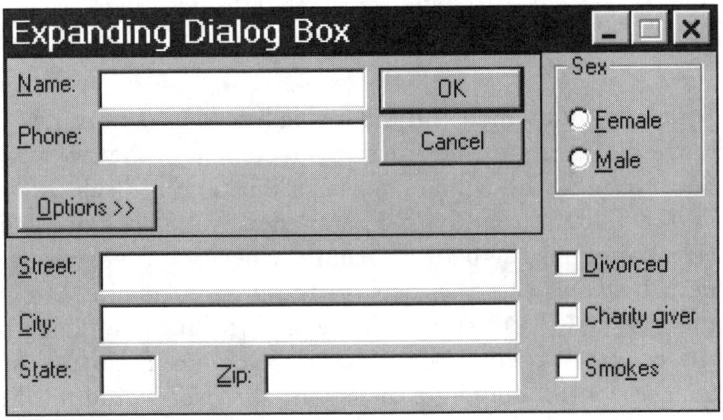

Figure 3.5 *The final dialog box with the default box.*

The ExpandBox Function

The function that is responsible for expanding and shrinking the dialog box is called ExpandBox. This function is in the **ExpndBox.C** source file and has the following prototype:

```
void ExpandBox (BOOL fExpand, HWND hwnd, int nIDDefaultBox);
```

The first parameter, fExpand, tells the function whether you want to expand or shrink the dialog box. Pass TRUE if you want to expand it. The second parameter, hwnd, is the handle to the dialog box itself. The third parameter, nIDDefaultBox, is the ID to the default box window (the Static window with the SS_BLACKFRAME style).

When the dialog box is shrunk, all the controls that lie outside the default area must be disabled. This is done by cycling through all the dialog box's child windows with the following loop:

```
// Retrieve coordinates for the default child window.
GetWindowRect(hwndDefaultBox, &rcDefaultBox);

// Enable/disable all child windows outside of the default box.
hwndChild = GetFirstChild(hwnd);
for (; hwndChild != NULL; hwndChild = GetNextSibling(hwndChild)) {

    // Get rectangle occupied by child window in screen coordinates.
    GetWindowRect(hwndChild, &rcChild);
```

137

```
    if (!IntersectRect(&rcIntersection, &rcChild, &rcShrinkBox))
        EnableWindow(hwndChild, fExpand);
}
```

For each child window in the dialog box, it is determined if its rectangle intersects the default box's rectangle. If the two windows do not intersect, the window is either enabled or disabled, depending on the value of the fExpand parameter. It is very important to disable the clipped windows because, when the user presses the Tab key, Windows sets the focus to the next enabled control that has the WS_TABSTOP style. Although shrinking the dialog box clips the controls beyond the default area, they are still enabled. A clipped control could get focus, but the user would not be able to see it. By disabling these controls, ExpandBox ensures that the Tab key allows the user to traverse only the controls in the default area.

After the child controls have been enabled or disabled, ExpandBox expands the dialog box or shrinks it depending on the fExpand parameter. ExpandBox can always determine what size the dialog box should be when it is shrinking because it can query the location of the default box. However, ExpandBox cannot easily determine what size the dialog box should be when it is expanded. So, in order for ExpandBox to expand the dialog box, it must somehow save the initial dimensions of the dialog box just before it shrinks the dialog box for the first time. These initial dimensions are stored in the shrink box's GWL_USERDATA extra bytes value (the width in the low-word and the height in the high-word). ExpandBox's code to shrink the dialog box follows:

```
GetWindowRect(hwnd, &rcWnd);
if (GetWindowLong(hwnd, GWL_USERDATA) == 0) {

    // This is the first time we are being called to shrink the dialog
    // box. The dialog box is currently in its expanded size, and we must
    // save the expanded width and height so that it can be restored
    // later when the dialog box is expanded.
    SetWindowLong(hwndDefaultBox, GWL_USERDATA,
        MAKELONG(rcWnd.right - rcWnd.left, rcWnd.bottom - rcWnd.top));

    // We hide the default box here so that it is not visible.
    ShowWindow(hwndDefaultBox, SW_HIDE);
}

// Shrink the dialog box so that it encompasses everything from the top-
// left up to and including the default box.
```

```
SetWindowPos(hwnd, NULL, 0, 0,
   rcDefaultBox.right - rcWnd.left, rcDefaultBox.bottom - rcWnd.top,
   SWP_NOZORDER | SWP_NOMOVE);
```

The preceding code first checks to see if the value of the shrink box's GWL_USERDATA value is zero. If it is, we know that this is the first time that the dialog box is being shrunk, and we store the dimensions of the full-size dialog box. Also, if this is the first time the dialog box is shrunk, the default box is hidden so that the user does not see it when the dialog box is displayed on the screen. The last line in the preceding code shrinks the dialog box so that its right and bottom edges line up with the right and bottom edges of the default box.

The code to expand the dialog box is much simpler. All it has to do is retrieve the original dimensions of the dialog box from the default box's GWL_USERDATA extra bytes and call SetWindowPos:

```
// Expand the dialog box by restoring it to its original size.
DWORD dwDims = GetWindowLong(hwndDefaultBox, GWL_USERDATA);
SetWindowPos(hwnd, NULL, 0, 0,
   LOWORD(dwDims), HIWORD(dwDims), SWP_NOZORDER | SWP_NOMOVE);

// Make sure that the entire dialog box is visible on the user's screen.
SendMessage(hwnd, DM_REPOSITION, 0, 0);
```

The call to SendMessage at the end ensures that the entire dialog box is visible on the user's screen. Imagine what would happen if the dialog box was in the shrunken state at the lower-right corner of the user's screen, and the user pressed the Options button. When the dialog box expanded, some of its controls would be off the right or bottom of the screen, and the user would have to move the dialog box in order to see these controls. By sending the new DM_REPOSITION message to the dialog box, the dialog box automatically adjusts its location so that it is completely on the users screen.

Now, the ExpandBox function is called from two locations: the first is inside the DlgXpnd_OnInitDialog function. DlgXpnd_OnInitDialog calls ExpandBox in order to shrink the dialog box. Remember that the dialog box is first presented in the shrunken state. So, an initial call to ExpandBox is necessary to shrink the dialog box. This call also saves the initial size of the dialog box so that it can be expanded later.

The second call to ExpandBox occurs in the DlgXpnd_ OnCommand function and is called when the user clicks the Options button in the dialog box. While processing the button click notification, DlgXpnd_OnCommand determines whether the dialog box is currently in the shrunken or expanded state and then calls ExpandBox to change the state of the dialog box.

DlgXpnd.ICO

Listing 3.1 *DlgXpnd.C*

```
/****************************************************************************
Module name: DlgXpnd.c
Written by: Jeffrey Richter
Notices: Copyright (c) 1995 Jeffrey Richter
Purpose: Demonstrates Expanding/Collapsing dialog box.
****************************************************************************/


#include "..\Win95ADG.h"          /* See Appendix A for details */
#include <windows.h>
#include <windowsx.h>
#pragma warning(disable: 4001)     /* Single line comment */
#include "ExpndBox.h"
#include "resource.h"


//////////////////////////////////////////////////////////////////////////


BOOL DlgXpnd_OnInitDialog (HWND hwnd, HWND hwndFocus, LPARAM lParam) {

   // During initialization, before any windows are shown, shrink the dialog
   // box so that only the default portion is shown.
   ExpandBox(FALSE, hwnd, IDC_DEFAULTBOX);

   adgSETDLGICONS(hwnd, IDI_DLGXPND, IDI_DLGXPND);
   return(TRUE);                   // Accept default focus window.
}


//////////////////////////////////////////////////////////////////////////


void DlgXpnd_OnCommand (HWND hwnd, int id, HWND hwndCtl, UINT codeNotify) {

   BOOL fExpanded;
   int nLen;
   TCHAR szText[20];

   switch (id) {

      case IDOK:
      case IDCANCEL:               // Allows dialog box to close
```

140

```
                    EndDialog(hwnd, id);
                    break;

                case IDC_OPTIONS:
                    if (codeNotify != BN_CLICKED)
                        break;

                    // Determine if the dialog is currently expanded.
                    nLen = Button_GetText(hwndCtl, szText, adgARRAY_SIZE(szText));
                    fExpanded = (szText[nLen - 1] == __TEXT('<'));

                    // User selected "Options >>" button, expand/shrink the dialog box.
                    ExpandBox(!fExpanded, hwnd, IDC_DEFAULTBOX);

                    // Set the focus to the desired control.
                    SetFocus(GetNextDlgTabItem(hwnd, hwndCtl, 0));

                    // Change the options button
                    lstrcpy(&szText[nLen - 2], fExpanded ? __TEXT(">>") : __TEXT("<<"));
                    Button_SetText(hwndCtl, szText);
                    break;
            }
        }


/////////////////////////////////////////////////////////////////////////////


BOOL WINAPI DlgXpnd_DlgProc (HWND hwnd, UINT uMsg,
    WPARAM wParam, LPARAM lParam) {

    switch (uMsg) {

        // Standard Window's messages
        adgHANDLE_DLGMSG(hwnd, WM_INITDIALOG, DlgXpnd_OnInitDialog);
        adgHANDLE_DLGMSG(hwnd, WM_COMMAND,    DlgXpnd_OnCommand);
    }
    return(FALSE);                    // We didn't process the message.
}


/////////////////////////////////////////////////////////////////////////////


int WINAPI WinMain (HINSTANCE hinstExe, HINSTANCE hinstPrev,
    LPSTR lpszCmdLine, int nCmdShow) {

    adgWARNIFUNICODEUNDERWIN95();
    adgVERIFY(-1 != DialogBox(hinstExe, MAKEINTRESOURCE(IDD_DLGXPAND),
        NULL, DlgXpnd_DlgProc));

    return(0);
}


///////////////////////////////// End of File /////////////////////////////////
```

Listing 3.2 *ExpndBox.C*

```
/****************************************************************************
Module name: ExpndBox.c
Written by: Jeffrey Richter
Notices: Copyright (c) 1995 Jeffrey Richter
Purpose: Expanding/shrinking dialog box toolkit functions.
****************************************************************************/


#include "..\Win95ADG.h"          /* See Appendix A for details */
#include <windows.h>
#include <windowsx.h>
#pragma warning(disable: 4001)     /* Single line comment */
#include "ExpndBox.h"
#pragma warning(disable: 4001)     /* Single line comment */


///////////////////////////////////////////////////////////////////////////


void ExpandBox (BOOL fExpand, HWND hwnd, int nIDDefaultBox) {

   RECT rcWnd, rcDefaultBox, rcChild, rcIntersection;
   HWND hwndChild, hwndDefaultBox = GetDlgItem(hwnd, nIDDefaultBox);

   // Retrieve coordinates for the default child window.
   GetWindowRect(hwndDefaultBox, &rcDefaultBox);

   // Enable/disable all child windows outside of the default box.
   hwndChild = GetFirstChild(hwnd);
   for (; hwndChild != NULL; hwndChild = GetNextSibling(hwndChild)) {

      // Get rectangle occupied by child window in screen coordinates.
      GetWindowRect(hwndChild, &rcChild);

      if (!IntersectRect(&rcIntersection, &rcChild, &rcDefaultBox))
         EnableWindow(hwndChild, fExpand);
   }

   if (!fExpand) {
      GetWindowRect(hwnd, &rcWnd);
      if (GetWindowLong(hwnd, GWL_USERDATA) == 0) {

         // This is the first time we are being called to shrink the dialog
         // box. The dialog box is currently in its expanded size and we must
         // save the expanded width and height so that it can be restored
         // later when the dialog box is expanded.
         SetWindowLong(hwndDefaultBox, GWL_USERDATA,
            MAKELONG(rcWnd.right - rcWnd.left, rcWnd.bottom - rcWnd.top));

         // We also hide the default box here so that it is not visible
         ShowWindow(hwndDefaultBox, SW_HIDE);
      }
```

```
    // Shrink the dialog box so that it encompasses everything from the top,
    // left up to and including the default box.
    SetWindowPos(hwnd, NULL, 0, 0,
        rcDefaultBox.right - rcWnd.left, rcDefaultBox.bottom - rcWnd.top,
        SWP_NOZORDER | SWP_NOMOVE);
  } else {

    // Expand the dialog box by restoring it to its original size.
    DWORD dwDims = GetWindowLong(hwndDefaultBox, GWL_USERDATA);
    SetWindowPos(hwnd, NULL, 0, 0,
        LOWORD(dwDims), HIWORD(dwDims), SWP_NOZORDER | SWP_NOMOVE);

    // Make sure that the entire dialog box is visible on the user's screen.
    SendMessage(hwnd, DM_REPOSITION, 0, 0);
  }
}


/////////////////////////////// End of File ///////////////////////////////
```

Listing 3.3 *ExpndBox.H*

```
/****************************************************************************
Module name: ExpndBox.h
Written by: Jeffrey Richter
Notices: Copyright (c) 1995 Jeffrey Richter
Purpose: Expanding/shrinking dialog box toolkit functions.
****************************************************************************/


void ExpandBox (BOOL fExpand, HWND hwnd, int nIDDefaultBox);


/////////////////////////////// End of File ///////////////////////////////
```

Listing 3.4 *DlgXpnd.RC*

```
//Microsoft Visual C++ generated resource script.
//
#include "resource.h"

#define APSTUDIO_READONLY_SYMBOLS
/////////////////////////////////////////////////////////////////////////////
//
// Generated from the TEXTINCLUDE 2 resource.
//
#include "windows.h"

/////////////////////////////////////////////////////////////////////////////
#undef APSTUDIO_READONLY_SYMBOLS
```

143

```
#ifdef APSTUDIO_INVOKED
//////////////////////////////////////////////////////////////////////
//
// TEXTINCLUDE
//

1 TEXTINCLUDE DISCARDABLE
BEGIN
    "resource.h\0"
END

2 TEXTINCLUDE DISCARDABLE
BEGIN
    "#include ""windows.h""\r\n"
    "\0"
END

3 TEXTINCLUDE DISCARDABLE
BEGIN
    "\r\n"
    "\0"
END


//////////////////////////////////////////////////////////////////////
#endif    // APSTUDIO_INVOKED


//////////////////////////////////////////////////////////////////////
//
// Dialog
//


IDD_DLGXPAND DIALOG DISCARDABLE  -32768, 5, 244, 110
STYLE WS_MINIMIZEBOX | WS_VISIBLE | WS_CAPTION | WS_SYSMENU
CAPTION "Dialog Expand"
FONT 8, "MS Sans Serif"
BEGIN
    LTEXT           "&Name:",IDC_STATIC,4,4,22,8
    EDITTEXT        IDC_NAME,32,4,92,13,ES_AUTOHSCROLL
    LTEXT           "&Phone:",IDC_STATIC,4,20,24,8
    EDITTEXT        IDC_PHONE,32,20,92,13,ES_AUTOHSCROLL
    PUSHBUTTON      "&Options >>",IDC_OPTIONS,4,40,48,14
    LTEXT           "&Street:",IDC_STATIC,4,60,23,8
    EDITTEXT        IDC_STREET,32,60,144,13,ES_AUTOHSCROLL
    LTEXT           "&City:",IDC_STATIC,4,78,16,8
    EDITTEXT        IDC_CITY,32,76,144,13,ES_AUTOHSCROLL
    LTEXT           "S&tate:",IDC_STATIC,4,92,21,8
    EDITTEXT        IDC_STATE,32,92,20,13,ES_AUTOHSCROLL
    LTEXT           "&Zip:",IDC_STATIC,72,94,14,8
    EDITTEXT        IDC_ZIP,88,92,88,13,ES_AUTOHSCROLL
    GROUPBOX        "Sex",IDC_STATIC,188,0,52,44
    CONTROL         "&Female",IDC_FEMALE,"Button",BS_AUTORADIOBUTTON |
                    WS_TABSTOP,192,16,35,10
    CONTROL         "&Male",IDC_MALE,"Button",BS_AUTORADIOBUTTON |
                    WS_TABSTOP,192,28,27,10
```

```
        CONTROL        "&Divorced",IDC_DIVORCED,"Button",BS_AUTOCHECKBOX |
                       WS_TABSTOP,188,60,41,10
        CONTROL        "Charity &giver",IDC_CHARITYGIVER,"Button",
                       BS_AUTOCHECKBOX | WS_TABSTOP,188,76,52,10
        CONTROL        "Smo&kes",IDC_SMOKES,"Button",BS_AUTOCHECKBOX |
                       WS_TABSTOP,188,92,37,10
        CONTROL        "",IDC_DEFAULTBOX,"Static",SS_BLACKFRAME,0,0,184,56
        DEFPUSHBUTTON  "OK",IDOK,128,4,50,14
        PUSHBUTTON     "Cancel",IDCANCEL,128,20,50,14
END


/////////////////////////////////////////////////////////////////////////
//
// Icon
//


IDI_DLGXPND             ICON    DISCARDABLE     "DlgXpnd.ico"

#ifndef APSTUDIO_INVOKED
/////////////////////////////////////////////////////////////////////////
//
// Generated from the TEXTINCLUDE 3 resource.
//



/////////////////////////////////////////////////////////////////////////
#endif    // not APSTUDIO_INVOKED
```

Listing 3.5 *Resource.H*

```
//{{NO_DEPENDENCIES}}
// Microsoft Visual C++ generated include file.
// Used by DlgXpnd.rc
//
#define IDC_STATIC                    -1
#define IDD_DLGXPAND                  101
#define IDI_DLGXPND                   102
#define IDC_NAME                      1000
#define IDC_PHONE                     1006
#define IDC_OPTIONS                   1007
#define IDC_STREET                    1008
#define IDC_CITY                      1009
#define IDC_STATE                     1010
#define IDC_ZIP                       1011
#define IDC_DIVORCED                  1012
#define IDC_CHARITYGIVER              1013
#define IDC_SMOKES                    1014
#define IDC_FEMALE                    1015
#define IDC_MALE                      1016
#define IDC_DEFAULTBOX                1029
```

```
// Next default values for new objects
//
#ifdef APSTUDIO_INVOKED
#ifndef APSTUDIO_READONLY_SYMBOLS
#define _APS_NEXT_RESOURCE_VALUE        103
#define _APS_NEXT_COMMAND_VALUE         40001
#define _APS_NEXT_CONTROL_VALUE         1000
#define _APS_NEXT_SYMED_VALUE           101
#endif
#endif
```

Modalless Dialog Box Technique

When you use a modal dialog box, you call the DialogBoxParam function, and then the controls in the dialog box are initialized. This sounds simple, but how does the dialog box know the values to use to initialize its controls? When, the user changes values in the dialog box's controls and presses the OK button, the dialog box reads the contents of the controls and somehow notifies the application of the new values. This communication between the application and the dialog box is very inconvenient. Usually, the communication is done as follows:

1. The application defines a data structure that contains members representing the data that should be shown to the user in the dialog box.

2. The application allocates one of these data structures (possibly on the stack as a local variable) and initializes its members.

3. The application calls DialogBoxParam and passes the address to the initialized structure as the last parameter (lParamInit).

4. When the dialog box window receives the WM_INITDIALOG message, the lParam parameter is the address of the data structure passed to DialogBoxParam. The Dlg_OnInitDialog function can now access the members of the structure and initialize the dialog box's controls appropriately.

5. Before Dlg_OnInitDialog returns, it saves the address of the data structure in the dialog box's GWL_USERDATA extra bytes, which is needed for step 6.

At this point, the dialog box is visible to the user and all the controls have been initialized. When the user is finished changing various settings, the user presses the OK button. At this point, the dialog box must communicate the modified settings back to the application.

6. When the Dlg_OnCommand function receives the OK button notification, the function retrieves the address to the applications data structure. Note that this address was saved in the dialog box's GWL_USERDATA extra bytes in step 5.

7. Then, the code gets the current values from the controls and sets the members of the data structure to reflect the controls current values.

8. Finally, Dlg_OnCommand calls the EndDialog function in order to dismiss the dialog box, allowing the user to work with the rest of the application.

After the dialog box is dismissed, the thread's call to DialogBoxParam returns, and the user's new values can be seen by examining the members of the data structure. This is an awful lot of work to go through in order to use a modal dialog box. In the early days of Windows programming, this procedure was even more difficult. Back in the early days, there was no DialogBoxParam function and there were no GWL_USERDATA extra bytes. So, the data structure had to be a global variable that was equally accessible to the application as well as the dialog box function.

Today, even though the Windows API has come a long way, these steps are still rather tedious, and better techniques are welcome. In this section, I present a technique of my own, called a modalless dialog box, that makes communicating with dialog boxes more convenient.

The modalless dialog box is a cross between a modal dialog box and a modeless dialog box. To the operating system, this is a modeless dialog box. To the user, this dialog box operates just like a modal dialog box. To the programmer, the dialog box is created and destroyed like a modeless dialog box but it is displayed and hidden like a modal dialog box.

The real problem with modal dialog boxes is that they are destroyed, along with their contents when the user presses the OK button. However, if we create a modeless dialog box and hide it only when the user presses the OK button, the dialog box is not destroyed and the application can easily query the dialog box's controls for their updated values.

The Modalless Dialog Box Application

The Modalless Dialog Box application (**DlgMdlls.EXE**), shown in Listings 3.6-3.11, (starting on page 153) demonstrates how to create and use a modalless dialog box. When you invoke the application, the main application window appears as shown in Figure 3.6 :

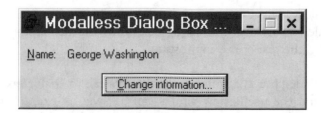

Figure 3.6 *The Modalless Dialog Box application.*

This window shows the current name of George Washington. But, what you don't see is another modeless dialog box that is also created (without the WS_VISIBLE style) when the application starts. This window is initially hidden.

Now, if the user wants to change George Washington to a different name, all they have to do is click on the Change Information button to display the dialog box shown in Figure 3.7. This dialog box is a modalless dialog box, but it appears to the user as though it is a modal dialog box. With this dialog box, the user can enter in a different name and then click either the OK or Cancel buttons. If OK is selected, the main application window updates its dialog box to reflect the new name. Selecting Cancel has no affect other than dismissing (hiding) the modalless dialog box.

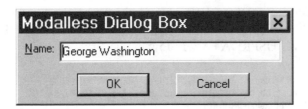

Figure 3.7 *The Change Information modalless dialog box.*

Table 3.2 describes the files used to create this application.

Table 3.2 *Files used to build the DlgMdlls application.*

File	Description
DlgMdlls.C	Contains WinMain and main window's dialog box and message cracker functions.
MdllsDlg.C	Contains dialog box and message cracker functions for the modalless dialog box.
Modalles.C	Contains a library of functions that make it much easier for you to construct modalless dialog boxes. You can use this file in your own applications.
Modalles.H	Contains prototypes for the functions contained in the **Modalles.C** file. Any source file that uses the library of functions in **Modalles.C**, must include this file.
DlgMdlls.RC	Contains dialog box template for main application window and its icons.
Resource.H	Contains IDs for all resources in the RC file.
DlgMdlls.ICO	Contains the icon for the main window.
DlgMdlls.MAK	Visual C++ project makefile.

When the **DlgMdlls.EXE** application starts, it creates a modal dialog box. This dialog box is the applications main window. When this dialog box receives a WM_INITDIALOG message, its DlgMdlls_OnInitDialog function calls the Modalless_CreateDlg library function. This function simply calls the CreateDialogParam function to create a hidden modalless dialog box and returns the handle of the parent window. This handle is then saved in the main application window's GWL_USERDATA window bytes:

```
HWND hwndMdllsDlg = Modalless_CreateDlg(GetWindowInstance(hwnd),
    MAKEINTRESOURCE(IDD_DLGMDLSDLG), hwnd, MdllsDlg_DlgProc, 0);
adgASSERT(IsWindow(hwndMdllsDlg));

// Save handle to modalless dialog box so that it can be shown later.
SetWindowLong(hwnd, GWL_USERDATA, (LONG) hwndMdllsDlg);
```

The modalless dialog box is destroyed when the user closes the application by calling the Modalless_DestroyDlg function (which calls DestroyWindow internally):

```
void DlgMdlls_OnCommand (HWND hwnd, int id, HWND hwndCtl, UINT codeNotify) {

  HWND hwndMdllsDlg = NULL;
  TCHAR szBuf[100];

  switch (id) {
    case IDCANCEL:                // Allows dialog box to close.
      // If the main window is dying, destroy the modalless dialog box. Of
      // course, the system would do this for us automatically, but its
      // better for us to explicitly do this instead.
      Modalless_DestroyDlg((HWND) GetWindowLong(hwnd, GWL_USERDATA));
      EndDialog(hwnd, id);
      break;
    .
    .
    .
```

Once a modalless dialog box is created, the functions that access it are similar to those for modal dialog boxes. Table 3.3 shows the modal dialog box functions and their equivalent modalless dialog box functions.

Table 3.3 *Modal and Modalless dialog box actions with their associated functions.*

Action	Modal dialog box function	Modalless dialog box function
Display the dialog box	DialogBoxParam	Modalless_ShowDlg
Dismiss the dialog box	EndDialog	Modalless_EndDlg

When the user clicks the Change Information button, the following code, contained in the DlgMdlls_OnCommand function, is executed:

```
// Get the handle to the modalless dialog box from the extra bytes.
hwndMdllsDlg = (HWND) GetWindowLong(hwnd, GWL_USERDATA);

// Initialize the edit control inside the modalless dialog box with
// the value from the main application window's static control.
GetDlgItemText(hwnd, IDC_NAME, szBuf, adgARRAY_SIZE(szBuf));
SetDlgItemText(hwndMdllsDlg, IDC_NAME, szBuf);

// Display the modalless dialog box to the user.
if (IDOK == Modalless_ShowDlg(hwndMdllsDlg)) {

   // If the user pressed the OK button, examine the modalless dialog
   // box's controls to get the user's modified values and update the
   // main window's data fields.
   GetDlgItemText(hwndMdllsDlg, IDC_NAME, szBuf, adgARRAY_SIZE(szBuf));
   SetDlgItemText(hwnd, IDC_NAME, szBuf);
}
```

This code retrieves the handle to the modalless dialog box from the main window's GWL_USERDATA window bytes, initializes the modalless dialog box's child controls with the current information, and then displays the modalless dialog box by calling the Modalless_ShowDlg function. If the user presses the OK button, Modalless_ShowDlg returns IDOK and the code above sets the main window's controls to reflect the user's modified values.

Let's look at the Modalless_ShowDlg function in more detail. This function requires the window handle to the modalless dialog box. This function makes the modeless dialog box behave like a modal dialog box. It does this by disabling the modalless dialog box's parent window, showing the modeless dialog box, and entering a GetMessage loop. The message loop follows:

```
// Execute a message loop until the "ModallessResult" property becomes
// associated with the modalless dialog box. This happens when the dialog
// box function calls the EndModalLessDlg function.
do {

   // Wait for a message and process it.
   GetMessage(&msg, NULL, 0, 0);
   if (!IsDialogMessage(hwnd, &msg)) {
      TranslateMessage(&msg);
      DispatchMessage(&msg);
   }
```

```
    // Get the value of "ModallessResult" property. If property does not
    // exist, GetProp returns zero.
    nResult = (int) GetProp(hwnd, g_szModallessResult);

    // Try to remove the property. If RemoveProp returns NULL, the property
    // is not associated with the window and the message loop must continue.
} while (RemoveProp(hwnd, g_szModallessResult) == NULL);
```

The message loop will not terminate until the modalless dialog box procedure calls the Modalless_EndDlg function. This function associates a property with the modalless dialog box. The GetMessage loop detects when this property exists and gets the value associated with this property. This is the value that the dialog box function wants to return to Modalless_ShowDlg's caller.

During the message loop, the GetProp function is called to see if Modalless_EndDlg has been called. If the value returned by GetProp is zero, it means that the property has not yet been associated with the window or that the nResult parameter to the Modalless_EndDlg function was zero. We can determine which of these cases it was by calling the RemoveProp function. If this function is unable to remove a property with the specified name, NULL is returned. This means that the message loop should not terminate. If the property was removed, the message loop terminates, the disabled parent window is enabled, the modalless dialog box is hidden, and the result from the GetProp function is returned to the application:

```
if (IsWindow(hwndOwner)) {

    // Allow the owner window to receive keyboard and mouse input.
    EnableWindow(hwndOwner, TRUE);
}

// Hide the modalless dialog box and return the result.
ShowWindow(hwnd, SW_HIDE);
return(nResult);
```

Now, lets talk about how the modalless dialog box initializes itself. When the dialog box is created with Modalless_CreateDlg, a WM_INITDIALOG message is sent to the dialog box procedure. This is the point at which any one-time initialization should be performed on the dialog box. When the Modalless_ShowDlg function displays the dialog box by calling ShowWindow, the system sends a WM_SHOWWINDOW message to the modalless dialog box procedure. This is the opportunity for the dialog box procedure to do any initialization before it is displayed. In the application, the keyboard focus is placed on the first child of the dialog box. This is what most users expect whenever a dialog box is displayed:

```
void MdllsDlg_OnShowWindow (HWND hwnd, BOOL fShow, UINT status) {

    if (fShow) {

        // The modalless dialog box is becoming visible. Make the first
        // WS_TABSTOP child window have the focus.
        SetFocus(GetNextDlgTabItem(hwnd, NULL, FALSE));
    }
}
```

When the user clicks the OK or Cancel button, the MdllsDlg_ OnCommand function calls Modalless_EndDlg:

```
BOOL WINAPI Modalless_EndDlg (HWND hwnd, int nResult) {

    // Setting the property also tells the mesasge loop to terminate.
    return(SetProp(hwnd, g_szModallessResult, (HANDLE) nResult));
}
```

This function uses a window property to associate a return value with the modalless dialog box. The first parameter is the handle of the dialog box; the second is the value to be returned to Modalless_ShowDlg's caller. Since an attempt to set a property can fail, Modalless_EndDlg's return value is FALSE if the property could not be associated and the dialog box will not be dismissed. This function is similar to the EndDialog function for modal dialog boxes.

DlgMdlls.ICO

Listing 3.6 *DlgMdlls.C*

```
/********************************************************************************
Module name: DlgMdlls.c
Written by: Jeffrey Richter
Notices: Copyright (c) 1995 Jeffrey Richter
Purpose: Application to demonstrate modalless dialog boxes.
********************************************************************************/


#include "..\Win95ADG.h"          /* See Appendix A for details */
#include <windows.h>
#include <windowsx.h>
#pragma warning(disable: 4001)     /* Single line comment */
#include "resource.h"
#include "Modalles.h"
#pragma warning(disable: 4001)     /* Single line comment */
```

```
///////////////////////////////////////////////////////////////////////////

// Dialog procedure for modalless dialog (contained in MdllsDlg.c)
extern BOOL WINAPI MdllsDlg_DlgProc (HWND hwnd, UINT uMsg,
   WPARAM wParam, LPARAM lParam);


///////////////////////////////////////////////////////////////////////////


BOOL DlgMdlls_OnInitDialog (HWND hwnd, HWND hwndFocus, LPARAM lParam) {

   HWND hwndMdllsDlg = Modalless_CreateDlg(GetWindowInstance(hwnd),
      MAKEINTRESOURCE(IDD_DLGMDLSDLG), hwnd, MdllsDlg_DlgProc, 0);
   adgASSERT(IsWindow(hwndMdllsDlg));

   // Save handle to modalless dialog box so it can be shown later
   SetWindowLong(hwnd, GWL_USERDATA, (LONG) hwndMdllsDlg);

   adgSETDLGICONS(hwnd, IDI_DLGMDLS, IDI_DLGMDLS);
   return(TRUE);                    // Accept default focus window.
}


///////////////////////////////////////////////////////////////////////////


void DlgMdlls_OnCommand (HWND hwnd, int id, HWND hwndCtl, UINT codeNotify) {

   HWND hwndMdllsDlg = NULL;
   TCHAR szBuf[100];

   switch (id) {

      case IDCANCEL:               // Allows dialog box to close
         // If the main window is dying, destroy the modalless dialog box. Of
         // course, the system would do this for us automatically, but its
         // better for us to explicitly do this instead.
         Modalless_DestroyDlg((HWND) GetWindowLong(hwnd, GWL_USERDATA));
         EndDialog(hwnd, id);
         break;

      case IDC_CHANGEINFO:

         // Get the handle to the modalless dialog box from the extra bytes.
         hwndMdllsDlg = (HWND) GetWindowLong(hwnd, GWL_USERDATA);

         // Initialize the edit control inside the modalless dialog box with
         // the value from the main application window's static control.
         GetDlgItemText(hwnd, IDC_NAME, szBuf, adgARRAY_SIZE(szBuf));
         SetDlgItemText(hwndMdllsDlg, IDC_NAME, szBuf);

         // Display the modalless dialog box to the user.
         if (IDOK == Modalless_ShowDlg(hwndMdllsDlg)) {
```

```
                    // If the user pressed the OK button, examine the modalless dialog
                    // box's controls to get the user's modified values and update the
                    // main window's data fields.
                    GetDlgItemText(hwndMdllsDlg, IDC_NAME, szBuf, adgARRAY_SIZE(szBuf));
                    SetDlgItemText(hwnd, IDC_NAME, szBuf);
                }
                break;
        }
    }


///////////////////////////////////////////////////////////////////////////////


BOOL WINAPI DlgMdlls_DlgProc (HWND hwnd, UINT uMsg,
    WPARAM wParam, LPARAM lParam) {

    switch (uMsg) {

        // Standard Window's messages
        adgHANDLE_DLGMSG(hwnd, WM_INITDIALOG, DlgMdlls_OnInitDialog);
        adgHANDLE_DLGMSG(hwnd, WM_COMMAND,    DlgMdlls_OnCommand);
    }
    return(FALSE);                     // We didn't process the message.
}


///////////////////////////////////////////////////////////////////////////////


int WINAPI WinMain (HINSTANCE hinstExe, HINSTANCE hinstPrev,
    LPSTR lpszCmdLine, int nCmdShow) {

    adgWARNIFUNICODEUNDERWIN95();
    adgVERIFY(-1 != DialogBox(hinstExe, MAKEINTRESOURCE(IDD_DLGMDLS),
        NULL, DlgMdlls_DlgProc));

    return(0);
}


////////////////////////////////// End of File //////////////////////////////////
```

Listing 3.7 *MdllsDlg.C*

```
/*****************************************************************************
Module name: MdllsDlg.c
Written by: Jeffrey Richter
Notices: Copyright (c) 1995 Jeffrey Richter
Purpose: Modalless dialog box.
*****************************************************************************/
```

```
#include "..\Win95ADG.h"          /* See Appendix A for details */
#include <windows.h>
#include <windowsx.h>
#pragma warning(disable: 4001)    /* Single line comment */
#include "resource.h"
#include "modalles.h"


/////////////////////////////////////////////////////////////////////////////


void MdllsDlg_OnShowWindow (HWND hwnd, BOOL fShow, UINT status) {

   if (fShow) {

      // The modalless dialog box is becoming visible. Make the first
      // WS_TABSTOP child window have the focus.
      SetFocus(GetNextDlgTabItem(hwnd, NULL, FALSE));
   }
}


/////////////////////////////////////////////////////////////////////////////


BOOL MdllsDlg_OnInitDialog (HWND hwnd, HWND hwndFocus, LPARAM lParam) {

   return(TRUE);                    // Accept default focus window.
}


/////////////////////////////////////////////////////////////////////////////


void MdllsDlg_OnCommand (HWND hwnd, int id, HWND hwndCtl, UINT codeNotify) {

   switch (id) {

      case IDOK:
      case IDCANCEL:                // Allows dialog box to close
         Modalless_EndDlg(hwnd, id);
         break;
   }
}


/////////////////////////////////////////////////////////////////////////////


BOOL WINAPI MdllsDlg_DlgProc (HWND hwnd, UINT uMsg,
   WPARAM wParam, LPARAM lParam) {

   switch (uMsg) {

      // Standard Window's messages
      adgHANDLE_DLGMSG(hwnd, WM_INITDIALOG, MdllsDlg_OnInitDialog);
      adgHANDLE_DLGMSG(hwnd, WM_COMMAND,    MdllsDlg_OnCommand);
```

```
        // NOTE: Normally, if a dialog box procedure processes a message it
        // returns TRUE and DefDlgProc does not do additional processing.
        // However, for the WM_SHOWWINDOW message, we need to do some processing
        // AND we also need the system to do its default processing (which
        // shows/hides the window). So, this message must have special handling.
        case WM_SHOWWINDOW:
            HANDLE_WM_SHOWWINDOW(hwnd, wParam, lParam, MdllsDlg_OnShowWindow);
            return(FALSE);              // Return FALSE to DefDlgProc.
    }
    return(FALSE);                      // We didn't process the message.
}



////////////////////////////////// End of File //////////////////////////////////
```

Listing 3.8 *Modalles.C*

```
/*****************************************************************************
Module name: Modalles.c
Written by: Jeffrey Richter
Notices: Copyright (c) 1995 Jeffrey Richter
Purpose: Modalless dialog box toolkit functions.
*****************************************************************************/


#include "..\Win95ADG.h"         /* See Appendix A for details */
#include <windows.h>
#include <windowsx.h>
#pragma warning(disable: 4001)    /* Single line comment */
#include "modalles.h"


///////////////////////////////////////////////////////////////////////////////


// Internal property string used to associate the dialog box's result value.
static TCHAR g_szModallessResult[] = __TEXT("ModallessResult");


///////////////////////////////////////////////////////////////////////////////


HWND WINAPI Modalless_CreateDlgA (HINSTANCE hinst, LPCSTR szTemplateName,
    HWND hwndOwner, DLGPROC pfnDlgProc, LPARAM lParamInit) {

    return(CreateDialogParamA(hinst, szTemplateName, hwndOwner,
        pfnDlgProc, lParamInit));
}
```

```
////////////////////////////////////////////////////////////////////////////


HWND WINAPI Modalless_CreateDlgW (HINSTANCE hinst, LPCWSTR szTemplateName,
   HWND hwndOwner, DLGPROC pfnDlgProc, LPARAM lParamInit) {

   return(CreateDialogParamW(hinst, szTemplateName, hwndOwner,
      pfnDlgProc, lParamInit));
}


////////////////////////////////////////////////////////////////////////////


BOOL WINAPI Modalless_DestroyDlg (HWND hwnd) {

   return(DestroyWindow(hwnd));
}


////////////////////////////////////////////////////////////////////////////


int WINAPI Modalless_ShowDlg (HWND hwnd) {

   HWND hwndOwner = GetParent(hwnd);
   int nResult = 0;
   MSG msg;

   if (IsWindow(hwndOwner)) {

      // Stop the owner window from receiving keyboard or mouse input.
      EnableWindow(hwndOwner, FALSE);
   }

   // Display the modalless dialog box by sending a WM_SHOWWINDOW message to
   // the dialog box function.
   ShowWindow(hwnd, SW_SHOW);

   // Execute a message loop until the "ModallessResult" property becomes
   // associated with the modalless dialog box. This happens when the dialog
   // box function calls the EndModalLessDlg function.
   do {

      // Wait for a message and process it.
      GetMessage(&msg, NULL, 0, 0);
      if (!IsDialogMessage(hwnd, &msg)) {
         TranslateMessage(&msg);
         DispatchMessage(&msg);
      }

      // Get the value of "ModallessResult" property. If property does not
      // exist, GetProp returns zero.
      nResult = (int) GetProp(hwnd, g_szModallessResult);
```

```
      // Try to remove the property. If RemoveProp returns NULL, the property
      // is not associated with the window and the message loop must continue.
      // The debug version of Windows 95 warns that the line below removes
      // a property that doesn't exist.  This is by design.
   } while (RemoveProp(hwnd, g_szModallessResult) == NULL);

   if (IsWindow(hwndOwner)) {

      // Allow the owner window to receive keyboard and mouse input.
      EnableWindow(hwndOwner, TRUE);
   }

   // Hide the modalless dialog box and return the result.
   ShowWindow(hwnd, SW_HIDE);
   return(nResult);
}


///////////////////////////////////////////////////////////////////////////


BOOL WINAPI Modalless_EndDlg (HWND hwnd, int nResult) {

   // Setting the property also tells the mesasge loop to terminate.
   return(SetProp(hwnd, g_szModallessResult, (HANDLE) nResult));
}


/////////////////////////////// End of File ///////////////////////////////
```

Listing 3.9 *Modalles.H*

```
/*****************************************************************************
Module name: Modalles.h
Written by: Jeffrey Richter
Notices: Copyright (c) 1995 Jeffrey Richter
Purpose: Modalless dialog box toolkit functions.
*****************************************************************************/


HWND WINAPI Modalless_CreateDlgA (HINSTANCE hinst, LPCSTR szTemplateName,
   HWND hwndOwner, DLGPROC pfnDlgProc, LPARAM lParamInit);

HWND WINAPI Modalless_CreateDlgW (HINSTANCE hinst, LPCWSTR szTemplateName,
   HWND hwndOwner, DLGPROC pfnDlgProc, LPARAM lParamInit);

#ifdef UNICODE
#define Modalless_CreateDlg Modalless_CreateDlgW
#else
#define Modalless_CreateDlg Modalless_CreateDlgA
#endif // !UNICODE
```

159

```
//////////////////////////////////////////////////////////////////////////

int  WINAPI Modalless_ShowDlg (HWND hwnd);
BOOL WINAPI Modalless_EndDlg (HWND hwnd, int nResult);
BOOL WINAPI Modalless_DestroyDlg (HWND hwnd);


//////////////////////////////// End of File ////////////////////////////////
```

Listing 3.10 *DlgMdlls.RC*

```
//Microsoft Visual C++ generated resource script.
//
#include "resource.h"

#define APSTUDIO_READONLY_SYMBOLS
//////////////////////////////////////////////////////////////////////////
//
// Generated from the TEXTINCLUDE 2 resource.
//
#include "windows.h"

//////////////////////////////////////////////////////////////////////////
#undef APSTUDIO_READONLY_SYMBOLS


#ifdef APSTUDIO_INVOKED
//////////////////////////////////////////////////////////////////////////
//
// TEXTINCLUDE
//

1 TEXTINCLUDE DISCARDABLE
BEGIN
    "resource.h\0"
END

2 TEXTINCLUDE DISCARDABLE
BEGIN
    "#include ""windows.h""\r\n"
    "\0"
END

3 TEXTINCLUDE DISCARDABLE
BEGIN
    "\r\n"
    "\0"
END

//////////////////////////////////////////////////////////////////////////
#endif  // APSTUDIO_INVOKED
```

160

```
///////////////////////////////////////////////////////////////////////////
//
// Dialog
//

IDD_DLGMDLS DIALOG DISCARDABLE  -32768, 5, 196, 44
STYLE WS_MINIMIZEBOX | WS_VISIBLE | WS_CAPTION | WS_SYSMENU
CAPTION "Modalless Dialogs"
FONT 8, "MS Sans Serif"
BEGIN
    LTEXT           "&Name:",IDC_STATIC,4,8,22,8
    LTEXT           "George Washington",IDC_NAME,32,8,160,8
    DEFPUSHBUTTON   "&Change information...",IDC_CHANGEINFO,56,24,88,14
END

IDD_DLGMDLSDLG DIALOG DISCARDABLE  0, 0, 186, 42
STYLE DS_MODALFRAME | WS_POPUP | WS_CAPTION | WS_SYSMENU
CAPTION "Modalless Dialog Box"
FONT 8, "MS Sans Serif"
BEGIN
    LTEXT           "&Name:",IDC_STATIC,4,4,22,8
    EDITTEXT        IDC_NAME,28,4,152,13,ES_AUTOHSCROLL
    DEFPUSHBUTTON   "OK",IDOK,40,24,50,14
    PUSHBUTTON      "Cancel",IDCANCEL,108,24,50,14
END


///////////////////////////////////////////////////////////////////////////
//
// Icon
//

IDI_DLGMDLS             ICON    DISCARDABLE     "DlgMDlls.ico"

#ifndef APSTUDIO_INVOKED
///////////////////////////////////////////////////////////////////////////
//
// Generated from the TEXTINCLUDE 3 resource.
//


///////////////////////////////////////////////////////////////////////////
#endif    // not APSTUDIO_INVOKED
```

Listing 3.11 *Resource.H*

```
//{{NO_DEPENDENCIES}}
// Microsoft Visual C++ generated include file.
// Used by DlgMdlls.rc
//
#define IDD_DLGMDLS                 101
```

```
#define IDI_DLGMDLS                    102
#define IDD_DLGMDLSDLG                 113
#define IDC_NAME                       1000
#define IDC_CHANGEINFO                 1001
#define IDC_STATIC                     -1

// Next default values for new objects
//
#ifdef APSTUDIO_INVOKED
#ifndef APSTUDIO_READONLY_SYMBOLS
#define _APS_NEXT_RESOURCE_VALUE       103
#define _APS_NEXT_COMMAND_VALUE        40001
#define _APS_NEXT_CONTROL_VALUE        1002
#define _APS_NEXT_SYMED_VALUE          101
#endif
#endif
```

Dynamic Dialog Box Technique

Sometimes it is necessary to design dialog boxes while the application is running. For example, a database application may allow the user to design the entry form and then create a dialog box based on this form for adding records to the database. Another example is the Visual C++ dialog box editor itself. The editor allows the user to create a dialog box visually and test the dialog without compiling any resources whatsoever. The dynamic dialog box technique demonstrates how dialog box templates can be created at run time.

The Win32 API offers two functions for creating dialog boxes at run time. DialogBoxIndirectParam creates modal dialog boxes:

```
int DialogBoxIndirectParam(HINSTANCE hinst, LPCDLGTEMPLATE lpDlgTemplate,
    HWND hwndOwner, DLGPROC pfnDlgProc, LPARAM lParamInit);
```

while CreateDialogIndirectParam creates modeless dialog boxes:

```
HWND CreateDialogIndirectParam(HINSTANCE hinst, LPCDLGTEMPLATE lpDlgTemplate,
    HWND hwndOwner, DLGPROC pfnDlgProc, LPARAM lParamInit);
```

Dynamic dialog boxes are created by building a dialog box template in a memory block and passing the address of this memory block in the lpDlgTemplate parameter to either of these two functions.

Immediately after the functions return, you can free the memory block. In Chapter 2, the Designing the Appearance of a Dialog Box section described what the binary image of a dialog box template looks like. In that section, I discussed how you could use Visual C++ to design a dialog box. Then, using the resource compiler, the script template is converted into a binary template and is embedded into the EXE file's image.

Since I already presented that discussion, it is very easy to see how a dialog box template could be created at run time. All we have to do is allocate a block of memory and populate this memory with a DLGTEMPLATEEX structure, an optional FONTINFOEX structure, and zero or more DLGITEMTEMPLATEEX structures (one for each child window). You may want to refer to the aforementioned section in Chapter 2 to refresh your memory. Once the memory block has been initialized, one of the dialog box functions may be called.

The Dynamic Dialog Box Application

The Dynamic Dialog Box application (**DlgDyn.EXE**), shown in Listings 3.12-3.17, (starting on page 169) demonstrates how to prepare dynamic dialog box templates at run time so that dialog boxes can be presented to the user. When you invoke the application, the main application window appears.

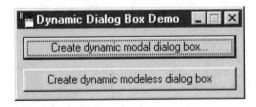

Figure 3.8 *The Dynamic Dialog Box application.*

When you select either button, a dynamic dialog box template is created in memory and is then presented on the screen. If you select the Create Dynamic Modal Dialog Box button, the template is used to produce a modal dialog box (shown in Figure 3.9), and the Create Dynamic Modeless Dialog Box button creates a modeless dialog box (shown in Figure 3.10). While the modeless dialog box is visible, the Create Dynamic Modeless Dialog Box button changes to a Destroy Dynamic Modeless Dialog Box button. You can use this button to remove the modeless dialog box.

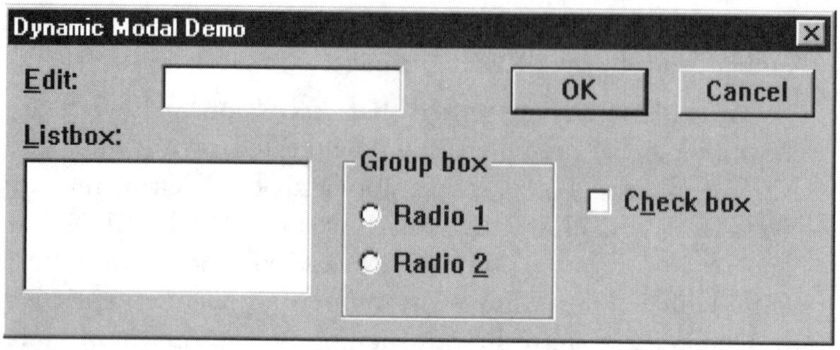

Figure 3.9 *The dynamic modal dialog box.*

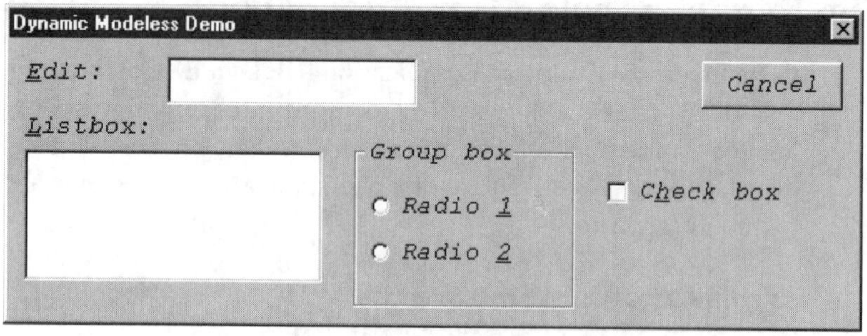

Figure 3.10 *The dynamic modeless dialog box.*

Table 3.4 describes the files used to create this application.

When you select the Create a Dynamic Modal Dialog Box button, the DlgDyn_OnCommand function (in **DlgDyn.C**) executes the following code:

```
case IDC_MODAL:
    pDlgTemplate = BuildDynamicDlgBox(FALSE);
    adgASSERT(pDlgTemplate);
    adgASSERT(-1 != DialogBoxIndirect(GetWindowInstance(hwnd),
        pDlgTemplate, hwnd, DynDlg_DlgProc));
    DlgTemplate_Free(pDlgTemplate);
    break;
```

Table 3.4 *Files used to build the DlgDyn application.*

File	Description
DlgDyn.C	Contains WinMain and main window's dialog box and message cracker functions.
DynDlg.C	Contains dialog box and message cracker functions for the dynamically created modal and modeless dialog boxes.
DlgTmplt.C	Contains a library of functions that make it much easier for you to construct dynamic dialog box templates in memory. You can use this file in your own applications.
DlgTmplt.H	Contains prototypes for the functions contained in the **DlgTmplt.C** file. Any source file that uses the library of functions in **DlgTmplt.C** must include this file.
DlgDyn.RC	Contains dialog box template for main application window and its icons.
Resource.H	Contains ID for all resources in the **DlgDyn.RC** file.
DlgDyn.ICO	Contains the icon for the main window.
DlgDyn.MAK	Visual C++ project makefile.

The BuildDynamicDlgBox function (in the **DynDlg.C** file) performs all the work to create the dialog box template in memory. It allocates a block of memory and initializes the block with a DLGTEMPLA-TEEX structure, an optional FONTINFOEX structure, and a series of DLGITEMTEMPLATEEX structures. The BuildDynamicDlgBox function accesses a set of data structures that describes the attributes of the dialog box and all its child windows. The BuildDynamicDlgBox function creates a template for both a modal dialog box and a modeless dialog box. If you want the template for a modal dialog box, pass FALSE to BuildDynamicDlgBox; pass TRUE for a modeless dialog box template.

If BuildDynamicDlgBox is successful, it returns the memory address of the template. This memory address is then passed to DialogBoxIndirect, which parses the memory block, creates the parent window and all the child windows, and then enters its internal GetMessage loop, waiting for the dialog box procedure to call the

EndDialog function. After the user dismisses the dialog box, DlgTemplate_Free (contained in **DlgTmplt.C**) is called to free the memory block.

The code to create the modeless dialog box is almost identical to the preceding code except that CreateDialogIndirect is called instead of DialogBoxIndirect. Also, the handle to the modeless dialog box is saved in the main window's GWL_USERDATA extra bytes so that the modeless dialog box can be destroyed when the user clicks the Destroy Dynamic Modeless Dialog Box button.

Building the Dialog Box Template

The BuildDynamicDlgBox function calls various functions in the **DlgTmplt.C** file to create the dialog box template. The only parameter to this function is a Boolean value, fModeless, which specifies whether a modal or modeless dialog box is to be created. BuildDynamicDlgBox first calls the DlgTemplate_Create function (contained in **DlgTmplt.C**):

```
// Create the dynamic dialog box header information.
if (fModeless) {

    pDlgTemplate = DlgTemplate_Create(
        WS_BORDER | WS_CAPTION | WS_DLGFRAME | WS_SYSMENU | WS_VISIBLE |
        WS_POPUP | DS_SETFONT, 0, 0, 6, 26, 216, 72, __TEXT(""), __TEXT(""),
        __TEXT("Dynamic Modeless Demo"), 12, FW_NORMAL, TRUE,
        __TEXT("Courier New"));
} else {

    pDlgTemplate = DlgTemplate_Create(
        WS_BORDER | WS_CAPTION | WS_DLGFRAME | WS_SYSMENU | WS_VISIBLE |
        WS_POPUP, 0, 0, 6, 26, 216, 72, __TEXT(""), __TEXT(""),
        __TEXT("Dynamic Modal Demo"), 0, 0, 0, NULL);
}
```

DlgTemplate_Create allocates a block of memory large enough to hold a DLGTEMPLATEEX data structure, an optional FONTIN-FOEX structure (if the DS_SETFONT style is specified), and the window's menu, class, and caption strings. The address of this memory block is returned.

Because the DS_SETFONT flag is specified when the modeless dialog box is created, the last four parameters (12, FW_NORMAL, TRUE, and Courier New) indicate the font that should be used when the dialog box is created. The DS_SETFONT flag is not specified for the modal dialog box, so DlgTemplate_Create ignores the last four parameters. The number of controls that appears in the dialog box template is not specified to DlgTemplate_Create; it is set to zero initially and is incremented with each call to the DlgTemplate_ AddControl function.

Once the DLGTEMPLATEEX structure has been placed in the memory block, the individual controls are appended. BuildDynamic-DlgBox uses the following data structure to create those controls:

```
// The table that describes the dialog box controls follows.
#define MAXDLGITEMDATA (10)

static struct {
    short    x, y, cx, cy;
    DWORD    dwStyle, dwExStyle, dwHelpId;
    int      id;
    LPCTSTR  szClass, szText;
    WORD     wExtraDataCount;
    PBYTE    pbExtraData;
} DynDlgBoxData[] = {

    { 4, 4, 32, 12, (unsigned short) IDC_STATIC, SS_LEFT, 0,
        __TEXT("STATIC"), __TEXT("&Edit:"), 0, { 0 } },

    { 40, 4, 64, 12, IDC_EDITBOX,
        ES_LEFT | WS_BORDER | WS_TABSTOP | WS_GROUP, 0,
        __TEXT("EDIT"), __TEXT(""), 0, { 0 } },
    .
    .
    .
    // End of list marker (szClass must be null).
    { 0, 0, 0, 0, 0, 0, 0, NULL, NULL, 0, { 0 } }
};
```

DlgTemplate_AddControl is called once for each item in this data structure, and a new DLGITEMTEMPLATEEX structure is appended to the end of the memory block:

```
// Add each of the controls in the DynamicDlgBoxData array.
for (x = 0; DynDlgBoxData[x].szClass != NULL; x++) {

    // Do not add an OK button for a modeless dialog box.
    if (fModeless) {

        if (DynDlgBoxData[x].id == IDOK)
            continue;
    }

    fCtrlAddedOK = DlgTemplate_AddControl(&pDlgTemplate,
        DynDlgBoxData[x].x,
```

```
        DynDlgBoxData[x].y,
        DynDlgBoxData[x].cx,
        DynDlgBoxData[x].cy,
        DynDlgBoxData[x].id,
        DynDlgBoxData[x].dwStyle | WS_VISIBLE,
        DynDlgBoxData[x].dwExtendedStyle,
        DynDlgBoxData[x].szClass,
        DynDlgBoxData[x].szText,
        DynDlgBoxData[x].cbDataBytes,
        DynDlgBoxData[x].Data);

    if (!fCtrlAddedOK)
        break;
}
```

Because modeless dialog boxes usually don't have OK buttons, the preceding code does not call DlgTemplate_AddControl for this button.

Managing the Dialog Box Templates Memory Block

The functions that manage the block of memory are DlgTemplate_ CreateA, DlgTemplate_CreateW, DlgTemplate_AddControlA, DlgTemplate_AddControlW, and DlgTemplate_Free.

The DlgTemplate_CreateA and DlgTemplate_AddControlA functions are easy to discuss, so lets get them out of the way first. These functions accept ANSI strings, convert them to Unicode strings, and then they call their Unicode counterparts. It is the Unicode versions of these functions that perform the actual work; the ANSI versions are simply thunking layers. Remember that both Windows NT and Windows 95 expect all resources to be in Unicode, so implementing the bulk of the work in the Unicode functions makes the most sense.

DlgTemplate_CreateW performs the initial memory allocation. This allocation must be large enough to contain a DLGTEMPLA-TEEX structure and its three string fields: menu, class, and caption. If the dialog template includes the DS_SETFONT style, the memory block must be large enough to also include the FONTINFOEX structure, including its typeface string field.

After the memory block is allocated, DlgTemplate_CreateW fills the memory block with the values passed in the parameters to the function, and the cDlgItems member is initialized to zero. The address of the memory block is then returned to the caller.

168

DlgTemplate_AddControlW appends new controls to the end of a memory block that was created by DlgTemplate_CreateW. This function first calculates the number of bytes required to contain a DLGITEMTEMPLATEEX structure and its three variable-length fields: class name, caption, and initialization data bytes. Before the memory block can be enlarged, this function must determine the number of bytes already used; the C-Runtime's _msize function returns the current size of the memory block. Now, DlgTemplate_ AddControlW calls the C-Runtime's realloc function to increase the size of the block in order to accommodate the new control's information.

```
// Increase the size of the memory block to include the new dialog item.
nBytesBeforeAddingControl = _msize(*ppDlgTemplate);
pDlgTemplateNew = realloc(*ppDlgTemplate,
    nBytesBeforeAddingControl + nBytesForNewControl);
if (pDlgTemplateNew == NULL)
    return(FALSE);
```

Because realloc does not necessarily return the same memory address that was passed to it, DlgTemplate_AddControlW must notify the calling application of the new address. This is why DlgTemplate_ AddControlW's first parameter is a pointer to a template pointer instead of just a template pointer. The new memory address is returned by updating this pointer so that it now points to the new template.

With the memory block now large enough to hold the additional control, the new DLGITEMTEMPLATEEX structure is appended after the number of bytes used in the block. When a new control is added, the cDlgItems member in DLGTEMPLATEEX is incremented.

Once the application has added controls to the dialog box template, the DialogBoxIndirectParam and CreateDialogIndirectParam functions can use the memory block.

DlgDyn.ICO

Listing 3.12 *DlgDyn.C*

```
/**************************************************************************
Module name: DlgDyn.c
Written by: Jeffrey Richter
Notices: Copyright (c) 1995 Jeffrey Richter
Purpose: Demonstrates dynamic modeless and modal dialog boxes.
**************************************************************************/
```

169

```
#include "..\Win95ADG.h"          /* See Appendix A for details */
#include <windows.h>
#include <windowsx.h>
#pragma warning(disable: 4001)    /* Single line comment */
#include "resource.h"
#include "dlgtmplt.h"


///////////////////////////////////////////////////////////////////////////


// Function (contained in dyndlg.c) that demonstrates how to create a dynamic
// dialog box template.
extern PDLGTEMPLATEEX BuildDynamicDlgBox (BOOL fModeless);

// Dialog box procedure (contained in dyndlg.c) for both the modal and modeless
// dynamic dialog boxes.
extern BOOL WINAPI DynDlg_DlgProc (HWND hwnd, UINT uMsg,
   WPARAM wParam, LPARAM lParam);


///////////////////////////////////////////////////////////////////////////


// When a modeless dialog box is invoked from a modal dialog box, the modeless
// dialog box's keyboard interface will not function. This is because the
// GetMessage loop inside DialogBox does not call IsDialogMessage for the
// modeless dialog box. In order to get the modeless dialog box's keyboard
// interface working, I install a message filter (WH_MSGFILTER) hook. I store
// the dialog's window handle in the variable below so that the message filter
// hook function has access to the modeless dialog box.
HWND g_hwndModeless = NULL;

// This is hook handle that identifies the WH_MSGFITLER hook used to get
// keyboard processing to the modeless dialog box.
HHOOK g_hhookMsgFilter = NULL;


///////////////////////////////////////////////////////////////////////////


BOOL DlgDyn_OnInitDialog (HWND hwnd, HWND hwndFocus, LPARAM lParam) {

   adgSETDLGICONS(hwnd, IDI_DLGDYN, IDI_DLGDYN);
   return(TRUE);                     // Accept default focus window.
}


///////////////////////////////////////////////////////////////////////////


void DlgDyn_OnCommand (HWND hwnd, int id, HWND hwndCtl, UINT codeNotify) {

   PDLGTEMPLATEEX pDlgTemplate;
```

```
   switch (id) {

     case IDOK:
     case IDCANCEL:                 // Allows dialog box to close
       EndDialog(hwnd, id);
       break;

     case IDC_MODAL:
       pDlgTemplate = BuildDynamicDlgBox(FALSE);
       adgASSERT(pDlgTemplate != NULL);
       adgVERIFY(-1 != DialogBoxIndirect(GetWindowInstance(hwnd),
          (LPDLGTEMPLATE) pDlgTemplate, hwnd, DynDlg_DlgProc));
       DlgTemplate_Free(pDlgTemplate);
       break;

     case IDC_MODELESS:
       if (IsWindow(g_hwndModeless)) {

          // The modeless window is already up, let's destroy it.
          DestroyWindow(g_hwndModeless);
          g_hwndModeless = NULL;
       } else {

          // The modeless window is not up, let's create it.
          pDlgTemplate = BuildDynamicDlgBox(TRUE);
          adgASSERT(pDlgTemplate != NULL);
          g_hwndModeless = CreateDialogIndirect(GetWindowInstance(hwnd),
             (LPDLGTEMPLATE) pDlgTemplate, hwnd, DynDlg_DlgProc);
          adgASSERT(IsWindow(g_hwndModeless));
          DlgTemplate_Free(pDlgTemplate);
       }

       // Toggle the text in the button
       SetWindowText(hwndCtl, IsWindow(g_hwndModeless) ?
          __TEXT("Destroy dynamic modeless dialog box") :
          __TEXT("Create dynamic modeless dialog box"));
       break;
   }
}


///////////////////////////////////////////////////////////////////////////


BOOL WINAPI DlgDyn_DlgProc (HWND hwnd, UINT uMsg,
   WPARAM wParam, LPARAM lParam) {

   switch (uMsg) {

     // Standard Window's messages
     adgHANDLE_DLGMSG(hwnd, WM_INITDIALOG, DlgDyn_OnInitDialog);
     adgHANDLE_DLGMSG(hwnd, WM_COMMAND,    DlgDyn_OnCommand);
   }
   return(FALSE);                   // We didn't process the message.
}
```

171

```
//////////////////////////////////////////////////////////////////////////////

// This message filter hook function exists to enable the keyboard interface
// for the modeless dialog.
LRESULT WINAPI DlgDyn_MsgFilterProc (int nCode, WPARAM wParam, LPARAM lParam) {

   // This variable prevents infinite recursion caused by the call to
   // IsDialogMessage below (IsDialogMessage calls any installed message
   // filter hooks as its first order of business).
   static BOOL fRecurse = FALSE;
   LRESULT lResult;

   // If we are called recursively due to IsDialogMessage, we simply return.
   if (fRecurse) {

      // Returning FALSE tells the system that we want it to do its normal
      // processing for this message.  Ie., let IsDialogMessage do its stuff.
      // NOTE: We are not calling CallNextHookEx because we don't want the
      // same message to go through the same hook chain twice (although this
      // hook function will see it twice).
      return(FALSE);
   }

   // Here we unhook our hook and then rehook ourselves to guarantee that our
   // hook procedure is at the front of the hook chain. This is necessary
   // because any hook procedure before us in the hook chain would see each
   // message twice. By installing ourselves at the front of the chain we get
   // the message first the second time it goes through the hook chain and
   // can simply stop the message from continuing through the hook chain when
   // we are recursing because of IsDialogMessage.
   adgVERIFY(UnhookWindowsHookEx(g_hhookMsgFilter));
   g_hhookMsgFilter = SetWindowsHookEx(WH_MSGFILTER, DlgDyn_MsgFilterProc,
      NULL, GetCurrentThreadId());
   adgASSERT(g_hhookMsgFilter != NULL);

   // Call any other hooks in the chain. lResult is TRUE if the next hook
   // in the chain doesn't want any additional processing for the message.
   lResult = CallNextHookEx(g_hhookMsgFilter, nCode, wParam, lParam);

   // If the next hook in the chain wants to allow additional processing
   if (!lResult) {

      // Call IsDialogMessage, setting the static variable fRecurse to TRUE
      // to avoid infinite recursion.  If IsDialogMessage returns TRUE, the
      // message was processed and we DO NOT want normal processing for this
      // message.
      if (IsWindow(g_hwndModeless)) {
         fRecurse = TRUE;
         lResult = IsDialogMessage(g_hwndModeless, (PMSG) lParam);
         fRecurse = FALSE;
      }
   }
   return(lResult);
}
```

//

```
int WINAPI WinMain (HINSTANCE hinstExe, HINSTANCE hinstPrev,
   LPSTR lpszCmdLine, int nCmdShow) {

   adgWARNIFUNICODEUNDERWIN95();

   // Set message filter hook to enable keyboard interface processing for the
   // dynamic modeless dialog box.
   g_hhookMsgFilter = SetWindowsHookEx(WH_MSGFILTER, DlgDyn_MsgFilterProc,
      NULL, GetCurrentThreadId());
   adgASSERT(g_hhookMsgFilter != NULL);

   adgVERIFY(-1 != DialogBox(hinstExe, MAKEINTRESOURCE(IDD_DLGDYN),
      NULL, DlgDyn_DlgProc));

   // Clean up by unhooking our message filter hook
   adgVERIFY(UnhookWindowsHookEx(g_hhookMsgFilter));
   return(0);
}
```

/////////////////////////////// End of File ///////////////////////////////////

Listing 3.13 *DynDlg.C*

```
/***************************************************************************
Module name: DynDlg.c
Written by: Jeffrey Richter
Notices: Copyright (c) 1995 Jeffrey Richter
Purpose: Dynamic dialog box functions.
***************************************************************************/


#include "..\Win95ADG.h"          /* See Appendix A for details */
#include <windows.h>
#include <windowsx.h>
#pragma warning(disable: 4001)     /* Single line comment */
#include "DlgTmplt.h"
#include "Resource.h"


////////////////////////////////////////////////////////////////////////////


// Below is the table that describes the dialog box controls.
static struct {
   short   x, y, cx, cy;
   DWORD   dwStyle, dwExStyle, dwHelpId;
   int     id;
   LPCTSTR szClass, szText;
```

```
      WORD    wExtraDataCount;
      PBYTE   pbExtraData;
} DynDlgBoxData[] = {

   { 4, 4, 32, 12, SS_LEFT, 0, 0, IDC_STATIC,
      __TEXT("STATIC"), __TEXT("&Edit:"), 0, NULL },

   { 40, 4, 64, 12, ES_LEFT | WS_BORDER | WS_TABSTOP | WS_GROUP, 0, 0,
      IDC_EDITBOX, __TEXT("EDIT"), __TEXT(""), 0, NULL },

   { 4, 18, 40,  8, SS_LEFT, 0, 0, IDC_STATIC,
      __TEXT("STATIC"), __TEXT("&Listbox:"), 0, NULL },

   { 4, 28, 76, 41, LBS_NOTIFY | LBS_SORT | LBS_STANDARD |
      WS_BORDER | WS_VSCROLL | WS_TABSTOP | WS_GROUP, 0, 0,
      IDC_LISTBOX, __TEXT("LISTBOX"), __TEXT(""), 0, NULL },

   { 132,  4, 36, 12, BS_DEFPUSHBUTTON | WS_TABSTOP | WS_GROUP, 0, 0,
      IDOK, __TEXT("BUTTON"), __TEXT("OK"), 0, NULL },

   { 176,  4, 36, 12, BS_PUSHBUTTON | WS_TABSTOP | WS_GROUP, 0, 0,
      IDCANCEL, __TEXT("BUTTON"), __TEXT("Cancel"), 0, NULL },

   { 88, 24, 56, 44, BS_GROUPBOX | WS_GROUP, 0, 0, IDC_STATIC,
      __TEXT("BUTTON"), __TEXT("Group box"), 0, NULL },

   { 92, 36, 48, 12, BS_AUTORADIOBUTTON | WS_TABSTOP | WS_GROUP, 0, 0,
      IDC_RADIO1, __TEXT("BUTTON"), __TEXT("Radio &1"), 0, NULL },

   { 92, 48, 48, 12, BS_AUTORADIOBUTTON | WS_TABSTOP, 0, 0,
      IDC_RADIO2, __TEXT("BUTTON"), __TEXT("Radio &2"), 0, NULL },

   { 152, 32, 60, 12, BS_AUTOCHECKBOX | WS_TABSTOP | WS_GROUP, 0, 0,
      IDC_CHECKBOX, __TEXT("BUTTON"), __TEXT("C&heck box"), 0, NULL },

   // End of list marker (szClass must be null)
   { 0, 0, 0, 0, 0, 0, 0, 0, NULL, NULL, 0, NULL }
};


/////////////////////////////////////////////////////////////////////////////


PDLGTEMPLATEEX BuildDynamicDlgBox (BOOL fModeless) {

   PDLGTEMPLATEEX pDlgTemplate;
   int x;
   BOOL fCtrlAddedOK;

   // Create the dynamic dialog box header information.
   if (fModeless) {
      pDlgTemplate = DlgTemplate_Create(
         WS_BORDER | WS_CAPTION | WS_DLGFRAME | WS_SYSMENU | WS_VISIBLE |
         WS_POPUP | DS_SETFONT, 0, 0, 6, 26, 216, 72, __TEXT(""), __TEXT(""),
         __TEXT("Dynamic Modeless Demo"),
         12, FW_NORMAL, TRUE, __TEXT("Courier New"));
```

```
   } else {
      pDlgTemplate = DlgTemplate_Create(
         WS_BORDER | WS_CAPTION | WS_DLGFRAME | WS_SYSMENU | WS_VISIBLE |
         WS_POPUP, 0, 0, 6, 26, 216, 72, __TEXT(""), __TEXT(""),
         __TEXT("Dynamic Modal Demo"),
         0, 0, 0, NULL);
   }

   if (pDlgTemplate == NULL)
      return(NULL);

   // Add each of the controls in the DynamicDlgBoxData array.
   for (x = 0; DynDlgBoxData[x].szClass != NULL; x++) {

      // Do not add an OK button for a modeless dialog box.
      if (fModeless) {
         if (DynDlgBoxData[x].id == IDOK)
            continue;
      }

      fCtrlAddedOK = DlgTemplate_AddControl(&pDlgTemplate,
         DynDlgBoxData[x].x,
         DynDlgBoxData[x].y,
         DynDlgBoxData[x].cx,
         DynDlgBoxData[x].cy,
         DynDlgBoxData[x].id,
         DynDlgBoxData[x].dwHelpId,
         DynDlgBoxData[x].dwStyle | WS_VISIBLE,
         DynDlgBoxData[x].dwExStyle,
         DynDlgBoxData[x].szClass,
         DynDlgBoxData[x].szText,
         DynDlgBoxData[x].wExtraDataCount,
         DynDlgBoxData[x].pbExtraData);

      if (!fCtrlAddedOK)
         break;
   }

   // If insufficient memory, free what we have and return NULL to caller.
   if (!fCtrlAddedOK) {
      DlgTemplate_Free(pDlgTemplate);
      pDlgTemplate = NULL;
   }

   // Return the address of the dynamic dialog box information.
   return(pDlgTemplate);
}


///////////////////////////////////////////////////////////////////////////


BOOL DynDlg_OnInitDialog (HWND hwnd, HWND hwndFocus, LPARAM lParam) {

   return(TRUE);
}
```

```
/////////////////////////////////////////////////////////////////////////////

void DynDlg_OnCommand (HWND hwnd, int id, HWND hwndCtl, UINT codeNotify) {

   switch (id) {

      case IDOK:
      case IDCANCEL:                  // Allows dialog box to close

         // The processing in here to close the dialog box differs depending on
         // whether the dialog box is modal or modeless.

         // First we must determine if the dialog box is modal or modeless.
         // If there is an OK button, the dialog box is modal.
         if (IsWindow(GetDlgItem(hwnd, IDOK))) {
            // The dialog box is modal
            EndDialog(hwnd, id); // Close the dialog box
         } else {
            // The dialog box is modeless
            if (id == IDCANCEL) {
               // Don't destroy the dialog box if the user pressed Enter.

               // Simulate the user clicking the "Destroy dynamic modeless
               // dialog box" button in the parent window.
               FORWARD_WM_COMMAND(GetParent(hwnd), IDC_MODELESS,
                  GetDlgItem(GetParent(hwnd), IDC_MODELESS),
                  BN_CLICKED, PostMessage);
            }
         }
         break;
   }
}


/////////////////////////////////////////////////////////////////////////////


BOOL WINAPI DynDlg_DlgProc (HWND hwnd, UINT uMsg,
   WPARAM wParam, LPARAM lParam) {

   switch (uMsg) {

      // Standard Window's messages
      adgHANDLE_DLGMSG(hwnd, WM_INITDIALOG, DynDlg_OnInitDialog);
      adgHANDLE_DLGMSG(hwnd, WM_COMMAND,    DynDlg_OnCommand);
   }
   return(FALSE);                     // We didn't process the message.
}


///////////////////////////// End of File /////////////////////////////////////
```

Listing 3.14 *DlgTmplt.C*

```
/**********************************************************************
Module name: DlgTmplt.c
Written by: Jeffrey Richter
Notices: Copyright (c) 1995 Jeffrey Richter
Purpose: Dynamic Dialog Box template toolkit functions.
**********************************************************************/


#include "..\Win95ADG.h"          /* See Appendix A for details */
#include <windows.h>
#include <windowsx.h>
#pragma warning(disable: 4001)    /* Single line comment */
#include <malloc.h>
#include "DlgTmplt.h"


///////////////////////////////////////////////////////////////////////


#define NEXTDWORDBOUNDARY(p) ((PBYTE) ((DWORD) ((3 + (PBYTE) (p))) & ~3))
#define LENINWORDS(ByteLen)  ((ByteLen + sizeof(WORD)  - 1) & ~1)
#define LENINDWORDS(ByteLen) ((ByteLen + sizeof(DWORD) - 1) & ~3)


///////////////////////////////////////////////////////////////////////


// Macro to calculate number of bytes needed for a (unicode) string, including
// the zero terminating character.
#define BYTESFORSTRING(sz) (sizeof(WCHAR) * (1 + wcslen(sz)))


///////////////////////////////////////////////////////////////////////


BOOL ANSIToUnicode (PCSTR szStrA, PWSTR *pszStrW) {

   int nLenOfWideCharStr;
   BOOL fOK = FALSE;              // Assume failure

   *pszStrW = NULL;              // Assume failure
   if (szStrA == NULL) {

      // It is OK to have a NULL string.
      return(TRUE);
   }

   // Get the number of bytes needed for the wide version of the string.
   nLenOfWideCharStr = MultiByteToWideChar(CP_ACP, 0, szStrA, -1, NULL, 0);

   // Allocate memory to accomodate the size of the wide character string.
   *pszStrW = malloc(nLenOfWideCharStr * sizeof(WCHAR));
```

```
    if (*pszStrW != NULL) {

        // Convert the multi-byte string to a wide-character string.
        MultiByteToWideChar(CP_ACP, 0, szStrA, -1, *pszStrW, nLenOfWideCharStr);
        fOK = TRUE;
    }
    return(fOK);
}


/////////////////////////////////////////////////////////////////////////////


PDLGTEMPLATEEX DlgTemplate_CreateW (
    DWORD  dwStyle,
    DWORD  dwExStyle,
    DWORD  dwHelpId,
    short  x,  short y,            // In dialog-box units
    short  cx, short cy,           // In dialog-box units
    PCWSTR szMenuName,             // "" if no menu
    PCWSTR szClassName,            // "" if standard dialog box class
    PCWSTR szCaptionText,
    short  nPointSize,             // Only used if DS_SETFONT specified
    short  nWeight,                // Only used if DS_SETFONT specified
    short  fItalic,                // Only used if DS_SETFONT specified
    PCWSTR szTypeFace) {           // Only used if DS_SETFONT specified

    int            nBytesForNewTemplate;
    int            nMenuNameLen, nClassNameLen, nCaptionTextLen, nTypeFaceLen;
    PBYTE          pbDlgTemplate, pbDlgTypeFace;
    PDLGTEMPLATEEX pDlgTemplate;
    PFONTINFOEX    pFontInfo;

    // Calculate number of bytes required by following fields:
    nMenuNameLen    = BYTESFORSTRING(szMenuName);
    nClassNameLen   = BYTESFORSTRING(szClassName);
    nCaptionTextLen = BYTESFORSTRING(szCaptionText);

    // Block must be large enough to contain the following:
    nBytesForNewTemplate =
        adgMEMBEROFFSET(DLGTEMPLATEEX, bStartOfStrings) +
        nMenuNameLen +          // # bytes: menu name.
        nClassNameLen +         // # bytes: dialog class name.
        nCaptionTextLen;        // # bytes: dialog box caption.

    if (dwStyle & DS_SETFONT) {

        // Dialog box uses font other than System font.

        // Calculate # of bytes required for typeface name.
        nTypeFaceLen = BYTESFORSTRING(szTypeFace);

        // Block must be large enough to include font information.
        nBytesForNewTemplate +=
            adgMEMBEROFFSET(FONTINFOEX, bStartOfStrings) +
```

```
      nTypeFaceLen;          // # bytes for font typeface name.

} else {

   // Dialog box uses the System font.
   nTypeFaceLen = 0;

   // Block length does not change.
}

// Allocate an even number of DWORDs for alignment.
nBytesForNewTemplate = LENINDWORDS(nBytesForNewTemplate);

// Allocate block of memory for dialog template.
pDlgTemplate = (PDLGTEMPLATEEX) malloc(nBytesForNewTemplate);
if (pDlgTemplate == NULL)
   return(NULL);

// Set the members of the DLGTEMPLATE structure.
pDlgTemplate->wDlgVer      = 1;        // Always 1
pDlgTemplate->wSignature   = 0xFFFF;   // Always 0xFFFF
pDlgTemplate->dwHelpID     = dwHelpId;
pDlgTemplate->dwStyle      = dwStyle;
pDlgTemplate->dwExStyle    = dwExStyle;
pDlgTemplate->cDlgItems    = 0;        // AddControl increments this
pDlgTemplate->x            = x;
pDlgTemplate->y            = y;
pDlgTemplate->cx           = cx;
pDlgTemplate->cy           = cy;


// pbDlgTemplate points to start of variable part of DLGTEMPLATEEX.
pbDlgTemplate = (PBYTE) pDlgTemplate +
   adgMEMBEROFFSET(DLGTEMPLATEEX, bStartOfStrings);

// Append the menu name, class name, and caption text to block.
CopyMemory(pbDlgTemplate, szMenuName, nMenuNameLen);
pbDlgTemplate += nMenuNameLen;
CopyMemory(pbDlgTemplate, szClassName, nClassNameLen);
pbDlgTemplate += nClassNameLen;
CopyMemory(pbDlgTemplate, szCaptionText, nCaptionTextLen);
pbDlgTemplate += nCaptionTextLen;

if (dwStyle & DS_SETFONT) {

   // Dialog box uses font other than system font.

   // pFontInfo points to start of FONTINFOEX structure.
   pFontInfo = (PFONTINFOEX) pbDlgTemplate;

   // Set the members of the FONTINFO structure.
   pFontInfo->nPointSize = nPointSize;
   pFontInfo->nWeight    = nWeight;
   pFontInfo->fItalic    = fItalic;
```

179

```
        // szTypeFace points to start of the variable part of FONTINFOEX.
        pbDlgTypeFace = (PBYTE) pFontInfo +
            adgMEMBEROFFSET(FONTINFOEX, bStartOfStrings);

        // Append the typeface name to the block.
        CopyMemory(pbDlgTypeFace, szTypeFace, nTypeFaceLen);
    }

    return(pDlgTemplate);
}


////////////////////////////////////////////////////////////////////////////////


PDLGTEMPLATEEX DlgTemplate_CreateA (
    DWORD   dwStyle,
    DWORD   dwExStyle,
    DWORD   dwHelpId,
    short   x,  short y,            // In dialog-box units
    short   cx, short cy,           // In dialog-box units
    PCSTR   szMenuName,             // "" if no menu
    PCSTR   szClassName,            // "" if standard dialog box class
    PCSTR   szCaptionText,
    short   nPointSize,             // Only used if DS_SETFONT specified
    short   nWeight,                // Only used if DS_SETFONT specified
    short   fItalic,                // Only used if DS_SETFONT specified
    PCSTR   szTypeFace) {           // Only used if DS_SETFONT specified

    PDLGTEMPLATEEX pDlgTemplate = NULL;
    PWSTR szMenuNameW = NULL, szClassNameW = NULL;
    PWSTR szCaptionTextW = NULL, szTypeFaceW = NULL;

    // Allocate temporary Unicode buffers and convert ANSI strings to Unicode.
    if (ANSIToUnicode(szMenuName,    &szMenuNameW)    &&
        ANSIToUnicode(szClassName,   &szClassNameW)   &&
        ANSIToUnicode(szCaptionText, &szCaptionTextW) &&
        ANSIToUnicode(szTypeFace,    &szTypeFaceW)) {

        pDlgTemplate = DlgTemplate_CreateW(dwStyle, dwExStyle,
            dwHelpId, x, y, cx, cy, szMenuNameW, szClassNameW,
            szCaptionTextW, nPointSize, nWeight, fItalic, szTypeFaceW);
    }

    // Destroy temporary Unicode buffers.
    // NOTE: ANSI C states that it is OK to pass NULL to free.
    free(szTypeFaceW);
    free(szCaptionTextW);
    free(szClassNameW);
    free(szMenuNameW);

    return(pDlgTemplate);
}


////////////////////////////////////////////////////////////////////////////////
```

```
BOOL DlgTemplate_AddControlW (
   PDLGTEMPLATEEX* ppDlgTemplate,  // Returned from Create or AddControl
   short  x,  short y,             // In dialog-box units
   short  cx, short cy,            // In dialog-box units
   DWORD  id,
   DWORD  dwHelpId,
   DWORD  dwStyle,                 // WS_CHILD is automatically added
   DWORD  dwExStyle,
   PCWSTR szClass,
   PCWSTR szText,
   WORD   wExtraDataCount,
   PBYTE  pbExtraData) {           // Number of additional data bytes

   PDLGTEMPLATEEX pDlgTemplateNew; // If the memory block expands.
   int nBytesForNewControl;
   int nBytesBeforeAddingControl;
   PDLGITEMTEMPLATEEX pDlgItemTemplate;
   PBYTE pbDlgItemTemplate;

   // Calculate number of bytes required by following fields:
   int nClassLen = BYTESFORSTRING(szClass);
   int nTextLen  = BYTESFORSTRING(szText);

   // Block must be increased by to contain the following:
   nBytesForNewControl =
      adgMEMBEROFFSET(DLGITEMTEMPLATEEX, bStartOfStrings) +
      nClassLen +               // # bytes for control class
      nTextLen +                // # bytes for control text
      sizeof(WORD);             // 1 byte  for size in bytes of CreateParams
                                // data

   // Alignment padding to CreateParams data
   nBytesForNewControl = LENINDWORDS(nBytesForNewControl);
   nBytesForNewControl += wExtraDataCount; // # bytes for CreateParams data

   // Alignment padding to next DLGITEMTEMPLATEEX structure
   nBytesForNewControl = LENINDWORDS(nBytesForNewControl);

   // Increase the size of the memory block to include the new dialog item.
   nBytesBeforeAddingControl = _msize(*ppDlgTemplate);
   pDlgTemplateNew = realloc(*ppDlgTemplate,
      nBytesBeforeAddingControl + nBytesForNewControl);
   if (pDlgTemplateNew == NULL)
      return(FALSE);

   // Tell the caller the new address of the dialog template.
   *ppDlgTemplate = pDlgTemplateNew;

   // Increment the number of controls in the template.
   pDlgTemplateNew->cDlgItems++;

   // pDlgItemTemplate points to the start of the DLGITEMTEMPLATE being added.
   pDlgItemTemplate = (PDLGITEMTEMPLATEEX)
      (((PBYTE) pDlgTemplateNew) + nBytesBeforeAddingControl);

   // Set the members of the newly added DLGITEMTEMPLATE structure.
```

181

```
    pDlgItemTemplate->x          = x;
    pDlgItemTemplate->y          = y;
    pDlgItemTemplate->cx         = cx;
    pDlgItemTemplate->cy         = cy;
    pDlgItemTemplate->id         = id;
    pDlgItemTemplate->dwStyle    = dwStyle | WS_CHILD;
    pDlgItemTemplate->dwExStyle  = dwExStyle;
    pDlgItemTemplate->dwHelpID   = dwHelpId;

    // pbDlgTemplate points to the start of the variable part of the
    // DLGITEMTEMPLATEEX.
    pbDlgItemTemplate = (PBYTE) pDlgItemTemplate +
        adgMEMBEROFFSET(DLGITEMTEMPLATEEX, bStartOfStrings);

    // Append the strings for the control's class name and caption to the block.
    CopyMemory(pbDlgItemTemplate, szClass, nClassLen);
    pbDlgItemTemplate += nClassLen;
    CopyMemory(pbDlgItemTemplate, szText, nTextLen);
    pbDlgItemTemplate += nTextLen;

    // Append the control's extra data byte information.
    * (PWORD) pbDlgItemTemplate = wExtraDataCount;
    pbDlgItemTemplate += sizeof(WORD);

    // Append the control's CreateParams data bytes.
    CopyMemory(pbDlgItemTemplate, pbExtraData, wExtraDataCount);

    return(TRUE);
}


///////////////////////////////////////////////////////////////////////////


BOOL DlgTemplate_AddControlA (
    PDLGTEMPLATEEX* ppDlgTemplate,  // Returned from Create or AddControl
    short  x,   short y,            // In dialog-box units
    short  cx,  short cy,           // In dialog-box units
    DWORD  id,
    DWORD  dwHelpId,
    DWORD  dwStyle,                 // WS_CHILD is automatically added
    DWORD  dwExStyle,
    PCSTR  szClass,
    PCSTR  szText,
    WORD   wExtraDataCount,         // Number of additional data bytes
    PBYTE  pbExtraData) {           // Passed via CREATESTRUCT's pCreateParams

    BOOL fOK = FALSE;               // Assume failure
    PWSTR szClassW = NULL;
    PWSTR szTextW = NULL;

    // Allocate temporary Unicode buffers and convert ANSI strings to Unicode.
    if (ANSIToUnicode(szClass, &szClassW) &&
        ANSIToUnicode(szText, &szTextW)) {
```

182

```
      fOK = DlgTemplate_AddControlW(ppDlgTemplate, x, y, cx, cy, id, dwHelpId,
          dwStyle, dwExStyle, szClassW, szTextW, wExtraDataCount, pbExtraData);
   }

   // Destroy temporary Unicode buffers.
   // NOTE: ANSI C states that it is OK to pass NULL to free.
   free(szTextW);
   free(szClassW);

   return(fOK);
}


///////////////////////////////////////////////////////////////////////////////


BOOL DlgTemplate_Free (PDLGTEMPLATEEX pDlgTemplate) {

   free((PVOID) pDlgTemplate);
   return(TRUE);
}


/////////////////////////////// End of File /////////////////////////////////////
```

Listing 3.15 *DlgTmplt.H*

```
/******************************************************************************
Module name: DlgTmplt.h
Written by: Jeffrey Richter
Notices: Copyright (c) 1995 Jeffrey Richter
Purpose: Dynamic Dialog Box template toolkit functions.
******************************************************************************/

typedef struct { // dlttex
   WORD    wDlgVer;      // Always 1
   WORD    wSignature;   // Always 0xFFFF
   DWORD   dwHelpID;
   DWORD   dwExStyle;    // Such as WS_EX_TOPMOST
   DWORD   dwStyle;      // Such as WS_CAPTION
   WORD    cDlgItems;
   short   x;            // In pixels
   short   y;            // In pixels
   short   cx;           // In dialog box units
   short   cy;           // In dialog box units
   BYTE    bStartOfStrings;
   // Zero-terminated Unicode string for the menu name;
   // Zero-terminated Unicode string for the class name;
   // Zero-terminated Unicode string for the window title;
} DLGTEMPLATEEX, *PDLGTEMPLATEEX;
```

```
typedef struct {
    short   nPointSize;
    short   nWeight;        // Such as FW_NORMAL
    short   fItalic;        // TRUE or FALSE
    BYTE    bStartOfStrings;
    // Zero-terminated Unicode string for the font name;
} FONTINFOEX, *PFONTINFOEX;


typedef struct {
    DWORD   dwHelpID;
    DWORD   dwExStyle;      // Such as WS_EX_CONTROLPARENT
    DWORD   dwStyle;        // Such as WS_TABSTOP
    short   x;              // In dialog box units
    short   y;              // In dialog box units
    short   cx;             // In dialog box units
    short   cy;             // In dialog box units
    DWORD   id;
    BYTE    bStartOfStrings;
    // Zero-terminated Unicode string for the class name;
    // Zero-terminated Unicode string for the control title;
    // WORD    wExtraCount; // Usually 0
    // wExtraCount bytes of raw data;
} DLGITEMTEMPLATEEX, *PDLGITEMTEMPLATEEX;

PDLGTEMPLATEEX DlgTemplate_CreateW (
    DWORD   dwStyle,
    DWORD   dwExStyle,
    DWORD   dwHelpId,
    short   x, short y,     // In dialog-box units
    short   cx, short cy,   // In dialog-box units
    PCWSTR szMenuName,      // "" if no menu
    PCWSTR szClassName,     // "" if standard dialog box class
    PCWSTR szCaptionText,
    short   nPointSize,     // Only used if DS_SETFONT specified
    short   nWeight,        // Only used if DS_SETFONT specified
    short   fItalic,        // Only used if DS_SETFONT specified
    PCWSTR szTypeFace);     // Only used if DS_SETFONT specified


PDLGTEMPLATEEX DlgTemplate_CreateA (
    DWORD   dwStyle,
    DWORD   dwExStyle,
    DWORD   dwHelpId,
    short   x, short y,     // In dialog-box units
    short   cx, short cy,   // In dialog-box units
    PCSTR szMenuName,       // "" if no menu
    PCSTR szClassName,      // "" if standard dialog box class
    PCSTR szCaptionText,
    short   nPointSize,     // Only used if DS_SETFONT specified
    short   nWeight,        // Only used if DS_SETFONT specified
    short   fItalic,        // Only used if DS_SETFONT specified
```

```
    PCSTR  szTypeFace);   // Only used if DS_SETFONT specified

#ifdef UNICODE
#define DlgTemplate_Create DlgTemplate_CreateW
#else
#define DlgTemplate_Create DlgTemplate_CreateA
#endif // !UNICODE


///////////////////////////////////////////////////////////////////////////


BOOL DlgTemplate_AddControlW (
    PDLGTEMPLATEEX* ppDlgTemplate, // Returned from Create or AddControl
    short  x,  short y,            // In dialog-box units
    short  cx, short cy,           // In dialog-box units
    DWORD  id,
    DWORD  dwHelpId,
    DWORD  dwStyle,                // WS_CHILD is automatically added
    DWORD  dwExStyle,
    PCWSTR szClass,
    PCWSTR szText,
    WORD   wExtraDataCount,        // Number of additional data bytes
    PBYTE  pbExtraData);           // Passed via CREATESTRUCT's pCreateParams

BOOL DlgTemplate_AddControlA (
    PDLGTEMPLATEEX* ppDlgTemplate, // Returned from Create or AddControl
    short  x,  short y,            // In dialog-box units
    short  cx, short cy,           // In dialog-box units
    DWORD  id,
    DWORD  dwHelpId,
    DWORD  dwStyle,                // WS_CHILD is automatically added
    DWORD  dwExStyle,
    PCSTR  szClass,
    PCSTR  szText,
    WORD   wExtraDataCount,        // Number of additional data bytes
    PBYTE  pbExtraData);           // Passed via CREATESTRUCT's pCreateParams

#ifdef UNICODE
#define DlgTemplate_AddControl DlgTemplate_AddControlW
#else
#define DlgTemplate_AddControl DlgTemplate_AddControlA
#endif // !UNICODE


///////////////////////////////////////////////////////////////////////////


BOOL DlgTemplate_Free (PVOID pvTemplate);


///////////////////////////// End of File /////////////////////////////////
```

185

Listing 3.16 *DlgDyn.RC*

```
//Microsoft Visual C++ generated resource script.
//
#include "resource.h"

#define APSTUDIO_READONLY_SYMBOLS
/////////////////////////////////////////////////////////////////////////////
//
// Generated from the TEXTINCLUDE 2 resource.
//
#include "windows.h"

/////////////////////////////////////////////////////////////////////////////
#undef APSTUDIO_READONLY_SYMBOLS


#ifdef APSTUDIO_INVOKED
/////////////////////////////////////////////////////////////////////////////
//
// TEXTINCLUDE
//

1 TEXTINCLUDE DISCARDABLE
BEGIN
    "resource.h\0"
END

2 TEXTINCLUDE DISCARDABLE
BEGIN
    "#include ""windows.h""\r\n"
    "\0"
END

3 TEXTINCLUDE DISCARDABLE
BEGIN
    "\r\n"
    "\0"
END


/////////////////////////////////////////////////////////////////////////////
#endif    // APSTUDIO_INVOKED


/////////////////////////////////////////////////////////////////////////////
//
// Dialog
//

IDD_DLGDYN DIALOG DISCARDABLE  -32768, 5, 156, 42
STYLE WS_MINIMIZEBOX | WS_VISIBLE | WS_CAPTION | WS_SYSMENU
CAPTION "Dynamic Dialogs"
FONT 8, "MS Sans Serif"
BEGIN
```

```
    DEFPUSHBUTTON    "Create dynamic modal dialog box...",IDC_MODAL,4,4,148,
                     14
    PUSHBUTTON       "Create dynamic modeless dialog box",IDC_MODELESS,4,24,
                     148,14
END


/////////////////////////////////////////////////////////////////////////
//
// Icon
//

IDI_DLGDYN              ICON    DISCARDABLE    "DlgDyn.ico"

#ifndef APSTUDIO_INVOKED
/////////////////////////////////////////////////////////////////////////
//
// Generated from the TEXTINCLUDE 3 resource.
//


/////////////////////////////////////////////////////////////////////////
#endif    // not APSTUDIO_INVOKED
```

Listing 3.17 *Resource.H*

```
//{{NO_DEPENDENCIES}}
// Microsoft Visual C++ generated include file.
// Used by DlgDyn.rc
//
#define IDD_DLGDYN                  101
#define IDC_EDITBOX                 101
#define IDI_DLGDYN                  102
#define IDC_LISTBOX                 102
#define IDC_RADIO1                  103
#define IDC_RADIO2                  104
#define IDC_CHECKBOX                105
#define IDC_MODAL                   1000
#define IDC_MODELESS                1001
#define IDC_STATIC                  -1

// Next default values for new objects
//
#ifdef APSTUDIO_INVOKED
#ifndef APSTUDIO_READONLY_SYMBOLS
#define _APS_NEXT_RESOURCE_VALUE    103
#define _APS_NEXT_COMMAND_VALUE     40001
#define _APS_NEXT_CONTROL_VALUE     1001
#define _APS_NEXT_SYMED_VALUE       106
#endif
#endif
```

The Layout Dialog Box Technique

Users very often find that the dialog boxes they use are too small to suit their needs. In some cases, dialog controls are unable to even display their full text. One wonders why the standard File Open dialog box isn't resizeable, so that users can see more files and folders. Wouldn't it be great if, when a user resized a dialog box, all the controls repositioned and resized themselves to make the dialog box more effective?

It can happen. Right click on My Computer on the Windows 95 desktop. A pop-up menu from which you can select the Find menu option appears, as shown in Figure 3.11. Choosing the Find option presents the dialog box shown in Figure 3.12. The Windows 95 file finder dialog box happens to be resizeable. If you grab the right side of the dialog, you can stretch the file finder so that it looks like the screen shown in Figure 3.13.

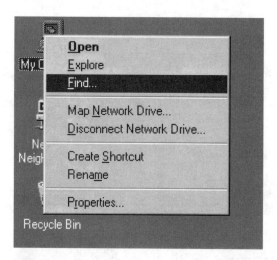

Figure 3.11 *Selecting the Windows 95 file finder.*

Giving the user the ability to resize a dialog box like this can be very useful. Controls such as comboboxes, listboxes, and edit controls can be much easier to work with if you can make them larger or smaller by resizing the dialog box that contains them.

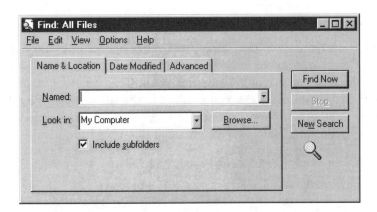

Figure 3.12 *The Windows 95 file finder.*

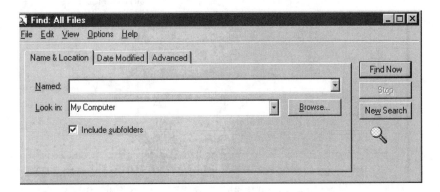

Figure 3.13 *The Windows 95 file finder resized.*

Windows offers the Win32 programmer very little support to help you create reorganizing dialog boxes. Of course, you can always add the WS_THICKFRAME style to a dialog box window so that the user can resize it. But unfortunately, you must write a good deal of code in your window procedures OnSize message handler, which repositions the dialog box's child controls whenever the dialog is sized. Writing this code can be time consuming. What's more, the resulting code can be inflexible, difficult to maintain, and error-prone. The Layout technique presented here provides a data-driven alternative. It enables you to rearrange your dialog box's child controls by specifying a small set of rules rather than by writing code.

Using Layout

To use Layout, you implement the OnSize handler for your dialog box by simply passing your dialog box's window handle and a list of rules to the function Layout_ComputeLayout. This function positions the children of your dialog box according to the rules you specify. If there is a problem with your rule set, Layout produces an assertion. Here is a simple example of an OnSize handler that uses Layout:

```
void SomeClass_OnSize (HWND hwnd, UINT state, int cx, int cy) {

    static RULE rules[] = {

        // Action     Act-on                    Relative-to            Offset
        // ------     ------                    --------------         --------

        { lMOVE,    lTOP   (IDC_B2),            lBOTTOM (IDC_B1),        +8  },
        { lMOVE,    lRIGHT (IDC_B1),            lRIGHT  (lPARENT),       -8  },
        { lMOVE,    lLEFT  (IDC_B2),            lLEFT   (IDC_B1),        +0  },
        { lVCENTER, lGROUP (IDC_B1, IDC_B2),    lCHILD  (lPARENT),       +0  },
        { lEND                                                              }

    };

    // Place the dialog box's child controls according to the rules. If there
    // is a problem with the rules, Layout_ComputeLayout will assert.
    Layout_ComputeLayout(hwnd, rules);
}
```

When the SomeClass_OnSize handler is called initially, the Layout_ComputeLayout function places the child controls IDC_B1 and IDC_B2 so that the dialog box looks like the one shown in Figure 3.14. Then, if you stretch the dialog vertically, SomeClass_OnSize places the controls so that the dialog box looks like the one in Figure 3.15. If you stretch the dialog box horizontally, it looks like the one shown in Figure 3.16. And if you stretch it in both directions, it looks like the dialog box in Figure 3.17.

Figure 3.14 *The original dialog box.*

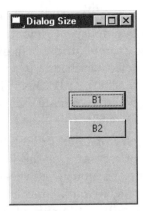

Figure 3.15 *The dialog box stretched vertically.*

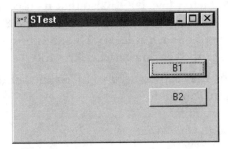

Figure 3.16 *The dialog box stretched horizontally.*

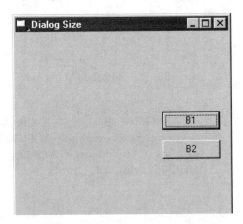

Figure 3.17 *The dialog box stretched both ways.*

191

To get the behavior described previously, the OnSize handler must pass an array of rules to the Layout_ComputeLayout function. Each rule is specified by filling in a RULE structure with the help of some macros defined in **Layout.H**. The first field of each rule is an action which can be: lSTRETCH, lMOVE, lHCENTER, or lVCENTER. The last rule in the list should have action lEND to terminate the list. The ordering of rules in the array makes no difference.

When defining a rule, a side is the left, top, right or bottom edge of a control; a metric is either a side of a control or the width or height of one; and a part is either a metric or a group of controls. Each rule has a part to act on and a part to act relative to. For example, in the preceding code, the first rule acts on the top side of control IDC_B2 (button 2), and it acts relative to the bottom side of control IDC_B1 (button 1). Since the action for this rule is lMOVE, the result of applying the rule would be to move IDC_B2 so that its top side is 8 vertical dialog units below the bottom side of IDC_B1. The 8 dialog unit come from the last field of each rule, which specifies an offset that can be used to fine-tune the spacing between controls.

The full list of macros that can be used to fill in the act-on and relative-to fields is given in Table 3.5.

Table 3.5 *Part macros supported by Layout.*

Part	Description
lLEFT(idc) lTOP(idc) lRIGHT(idc) lBOTTOM(idc)	Specifies a side of control idc.
lWIDTH(idc) lHEIGHT(idc)	Specifies the width/height of control idc.
lWIDTHOF(idc, percent) lHEIGHTOF(idc, percent)	Specifies a percentage of the width/height of control idc. For example, lWIDTHOF (IDC_B1, 33) would specify 33% of the width of control IDC_B1.

continued...

Part	Description
lCHILD(idc)	Specifies the control idc.
lGROUP(idcFirst, idcLast)	Specifies the group of all controls whose id values are between idcFirst and idcLast, inclusive.

Notice that the second rule in the preceding example acts relative to the right-hand side of a control called lPARENT. The lPARENT identifier is a special value that is used to reference the metrics of the parent dialog box. So the second rule can be read as "position the right side of control IDC_B1 so that it is 8 dialog box units from the right-hand side of the parent dialog box", and no matter how the user stretches the dialog box, IDC_B1 will always be placed 8 dialog box units from the right-hand side of the dialog box.

The third rule simply aligns the left side of IDC_B2 with the left side of IDC_B1. We could achieve the same effect by positioning IDC_B2 with the same rule as IDC_B1, but by making IDC_B2 relative to IDC_B1, IDC_B2 will follow IDC_B1, wherever we should choose to move it.

The fourth and final rule vertically centers IDC_B1 and IDC_B2, as a group, with respect to lPARENT (the height of the dialog box). To center the group, Layout first applies the rule to position IDC_B2 underneath IDC_B1; then, it computes the bounding rectangle for the group (both controls) and centers that rectangle, moving each control in the group accordingly.

The four Layout actions are defined in Table 3.6.

Table 3.6 *Action macros supported by Layout.*

Action	Meaning
lSTRETCH	Stretch one metric of a control based on a metric of another control. Only one metric of the control is changed, so the control will be stretched to a new width/height rather than moved. If you stretch the left side of a control, the right side will stay fixed, and vice versa. If you stretch the width of a control, the control will be given the new width, but neither the left nor the right side will be explicitly positioned. Stretching the width/height of a control can be useful when you want to size a control that has other rules for centering or positioning.

continued...

| lMOVE | The control maintains its size, but one side of the control is moved relative to a metric of another control. Typically, this is something like move the left side of control A next to the right side of control B. But notice that you could actually move one side of a control relative to the width/height of another control. This can be useful when positioning a control relative to the width/height of the parent dialog box. For example, lMOVE, lLEFT(IDC_B1), lWIDTHOF(lPARENT, 33), 0 would move IDC_B1 so that its left side would be at one-third of the width of the parent dialog box. |
| lHCENTER lVCENTER | A group of controls is centered with respect to a single control. If you specify lHCENTER, centering is horizontal. If you specify lVCENTER, centering is vertical. Very often, centering is relative to lPARENT, but this is not a requirement. In fact, the DlgSize application presented in this chapter vertically centers a group of two buttons relative to an edit control. |

Now that you know how to use Layout, you may want to try some experiments by modifying the rules in the DlgSize application which is described in the next section.

The Implementation of Layout

The basic algorithm for Layout works roughly as follows:

1. Create a list of child controls for the dialog box being laid out, initially marking the metrics of each child as known.

2. Traverse the list of rules, marking the metrics of children that are affected by rules as unknown. Layout's goal is to discover values for these unknown quantities based on the values of quantities that are known. It is important to note that all six metrics of the parent dialog box (lPARENT) are always known. Known quantities, such as the metrics of the parent dialog box and any fixed sides of child controls, provide a way for the rule system to "bottom out."

3. Traverse the list of rules, converting offset values from dialog box units to pixels and marking each rule as unapplied.

4. Repeatedly loop through the whole list of rules, attempting to apply each unapplied rule, until a complete pass is made without successfully applying a rule. At this point, we can make no more progress, so we are finished. If there are rules

that were not applied, or if any children still have unknown metrics, Layout has failed to find a solution, and it asserts.

5. If all the rules were successfully applied, and all four sides of each child are known, we have succeeded, and we can move all the children to their new locations simultaneously with DeferWindowPos.

Because this is a book about Windows and not about layout algorithms, I have intentionally glossed over the implementation details of Layout. If you are interested in understanding exactly how Layout works, read the code and comments in **Layout.C** and **Layout.H** thoroughly. When you have done this, create a simple set of rules and trace through Layout in the debugger.

Before we move on to the DlgSize application, I want to go over the Windows-related portions of the Layout implementation. In the first step of the algorithm, the child list is created by enumerating the children of the dialog box with the macros GetFirstChild and GetNextSibling, which are defined in **WindowsX.H**. These macros simply use the GetTopWindow and GetWindow functions to get the child window with the highest z-order, and the next sibling window in the window list, respectively. Enumerating the children of a window is a common task, so you will probably find that these macros come in handy in your own applications.

In the third step, we convert offset values from dialog box units to pixels using a function called adgMapDialogRect. Because I wanted Layout to work for any window (not just dialog boxes), I could not use MapDialogRect because, unfortunately, MapDialogRect is one of those rare dialog functions that truly works only on dialog boxes. adgMapDialogRect first checks the GCW_ATOM value of the windows class to see if it is 32770, the atom value of the Windows dialog box class. If the window is a dialog box, we simply call MapDialogRect. If the window is not a dialog, we must emulate the quirky mapping algorithm that Windows uses internally in MapDialog Rect. The MapDialogRect function computes an average character width by getting the text extent of a string containing all the lowercase and uppercase letters (a to z and A to Z).[1] MapDialogRect takes this extent and divides by the length of the string to obtain the average character width

---

[1]This algorithm is used regardless of the language version of Windows.

(rounding up). Given the average character width, cxChar, it is a simple matter to map a rectangle from dialog box units to pixels:

```
SetRect(prc,
     prc->left * cxChar / 4, prc->right  * cxChar / 4,
     prc->top  * cyChar / 8, prc->bottom * cyChar / 8);
```

In the final step of the algorithm, Layout uses BeginDeferWindowPos to create a list of windows to be moved. It adds positioning information to this list with DeferWindowPos and then calls EndDeferWindowPos to move all the windows simultaneously. When you have several windows to move, using DeferWindowPos is more efficient than calling SetWindowPos for each window.

The DlgSize Application

The DlgSize application (**DlgSize.EXE**), shown in Listings 3.18-3.22, (starting on page 199) demonstrates how to use the Layout technique to reposition the children of a sizeable dialog box. When you invoke the application, the main application window appears "Figure 3.18." DlgSize has several child controls: three buttons, two edit controls, two static controls and a groupbox. These controls are not functional—they are present only for the purposes of demonstration. When the DlgSize dialog is resized, the Layout technique is used to rearrange the controls. When resized both horizontally and vertically, DlgSize looks like the dialog box shown in Figure 3.19.

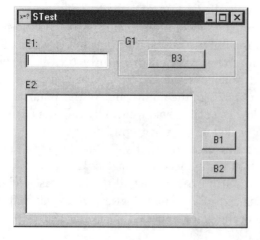

Figure 3.18 *The DlgSize application.*

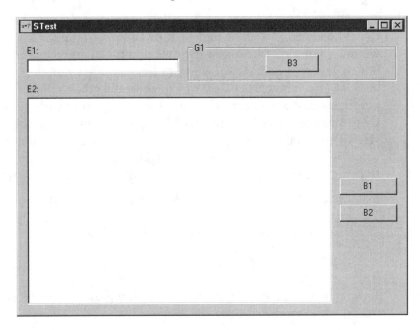

Figure 3.19 *The DlgSize application resized.*

Table 3.7 describes the files used to create this application.

Table 3.7 *Files used to build the DlgSize application.*

File	Description
DlgSize.C	Contains WinMain and main window's dialog box and message cracker functions.
Layout.C	Contains a library of functions that make it much easier for you to dynamically layout a dialog box's child windows. You can use this file in your own applications.
Layout.H	Contains prototypes for the functions contained in the **Layout.C** file. Any source file that uses the library of functions in **Layout.C** must include this file.
DlgSize.RC	Contains the dialog box template for the main application window and its icons.
Resource.H	Contains IDs for all resources in the RC file.
DlgSize.ICO	Contains the icon for the main window.
DlgSize.MAK	Visual C++ project makefile.

The DlgSize_OnSize message handler (in DlgSize.C) repositions all the child controls with a single call to Layout_ComputeLayout. But we must put a restriction on this: we don't want the DlgSize dialog box to get too small. If DlgSize were too small, Layout would assert because DlgSize's particular set of rules would give some windows a negative size.[2] To prevent this situation, we restrict the user's ability to size the dialog box too small. This is done by saving the initial size of the dialog box in GWL_USERDATA and then using this value, when the window is about to be sized, to specify a minimum tracking size in response to a WM_GETMINMAXINFO message:

```
void DlgSize_OnGetMinMaxInfo (HWND hwnd, LPMINMAXINFO lpMinMaxInfo) {

    // Override the default minimum tracking size with our own size, which was
    // computed and saved in GWL_USERDATA in OnInitDialog.
    lpMinMaxInfo->ptMinTrackSize = * (POINT*)
        GetWindowLong(hwnd, GWL_USERDATA);
}
```

This technique prevents the user from making the dialog box smaller than its original size.

Other Applications of Layout

Although we have discussed only the uses of Layout with respect to OnSize handlers, there is no reason you can't use Layout in other message handlers, for other purposes. For example, sometimes dialog boxes dynamically create child controls (for one reason or another) with CreateWindowEx. This can be cumbersome because you need to compute the locations of your controls "by hand". But if you use Layout, you can create the controls with zero size and then use Layout rules to position/size them.

---

[2]In particular, if DlgSize's dialog box were too small, the rule: lSTRETCH, lRIGHT (IDC_E2), lLEFT (IDC_B1), -8 would cause IDC_E2 to have a negative width. This would happen because IDC_B1 is of fixed width and is positioned 8 dialog box units from the right-hand side of the dialog box. If the dialog box were very narrow, the left side of IDC_B1 would have to extend beyond the left side of IDC_E2, and the right-hand side of IDC_E2 would follow, causing IDC_E2 to have a negative width. In practice, the best way to determine if you have a problem like this in your rule set is to simply try it out. If making your dialog box too small causes assertions in Layout or results in something less than aesthetic, you may need to restrict the sizing of your dialog box in some way.

Another interesting set of possibilities lies in using Layout to reposition controls conditionally. You could have two (or more) different rule sets that change the appearance of a dialog box based on some condition (such as the hide/show state of a control or the check state of a checkbox). Keep in mind that rule lists don't have to be static; you can modify one or more rules based on a condition or even create a rule list dynamically.

DlgSize.ICO

Listing 3.18 *DlgSize.C*

```
/********************************************************************
Module name: DlgSize.c
Written by: Jonathan W. Locke
Notices: Copyright (c) 1995 Jeffrey Richter
Purpose: Example to demonstrate use of the layout algorithm (see Layout.c)
********************************************************************/


#include "..\Win95ADG.h"          /* See Appendix A for details */
#include <windows.h>
#include <windowsx.h>
#pragma warning(disable: 4001)     /* Single line comment */
#include "Resource.h"
#include "Layout.h"


///////////////////////////////////////////////////////////////////


void DlgSize_OnSize (HWND hwnd, UINT state, int cx, int cy) {

  static RULE rules[] = {

    // Action    Act-on                   Relative-to          Offset
    // ------    ------                    -----------          ------

     { lMOVE,    lRIGHT (IDC_B1),          lRIGHT  (lPARENT),     -8 },
     { lSTRETCH, lWIDTH (IDC_B1),          lWIDTHOF(lPARENT, 15), +0 },
     { lMOVE,    lTOP   (IDC_B2),          lBOTTOM (IDC_B1),      +8 },
     { lMOVE,    lLEFT  (IDC_B2),          lLEFT   (IDC_B1),      +0 },
     { lSTRETCH, lWIDTH (IDC_B2),          lWIDTH  (IDC_B1),      +0 },
     { lVCENTER, lCHILD (IDC_B3),          lCHILD  (IDC_G1),      +2 },
     { lHCENTER, lCHILD (IDC_B3),          lCHILD  (IDC_G1),      +0 },
     { lVCENTER, lGROUP (IDC_B1, IDC_B2),  lCHILD  (IDC_E2),      +0 },
     { lSTRETCH, lWIDTH (IDC_E1),          lWIDTHOF(IDC_E2, 50),  +0 },
     { lSTRETCH, lBOTTOM(IDC_E2),          lBOTTOM (lPARENT),     -8 },
     { lSTRETCH, lRIGHT (IDC_E2),          lLEFT   (IDC_B1),      -8 },
     { lMOVE,    lLEFT  (IDC_G1),          lRIGHT  (IDC_E1),      +8 },
     { lSTRETCH, lRIGHT (IDC_G1),          lRIGHT  (lPARENT),     -8 },
```

```
      {  1END                                                        }
   };

   // Place the dialog's child controls according to the rules. If there is
   // a problem with the rules, Layout_ComputeLayout will assert.
   Layout_ComputeLayout(hwnd, rules);
}


//////////////////////////////////////////////////////////////////////////


BOOL DlgSize_OnInitDialog (HWND hwnd, HWND hwndFocus, LPARAM lParam) {

   RECT rc;
   POINT *pptMin;

   adgSETDLGICONS(hwnd, IDI_LAYOUT, IDI_LAYOUT);

   // Save the initial width/height of the dialog in the GWL_USERDATA extra
   // bytes. We use this information later in DlgSize_OnGetMinMaxInfo to ensure
   // that the dialog is not sized smaller than the initial size.
   GetWindowRect(hwnd, &rc);
   pptMin = malloc(sizeof (POINT));
   if (pptMin) {
      pptMin->x = rc.right - rc.left;
      pptMin->y = rc.bottom - rc.top;
   }
   SetWindowLong(hwnd, GWL_USERDATA, (LONG) pptMin);
   return(TRUE);                     // Accept default focus window.
}


//////////////////////////////////////////////////////////////////////////


void DlgSize_OnDestroy(HWND hwnd) {

   // Free the minimum tracking size data that is stored in GWL_USERDATA. If
   // malloc fails in OnInitDialog, this value may be NULL, but this is okay
   // because ANSI C states that free is defined to ignore NULL pointers.
   free((void*) GetWindowLong(hwnd, GWL_USERDATA));
}


//////////////////////////////////////////////////////////////////////////


void DlgSize_OnGetMinMaxInfo (HWND hwnd, LPMINMAXINFO lpMinMaxInfo) {

   // Override the default minimum tracking size with our own size, which was
```

```
        // computed and saved in GWL_USERDATA in OnInitDialog.
        lpMinMaxInfo->ptMinTrackSize = *(POINT*) GetWindowLong(hwnd, GWL_USERDATA);
}


///////////////////////////////////////////////////////////////////////////


void DlgSize_OnCommand (HWND hwnd, int id, HWND hwndCtl, UINT codeNotify) {

    switch (id) {
        case IDCANCEL:                  // Allows dialog box to close
            EndDialog(hwnd, id);
            break;
    }
}


///////////////////////////////////////////////////////////////////////////


BOOL WINAPI DlgSize_DlgProc (HWND hwnd, UINT uMsg,
    WPARAM wParam, LPARAM lParam) {

    switch (uMsg) {

        // Standard Windows messages
        adgHANDLE_DLGMSG(hwnd, WM_INITDIALOG,   DlgSize_OnInitDialog);
        adgHANDLE_DLGMSG(hwnd, WM_COMMAND,      DlgSize_OnCommand);
        adgHANDLE_DLGMSG(hwnd, WM_SIZE,         DlgSize_OnSize);
        adgHANDLE_DLGMSG(hwnd, WM_GETMINMAXINFO, DlgSize_OnGetMinMaxInfo);
        adgHANDLE_DLGMSG(hwnd, WM_DESTROY,      DlgSize_OnDestroy);
    }
    return(FALSE);                      // We didn't process the message.
}


///////////////////////////////////////////////////////////////////////////


int WINAPI WinMain (HINSTANCE hinstExe, HINSTANCE hinstPrev,
    LPSTR lpszCmdLine, int nCmdShow) {

    adgWARNIFUNICODEUNDERWIN95();
    adgVERIFY(-1 != DialogBox(hinstExe, MAKEINTRESOURCE(IDD_LAYOUT),
        NULL, DlgSize_DlgProc));

    return(0);
}


///////////////////////////// End of File /////////////////////////////////
```

Listing 3.19 *Layout.C*

```
/************************************************************************
Module name: Layout.c
Written by: Jonathan W. Locke
Notices: Copyright (c) 1995 Jeffrey Richter
Purpose: Implementation of a layout algorithm which positions controls
         in a window based on a set of rules.
*************************************************************************/


#include "..\Win95ADG.h"        /* See Appendix A for details */
#include <windows.h>
#include <windowsx.h>
#pragma warning(disable: 4001)   /* Single line comment */
#include "Layout.h"


//////////////////////// ID for Child List Terminator ////////////////////////


#define IDC_LASTCHILD 0x10001    // Special child id for last child in list.
                                 // Guaranteed not to be used because you
                                 // cannot have control ids above 0xffff.


//////////////////////////////////// Limits //////////////////////////////////


#define NUMPARTS    7            // There are 7 parts: left, top, right,
                                 // bottom, width, height and group
#define NUMMETRICS  6            // There are 6 metrics: left, top, right,
                                 // bottom, width and height.
#define NUMSIDES    4            // There are 4 sides: left, top, right and
                                 // bottom.


//////////////////////// Macros for Asserting Part Types //////////////////////


#define ISPART(n)   adgINRANGE(lpLEFT, (n), lpGROUP)
#define ISMETRIC(n) adgINRANGE(lpLEFT, (n), lpHEIGHT)
#define ISSIDE(n)   adgINRANGE(lpLEFT, (n), lpBOTTOM)


//////////////////////////////// Metric Flags ////////////////////////////////


typedef enum {
   UNKNOWN,                      // Metric is unknown
   KNOWN                         // Metric is known
} MFLAG;


//////////////////////////////// Rule States /////////////////////////////////
```

```
enum {
   UNAPPLIED,                         // Rule has not been applied
   APPLIED                            // Rule has been applied
};



//////////////////////////// Definition of a Child Control ////////////////////////////


typedef struct tagCHILD {
   int idc;                           // Control id (lPARENT represents parent)
   union {                            // Child has either a list of metrics:
      int anMetric[NUMMETRICS];       //    left, top, right, bottom, width, height
      struct {                        // or a RECT, a width and a height:
         RECT rc;                     //    RECT (left, top, right, bottom)
         int nWidth;                  //    width
         int nHeight;                 //    height
      };                              // depending on which is more readable in
   };                                 // a given context.
   BOOL fFixed;                       // TRUE if child doesn't need to be placed
   MFLAG afMetric[NUMMETRICS];        // Metric flags (KNOWN or UNKNOWN)
} CHILD;



//////////////////////////// Local Function Prototypes ////////////////////////////


BOOL adgMapDialogRect (HWND hwndParent, PRECT prc);

int Layout_GetOppositeSide (int nSide);
int Layout_GetOtherUnknownMetric (int nUnknownMetric);
BOOL Layout_MetricIsVertical (int nMetric);
void Layout_SolveChild (CHILD* pChild);
CHILD* Layout_FindChild (CHILD* pChildList, int idcChild);
CHILD* Layout_CreateChildList (HWND hwndParent, int* pnChildren);
void Layout_ConvertDlgUnits (HWND hwndParent, RULE* pRules, CHILD* pChildList);
void Layout_MarkUnknowns (HWND hwndParent, RULE* pRules, CHILD* pChildList);
BOOL Layout_CheckChild (CHILD* pChild);
BOOL Layout_ApplyRule (HWND hwndParent, RULE* pRules,
   CHILD* pChildList, RULE* pRule);
BOOL Layout_ApplyRules (HWND hwndParent, RULE* pRules, CHILD* pChildList);


//////////////////////////////////////////////////////////////////////////////////


// A MapDialogRect function that works for non-dialog windows.
BOOL adgMapDialogRect (HWND hwndParent, PRECT prc) {

   HDC hdc;
   SIZE size;
   int cxChar, cyChar;
   HFONT hfont, hfontOriginal;

   // This is the set of characters that Windows uses to compute the average
```

```
    // character width.
    static TCHAR szChars[] =
        __TEXT("abcdefghijklmnopqrstuvwxyzABCDEFGHIJKLMNOPQRSTUVWXYZ");

    // Check assumptions.
    adgASSERT(IsWindow(hwndParent));
    adgASSERT(prc);

    // If the window is a dialog, just use MapDialogRect.
    if (GetClassWord(hwndParent, GCW_ATOM) == 32770)
        return(MapDialogRect(hwndParent, prc));

    // Get a device context and select the window's font into it.
    hdc = GetDC(hwndParent);
    hfont = GetWindowFont(hwndParent);
    if (hfont != NULL)
        hfontOriginal = SelectFont(hdc, hfont);

    // Unfortunately, we cannot use GetTextMetrics to get the average character
    // width because the TEXTMETRIC structure's tmAveCharWidth member is
    // incorrect for proportional fonts. So, instead we compute the average
    // character width ourselves using the same technique employed by Windows
    // itself:  We pass "a-zA-Z" to GetTextExtentPoint and average, rounding up.
    // (NOTE: We do not call GetTextExtentPoint32 because this function corrects
    // an error that Windows relies on)
    GetTextExtentPoint(hdc, szChars, adgARRAY_SIZE(szChars), &size);
    cyChar = size.cy;
    cxChar = ((size.cx / (adgARRAY_SIZE(szChars) / 2)) + 1) / 2;

    // Restore any original font and then release the device context.
    if (hfont != NULL)
        SelectFont(hdc, hfontOriginal);
    ReleaseDC(hwndParent, hdc);

    // Map rectangle prc based on the font dimensions (cxChar by cyChar).
    SetRect(prc,
        prc->left  * cxChar / 4, prc->top    * cyChar / 8,
        prc->right * cxChar / 4, prc->bottom * cyChar / 8);
    return(TRUE);
}


/////////////////////////////////////////////////////////////////////////////


int Layout_GetOppositeSide (int nSide) {

    int nOppositeSide;

    // Check assumptions.
    adgASSERT(ISSIDE(nSide));

    switch (nSide) {
        case lpLEFT:
            nOppositeSide = lpRIGHT;
            break;
```

```
      case lpRIGHT:
         nOppositeSide = lpLEFT;
         break;

      case lpTOP:
         nOppositeSide = lpBOTTOM;
         break;

      case lpBOTTOM:
         nOppositeSide = lpTOP;
         break;

      default:                         // Invalid side
         adgFAIL(__TEXT("Invalid side"));
         break;
   }
   return(nOppositeSide);
}


///////////////////////////////////////////////////////////////////////////


int Layout_GetOtherUnknownMetric (int nUnknownMetric) {

   int nOtherUnknownMetric = 0;

   // Check assumptions.
   adgASSERT(ISMETRIC(nUnknownMetric));

   switch (nUnknownMetric) {
      case lpLEFT:
      case lpRIGHT:
         nOtherUnknownMetric = lpWIDTH;
         break;

      case lpTOP:
      case lpBOTTOM:
         nOtherUnknownMetric = lpHEIGHT;
         break;

      case lpWIDTH:
         nOtherUnknownMetric = lpRIGHT;
         break;

      case lpHEIGHT:
         nOtherUnknownMetric = lpBOTTOM;
         break;

      default:
         adgFAIL(__TEXT("Invalid metric"));
         break;
   }
   return(nOtherUnknownMetric);
}
```

```
/////////////////////////////////////////////////////////////////////////////

BOOL Layout_MetricIsVertical (int nMetric) {

    BOOL fMetricIsVertical = FALSE;

    // Check assumptions.
    adgASSERT(ISMETRIC(nMetric));

    switch (nMetric) {
      case lpLEFT:
      case lpRIGHT:
      case lpWIDTH:
          fMetricIsVertical = FALSE;
          break;

      case lpTOP:
      case lpBOTTOM:
      case lpHEIGHT:
          fMetricIsVertical = TRUE;
          break;

      default:
          adgFAIL(__TEXT("Invalid metric"));
          break;
    }
    return(fMetricIsVertical);
}


/////////////////////////////////////////////////////////////////////////////


void Layout_SolveChild (CHILD* pChild) {

    int i;

    // Check assumptions.
    adgASSERT(pChild);

    // Loop through all six metrics of a child, computing values for unknown
    // metrics from values of known metrics (if any).
    for (i = 0; i < NUMMETRICS; i++) {

        // If this metric of the child is unknown, see if it can be computed in
        // terms of other metrics which we do know.
        if (pChild->afMetric[i] == UNKNOWN) {

            // Compute left/top as right/bottom - width/height
            if (i < 2) {
                if ((pChild->afMetric[i + 2] == KNOWN) &&
                    (pChild->afMetric[i + 4] == KNOWN)) {
                    pChild->anMetric[i] = pChild->anMetric[i + 2] -
                        pChild->anMetric[i + 4];
```

```
                pChild->afMetric[i] = KNOWN;
            }
        }
        // Compute right/bottom as left/top + width/height
        else if (i < 4) {
            if ((pChild->afMetric[i - 2] == KNOWN) &&
                (pChild->afMetric[i + 2] == KNOWN)) {
                pChild->anMetric[i] = pChild->anMetric[i - 2] +
                    pChild->anMetric[i + 2];
                pChild->afMetric[i] = KNOWN;
            }
        }
        // Compute width/height as right/bottom - left/top
        else {
            if ((pChild->afMetric[i - 2] == KNOWN) &&
                (pChild->afMetric[i - 4] == KNOWN)) {
                pChild->anMetric[i] = pChild->anMetric[i - 2] -
                    pChild->anMetric[i - 4];
                pChild->afMetric[i] = KNOWN;
            }
        }
    }
    }
}


//////////////////////////////////////////////////////////////////////////////


CHILD* Layout_FindChild (CHILD* pChildList, int idcChild) {

    CHILD *pChild;

    // Check assumptions.
    adgASSERT(pChildList);
    adgASSERT(adgINRANGE(0, idcChild, IDC_LASTCHILD));

    // Traverse the child list looking for an id
    for (pChild = pChildList; pChild->idc != IDC_LASTCHILD; pChild++) {

        // If we find idcChild, we solve the child for unknowns and return it
        if (pChild->idc == idcChild) {
            Layout_SolveChild(pChild);
            return(pChild);
        }
    }
    adgFAIL(__TEXT("Child not found in child list"));
    return(NULL);
}


//////////////////////////////////////////////////////////////////////////////


CHILD* Layout_CreateChildList (HWND hwndParent, int* pnChildren) {
```

```
int i;
HWND hwnd, hwndFirst;
CHILD* pChild, *pChildList;

// Check assumptions.
adgASSERT(IsWindow(hwndParent));
adgASSERT(pnChildren);

// Count the number of child windows in hwndParent.
hwndFirst = hwnd = GetFirstChild(hwndParent);
for (*pnChildren = 0; IsWindow(hwnd); hwnd = GetNextSibling(hwnd))
   (*pnChildren)++;
if (*pnChildren == 0)
   return(NULL);

// Allocate memory for the CHILD list. This list will have an entry for
// each child of the dialog, plus a CHILD structure for the parent window
// (lPARENT) and one which acts as a list terminator (IDC_LASTCHILD).
pChildList = malloc((*pnChildren + 2) * sizeof(CHILD));
adgASSERT(pChildList);
if (!pChildList)
   return(NULL);
pChild = pChildList;

// Add the special-case parent 'CHILD' structure
pChild->idc = lPARENT;
GetClientRect(hwndParent, &pChild->rc);
for (i = 0; i < NUMSIDES; i++)
   pChild->afMetric[i] = KNOWN;
pChild->afMetric[lpWIDTH] = pChild->afMetric[lpHEIGHT] = UNKNOWN;
Layout_SolveChild(pChild);
pChild++;

// Add all the real children of the dialog to the list
hwnd = hwndFirst;
for (; IsWindow(hwnd); hwnd = GetNextSibling(hwnd)) {

   // Get child's id and bounding rectangle in client coordinates
   pChild->idc = GetWindowID(hwnd);
   GetWindowRect(hwnd, &pChild->rc);
   MapWindowRect(HWND_DESKTOP, hwndParent, &pChild->rc);
   for (i = 0; i < NUMSIDES; i++)
      pChild->afMetric[i] = KNOWN;

   // Solve for the width and height.
   pChild->afMetric[lpWIDTH] = pChild->afMetric[lpHEIGHT] = UNKNOWN;
   Layout_SolveChild(pChild);

   // All children are fixed, initially.
   pChild->fFixed = TRUE;
   pChild++;
}

// Terminate and return the list.
pChild->idc = IDC_LASTCHILD;
```

```
    return(pChildList);
}


/////////////////////////////////////////////////////////////////////////


void Layout_ConvertDlgUnits (HWND hwndParent, RULE* pRules, CHILD*
pChildList) {

    RECT rc = { 0, 0, 0, 0 };
    BOOL fVertical;
    RULE* pRule;

    // Check assumptions.
    adgASSERT(IsWindow(hwndParent));
    adgASSERT(pRules);
    adgASSERT(pChildList);

    // Traverse the rules list
    for (pRule = pRules; pRule->Action != lEND; pRule++) {

        // Simultaneously map the rule's offset value, vertically and
        // horizontally, from dialog units to pixels.
        rc.right = rc.bottom = pRule->nOffset;
        adgMapDialogRect(hwndParent, &rc);

        // Determine if the current rule affects horizontal or vertical
        // coordinates. We need to know this because dialog unit space is not
        // isometric (horizontal and vertical dialog units are not equivalent).
        switch (pRule->Action) {

            case lVCENTER:
                fVertical = TRUE;
                break;

            case lHCENTER:
                fVertical = FALSE;
                break;

            case lMOVE:
            case lSTRETCH:
                fVertical = Layout_MetricIsVertical(pRule->ActOn.nMetric);
                break;

            default:
                adgFAIL(__TEXT("Invalid action"));
                break;
        }

        // Take the correct mapped value based on the rule being applied
        pRule->nPixelOffset = fVertical ? rc.bottom : rc.right;
    }
}
```

```
/////////////////////////////////////////////////////////////////////////////

void Layout_MarkUnknowns (HWND hwndParent, RULE* pRules, CHILD* pChildList) {

    RULE* pRule;
    CHILD* pChildActOn;
    HWND hwnd;
    int nOtherUnknown, nOppositeSide, idc, idcFirst, idcLast;

    // Check assumptions.
    adgASSERT(IsWindow(hwndParent));
    adgASSERT(pRules);
    adgASSERT(pChildList);

    // Traverse the rule list, marking unknowns in the child list.
    for (pRule = pRules; pRule->Action != lEND; pRule++) {

        // Set metric flags based on the rule's proposed action
        switch (pRule->Action) {

            case lSTRETCH:              // Metric should be stretched

                // Find the child to be acted upon
                pChildActOn = Layout_FindChild(pChildList, pRule->ActOn.idc);
                adgASSERT(pChildActOn);

                // Since the child is going to be acted upon, it is no longer fixed.
                pChildActOn->fFixed = FALSE;

                // The part being acted on must be a metric.
                adgASSERT(ISMETRIC(pRule->ActOn.nMetric));

                // The metric being stretched must be unknown.
                pChildActOn->afMetric[pRule->ActOn.nMetric] = UNKNOWN;

                // If the left/top or right/bottom is unknown, so is the
                // width/height. If the width/height is unknown, then the
                // right/bottom is also unknown.
                nOtherUnknown = Layout_GetOtherUnknownMetric(pRule->ActOn.nMetric);
                pChildActOn->afMetric[nOtherUnknown] = UNKNOWN;
                break;

            case lMOVE:                 // Control should be moved

                // Find the child to be acted upon
                pChildActOn = Layout_FindChild(pChildList, pRule->ActOn.idc);
                adgASSERT(pChildActOn);

                // Since the child is going to be acted upon, it is no longer fixed.
                pChildActOn->fFixed = FALSE;

                // The part being acted upon must be a side.
                adgASSERT(ISSIDE(pRule->ActOn.nSide));
```

```
            // The side being moved is unknown.
            pChildActOn->afMetric[pRule->ActOn.nSide] = UNKNOWN;

            // So is the opposite side. But, the width/height remains known.
            // (Actually, this is the primary reason for having six metrics).
            nOppositeSide = Layout_GetOppositeSide(pRule->ActOn.nSide);
            pChildActOn->afMetric[nOppositeSide] = UNKNOWN;
            break;

        case lVCENTER:          // Vertically center control/group
        case lHCENTER:          // Horizontally center control/group

            // We must be centering a group of one or more controls.
            adgASSERT(pRule->ActOn.nPart == lpGROUP);

            // Go through the group of one or more controls
            idcFirst = pRule->ActOn.idcFirst;
            idcLast = pRule->ActOn.idcLast;
            adgASSERT(idcFirst <= idcLast);
            hwnd = GetFirstChild(hwndParent);
            for (; IsWindow(hwnd); hwnd = GetNextSibling(hwnd)) {
                idc = GetWindowID(hwnd);
                if (adgINRANGE(idcFirst, idc, idcLast)) {

                    // Find the child to be acted upon and set the appropriate
                    // sides to unknown. Width is still known.
                    pChildActOn = Layout_FindChild(pChildList, idc);
                    if (pRule->Action == lHCENTER) {
                        pChildActOn->afMetric[lpLEFT] = UNKNOWN;
                        pChildActOn->afMetric[lpRIGHT] = UNKNOWN;
                    } else {
                        pChildActOn->afMetric[lpTOP] = UNKNOWN;
                        pChildActOn->afMetric[lpBOTTOM] = UNKNOWN;
                    }

                    // Child acted upon is no longer fixed.
                    pChildActOn->fFixed = FALSE;
                }
            }
            break;

        default:
            adgFAIL(__TEXT("Invalid action"));
            break;
    }
  }
 }
}


////////////////////////////////////////////////////////////////////////////


BOOL Layout_CheckChild (CHILD* pChild) {
```

```
      static TCHAR* pszMetric[] = {
         __TEXT("left"),   __TEXT("top"),    __TEXT("right"),
         __TEXT("bottom"), __TEXT("width"),  __TEXT("height")
      };

      int i;
      BOOL fOK = TRUE;
      TCHAR sz[80];

      // Check assumptions.
      adgASSERT(pChild);

      // Any unknown metric indicates a problem with the rules, so we 'assert'.
      for (i = 0; i < NUMMETRICS; i++) {
         if (pChild->afMetric[i] == UNKNOWN) {
            wsprintf(sz, __TEXT("Layout couldn't find %s of id=%d"),
               pszMetric[i], pChild->idc);
            adgMB(sz);
            fOK = FALSE;
         }
      }
      return(fOK);
}


//////////////////////////////////////////////////////////////////////////////


BOOL Layout_ApplyRule (HWND hwndParent, RULE* pRules,
   CHILD* pChildList, RULE* pRule) {

   CHILD* pChildRelTo, *pChildActOn, ChildRelTo;
   CHILD* pChild, *pChildListNew, *pSrc, *pDest;
   int nRules, nMetric, nChildren;
   int idcFirst, idcLast, nOffset, nCentered;
   RECT rcBounds;
   HWND hwnd, hwndFirst;
   RULE *pr, *prn, *prNew;

   // Check assumptions.
   adgASSERT(IsWindow(hwndParent));
   adgASSERT(pRules);
   adgASSERT(pChildList);
   adgASSERT(pRule);

   // Find the child and part(s) that we are going to act relative to
   pChildRelTo = Layout_FindChild(pChildList, pRule->RelTo.idc);
   adgASSERT(pChildRelTo);

   switch (pRule->RelTo.nPart) {

      case lpLEFT:
      case lpTOP:
      case lpRIGHT:
      case lpBOTTOM:
```

```
    case lpWIDTH:
    case lpHEIGHT:

        // We can't apply a rule relative to a metric that is unknown.
        if (pChildRelTo->afMetric[pRule->RelTo.nMetric] == UNKNOWN)
            return(FALSE);
        break;

    case lpGROUP:

        // We can't apply a rule relative to a control unless we know its
        // left/top and right/bottom sides (for centering).
        adgASSERT(pRule->RelTo.idcFirst == pRule->RelTo.idcLast);
        adgASSERT((pRule->Action == lHCENTER) || (pRule->Action == lVCENTER));
        if (pRule->Action == lHCENTER) {
            if ((pChildRelTo->afMetric[lpLEFT] == UNKNOWN) ||
                (pChildRelTo->afMetric[lpRIGHT] == UNKNOWN))
                return(FALSE);
        } else {
            if ((pChildRelTo->afMetric[lpTOP] == UNKNOWN) ||
                (pChildRelTo->afMetric[lpBOTTOM] == UNKNOWN))
                return(FALSE);
        }
        break;
}

// Make a local copy of the child we are relative to. We need to do this
// because we may need to apply a percentage to the width/height metrics
// and we don't want to modify the actual child list.
ChildRelTo = *pChildRelTo;

// Use percentage to modify the width/height of the child we are relative to
if ((pRule->RelTo.nMetric == lpWIDTH) ||
    (pRule->RelTo.nMetric == lpHEIGHT)) {

    ChildRelTo.anMetric[pRule->RelTo.nMetric] *= pRule->RelTo.nPercent;
    ChildRelTo.anMetric[pRule->RelTo.nMetric] /= 100;
    Layout_SolveChild(&ChildRelTo);
}

// Apply our rule based on the action field
switch (pRule->Action) {

    case lSTRETCH:                    // Metric should be stretched

        // The part being acted on must be a metric. If it is a width/height
        // metric, it must be 100% of the width/height.
        adgASSERT(ISMETRIC(pRule->ActOn.nMetric));
        adgASSERT(ISSIDE(pRule->ActOn.nSide) ||
            (pRule->ActOn.nPercent == 100));

        // The part being acted relative to must be a metric.
        adgASSERT(ISMETRIC(pRule->RelTo.nMetric));

        // Find the child being acted on and stretch the specified metric.
```

```
            pChildActOn = Layout_FindChild(pChildList, pRule->ActOn.idc);
            adgASSERT(pChildActOn);
            pChildActOn->anMetric[pRule->ActOn.nMetric] =
                ChildRelTo.anMetric[pRule->RelTo.nMetric] + pRule->nPixelOffset;
            pChildActOn->afMetric[pRule->ActOn.nMetric] = KNOWN;
            Layout_SolveChild(pChildActOn);
            pRule->fState = APPLIED;
            return(TRUE);

        case lMOVE:                     // Whole control should be moved

            // The part being moved must be a side.
            adgASSERT(ISSIDE(pRule->ActOn.nSide));

            // The part that is being acted relative to must be a metric.
            adgASSERT(ISMETRIC(pRule->RelTo.nMetric));

            // Find the child being acted on and move the specified side.
            pChildActOn = Layout_FindChild(pChildList, pRule->ActOn.idc);
            adgASSERT(pChildActOn);
            pChildActOn->anMetric[pRule->ActOn.nSide] =
                ChildRelTo.anMetric[pRule->RelTo.nMetric] + pRule->nPixelOffset;
            pChildActOn->afMetric[pRule->ActOn.nSide] = KNOWN;
            Layout_SolveChild(pChildActOn);
            pRule->fState = APPLIED;
            return(TRUE);

        case lVCENTER:                  // Vertically center a control/group
        case lHCENTER:                  // Horizontally center a control/group

            // We can only center a group of one or more controls relative to
            // another control (a single control is a 'group' of one control).
            adgASSERT(pRule->ActOn.nPart == lpGROUP);
            adgASSERT(pRule->RelTo.nPart == lpGROUP);
            adgASSERT(pRule->RelTo.idcFirst == pRule->RelTo.idcLast);

            // First id in group must be less than or equal to the last id
            idcFirst = pRule->ActOn.idcFirst;
            idcLast = pRule->ActOn.idcLast;
            adgASSERT(idcFirst <= idcLast);

            // Ensure that the width/height is known for each control in the
            // group before proceeding with any centering.
            hwndFirst = GetFirstChild(hwndParent);
            for (hwnd = hwndFirst; IsWindow(hwnd); hwnd = GetNextSibling(hwnd)) {
                int idc = GetWindowID(hwnd);
                if (adgINRANGE(idcFirst, idc, idcLast)) {
                    pChildActOn = Layout_FindChild(pChildList, idc);
                    if (pRule->Action == lHCENTER) {
                        if (pChildActOn->afMetric[lpWIDTH] == UNKNOWN)
                            return(FALSE);
                    } else {
                        if (pChildActOn->afMetric[lpHEIGHT] == UNKNOWN)
                            return(FALSE);
                    }
```

```
        }
    }

    // Create a new list of rules which contains the subset of rules
    // which act on controls in the centered group.
    for (nRules = 0, pr = pRules; pr->Action != lEND; pr++)
        nRules++;
    nRules++;
    prNew = _alloca(nRules * sizeof(RULE));
    prn = prNew;
    for (pr = pRules; pr->Action != lEND; pr++) {
        if (adgINRANGE(idcFirst, pr->ActOn.idc, idcLast)) {
            if (pRule->Action == lHCENTER) {
                if ((pr->ActOn.nPart == lpLEFT) ||
                    (pr->ActOn.nPart == lpRIGHT)) {
                    *prn++ = *pr;
                }
            } else {
                if ((pr->ActOn.nPart == lpTOP) ||
                    (pr->ActOn.nPart == lpBOTTOM)) {
                    *prn++ = *pr;
                }
            }
        }
    }
    prn->Action = lEND;

    // Make a local copy of the child list and set everything to KNOWN.
    nChildren = 0;
    for (pChild = pChildList; pChild->idc != IDC_LASTCHILD; pChild++)
        nChildren++;
    nChildren++;
    pChildListNew = _alloca(nChildren * sizeof(CHILD));
    MoveMemory(pChildListNew, pChildList, nChildren * sizeof(CHILD));
    for (pChild = pChildListNew; pChild->idc != IDC_LASTCHILD; pChild++)
        for (nMetric = 0; nMetric < NUMMETRICS; nMetric++)
            pChild->afMetric[nMetric] = KNOWN;

    // Solve for the children being centered as a sub-problem.
    if (!Layout_ApplyRules (hwndParent, prNew, pChildListNew)) {
        adgFAIL(__TEXT("Unable to apply rules to centered children"));
        return(FALSE);
    }

    // Compute the bounding rectangle of the group
    SetRectEmpty(&rcBounds);
    hwndFirst = GetFirstChild(hwndParent);
    for (hwnd = hwndFirst; IsWindow(hwnd); hwnd = GetNextSibling(hwnd)) {
        int idc = GetWindowID(hwnd);
        if (adgINRANGE(idcFirst, idc, idcLast)) {
            pChildActOn = Layout_FindChild(pChildListNew, idc);
            UnionRect(&rcBounds, &rcBounds, &pChildActOn->rc);
        }
    }
```

```
// Find the offset required to center the group's bounding rectangle
// against the control we are relative to.
if (pRule->Action == lHCENTER) {
    nCentered = ChildRelTo.anMetric[lpLEFT] +
        ((ChildRelTo.anMetric[lpWIDTH] -
        (rcBounds.right - rcBounds.left)) / 2);
    nOffset = nCentered - rcBounds.left;
} else {
    nCentered = ChildRelTo.anMetric[lpTOP] +
        ((ChildRelTo.anMetric[lpHEIGHT] -
        (rcBounds.bottom - rcBounds.top)) / 2);
    nOffset = nCentered - rcBounds.top;
}


// Add in any additional offset from the rule.
nOffset += pRule->nPixelOffset;

// Go through the new child list, moving each control.
adgASSERT(pRule->ActOn.idcFirst <= pRule->ActOn.idcLast);
for (hwnd = hwndFirst; IsWindow(hwnd); hwnd = GetNextSibling(hwnd)) {
    int idc = GetWindowID(hwnd);
    if (adgINRANGE(idcFirst, idc, idcLast)) {
        pChildActOn = Layout_FindChild(pChildListNew, idc);
        if (pRule->Action == lHCENTER) {
            pChildActOn->anMetric[lpLEFT]  += nOffset;
            pChildActOn->anMetric[lpRIGHT] += nOffset;
        } else {
            pChildActOn->anMetric[lpTOP]    += nOffset;
            pChildActOn->anMetric[lpBOTTOM] += nOffset;
        }
    }
}


// Now modify the real child list based on pChildListNew.
for (pSrc = pChildListNew, pDest = pChildList;
    pSrc->idc != IDC_LASTCHILD; pSrc++, pDest++) {

    if (adgINRANGE(idcFirst, pSrc->idc, idcLast)) {
        if (pRule->Action == lHCENTER) {
            pDest->anMetric[lpLEFT]  = pSrc->anMetric[lpLEFT];
            pDest->anMetric[lpRIGHT] = pSrc->anMetric[lpRIGHT];
            pDest->afMetric[lpLEFT]  = KNOWN;
            pDest->afMetric[lpRIGHT] = KNOWN;
        } else {
            pDest->anMetric[lpTOP]    = pSrc->anMetric[lpTOP];
            pDest->anMetric[lpBOTTOM] = pSrc->anMetric[lpBOTTOM];
            pDest->afMetric[lpTOP]    = KNOWN;
            pDest->afMetric[lpBOTTOM] = KNOWN;
        }
    }
}

pRule->fState = APPLIED;
return(TRUE);
```

```
        default:
            adgFAIL(__TEXT("Invalid action"));
            return(FALSE);
    }
}


/////////////////////////////////////////////////////////////////////////////


BOOL Layout_ApplyRules (HWND hwndParent, RULE* pRules, CHILD* pChildList) {

    RULE* pRule;
    BOOL fAppliedAtLeastOneRule, fOK = TRUE;

    // Check assumptions.
    adgASSERT(IsWindow(hwndParent));
    adgASSERT(pRules);
    adgASSERT(pChildList);

    // Based on the list of rules, mark all unknown child metrics as UNKNOWN.
    Layout_MarkUnknowns(hwndParent, pRules, pChildList);

    // Traverse the rule list, converting offsets from dialog units to pixels.
    Layout_ConvertDlgUnits(hwndParent, pRules, pChildList);

    // Mark all the rules as unapplied before attempting to apply them.
    for (pRule = pRules; pRule->Action != lEND; pRule++)
        pRule->fState = UNAPPLIED;

    // Loop through the rule list for as long as we are able to apply at least
    // one rule (if we make a pass through the entire list, and we are unable
    // to apply any rule, we are finished).
    do {
        fAppliedAtLeastOneRule = FALSE;
        for (pRule = pRules; pRule->Action != lEND; pRule++) {
            if (pRule->fState != APPLIED) {
                if (Layout_ApplyRule(hwndParent, pRules, pChildList, pRule))
                    fAppliedAtLeastOneRule = TRUE;
            }
        }
    } while (fAppliedAtLeastOneRule);

    // Verify that all rules have been successfully applied.
    for (pRule = pRules; pRule->Action != lEND; pRule++) {
        adgASSERT(pRule->fState == APPLIED);
        if (pRule->fState != APPLIED)
            fOK = FALSE;
    }
    return(fOK);
}

/////////////////////////////////////////////////////////////////////////////
```

```
BOOL WINAPI Layout_ComputeLayout (HWND hwndParent, RULE* pRules) {

    HDWP hdwp;
    BOOL fOK = TRUE;
    CHILD* pChild, *pChildList;
    int nChildren;

    // Check assumptions.
    adgASSERT(IsWindow(hwndParent));
    adgASSERT(pRules);

    // Don't do anything to a minimized window.
    if (IsIconic(hwndParent))
        return(TRUE);

    // Enumerate all child windows of the dialog, allocating a CHILD structure
    // for each child, with all six metric flags set to KNOWN. To simplify
    // coding, we also add a special CHILD structure for the parent window with
    // the id lPARENT (defined in layout.h). If there are no children, or
    // memory cannot be allocated for the child list, we do nothing.
    pChildList = Layout_CreateChildList(hwndParent, &nChildren);
    if (pChildList == NULL)
        return(FALSE);
    if (nChildren == 0)
        return(TRUE);

    // Apply the rules from the rule list to solve for the locations of all the
    // child controls.
    if (!Layout_ApplyRules(hwndParent, pRules, pChildList)) {
        adgFAIL(__TEXT("Unable to apply rules"));
        return(FALSE);
    }

    // Simultaneously relocate all the children using DeferWindowPos.
    hdwp = BeginDeferWindowPos(0);
    adgASSERT(hdwp);

    // Move each child in the CHILD list.  We enumerate the child list starting
    // at pChildList + 1, because the first CHILD is lPARENT.
    for (pChild = pChildList + 1; pChild->idc != IDC_LASTCHILD; pChild++) {

        // Check child for any still-unsolved metrics. You may want to remove or
        // #ifdef out this check once your rules are known to be working.
        if (!Layout_CheckChild(pChild))
            fOK = FALSE;

        // Add child to DeferWindowPos list if it is not fixed.
        if (!pChild->fFixed) {
            HWND hwndChild = GetDlgItem(hwndParent, pChild->idc);
            adgASSERT(pChild->anMetric[lpWIDTH] >= 0);
            adgASSERT(pChild->anMetric[lpHEIGHT] >= 0);
            hdwp = DeferWindowPos(hdwp, hwndChild, NULL,
                pChild->anMetric[lpLEFT], pChild->anMetric[lpTOP],
                pChild->anMetric[lpWIDTH], pChild->anMetric[lpHEIGHT],
                SWP_NOZORDER);
            adgASSERT(hdwp);
```

```
            // Invalidation is necessary here because some controls (edit
            // controls in particular) don't repaint correctly under Windows NT
            // when they are moved with DeferWindowPos.
            InvalidateRect(hwndChild, NULL, TRUE);
        }
    }

    // It is this function call which actually moves all the windows.
    EndDeferWindowPos(hdwp);

    // Free the allocated list of CHILD structures
    free(pChildList);
    return(fOK);
}


///////////////////////////////// End of File /////////////////////////////////
```

Listing 3.20 *Layout.H*

```
/*****************************************************************************
Module name: Layout.h
Written by: Jonathan W. Locke
Notices: Copyright (c) 1995 Jeffrey Richter
Purpose: Header file with external interface of layout algorithm.
*****************************************************************************/


//////////////////////////// Special Parent Identifier ////////////////////////


#define lPARENT 0x10000         // Special CHILD id for parent - this id is
                                // guaranteed not to be used because you
                                // cannot have control ids above 0xffff.


///////////////////////////////// Layout Actions //////////////////////////////


typedef enum {
    lSTRETCH,                   // Metric should be stretched
    lMOVE,                      // Control should be moved
    lVCENTER,                   // Vertically center control/group
    lHCENTER,                   // Horizontally center control/group
    lEND.                       // Special flag for end of list
} lACTION;


///////////////////////////////// Layout Part Types ///////////////////////////


typedef enum {
    lpLEFT  = 0,                // Left side of control
    lpTOP   = 1,                // Top side of control
```

219

```
    lpRIGHT  = 2,                    // Right side of control
    lpBOTTOM = 3,                    // Bottom side of control
    lpWIDTH  = 4,                    // Width of control
    lpHEIGHT = 5,                    // Height of control
    lpGROUP  = 6,                    // Group of one or more controls
} lPART;


/////////////////////////// Macros for Defining Rules ///////////////////////////


//                          Part,        Control id    Percentage
//                          metric       or first id   of control or
//      Macro               or side      in group      last id in group
//      -----               -------      -----------   ----------------
#define lLEFT(idc)          lpLEFT,      idc,          0
#define lTOP(idc)           lpTOP,       idc,          0
#define lRIGHT(idc)         lpRIGHT,     idc,          0
#define lBOTTOM(idc)        lpBOTTOM,    idc,          0
#define lWIDTH(idc)         lpWIDTH,     idc,          100
#define lHEIGHT(idc)        lpHEIGHT,    idc,          100
#define lWIDTHOF(idc, percent)  lpWIDTH,  idc,         percent
#define lHEIGHTOF(idc, percent) lpHEIGHT, idc,         percent
#define lCHILD(idc)         lpGROUP,     idc,          idc
#define lGROUP(idcFirst, idcLast) lpGROUP, idcFirst,   idcLast


/////////////////////////// Definition of an Action ///////////////////////////


typedef struct {
  union {
    int nPart;                  // Name used only for group oriented actions
    int nMetric;                // Name used only for metric oriented actions
    int nSide;                  // Name used only for side oriented actions
  };
  union {
    int idc;                    // Used for all actions except group actions
    int idcFirst;               // Used for group actions
  };
  union {
    int nPercent;               // Used only for width/height actions
    int idcLast;                // Used for group actions
  };
} lACTIONINFO;


/////////////////////////// Definition of a Rule ///////////////////////////


typedef struct {
  lACTION Action;               // Layout action to take
  lACTIONINFO ActOn;            // Data describing the part to act on
  lACTIONINFO RelTo;            // Data for the part to position relative to
  int nOffset;                  // Additional offset (in dialog units)
```

```
    UINT fState;                    // INTERNAL USE: Rule application state flag
    int nPixelOffset;               // INTERNAL USE: nOffset converted to pixels
} RULE;


/////////////////////////// Prototype for Layout  ///////////////////////////


BOOL WINAPI Layout_ComputeLayout (HWND hwndDlg, RULE* pRules);


/////////////////////////////// End of File //////////////////////////////////
```

Listing 3.21 *DlgSize.RC*

```
//Microsoft Visual C++ generated resource script.
//
#include "resource.h"

#define APSTUDIO_READONLY_SYMBOLS
/////////////////////////////////////////////////////////////////////////////
//
// Generated from the TEXTINCLUDE 2 resource.
//
#include <windows.h>

/////////////////////////////////////////////////////////////////////////////
#undef APSTUDIO_READONLY_SYMBOLS


#ifdef APSTUDIO_INVOKED
/////////////////////////////////////////////////////////////////////////////
//
// TEXTINCLUDE
//

1 TEXTINCLUDE DISCARDABLE
BEGIN
    "resource.h\0"
END

2 TEXTINCLUDE DISCARDABLE
BEGIN
    "#include <windows.h>\r\n"
    "\0"
END

3 TEXTINCLUDE DISCARDABLE
BEGIN
    "\r\n"
    "\0"
END
```

```
///////////////////////////////////////////////////////////////////////////
#endif    // APSTUDIO_INVOKED


///////////////////////////////////////////////////////////////////////////
//
// Dialog
//

IDD_LAYOUT DIALOG DISCARDABLE  -32768, 5, 198, 154
STYLE WS_MINIMIZEBOX | WS_MAXIMIZEBOX | WS_VISIBLE | WS_CAPTION | WS_SYSMENU
|
    WS_THICKFRAME
CAPTION "Dialog Size"
FONT 8, "MS Sans Serif"
BEGIN
    LTEXT           "E1:",IDC_STATIC,7,10,29,8
    EDITTEXT        IDC_E1,7,21,64,12,ES_AUTOHSCROLL
    GROUPBOX        "G1",IDC_G1,83,8,105,32
    PUSHBUTTON      "B3",IDC_B3,112,19,49,14
    CONTROL         "E2:",IDC_STATIC,"Static",SS_LEFTNOWORDWRAP | WS_GROUP,7,
                    42,45,8
    EDITTEXT        IDC_E2,7,53,128,73,ES_AUTOHSCROLL
    PUSHBUTTON      "B1",IDC_B1,32,129,49,14
    PUSHBUTTON      "B2",IDC_B2,74,133,49,14
END


///////////////////////////////////////////////////////////////////////////
//
// Icon
//

IDI_LAYOUT              ICON    DISCARDABLE     "DlgSize.ico"

#ifndef APSTUDIO_INVOKED
///////////////////////////////////////////////////////////////////////////
//
// Generated from the TEXTINCLUDE 3 resource.
//


///////////////////////////////////////////////////////////////////////////
#endif    // not APSTUDIO_INVOKED
```

Listing 3.22 *Resource.H*

```
//{{NO_DEPENDENCIES}}
// Microsoft Visual C++ generated include file.
// Used by DLGSIZE.RC
//
#define IDD_LAYOUT                      101
```

```
#define IDI_LAYOUT                    102
#define IDC_B1                        1001
#define IDC_B2                        1002
#define IDC_B3                        1003
#define IDC_E1                        2001
#define IDC_E2                        2002
#define IDC_G1                        3001
#define IDC_STATIC                    -1

// Next default values for new objects
//
#ifdef APSTUDIO_INVOKED
#ifndef APSTUDIO_READONLY_SYMBOLS
#define _APS_NEXT_RESOURCE_VALUE      103
#define _APS_NEXT_COMMAND_VALUE       40001
#define _APS_NEXT_CONTROL_VALUE       3002
#define _APS_NEXT_SYMED_VALUE         101
#endif
#endif
```

CHAPTER FOUR

Custom Controls

The Windows built-in control classes provide standard elements of the user interface. Microsoft endowed these controls with many features so that they would be suitable for use in almost any application. This set of controls has been extended, both in Windows 95 and Windows NT 3.51, to include even more control classes. What's more, you can subclass or superclass (see Chapter 5) any of these controls to modify their default appearance and behavior. Yet there may still be occasions when none of the supplied controls, however customized, has the features your application requires. The solution is to design and implement your own controls. These custom controls may be used in dialog boxes or as stand-alone windows.

In this chapter, we'll create two custom controls. The first control, legend (shown in Figure 4.1), is familiar to everyone. It is designed to be used in the legend of a map, graph, or chart to designate the meaning of each part of the diagram. The legend control is simply a large or small box drawn to the left of a text string. The box is filled with a brush and optionally surrounded by a 1-pixel-wide frame.

The second control is a bargraph control (see Figure 4.2). As you might expect, it draws a graph of several values, where each value is represented by a bar. Unlike the legend control, the bargraph control accepts mouse and keyboard input from the user. When the user selects a bar using the mouse or keyboard, bargraph sends a notification message to its parent telling it which bar was chosen. In response to this message, the parent can then do something such as provide more information about the bar.

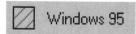

Figure 4.1 *Legend custom control.*

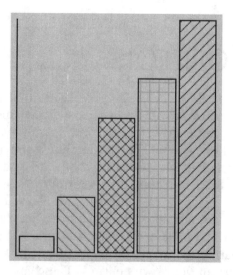

Figure 4.2 *Bargraph custom control.*

Rules of Thumb for Designing Custom Controls

Designing custom controls and designing a class for an application's main window are similar activities. However, controls are slightly more difficult to design because most controls must be designed so that several instances can exist at one time.

A control should also be designed so that its capabilities can be easily enhanced in the future. As you write other applications, you will hear yourself saying, "I could use that control here if it only had (fill in the desired feature)." You will find that adding new features to your control for one application will generally enhance the other applications that already use the control. But watch out for overdesigning your controls or adding features that you speculate might be useful someday. It is much better to start with a simple design and add to it as necessary. Do not add features to a control if the features are useful only to a single application. Instead, add the needed special features by subclassing or superclassing the control.

One of the most important design issues to keep in mind when implementing a custom control is that it generally should not use any global or static variables. Unlike application windows, controls are usually created in bunches. For application windows, if several instances of the same application are running, each has its own address space containing a separate copy of its global and static variables. This is not true for controls. An application may create several controls of the same class, each of which is running in the same address space, sharing the same static and global variables with all the others. Because a single copy of these variables is being shared among all instances of the control, changes made to these variables will affect all controls of the same class. This is usually undesirable. For example, if windows created from the edit class stored their text in a global variable, all edit windows created by the threads of a given process would contain and display the same text.

A custom control should have a cleanly designed programmatic interface that details all the capabilities of the control and relates how the programmer can manage the control's actions. Designing the programmer's interface involves creating a list of #defined values, which should be placed in a header file for the control. Any application that is going to use the control must include this header file. In addition to #defined values, a control's header file can contain function prototypes, structures, typedefs, macros, message APIs, and message crackers that might be helpful to someone using the control. As a general rule, the header file should not contain implementation details of the control. Such details are distracting to someone using the control and are probably subject to change.

The Anatomy of a Custom Control

Window Styles

Each control class may have specific window styles associated with it. These styles allow the programmer to fine-tune the control's behavior and appearance. A window's style is specified by the dwStyle parameter passed to the CreateWindowEx function.

The high 16 bits are used for window styles that are common to all window classes. These system-defined bits include the WS_BORDER, WS_VISIBLE, and WS_POPUP styles, to name just a few. The low 16 bits are specific to each class. For example, all the styles specific to the button class begin with BS_, and all the styles specific to the listbox class begin with LBS_. When you design a custom control, you also define any styles that can be used in these low 16 bits to modify the control's appearance or behavior.

Custom Window Messages

Each custom control may define messages specific to its window class. The first class-specific message should be defined as (WM_ USER + 0). The next should be (WM_USER + 1) and so on. Like the window styles, these messages should be listed in the control's header file.

Comments should detail what the message does, what the return value means (if anything), and the values of the wParam and lParam parameters. For example, the LB_DELETESTRING message for the listbox class requires that the wParam parameter contain the index of the string to be deleted. The lParam parameter is not used. The return value from this message is the number of strings remaining or LB_ERR if an error occurred. If this information is documented in the custom control's header file, it will be easier for a programmer to use your control.

Parent Notification

The last part of the programmer's interface deals with parent notification. When an action takes place in a child control that the parent window might want to know about, the child sends it a notification message. There are two system-defined notification messages. The simplest and most commonly used is WM_COMMAND. Many of the built-in Windows controls that you are already familiar with use WM_COMMAND for parent notifications. For example, when you click on a button, the built-in Windows button class sends a WM_COMMAND message to its parent, with a notification code of BN_CLICKED. The alternative to WM_COMMAND is WM_NOTIFY. WM_NOTIFY is somewhat more involved than WM_COMMAND, but it has more flexibility because it allows you to send more than just a notification code. In fact, you can send any kind of information you want. Although this can be advantageous in certain situations, you should feel free to use the simpler syntax of WM_COMMAND if it is sufficient for your needs.

WM_COMMAND

To support WM_COMMAND notifications, you will want to add a list of notification codes to your control's header file. Each code is a unique 16-bit value that you are free to choose. When your control notifies its parent of an action by sending a WM_COMMAND message, wParam should contain the control's ID in the low word and your control's notification code in the high word, while lParam should simply hold the control's window handle.

To make it easier to send WM_COMMAND messages, use the following function:

```
void NotifyParent (HWND hwndControl, WORD wNotifyCode) {

   SendMessage(GetParent(hwndControl), WM_COMMAND,
      MAKEWPARAM(GetWindowID(hwndControl), wNotifyCode),
      (LPARAM) hwndControl);
}
```

Alternatively, use the FORWARD_WM_COMMAND macro from the **WindowsX.H** include file:

```
void NotifyParent (HWND hwndControl, WORD wNotifyCode) {

   FORWARD_WM_COMMAND(GetParent(hwndControl),
      GetWindowID(hwndControl), hwndControl, wNotifyCode, SendMessage);
}
```

Both of these functions send a WM_COMMAND message, with the proper parameters, to the control's parent window. In both cases, the return value of NotifyParent is void because WM_COMMAND messages are defined as having no meaningful return value. In fact, the FORWARD_WM_COMMAND message cracker casts its result to void, making a return value impossible. If you need to receive a response from a notification message, you should use WM_NOTIFY.

WM_NOTIFY

WM_COMMAND is great if all you need to send is a simple notification code. But sometimes you need more flexibility. This is where WM_NOTIFY (not to be confused with WM_PARENT NOTIFY!) comes in. The wParam of WM_NOTIFY is the identifier of the control sending the notification, and lParam points to an arbitrarily complex structure whose only requirement is that it have an NMHDR structure as its first member. NMHDR is defined in **WinUser.H** to have the following members:

```
typedef struct tagNMHDR {
   HWND hwndFrom;  // Window handle of the control that sent the notification
   UINT idFrom;    // Identifier of the control that sent the notification
   UINT code;      // Notification code (user defined or NM_* from
CommCtrl.H)
} NMHDR;
typedef NMHDR FAR * LPNMHDR;
```

The hwndFrom and idFrom fields contain the window handle and identifier of the window that sent the notification. The code field contains a unique identifier that can be used to distinguish different notifications from the same control. **CommCtrl.H** defines some generic notification codes between NM_FIRST and NM_LAST (see below), and the common controls each define their own special notification codes.

```
// Generic WM_NOTIFY notification codes

#define NM_OUTOFMEMORY     (NM_FIRST-1)
#define NM_CLICK           (NM_FIRST-2)
#define NM_DBLCLK          (NM_FIRST-3)
#define NM_RETURN          (NM_FIRST-4)
#define NM_RCLICK          (NM_FIRST-5)
#define NM_RDBLCLK         (NM_FIRST-6)
#define NM_SETFOCUS        (NM_FIRST-7)
#define NM_KILLFOCUS       (NM_FIRST-8)

// WM_NOTIFY codes (NMHDR.code values) are not required
// to be in seperate ranges, but establishing these ranges makes
// validation and debugging easier.

#define NM_FIRST    (0U- 0U) // Generic to all controls
#define NM_LAST     (0U- 99U)
```

You are free to use any of the generic notification codes or to define your own. No specific numeric range is assigned for user-defined notification codes, but **CommCtrl.H** uses the highest numbers for itself,[1] so you should number your notification codes upward starting at 1. This will make your values unique and easy to recognize in the debugger.

---

[1]**CommCtrl.H** accomplishes this by subtracting ascending ordinals from an unsigned zero value. NM_OUTOFMEMORY is defined as (NM_FIRST-1), which is 0U-1 or 0xFFFFFFFF and NM_CLICK is (NM_FIRST-2), which is or 0U-2 or 0xFFFFFFFE.

Notice that the idFrom field contains the same information as wParam. The documentation does not give an explicit reason for this duplication. However, parents handling a notification message may have a reason to prefer one location over the other. If a handler wants to pass an NMHDR pointer to another routine, the idFrom value will be available to that routine. On the other hand, it may be convenient for a handler to switch directly on the wParam value, avoiding the additional syntax and pointer dereference required to access idFrom. Because you cannot predict which value will be used by your control's parent, you must be sure to send your control's ID in both places.

It is important to note that you should send WM_NOTIFY messages instead of posting them. If you use SendMessage you can declare your notification structure on the stack and pass a pointer to it in lParam. Since SendMessage is a synchronous function, it will not return until your message has been processed. But if you put a pointer to a stack variable in lParam and call PostMessage, you are inviting disaster. PostMessage is asynchronous and will put your message in the appropriate queue and return immediately. That posted message will not be processed until after your function returns,[2] at which point your stack frame will have been destroyed and the lParam of your queued message will be an invalid pointer.

To respond to a WM_NOTIFY message, you can use the message cracker HANDLE_WM_NOTIFY, which is defined in **CommCtrl.H**. In your OnNotify handler, you simply switch on the identifier of the control that sent the notification, and then cast the NMHDR pointer to the appropriate type of structure pointer based on the notification code. You are then free to access any additional information that was sent. Like WM_COMMAND, WM_NOTIFY is defined as having no return value. So we must declare OnNotify as returning void, as in the following code fragment. Notice, however, that you can still return a value from the notification by simply storing the return value in your user-defined structure.

---

[2]This is true unless it is posted to your own thread's queue, and you happen to enter a message loop before returning.

```
#include <commctrl.h>
```

```
////////////////////////////////////////////////////////////////////////////
```

```
typedef struct {
   NMHDR nmh;
   int nData;
   DWORD dwReturnValue;
} WHATEVER_NOTIFY;
```

```
////////////////////////////////////////////////////////////////////////////
```

```
void Dlg_OnNotify (HWND hwnd, int idCtl, NMHDR* pnmh) {

   WHATEVER_NOTIFY* pwhatever;

   switch (idCtl) {
      case IDC_WHATEVER:
      if (pnmh->code == NM_CLICK) {
         pwhatever = (WHATEVER_NOTIFY*) pnmh;
         pwhatever->dwReturnValue = Dlg_DoWhatever(pwhatever->nData);
      }
      break;
   }
}
```

```
////////////////////////////////////////////////////////////////////////////
```

```
BOOL WINAPI Dlg_Proc (HWND hwnd, UINT uMsg, WPARAM wParam, LPARAM lParam) {

   switch (uMsg) {
      .

      .
      adgHANDLE_DLGMSG(hwnd, WM_NOTIFY, Dlg_OnNotify);
   }
   return(FALSE);
}
```

Implementing Your Custom Control

Once the programmer's interface has been designed and the control's header file created, you need to determine what information, if any, the control will need to store internally. For example, each listbox control must remember the number of items in the list, which item is selected, and which item is displayed at the top of the box, as well as other information.

To store this kind of information, which must be maintained separately for each instance of your control, you should use the window extra bytes. Although it is possible to use window properties to associate information with a window, using the window extra bytes is preferred due to the memory consumption and performance overhead of window properties. Under no circumstances should you use the GWL_USERDATA window long value when implementing a control class. This value is specifically reserved for programmers using your control.

If a small amount of storage is required, the control's window extra bytes can be used directly. This technique is efficient and convenient, but you should be careful not to abuse it. To discourage excessive use of the extra bytes, the debug build of Windows 95 issues a warning if you register a class with more than 40 extra bytes. To maintain a large amount of information, you should allocate a block of memory and store a pointer to this block in the extra bytes instead. The legend control, being simpler, uses the first approach. The bargraph control is somewhat more complex and demonstrates the second approach.

Designing the Legend Programmer's Interface

The legend control is a display-only control much like the familiar Windows static control. As such, legend accepts no mouse or keyboard input. The visual appearance of legend is configured through the use of class-specific window styles and messages. The text that appears to the right of legend's box is retrieved from the control's window text.

Legend defines three class-specific window styles:

```
#define LS_SMALLBOX     0x00000000
#define LS_BIGBOX       0x00000001
#define LS_BOXBORDER    0x00000002
```

Although each of these style options could be managed through class-specific messages, it is generally more convenient to use style bits to configure the most common features of a control. But some day you will run out of style bits (since there are only 16 available), whereupon you will need to find an alternative method to configure your control's style. At this point, class-specific messages to get and set each style option are a pretty good workaround. Another common approach is to define a message that lets you get and set your own private style bits stored in the window's extra bytes. Four extra bytes is enough storage for 32 more style bits, which is usually more than enough.

The first two legend styles allow the programmer to configure the size of legend's box. The third style can be used to put a border around the box. The combination of the LS_BIGBOX and LS_BOXBORDER bits gives us four possible styles for legend, as seen in Figure 4.3.

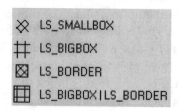

Figure 4.3 *Legend window styles.*

Although the styles of most controls are single Boolean bits, nothing prevents you from using several style bits together to form a numeric value. The windows button class does just this:

```
#define BS_PUSHBUTTON        0x00000000L
#define BS_DEFPUSHBUTTON     0x00000001L
#define BS_CHECKBOX          0x00000002L
#define BS_AUTOCHECKBOX      0x00000003L
#define BS_RADIOBUTTON       0x00000004L
#define BS_3STATE            0x00000005L
#define BS_AUTO3STATE        0x00000006L
#define BS_GROUPBOX          0x00000007L
#define BS_USERBUTTON        0x00000008L
#define BS_AUTORADIOBUTTON   0x00000009L
#define BS_OWNERDRAW         0x0000000BL
```

Windows is able to extract the type of a button from the button's style bits by simply bitwise ANDing with the mask value 0x0000000F. The result of this operation is one of the BS_* values already listed.

Legend defines six class-specific messages. Class-specific messages must be defined within the range of WM_USER to 0x7FFF. In

WinUser.H, WM_USER is defined as 0x0400. The first two legend messages are accessors that allow the programmer to get and set the brush being used to fill legend's box:

```
// Purpose: Sets the brush used to fill legend's box. The brush is used only by
//          the control. It is owned by the caller. The caller must create
//          and destroy the brush.
// wParam:  HBRUSH hbrNew - New brush
// lParam:  N/A
// Returns: void
#define LM_SETBOXBRUSH    (WM_USER + 0)

// Purpose: Returns HBRUSH being used to fill legend's box.
// wParam:  N/A
// lParam:  N/A
// Returns: HBRUSH - Current box brush
#define LM_GETBOXBRUSH    (WM_USER + 1)
```

An application must configure each legend control it creates by telling it what brush to fill its box with. For example, you could make the legend control fill its box with a blue, backward-slanting hatch pattern:

```
HBRUSH hbr = CreateHatchBrush(HS_BDIAGONAL, RGB(0, 0, 255));
SendDlgItemMessage(hdlg, IDC_LEGEND, LM_SETBOXBRUSH, (WPARAM) hbr, 0);
```

Should an application need to know what brush is being used by a legend control, it can send an LM_GETBOXBRUSH message:

```
HBRUSH hbr = (HBRUSH) SendDlgItemMessage(hdlg, LM_GETBOXBRUSH, 0, 0);
```

The other four legend messages allow the programmer to get and set the background and text colors to be used when drawing the control. All new custom controls should use this method rather than attempting to provide a WM_CTLCOLOR* interface. The WM_CTL-COLOR* scheme is used by the built-in controls, but the new common controls use accessor messages to get and set color values.

```
// Purpose: Sets the background color of a legend control.
// wParam:  N/A
// lParam:  COLORREF crNew - New background color
// Returns: void
#define LM_SETBKCOLOR     (WM_USER + 2)

// Purpose: Gets the background color of a legend control.
// wParam:  N/A
```

```
// lParam:  N/A
// Returns: COLORREF - Current background color
#define LM_GETBKCOLOR   (WM_USER + 3)

// Purpose: Sets the text color of a legend control.
// wParam:  N/A
// lParam:  COLORREF crNew - New text color
// Returns: void
#define LM_SETTEXTCOLOR   (WM_USER + 4)

// Purpose: Gets the text color of a legend control.
// wParam:  N/A
// lParam:  N/A
// Returns: COLORREF - Current text color
#define LM_GETTEXTCOLOR   (WM_USER + 5)
```

In addition to message definitions, **Legend.H** defines a set of message API macros and message crackers. These macros are defined in the same way that **WindowsX.H** defines them for the Windows system messages. It is good programming practice to use these macros whenever possible. They will make your code more readable and easier to maintain.

Although the examples thus far have demonstrated how messages would be sent to the legend control if it were part of a dialog box, any custom control may be created outside of a dialog box by using the CreateWindowEx function. The legend control can then be manipulated with SendMessage or SendDlgItemMessage, passing as the first parameter the window handle of the control, as returned by CreateWindowEx.

Writing Some Legendary Code

The first step in creating legend is to write the functions that register and unregister the legend window class. The Legend_RegisterClass function registers the legend window class by making a call to RegisterClassEx. Legend_RegisterClass must be called by the programmer before any legend windows can be created. When the programmer is done using the legend window class, the Legend_UnregisterClass function unregisters the window class by calling UnregisterClass.

```
// ANSI/Unicode declarations for legend's window class name
#define WC_LEGENDA "Legend"
#define WC_LEGENDW L"Legend"
#ifdef UNICODE
#define WC_LEGEND WC_LEGENDW
#else
```

```
#define WC_LEGEND WC_LEGENDA
#endif


/////////////////////////////////////////////////////////////////////////////


// The following structure is for the window extra bytes.
// For more information, see the macros presented in appendix A.
typedef struct tagLEGEND_WNDEXTRABYTES {
    HFONT hfont;           // Font to use for legend text
    HBRUSH hbr;            // Brush to fill legend's box with
    COLORREF crBk;         // Background color
    COLORREF crText;       // Text color
} LEGEND_WNDEXTRABYTES;


/////////////////////////////////////////////////////////////////////////////


ATOM WINAPI Legend_RegisterClass (HINSTANCE hinst, BOOL fGlobalClass) {

    WNDCLASSEX wc;

    adgINITSTRUCT(wc, TRUE);
    wc.style          = CS_HREDRAW | CS_VREDRAW;
    wc.lpfnWndProc    = Legend_WndProc;
    wc.cbWndExtra     = sizeof(LEGEND_WNDEXTRABYTES);
    wc.hInstance      = hinst;
    wc.hCursor        = LoadCursor(NULL, IDC_ARROW);
    wc.lpszClassName  = WC_LEGEND;

    if (fGlobalClass)
        wc.style |= CS_GLOBALCLASS;

    return(RegisterClassEx(&wc));
}


/////////////////////////////////////////////////////////////////////////////


BOOL WINAPI Legend_UnregisterClass (HINSTANCE hinst) {

    return(UnregisterClass(WC_LEGEND, hinst));
}
```

If legend were implemented in a DLL, you would probably want to register the legend window class automatically when the DLL is loaded into the process's address space. This can be done by making a call to Legend_RegisterClass when DllMain is called with an fdwReason of DLL_PROCESS_ATTACH and by calling Legend_UnregisterClass when DllMain is called with DLL_PROCESS_DETACH.

```
BOOL WINAPI DllMain (HINSTANCE hinstDll, DWORD fdwReason, LPVOID lpvReserved) {

   BOOL fOK = TRUE;
   switch (fdwReason) {

      case DLL_PROCESS_ATTACH:
         fOK = (Legend_RegisterClass(hinstDll, TRUE) != INVALID_ATOM);
         adgASSERT(fOK);
         break;

      case DLL_PROCESS_DETACH:
         Legend_UnregisterClass(hinstDll);
         break;
   }
   return(fOK);
}
```

We pass TRUE as the second parameter to Legend_RegisterClass because we want to specify that the window class be registered with CS_GLOBAL-CLASS style. The CS_GLOBALCLASS style bit enables other modules in your address space to use your window class. If you don't specify CS_GLOBALCLASS, Windows will compare the HINSTANCE that was used to register the class with the HINSTANCE passed to CreateWindowEx each time you create a window. If the instance handles don't match, window creation will fail. CS_GLOBALCLASS turns off this checking so that any module in your process's address space can use your class without restriction.

Specifying the CS_HREDRAW and CS_VREDRAW styles causes Windows to invalidate the entire window whenever its size changes. If these styles are not included, Windows does not invalidate any part of the window when the window is made smaller and invalidates only the uncovered area when the window is made larger. Because legend controls should be completely redrawn whenever the size of the window is changed, these two styles are specified. Note, however, that the size of a legend control, like most dialog box controls, usually does not change after it is created.

Because most custom controls maintain some internal information, the cbWndExtra member of the WNDCLASSEX structure is usually not zero. This reserves internal space for each control, which can be accessed with GetWindowWord/Long and SetWindowWord/Long. The legend control must maintain a brush handle to fill its box, a font handle to draw its text, and two COLORREF values to specify the control's text and background colors. Because each of these values is 32 bits (4 bytes), a total of 16 extra bytes is necessary for legend control windows.

Very often, programmers hard-wire the number of extra bytes required and the offsets to access each value by using #defines:

```
#define CBWNDEXTRA      (16) // Total number of bytes required
#define GWL_FONT        (0)  // Offset of font handle (BYTE 0)
#define GWL_BOXBRUSH    (4)  // Offset of brush handle (BYTE 4)
#define GWL_CRBK        (8)  // Offset of background color (BYTE 8)
#define GWL_CRTEXT      (12) // Offset of text color (BYTE 12)
```

Although this method works, I don't recommend it. It is very error-prone to hand-calculate sizes and offsets. And when you finally do make a mistake in these calculations, the resulting bug is likely to be difficult to find. What's more, every time you change the data you are storing, you will have to remember to adjust your calculations. Appendix A details a set of macros (defined in **Win95ADG.H**), which relieve this burden and ensure that the offsets are computed correctly. To use these macros, we define a structure that has the data members we want at the top of **Legend.C**. Then we simply set cbWndExtra to the sizeof that structure. When we want to access these bytes, we use the adgGET/SETWINDOWLONG macros, which automatically compute the correct byte offsets and pass them to Get/SetWindowLong.[3]

```
// The following structure is for the window extra bytes.
// For more information, see the macros presented in Appendix A.
typedef struct tagLEGEND_WNDEXTRABYTES {
    HFONT hfont;         // Font to use for legend text
    HBRUSH hbr;          // Brush to fill legend's box with
    COLORREF crBk;       // Background color
    COLORREF crText;     // Text color
} LEGEND_WNDEXTRABYTES;
 .
 .
 .
// Set the font in the window extra bytes.
adgSETWINDOWLONG(hwnd, LEGEND_WNDEXTRABYTES, hfont, hfontNew);
 .
 .
 .
// Get the font from the window extra bytes
HFONT hfontCur = (HFONT) adgGETWINDOWLONG(hwnd, LEGEND_WNDEXTRABYTES, hfont);
```

---

[3]In a 32-bit computing environment, it is usually best to use 32-bit values. For the sake of completeness, however, there are a pair of macros, adgGET/SETWINDOWWORD for accessing 16-bit window extra byte values. If you use 16-bit values in the hopes of reducing the number of window extra bytes needed by your control, you will probably need to use a compiler switch or pragma to ensure that your WNDEXTRABYTES structure is packed with 16-bit alignment.

The last member of note in the WNDCLASSEX structure is hbrBackground. When BeginPaint is called, Windows sends a WM_ERASEBKGND message to the window procedure.[4] Normally, window procedures pass this message directly to the DefWindowProc function for processing. If the hbrBackground member's value is NULL, DefWindowProc doesn't paint the window's background and returns zero, indicating that the background has not been erased. Because the WM_PAINT message in the legend control's window procedure draws the whole window, including its background, painting the window is faster if DefWindowProc doesn't also paint the background. Furthermore, if DefWindowProc were allowed to erase the background, the nonbackground features of legend would flicker because they would be temporarily erased before being repainted again in WM_PAINT. By centralizing all painting activities in WM_PAINT (and doing this painting carefully), we avoid this situation and legend controls won't flicker no matter how frequently they are asked to repaint.

Before the legend class is unregistered with Legend_UnregisterClass, it is the application's responsibility to ensure that all legend windows have be destroyed.

Special Messages for Custom Controls

Legend's window procedure, Legend_WndProc, is almost identical to any other window procedure except that it processes two additional messages: WM_SETFONT and WM_GETFONT. If legend accepted keyboard or mouse input, it might also choose to handle one or more of WM_GETDLGCODE, WM_SETFOCUS, or WM_KILLFOCUS. Later in this chapter, the bargraph control, which accepts keyboard and mouse input, will demonstrate these messages.

The special messages WM_SETFONT and WM_GETFONT allow an application to specify a font that a control should use when displaying text. When an application sets a control's font by sending it a WM_SETFONT message, the wParam parameter must contain the handle of a valid font. This font must remain valid for the lifetime of the control. The lParam parameter should be TRUE if the application wants the control to be repainted and FALSE if the control should not be repainted. Because DefWindowProc provides no default handling for WM_SETFONT, we must implement a Legend_OnSetFont handler that stores the font handle in the window extra bytes.

---

[4]Unless you called *InvalidateRect* with the *fErase* parameter, set to FALSE.

```
void WINAPI Legend_OnSetFont (HWND hwnd, HFONT hfontNew, BOOL fRedraw) {

    adgASSERT((hfontNew == NULL) || (OBJ_FONT == GetObjectType(hfontNew)));
    adgSETWINDOWLONG(hwnd, LEGEND_WNDEXTRABYTES, hfont, hfontNew);
    if (fRedraw)
        InvalidateRect(hwnd, NULL, FALSE);
}
```

An application can also ask a control which font it is using by sending it a WM_GETFONT message. Legend processes this message by simply returning the font handle that was stored in the window extra bytes by Legend_OnSetFont:

```
HFONT WINAPI Legend_OnGetFont (HWND hwnd) {

    return((HFONT) adgGETWINDOWLONG(hwnd, LEGEND_WNDEXTRABYTES, hfont));
}
```

One additional special message processed by many controls is the WM_ENABLE message. This message is sent to a window when it has been enabled or disabled. When a window is disabled, Windows no longer sends keyboard or mouse messages to it. Usually, a disabled window repaints itself in a grayed state to give the user a visual indication that the control is not usable.

To keep a control's appearance consistent with its state, the control calls InvalidateRect upon receiving a WM_ENABLE message to force the control to be repainted. When the control later receives the WM_PAINT message, it calls IsWindowEnabled to see if it is enabled and paints itself accordingly. As an exercise, you might want to modify the bargraph control presented in the next section so that it responds to WM_ENABLE.

Painting a Legend

Most of the work done by the legend control is in the WM_PAINT message. Painting starts with a call to BeginPaint:

```
void Legend_OnPaint (HWND hwnd) {

    PAINTSTRUCT ps;
    .
    .
    .
    // Start painting.
    BeginPaint(hwnd, &ps);
```

241

Then we set the control's background and text colors based on the current settings in the window extra bytes:

```
void Legend_OnPaint (HWND hwnd) {
    .
    .
    .
    // Set background and text colors.
    SetBkColor(ps.hdc, Legend_GetBkColor(hwnd));
    SetTextColor(ps.hdc, Legend_GetTextColor(hwnd));
```

The message handlers to get and set the text and background colors of the legend control are implemented using the window extra byte macros (see Appendix A):

```
void WINAPI Legend_OnSetBkColor (HWND hwnd, COLORREF crBkNew) {

    adgSETWINDOWLONG(hwnd, LEGEND_WNDEXTRABYTES, crBk, crBkNew);
    InvalidateRect(hwnd, NULL, TRUE);
}


/////////////////////////////////////////////////////////////////////////////


COLORREF WINAPI Legend_OnGetBkColor (HWND hwnd) {

    return((COLORREF) adgGETWINDOWLONG(hwnd, LEGEND_WNDEXTRABYTES, crBk));
}


/////////////////////////////////////////////////////////////////////////////


void WINAPI Legend_OnSetTextColor (HWND hwnd, COLORREF crTextNew) {

    adgSETWINDOWLONG(hwnd, LEGEND_WNDEXTRABYTES, crText, crTextNew);
    InvalidateRect(hwnd, NULL, TRUE);
}


/////////////////////////////////////////////////////////////////////////////


COLORREF WINAPI Legend_OnGetTextColor (HWND hwnd) {

    return((COLORREF) adgGETWINDOWLONG(hwnd, LEGEND_WNDEXTRABYTES, crText));
}
```

Now that we have our colors straight, we are ready to continue with our preparations to paint the control. The next thing we need to do is get the size of our client area. Then, using this client area, we compute the size of legend's box. First, we compute the maximum box size by making a square that is the full height of our client area and the same size in width. Then we make the box smaller by an amount determined by the presence or absence of the LS_BIGBOX style bit. The box is deflated with a call to InflateRect, passing negative values for both the xAmt and yAmt parameters. We arbitrarily shrink the box by 1/6th if LS_BIGBOX is set and 1/4th if it is not.

```
void Legend_OnPaint (HWND hwnd) {

    RECT rcBox, rcClient;
    int nBoxSide, nShrinkBox;
    .
    .
    .
    // Calculate the size of our legend box based on the client rect and the
    // window style. If the LS_BIGBOX window style is set, then we shrink the
    // box area by 1/6th of its size; otherwise, we shrink it by 1/4th. These
    // values were arbitrarily determined to look good through experimentation.
    GetClientRect(hwnd, &rcClient);
    nBoxSide = rcClient.bottom;
    SetRect(&rcBox, 0, 0, nBoxSide, nBoxSide);
    nShrinkBox = -(nBoxSide / (GetWindowStyle(hwnd) & LS_BIGBOX ? 6 : 4));
    InflateRect(&rcBox, nShrinkBox, nShrinkBox);
```

If the legend control has the LS_BOXBORDER style, we draw a frame around the box and then deflate the box rectangle by 1 pixel so that filling the rectangle won't overwrite the frame.

```
void Legend_OnPaint (HWND hwnd) {

    PAINTSTRUCT ps;
    RECT rcBox;
    .
    .
    .
    // If we have a border around the box, draw it and shrink rcBox by one.
    if (GetWindowStyle(hwnd) & LS_BOXBORDER) {
        HBRUSH hbrFrame = CreateSolidBrush(GetTextColor(ps.hdc));
        FrameRect(ps.hdc, &rcBox, hbrFrame);
        DeleteBrush(hbrFrame);
        InflateRect(&rcBox, -1, -1);
    }
```

Now we are ready to fill the box. We retrieve the brush handle to fill the box by using the message API macro Legend_GetBoxBrush. Notice that we could simply use the adgGETWINDOWLONG macro to get the brush handle directly, but this is not particularly good programming practice because doing that makes our code dependent on implementation details that we may want to change. Finally, we reset the brush's origin to (0, 0) by calling SetBrush-OrgEx and fill the box rectangle with a call to PatBlt.

If we didn't reset the brush origin, it would be possible for a repaint of a portion of our control to misalign with a part of the control that is already painted. You can see this problem in action by commenting out the SetBrushOrgEx line in legend's OnPaint. Once you have done this, recompile and run the example program **CustCntl.EXE**. Move the main dialog box just a pixel or two down and to the right and use any draggable window to invalidate just a portion of any of the legend controls. When the control redraws, it will redraw just the obscured part of the control and you will see that the brush hash marks don't line up. If you comment the SetBrushOrgEx line back in and recompile, the problem goes away.

```
HBRUSH WINAPI Legend_OnGetBoxBrush (HWND hwnd) {

    // Return the current brush handle stored in the window extra bytes
    return((HBRUSH) adgGETWINDOWLONG(hwnd, LEGEND_WNDEXTRABYTES, hbr));
}


/////////////////////////////////////////////////////////////////////////////


void Legend_OnPaint (HWND hwnd) {

    PAINTSTRUCT ps;
    RECT rcBox;
    HBRUSH hbrOriginal;
    .
    .
    .
    // Fill the box with the appropriate brush.
    SetBrushOrgEx(ps.hdc, 0, 0, NULL);
    hbrOriginal = SelectBrush(ps.hdc, Legend_GetBoxBrush(hwnd));
    PatBlt(ps.hdc, rcBox.left, rcBox.top, rcBox.right - rcBox.left,
        rcBox.bottom - rcBox.top, PATCOPY);
    SelectBrush(ps.hdc, hbrOriginal);
```

We are done drawing the box now, so we exclude the area we have drawn from the clipping region of our device context. This trick is used so that we can call ExtTextOut in the next step to draw the text and fill the control's background at the same time. By painting in this way, we prevent our control from flickering.

```
void Legend_OnPaint (HWND hwnd) {

    PAINTSTRUCT ps;
    RECT rcBox;
    .
    .
    .
    // If we drew a border, restore rcBox to it's original size.
    if (GetWindowStyle(hwnd) & LS_BOXBORDER)
        InflateRect(&rcBox, 1, 1);

    // Exclude rcBox (everything we have drawn so far) from the clipping region
    // so that we can use ExtTextOut to fill in the control's background and draw
    // the text at the same time without blinking.
    ExcludeClipRect(ps.hdc, rcBox.left, rcBox.top, rcBox.right, rcBox.bottom);
```

Now we are ready to draw the text to the right of the box. Because
we don't know how long that text might be, we must dynamically
allocate a buffer to hold the text. The size of the buffer is determined by calling GetWindowTextLength, adding one for the terminating zero, and then multiplying by sizeof(TCHAR) to convert
from characters to bytes. The _alloca intrinsic function that is used
to allocate our text buffer is a non-standard compiler feature that
allocates memory directly from the stack. Any memory allocated
with _alloca is automatically freed when your function returns.

```
void Legend_OnPaint (HWND hwnd) {

    int nTextLength;
    LPTSTR psz;
    .
    .
    .
    // Allocate a buffer of sufficient size to hold the window text and then
    // call GetWindowText to retrieve it. The _alloca function allocates
    // storage from the stack. This memory is automatically freed when our
    // function returns.
    nTextLength = GetWindowTextLength(hwnd);
    psz = _alloca((nTextLength + 1) * sizeof(TCHAR));
    GetWindowText(hwnd, psz, nTextLength + 1);
```

Next, we get the window's font with GetWindowFont, a macro
defined in **WindowsX.H** as:

```
#define GetWindowFont(hwnd) FORWARD_WM_GETFONT((hwnd), SendMessage)
```

This macro ultimately results in a call to Legend_OnGetFont to get
the HFONT stored in the window extra bytes. We select this font
into the device context and then call GetTextExtentPoint32 to

determine the dimensions, in pixels, of our window text string. We use this information to vertically center our ExtTextOut output.

The SDK documentation gives the following prototype for the ExtTextOut function:

```
BOOL ExtTextOut(hdc, X, Y, fuOptions, lprc, lpszString, cbCount, lpDx)
HDC hdc;               // Handle of device context
int X;                 // X-coordinate of reference point
int Y;                 // Y-coordinate of reference point
UINT fuOptions;        // Text-output options
CONST RECT* lprc;      // Optional clipping and/or opaquing rectangle
LPCTSTR lpszString;    // Address of string
UINT cbCount;          // String length
CONST INT* lpDx;       // Address of array of intercharacter spacing values
```

The first parameter we pass to ExtTextOut is the handle to our device context. The second and third parameters specify the vertically centered x- and y-coordinates where our string is to be placed. The fourth parameter specifies that the background color should be used to fill the clipping/opaquing rectangle (ETO_OPAQUE) and that no text should be drawn outside the rectangle (ETO_CLIPPED). The fifth parameter is the address of the clipping/opaquing rectangle to be used (in this case, our whole client area). The sixth and seventh parameters specify the string to ouput and its length in characters. And the eighth and final parameter is NULL, indicating that we want Windows to use normal spacing between characters.

```
void Legend_OnPaint (HWND hwnd) {

    PAINTSTRUCT ps;
    RECT rcClient;
    int nBoxSide, nTextLength;
    HFONT hfont, hfontOriginal = NULL;
    SIZE size;
    TCHAR* psz;
    .
    .
    .
    // Draw the window text, vertically centered, to the right of the box.
    // ETO_OPAQUE causes the background to be filled with the current
    // background color at the same time. The arbitrary offset of (nBoxSide / 3)
    // is used to add some padding space between the box and the text string.
    hfont = GetWindowFont(hwnd);
    if (hfont != NULL)
        hfontOriginal = SelectFont(ps.hdc, hfont);
    GetTextExtentPoint32(ps.hdc, psz, nTextLength, &size);
    ExtTextOut(ps.hdc, nBoxSide + (nBoxSide / 3),
        (rcClient.bottom - size.cy) / 2, ETO_OPAQUE | ETO_CLIPPED,
```

```
        &rcClient, psz, nTextLength, NULL);
    if (hfont != NULL)
        SelectFont(ps.hdc, hfontOriginal);
```

Just before Legend_OnPaint returns, we release our device context by calling EndPaint.

Designing the Bargraph Control

Although many applications have the need to display bar graphs, Windows itself does not implement a bar graph control.

The bargraph control shows two axes on its left and bottom sides, between which are shown a series of vertical bars, each filled with a particular brush and each representing a particular value. In addition to displaying a set of values, the bargraph control accepts keyboard and mouse input, enabling the user to choose any bar in the graph. Choosing a bar generates a notification message to the parent of the control, allowing that parent to perform an action. For instance, clicking on a bar might take the user to a particular value in a spreadsheet, or it might display some detailed information about the bar.

The programmer must tell the bargraph control what brush and what value to use for each bar in the graph. For example, an application might choose to fill the first bar with a solid blue brush and to make that bar 100 units high. To determine the scale of the bars in the graph, the programmer must also tell the bargraph control how high the whole graph is in units. If our first bar is 100 units high and other bars in the same graph are as high as 900 units, we might choose 1000 units for the height of the whole graph.

Designing the Bargraph Programmer's Interface

Unlike the legend control, bargraph doesn't have any class-specific window styles. So our first step in designing the programmer's interface for bargraph is to define a set of class-specific window messages.

```
// Purpose: Sets the array of BAR structures for the control. The brush in
//          each BAR structure is only used by the control. It is owned by
//          the caller. Therefore, the caller must create and destroy the
//          brush handle.
// wParam:  UINT cBars - Number of BAR structures in array
```

```
// lParam:  BAR* pbar - Pointer to first BAR in array
// Returns: void
#define BGM_SETBARS     (WM_USER + 0)


// Purpose: Gets pointer to BAR array for control.
// wParam:  N/A
// lParam:  N/A
// Returns: BAR* - Pointer to first BAR in array
#define BGM_GETBARS     (WM_USER + 1)


// Purpose: Gets number of BAR structures in array.
// wParam:  N/A
// lParam:  N/A
// Returns: UINT - Number of BARs
#define BGM_GETCOUNT    (WM_USER + 2)


// Purpose: Sets the current graph height (in user-defined units).
// wParam:  UINT nHeight - New graph height
// lParam:  N/A
// Returns: void
#define BGM_SETHEIGHT   (WM_USER + 3)


// Purpose: Gets the current graph height (in user-defined units).
// wParam:  N/A
// lParam:  N/A
// Returns: UINT - Current graph height
#define BGM_GETHEIGHT   (WM_USER + 4)


// Purpose: Sets the background color of a bargraph control.
// wParam:  N/A
// lParam:  COLORREF crNew - New background color
// Returns: void
#define BGM_SETBKCOLOR  (WM_USER + 5)


// Purpose: Gets the background color of a bargraph control.
// wParam:  N/A
// lParam:  N/A
// Returns: COLORREF - Current background color
#define BGM_GETBKCOLOR  (WM_USER + 6)


// Purpose: Sets the text color of a bargraph control.
// wParam:  N/A
// lParam:  COLORREF crNew - New text color
// Returns: void
#define BGM_SETTEXTCOLOR (WM_USER + 7)


// Purpose: Gets the text color of a bargraph control.
// wParam:  N/A
// lParam:  N/A
// Returns: COLORREF - Current text color
#define BGM_GETTEXTCOLOR (WM_USER + 8)
```

The BGM_SETHEIGHT and BGM_GETHEIGHT messages are provided to permit the programmer to specify the vertical scale of a bargraph. By default, bargraph assumes that bars will be drawn on a scale of 0 to 100 units. So, a bar shown by bargraph that is 50 units high will consume about 50% of the vertical height of the control, as shown in Figure 4.4.

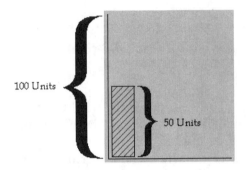

Figure 4.4 *A 50-unit bar in a graph with a height of 100 units.*

If instead we wanted that same 50-unit-high bar to be the full height of the control, we could send the following message:

```
SendDlgItemMessage(hdlg, IDC_BARGRAPH, BGM_SETHEIGHT, 50, 0);
```

Or we could use the message API defined in **Bargraph.H**:

```
BarGraph_SetHeight(GetDlgItem(hdlg, IDC_BARGRAPH), 50);
```

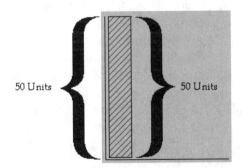

Figure 4.5 *A 50-unit-high bar in a graph with a height of 50 units.*

Upon receiving the BGM_SETHEIGHT message, the control automatically repaints. This time our 50-unit-high bar is painted so that it reaches all the way to the top of the control (as seen in Figure 4.5).

The BGM_SETBARS and BGM_GETBARS messages allow the programmer to get and set a pointer to an array of BAR structures. This array of BARs is used at paint time to draw the bar graph. A BAR is defined in **Bargraph.H** as:

```
// BAR structure defines each bar in the bar graph.
typedef struct {
    UINT nHeight;           // Height of bar in user-defined units
    HBRUSH hbr;             // Brush to fill bar with
} BAR;
```

The nHeight member of a BAR defines the height of that bar (on a scale from 0 to the height of the graph). The hbr member is the brush handle that will be used to fill the interior of the bar. The BGM_SETBARS message expects the number of bars in wParam and a pointer to the first BAR in the caller's array in lParam.

Our implementation expects the caller to manage the memory for the array of BAR structures and the HBRUSH handles used to fill each bar. Although this approach puts more burden on the caller, it has several advantages over other possible implementations. Most importantly, the bargraph control doesn't have to get involved in the creation or management of the BAR array or its HBRUSH members. This makes bargraph very flexible because the programmer can determine how the array is constructed and where the HBRUSHes come from. It is no problem if a programmer wants to cache HBRUSHes or simply use the same HBRUSH handle for several BARs. What's more, the programmer is free to use a variety of means to construct brushes, including CreateSolidBrush, CreateBrushIndirect, CreatePatternBrush, CreateDIBPatternBrush, CreateDIBPatternBrushPt and CreateHatch Brush (not to mention GetStockObject!). The moral of the story is that if your interface makes too many assumptions about how it will be used, it loses flexibility. For example, if bargraph had assumed that you always wanted to fill your bars with solid RGB colors, the resulting interface would have been simpler, but bargraph would be unable to display bars with hatches or fill patterns.

As long as we are pondering implementation strategy, it is interesting to note the almost limitless flexibility that notification messages can give to a control. For example, it would be fairly trivial for bargraph to send a notification message, call it BGN_BARPAINT, to its parent each time it painted a bar, giving the index of the bar being drawn and the bounding rectangle to draw in. If the parent wanted to, it could respond to BGN_BARPAINT notifications and take over the painting of one or more bars in the graph. You can probably imagine dozens of ways that the parent could respond to BGN_BARPAINT, resulting in an equal number of unique and interesting looking bar graphs.

Although we won't implement BGN_BARPAINT, we do need to implement another notification message. This notification will tell the parent when a bar is clicked on with the mouse or chosen with the keyboard interface. The message we will use to implement this notification is WM_NOTIFY, which is already defined by **WinUser.H**. To complete our header file and our design of bargraph, we need only to define a structure for our notification data which can be passed in the lParam of a WM_NOTIFY message. We will talk more about WM_NOTIFY in the next section, when we write the code for BarGraph_NotifyParent.

```
// The following is the BARGRAPH_NOTIFY structure sent to the parent in the
// lParam of a WM_NOTIFY message. The NMHDR structure can be found in WinUser.H.
typedef struct {
    NMHDR nmh;              // Notify message header
    UINT uBar;              // Index of bar in graph
} BARGRAPH_NOTIFY;
```

Implementing the Code for Bargraph

To start with, BarGraph_RegisterClass and BarGraph_Unregister-Class are essentially identical to the legend functions that do the same thing. However, because our bargraph control is more complex than legend, we will take a different approach to instance data storage. Instead of storing data directly in the window extra bytes, we will store a pointer to an allocated structure. This structure will contain the control's instance data. We define the structure, THIS-DATA, along with two macros to access the THISDATA pointer stored in the window extra bytes, as follows:

```
typedef struct {
    UINT nHeight;          // Bar graph's height (in user-defined units)
    UINT cBars;            // Number of bars in the graph
    BAR* pbar;             // Array of bars to draw
    UINT nSelectedBar;     // Bar to highlight when focused
    UINT nMouseDownBar;    // Bar where mouse button went down
    UINT nCancelBar;       // Bar to reselect if choice is canceled
    COLORREF crBk;         // Background color
    COLORREF crText;       // Text color
} THISDATA;
```

```
///////////////////////////////////////////////////////////////////////////

// The following structure is for the window extra bytes.
// For more information, see the macros presented in Appendix A.
typedef struct {
   THISDATA* pthis;
} BARGRAPH_WNDEXTRABYTES;


///////////////////////////////////////////////////////////////////////////

// Macros to get and set the THISDATA pointer stored in the window extra bytes
#define GETTHISDATA(hwnd) \
   ((THISDATA*) adgGETWINDOWLONG(hwnd, BARGRAPH_WNDEXTRABYTES, pthis))
#define SETTHISDATA(hwnd, pthisNew) \
   adgSETWINDOWLONG(hwnd, BARGRAPH_WNDEXTRABYTES, pthis, pthisNew);
```

In our BarGraph_OnCreate function, we allocate space for a THIS-
DATA structure and set a pointer to it into the window extra bytes
with the SETTHISDATA macro. If the allocation fails, we return
FALSE from BarGraph_OnCreate and our window is destroyed. Later,
when we want to retrieve our THISDATA pointer again, we can use
the GETTHISDATA macro. When the window is destroyed, our
BarGraph_OnDestroy function frees the memory allocated for the
THISDATA structure. Notice that this code does not check to see if
the pointer is NULL.[5] This is okay because ANSI C states that it is
valid to pass NULL to free, which is defined to ignore NULL pointers.

```
BOOL BarGraph_OnCreate (HWND hwnd, CREATESTRUCT* pcs) {

   // Allocate memory for a THISDATA structure and store a pointer to it in
   // the window extra bytes.
   THISDATA* pthis = malloc(sizeof(THISDATA));
   adgASSERT(pthis != NULL);
   SETTHISDATA(hwnd, pthis);

   // If our allocation succeeds, we set some default values.
   if (pthis != NULL) {
      BarGraph_SetHeight(hwnd, 100);
      BarGraph_SetBars(hwnd, 0, NULL);
      BarGraph_SetBkColor(hwnd, GetSysColor(COLOR_3DFACE));
      BarGraph_SetTextColor(hwnd, GetSysColor(COLOR_WINDOWTEXT));
      pthis->nSelectedBar = 0;
   }
```

---

[5]The THISDATA pointer can be NULL if malloc fails in BarGraph_
OnCreate.

```
   // If our allocation fails, we return FALSE, and the window is destroyed.
   return(pthis != NULL);
}


/////////////////////////////////////////////////////////////////////////


void BarGraph_OnDestroy (HWND hwnd) {

   // NOTE: ANSI C states that it is OK to pass NULL to free.
   // This can happen if malloc fails in BarGraph_OnCreate.
   THISDATA* pthis = GETTHISDATA(hwnd);
   free(pthis);
}
```

Now, to implement the BarGraph_OnGetHeight and BarGraph_
OnSetHeight accessor functions, we simply use GETTHISDATA to
retrieve the THISDATA pointer, which we stashed away in the
window extra bytes.

```
UINT WINAPI BarGraph_OnGetHeight (HWND hwnd) {

   return(GETTHISDATA(hwnd)->nHeight);
}


/////////////////////////////////////////////////////////////////////////


void WINAPI BarGraph_OnSetHeight (HWND hwnd, UINT nHeightNew) {

   GETTHISDATA(hwnd)->nHeight = nHeightNew;

   // Our data changed, so we need to force a repaint.
   InvalidateRect(hwnd, NULL, TRUE);
}
```

Painting Bargraph

Painting bargraph is actually very similar to painting legend. The
main difference between legend's OnPaint routine and bargraph's
is that bargraph draws several rectangles instead of just one square.
To store the heights of each bar and the brushes to fill them, we
implement BarGraph_OnSetBars, BarGraph_OnGetBars, and
BarGraph_OnGetCount. Once again, we use the GETTHISDATA
macro to access the pointer to our control's THISDATA structure.

```
BAR* WINAPI BarGraph_OnGetBars (HWND hwnd) {

    return(GETTHISDATA(hwnd)->pbar);
}
```

`//////////////////////////////////////////////////////////////////////////`

```
UINT WINAPI BarGraph_OnGetCount (HWND hwnd) {

    return(GETTHISDATA(hwnd)->cBars);
}
```

`//////////////////////////////////////////////////////////////////////////`

```
void WINAPI BarGraph_OnSetBars (HWND hwnd, UINT cBars, BAR* pbar) {

    THISDATA* pthis;
    pthis = GETTHISDATA(hwnd);
    pthis->pbar = pbar;
    pthis->cBars = cBars;
    pthis->nSelectedBar = 0;

    // Our data changed, so we need to force a repaint.
    InvalidateRect(hwnd, NULL, TRUE);
}
```

In BarGraph_OnPaint we simply loop through and draw each bar in the BAR array. To draw a single bar, we must compute its bounding rectangle by calling a function, BarGraph_GetBarRect, which we will define next. Filling and framing this bounding rectangle is accomplished using the same functions that legend used to draw its box.

```
UINT bar;
RECT rcBar;
for (bar = 0; bar < pthis->cBars; bar++) {
    BarGraph_GetBarRect(hwnd, i, &rcBar);
    // Draw the bar designated by the rectangle rcBar.
}
```

Of course there is more to bargraph's OnPaint than this, but there's really nothing new here that you didn't already learn from legend's OnPaint routine. The only hard thing about BarGraph_OnPaint is implementing BarGraph_GetBarRect:

```
RECT* BarGraph_GetBarRect (HWND hwnd, UINT n, RECT* prc) {

    RECT rcClient;
    THISDATA* pthis = GETTHISDATA(hwnd);
```

```
    int cxClient, cyClient;

    // Check window handle, RECT pointer, and the value of n.
    adgASSERT(IsWindow(hwnd));
    adgASSERT(prc != NULL);
    adgASSERT(n < pthis->cBars);

    // Get the size of the client area but don't include the axes lines on the
    // left and bottom.
    GetClientRect(hwnd, &rcClient);
    rcClient.left++;
    rcClient.bottom--;
    cxClient = rcClient.right - rcClient.left;
    cyClient = rcClient.bottom - rcClient.top;

    // This arbitrary value defines the spacing in pixels between bars.
    #define BARSPACING 2

    // Find the left and right sides of bar n.
    #define BARTOCLIENT(uBar) (rcClient.left + \
        (int) (((__int64) cxClient * (uBar)) / pthis->cBars))
    prc->left = BARTOCLIENT(n) + BARSPACING;
    prc->right = BARTOCLIENT(n + 1);
    #undef BARTOCLIENT

    // Set the top based on the height of the bar and the height of the bar
    // graph (in user-defined units). Set the bottom to be the bottom of the
    // client area (minus BARSPACING to leave space between the bottom axis
    // line and the bottom of each bar).
    prc->top = rcClient.bottom -
        (int) (((__int64) cyClient * pthis->pbar[n].nHeight) / pthis->nHeight);
    prc->bottom = rcClient.bottom - BARSPACING;
    #undef BARSPACING

    return(prc);
}
```

This routine isn't really all that complicated, but it did require a little planning. To start solving this problem, it's best to think in one dimension at a time. First, let's figure out how to compute the left and right sides of bar n, and then we'll worry about the top and bottom sides.

Before we can compute anything, we need to get the client area. Our client area is cxClient pixels wide and cyClient pixels high and has an top-left corner of (rcClient.left, rcClient.top). This area is shrunk slightly by the preceding code so that our bars won't overlap the axes, which have already been drawn on the left and bottom sides of the graph by BarGraph_OnPaint.

Now, if we have pthis->cBars bars in our graph, and we have cxClient pixels to work with, the left side (prc->left) of bar uBar can be found by creating a simple proportion:

```
uBar / pthis->cBars = prc->left / cxClient
```

and then solving for prc->left:

```
prc->left = (uBar / pthis->cBars) * cxClient
```

Adding the left side of our client area, we *could* implement this exactly as we solved it.

```
prc->left = rcClient.left + ((uBar / pthis->cBars) * cxClient);
```

But this implementation has two serious flaws. The first problem occurs because we are using integer arithmetic. Dividing uBar (which ranges between 0 and (pthis->cBars - 1)) by pthis->cBars gives us a fractional value somewhere between 0 and 1. But we are using integers, so this value always is rounded down to zero! To circumvent this problem, we need to rewrite the equation so that the multiplication happens first.

```
prc->left = rcClient.left + ((cxClient * uBar) / pthis->cBars);
```

Now we won't lose precision when we divide because the division will happen last.

Now for the other, more subtle, problem. What if (cxClient * uBar) is too large to be held in a 32-bit integer? Admittedly this overflow situation seems pretty far fetched in solving for prc->left, but what about the y dimension of our graph where the units are arbitrarily determined by the programmer?

```
prc->top = rcClient.bottom -
    ((cyClient * pthis->pbar[n].nHeight) / pthis->nUnits);
```

If we take cyClient to be 2048 pixels (pretty extreme, but possible) then pthis>pbar[n].nHeight is restricted to $(2 \wedge 32) / 2048$ or 2,097,152 units. This is a potential bug for anyone who isn't aware that the argument to BarGraph_OnSetHeight is really restricted to values less than 2,097,152. Any value larger than this will result in an overflow, causing bargraph to paint incorrectly!

We could choose to ignore this problem and document the limitation instead, but it is easy enough to fix the problem by using 64-bit integers to prevent multiplication overflow.

```
prc->left = (__int64) cxClient * uBar / pthis->cBars;
prc->top = (__int64) cyClient * pthis->pbar[n].nHeight / pthis->nUnits;
```

The rest of BarGraph_GetBarRect is trivial. We use our formula to write a macro called BARTOCLIENT, which uses 64-bit integers to find the left side of a bar in pixels. Then, we simply use the macro twice to find the left and right sides of the bar we are being asked to compute, using BARSPACING to add some padding between bars.

```
// This arbitrary value defines the spacing in pixels between bars.

#define BARSPACING 2

// Find the left and right sides of bar n.
#define BARTOCLIENT(uBar) (rcClient.left + \
    (int) (((__int64) cxClient * (uBar)) / pthis->cBars))
prc->left = BARTOCLIENT(n) + BARSPACING;
prc->right = BARTOCLIENT(n + 1);
#undef BARTOCLIENT
```

Finally, we use 64-bit integers again to compute the top and bottom sides of the bar rectangle:

```
// Set the top based on the height of the bar and the height of the bar
// graph (in user-defined units). Set the bottom to be the bottom of the
// client area (minus BARSPACING to leave space between the bottom axis
// line and the bottom of each bar).
prc->top = rcClient.bottom -
    (int) (((__int64) cyClient * pthis->pbar[n].nHeight) / pthis->nHeight);
prc->bottom = rcClient.bottom - BARSPACING;
#undef BARSPACING
```

Choosing a Bar

Bargraph allows the user to choose a bar by either clicking with the mouse or using a keyboard interface. The keyboard interface requires that the user first set focus to the bargraph control with the Tab key. Then, the Left and Right arrow keys cycle through the bars, highlighting each in turn. Pressing the Space bar or Return key chooses the bar that is currently highlighted.

The mouse interface is implemented by trapping WM_LBUTTON-DOWN and WM_LBUTTONUP messages. If the left mouse button goes down inside our control, we receive a WM_LBUTTONDOWN message. When this happens, we determine which bar the cursor is in. We save this value in the instance variables nMouseDownBar and nSelectedBar, first saving the original nSelectedBar in the instance variable nCancelBar. These variables are used in BarGraph_OnLButtonUp and BarGraph_OnMouseMove to handle the case where a user wants to cancel a bar selection. To make the bar that was clicked on visible to the user, we invalidate our control and take the focus so that WM_PAINT highlights nSelectedBar. Finally, we capture the mouse so that we receive the WM_LBUTTONUP message that is sent when the mouse button is released (regardless of whether the mouse has left our window or not).

```
void BarGraph_OnLButtonDown (HWND hwnd, BOOL fDoubleClick, int x, int y,
    UINT keyFlags) {

    UINT bar = BarGraph_BarFromPoint(hwnd, x, y);
    if (bar != INVALID_BAR) {

        // If the user clicked on a valid bar, set nMouseDownBar and
        // nSelectedBar to the bar that was clicked on, saving the original
        // nSelectedBar in nCancelBar so that we can restore the old selection if
        // the user cancels. Then we force a repaint and set focus and mouse
        // capture.
        GETTHISDATA(hwnd)->nMouseDownBar = bar;
        GETTHISDATA(hwnd)->nCancelBar = GETTHISDATA(hwnd)->nSelectedBar;
        GETTHISDATA(hwnd)->nSelectedBar = bar;
        InvalidateRect(hwnd, NULL, FALSE);
        SetFocus(hwnd);
        SetCapture(hwnd);
    }
}
```

To determine what bar the cursor is in, we create a function, BarGraph_BarFromPoint, which simply calls PtInRect with the bounding rectangle of each bar in the graph. If PtInRect returns TRUE, indicating that the cursor lies inside the bounding rectangle, we return the index of the bar. If the loop terminates without returning the index of a bar, we return INVALID_BAR to indicate failure. Naturally, the bounding rectangle is determined by the same function that BarGraph_OnPaint used to fill each bar, BarGraph_ GetBarRect. Thinking ahead when we implemented BarGraph_ OnPaint has paid off!

```
#define INVALID_BAR ((UINT)-1)


/////////////////////////////////////////////////////////////////////////////


UINT BarGraph_BarFromPoint (HWND hwnd, int x, int y) {
```

```
UINT bar;
RECT rcBar;
THISDATA* pthis = GETTHISDATA(hwnd);
POINT pt;
pt.x = x;
pt.y = y;

// If point (x, y) is inside a bar, return the index of that bar.
for (bar = 0; bar < pthis->cBars; bar++)
    if (PtInRect(BarGraph_GetBarRect(hwnd, bar, &rcBar), pt))
        return(bar);

// Failed. Point (x, y) is not inside any bar in the graph.
return(INVALID_BAR);
}
```

Because we set the mouse capture in BarGraph_OnLButtonDown, we receive all WM_MOUSEMOVE messages in BarGraph_OnMouse-Move, regardless of where the mouse is positioned. On each mouse move, we highlight either nMouseDownBar or nCancelBar, depending on whether the mouse is still inside the original nMouseDownBar. When the mouse button is released, we release capture and check the cursor to see if it is still inside nMouseDownBar. If it is, we change the selected bar and notify the parent that a bar has been chosen.

```
void BarGraph_OnLButtonUp (HWND hwnd, int x, int y, UINT keyFlags) {

    // We respond to a mouse button up only if we set capture previously
    // on a mouse button down.
    if (GetCapture() == hwnd) {

        // Get the bar we were over when the button was released.
        UINT bar = BarGraph_BarFromPoint(hwnd, x, y);

        // Releasing capture generates a WM_CAPTURECHANGED message, which sets
        // nSelectedBar to nCancelBar (canceling the selection by default).
        ReleaseCapture();

        // Check if the user let up the mouse on the same bar it went down on.
        if (bar == GETTHISDATA(hwnd)->nMouseDownBar) {

            // Change the currently selected bar.
            GETTHISDATA(hwnd)->nSelectedBar = bar;
            InvalidateRect(hwnd, NULL, FALSE);

            // Tell the parent which bar was clicked on.
            BarGraph_NotifyParent(hwnd, NM_CLICK, bar);
        }
    }
}
```

Here is one small but important note about mouse capture: focus and mouse capture are independent of each other. You don't need one to have the other. This means that any time you capture the mouse with GetCapture, you should be prepared to release capture again in OnKillFocus. Still having the mouse input captured when another control has assumed the input focus can be very confusing to the user and is probably a bug just waiting to happen. How can you lose the focus while you have the mouse captured? All the user has to do is press the Tab key.

Besides being prepared to lose the focus at any time, your control should also be prepared to lose the mouse capture at any time. Here are a few events that can result in your thread losing the mouse capture:

- A message box or dialog box can pop up.
- The user can Alt+Tab to another window.
- The user can type Ctrl+Esc to bring up the start menu (the task list under Windows NT).
- Another window created by your thread can call SetCapture.

Although these scenarios may seem obscure, they do happen. Just image how frustrating the resulting problems would be for a novice user. Luckily, Windows sends us a WM_CAPTURECHANGED message[6] just after releasing our mouse capture.

We can prevent all the aforementioned problems by implementing BarGraph_OnKillFocus and BarGraph_OnCaptureChanged as follows:

```
void BarGraph_OnKillFocus (HWND hwnd, HWND hwndNewFocus) {

    // If we have the capture, release it.
    if (GetCapture() == hwnd)
      ReleaseCapture();

    // Remove the focus indicator by causing a repaint.
    InvalidateRect(hwnd, NULL, FALSE);
}


/////////////////////////////////////////////////////////////////////////////


void BarGraph_OnCaptureChanged (HWND hwnd, HWND hwndNewCapture) {

    // If we are losing the capture, cancel the current selection.
    GETTHISDATA(hwnd)->nSelectedBar = GETTHISDATA(hwnd)->nCancelBar;
    InvalidateRect(hwnd, NULL, FALSE);
}
```

---

[6]Windows NT 3.51 does not support this message, but Windows NT will in future releases.

In addition to handling WM_KILLFOCUS, we also need to handle WM_SETFOCUS. All we need to do in BarGraph_OnSetFocus is invalidate our window. Later, when BarGraph_OnPaint is called, it notices that GetFocus returns the control's hwnd, indicating that the control has the input focus, and it repaints accordingly.

The last function we need to implement for mouse support is BarGraph_NotifyParent, which simply packs information into a BAR-GRAPH_NOTIFY structure and sends it to the parent window as the lParam of a WM_NOTIFY message. The NMHDR members of BAR-GRAPH_NOTIFY are packed with the window handle of the control, the control's identifier, and the code passed to BarGraph_NotifyParent. For this parameter, we use the generic NM_CLICK notify code defined in **CommCtrl.H**. The only other member we need to set is uBar (which is the reason we can't simply use WM_COMMAND to begin with), which is set to the value passed in.

```
void BarGraph_NotifyParent (HWND hwndCtl, UINT code, UINT uBar) {

    BARGRAPH_NOTIFY bgn;
    adgASSERT(IsWindow(hwndCtl));
    bgn.nmh.hwndFrom = hwndCtl;
    bgn.nmh.idFrom = GetWindowID(hwndCtl);
    bgn.nmh.code = code;
    bgn.uBar = uBar;
    FORWARD_WM_NOTIFY(GetParent(hwndCtl), bgn.nmh.idFrom, &bgn, SendMessage);
}
```

WM_GETDLGCODE

Windows periodically sends WM_GETDLGCODE messages to windows that are in a dialog box. These messages are actually sent for two quite different reasons:

- to query the type of a control
- to determine what keys a control is interested in processing

In either case, a control must respond with one or more DLGC_* identifiers (defined in **WinUser.H**) ORed together. If the lParam parameter is zero, WM_GETDLGCODE was sent to query the type of your control. If lParam is nonzero, WM_GETDLGCODE was sent by IsDialogMessage in response to a keyboard message and lParam holds a pointer to the MSG structure for that keyboard message.

The first group of DLGC_* codes (shown in Table 4.1) is used to identify a control as a certain type. These DLGC_* bits determine how Windows handles the control in terms of special dialog-box behaviors. For example, default push buttons are given their special dialog-box behavior because they set the DLGC_DEFPUSHBUTTON bit in their response to WM_GETDLGCODE.

Table 4.1 *DLGC_* Values Used to Determine the Type of a Control.*

Identifier	Value	Meaning
DLGC_BUTTON	0x2000	Control is to be treated like a button. All BS_* styles of the Windows button class return this bit with the exception of BS_GROUPBOX, which returns DLGC_STATIC because it is not checkable.
DLGC_DEFPUSHBUTTON	0x0010	Control is to be treated as a default push button. Buttons with BS_DEFPUSHBUTTON style always return a code with this bit set.
DLGC_UNDEFPUSHBUTTON	0x0020	Control is to be treated as a normal push button. If your control is not a default push button but you want push-button behavior, you must set this bit. This bit is returned by all buttons with a style of BS_PUSHBUTTON.
DLGC_RADIOBUTTON	0x0040	Control is to be treated as a radio button. Windows uses this bit to determine which controls in a group are radio buttons. The BS_AUTORADIOBUTTON and arrow keys behaviors rely on this bit.

Identifier	Value	Meaning
DLGC_STATIC	0x0100	Control doesn't process any keys. Controls that return DLGC_STATIC are considered when handling mnemonics (the underscored characters that let you jump from control to control in a dialog box). Controls that simply return 0 or that do not handle WM_GETDLGCODE are not considered when searching for mnemonics.
DLGC_HASSETSEL	0x0008	Control processes EM_SETSEL messages. Controls that set this bit are sent an EM_SETSEL message when they receive focus, selecting their entire contents.

The second group of DLGC_* codes (shown in Table 4.2) is used to tell Windows what keys your control wants to process. If the user presses a key while a dialog box is active, IsDialogMessage receives the key and sends a WM_GETDLGCODE message to the window that currently has the input focus. This gives the control a chance to tell Windows not to perform its default handling and instead to send the keyboard message directly to the control. If lParam is nonzero, it will point to the MSG structure for the current keyboard message. You can use this MSG structure to decide what DLGC_* code to return based on what key was pressed. You may also choose to simply return a set of one or more DLGC_* codes unconditionally.

Consider an example. If the edit control's window procedure responded to the WM_GETDLGCODE message in this way

```
UINT uNormalEditDlgCodes = DLGC_HASSETSEL | DLGC_WANTCHARS | DLGC_WANTARROWS;
return (uNormalEditDlgCodes | DLGC_WANTTAB);
```

the edit control would continue to work as always, but the Tab key would be sent to the control, and Windows would not change the input focus to the next control, as would ordinarily be expected.

Bargraph's keyboard interface requires that we receive the arrow keys, the Spacebar and the Return key. We do this by returning DLGC_WANTMESSAGE if we get a WM_KEYDOWN for either the Spacebar or the Return key. In addition, we always ask Windows for the arrow keys.

Because bargraph takes over processing of the Return key, Windows will not do any default push-button handling while a bargraph control has focus. You can verify this by adding a default push button to the CustCntl application.

```
UINT BarGraph_OnGetDlgCode (HWND hwnd, LPMSG lpmsg) {

    // We want to process the arrow keys unconditionally.
    UINT uRet = DLGC_WANTARROWS;

    // If lpmsg is not NULL, it points to the keyboard message that generated
    // the current WM_GETDLGCODE message.
    if (lpmsg != NULL) {

        // We want to override the default processing if the keyboard message
        // is a WM_KEYDOWN produced by the VK_RETURN or VK_SPACE key.
        if (lpmsg->message == WM_KEYDOWN)
            if ((lpmsg->wParam == VK_RETURN) || (lpmsg->wParam == VK_SPACE))
                uRet |= DLGC_WANTMESSAGE;
    }
    return(uRet);
}
```

Table 4.2 *DLGC_* Values Used to Determine Which Keys a Control Wants to Process.*

Identifier	Value	Meaning
DLGC_WANTARROWS	0x0001	Control processes the arrow keys. Control receives WM_KEYUP and WM_KEYDOWN messages for the VK_LEFT, VK_RIGHT, VK_UP, and VK_DOWN keys. While the control has focus, default handling of the arrow keys is disabled.
DLGC_WANTTAB	0x0002	Control processes the Tab key. Control receives a WM_KEYUP, WM_KEYDOWN and WM_CHAR message for the VK_TAB key. Default handling of the Tab key is disabled while the control has focus. This means that you cannot tab out of the control!

Identifier	Value	Meaning
DLGC_WANTALLKEYS	0x0004	Control processes all keys. The control receives WM_KEYUP, WM_KEYDOWN, and WM_CHAR messages for all keys. Mnemonic handling and default processing for the arrow key and the, Tab, Return and Esc keys are all turned off. While this control has focus, all dialog box behavior will cease, with the exception of mnemonics that are entered with the Alt key held down.
DLGC_WANTMESSAGE	0x0004	Control wants to process a particular message. This is just a different name for DLGC_WANTALLKEYS. However, the different name is justified because DLGC_WANTALLKEYS is meant to be used when you literally want all keyboard messages (unconditionally), whereas DLGC_WANTMESSAGE is intended to be used when a control wants to conditionally take over the processing for a particular keyboard message. The keyboard message that caused the WM_ GETDLGCODE to be sent is available in the *lpmsg* parameter of the *OnGetDlgCode* message handler. If this message is one that you want to receive, you can return DLGC_WANTMESSAGE, and it will be sent to you. The *lpmsg* parameter will be NULL if WM_GETDLGCODE was not sent in response to a keyboard message.

continued...

Identifier	Value	Meaning
DLGC_WANTCHARS	0x0080	Control handles WM_CHAR messages. A control that returns this bit receives WM_CHAR messages. This does not include any of the special keys such as the arrow keys and the Return, Escape or Tab keys. Because the control takes over processing of character messages, dialog box mnemonics are turned off. (You must use the Alt key to access the mnemonic, as in an edit control.)

We now receive arrow keys in our BarGraph_OnKey function. When we get a VK_LEFT or VK_RIGHT key, we decrement or increment the selected bar, implementing "wrap-around" if we go left when the selected bar is at the far left or right when the selected bar is at the far right. If we get a VK_SPACE or VK_RETURN key, we notify our parent window of the user's choice by calling the same BarGraph_NotifyParent function that we used in BarGraph_OnLButtonUp.

```
void BarGraph_OnKey (HWND hwnd, UINT vk, BOOL fDown, int cRepeat, UINT flags) {

    if (fDown) {

        THISDATA* pthis = GETTHISDATA(hwnd);

        switch (vk) {

            case VK_LEFT:
            case VK_RIGHT:

                // Select the next bar to the left or right and wrap if need be
                pthis->nSelectedBar += ((vk == VK_LEFT) ? (pthis->cBars - 1) : 1);
                pthis->nSelectedBar %= pthis->cBars;
                InvalidateRect(hwnd, NULL, TRUE);
                break;

            case VK_RETURN:
            case VK_SPACE:
                BarGraph_NotifyParent(hwnd, NM_CLICK, pthis->nSelectedBar);
                break;
        }
    }
}
```

266

The Custom Control Application

The CustCntl application (**CustCntl.EXE**), shown in Listings 4.1-4.9, (starting on page 269) demonstrates one possible use for the legend and bargraph custom controls. When you invoke the application, the main application window shown in Figure 4.6 appears.

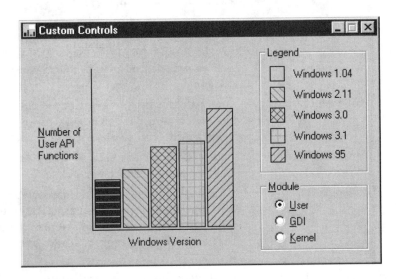

Figure 4.6 *The custom control application.*

As you can see, CustCntl graphs the number of API functions exported from User, GDI and Kernel for each major release of Windows to date. The graph depicts the total number of exports for each module rather than the subset that is documented by the Windows SDK. Nonetheless, by running CustCntl, you can see for yourself just how much the Windows operating system has grown since the days of Windows 1.0!

Table 4.3 describes the files used to create this application.

Table 4.3 *Files used to build the CustCntl application.*

File	Description
CustCntl.C	Contains *WinMain* and main window's dialog box and message cracker functions.

continued...

File	Description
Legend.C	Contains the implementation of the legend custom control. You can use this file in your own applications or modify it to suit your needs.
Legend.MSG	MsgCrack input file used to create **Legend.H** (see Appendix B for details).
Legend.H	Contains the window styles, messages, message APIs, message crackers and function prototypes for the legend custom control. Any source file that uses the legend custom control must include this file.
BarGraph.C	Contains the implementation of the bargraph custom control. You can use this file in your own applications or modify it to suit your needs.
BarGraph.MSG	MsgCrack input file used to create **BarGraph.H** (See Appendix B for details).
BarGraph.H	Contains the window styles, messages, message APIs, message crackers, and function prototypes for the bargraph custom control. Any source file that uses the bargraph custom control must include this file.
CustCntl.RC	Contains the dialog box template for the main application window and its icons.
Resource.H	Contains IDs for all resources in the RC file.
CustCtnl.ICO	Contains the icon for the main window.
CustCntl.MAK	Visual C++ project makefile.

The implementation of CustCntl is pretty cut-and-dry, so we won't go into it in much detail. The first step we take is to implement for our application a WinMain that registers the legend and bargraph control classes and invokes the main application dialog box containing the controls.

```
int WINAPI WinMain (HINSTANCE hinstExe, HINSTANCE hinstPrev,
   LPSTR lpszCmdLine, int nCmdShow) {

   // Register the legend and bar graph control classes.
   ATOM atomLegend = Legend_RegisterClass(hinstExe, FALSE);
   ATOM atomBarGraph = BarGraph_RegisterClass(hinstExe, FALSE);
```

```
    // Check that class registration succeeded.
    if ((atomLegend != INVALID_ATOM) && (atomBarGraph != INVALID_ATOM)) {

        // Create the application window.
        adgVERIFY(-1 != DialogBox(hinstExe, MAKEINTRESOURCE(IDD_CUSTCNTL),
            NULL, CustCntl_DlgProc));
    }

    // Unregister window classes.
    if (atomLegend != INVALID_ATOM)
        Legend_UnregisterClass(hinstExe);
    if (atomBarGraph != INVALID_ATOM)
        BarGraph_UnregisterClass(hinstExe);

    return(0);
}
```

The rest of the code for CustCntl basically talks to the controls in
the dialog box through our bargraph and legend API functions. In
our CustCntl_OnInitDialog, we allocate an array of BAR structures
for the bargraph control and assign a brush and a height to each
BAR in the array. These same brushes are also assigned to the corresponding legend controls. In our CustCntl_OnDestroy function, we
delete the brushes and free the BAR array.

To handle user input notifications, we implement a handler for
any WM_NOTIFY messages that might be sent from the bargraph
control. This handler simply puts up a message box displaying more
information about the bar that was clicked on. We also implement
a CustCntl_OnCommand handler so that when someone clicks on
one of the radio buttons in the dialog box we can change the heights
of the bar graph bars to reflect the chosen Windows module.

Listing 4.1 *CustCntl.C*

CustCntl.ICO

```
/*****************************************************************************
Module name: CustCntl.c
Written by: Jonathan Locke
Notices: Copyright (c) 1995 Jeffrey Richter
Purpose: Application to demonstrate use of bar graphs and legends.
*****************************************************************************/


#include "..\Win95ADG.h"        /* See Appendix A for details */
#include <windows.h>
#include <windowsx.h>
#pragma warning(disable: 4001)  /* Single line comment */
```

```
#include <commctrl.h>
#include <stdio.h>
#include <tchar.h>
#include "Resource.h"
#include "Legend.h"
#include "BarGraph.h"


//////////////////////////////////////////////////////////////////////


// IDs of first and last legend controls and total number of legends
#define FIRST_LEGEND   IDC_LEGEND0
#define LAST_LEGEND    IDC_LEGEND4
#define NUM_LEGENDS    (LAST_LEGEND - FIRST_LEGEND + 1)


//////////////////////////////////////////////////////////////////////


// The height of our API graph (in units of 1 API function)
#define APIGRAPH_HEIGHT 750


//////////////////////////////////////////////////////////////////////


void CustCntl_SetBars (HWND hwnd, int nIDC) {

   int i;
   HWND hwndBarGraph = GetDlgItem(hwnd, IDC_BARGRAPH);
   int cBars = BarGraph_GetCount(hwndBarGraph);
   BAR* pbar = BarGraph_GetBars(hwndBarGraph);

   //    Windows Version      1.04 2.11 3.0  3.1  '95
   //                         ---- ---- ---- ---- ----
   int anAPICallsUser[] =   { 236, 283, 387, 413, 563 };
   int anAPICallsKernel[] = { 103, 141, 192, 233, 707 };
   int anAPICallsGDI[] =    { 183, 213, 235, 283, 332 };

   if (pbar) {

      int *pnAPICalls = NULL;

      switch (nIDC) {

         case IDC_GDI:
            pnAPICalls = anAPICallsGDI;
            SetDlgItemText(hwnd, IDC_APILABEL,
               __TEXT("&Number of GDI API Functions"));
            break;

         case IDC_USER:
            pnAPICalls = anAPICallsUser;
            SetDlgItemText(hwnd, IDC_APILABEL,
```

```
              __TEXT("&Number of User API Functions"));
         break;

      case IDC_KERNEL:
         pnAPICalls = anAPICallsKernel;
         SetDlgItemText(hwnd, IDC_APILABEL,
            __TEXT("&Number of Kernel API Functions"));
         break;
   }

   // Change the heights of each bar.
   for (i = 0; i < cBars; i++)
      pbar[i].nHeight = pnAPICalls[i];

   // Set the bar graph's bars to our new bars.
   BarGraph_SetBars(hwndBarGraph, cBars, pbar);
   }
}


/////////////////////////////////////////////////////////////////////////////


BOOL CustCntl_OnInitDialog (HWND hwnd, HWND hwndFocus, LPARAM lParam) {

   int i;
   HWND hwndBarGraph;
   int cBars;
   BAR* pbar;

   LOGBRUSH alb[] = {
      { BS_HATCHED, RGB(0, 255, 255), HS_HORIZONTAL },
      { BS_HATCHED, RGB(255, 0, 255), HS_FDIAGONAL },
      { BS_HATCHED, RGB(255, 0, 0),   HS_DIAGCROSS },
      { BS_HATCHED, RGB(0, 255, 0),   HS_CROSS    },
      { BS_HATCHED, RGB(0, 0, 255),   HS_BDIAGONAL }
   };

   cBars = NUM_LEGENDS;
   pbar = malloc(sizeof(BAR) * cBars);
   adgASSERT(pbar);
   hwndBarGraph = GetDlgItem(hwnd, IDC_BARGRAPH);
   if (pbar != NULL) {

      // Set brushes of legend controls and bar graph bars. Set heights to
      // zero for now.
      for (i = 0; i < cBars; i++) {
         pbar[i].hbr = CreateBrushIndirect(&alb[i]);
         pbar[i].nHeight = 0;
         if (pbar[i].hbr != NULL) {
            Legend_SetBoxBrush(GetDlgItem(hwnd, FIRST_LEGEND + i),
               pbar[i].hbr);
         }
      }
```

```
            // Set the array of bars for our API bar graph and specify the height
            // (in units of one API) of the graph.
            BarGraph_SetBars(hwndBarGraph, cBars, pbar);
            BarGraph_SetHeight(hwndBarGraph, APIGRAPH_HEIGHT);

            // Initially, select the IDC_USER radio button and set the bar graph's
            // bars based on this selection.
            CheckRadioButton(hwnd, IDC_USER, IDC_KERNEL, IDC_USER);
            CustCntl_SetBars(hwnd, IDC_USER);
        } else {

            // If memory allocation failed, then end the dialog box before it has a
            // chance to show up on the screen.
            BarGraph_SetBars(hwndBarGraph, 0, NULL);
            EndDialog(hwnd, FALSE);
        }
        adgSETDLGICONS(hwnd, IDI_CUSTCNTL, IDI_CUSTCNTL);
        return(TRUE);              // Accept default focus window.
}


///////////////////////////////////////////////////////////////////////////////


void CustCntl_OnDestroy (HWND hwnd) {

    int i;

    // Destroy the brushes assigned to each control.
    for (i = 0; i < NUM_LEGENDS; i++) {

        HBRUSH hbr = Legend_GetBoxBrush(GetDlgItem(hwnd, FIRST_LEGEND + i));
        if (hbr != NULL)
            DeleteObject(hbr);
    }

    // Destroy the array of BAR structures allocated in CustCntl_OnInitDialog.
    // It is valid to pass NULL to free, which can occur if the malloc in
    // OnInitDialog fails.
    free(BarGraph_GetBars(GetDlgItem(hwnd, IDC_BARGRAPH)));
}


///////////////////////////////////////////////////////////////////////////////


// Simple routine to get rid of accelerator characters in psrc by removing ALL
// ampersands (including '&&' escapes).
void RemoveAccelerators (PTSTR psrc) {

    PTSTR pdest = psrc;
    for (; *psrc; psrc++) {
        if (*psrc != __TEXT('&'))
            *pdest++ = *psrc;
    }
```

```
    *pdest = 0;
}


/////////////////////////////////////////////////////////////////////////////


// For a set of radio buttons with ids between idcFirst and idcLast,
// inclusive, return the first radio button that is checked. This handy
// function could be used in any application.
int GetRadioCheck (HWND hwnd, int idcFirst, int idcLast) {

    int idc;
    for (idc = idcFirst; idc <= idcLast; idc++) {
        if (IsDlgButtonChecked(hwnd, idc))
            return(idc);
    }
    return(-1);
}


/////////////////////////////////////////////////////////////////////////////


LRESULT CustCntl_OnNotify (HWND hwnd, int idCtl, NMHDR* pnmh) {

    BARGRAPH_NOTIFY* pbgn;

    switch (idCtl) {

        case IDC_BARGRAPH:
            pbgn = (BARGRAPH_NOTIFY*) pnmh;
            if (pbgn->nmh.code == NM_CLICK) {

                TCHAR sz[256];
                TCHAR szWindowsVersion[64];
                TCHAR szModule[64];
                int idcModule;

                // Get the name of the Windows version that was chosen.
                GetDlgItemText(hwnd, IDC_LEGEND0 + pbgn->uBar, szWindowsVersion,
                    adgARRAY_SIZE(szWindowsVersion));
                RemoveAccelerators(szWindowsVersion);

                // Get the name of the currently selected module.
                szModule[0] = 0;
                idcModule = GetRadioCheck(hwnd, IDC_USER, IDC_KERNEL);
                adgASSERT(idcModule != -1);
                if (idcModule != -1) {
                    GetDlgItemText(hwnd, idcModule, szModule,
                        adgARRAY_SIZE(szModule));
                    RemoveAccelerators(szModule);
                }

                // Format and display our message to the user.
```

273

```
            wsprintf(sz,
                __TEXT("You picked bar #%d.\r\n")
                __TEXT("%s %s - %d API calls."),
                pbgn->uBar + 1,
                szWindowsVersion,
                szModule,
                BarGraph_GetBars(GetDlgItem(hwnd, idCtl))[pbgn->uBar]);
            MessageBox(hwnd, sz, __TEXT("Notification"), MB_OK);
        }
        break;
    }
    return(0);
}


//////////////////////////////////////////////////////////////////////////////


void CustCntl_OnCommand (HWND hwnd, int id, HWND hwndCtl, UINT codeNotify) {

    switch (id) {

        case IDC_KERNEL:
        case IDC_USER:
        case IDC_GDI:
            CustCntl_SetBars(hwnd, id);
            break;

        case IDCANCEL:          // Allows dialog box to close
            EndDialog(hwnd, id);
            break;
    }
}


//////////////////////////////////////////////////////////////////////////////


// This function processes messages sent to CustCntl's dialog box.
BOOL WINAPI CustCntl_DlgProc (HWND hwnd, UINT uMsg,
    WPARAM wParam, LPARAM lParam) {

    switch (uMsg) {

        // Standard Window's messages
        adgHANDLE_DLGMSG(hwnd, WM_INITDIALOG, CustCntl_OnInitDialog);
        adgHANDLE_DLGMSG(hwnd, WM_DESTROY,    CustCntl_OnDestroy);
        adgHANDLE_DLGMSG(hwnd, WM_COMMAND,    CustCntl_OnCommand);
        adgHANDLE_DLGMSG(hwnd, WM_NOTIFY,     CustCntl_OnNotify);
    }
    return(FALSE);          // We didn't process the message.
}


//////////////////////////////////////////////////////////////////////////////
```

```
int WINAPI WinMain (HINSTANCE hinstExe, HINSTANCE hinstPrev,
   LPSTR lpszCmdLine, int nCmdShow) {

   // Register the legend and bar graph control classes.
   ATOM atomLegend = Legend_RegisterClass(hinstExe, FALSE);
   ATOM atomBarGraph = BarGraph_RegisterClass(hinstExe, FALSE);


   adgWARNIFUNICODEUNDERWIN95();

   // Check whether class registration succeeded.
   if ((atomLegend != INVALID_ATOM) && (atomBarGraph != INVALID_ATOM)) {

      // Create the application window.
      adgVERIFY(-1 != DialogBox(hinstExe, MAKEINTRESOURCE(IDD_CUSTCNTL),
         NULL, CustCntl_DlgProc));
   }

   // Unregister window classes.
   if (atomLegend != INVALID_ATOM)
      Legend_UnregisterClass(hinstExe);
   if (atomBarGraph != INVALID_ATOM)
      BarGraph_UnregisterClass(hinstExe);

   return(0);
}

//////////////////////////////// End of File ////////////////////////////////////
```

Listing 4.2 *Legend.C*

```
/*****************************************************************************
Module name: Legend.c
Written by: Jonathan Locke
Notices: Copyright (c) 1995 Jeffrey Richter
Purpose: Legend custom control implementation file.
*****************************************************************************/


#include "..\Win95ADG.h"          /* See Appendix A for details */
#include <windows.h>
#include <windowsx.h>
#pragma warning(disable: 4001)  /* Single line comment */
#include <stdio.h>
#include <tchar.h>
#include "Legend.h"


///////////////////////////////////////////////////////////////////////////


// The following structure is for the window extra bytes.
```

275

```
// For more information, see the macros presented in Appendix A.
typedef struct {
   HFONT hfont;            // Font to use for legend text
   HBRUSH hbr;             // Brush to fill legend's box with
   COLORREF crBk;          // Background color
   COLORREF crText;        // Text color
} LEGEND_WNDEXTRABYTES;


/////////////////////////////////////////////////////////////////////////////


BOOL Legend_OnCreate (HWND hwnd, CREATESTRUCT* pCreateStruct) {

   COLORREF crBk;
   HWND hwndParent = GetParent(hwnd);

   // Initialize default attributes
   SetWindowFont(hwnd, NULL, FALSE);

   // If our control's parent window is a dialog, get our default background
   // color with WM_CTLCOLORDLG, otherwise assume GetSysColor(COLOR_WINDOW).
   if (GetClassWord(hwndParent, GCW_ATOM) == 32770) {

      LOGBRUSH lb;
      HDC hdc = GetDC(hwndParent);
      HBRUSH hbr = (HBRUSH)SendMessage(hwndParent, WM_CTLCOLORDLG,
         (WPARAM)hdc, (LPARAM)hwndParent);
      ReleaseDC(hwndParent, hdc);
      GetObject(hbr, sizeof lb, (LPVOID)&lb);
      crBk = lb.lbColor;
   } else {
      crBk = GetSysColor(COLOR_WINDOW);
   }

   Legend_SetBkColor(hwnd, crBk);
   Legend_SetBoxBrush(hwnd, GetStockObject(DKGRAY_BRUSH));
   Legend_SetTextColor(hwnd, GetSysColor(COLOR_WINDOWTEXT));
   return(TRUE);
}


/////////////////////////////////////////////////////////////////////////////


void WINAPI Legend_OnSetFont (HWND hwnd, HFONT hfontNew, BOOL fRedraw) {

   adgASSERT((hfontNew == NULL) || (OBJ_FONT == GetObjectType(hfontNew)));
   adgSETWINDOWLONG(hwnd, LEGEND_WNDEXTRABYTES, hfont, hfontNew);
   if (fRedraw)
      InvalidateRect(hwnd, NULL, FALSE);
}


/////////////////////////////////////////////////////////////////////////////
```

```
HFONT WINAPI Legend_OnGetFont (HWND hwnd) {

    return((HFONT) adgGETWINDOWLONG(hwnd, LEGEND_WNDEXTRABYTES, hfont));
}


///////////////////////////////////////////////////////////////////////////


void Legend_OnPaint (HWND hwnd) {

    RECT rcClient, rcBox;
    PAINTSTRUCT ps;
    HFONT hfont, hfontOriginal = NULL;
    HBRUSH hbrOriginal;
    SIZE size;
    LPTSTR psz;
    int nTextLength, nBoxSide, nShrinkBox;

    // Start painting.
    BeginPaint(hwnd, &ps);

    // Set background and text colors.
    SetBkColor(ps.hdc, Legend_GetBkColor(hwnd));
    SetTextColor(ps.hdc, Legend_GetTextColor(hwnd));

    // Calculate the size of our legend box based on the client rect and the
    // window style. If the LS_BIGBOX window style is set, then we shrink the
    // box area by 1/6th of its size; otherwise, we shrink it by 1/4th. These
    // values were arbitrarily determined to look good through experimentation.
    GetClientRect(hwnd, &rcClient);
    nBoxSide = rcClient.bottom;
    SetRect(&rcBox, 0, 0, nBoxSide, nBoxSide);
    nShrinkBox = -(nBoxSide / (GetWindowStyle(hwnd) & LS_BIGBOX ? 6 : 4));
    InflateRect(&rcBox, nShrinkBox, nShrinkBox);

    // If we have a border around the box, draw it and shrink rcBox by one.
    if (GetWindowStyle(hwnd) & LS_BOXBORDER) {
        HBRUSH hbrFrame = CreateSolidBrush(GetTextColor(ps.hdc));
        FrameRect(ps.hdc, &rcBox, hbrFrame);
        DeleteBrush(hbrFrame);
        InflateRect(&rcBox, -1, -1);
    }

    // Fill the box with the appropriate brush.
    SetBrushOrgEx(ps.hdc, 0, 0, NULL);
    hbrOriginal = SelectBrush(ps.hdc, Legend_GetBoxBrush(hwnd));
    PatBlt(ps.hdc, rcBox.left, rcBox.top, rcBox.right - rcBox.left,
        rcBox.bottom - rcBox.top, PATCOPY);
    SelectBrush(ps.hdc, hbrOriginal);

    // If we drew a border, restore rcBox to it's original size.
    if (GetWindowStyle(hwnd) & LS_BOXBORDER)
        InflateRect(&rcBox, 1, 1);
```

```
        // Exclude rcBox (everything we have drawn so far) from the clipping region
        // so that we can use ExtTextOut to fill in the control's background and draw
        // the text at the same time without blinking.
        ExcludeClipRect(ps.hdc, rcBox.left, rcBox.top, rcBox.right, rcBox.bottom);

        // Allocate a buffer of sufficient size to hold the window text and then
        // call GetWindowText to retrieve it. The _alloca function allocates
        // storage from the stack. This memory is automatically freed when our
        // function returns.
        nTextLength = GetWindowTextLength(hwnd);
        psz = _alloca((nTextLength + 1) * sizeof(TCHAR));
        GetWindowText(hwnd, psz, nTextLength + 1);

        // Draw the window text, vertically centered, to the right of the box.
        // ETO_OPAQUE causes the background to be filled with the current
        // background color at the same time. The arbitrary offset of (nBoxSide / 3)
        // is used to add some padding space between the box and the text string.
        hfont = GetWindowFont(hwnd);
        if (hfont != NULL)
            hfontOriginal = SelectFont(ps.hdc, hfont);
        GetTextExtentPoint32(ps.hdc, psz, nTextLength, &size);
        ExtTextOut(ps.hdc, nBoxSide + (nBoxSide / 3),
            (rcClient.bottom - size.cy) / 2, ETO_OPAQUE | ETO_CLIPPED,
            &rcClient, psz, nTextLength, NULL);
        if (hfont != NULL)
            SelectFont(ps.hdc, hfontOriginal);

        // Done painting.
        EndPaint(hwnd, &ps);
    }


///////////////////////////////////////////////////////////////////////////


void Legend_OnSetText (HWND hwnd, LPCTSTR lpszText) {

    // We must call DefWindowProc here instead of SetWindowText because
    // SetWindowText sends a WM_SETTEXT message, which results in infinite
    // recursion. DefWindowProc actually sets the text.
    FORWARD_WM_SETTEXT(hwnd, lpszText, DefWindowProc);

    // Force control to redraw with new text.
    InvalidateRect(hwnd, NULL, FALSE);
    }


///////////////////////////////////////////////////////////////////////////


void WINAPI Legend_OnSetBoxBrush (HWND hwnd, HBRUSH hbrNew) {

    // Check window and brush handles for validity.
    adgASSERT(OBJ_BRUSH == GetObjectType(hbrNew));

    // Set the new brush and trigger a repaint.
```

```
   adgSETWINDOWLONG(hwnd, LEGEND_WNDEXTRABYTES, hbr, hbrNew);
   InvalidateRect(hwnd, NULL, FALSE);
}


/////////////////////////////////////////////////////////////////////////


HBRUSH WINAPI Legend_OnGetBoxBrush (HWND hwnd) {

   // Return the current brush handle stored in the window extra bytes.
   return((HBRUSH) adgGETWINDOWLONG(hwnd, LEGEND_WNDEXTRABYTES, hbr));
}


/////////////////////////////////////////////////////////////////////////


void WINAPI Legend_OnSetBkColor (HWND hwnd, COLORREF crBkNew) {

   adgSETWINDOWLONG(hwnd, LEGEND_WNDEXTRABYTES, crBk, crBkNew);
   InvalidateRect(hwnd, NULL, TRUE);
}


/////////////////////////////////////////////////////////////////////////


COLORREF WINAPI Legend_OnGetBkColor (HWND hwnd) {

   return((COLORREF) adgGETWINDOWLONG(hwnd, LEGEND_WNDEXTRABYTES, crBk));
}


/////////////////////////////////////////////////////////////////////////


void WINAPI Legend_OnSetTextColor (HWND hwnd, COLORREF crTextNew) {

   adgSETWINDOWLONG(hwnd, LEGEND_WNDEXTRABYTES, crText, crTextNew);
   InvalidateRect(hwnd, NULL, TRUE);
}


/////////////////////////////////////////////////////////////////////////


COLORREF WINAPI Legend_OnGetTextColor (HWND hwnd) {

   return((COLORREF) adgGETWINDOWLONG(hwnd, LEGEND_WNDEXTRABYTES, crText));
}


/////////////////////////////////////////////////////////////////////////
```

279

```
LRESULT WINAPI Legend_WndProc (HWND hwnd, UINT uMsg,
   WPARAM wParam, LPARAM lParam) {

   switch (uMsg) {

      // Standard Windows messages
      HANDLE_MSG(hwnd, WM_CREATE,       Legend_OnCreate);
      HANDLE_MSG(hwnd, WM_PAINT,        Legend_OnPaint);
      HANDLE_MSG(hwnd, WM_SETTEXT,      Legend_OnSetText);
      HANDLE_MSG(hwnd, WM_SETFONT,      Legend_OnSetFont);
      HANDLE_MSG(hwnd, WM_GETFONT,      Legend_OnGetFont);

      // Legend control class-specific messages
      HANDLE_MSG(hwnd, LM_SETBOXBRUSH,  Legend_OnSetBoxBrush);
      HANDLE_MSG(hwnd, LM_GETBOXBRUSH,  Legend_OnGetBoxBrush);
      HANDLE_MSG(hwnd, LM_SETBKCOLOR,   Legend_OnSetBkColor);
      HANDLE_MSG(hwnd, LM_GETBKCOLOR,   Legend_OnGetBkColor);
      HANDLE_MSG(hwnd, LM_SETTEXTCOLOR, Legend_OnSetTextColor);
      HANDLE_MSG(hwnd, LM_GETTEXTCOLOR, Legend_OnGetTextColor);
   }
   return(DefWindowProc(hwnd, uMsg, wParam, lParam));
}


/////////////////////////////////////////////////////////////////////////


ATOM WINAPI Legend_RegisterClass (HINSTANCE hinst, BOOL fGlobalClass) {

   WNDCLASSEX wc;

   adgINITSTRUCT(wc, TRUE);
   wc.style          = CS_HREDRAW | CS_VREDRAW;
   wc.lpfnWndProc    = Legend_WndProc;
   wc.cbWndExtra     = sizeof(LEGEND_WNDEXTRABYTES);
   wc.hInstance      = hinst;
   wc.hCursor        = LoadCursor(NULL, IDC_ARROW);
   wc.lpszClassName  = WC_LEGEND;

   if (fGlobalClass)
      wc.style |= CS_GLOBALCLASS;

   return(RegisterClassEx(&wc));
}


/////////////////////////////////////////////////////////////////////////


BOOL WINAPI Legend_UnregisterClass (HINSTANCE hinst) {

   return(UnregisterClass(WC_LEGEND, hinst));
}


///////////////////////////// End of File /////////////////////////////////
```

Listing 4.3 *Legend.MSG*

```
// Module name: Legend.msg
// Written by: Jonathan Locke
// Notices: Copyright (c) 1995 Jeffrey Richter
// Purpose: 'MsgCrack' input file for legend control.

MessageBase WM_USER
MessageClass Legend

Message LM_SETBOXBRUSH SetBoxBrush \
 - Sets the brush used to fill legend's box. The brush is only used by the\
 control. It is owned by the caller. The caller must create and destroy\
 the brush.
wParam HBRUSH hbrNew - New brush
.

Message LM_GETBOXBRUSH GetBoxBrush \
 - Returns HBRUSH being used to fill legend's box.
Returns HBRUSH - Current box brush
.

Message LM_SETBKCOLOR SetBkColor \
 - Sets the background color of a legend control.
lParam COLORREF crNew - New background color
.

Message LM_GETBKCOLOR GetBkColor \
 - Gets the background color of a legend control.
Returns COLORREF - Current background color
.

Message LM_SETTEXTCOLOR SetTextColor \
 - Sets the text color of a legend control.
lParam COLORREF crNew - New text color
.

Message LM_GETTEXTCOLOR GetTextColor \
 - Gets the text color of a legend control.
Returns COLORREF - Current text color
.
```

Listing 4.4 *Legend.H*

```
/***************************************************************************
Module name: Legend.h
Written by: Jonathan Locke
Notices: Copyright (c) 1995 Jeffrey Richter
Purpose: Legend custom control header file.
***************************************************************************/
```

281

```
////////////////////////////// Class Name //////////////////////////////////


// ANSI/Unicode declarations for legend's window class name
#define WC_LEGENDA "Legend"
#define WC_LEGENDW L"Legend"
#ifdef UNICODE
#define WC_LEGEND WC_LEGENDW
#else
#define WC_LEGEND WC_LEGENDA
#endif



/////////////////////// Class-Specific Window Styles ///////////////////////////


#define LS_SMALLBOX      0x00000000
#define LS_BIGBOX        0x00000001
#define LS_BOXBORDER     0x00000002



////////////////////////////// Class Registration ////////////////////////////////


// Register and unregister the legend window class.
ATOM WINAPI Legend_RegisterClass(HINSTANCE hinst, BOOL fGlobalClass);
BOOL WINAPI Legend_UnregisterClass(HINSTANCE hinst);



/////////////////////////////// Parent Notification //////////////////////////////


// Legend controls have no class-specific notification codes at this time.



/////////////////////// Class-Specific Window Messages ///////////////////////////


//{{adgMSGCRACK_MESSAGES

// Purpose: Sets the brush used to fill legend's box. The brush is used only by
//          the control. It is owned by the caller. The caller must create
//          and destroy the brush.
// wParam:  HBRUSH hbrNew - New brush
// lParam:  N/A
// Returns: void
#define LM_SETBOXBRUSH    (WM_USER + 0)

// Purpose: Returns HBRUSH being used to fill legend's box.
// wParam:  N/A
// lParam:  N/A
// Returns: HBRUSH - Current box brush
#define LM_GETBOXBRUSH    (WM_USER + 1)

// Purpose: Sets the background color of a legend control.
```

```
// wParam:  N/A
// lParam:  COLORREF crNew - New background color
// Returns: void
#define LM_SETBKCOLOR    (WM_USER + 2)

// Purpose: Gets the background color of a legend control.
// wParam:  N/A
// lParam:  N/A
// Returns: COLORREF - Current background color
#define LM_GETBKCOLOR    (WM_USER + 3)

// Purpose: Sets the text color of a legend control.
// wParam:  N/A
// lParam:  COLORREF crNew - New text color
// Returns: void
#define LM_SETTEXTCOLOR    (WM_USER + 4)

// Purpose: Gets the text color of a legend control.
// wParam:  N/A
// lParam:  N/A
// Returns: COLORREF - Current text color
#define LM_GETTEXTCOLOR    (WM_USER + 5)

//}}adgMSGCRACK_MESSAGES


///////////////////////// Legend Control Message APIs /////////////////////////


//{{adgMSGCRACK_APIS

#define Legend_SetBoxBrush(hwnd, hbrNew) \
   ((void)SendMessage((hwnd), LM_SETBOXBRUSH, (WPARAM)(DWORD)(hbrNew), 0))

#define Legend_GetBoxBrush(hwnd) \
   ((HBRUSH )SendMessage((hwnd), LM_GETBOXBRUSH, 0, 0))

#define Legend_SetBkColor(hwnd, crNew) \
   ((void)SendMessage((hwnd), LM_SETBKCOLOR, 0, (LPARAM)(DWORD)(crNew)))

#define Legend_GetBkColor(hwnd) \
   ((COLORREF )SendMessage((hwnd), LM_GETBKCOLOR, 0, 0))

#define Legend_SetTextColor(hwnd, crNew) \
   ((void)SendMessage((hwnd), LM_SETTEXTCOLOR, 0, (LPARAM)(DWORD)(crNew)))

#define Legend_GetTextColor(hwnd) \
   ((COLORREF )SendMessage((hwnd), LM_GETTEXTCOLOR, 0, 0))

//}}adgMSGCRACK_APIS


////////////////////////////// Message Crackers //////////////////////////////


//{{adgMSGCRACK_CRACKERS
```

```
// void Cls_OnSetBoxBrush(HWND hwnd, HBRUSH hbrNew)
#define HANDLE_LM_SETBOXBRUSH(hwnd, wParam, lParam, fn) \
   ((fn)((hwnd), (HBRUSH)(wParam)), 0)
#define FORWARD_LM_SETBOXBRUSH(hwnd, hbrNew, fn) \
   (void)((fn)((hwnd), LM_SETBOXBRUSH, (WPARAM)(DWORD)(hbrNew), 0))

// HBRUSH Cls_OnGetBoxBrush(HWND hwnd)
#define HANDLE_LM_GETBOXBRUSH(hwnd, wParam, lParam, fn) \
   (LRESULT)(fn)((hwnd))
#define FORWARD_LM_GETBOXBRUSH(hwnd, fn) \
   (HBRUSH )((fn)((hwnd), LM_GETBOXBRUSH, 0, 0))

// void Cls_OnSetBkColor(HWND hwnd, COLORREF crNew)
#define HANDLE_LM_SETBKCOLOR(hwnd, wParam, lParam, fn) \
   ((fn)((hwnd), (COLORREF)(lParam)), 0)
#define FORWARD_LM_SETBKCOLOR(hwnd, crNew, fn) \
   (void)((fn)((hwnd), LM_SETBKCOLOR, 0, (LPARAM)(DWORD)(crNew)))

// COLORREF Cls_OnGetBkColor(HWND hwnd)
#define HANDLE_LM_GETBKCOLOR(hwnd, wParam, lParam, fn) \
   (LRESULT)(fn)((hwnd))
#define FORWARD_LM_GETBKCOLOR(hwnd, fn) \
   (COLORREF )((fn)((hwnd), LM_GETBKCOLOR, 0, 0))

// void Cls_OnSetTextColor(HWND hwnd, COLORREF crNew)
#define HANDLE_LM_SETTEXTCOLOR(hwnd, wParam, lParam, fn) \
   ((fn)((hwnd), (COLORREF)(lParam)), 0)
#define FORWARD_LM_SETTEXTCOLOR(hwnd, crNew, fn) \
   (void)((fn)((hwnd), LM_SETTEXTCOLOR, 0, (LPARAM)(DWORD)(crNew)))

// COLORREF Cls_OnGetTextColor(HWND hwnd)
#define HANDLE_LM_GETTEXTCOLOR(hwnd, wParam, lParam, fn) \
   (LRESULT)(fn)((hwnd))
#define FORWARD_LM_GETTEXTCOLOR(hwnd, fn) \
   (COLORREF )((fn)((hwnd), LM_GETTEXTCOLOR, 0, 0))

//}}adgMSGCRACK_CRACKERS


/////////////////////////////// End of File ///////////////////////////////
```

Listing 4.5 *BarGraph.C*

```
/*****************************************************************************
Module name: BarGraph.c
Written by: Jonathan Locke
Notices: Copyright (c) 1995 Jeffrey Richter
Purpose: BarGraph custom control implementation file.
*****************************************************************************/


#include "..\Win95ADG.h"          /* See Appendix A for details */
#include <windows.h>
```

```
#include <windowsx.h>
#pragma warning(disable: 4001)      /* Single line comment */
#include <stdio.h>
#include <tchar.h>
#include <commctrl.h>
#include "BarGraph.h"


//////////////////////////////////////////////////////////////////////////


typedef struct {
   UINT nHeight;                    // Bar graph's height (in user-defined units)
   UINT cBars;                      // Number of bars in the graph
   BAR* pbar;                       // Array of bars to draw
   UINT nSelectedBar;               // Bar to highlight when focused
   UINT nMouseDownBar;              // Bar where mouse button went down
   UINT nCancelBar;                 // Bar to reselect if choice is canceled
   COLORREF crBk;                   // Background color
   COLORREF crText;                 // Text color
} THISDATA;


//////////////////////////////////////////////////////////////////////////


// The following structure is for the window extra bytes.
// For more information, see the macros presented in appendix A.
typedef struct {
   THISDATA* pthis;
} BARGRAPH_WNDEXTRABYTES;


//////////////////////////////////////////////////////////////////////////


// Macros to get and set the THISDATA pointer stored in the window extra bytes
#define GETTHISDATA(hwnd) \
   ((THISDATA*) adgGETWINDOWLONG(hwnd, BARGRAPH_WNDEXTRABYTES, pthis))
#define SETTHISDATA(hwnd, pthisNew) \
   adgSETWINDOWLONG(hwnd, BARGRAPH_WNDEXTRABYTES, pthis, pthisNew);


//////////////////////////////////////////////////////////////////////////


#define INVALID_BAR ((UINT)-1)


//////////////////////////////////////////////////////////////////////////


BOOL BarGraph_OnCreate (HWND hwnd, CREATESTRUCT* pcs) {

   COLORREF crBk;
   HWND hwndParent = GetParent(hwnd);
```

285

```
   // Allocate memory for a THISDATA structure and store a pointer to it in
   // the window extra bytes.
   THISDATA* pthis = malloc(sizeof(THISDATA));
   adgASSERT(pthis != NULL);
   SETTHISDATA(hwnd, pthis);

   // If our control's parent window is a dialog, get our default background
   // color with WM_CTLCOLORDLG, otherwise assume GetSysColor(COLOR_WINDOW).
   if (GetClassWord(hwndParent, GCW_ATOM) == 32770) {

      LOGBRUSH lb;
      HDC hdc = GetDC(hwndParent);
      HBRUSH hbr = (HBRUSH)SendMessage(hwndParent, WM_CTLCOLORDLG,
         (WPARAM)hdc, (LPARAM)hwndParent);
      ReleaseDC(hwndParent, hdc);
      GetObject(hbr, sizeof lb, (LPVOID)&lb);
      crBk = lb.lbColor;
   } else {
      crBk = GetSysColor(COLOR_WINDOW);
   }

   // If our allocation succeeds, we set some default values
   if (pthis != NULL) {
      BarGraph_SetHeight(hwnd, 100);
      BarGraph_SetBars(hwnd, 0, NULL);
      BarGraph_SetBkColor(hwnd, crBk);
      BarGraph_SetTextColor(hwnd, GetSysColor(COLOR_WINDOWTEXT));
      pthis->nSelectedBar = 0;
   }

   // If our allocation fails, we return FALSE, and the window is destroyed.
   return(pthis != NULL);
}


/////////////////////////////////////////////////////////////////////////////


void BarGraph_OnDestroy (HWND hwnd) {

   // NOTE: ANSI C states that it is OK to pass NULL to free.
   // This can happen if malloc fails in BarGraph_OnCreate.
   THISDATA* pthis = GETTHISDATA(hwnd);
   free(pthis);
}


/////////////////////////////////////////////////////////////////////////////


UINT BarGraph_OnGetDlgCode (HWND hwnd, LPMSG lpmsg) {

   // We want to process the arrow keys unconditionally.
   UINT uRet = DLGC_WANTARROWS;

   // If lpmsg is not NULL, it points to the keyboard message that generated
```

```
        // the current WM_GETDLGCODE message.
        if (lpmsg != NULL) {

            // We want to override the default processing if the keyboard message is
            // a WM_KEYDOWN produced by the VK_RETURN or VK_SPACE key.
            if (lpmsg->message == WM_KEYDOWN)
                if ((lpmsg->wParam == VK_RETURN) || (lpmsg->wParam == VK_SPACE))
                    uRet |= DLGC_WANTMESSAGE;
        }
        return(uRet);
}


/////////////////////////////////////////////////////////////////////////////


RECT* BarGraph_GetBarRect (HWND hwnd, UINT n, RECT* prc) {

    RECT rcClient;
    THISDATA* pthis = GETTHISDATA(hwnd);
    int cxClient, cyClient;

    // Check window handle, RECT pointer, and the value of n
    adgASSERT(IsWindow(hwnd));
    adgASSERT(prc != NULL);
    adgASSERT(n < pthis->cBars);

    // Get the size of the client area but don't include the axes lines on the
    // left and bottom.
    GetClientRect(hwnd, &rcClient);
    rcClient.left++;
    rcClient.bottom--;
    cxClient = rcClient.right - rcClient.left;
    cyClient = rcClient.bottom - rcClient.top;

    // This arbitrary value defines the spacing in pixels between bars
    #define BARSPACING 2

    // Find the left and right sides of bar n.
    #define BARTOCLIENT(uBar) (rcClient.left + \
        (int) (((__int64) cxClient * (uBar)) / pthis->cBars))
    prc->left = BARTOCLIENT(n) + BARSPACING;
    prc->right = BARTOCLIENT(n + 1);
    #undef BARTOCLIENT

    // Set the top based on the height of the bar and the height of the bar
    // graph (in user-defined units). Set the bottom to be the bottom of the
    // client area (minus BARSPACING to leave space between the bottom axis
    // line and the bottom of each bar).
    prc->top = rcClient.bottom -
        (int) (((__int64) cyClient * pthis->pbar[n].nHeight) / pthis->nHeight);
    prc->bottom = rcClient.bottom - BARSPACING;
    #undef BARSPACING


    return(prc);
}
```

```
///////////////////////////////////////////////////////////////////////////

UINT BarGraph_BarFromPoint (HWND hwnd, int x, int y) {

   UINT bar;
   RECT rcBar;
   THISDATA* pthis = GETTHISDATA(hwnd);
   POINT pt;
   pt.x = x;
   pt.y = y;

   // If point (x, y) is inside a bar, return the index of that bar.
   for (bar = 0; bar < pthis->cBars; bar++)
     if (PtInRect(BarGraph_GetBarRect(hwnd, bar, &rcBar), pt))
       return(bar);

   // Failed.  Point (x, y) is not inside any bar in the graph.
   return(INVALID_BAR);
}


///////////////////////////////////////////////////////////////////////////


void BarGraph_NotifyParent (HWND hwndCtl, UINT code, UINT uBar) {

   BARGRAPH_NOTIFY bgn;
   adgASSERT(IsWindow(hwndCtl));
   bgn.nmh.hwndFrom = hwndCtl;
   bgn.nmh.idFrom = GetWindowID(hwndCtl);
   bgn.nmh.code = code;
   bgn.uBar = uBar;
   FORWARD_WM_NOTIFY(GetParent(hwndCtl), bgn.nmh.idFrom, &bgn, SendMessage);
}


///////////////////////////////////////////////////////////////////////////


void BarGraph_OnLButtonDown (HWND hwnd, BOOL fDoubleClick, int x, int y,
   UINT keyFlags) {

   UINT bar = BarGraph_BarFromPoint(hwnd, x, y);
   if (bar != INVALID_BAR) {

      // If the user clicked on a valid bar, set nMouseDownBar and
      // nSelectedBar to the bar that was clicked on, saving the original
      // nSelectedBar in nCancelBar so that we can restore the old selection
      // if the user cancels. Then we force a repaint and set focus and mouse
      // capture.
      GETTHISDATA(hwnd)->nMouseDownBar = bar;
      GETTHISDATA(hwnd)->nCancelBar = GETTHISDATA(hwnd)->nSelectedBar;
      GETTHISDATA(hwnd)->nSelectedBar = bar;
      InvalidateRect(hwnd, NULL, FALSE);
      SetFocus(hwnd);
```

```
        SetCapture(hwnd);
    }
}


/////////////////////////////////////////////////////////////////////////////


void BarGraph_OnLButtonUp (HWND hwnd, int x, int y, UINT keyFlags) {

    // We will only respond to a mouse button up if we set capture previously
    // on a mouse button down.
    if (GetCapture() == hwnd) {

        // Get the bar we were over when the button was released.
        UINT bar = BarGraph_BarFromPoint(hwnd, x, y);

        // Releasing capture generates a WM_CAPTURECHANGED message, which sets
        // nSelectedBar to nCancelBar (canceling the selection by default).
        ReleaseCapture();

        // Check if the user let up the mouse on the same bar it went down on.
        if (bar == GETTHISDATA(hwnd)->nMouseDownBar) {

            // Change the currently selected bar.
            GETTHISDATA(hwnd)->nSelectedBar = bar;
            InvalidateRect(hwnd, NULL, FALSE);

            // Tell the parent which bar was clicked on.
            BarGraph_NotifyParent(hwnd, NM_CLICK, bar);
        }
    }
}


/////////////////////////////////////////////////////////////////////////////


void BarGraph_OnMouseMove (HWND hwnd, int x, int y, UINT keyFlags) {

    // If the mouse moves while we have capture
    if (GetCapture() == hwnd) {

        // Get the bar we are currently over.
        UINT bar = BarGraph_BarFromPoint(hwnd, x, y);
        UINT nSelectedBar = GETTHISDATA(hwnd)->nSelectedBar;

        // Check if the mouse is over the same bar the button went down on.
        if (bar == GETTHISDATA(hwnd)->nMouseDownBar) {

            // Highlight the bar we are over, if need be, to indicate that
            // releasing the mouse button will choose the current bar.
            if (nSelectedBar != bar) {
                GETTHISDATA(hwnd)->nSelectedBar = bar;
                InvalidateRect(hwnd, NULL, FALSE);
            }
```

```
        }
        else
        {
            // Since the user isn't over the bar where the mouse went down,
            // releasing the mouse button would be a cancel operation. So, we
            // highlight the cancel bar to indicate this, if need be.
            if (nSelectedBar != GETTHISDATA(hwnd)->nCancelBar) {
                GETTHISDATA(hwnd)->nSelectedBar = GETTHISDATA(hwnd)->nCancelBar;
                InvalidateRect(hwnd, NULL, FALSE);
            }
        }
    }
}


//////////////////////////////////////////////////////////////////////////////


void BarGraph_OnSetFocus (HWND hwnd, HWND hwndOldFocus) {

    // Cause a repaint so the focus indicator will be drawn.
    InvalidateRect(hwnd, NULL, FALSE);
}


//////////////////////////////////////////////////////////////////////////////


void BarGraph_OnKillFocus (HWND hwnd, HWND hwndNewFocus) {

    // If we have the capture, release it.
    if (GetCapture() == hwnd)
        ReleaseCapture();

    // Remove the focus indicator by causing a repaint.
    InvalidateRect(hwnd, NULL, FALSE);
}


//////////////////////////////////////////////////////////////////////////////


void BarGraph_OnCaptureChanged(HWND hwnd, HWND hwndNewCapture) {

    // If we are losing the capture, cancel the current selection.
    GETTHISDATA(hwnd)->nSelectedBar = GETTHISDATA(hwnd)->nCancelBar;
    InvalidateRect(hwnd, NULL, FALSE);
}


//////////////////////////////////////////////////////////////////////////////


void BarGraph_OnKey (HWND hwnd, UINT vk, BOOL fDown, int cRepeat, UINT flags) {

    if (fDown) {
```

```
        THISDATA* pthis = GETTHISDATA(hwnd);

    switch (vk) {

        case VK_LEFT:
        case VK_RIGHT:

            // Select the next bar to the left or right and wrap if need be
            pthis->nSelectedBar += ((vk == VK_LEFT) ? (pthis->cBars - 1) : 1);
            pthis->nSelectedBar %= pthis->cBars;
            InvalidateRect(hwnd, NULL, FALSE);
            break;

        case VK_RETURN:
        case VK_SPACE:
            BarGraph_NotifyParent(hwnd, NM_CLICK, pthis->nSelectedBar);
            break;
    }
  }
}


/////////////////////////////////////////////////////////////////////////////


void BarGraph_OnPaint (HWND hwnd) {

    PAINTSTRUCT ps;
    UINT bar;
    RECT rcClient, rcBar;
    HBRUSH hbrFrame, hbrOriginal, hbrBk;
    THISDATA* pthis = GETTHISDATA(hwnd);
    BOOL fHighlight;
    HPEN hpen, hpenOriginal;

    // Start painting.
    BeginPaint(hwnd, &ps);

    // Draw left and bottom axes of bar graph.
    GetClientRect(hwnd, &rcClient);
    hpen = CreatePen(PS_SOLID, 1, BarGraph_GetTextColor(hwnd));
    hpenOriginal = SelectObject(ps.hdc, hpen);
    MoveToEx(ps.hdc, rcClient.left, rcClient.top, NULL);
    LineTo(ps.hdc, rcClient.left, rcClient.bottom - 1);
    LineTo(ps.hdc, rcClient.right, rcClient.bottom - 1);
    SelectObject(ps.hdc, hpenOriginal);
    DeleteObject(hpen);
    rcClient.left++;
    rcClient.bottom--;

    // Draw each bar in the graph.
    for (bar = 0; bar < pthis->cBars; bar++) {

        // Get the bar's rectangle.
        BarGraph_GetBarRect(hwnd, bar, &rcBar);
```

```
        // Frame the rectangle.
        hbrFrame = CreateSolidBrush (BarGraph_GetTextColor(hwnd));
        FrameRect(ps.hdc, &rcBar, hbrFrame);
        DeleteBrush(hbrFrame);
        InflateRect(&rcBar, -1, -1);

        // Fill the bar with the appropriate brush. If the bar we are drawing is
        // the bar to highlight when we are focused (nSelectedBar), and we have
        // the focus, we use COLOR_HIGHLIGHT as the background color. Otherwise,
        // we use BarGraph_GetBkColor(hwnd).
        fHighlight = ((bar == pthis->nSelectedBar) && (GetFocus() == hwnd));
        SetBkColor(ps.hdc, fHighlight ? GetSysColor(COLOR_HIGHLIGHT) :
            BarGraph_GetBkColor(hwnd));
        SetBrushOrgEx(ps.hdc, 0, 0, NULL);
        hbrOriginal = SelectBrush(ps.hdc, pthis->pbar[bar].hbr);
        PatBlt(ps.hdc, rcBar.left, rcBar.top, rcBar.right - rcBar.left,
            rcBar.bottom - rcBar.top, PATCOPY);
        SelectBrush(ps.hdc, hbrOriginal);

        // Inflate rect back.
        InflateRect(&rcBar, 1, 1);

        // Exclude the bar from the clipping region.
        ExcludeClipRect(ps.hdc, rcBar.left, rcBar.top, rcBar.right, rcBar.bottom);
    }

    // Fill the client area with the background color.
    hbrBk = CreateSolidBrush(BarGraph_GetBkColor(hwnd));
    SetBrushOrgEx(ps.hdc, 0, 0, NULL);
    hbrOriginal = SelectBrush(ps.hdc, hbrBk);
    PatBlt(ps.hdc, rcClient.left, rcClient.top, rcClient.right - rcClient.left,
        rcClient.bottom - rcClient.top, PATCOPY);
    SelectBrush(ps.hdc, hbrOriginal);
    DeleteObject(hbrBk);

    // Done painting.
    EndPaint(hwnd, &ps);
}


//////////////////////////////////////////////////////////////////////////


BAR* WINAPI BarGraph_OnGetBars (HWND hwnd) {

    return(GETTHISDATA(hwnd)->pbar);
}


//////////////////////////////////////////////////////////////////////////


UINT WINAPI BarGraph_OnGetCount (HWND hwnd) {

    return(GETTHISDATA(hwnd)->cBars);
}
```

```
//////////////////////////////////////////////////////////////////////////

void WINAPI BarGraph_OnSetBars (HWND hwnd, UINT cBars, BAR* pbar) {

   THISDATA* pthis;
   pthis = GETTHISDATA(hwnd);
   pthis->pbar = pbar;
   pthis->cBars = cBars;
   pthis->nSelectedBar = 0;

   // Our data changed, so we need to force a repaint.
   InvalidateRect(hwnd, NULL, FALSE);
}


//////////////////////////////////////////////////////////////////////////


UINT WINAPI BarGraph_OnGetHeight (HWND hwnd) {

   return(GETTHISDATA(hwnd)->nHeight);
}


//////////////////////////////////////////////////////////////////////////


void WINAPI BarGraph_OnSetHeight (HWND hwnd, UINT nHeightNew) {

   GETTHISDATA(hwnd)->nHeight = nHeightNew;

   // Our data changed, so we need to force a repaint.
   InvalidateRect(hwnd, NULL, FALSE);
}


//////////////////////////////////////////////////////////////////////////


void WINAPI BarGraph_OnSetBkColor (HWND hwnd, COLORREF cr) {

   GETTHISDATA(hwnd)->crBk = cr;
   InvalidateRect(hwnd, NULL, FALSE);
}


//////////////////////////////////////////////////////////////////////////


COLORREF WINAPI BarGraph_OnGetBkColor (HWND hwnd) {

   return(GETTHISDATA(hwnd)->crBk);
}


//////////////////////////////////////////////////////////////////////////
```

```
void WINAPI BarGraph_OnSetTextColor (HWND hwnd, COLORREF cr) {

   GETTHISDATA(hwnd)->crText = cr;
   InvalidateRect(hwnd, NULL, FALSE);
}


/////////////////////////////////////////////////////////////////////////


COLORREF WINAPI BarGraph_OnGetTextColor (HWND hwnd) {

   return(GETTHISDATA(hwnd)->crText);
}


/////////////////////////////////////////////////////////////////////////


LRESULT WINAPI BarGraph_WndProc (HWND hwnd, UINT uMsg,
   WPARAM wParam, LPARAM lParam) {

   switch (uMsg) {

      // Standard window messages
      HANDLE_MSG(hwnd, WM_CREATE,         BarGraph_OnCreate);
      HANDLE_MSG(hwnd, WM_DESTROY,        BarGraph_OnDestroy);
      HANDLE_MSG(hwnd, WM_GETDLGCODE,     BarGraph_OnGetDlgCode);
      HANDLE_MSG(hwnd, WM_PAINT,          BarGraph_OnPaint);
      HANDLE_MSG(hwnd, WM_LBUTTONDOWN,    BarGraph_OnLButtonDown);
      HANDLE_MSG(hwnd, WM_LBUTTONUP,      BarGraph_OnLButtonUp);
      HANDLE_MSG(hwnd, WM_MOUSEMOVE,      BarGraph_OnMouseMove);
      HANDLE_MSG(hwnd, WM_SETFOCUS,       BarGraph_OnSetFocus);
      HANDLE_MSG(hwnd, WM_KILLFOCUS,      BarGraph_OnKillFocus);
      HANDLE_MSG(hwnd, WM_CAPTURECHANGED, BarGraph_OnCaptureChanged);
      HANDLE_MSG(hwnd, WM_KEYDOWN,        BarGraph_OnKey);

      // Control-specific messages
      HANDLE_MSG(hwnd, BGM_SETBARS,       BarGraph_OnSetBars);
      HANDLE_MSG(hwnd, BGM_GETBARS,       BarGraph_OnGetBars);
      HANDLE_MSG(hwnd, BGM_GETCOUNT,      BarGraph_OnGetCount);
      HANDLE_MSG(hwnd, BGM_SETHEIGHT,     BarGraph_OnSetHeight);
      HANDLE_MSG(hwnd, BGM_GETHEIGHT,     BarGraph_OnGetHeight);
      HANDLE_MSG(hwnd, BGM_SETBKCOLOR,    BarGraph_OnSetBkColor);
      HANDLE_MSG(hwnd, BGM_GETBKCOLOR,    BarGraph_OnGetBkColor);
      HANDLE_MSG(hwnd, BGM_SETTEXTCOLOR,  BarGraph_OnSetTextColor);
      HANDLE_MSG(hwnd, BGM_GETTEXTCOLOR,  BarGraph_OnGetTextColor);

   }
   return(DefWindowProc(hwnd, uMsg, wParam, lParam));
}


/////////////////////////////////////////////////////////////////////////
```

```
ATOM WINAPI BarGraph_RegisterClass (HINSTANCE hinst, BOOL fGlobalClass) {

   WNDCLASSEX wc;

   adgINITSTRUCT(wc, TRUE);
   wc.style          = CS_HREDRAW | CS_VREDRAW;
   wc.lpfnWndProc    = BarGraph_WndProc;
   wc.cbWndExtra     = sizeof(BARGRAPH_WNDEXTRABYTES);
   wc.hInstance      = hinst;
   wc.hCursor        = LoadCursor(NULL, IDC_ARROW);
   wc.lpszClassName  = WC_BARGRAPH;

   if (fGlobalClass)
      wc.style |= CS_GLOBALCLASS;

   return(RegisterClassEx(&wc));
}


///////////////////////////////////////////////////////////////////////////


BOOL WINAPI BarGraph_UnregisterClass (HINSTANCE hinst) {

   return(UnregisterClass(WC_BARGRAPH, hinst));
}


/////////////////////////////////// End of File ///////////////////////////////////
```

Listing 4.6 *BarGraph.MSG*

```
// Module name: BarGraph.msg
// Written by: Jonathan Locke
// Notices: Copyright (c) 1995 Jeffrey Richter
// Purpose: 'MsgCrack' input file for BarGraph control.

MessageBase WM_USER
MessageClass BarGraph

Message BGM_SETBARS SetBars \
 - Sets the array of BAR structures for the control. The brush in each BAR\
   structure is only USED by the control. It is OWNED by the caller. Therefore,\
   the caller must create and destroy the brush handle.
wParam UINT cBars - Number of BAR structures in array
lParam BAR* pbar - Pointer to first BAR in array
 .

Message BGM_GETBARS GetBars \
```

```
  - Gets pointer to BAR array for control.
Returns BAR* - Pointer to first BAR in array
.

Message BGM_GETCOUNT GetCount \
 - Gets number of BAR structures in array
Returns UINT - Number of BARs
.

Message BGM_SETHEIGHT SetHeight \
 - Sets the current graph height (in user-defined units)
wParam UINT nHeight - New graph height
.

Message BGM_GETHEIGHT GetHeight \
 - Gets the current graph height (in user-defined units)
Returns UINT - Current graph height
.

Message BGM_SETBKCOLOR SetBkColor \
 - Sets the background color of a bargraph control.
lParam COLORREF crNew - New background color
.

Message BGM_GETBKCOLOR GetBkColor \
 - Gets the background color of a bargraph control.
Returns COLORREF - Current background color
.

Message BGM_SETTEXTCOLOR SetTextColor \
 - Sets the text color of a bargraph control.
lParam COLORREF crNew - New text color
.

Message BGM_GETTEXTCOLOR GetTextColor \
 - Gets the text color of a bargraph control.
Returns COLORREF - Current text color
.
```

Listing 4.7 *BarGraph.H*

```
/*****************************************************************************
Module name: BarGraph.h
Written by: Jonathan Locke
Notices: Copyright (c) 1995 Jeffrey Richter
Purpose: Bargraph custom control header file.
*****************************************************************************/

/////////////////////////////// Class Name ///////////////////////////////
```

```
// ANSI/Unicode declarations for bargraph's window class name
#define WC_BARGRAPHA "BarGraph"
#define WC_BARGRAPHW L"BarGraph"

#ifdef UNICODE
#define WC_BARGRAPH WC_BARGRAPHW
#else
#define WC_BARGRAPH WC_BARGRAPHA
#endif


///////////////////////// Class-Specific Window Styles //////////////////////////


// Bargraph controls don't have any class-specific window styles at this time.


/////////////////////////////// Class Registration //////////////////////////////


// Register and unregister the bargraph window class.
ATOM WINAPI BarGraph_RegisterClass (HINSTANCE hinst, BOOL fGlobalClass);
BOOL WINAPI BarGraph_UnregisterClass (HINSTANCE hinst);


/////////////////////////////// Parent Notification //////////////////////////////


// The following is the BARGRAPH_NOTIFY structure sent to the parent in the
// lParam of a WM_NOTIFY message. The NMHDR structure can be found in
// WinUser.H.
typedef struct tagBARGRAPH_NOTIFY {
   NMHDR nmh;            // Notify message header
   UINT uBar;            // Index of bar in graph
} BARGRAPH_NOTIFY;


//////////////////////////////// Definition of a Bar ////////////////////////////


// BAR structure defines each bar in the bar graph.
typedef struct tagBAR {
   UINT nHeight;        // Height of bar in user-defined units
   HBRUSH hbr;          // Brush to fill bar with
} BAR;


/////////////////////// Class-Specific Window Messages ///////////////////////////


//{{adgMSGCRACK_MESSAGES

// Purpose: Sets the array of BAR structures for the control. The brush in each
//          BAR structure is only used by the control. It is owned by the
```

297

```
//          caller. Therefore, the caller must create and destroy the brush
//          handle.
// wParam:  UINT cBars - Number of BAR structures in array
// lParam:  BAR* pbar - Pointer to first BAR in array
// Returns: void
#define BGM_SETBARS      (WM_USER + 0)


// Purpose: Gets pointer to BAR array for control.
// wParam:  N/A
// lParam:  N/A
// Returns: BAR* - Pointer to first BAR in array
#define BGM_GETBARS      (WM_USER + 1)


// Purpose: Gets number of BAR structures in array.
// wParam:  N/A
// lParam:  N/A
// Returns: UINT - Number of BARs
#define BGM_GETCOUNT     (WM_USER + 2)


// Purpose: Sets the current graph height (in user-defined units).
// wParam:  UINT nHeight - New graph height
// lParam:  N/A
// Returns: void
#define BGM_SETHEIGHT    (WM_USER + 3)


// Purpose: Gets the current graph height (in user-defined units).
// wParam:  N/A
// lParam:  N/A
// Returns: UINT - Current graph height
#define BGM_GETHEIGHT    (WM_USER + 4)


// Purpose: Sets the background color of a bargraph control.
// wParam:  N/A
// lParam:  COLORREF crNew - New background color
// Returns: void
#define BGM_SETBKCOLOR   (WM_USER + 5)


// Purpose: Gets the background color of a bargraph control.
// wParam:  N/A
// lParam:  N/A
// Returns: COLORREF - Current background color
#define BGM_GETBKCOLOR   (WM_USER + 6)


// Purpose: Sets the text color of a bargraph control.
// wParam:  N/A
// lParam:  COLORREF crNew - New text color
// Returns: void
#define BGM_SETTEXTCOLOR   (WM_USER + 7)


// Purpose: Gets the text color of a bargraph control.
// wParam:  N/A
// lParam:  N/A
// Returns: COLORREF - Current text color
#define BGM_GETTEXTCOLOR   (WM_USER + 8)

//}}adgMSGCRACK_MESSAGES
```

```
/////////////////////// Bargraph Control Message APIs ////////////////////////


//{{adgMSGCRACK_APIS

#define BarGraph_SetBars(hwnd, cBars, pbar) \
    ((void)SendMessage((hwnd), BGM_SETBARS, (WPARAM)(DWORD)(cBars),
(LPARAM)(DWORD)(pbar)))

#define BarGraph_GetBars(hwnd) \
    ((BAR* )SendMessage((hwnd), BGM_GETBARS, 0, 0))

#define BarGraph_GetCount(hwnd) \
    ((UINT )SendMessage((hwnd), BGM_GETCOUNT, 0, 0))

#define BarGraph_SetHeight(hwnd, nHeight) \
    ((void)SendMessage((hwnd), BGM_SETHEIGHT, (WPARAM)(DWORD)(nHeight), 0))

#define BarGraph_GetHeight(hwnd) \
    ((UINT )SendMessage((hwnd), BGM_GETHEIGHT, 0, 0))

#define BarGraph_SetBkColor(hwnd, crNew) \
    ((void)SendMessage((hwnd), BGM_SETBKCOLOR, 0, (LPARAM)(DWORD)(crNew)))

#define BarGraph_GetBkColor(hwnd) \
    ((COLORREF )SendMessage((hwnd), BGM_GETBKCOLOR, 0, 0))

#define BarGraph_SetTextColor(hwnd, crNew) \
    ((void)SendMessage((hwnd), BGM_SETTEXTCOLOR, 0, (LPARAM)(DWORD)(crNew)))

#define BarGraph_GetTextColor(hwnd) \
    ((COLORREF )SendMessage((hwnd), BGM_GETTEXTCOLOR, 0, 0))

//}}adgMSGCRACK_APIS


//////////////////////////// Message Crackers /////////////////////////////////


//{{adgMSGCRACK_CRACKERS

// void Cls_OnSetBars (HWND hwnd, UINT cBars, BAR* pbar)
#define HANDLE_BGM_SETBARS(hwnd, wParam, lParam, fn) \
    ((fn)((hwnd), (UINT)(wParam), (BAR*)(lParam)), 0)
#define FORWARD_BGM_SETBARS(hwnd, cBars, pbar, fn) \
    (void)((fn)((hwnd), BGM_SETBARS, (WPARAM)(DWORD)(cBars),
(LPARAM)(DWORD)(pbar)))

// BAR* Cls_OnGetBars(HWND hwnd)
#define HANDLE_BGM_GETBARS(hwnd, wParam, lParam, fn) \
    (LRESULT)(fn)((hwnd))
#define FORWARD_BGM_GETBARS(hwnd, fn) \
    (BAR* )((fn)((hwnd), BGM_GETBARS, 0, 0))

// UINT Cls_OnGetCount(HWND hwnd)
#define HANDLE_BGM_GETCOUNT(hwnd, wParam, lParam, fn) \
```

```
    (LRESULT)(fn)((hwnd))
#define FORWARD_BGM_GETCOUNT(hwnd, fn) \
    (UINT)((fn)((hwnd), BGM_GETCOUNT, 0, 0))

// void Cls_OnSetHeight (HWND hwnd, UINT nHeight)
#define HANDLE_BGM_SETHEIGHT(hwnd, wParam, lParam, fn) \
    ((fn)((hwnd), (UINT)(wParam)), 0)
#define FORWARD_BGM_SETHEIGHT(hwnd, nHeight, fn) \
    (void)((fn)((hwnd), BGM_SETHEIGHT, (WPARAM)(DWORD)(nHeight), 0))

// UINT Cls_OnGetHeight (HWND hwnd)
#define HANDLE_BGM_GETHEIGHT(hwnd, wParam, lParam, fn) \
    (LRESULT)(fn)((hwnd))
#define FORWARD_BGM_GETHEIGHT(hwnd, fn) \
    (UINT )((fn)((hwnd), BGM_GETHEIGHT, 0, 0))

// void Cls_OnSetBkColor (HWND hwnd, COLORREF crNew)
#define HANDLE_BGM_SETBKCOLOR(hwnd, wParam, lParam, fn) \
    ((fn)((hwnd), (COLORREF)(lParam)), 0)
#define FORWARD_BGM_SETBKCOLOR(hwnd, crNew, fn) \
    (void)((fn)((hwnd), BGM_SETBKCOLOR, 0, (LPARAM)(DWORD)(crNew)))

// COLORREF Cls_OnGetBkColor (HWND hwnd)
#define HANDLE_BGM_GETBKCOLOR(hwnd, wParam, lParam, fn) \
    (LRESULT)(fn)((hwnd))
#define FORWARD_BGM_GETBKCOLOR(hwnd, fn) \
    (COLORREF )((fn)((hwnd), BGM_GETBKCOLOR, 0, 0))

// void Cls_OnSetTextColor (HWND hwnd, COLORREF crNew)
#define HANDLE_BGM_SETTEXTCOLOR(hwnd, wParam, lParam, fn) \
    ((fn)((hwnd), (COLORREF)(lParam)), 0)
#define FORWARD_BGM_SETTEXTCOLOR(hwnd, crNew, fn) \
    (void)((fn)((hwnd), BGM_SETTEXTCOLOR, 0, (LPARAM)(DWORD)(crNew)))

// COLORREF Cls_OnGetTextColor(HWND hwnd)
#define HANDLE_BGM_GETTEXTCOLOR(hwnd, wParam, lParam, fn) \
    (LRESULT)(fn)((hwnd))
#define FORWARD_BGM_GETTEXTCOLOR(hwnd, fn) \
    (COLORREF )((fn)((hwnd), BGM_GETTEXTCOLOR, 0, 0))

//}}adgMSGCRACK_CRACKERS


//////////////////////////////// End of File /////////////////////////////////
```

Listing 4.8 *CustCntl.RC*

```
// Microsoft Visual C++-generated resource script
//
#include "resource.h"

#define APSTUDIO_READONLY_SYMBOLS
```

```
///////////////////////////////////////////////////////////////////////
//
// Generated from the TEXTINCLUDE 2 resource.
//
#include "windows.h"


///////////////////////////////////////////////////////////////////////
#undef APSTUDIO_READONLY_SYMBOLS


///////////////////////////////////////////////////////////////////////
//
// Icon
//

IDI_CUSTCNTL            ICON    DISCARDABLE      "CUSTCNTL.ICO"

///////////////////////////////////////////////////////////////////////
//
// Dialog box
//

IDD_CUSTCNTL DIALOG DISCARDABLE  0x8000, 5, 272, 154
STYLE WS_MINIMIZEBOX | WS_VISIBLE | WS_CAPTION | WS_SYSMENU
CAPTION "Custom Controls"
FONT 8, "MS Sans Serif"
BEGIN
    LTEXT          "&Number of User API Functions",IDC_APILABEL,12,59,37,40,
                   NOT WS_GROUP
    CONTROL        "",IDC_BARGRAPH,"BarGraph",WS_TABSTOP,53,20,107,111
    CTEXT          "Windows Version",IDC_STATIC,53,135,109,9,NOT WS_GROUP
    CONTROL        "Windows 1.04",IDC_LEGEND0,"Legend",0x3,187,18,71,14
    CONTROL        "Windows 2.11",IDC_LEGEND1,"Legend",0x3,187,32,71,14
    CONTROL        "Windows 3.0",IDC_LEGEND2,"Legend",0x3,187,46,71,14
    CONTROL        "Windows 3.1",IDC_LEGEND3,"Legend",0x3,187,60,71,14
    CONTROL        "Windows 95",IDC_LEGEND4,"Legend",0x3,187,73,71,14
    GROUPBOX       "Legend",IDC_STATIC,181,6,83,87
    GROUPBOX       "&Module",IDC_STATIC,181,98,83,48
    CONTROL        "&User",IDC_USER,"Button",BS_AUTORADIOBUTTON | WS_GROUP,
                   191,110,32,10
    CONTROL        "&GDI",IDC_GDI,"Button",BS_AUTORADIOBUTTON,191,121,31,10
    CONTROL        "&Kernel",IDC_KERNEL,"Button",BS_AUTORADIOBUTTON,191,132,
                   35,10
END


#ifdef APSTUDIO_INVOKED
///////////////////////////////////////////////////////////////////////
//
// TEXTINCLUDE
//

1 TEXTINCLUDE DISCARDABLE
BEGIN
    "resource.h\0"
END
```

```
2 TEXTINCLUDE DISCARDABLE
BEGIN
    "#include ""windows.h""\r\n"
    "\r\n"
    "\0"
END

3 TEXTINCLUDE DISCARDABLE
BEGIN
    "\r\n"
    "\0"
END

/////////////////////////////////////////////////////////////////////////////
#endif    // APSTUDIO_INVOKED


#ifndef APSTUDIO_INVOKED
/////////////////////////////////////////////////////////////////////////////
//
// Generated from the TEXTINCLUDE 3 resource.
//


/////////////////////////////////////////////////////////////////////////////
#endif    // not APSTUDIO_INVOKED
```

Listing 4.9 *Resource.H*

```
//{{NO_DEPENDENCIES}}
// Microsoft Visual C++-generated include file
// Used by CUSTCNTL.RC
//
#define IDI_CUSTCNTL              102
#define IDD_CUSTCNTL              103
#define IDC_LEGEND0               1000
#define IDC_LEGEND1               1001
#define IDC_LEGEND2               1002
#define IDC_LEGEND3               1003
#define IDC_LEGEND4               1004
#define IDC_BARGRAPH              1005
#define IDC_USER                  1006
#define IDC_GDI                   1007
#define IDC_KERNEL                1008
#define IDC_APILABEL              1009
#define IDC_BUTTON1               1010
#define IDC_STATIC                -1

// Next default values for new objects
//
#ifdef APSTUDIO_INVOKED
```

```
#ifndef APSTUDIO_READONLY_SYMBOLS
#define _APS_NEXT_RESOURCE_VALUE        104
#define _APS_NEXT_COMMAND_VALUE         40001
#define _APS_NEXT_CONTROL_VALUE         1011
#define _APS_NEXT_SYMED_VALUE           101
#endif
#endif
```

CHAPTER FIVE

Window Subclassing and Superclassing

Microsoft Windows supplies a number of ready-to-use window classes, including listboxes, comboboxes, and scrollbars. These controls are intended to be general and feature-laden enough for use in any application. Sometimes, however, you may wish that these controls had slightly different behavior.

One solution to this problem is to design your own control from scratch (as discussed in Chapter 4). This task is usually significant; however, it would be nice if the source code to the Windows built-in controls was freely available. Unfortunately, Microsoft does not distribute these sources. So we must take a different approach to this problem. Window subclassing and superclassing come to the rescue here and save us from reinventing the wheel.

Subclassing and superclassing can also be used on your own window classes, including application windows and custom controls that you create. However, using subclassing and superclassing on your own code is usually not necessary because you have easy access to your own source code and you can easily modify your own source code to do exactly what you desire.

How Window Subclassing Works

When registering a window class, you fill in the members of the WNDCLASSEX structure and pass the address of the structure to the RegisterClassEx function. Of course, before calling RegisterClassEx, you must initialize the lpfnWndProc member of the WNDCLASS-EX structure to point to the address of the class's window procedure. This procedure processes messages pertaining to all windows of this class. Before RegisterClassEx returns, the system allocates an internal block of memory that contains information about the window class. The class's window procedure address is part of this block.

Whenever a new window is created, the system allocates another internal block of memory containing information specific to the new window. When the system allocates and initializes the block of memory for this window, the system copies the class's window procedure address from the class's internal memory block into the window's internal memory block. When a message is dispatched to a window procedure, the system examines the value of the window procedure in the window's memory block and calls the function whose address is stored there. The system does not use the window procedure address stored in the window class's memory block when dispatching a message to a window. The window procedure address stored in the class's memory block is there only so that it can be copied when a window is created—the system does not use this address for any other purpose.

To subclass a window, you change the window procedure address in the window's memory block to point to a new window procedure. Because the address is changed in one window's memory block, it does not affect any other windows created from the same class. If the system did not give each window instance its own copy of the window procedure address, then changing the class's address would alter the behavior of all windows in the class. If this were the case, subclassing a single edit control so that it no longer accepts digits would cause all edit controls used within a single process to stop accepting digits. This is certainly not desirable.

Once you have changed the window procedure address in the window's memory block, all messages destined for the window are sent to the function at this new address. This function must look exactly like a standard window procedure. In other words, its prototype must have an identical prototype:

```
LRESULT WINAPI SubClassWndProc (HWND hwnd, UINT uMsg,
    WPARAM wParam, LPARAM lParam);
```

Once the message destined for the original window procedure has been sent to your procedure, you may do one of the following:

■ Pass it to the original procedure. This option is used for most messages. The reason for subclassing is usually to alter the behavior of a window only slightly. For this reason, most messages are passed to the original procedure so that the default behavior for this window class can be performed.

■ Stop the message from being passed to the original procedure. For example, if you want an edit control to stop accepting digits, you examine WM_CHAR messages, check to see if the character (wParam parameter) is between '0' and '9', and, if it is, immediately return from the SubClassWndProc function. If the character is not a digit, you pass the message to the original window procedure for edit controls. An example, which alters an edit control like this, appears later in this chapter.

■ Alter the message before sending it. If you want a combobox to accept only uppercase characters, examine each WM_CHAR message and convert the key (contained in wParam) to uppercase (using the CharUpper function) before passing the message to the original procedure.

Here is an example of how to subclass a window:

```
static LPCSTR g_szSubclassWndProcOrig = "SubclassWndProcOrig";

int WINAPI WinMain (HINSTANCE hinstExe, HINSTANCE hinstPrev,
   LPSTR lpszCmdLine, int nCmdShow) {

   HWND hwndEdit = CreateWindowEx(0, "EDIT", "", WS_CHILD,
      10, 20, 100, 16, hWndParent, NULL, hInstance, OL);

   // Change the window procedure address associated with this one edit control.
   pfnWndProcOrig = SubclassWindow(hwndEdit, Edit_SubClassWndProc);

   // Associate the original window procedure address with the window.
   SetProp(hwndEdit, g_szSubclassWndProcOrig, (HANDLE) (DWORD) pfnWndProcOrig);

   // All messages destined for hwndEdit are sent to
   // Edit_SubClassWndProc instead.
}
   .
   .
   .
LRESULT WINAPI Edit_SubClassWndProc (HWND hwnd, UINT uMsg,
```

```
        WPARAM wParam, LPARAM lParam) {

   LRESULT lResult = 0;
   BOOL fCallOrigWndProc = TRUE;


   switch (uMsg) {

      // Some cases set fCallOrigWndProc to FALSE.
      .
      .
      .
   }
   if (fCallOrigWndProc)
      lResult = CallWindowProc(
         (WNDPROC) (DWORD) GetProp(hwnd, g_szSubclassWndProcOrig),
         hwnd, uMsg, wParam, lParam);

   return(lResult);
}
```

The only information required to subclass a window is its window handle. Notice that I have used the SubclassWindow macro to perform the window subclassing. This macro is defined in **WindowsX.H** as follows:

```
#define SubclassWindow(hwnd, lpfn) \
      ((WNDPROC)SetWindowLong((hwnd), GWL_WNDPROC, \
      (LPARAM)(WNDPROC)(lpfn)))
```

You can see that, aside from some casting, this macro simply calls SetWindowLong, changing the address of the window's window procedure. Of course, this means that the function address passed to SubclassWindow must identify a function that is contained in the process's address space. In Win32 it is not possible to subclass a window using a window procedure that is contained in another process's address space.[1] The return value from SetWindowLong is the address of the original window procedure. This window procedure is saved in a window property that is associated with the subclassed window.

---

[1] If you are interested in creating applications that subclass windows created by other applications, see the "Breaking Though Process Boundary Walls" chapter in my book *Advanced Windows*, published by Microsoft Press, 1995.

The function you write to intercept messages is identical in form to a window procedure. The only difference is that you pass the messages to the original window procedure instead of calling DefWindowProc. To have the original window perform its normal operations for a particular message, you must use the CallWindowProc function. This function is passed to the address of the original window procedure, the window handle (hwnd), the message (uMsg), and the two standard parameters (wParam and lParam).

Notice that the address of the original window procedure is obtained by accessing the window's property using the GetProp function. I thought long and hard before recommending window properties for storing the original window procedure address in a window property. Unfortunately, there are not many good places to save the original procedure. However, I will list some ideas that I've had and explain the advantages and disadvantages of each one.

- Because you subclass individual windows, it makes sense to associate the original window procedure with the window itself. So, one idea is to store the original window procedure address in the window's GWL_USERDATA bytes. I would recommend this idea highly except that it has a really big downside. Since you are subclassing a window, you should not use the GWL_USERDATA bytes because you don't know how the original window procedure uses these bytes. The "Associating Additional Data with a Subclassed Window" section, which appears a little later in this chapter, discusses more of these issues.

- So next I thought about saving the original window procedure in a global variable. This option is fast but not flexible. For example, if you have several windows to subclass, you need a global variable for each one. Or, if you are subclassing several windows of a single class, you could save the original window procedure once for all window instances of the class. I feel that global variables are the root of all evil and should be avoided whenever possible.

- When I wrote this chapter, I planned to recommend an approach like this:

```
int WINAPI WinMain (HINSTANCE hinstExe, HINSTANCE hinstPrev,
   LPSTR lpszCmdLine, int nCmdShow) {

   HWND hwndEdit = CreateWindowEx(0, "EDIT", "", WS_CHILD,
      10, 20, 100, 16, hWndParent, NULL, hInstance, OL);

   // Change the window procedure address associated with this one edit control.
   SubclassWindow(hwndEdit, Edit_SubClassWndProc);

   // All messages destined for hwndEdit are sent to
   // Edit_SubClassWndProc instead.
}
   .
   .
   .

LRESULT WINAPI Edit_SubClassWndProc (HWND hwnd, UINT uMsg,
   WPARAM wParam, LPARAM lParam) {

   LRESULT lResult = 0;
   BOOL fCallOrigWndProc = TRUE;

   switch (uMsg) {

      // Some cases set fCallOrigWndProc to FALSE.
      .
      .
      .
   }
   if (fCallOrigWndProc)
      lResult = CallWindowProc(GetClassLong(hwnd, GCL_WNDPROC),
         hwnd, uMsg, wParam, lParam);

   return(lResult);
}
```

Notice that this approach eliminates the global variable. For the call to CallWindowProc, I call GetClassLong using the GCL_WND-PROC identifier. Remember that the SubclassWindow macro changes the window procedure address for a specific window using the SetWindowLong function. The original window procedure address is still accessible by querying the window class information. However, I decided not to recommend this approach because all this chapter's technical reviewers hated it. They hated it because many utility applications on the market today subclass various windows. So, there may be a window in the system that is subclassed several times over.

Windows allows this to happen, but the additional subclass window procedures will not get their chance to process the messages if any of the subclass window procedures use this technique.

After reviewing all these ideas, it seemed obvious that using window properties was by far the best solution. The only disadvantage is that accessing properties is slower than any of the methods listed here. However, I spoke to some Microsoft developers who worked on Windows 95 and Windows NT, and they told me that the overhead of properties would not be too bad. They also told me that MFC, the control 3-D library, and the common dialog boxes all use properties to save the subclassed window's original window procedure. If you are concerned about performance, you can use a shorter property name or even call SetProp and GetProp using an atom value.

Another problem with all these techniques is that a subclass chain can easily be broken. For example, a window may be subclassed by code in DLL-A, and then the subclassed window may be subclassed again by code in DLL-B. Windows allows this technique, which actually works quite well. When a message is dispatched to the window, DLL-B's subclass window procedure receives the message. When it passes the window message on, the message is passed to the subclass procedure in DLL-A. This transfer happens because, when the code in DLL-B calls SubclassWindow, the return value is the address of the subclass procedure contained in DLL-A. Of course, if the code in DLL-B doesn't save the original window procedure and instead uses the last technique described here, the chain is broken and the subclass procedure in DLL-A is not called. This is precisely the reason why this final technique is discouraged.

Now look at what happens if the code in DLL-A wants to un-subclass a window. When the code attempts to un-subclass the window, it attempts to call SubclassWindow macro again passing in the address of what DLL-A thinks is the original window procedure—this is the address of the window class's window procedure. So, from now on, all messages destined for the window are directed back to the class's window procedure. But this is not what we wanted to happen! The DLL-B still wants to subclass the window but will no longer be intercepting the messages—the window subclass chain is broken.

Unfortunately, we cannot solve this problem. What is needed is for the operating system to offer more support to allow window subclassers to remove themselves from the chain gracefully.

Creating New Window Messages for the Subclassed Window

Often, when we subclass a window, we would like to define some new window messages that we can send to the window. Let's say that we create an edit window that accepts only numbers (using the new ES_NUMBER window style). Then, we subclass this edit window to alter its behavior slightly. For example, we might want to define a new window message, EM_ADDNUM, that we can send to our subclassed window to make adding a value to the number shown in the subclassed edit window very easy.

How should we define this EM_ADDNUM message? Normally, if we were implementing a window class entirely by ourselves, we would define our class-specific window messages starting with WM_USER. For example, the EM_ADDNUM message might be defined as

```
#define EM_ADDNUM       (WM_USER + 0)
```

But, when we are subclassing a window that was originally created from a class that we did not implement ourselves, we cannot simply create new window messages starting at WM_USER. All the new common controls, like trackbars, have their class-specific messages starting at WM_USER. For example, the trackbar class's TBM_GETPOS message is defined as

```
#define TBM_GETPOS          (WM_USER)
```

If we subclass a trackbar window and define our own message with a value of WM_USER + 0, our subclass procedure intercepts the message and processes the message our way. Any code that is expecting to send the TBM_GETPOS message in order to retrieve size information will be in for a big surprise!

So, you can start defining your messages at WM_USER + 500. But, this isn't really a safe approach because we don't know if Microsoft has created any undocumented (WM_USER + x) messages specific for the control. If we add our own user message starting at WM_USER + 500, it could conflict with an undocumented message recognized by the trackbar class. Actually, choosing any value would be tempting fate.

Fortunately, there are two ways to solve this problem. The first way is to use the RegisterWindowMessage function described in Chapter 1. This function creates a new message that is unique as long as the string we pass to it is also unique. Whenever we call Register WindowMessage, we know that the integer value returned identifies a message that is ignored by any and all window procedures that have not also requested to register the same string message.

The second way to solve this problem is much easier. Starting with Windows 95, Microsoft has declared that all third-party window class procedures must ignore messages that range from WM_APP to 0xBFFF inclusive where WM_APP is defined in **WinUser.H** as

```
#define WM_APP      0x8000
```

This means that Microsoft guarantees that all the system global window classes and all the new common controls will ignore messages in this range. It also means that any other companies that produce controls should also be ignoring messages in this range. You should definitely check with the vendor of any controls you use to make sure that they do not process any messages above WM_APP.

Because these classes ignore messages in this range, we can safely define our EM_ADDNUM message for our subclassed edit window as

```
#define EM_ADDNUM   (WM_APP + 0)
```

Now, when we send this message to a subclassed edit window, it will know beyond a shadow of a doubt that we want it to add a number to the value shown in the edit control.

Associating Additional Data with a Subclassed Window

Another problem with subclassing windows is that associating additional data with the window is difficult. For example, we might like to associate a valid numeric range with our subclassed edit window. Because we did not register the edit window class ourselves, we have no way to add additional class and/or window extra bytes. In addition, because subclassing requires that a window instance already exist before we can subclass it, increasing the number of class or window extra bytes is also impossible.

The best way to associate data with a subclassed window is to use window properties, as explained in Chapter 1. You could also use the GWL_USERDATA bytes to store an address of a data structure that contains some additional data, but this is not a good idea. The GWL_USERDATA bytes are supposed to be available for the application that creates and manipulates the window. Since your subclass procedure doesn't create the window but acts very much like a window procedure, you should not touch the GWL_USERDATA bytes. Window properties are the only robust solution.

Of course, if you know that the users of your subclassed window will not touch the GWL_USERDATA bytes, you certainly can use them, but you will be sacrificing some flexibility that you may desire in the future.

The NoDigits Application

The NoDigits application (**NoDigits.EXE**), shown in Listings 5.1-5.4, (starting on page 317) demonstrates how to subclass two edit control windows. When you invoke the application, the main application window (shown in Figure 5.1) appears. This window contains three edit controls and two buttons. The first edit control uses the standard, built-in window procedure while the other two edit controls are subclassed. The subclass procedure intercepts all characters that are being sent to the edit control. However, if the character is a digit, the subclass window procedure does not call the original window procedure. Instead, it beeps and simply returns.

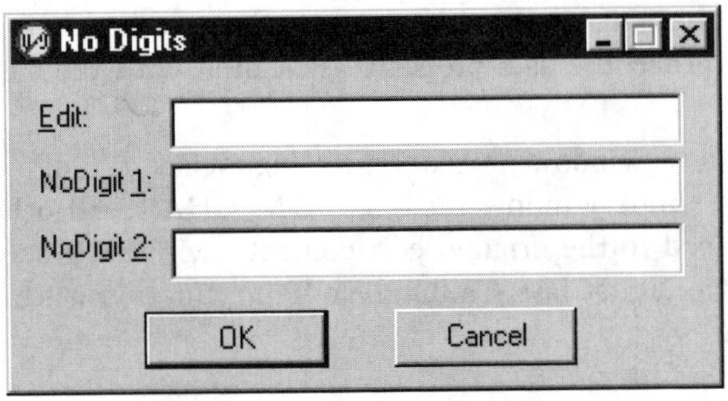

Figure 5.1 *The NoDigits application.*

Table 5.1 describes the files used to create this application.

Table 5.1 *Files used to build the NoDigits application.*

File	Description
NoDigits.C	Contains WinMain and main window's dialog box and message cracker functions.
NoDigCls.C	Contains the subclass window procedure that turns an edit control into a NoDigits control.
NoDigits.RC	Contains dialog-box template for main application window and its icons.
Resource.H	Contains IDs for all resources in the RC file.
NoDigits.ICO	Contains the icon for the main window.
NoDigits.MAK	Visual C++ project makefile.

When the **NoDigits.EXE** application starts, it creates a dialog box from a template that contains three edit controls and two buttons. When the dialog-box procedure receives a WM_INITDIALOG message, the NoDigits_OnInitDialog function subclasses two of the edit windows by calling the NoDigitsClass_Convert- Edit function:

```
NoDigitsClass_ConvertEdit(GetDlgItem(hwnd, IDC_NODIGITS1));
NoDigitsClass_ConvertEdit(GetDlgItem(hwnd, IDC_NODIGITS2));
```

The NoDigitsClass_ConvertEdit function is implemented in the **NoDigCls.C** file but is prototyped in the **NoDigits.C** file. This function simply calls the SubclassWindow macro and saves the returned original window procedure as a property associated with the subclassed window.

The subclass window procedure, NoDigitsClass_WndProc, intercepts only a single window message, WM_CHAR. All other messages are passed to the original edit control's window procedure by calling the NoDigitsClass_CallOrigWndProc function at the end of the function:

```
LRESULT WINAPI NoDigitsClass_WndProc (HWND hwnd, UINT uMsg,
   WPARAM wParam, LPARAM lParam) {

   switch (uMsg) {
      HANDLE_MSG(hwnd, WM_CHAR, NoDigitsClass_OnChar);
   }
   return(NoDigitsClass_CallOrigWndProc(hwnd, uMsg, wParam, lParam));
}
```

The NoDigitsClass_CallOrigWndProc function is implemented as follows:

```
LRESULT NoDigitsClass_CallOrigWndProc (HWND hwnd, UINT uMsg,
   WPARAM wParam, LPARAM lParam) {

   // Call the base class's window procedure.  It was saved as a window
   // property by the NoDigitsClass_ConvertEdit function.
   return(CallWindowProc(
           (WNDPROC) (DWORD) GetProp(hwnd, g_szNoDigitsClassWndProcOrig),
           hwnd, uMsg, wParam, lParam));
}
```

It has the same prototype as any other window procedure, but it calls the CallWindowProc function to forward messages to the original window procedure. CallWindowProc's first parameter is the address of the window procedure we wish to forward the message to. It's easy for the NoDigitsClass_WndProc function to get the address of the edit control's original window procedure. It does this by calling the GetProp function passing the same string that was passed to SetProp inside the NoDigitsClass_ConvertEdit function.

Now, we'll discuss how digits are prevented from being entered into the edit control after it's subclassed. As mentioned earlier, the subclass function performs some additional processing for the WM_CHAR message only. Whenever NoDigitsClass_WndProc

receives a WM_CHAR message, it calls the NoDigitsClass_OnChar
function:

```
void NoDigitsClass_OnChar (HWND hwnd, TCHAR ch, int cRepeat) {

   if (adgINRANGE(__TEXT('0'), ch, __TEXT('9'))) {

      // Beep when a digit is received.
      MessageBeep(0);
   } else {

      // Allow nondigits to pass through to the original window procedure.
      FORWARD_WM_CHAR(hwnd, ch, cRepeat, NoDigitsClass_CallOrigWndProc);
   }
}
```

The first thing that this function does is determine if the character
passed to it is a digit. If the character is a digit, MessageBeep is
called so that the user is given some indication that the window
does not accept digits. However, if the character is not a digit, the
WM_CHAR message is forwarded to the edit control's original window procedure by using the FORWARD_WM_CHAR macro. The
last parameter is the address of the function that we wish to forward the message to, NoDigitsClass_CallOrigWndProc.

Listing 5.1 *NoDigits.C*

NoDigits.ICO

```
/******************************************************************************
Module name: NoDigits.c
Written by: Jeffrey Richter
Notices: Copyright (c) 1995 Jeffrey Richter
Purpose: Demonstrates how to subclass a window
******************************************************************************/

#include "..\Win95ADG.h"          /* See Appendix A for details. */
#include <Windows.h>
#include <WindowsX.h>
#pragma warning(disable: 4001)     /* Single-line comment */
#include "resource.h"


///////////////////////////////////////////////////////////////////////////


// Function that converts an edit window to a NoDigitsClass window
// by subclassing the edit window
BOOL WINAPI NoDigitsClass_ConvertEdit (HWND hwnd, BOOL fSubclass);


///////////////////////////////////////////////////////////////////////////
```

```
BOOL NoDigits_OnInitDialog (HWND hwnd, HWND hwndFocus, LPARAM lParam) {

   adgSETDLGICONS(hwnd, IDI_SUBCLASS, IDI_SUBCLASS);

   // Turn the regular edit windows into NoDigits windows by subclassing them.
   NoDigitsClass_ConvertEdit(GetDlgItem(hwnd, IDC_NODIGITS1), TRUE);
   NoDigitsClass_ConvertEdit(GetDlgItem(hwnd, IDC_NODIGITS2), TRUE);

   return(TRUE);  // Accepts default focus window.
}


/////////////////////////////////////////////////////////////////////////////


void NoDigits_OnCommand (HWND hwnd, int id, HWND hwndCtl, UINT codeNotify) {

   switch (id) {
      case IDCANCEL:                  // Allows dialog box to close.

         // Turn the NoDigits windows back into regular Edit windows.
         NoDigitsClass_ConvertEdit(GetDlgItem(hwnd, IDC_NODIGITS1), FALSE);
         NoDigitsClass_ConvertEdit(GetDlgItem(hwnd, IDC_NODIGITS2), FALSE);
         EndDialog(hwnd, id);
         break;
   }
}


/////////////////////////////////////////////////////////////////////////////


BOOL WINAPI NoDigits_DlgProc (HWND hwnd, UINT uMsg,
   WPARAM wParam, LPARAM lParam) {

   switch (uMsg) {

      // Standard Window's messages
      adgHANDLE_DLGMSG(hwnd, WM_INITDIALOG, NoDigits_OnInitDialog);
      adgHANDLE_DLGMSG(hwnd, WM_COMMAND,    NoDigits_OnCommand);
   }
   return(FALSE);                     // We didn't process the message.
}


/////////////////////////////////////////////////////////////////////////////


int WINAPI WinMain (HINSTANCE hinstExe, HINSTANCE hinstPrev,
   LPSTR lpszCmdLine, int nCmdShow) {

   adgWARNIFUNICODEUNDERWIN95();
   adgVERIFY(-1 != DialogBox(hinstExe, MAKEINTRESOURCE(IDD_NODIGITS),
      NULL, NoDigits_DlgProc));
```

```
      return(0);
}


///////////////////////////// End of File /////////////////////////////////
```

Listing 5.2 *NoDigCls.C*

```
/**************************************************************************
Module name: NoDigCls.c
Written by: Jeffrey Richter
Notices: Copyright (c) 1995 Jeffrey Richter
Purpose: NoDigits subclass child control implementation file
**************************************************************************/


#include "..\Win95ADG.h"          /* See Appendix A for details. */
#include <Windows.h>
#include <WindowsX.h>
#pragma warning(disable: 4001)     /* Single-line comment */
#include "resource.h"


//////////////////////////////////////////////////////////////////////////


static LPCTSTR g_szNoDigitsClassWndProcOrig =
   __TEXT("NoDigitsClassWndProcOrig");


//////////////////////////////////////////////////////////////////////////


// The sole purpose of this function is to call the base class's window
// procedure. When using the FORWARD_* message crackers, a function like
// this one is necessary because the last parameter to a FORWARD_* message
cracker
// is a function with the standard WNDPROC function prototype, whereas
// CallWindowProc requires a fifth parameter - the address of the window
// procedure to call.
LRESULT NoDigitsClass_CallOrigWndProc (HWND hwnd, UINT uMsg,
   WPARAM wParam, LPARAM lParam) {

   // Call the base class's window procedure.  It was saved as a window
   // property by the NoDigitsClass_ConvertEdit function.
   return(CallWindowProc(
     (WNDPROC) (DWORD) GetProp(hwnd, g_szNoDigitsClassWndProcOrig),
     hwnd, uMsg, wParam, lParam));
}
```

319

```
//////////////////////////////////////////////////////////////////////////

void NoDigitsClass_OnChar (HWND hwnd, TCHAR ch, int cRepeat) {

   if (adgINRANGE(__TEXT('0'), ch, __TEXT('9'))) {

      // Beep when a digit is received.
      MessageBeep(0);
   } else {

      // Allow nondigits to pass through to the original window procedure.
      FORWARD_WM_CHAR(hwnd, ch, cRepeat, NoDigitsClass_CallOrigWndProc);
   }
}


//////////////////////////////////////////////////////////////////////////


// This function processes all messages sent to the NoDigits windows.
LRESULT WINAPI NoDigitsClass_WndProc (HWND hwnd, UINT uMsg,
   WPARAM wParam, LPARAM lParam) {

   switch (uMsg) {
      HANDLE_MSG(hwnd, WM_CHAR, NoDigitsClass_OnChar);
   }
   return(NoDigitsClass_CallOrigWndProc(hwnd, uMsg, wParam, lParam));
}


//////////////////////////////////////////////////////////////////////////


// Function that converts an edit window to a NoDigitsClass window
// by subclassing the edit window.
BOOL WINAPI NoDigitsClass_ConvertEdit (HWND hwnd, BOOL fSubclass) {

   BOOL fOk = FALSE;

   if (fSubclass) {
      fOk = SetProp(hwnd, g_szNoDigitsClassWndProcOrig,
         (HANDLE) (DWORD) SubclassWindow(hwnd, NoDigitsClass_WndProc));
   } else {
      WNDPROC wp = (WNDPROC) (DWORD)
         RemoveProp(hwnd, g_szNoDigitsClassWndProcOrig);
      SubclassWindow(hwnd, wp);
      fOk = (wp != NULL);
   }
   return(fOk);
}


/////////////////////////////// End of File /////////////////////////////////
```

Listing 5.3 *NoDigits.RC*

```
//Microsoft Visual C++-generated resource script
//
#include "resource.h"

#define APSTUDIO_READONLY_SYMBOLS
/////////////////////////////////////////////////////////////////////////////
//
// Generated from the TEXTINCLUDE 2 resource
//
#include "afxres.h"


/////////////////////////////////////////////////////////////////////////////
#undef APSTUDIO_READONLY_SYMBOLS

/////////////////////////////////////////////////////////////////////////////
// English (United States) resources

#if !defined(AFX_RESOURCE_DLL) || defined(AFX_TARG_ENU)

/////////////////////////////////////////////////////////////////////////////
//
// Icon
//

IDI_SUBCLASS            ICON    DISCARDABLE     "NoDigits.Ico"


/////////////////////////////////////////////////////////////////////////////
//
// Dialog
//

IDD_SUBCLASS DIALOG DISCARDABLE  0x8000, 5, 184, 80
STYLE WS_MINIMIZEBOX | WS_VISIBLE | WS_CAPTION | WS_SYSMENU
CAPTION "NoDigits Edit Control"
FONT 8, "MS Sans Serif"
BEGIN
    LTEXT           "&Edit:",IDC_STATIC,4,4,15,8
    EDITTEXT        IDC_EDIT,40,4,140,13,ES_AUTOHSCROLL
    LTEXT           "NoDigit &1:",IDC_STATIC,4,20,32,8
    EDITTEXT        IDC_NODIGITS1,40,20,140,13,ES_AUTOHSCROLL
    LTEXT           "NoDigit &2:",IDC_STATIC,4,36,32,8
    EDITTEXT        IDC_NODIGITS2,40,36,140,13,ES_AUTOHSCROLL
    DEFPUSHBUTTON   "OK",1,32,60,50,14
    PUSHBUTTON      "Cancel",2,100,60,50,14
END


#ifdef APSTUDIO_INVOKED
/////////////////////////////////////////////////////////////////////////////
//
// TEXTINCLUDE
//
```

```
1 TEXTINCLUDE DISCARDABLE
BEGIN
    "resource.h\0"
END

2 TEXTINCLUDE DISCARDABLE
BEGIN
    "#include ""afxres.h""\r\n"
    "\0"
END

3 TEXTINCLUDE DISCARDABLE
BEGIN
    "\r\n"
    "\0"
END

/////////////////////////////////////////////////////////////////////////
#endif    // APSTUDIO_INVOKED


/////////////////////////////////////////////////////////////////////////
//
// DESIGNINFO
//


#endif    // English (United States) resources
/////////////////////////////////////////////////////////////////////////


#ifndef APSTUDIO_INVOKED
/////////////////////////////////////////////////////////////////////////
//
// Generated from the TEXTINCLUDE 3 resource.
//


/////////////////////////////////////////////////////////////////////////
#endif    // not APSTUDIO_INVOKED
```

Listing 5.4 *Resource.H*

```
//{{NO_DEPENDENCIES}}
// Microsoft Visual C++-generated include file
// Used by NoDigits.RC
//
#define IDD_NODIGITS                    104
#define IDD_SUBCLASS                    104
#define IDI_NODIGITS                    105
```

```
#define IDI_SUBCLASS                    105
#define IDC_EDIT                        1000
#define IDC_NODIGITS1                   1004
#define IDC_NODIGITS2                   1005
#define IDC_STATIC                      -1


// Next default values for new objects
//
#ifdef APSTUDIO_INVOKED
#ifndef APSTUDIO_READONLY_SYMBOLS
#define _APS_NEXT_RESOURCE_VALUE        101
#define _APS_NEXT_COMMAND_VALUE         40001
#define _APS_NEXT_CONTROL_VALUE         1002
#define _APS_NEXT_SYMED_VALUE           101
#endif
#endif
```

How Window Superclassing Works

Window superclassing is similar to window subclassing. Again, we are associating a different window procedure address with a window to alter the window's behavior slighlty. With window superclassing, however, you create a new window class that has altered behavior whereas with subclassing you alter the behavior of a single window. Superclassing is most useful if you intend to create several windows, all with slightly altered behavior. There are some other differences between subclassing and superclassing that I will discuss later.

Creating a superclass is accomplished by registering a new window class. For example, let's say that your application needs to create several edit windows where each of the windows can accept only letters. You could create all the windows and then subclass each one individually in order to get the desired effect, or, alternatively, you could use window superclassing.

For window superclassing, you must create a superclass window procedure that is almost identical to a window subclass procedure. The prototype is the same, and the way that you intercept messages is the same. In fact, the only difference is in how you call the original window procedure.

Here is an example of how to create a superclass.

```
// Store the address of the original window procedure.
WNDPROC g_pfnWndProcOrig;
```

```
   .
   .
   .

int WINAPI WinMain (HINSTANCE hinstExe, HINSTANCE hinstPrev,
  LPSTR lpszCmdLine, int nCmdShow) {

  WNDCLASSEX wc;
  adgINITSTRUCT(wc, TRUE);

  // Get all the information about the original window class
  GetClassInfoEx(NULL, "EDIT", &wc);

  // Save the original window procedure address so that the
  // Edit_SuperClassWndProc can use it.
  g_pfnWndProcOrig = wc.lpfnWndProc;

  // Our new class must have a new class name.
  wc.lpszClassName = "NoDigits";

  // Our new class is registered by our module.
  wc.hInstance = hinstExe;

  // Our new class has a different window procedure address.
  wc.lpfnWndProc = NoDigitsClass_SuperClassWndProc;

  // Register our new window class.
  RegisterClassEx(&wc);

  // At this point we can create windows of the NoDigits window class.
  // All messages that go to these windows are sent to the
  // NoDigitsClass_SuperClassWndProc first where we can decide if we
  // want to pass them on to g_pfnWndProcOrig.
  .
  .
  .
}


LRESULT WINAPI NoDigitsClass_SuperClassWndProc (HWND hwnd, UINT uMsg,
  WPARAM wParam, LPARAM lParam) {

  LRESULT lResult = 0;
  BOOL fCallOrigWndProc = TRUE;

  switch (uMsg) {
    .
    .
    .
  }
  if (fCallOrigWndProc)
    lResult = CallWindowProc(g_pfnWndProcOrig,
      hwnd, uMsg, wParam, lParam);

  return(lResult);
}
```

Many more steps are necessary to create a superclass than to subclass a window. The process of superclassing a window begins with a call to the GetClassInfoEx function passing it the name of the desired base class. This fills a WNDCLASSEX structure with the statistics regarding the base class. This WNDCLASSEX structure serves as a starting point for the new window class.

Once you have the base class's information, it is very important to save the value of the lpfnWndProc member (usually in a global variable as in the example but later I'll present another method). This value is the address of the base class window procedure. This variable will be used later in the superclass window procedure as the first parameter to the CallWindowProc function.

The next step is to give the new class a name by setting the lpszClassName member to the new name for the class. The value of the hInstance member should be set to the value of hinstExe that was passed to WinMain or the value of hinstDll passed to a DLL's DllMain function. This value lets the system know which module (EXE or DLL file image) in the process's address space is registering the new window class. Finally, the lpfnWndProc member of the WNDCLASSEX structure is changed to the address of the superclass window procedure.

Because a new window class is being registered, you can increase the values of the cbClsExtra and cbWndExtra members of the WND-CLASSEX structure. These additional bytes may be used by your superclass function and are a big advantage of superclassing over subclassing. But be careful when using the class or window extra bytes for a superclassed window class. The base class window procedure is written with the assumption that the class extra bytes from zero to cbClsExtra – 1 and the window extra bytes from zero to cbWndExtra – 1 are for its own use. The superclass window procedure must not access the class and window extra bytes within these ranges unless it knows exactly how they are used by the base class.

If the superclass window procedure is going to add class and window extra bytes, it must save the original values of the cbClsExtra and cbWndExtra members of the WNDCLASSEX structure, usually in global variables, before changing the values of those members. When the superclass window procedure accesses any of the window extra bytes, it must add the original value of cbWndExtra to the index so that it does not reference the window extra bytes used by the base class. Here is an example of how to prepare and access additional window bytes added to the superclass.

```
// Global variables to save the number of class extra bytes, the
// window extra bytes, and the window procedure address of the
// listbox base class
int g_cbClsExtraOrig, g_cbWndExtraOrig;
WNDPROC g_pfnWndProcOrig;

// Index into window extra bytes where our edit data can be found.
// These data follow the data required by the base class.
#define GWL_NODIGITSDATA        (g_cbWndExtraOrig + 0)
.
.
.
ATOM WINAPI NoDigitsClass_RegisterClass (void) {

    WNDCLASSEX wc;
    GetClassInfoEx(NULL, "Edit", &wc);

    // Save the information we need later in global variables.
    g_cbClsExtraOrig = wc.cbClsExtra;
    g_cbWndExtraOrig = wc.cbWndExtra;
    g_pfnWndProcOrig = wc.lpfnWndProc;

    // Add four window extra bytes to account for our additional edit data.
    wc.cbWndExtra += sizeof(LONG);

    // Change the lpfnWndProc, lpszClassName, and hInstance members, too.
    .
    .
    .
    // Register the new window class.
    return(RegisterClassEx(&wc));
}


LRESULT WINAPI NoDigitsClass_SuperClassWndProc (HWND hwnd, UINT uMsg,
    WPARAM wParam, LPARAM lParam) {

    int nNoDigitsData;
    .
    .
    .
    // Retrieve our data from the added window extra bytes.
```

```
nNoDigitsData = GetWindowLong(hwnd, GWL_NODIGITSDATA);
.
.
.
// Call base class window procedure for remainder of processing.
return(CallWindowProc(g_pfnWndProcOrig,
    hwnd, uMsg, wParam, lParam));
}
```

Of course, it is possible to associate data with a superclassed window via window properties as explained in Chapter 1 and earlier in this chapter for subclassed windows. However, it is always better to store information in window extra bytes because properties require more data space and take more time to access.

The lpszMenuName member of WNDCLASSEX may also be changed to give the new class a new menu. If a new menu is used, the IDs for the menu options should correspond to the IDs in the "standard" menu for the base class. This new menu is not necessary if the superclass window procedure processes the WM_COMMAND message in its entirety and does not pass this message to the base class window procedure.

The remaining members of the WNDCLASSEX structure—style, hIcon, hCursor, hbrBackground, and hIconSm—may be changed in any way you desire. For example, if you want your new window class to use a different mouse cursor or a different icon, you can change the hCursor and hIcon members of the WNDCLASSEX structure accordingly. Finally, call the RegisterClassEx function to inform Windows of the new class.

The main difference between subclassing and superclassing is that subclassing alters the behavior of an existing window, while superclassing creates a new window class where all windows created by the class have altered behavior. It is better to use superclassing when you wish to create several windows whose behavior differs slightly from an existing window class. This is because it is easier to register a new class, give it a new name, and create windows of this new class than it is to create all the desired windows and use the SetWindowLong function or SubclassWindow macro to change the address of each of their window procedures.

Superclassing is used quite frequently when you want to create a dialog box that contains several superclassed controls. When a dialog box is created, CreateDialogIndirectParam goes through the dialog-box template and creates a window using the parameters specified on each CONTROL line in the template. If the template contains several listbox windows that require altered behavior, it is much easier to specify "NewListBox" in each CONTROL line of the template. With window subclassing, the system would have to create all the listbox windows before you could subclass these windows, one at a time, during the processing of the WM_INITDIALOG message. This is a very tedious process.

Another advantage of superclassing is that the superclass window procedure performs its own initialization for the window. This is because Windows knows about the superclass window procedure from the class memory block before a window is created. When the window is created, the superclass window procedure receives the WM_NCCREATE and WM_CREATE messages. During the processing of these messages, the superclass window procedure may initialize its class or window extra bytes or do any other processing it desires.

Both of these messages should be passed to the base class window procedure, whether the superclass window procedure processes them or not. Windows must perform initialization for each window in response to WM_NCCREATE. If this message wasn't passed to the original window procedure, DefWindowProc would never be called, and the window would not be initialized properly. By passing the WM_NCCREATE message to the base class procedure, we ensure that DefWindowProc eventually is called. Similarly, the WM_CREATE message should also be passed to the base class window procedure.

Unfortunately, defining new window messages for superclassed windows involves the same problems that you have for subclassed windows. To define new window messages, you must either use the RegisterWindowMessage function or define your messages starting with WM_APP.

Table 5.2 summarizes the differences between window subclassing and superclassing.

Table 5.2 *Comparison of window subclassing versus superclassing.*

Subclassing	Superclassing
Recommended if few windows need to have altered behavior.	Recommended if many windows need to have the same type of altered behavior.
No new window class is registered.	A new window class must be registered.
Subclass function may not use any class or window extra bytes.	Superclass function may use additional class and window extra bytes.
Window must have been created before it can be subclassed.	Superclassing does not require that a window be created first.
Subclassed windows cannot intercept the window's initialization messages (WM_NCCREATE and WM_CREATE).	Superclassed windows can intercept the window's initialization messages (WM_NCCREATE and WM_CREATE).
Executes a little slower and uses slightly more memory if you use properties to store the address of the original window procedure.	Executes more quickly and uses less memory if you use a global or class extra bytes to store the address of the original window procedure.

The Arcade Application

The Arcade application (**Arcade.EXE**), shown in Listings 5.5-5.12, (starting on page 343) demonstrates how to create an animated button class, AniBtn, by superclassing the standard button class. The new AniBtn class works almost identically to the standard button class except that it takes advantage of the new imagelist controls to create buttons that have animated icon images instead of boring, old text. When you invoke the application, the main application window shown in Figure 5.2 appears. Of course, the figure does not show that the buttons are animated; you must run the program yourself to see the animation in action.

Figure 5.2 *The Arcade application.*

This window allows the user to select a game to play. Only two games are available: Pong and Tetris. What makes Arcade's user-interface exciting is that the buttons for the games are animated. This way, the user gets a better idea of what the game is like before making a selection.

Table 5.3 describes the files used to create this application.

Table 5.3 *Files used to build the Arcade application.*

File	Description
Arcade.C	Contains WinMain and main window's dialog box and message cracker functions.
AniBtn.C	Contains the superclass window procedure that turns a button into an AniBtn control.
AniBtn.H	Contains function prototypes and message macros for AniBtn controls.
AniBtn.MSG	MsgCrack input file used to create **AniBtn.H** (see Appendix B for details).
SuperCls.C	Contains functions to make superclassing easier. You can use this library in your own applications.
SuperCls.H	Contains prototypes for the functions contained in the **SuperCls.C** file. Any source file that uses the library of functions in **SuperCls.C** must include this file.
Arcade.RC	Contains dialog box template for main application window and its icons.
Resource.H	Contains IDs for all resources in the RC file.

Arcade.ICO	Contains the icon for the main window.
Pong1.ICO to Pong6.ICO	Contains the icon used to animate the Pong button.
Tetris1.ICO to Tetris7.ICO	Contains the icon used to animate the Tetris button.
AniBtn.MAK	Visual C++ project makefile.

When **Arcade.EXE** is invoked, the WinMain function (in **Arcade.C**) first calls the AniBtn_RegisterClass function (in **AniBtn.C**) to register the AniBtn window class. The Arcade application itself does not need to know that the AniBtn window class is actually a superclass of the built-in button window class. Registering the AniBtn class in this way makes it seem like we are registering a custom control just like we did in Chapter 4.

The AniBtn_RegisterClass function returns the atom value of the newly registered window class. WinMain simply examines this value to see if it is INVALID_ATOM, and if it is, the process terminates. However, if the AniBtn class is registered successfully, WinMain calls DialogBox in order to present the application's user-interface.

When viewed using Visual C++, Arcade's dialog box looks like the one shown in Figure 5.3. This template contains three controls: one static control and two AniBtn controls. Because the AniBtn controls are user-defined window classes, Visual C++ cannot show much detailed information about them. In Figure 5.3, they simply look like dark-grey rectangles. When you look at the property windows for user-defined classes, you'll notice that only a few settings are shown (see Figure 5.4). In particular the window styles are shown as a 32-bit hexadecimal value. This certainly makes it inconvenient to work with nonstandard window classes in Visual C++, but at least we can do it.

Now, after the dialog box and all its child windows have been created, the dialog-box procedure receives a WM_INITDIALOG message. The code to process this message is in Arcade_OnInitDialog. It is inside this function where we create an imagelist and fill it with the list of icons used to animate the Pong and Tetris buttons.

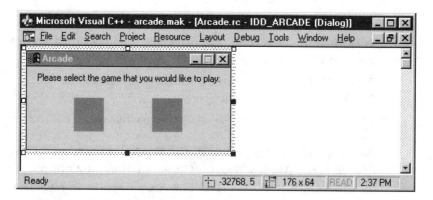

Figure 5.3 *The Arcade dialog box resource.*

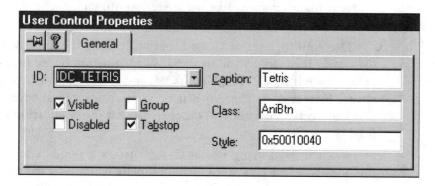

Figure 5.4 *Properties of a user-defined class.*

```
BOOL Arcade_OnInitDialog (HWND hwnd, HWND hwndFocus, LPARAM lParam) {

   // Create and set the imagelists for both buttons.
   // NOTE: When an AniBtn is destroyed, it destroys the imagelist.
   HINSTANCE hinstRes = GetWindowInstance(hwnd);
   HIMAGELIST himl;

   // Initialize the Pong AniBtn.
   himl = Arcade_MakeImageList(hinstRes, IDI_PONG1, IDI_PONG2,
      IDI_PONG3, IDI_PONG4, IDI_PONG5, IDI_PONG6, 0);
   adgASSERT(himl != NULL);
   AniBtn_SetImageList(GetDlgItem(hwnd, IDC_PONG), himl);
   AniBtn_SetTimer(GetDlgItem(hwnd, IDC_PONG), 250);

   // Initialize the Tetris AniBtn.
   himl = Arcade_MakeImageList(hinstRes, IDI_TETRIS1, IDI_TETRIS2,
      IDI_TETRIS3, IDI_TETRIS4, IDI_TETRIS5, IDI_TETRIS6, IDI_TETRIS7, 0);
   adgASSERT(himl != NULL);
```

```
AniBtn_SetImageList(GetDlgItem(hwnd, IDC_TETRIS), himl);
AniBtn_SetTimer(GetDlgItem(hwnd, IDC_TETRIS), 500);

adgSETDLGICONS(hwnd, IDI_ARCADE, IDI_ARCADE);

return(TRUE);  // Accept default focus window.
}
```

The bulk of the code to create and initialize the imagelist control is in
Arcade_MakeImageList. The variable argument function is straightforward. It takes an HINSTANCE, which identifies the module containing the icons to retrieve, and a set of icon IDs (an ID of zero terminates
the list). The function then calls ImageList_Create to create the new
imagelist control and then calls LoadIcon and ImageList_AddIcon once
for each ID passed to Arcade_MakeImageList. The handle of the resulting imagelist is returned back to Arcade_OnInitDialog:

```
HIMAGELIST Arcade_MakeImageList (HINSTANCE hinstRes, int idi, ...) {

    va_list args;
    HIMAGELIST himl = ImageList_Create(
        GetSystemMetrics(SM_CXICON), GetSystemMetrics(SM_CYICON),
        ILC_MASK, 5, 5);
    adgASSERT(himl != NULL);

    va_start(args, idi);
    while (idi != 0) {
        ImageList_AddIcon(himl, LoadIcon(hinstRes, MAKEINTRESOURCE(idi)));
        idi = va_arg(args, int);
    }
    va_end(args);
    return(himl);
}
```

This imagelist handle must now be selected into the proper AniBtn.
We use the AniBtn_SetImageList macro defined in **AniBtn.H** to
send the ABM_SETIMAGELIST message to the AniBtn window. We
must also tell the AniBtn window the speed at which it should animate the icons. This is done using the AniBtn_ SetTimer macro to
send an ABM_SETTIMER message.

The only thing left of interest in **Arcade.C** is the Arcade_
OnCommand function. When the user selects either the Pong or
Tetris animated button, this function is called and the proper game
is then executed. In the Arcade application, a message box appears
(see Figure 5.5).

Figure 5.5 *What happens if you play Pong.*

The AniBtn Window Class

Let's turn our attention to the AniBtn class and how it is implemented. The code can be found in the **AniBtn.C** file, and the messages and macros for working with the new class can be found in the **AniBtn.H** file.

Each AniBtn window needs to maintain some additional data. Specifically, each AniBtn window is required to store three data elements: the handle to its imagelist, the index of the icon in the imagelist that is to be shown next, and the timer interval that must pass before swapping images. If we were implementing an AniBtn class from scratch instead of superclassing a button control, we would have no problem determining where to store this information: we would store it in the window's extra bytes.

Recall that I said earlier in this chapter, that it is possible to add class and window extra bytes when superclassing a window. It's just that doing this is difficult because you have to make absolutely sure that you do not corrupt any class and window extra bytes that are allocated and used by the base class. This is not an easy thing to do. However, I have created a library of functions that make this significantly easier. These functions are contained in the **SuperCls.C** file and prototyped in the **SuperCls.H** file. Whenever you see a function that starts with the SuperCls_ prefix, be aware that this function is in the **SuperCls.C** library source file. I will discuss this library in detail in the next section.

The first thing we see in the **AniBtn.C** file is a data structure that defines the data members that we are going to store in each AniBtn's window extra bytes:

```
typedef struct {
   HIMAGELIST himl;      // Handle of image lList containing images
   int iImage;           // Index of image in himl to show next
   int nTimeout;         // Image change interval
} ANIBTN_WNDEXTRABYTES;
```

When the AniBtn_RegisterClass function is called by **Arcade.C**'s WinMain, the AniBtn window class is registered:

```
ATOM WINAPI AniBtn_RegisterClass (HINSTANCE hinst, BOOL fGlobalClass) {

   WNDCLASSEX wc;
   adgINITSTRUCT(wc, TRUE);
   if (!GetClassInfoEx(NULL, __TEXT("BUTTON"), &wc))
      return(INVALID_ATOM);

   // Give our new class a new name.
   wc.lpszClassName = WC_ANIBTN;

   // Our module is registering the class.
   wc.hInstance = hinst;

   // Make the new class a global class if the user desires.
   if (fGlobalClass)
      wc.style |= CS_GLOBALCLASS;

   // The following WNDCLASSEX members are not changed for AniBtn:
   //      hIcon, hIconSm, hCursor, hbrBackground, lpszMenuName.

   // Register the new window superclass.
   return(SuperCls_RegisterClassEx(&wc, AniBtn_WndProc,
      0, sizeof(ANIBTN_WNDEXTRABYTES)));
}
```

As you can see, this function first calls GetClassInfoEx in order to get the class information for the Windows' system-global button window class. Then, to register our new class, we must change the name of the class and the HINSTANCE. I also have some additional code that allows us to register the AniBtn class as an application-global class by combining the CS_GLOBALCLASS class style (as described in Chapter 4). After preparing the WNDCLASSEX structure, I registered the AniBtn class by calling the SuperCls_RegisterClassEx function contained in the **SuperCls.C** library file.

This function is similar to the Win32 RegisterClassEx function except that it performs some additional work in order to make it easy for the AniBtn code to use the superclass's class and window extra bytes. When you call SuperCls_RegisterClassEx, you must pass it the address of the WNDCLASSEX structure, the address of the super-class's window procedure (AniBtn_WndProc in this case), and the number of additional class and extra bytes that the superclass would like to have. The AniBtn class does not require any additional class extra bytes, but it does require some additional window extra bytes. The number of window extra bytes required is defined by the size of the ANIBTN_WNDEXTRABYTES data structure.

Like the Win32 RegisterClassEx function, SuperCls_Register-ClassEx returns the atom value of the registered class or INVALID_ATOM if the class could not be registered. This return value is passed back to the caller (Arcade's WinMain in this application).

Now, whenever an AniBtn window is created, all messages for that window are directed to the superclass window procedure, AniBtn_WndProc. This function intercepts just three of the standard window messages: WM_CREATE, WM_DESTROY, and WM_TIMER.

The AniBtn_OnCreate function is responsible for initializing the AniBtn window.

```
BOOL AniBtn_OnCreate (HWND hwnd, LPCREATESTRUCT lpCreateStruct) {

    AniBtn_SetTimer(hwnd, 250);     // Defaults to .25 seconds.

    // Make sure that the button base class is given the opportunity to
    // perform any needed cleanup.

    // NOTE: The return value for WM_CREATE is -1 if the window should not be
    // created and 0 if it should be created.  However, the OnCreate message
    // cracker expects TRUE to be returned if the window should be created and
    // FALSE if the window should not be created.
    return(-1 != FORWARD_WM_CREATE(hwnd, lpCreateStruct, AniBtn_CallBaseClass));
}
```

First, it calls SetTimer so that the AniBtn window periodically receives WM_TIMER messages, indicating that the image should be changed. By default, this timer is set to go off every quarter of a second. However, a user of an AniBtn window can change this by sending an ABM_SETTIMER message (discussed later) to the window.

After the timer is created, the AniBtn must complete the rest of its initialization. It is extremely important to remember that an AniBtn is a superclass of a button class. So, the button base class's window proce-dure must get an opportunity to do its initialization as well. This initialization is done using the FORWARD_WM_CREATE macro to send the WM_CREATE message to the AniBtn_CallBaseClass function:

```
LRESULT AniBtn_CallBaseClass (HWND hwnd, UINT uMsg,
    WPARAM wParam, LPARAM lParam) {

    return(CallWindowProc(SuperCls_GetWndProcBaseCls(hwnd),
        hwnd, uMsg, wParam, lParam));
}
```

This function must have the same prototype as a window procedure because all the FORWARD_* macros in **WindowsX.H** pass four parameters to the function that you pass to these macros. Once inside the AniBtn_CallBaseClass function, we call the base class's window procedure using the CallWindowProc function. The first parameter is the memory address of the function. Again, the functions that I supply in the **SuperCls.C** library help us out here. All we have to do is call the SuperCls_GetWndProcBaseClass function and it returns to us the Button's window procedure. The remaining four parameters to CallWindowProc are the standard parameters that get passed to any window procedure.

The AniBtn_OnDestroy function is responsible for cleaning up when an AniBtn window is destroyed:

```
void AniBtn_OnDestroy (HWND hwnd) {

    // If there is an imagelist associated with the button, destroy it.
    HIMAGELIST himl = AniBtn_GetImageList(hwnd);
    if (himl != NULL)
        ImageList_Destroy(himl);

    // Kill the timer associated with the button.
    KillTimer(hwnd, 1);

    // Make sure that the button base class is given the opportunity to
    // perform any needed cleanup.
    FORWARD_WM_DESTROY(hwnd, AniBtn_CallBaseClass);
}
```

There are just three things to clean up. First, if an imagelist has been associated with the AniBtn, the imagelist is destroyed by calling ImageList_Destroy. Second, the timer is killed. And third, the button base class procedure is called so that it can do any clean up that it has to. The AniBtn_OnTimer function is responsible for animating the icon in the button. It is called whenever the timer interval has expired.

```
void AniBtn_OnTimer (HWND hwnd, UINT id) {

    HIMAGELIST himl = AniBtn_GetImageList(hwnd);

    if (himl != NULL) {

        // Get the AniBtn's image index.
        int iImage = SuperCls_GetWindowLong(hwnd,
            adgMEMBEROFFSET(ANIBTN_WNDEXTRABYTES, iImage));

        // Change the AniBtn's icon.
        HICON hiconOld = (HICON) SendMessage(hwnd, BM_SETIMAGE, IMAGE_ICON,
            (LONG) ImageList_GetIcon(himl, iImage, ILD_NORMAL));

        // Destroy any old icon that is displayed.
        if (hiconOld != NULL)
            DestroyIcon(hiconOld);

        iImage = ++iImage % ImageList_GetImageCount(himl);
        SuperCls_SetWindowLong(hwnd,
            adgMEMBEROFFSET(ANIBTN_WNDEXTRABYTES, iImage), iImage);
    }
}
```

First, the function gets the handle of the imagelist associated with the AniBtn. If the handle is not NULL, it then looks into the AniBtn's window extra bytes to get the index of the icon that is to be displayed next. It gets the window extra bytes by calling the SuperCls_GetWindowLong function (described in the next section) and passing it the handle of the window and the offset of the member we're interested in from the ANIBTN_WNDEXTRABYTES structure.

Then, we create an icon that matches the image in the imagelist by calling ImageList_GetIcon and force the button to show the new icon by sending it a BM_SETIMAGE message. Sending this message to a button causes it to return the handle of the previously selected icon, which we delete (if it's not NULL).

Finally, the image index is incremented (wrapping it back to zero if necessary), and the new index is saved in the AniBtn's window extra bytes using the SuperCls_SetWindowLong function.

In addition to intercepting the three standard window messages, the AniBtn class defines four class-specific messages: ABM_SET-

TIMER, ABM_GETTIMER, ABM_SETIMAGELIST, and ABM_GETIMAGELIST. These messages are defined in the **AniBtn.MSG** file. This file is passed to the MsgCrack utility (described in Appendix B) to produce the message and define crackers that appear in the **AniBtn.H** file. All these messages are defined using the message base value of WM_APP. All four of these messages are handled by message handler functions. All four of the functions simply call SuperCls_SetWindowLong or SuperCls_GetWindowLong to change some data associated with the window. You can examine the code listing for the specific details.

The Window Superclassing Library

The **SuperCls.C** file contains a library of functions for superclassing that could easily be incorporated into your own applications. The functions in this module help you register new window super-classes and aid in the manipulation of any class and window extra bytes that you may add when superclassing a window class.

Some of the information obtained from the base class must be used when processing superclassed windows, including the number of class and window extra bytes and the address of the base class window procedure. Instead of storing this information in global variables, the SuperCls_RegisterClassEx function adds 12 bytes to the superclass's class extra bytes and stores the information there. This information is represented by the following data structure:

```
typedef struct {
   WNDPROC pfnWndProcBaseCls;   // Base class's window procedure
   int     cbClsExtraBaseCls;   // Class extra bytes for base class
   int     cbWndExtraBaseCls;   // Window extra bytes for base class
} SUPERCLS_BASECLSINFO;
```

The SuperCls_RegisterClassEx function follows:

```
ATOM WINAPI SuperCls_RegisterClassEx (
   PWNDCLASSEX pwc,             // lpfnWndClass member is base class WndProc
   WNDPROC pfnWndProcSuperCls,  // Address of superclass WndProc function
   int cbClsAdditional,         // # of class extra bytes for super class
   int cbWndAdditional) {       // # of window extra bytes for super class

   HWND hwnd;
   ATOM atomSuperClass;
   WNDPROC pfnWndProcBaseCls = pwc->lpfnWndProc;
   int cbClsExtraBaseCls     = pwc->cbClsExtra;
```

339

```
int cbWndExtraBaseCls      = pwc->cbWndExtra;

// Add to the cbClsExtra member the number of class extra bytes
// desired by the superclass plus the number of extra bytes
// required by the SUPERCLS_BASECLSINFO structure.
pwc->cbClsExtra += cbClsAdditional + sizeof(SUPERCLS_BASECLSINFO);

// Add to the cbWndExtra member the number of window extra bytes
// desired by the superclass.
pwc->cbWndExtra += cbWndAdditional;

// In order for the superclass window procedure to manipulate
// any of the superclass's class and window extra bytes successfully, the
// SUPERCLS_BASECLSINFO data members in the superclass's class extra bytes
// must be initialized first.  Because there is no Win32 function that
// allows us to change a class's extra bytes without creating a window
// first, we need to hack the solution.  This is done by registering the
// class using DefWindowProc as the window procedure.  After the class
// extra bytes have been initialized, DefWindowProc is replaced by the
// desired superclass window procedure.
pwc->lpfnWndProc = DefWindowProc;

// Register the superclass.
atomSuperClass = RegisterClassEx(pwc);
if (atomSuperClass == INVALID_ATOM)
   return(atomSuperClass);

// Now, we must complete the class's initialization by setting its
// class extra bytes.  Unfortunately, we must have a window handle in order
// to change a class's extra bytes.  So, we create a window of the class.
// This is a dummy window whose messages are processed by DefWindowProc.
hwnd = CreateWindowEx(0, MAKEINTATOM(atomSuperClass), NULL,
   0, 0, 0, 0, 0, NULL, NULL, pwc->hInstance, NULL);

if (!IsWindow(hwnd)) {

   // If the window could not be created, unregister the superclass
   // and return INVALID_ATOM to the caller.
   UnregisterClass(MAKEINTATOM(atomSuperClass), pwc->hInstance);
   atomSuperClass = INVALID_ATOM;
} else {

   // Initialize the data represented by the SUPERCLS_BASECLSINFO structure.
   SetClassLong(hwnd,
      SuperCls_BaseClsInfoIndex(pwc->cbClsExtra, pfnWndProcBaseCls),
      (LONG) pfnWndProcBaseCls);
   SetClassLong(hwnd,
      SuperCls_BaseClsInfoIndex(pwc->cbClsExtra, cbClsExtraBaseCls),
      cbClsExtraBaseCls);
   SetClassLong(hwnd,
      SuperCls_BaseClsInfoIndex(pwc->cbClsExtra, cbWndExtraBaseCls),
      cbWndExtraBaseCls);

   // Now, we can set the class's window procedure to point to the
   // desired superclass window procedure.
   SetClassLong(hwnd, GCL_WNDPROC, (LONG) pfnWndProcSuperCls);
```

```
      // NOTE: At this point, any windows of this class that are created
      // will have their messages processed by the proper superclass WndProc.

      // Because all the class extra bytes are set, we can destroy the dummy
      // window.  The WM_DESTROY/WM_NCDESTROY messages will be sent to
      // DefWindowProc because the call to SetClassLong above does NOT affect
      // the window procedure address that was associated with the dummy
      // window when it was created.
      DestroyWindow(hwnd);
   }

   // Return the atom of the registered class to the caller.
   return(atomSuperClass);
}
```

To register a new superclass, your application should first prepare a WNDCLASSEX structure by calling GetClassInfoEx. It should then change any of the WNDCLASSEX members necessary with the exception of the cbClsExtra, cbWndExtra, and lpfnWndProc members. These values are altered by the SuperCls_RegisterClassEx function. When SuperCls_RegisterClassEx is called, the first parameter is the address of the WNDCLASSEX structure followed by the address of the superclass's window procedure as well as the number of additional class and window extra bytes that you desire for the superclass.

Before registering the new window class, SuperCls_Register-ClassEx modifies the cbClsExtra and cbWndExtra members of the WNDCLASSEX structure by adding the number of class and window extra bytes that you desire. In addition, 12 more class extra bytes are added to make room for the SUPERCLS_BASECLSINFO structure. These bytes are referenced from the end of the class's extra bytes. Because the base class information is identical for all windows created of the new class, storing this information in the class extra bytes is much more efficient than saving the information in the window extra bytes.

Now, what we want to do is initialize the class extra bytes represented by the SUPERCLS_BASECLSINFO structure. We must do this before any windows of the superclass are created. This is a real problem because there is no Win32 function that allows you to alter a class's extra bytes without first having a window created of the desired class—a hack is in order here!

To initialize the class extra bytes properly, SuperCls_Register-ClassEx sets the WNDCLASSEX's lpfnWndProc member to

DefWindowProc before calling the Win32 RegisterClassEx function. As we all know, DefWindowProc is a safe window procedure that offers enough support to give minimal window functionality and nothing more. Therefore, we also know that DefWindowProc doesn't manipulate any class window extra bytes.

After SuperCls_RegisterClassEx registers the window class, we can call CreateWindowEx to create a dummy window. Technically, this window is created of the superclass window class, but the superclass's window procedure will not be called to process messages for this class; DefWindowProc is going to process the messages instead. If this dummy window is created successfully, SuperCls_Register- ClassEx calls the SetClassLong function three times in order to initialize the class extra bytes represented by the SUPERCLS_BASECLSINFO structure.

At this point, all the class extra bytes have been initialized, but the superclass's window procedure is still set to DefWindowProc. We need to change the superclass's window procedure address to the appropriate one by calling SetClassLong a fourth time using the GCL_WNDPROC identifier. Now, the superclass is all fixed up, the dummy window is destroyed, and the superclass's atom value is returned to the caller.

The remaining functions in **SuperCls.C** rely on the initialized class extra bytes. For example, the SuperCls_GetWndProcBaseClass function retrieves the base class's window procedure address by doing the following:

1. Determines the total number of class extra bytes by calling GetClassLong with the GCL_CBCLSEXTRA identifier.

2. Gets the offset that marks the beginning of the SUPERCLS_ BASECLSINFO structure. Because this structure is at the end of the class extra bytes, all we have to do is subtract the size of the structure from the total number of class extra bytes obtained in step 1.

3. Gets the offset of the pfnWndProcBaseCls member in the SUPERCLS_BASECLSINFO structure and adds this offset to the offset obtained in step 2.

4. Calls GetClassLong passing the index obtained in step 3. The value returned is the address of the base class's window procedure.

Getting and setting any of the superclass's class and window extra bytes is a similar process. Each of the functions follows.

```
WORD  SuperCls_SetClassWord(HWND hwnd, int nIndex, WORD wNewWord);
WORD  SuperCls_GetClassWord(HWND hwnd, int nIndex);
DWORD SuperCls_SetClassLong(HWND hwnd, int nIndex, DWORD dwNewLong);
DWORD SuperCls_GetClassLong(HWND hwnd, int nIndex);
WORD  SuperCls_SetWindowWord(HWND hwnd, int nIndex, WORD wNewWord);
WORD  SuperCls_GetWindowWord(HWND hwnd, int nIndex);
DWORD SuperCls_SetWindowLong(HWND hwnd, int nIndex, DWORD dwNewLong);
DWORD SuperCls_GetWindowLong(HWND hwnd, int nIndex);
```

First we must examine the appropriate members of the class's SUPERCLS_BASECLSINFO structure to get either the base offset of the superclass's class or window extra bytes. This offset, of course, skips over any of the class and window extra bytes that were reserved by the base window class. Then, the desired offset is added to the base and the Win32 function to get or set the extra bytes is called; the result is returned to the caller.

Most of this code in these functions is simply a matter of adding and subtracting various offsets. I will not go into the minute details of it here.

Listing 5.5 *Arcade.C*

Arcade.ICO

```
/*******************************************************************************
Module name: Arcade.c
Written by: Jeffrey Richter
Notices: Copyright (c) 1995 Jeffrey Richter
Purpose: AniBtn superclass child control implementation file.
*******************************************************************************/

#include "..\Win95ADG.h"          /* See Appendix A for details */
#include <Windows.h>
#include <Windowsx.h>
#pragma warning(disable: 4001)    /* Single- line comment */
#include <commctrl.h>
#include <stdarg.h>
#include "AniBtn.h"
#include "resource.h"


////////////////////////////////////////////////////////////////////////////////


HIMAGELIST Arcade_MakeImageList (HINSTANCE hinstRes, int idi, ...) {
```

```
     va_list args;
     HIMAGELIST himl = ImageList_Create(
        GetSystemMetrics(SM_CXICON), GetSystemMetrics(SM_CYICON),
        ILC_MASK, 5, 5);
     adgASSERT(himl != NULL);

     va_start(args, idi);
     while (idi != 0) {
        ImageList_AddIcon(himl, LoadIcon(hinstRes, MAKEINTRESOURCE(idi)));
        idi = va_arg(args, int);
     }
     va_end(args);
     return(himl);
}


//////////////////////////////////////////////////////////////////////////


BOOL Arcade_OnInitDialog (HWND hwnd, HWND hwndFocus, LPARAM lParam) {

     // Create and set the imagelists for both buttons.
     // NOTE: When an AniBtn is destroyed, it destroys the imagelist.
     HINSTANCE hinstRes = GetWindowInstance(hwnd);
     HIMAGELIST himl;

     // Initialize the Pong AniBtn.
     himl = Arcade_MakeImageList(hinstRes, IDI_PONG1, IDI_PONG2,
        IDI_PONG3, IDI_PONG4, IDI_PONG5, IDI_PONG6, 0);
     adgASSERT(himl != NULL);
     AniBtn_SetImageList(GetDlgItem(hwnd, IDC_PONG), himl);
     AniBtn_SetTimer(GetDlgItem(hwnd, IDC_PONG), 250);

     // Initialize the Tetris AniBtn.
     himl = Arcade_MakeImageList(hinstRes, IDI_TETRIS1, IDI_TETRIS2,
        IDI_TETRIS3, IDI_TETRIS4, IDI_TETRIS5, IDI_TETRIS6, IDI_TETRIS7, 0);
     adgASSERT(himl != NULL);
     AniBtn_SetImageList(GetDlgItem(hwnd, IDC_TETRIS), himl);
     AniBtn_SetTimer(GetDlgItem(hwnd, IDC_TETRIS), 500);

     adgSETDLGICONS(hwnd, IDI_ARCADE, IDI_ARCADE);

     return(TRUE);  // Accepts default focus window.
}


//////////////////////////////////////////////////////////////////////////


void Arcade_OnCommand (HWND hwnd, int id, HWND hwndCtl, UINT codeNotify) {

     switch (id) {

        case IDCANCEL:                   // Allows dialog box to close.
           EndDialog(hwnd, id);
           break;
```

```
        case IDC_PONG:
            adgMB(__TEXT("Imagine Pong running here."));
            break;

        case IDC_TETRIS:
            adgMB(__TEXT("Imagine Tetris running here."));
            break;
    }
}


//////////////////////////////////////////////////////////////////////////


BOOL WINAPI Arcade_DlgProc (HWND hwnd, UINT uMsg,
    WPARAM wParam, LPARAM lParam) {

    switch (uMsg) {
        // Standard Window's messages
        adgHANDLE_DLGMSG(hwnd, WM_INITDIALOG, Arcade_OnInitDialog);
        adgHANDLE_DLGMSG(hwnd, WM_COMMAND, Arcade_OnCommand);
    }
    return(FALSE);
}


//////////////////////////////////////////////////////////////////////////


int WINAPI WinMain (HINSTANCE hinstExe, HINSTANCE hinstPrev,
    LPSTR lpszCmdLine, int nCmdShow) {


#ifndef WINDOWSNT_COMPATIBILITY
    OSVERSIONINFO VerInfo;
    adgINITSTRUCT(VerInfo, TRUE);
    GetVersionEx(&VerInfo);
    if ((VerInfo.dwPlatformId == VER_PLATFORM_WIN32_NT) &&
        (VerInfo.dwMajorVersion <= 3 && VerInfo.dwMinorVersion <= 51)) {
        adgMB(__TEXT("This program may not run properly on Windows NT because ")
            __TEXT("it requires that the BS_BITMAP style be supported by the ")
            __TEXT("Windows' Button class."));
    }
#endif

    adgWARNIFUNICODEUNDERWIN95();

    // Register the AniBtn control class.
    if (AniBtn_RegisterClass(hinstExe, FALSE) != INVALID_ATOM) {

        adgVERIFY(-1 != DialogBox(hinstExe,
            MAKEINTRESOURCE(IDD_ARCADE), NULL, Arcade_DlgProc));

        // Unregister window classes.
```

```
        AniBtn_UnregisterClass(hinstExe);
    }
    return(0);
}



/////////////////////////////////// End of File ////////////////////////////////
```

Listing 5.6 *AniBtn.C*

```
/*****************************************************************************
Module name: AniBtn.c
Written by: Jeffrey Richter
Notices: Copyright (c) 1995 Jeffrey Richter
Purpose: AniBtn superclass child control implementation file
*****************************************************************************/


#include "..\Win95ADG.h"          /* See Appendix A for details. */
#include <windows.h>
#include <windowsx.h>
#pragma warning(disable: 4001)     /* Single-line comment */
#include <commctrl.h>
#include "SuperCls.h"
#include "AniBtn.h"


///////////////////////////////////////////////////////////////////////////


// The imagelist code requires the ComCtl32.lib library.  Because
// VC++ 2.x doesn't link with ComCtl32.lib by default, I must force it.
#pragma comment(lib, "ComCtl32.lib")


///////////////////////////////////////////////////////////////////////////


typedef struct {
    HIMAGELIST himl;               // Handle of imagelist containing images
    int iImage;                    // Index of image in himl to show next
    int nTimeout;                  // Image change interval
} ANIBTN_WNDEXTRABYTES;


///////////////////////////////////////////////////////////////////////////


void WINAPI AniBtn_OnSetTimer (HWND hwnd, int nTimeout) {

    SuperCls_SetWindowLong(hwnd,
```

346

```
      adgMEMBEROFFSET(ANIBTN_WNDEXTRABYTES, nTimeout), nTimeout);
   SetTimer(hwnd, 1, nTimeout, NULL);
}


/////////////////////////////////////////////////////////////////////////////


int WINAPI AniBtn_OnGetTimer (HWND hwnd) {

   return(SuperCls_GetWindowLong(hwnd,
      adgMEMBEROFFSET(ANIBTN_WNDEXTRABYTES, nTimeout)));
}



/////////////////////////////////////////////////////////////////////////////


void WINAPI AniBtn_OnSetImageList (HWND hwnd, HIMAGELIST himl) {

   SuperCls_SetWindowLong(hwnd,
      adgMEMBEROFFSET(ANIBTN_WNDEXTRABYTES, himl), (LONG) himl);
   SuperCls_SetWindowLong(hwnd,
      adgMEMBEROFFSET(ANIBTN_WNDEXTRABYTES, iImage), 0);
}


/////////////////////////////////////////////////////////////////////////////


HIMAGELIST WINAPI AniBtn_OnGetImageList (HWND hwnd) {

   return((HIMAGELIST) SuperCls_GetWindowLong(hwnd,
      adgMEMBEROFFSET(ANIBTN_WNDEXTRABYTES, himl)));
}


/////////////////////////////////////////////////////////////////////////////


LRESULT AniBtn_CallBaseClass (HWND hwnd, UINT uMsg,
   WPARAM wParam, LPARAM lParam) {

   return(CallWindowProc(SuperCls_GetWndProcBaseCls(hwnd),
      hwnd, uMsg, wParam, lParam));
}


/////////////////////////////////////////////////////////////////////////////


BOOL AniBtn_OnCreate (HWND hwnd, LPCREATESTRUCT lpCreateStruct) {

   AniBtn_SetTimer(hwnd, 250);     // Default to .25 seconds.
```

```
    // Make sure that the button base class is given the opportunity to
    // perform any initialization that it needs to.
    // NOTE: The return value for WM_CREATE is -1 if the window should not be
    // created and 0 if it should be created.  However, the OnCreate message
    // cracker expects TRUE to be returned if the window should be created and
    // FALSE if the window should not be created.
    return(-1 != FORWARD_WM_CREATE(hwnd, lpCreateStruct, AniBtn_CallBaseClass));
}


/////////////////////////////////////////////////////////////////////////////


void AniBtn_OnDestroy (HWND hwnd) {

    // If there is an imagelist associated with the button, destroy it.
    HIMAGELIST himl = AniBtn_GetImageList(hwnd);
    if (himl != NULL)
        ImageList_Destroy(himl);

    // Kill the timer associated with the button.
    KillTimer(hwnd, 1);

    // Make sure that the button base class is given the opportunity to
    // perform any needed clean up.
    FORWARD_WM_DESTROY(hwnd, AniBtn_CallBaseClass);
}


/////////////////////////////////////////////////////////////////////////////


void AniBtn_OnTimer (HWND hwnd, UINT id) {

    HIMAGELIST himl = AniBtn_GetImageList(hwnd);

    if (himl != NULL) {

        // Get the AniBtn's image index.
        int iImage = SuperCls_GetWindowLong(hwnd,
            adgMEMBEROFFSET(ANIBTN_WNDEXTRABYTES, iImage));

        // Change the AniBtn's icon.
        HICON hiconOld = (HICON) SendMessage(hwnd, BM_SETIMAGE, IMAGE_ICON,
            (LONG) ImageList_GetIcon(himl, iImage, ILD_NORMAL));

        // Destroy any old icon that is displayed.
        if (hiconOld != NULL)
            DestroyIcon(hiconOld);

        iImage = ++iImage % ImageList_GetImageCount(himl);
        SuperCls_SetWindowLong(hwnd,
            adgMEMBEROFFSET(ANIBTN_WNDEXTRABYTES, iImage), iImage);
    }
}
```

```
/////////////////////////////////////////////////////////////////////////

LRESULT WINAPI AniBtn_WndProc (HWND hwnd, UINT uMsg,
  WPARAM wParam, LPARAM lParam) {

  switch (uMsg) {

    // Standard window messages
    HANDLE_MSG(hwnd, WM_CREATE,       AniBtn_OnCreate);
    HANDLE_MSG(hwnd, WM_DESTROY,      AniBtn_OnDestroy);
    HANDLE_MSG(hwnd, WM_TIMER,        AniBtn_OnTimer);

    // Control-specific messages
    HANDLE_MSG(hwnd, ABM_SETTIMER,    AniBtn_OnSetTimer);
    HANDLE_MSG(hwnd, ABM_GETTIMER,    AniBtn_OnGetTimer);
    HANDLE_MSG(hwnd, ABM_SETIMAGELIST, AniBtn_OnSetImageList);
    HANDLE_MSG(hwnd, ABM_GETIMAGELIST, AniBtn_OnGetImageList);
  }

  return(AniBtn_CallBaseClass(hwnd, uMsg, wParam, lParam));
}


/////////////////////////////////////////////////////////////////////////



ATOM WINAPI AniBtn_RegisterClass (HINSTANCE hinst, BOOL fGlobalClass) {

  WNDCLASSEX wc;
  adgINITSTRUCT(wc, TRUE);
  if (!GetClassInfoEx(NULL, __TEXT("BUTTON"), &wc))
    return(INVALID_ATOM);

  // Calling InitCommonControls isn't strictly necessary because ImageLists
  // are not actually registered window classes, but for "correctness" we
  // call this function here anyway.
  InitCommonControls();

  // Give our new class a new name.
  wc.lpszClassName = WC_ANIBTN;

  // Our module is registering the class.
  wc.hInstance = hinst;

  // Make the new class a global class if the user desires.
  if (fGlobalClass)
    wc.style |= CS_GLOBALCLASS;

  // The following WNDCLASSEX members are not changed for AniBtn:
  //      hIcon, hIconSm, hCursor, hbrBackground, lpszMenuName.

  // Register the new window superclass.
  return(SuperCls_RegisterClassEx(&wc, AniBtn_WndProc,
```

```
      0, sizeof(ANIBTN_WNDEXTRABYTES)));
}


////////////////////////////////////////////////////////////////////////////


BOOL WINAPI AniBtn_UnregisterClass (HINSTANCE hinst) {

   return(UnregisterClass(WC_ANIBTN, hinst));
}


//////////////////////////// End of File //////////////////////////////////
```

Listing 5.7 *AniBtn.H*

```
/****************************************************************************
Module name: AniBtn.h
Written by: Jeffrey Richter
Notices: Copyright (c) 1995 Jeffrey Richter
Purpose: AniBtn superclass child control header file
****************************************************************************/


///////////////////////////////// Class Name ////////////////////////////////


#define WC_ANIBTNA  "AniBtn"
#define WC_ANIBTNW  L"AniBtn"

#ifdef UNICODE
#define WC_ANIBTN WC_ANIBTNW
#else
#define WC_ANIBTN WC_ANIBTNA
#endif


////////////////////////////// Class Registration /////////////////////////////


// Register and unregister the AniBtn window class.
ATOM WINAPI AniBtn_RegisterClass (HINSTANCE hinst, BOOL fGlobalClass);
BOOL WINAPI AniBtn_UnregisterClass (HINSTANCE hinst);


////////////////////////// Class-Specific Window Styles ////////////////////////


// NOTE: Superclassed classes cannot have any class-specific window styles.


/////////////////////////// Parent Notification Codes /////////////////////////
```

350

```
// AniBtn controls have no class-specific notification codes at this time.


/////////////////////// Class-Specific Window Messages //////////////////////////


// NOTE: We must select a value for ABM_FIRSTMSG that is guaranteed not to
// conflict with other messages.  If the application defines other WM_APP
// messages, the following line will have to change.  Similarly, if the
// application uses other superclasses or subclasses, their message ranges
// must not overlap!
#define ABM_FIRSTMSG    (WM_APP + 0)

//{{adgMSGCRACK_MESSAGES

// Purpose: Sets the timer interval between image changes.
// wParam:  int nTimeout - New timer interval in milliseconds
// lParam:  N/A
// Returns: void
#define ABM_SETTIMER          (ABM_FIRSTMSG + 0)

// Purpose: Gets the timer interval between image changes.
// wParam:  N/A
// lParam:  N/A
// Returns: int - Current timer interval in milliseconds
#define ABM_GETTIMER          (ABM_FIRSTMSG + 1)

// Purpose: Sets the imagelist that contains the set of images.
// wParam:  HIMAGELIST himl - New imagelist containing images
// lParam:  N/A
// Returns: void
#define ABM_SETIMAGELIST      (ABM_FIRSTMSG + 2)

// Purpose: Gets the imagelist that contains the set of images.
// wParam:  N/A
// lParam:  N/A
// Returns: HIMAGELIST - Current imagelist containing images
#define ABM_GETIMAGELIST      (ABM_FIRSTMSG + 3)

//}}adgMSGCRACK_MESSAGES


///////////////////////////////// Message APIs ////////////////////////////////////


//{{adgMSGCRACK_APIS

#define AniBtn_SetTimer(hwnd, nTimeout) \
   ((void)SendMessage((hwnd), ABM_SETTIMER, (WPARAM)(DWORD)(nTimeout), 0))

#define AniBtn_GetTimer(hwnd) \
   ((int )SendMessage((hwnd), ABM_GETTIMER, 0, 0))

#define AniBtn_SetImageList(hwnd, himl) \
   ((void)SendMessage((hwnd), ABM_SETIMAGELIST, (WPARAM)(DWORD)(himl), 0))
```

```
#define AniBtn_GetImageList(hwnd) \
   ((HIMAGELIST )SendMessage((hwnd), ABM_GETIMAGELIST, 0, 0))

//}}adgMSGCRACK_APIS


/////////////////////////////// Message Crackers ///////////////////////////////


// The following message crackers are available for use in subclassing and
// superclassing the AniBtn control.

//{{adgMSGCRACK_CRACKERS

// void Cls_OnSetTimer (HWND hwnd, int nTimeout)
#define HANDLE_ABM_SETTIMER(hwnd, wParam, lParam, fn) \
   ((fn)((hwnd), (int)(wParam)), 0)
#define FORWARD_ABM_SETTIMER(hwnd, nTimeout, fn) \
   (void)((fn)((hwnd), ABM_SETTIMER, (WPARAM)(DWORD)(nTimeout), 0))

// int  Cls_OnGetTimer (HWND hwnd)
#define HANDLE_ABM_GETTIMER(hwnd, wParam, lParam, fn) \
   (LRESULT)(fn)((hwnd))
#define FORWARD_ABM_GETTIMER(hwnd, fn) \
   (int )((fn)((hwnd), ABM_GETTIMER, 0, 0))

// void Cls_OnSetImageList (HWND hwnd, HIMAGELIST himl)
#define HANDLE_ABM_SETIMAGELIST(hwnd, wParam, lParam, fn) \
   ((fn)((hwnd), (HIMAGELIST)(wParam)), 0)
#define FORWARD_ABM_SETIMAGELIST(hwnd, himl, fn) \
   (void)((fn)((hwnd), ABM_SETIMAGELIST, (WPARAM)(DWORD)(himl), 0))

// HIMAGELIST  Cls_OnGetImageList (HWND hwnd)
#define HANDLE_ABM_GETIMAGELIST(hwnd, wParam, lParam, fn) \
   (LRESULT)(fn)((hwnd))
#define FORWARD_ABM_GETIMAGELIST(hwnd, fn) \
   (HIMAGELIST )((fn)((hwnd), ABM_GETIMAGELIST, 0, 0))

//}}adgMSGCRACK_CRACKERS


/////////////////////////////// End of File ///////////////////////////////
```

Listing 5.8 *AniBtn.MSG*

```
// Module name: AniBtn.msg
// Written by: Jeffrey Richter
// Notices: Copyright (c) 1995 Jeffrey Richter
// Purpose: 'MsgCrack' input file for AniBtn

MessageBase ABM_FIRSTMSG
```

```
MessageClass AniBtn

Message ABM_SETTIMER SetTimer \
 - Sets the timer interval between image changes.
wParam int nTimeout - New timer interval in milliseconds
.


Message ABM_GETTIMER GetTimer \
 - Gets the timer interval between image changes.
Returns int - Current timer interval in milliseconds
.


Message ABM_SETIMAGELIST SetImageList \
 - Sets the imagelist that contains the set of images.
wParam HIMAGELIST himl - New imagelist containing images
.


Message ABM_GETIMAGELIST GetImageList \
 - Gets the imagelist that contains the set of images.
Returns HIMAGELIST - Current imagelist containing images
.
```

Listing 5.9 *SuperCls.C*

```
/******************************************************************************
Module name: SuperCls.c
Written by: Jeffrey Richter
Notices: Copyright (c) 1995 Jeffrey Richter
Purpose: Utility functions to help with window superclassing.
******************************************************************************/


#include "..\Win95ADG.h"          /* See Appendix A for details. */
#include <Windows.h>
#include <WindowsX.h>
#pragma warning(disable: 4001)     /* Single-line comment */
#include "SuperCls.h"


///////////////////////////////////////////////////////////////////////////


// Enough class extra bytes are added to the superclass to accommodate
// the data represented by the following structure. These additional data make
it
// easier for a superclass to add class and window extra bytes of its own to
// the superclass. After the superclass has been registered, using the
// functions in this module, the layout of the superclass's extra bytes is as
// follows:
//
// Range:    0 to (cbClsExtraBaseCls - 1)
```

```
// Contents: Base class's class extra bytes
// Range:    cbClsExtraBaseCls to (GCL_CBCLSEXTRA - SUPERCLS_BASECLSINFO - 1)
// Contents: Additional class extra bytes desired by superclass
// Range:    (GCL_CBCLSEXTRA - SUPERCLS_BASECLSINFO) to (GCL_CBCLSEXTTA - 1)
// Contents: Data represented by the following SUPERCLS_BASECLSINFO structure
//
typedef struct {
    WNDPROC pfnWndProcBaseCls;     // Base class's window procedure
    int     cbClsExtraBaseCls;     // Class extra bytes for base class
    int     cbWndExtraBaseCls;     // Window extra bytes for base class
} SUPERCLS_BASECLSINFO;


////////////////////////////////////////////////////////////////////////////


// Helper macro is used to get the offset of a SUPERCLS_BASECLSINFO member from
// within the class's extra bytes.
#define SuperCls_BaseClsInfoIndex(cbClsTotal, member)    \
    (cbClsTotal - sizeof(SUPERCLS_BASECLSINFO) +         \
    adgMEMBEROFFSET(SUPERCLS_BASECLSINFO, member))


////////////////////////////////////////////////////////////////////////////


ATOM WINAPI SuperCls_RegisterClassEx (
    PWNDCLASSEX pwc,              // lpfnWndClass member is base class WndProc.
    WNDPROC pfnWndProcSuperCls,   // Address of superclass WndProc function
    int cbClsAdditional,          // # of class extra bytes for super class
    int cbWndAdditional) {        // # of window extra bytes for super class

    HWND hwnd;
    ATOM atomSuperClass;
    WNDPROC pfnWndProcBaseCls = pwc->lpfnWndProc;
    int cbClsExtraBaseCls     = pwc->cbClsExtra;
    int cbWndExtraBaseCls     = pwc->cbWndExtra;

    // Add to the cbClsExtra member the number of class extra bytes
    // desired by the superclass plus the number of extra bytes
    // required by the SUPERCLS_BASECLSINFO structure.
    pwc->cbClsExtra += cbClsAdditional + sizeof(SUPERCLS_BASECLSINFO);

    // Add to the cbWndExtra member the number of window extra bytes
    // desired by the superclass.
    pwc->cbWndExtra += cbWndAdditional;

    // In order for the superclass window procedure to manipulate
    // any of the superclass's class and window extra bytes successfully, the
    // SUPERCLS_BASECLSINFO data members in the superclass's class extra bytes
    // must be initialized first.  Because there is no Win32 function that
    // allows us to change a class's extra bytes without creating a window
    // first, we need to hack the solution.  This is done by registering the
    // class using DefWindowProc as the window procedure.  After the class
    // extra bytes have been initialized, DefWindowProc is replaced by the
```

```
      // desired superclass window procedure.
      pwc->lpfnWndProc = DefWindowProc;

      // Register the superclass.
      atomSuperClass = RegisterClassEx(pwc);
      if (atomSuperClass == INVALID_ATOM)
         return(atomSuperClass);

      // Now, we must complete the class's initialization by setting its
      // class extra bytes.  Unfortunately, we must have a window handle
      // to change a class's extra bytes.  So, we create a window of the class.
      // This is a dummy window whose messages are processed by DefWindowProc.
      hwnd = CreateWindowEx(0, MAKEINTATOM(atomSuperClass), NULL,
         0, 0, 0, 0, 0, NULL, NULL, pwc->hInstance, NULL);

      if (!IsWindow(hwnd)) {

         // If the window could not be created, unregister the superclass
         // and return INVALID_ATOM to the caller.
         UnregisterClass(MAKEINTATOM(atomSuperClass), pwc->hInstance);
         atomSuperClass = INVALID_ATOM;
      } else {

         // Initialize the data represented by the SUPERCLS_BASECLSINFO structure.
         SetClassLong(hwnd,
            SuperCls_BaseClsInfoIndex(pwc->cbClsExtra, pfnWndProcBaseCls),
               (LONG) pfnWndProcBaseCls);
         SetClassLong(hwnd,
            SuperCls_BaseClsInfoIndex(pwc->cbClsExtra, cbClsExtraBaseCls),
               cbClsExtraBaseCls);
         SetClassLong(hwnd,
            SuperCls_BaseClsInfoIndex(pwc->cbClsExtra, cbWndExtraBaseCls),
               cbWndExtraBaseCls);

         // Now, we can set the class's window procedure to point to the
         // desired superclass window procedure.
         SetClassLong(hwnd, GCL_WNDPROC, (LONG) pfnWndProcSuperCls);

         // NOTE: At this point, any windows of this class that are created
         // will have their messages processed by the proper superclass WndProc.

         // Because all the class extra bytes are set, we can destroy the dummy
         // window.  The WM_DESTROY/WM_NCDESTROY messages will be sent to
         // DefWindowProc because the call to SetClassLong above does NOT affect
         // the window procedure address that was associated with the dummy
         // window when it was created.
         DestroyWindow(hwnd);
      }

      // Return the atom of the registered class to the caller.
      return(atomSuperClass);
}


//////////////////////////////////////////////////////////////////////////////


WNDPROC WINAPI SuperCls_GetWndProcBaseCls (HWND hwnd) {
```

```
   // Return the address of the base class's WndProc from the superclass's
   // extra bytes.
   return((WNDPROC) GetClassLong(hwnd,
      SuperCls_BaseClsInfoIndex(GetClassLong(hwnd, GCL_CBCLSEXTRA),
         pfnWndProcBaseCls)));
}


//////////////////////////////////////////////////////////////////////////


// Function used internally by Get/SetClassWord/Long functions
static int SuperCls_ClassByteIndex (HWND hwnd, int nIndex) {

   int cbClsExtraIndexBaseCls, cbClsExtraBaseCls;

   // If nIndex is negative, the caller wants a Win32 predefined class
   // word/long value.
   if (nIndex < 0)
      return(nIndex);

   // Retrieve index into class extra bytes for the number of class extra
   // bytes used by the base class.
   cbClsExtraIndexBaseCls =
      SuperCls_BaseClsInfoIndex(GetClassLong(hwnd, GCL_CBCLSEXTRA),
         cbClsExtraBaseCls);

   // Retrieve number of class extra bytes used by the base class.
   cbClsExtraBaseCls = GetClassWord(hwnd, cbClsExtraIndexBaseCls);

   // Return (index + number) of class extra bytes used by base class.
   return(nIndex + cbClsExtraBaseCls);
}


///////////////////////// Set/GetClassWord/Long Functions /////////////////////////


WORD WINAPI SuperCls_SetClassWord (HWND hwnd, int nIndex, WORD wNewWord) {

   return(SetClassWord(hwnd,
      SuperCls_ClassByteIndex(hwnd, nIndex), wNewWord));
}


WORD WINAPI SuperCls_GetClassWord (HWND hwnd, int nIndex) {

   return(GetClassWord(hwnd,
      SuperCls_ClassByteIndex(hwnd, nIndex)));
}


DWORD WINAPI SuperCls_SetClassLong (HWND hwnd, int nIndex, DWORD dwNewLong) {

   return(SetClassLong(hwnd,
```

```
      SuperCls_ClassByteIndex(hwnd, nIndex), dwNewLong));
}


DWORD WINAPI SuperCls_GetClassLong (HWND hwnd, int nIndex) {

   return(GetClassLong(hwnd,
      SuperCls_ClassByteIndex(hwnd, nIndex)));
}


//////////////////////////////////////////////////////////////////////////


// Function used internally by Get/SetWindowWord/Long functions.
static int SuperCls_WindowByteIndex (HWND hwnd, int nIndex) {

   int cbWndExtraIndexBaseCls, cbWndExtraBaseCls;

   // If nIndex is negative, the caller wants a Win32 predefined window
   // word/long value.
   if (nIndex < 0)
      return(nIndex);

   // Retrieve index into class extra bytes for the number of window extra
   // bytes used by the base class.
   cbWndExtraIndexBaseCls =
      SuperCls_BaseClsInfoIndex(GetClassLong(hwnd, GCL_CBCLSEXTRA),
         cbWndExtraBaseCls);

   // Retrieve number of window extra bytes used by base class.
   cbWndExtraBaseCls = GetClassWord(hwnd, cbWndExtraIndexBaseCls);

   // Return (index + number) of window extra bytes used by base class.
   return(nIndex + cbWndExtraBaseCls);
}


//////////////////////// Set/GetWindowWord/Long Functions ////////////////////////


WORD WINAPI SuperCls_SetWindowWord (HWND hwnd, int nIndex, WORD wNewWord) {

   return(SetWindowWord(hwnd,
      SuperCls_WindowByteIndex(hwnd, nIndex), wNewWord));
}


WORD WINAPI SuperCls_GetWindowWord (HWND hwnd, int nIndex) {

   return(GetWindowWord(hwnd,
      SuperCls_WindowByteIndex(hwnd, nIndex)));
}


DWORD WINAPI SuperCls_SetWindowLong (HWND hwnd, int nIndex, DWORD dwNewLong) {
```

357

```
   return(SetWindowLong(hwnd,
      SuperCls_WindowByteIndex(hwnd, nIndex), dwNewLong)));
}



DWORD WINAPI SuperCls_GetWindowLong (HWND hwnd, int nIndex) {

   return(GetWindowLong(hwnd,
      SuperCls_WindowByteIndex(hwnd, nIndex)));
}



/////////////////////////////// End of File ///////////////////////////////
```

Listing 5.10 *SuperCls.H*

```
/****************************************************************************
Module name: SuperCls.h
Written by: Jeffrey Richter
Notices: Copyright (c) 1995 Jeffrey Richter
Purpose: Utility functions to help with window superclassing
****************************************************************************/


// Function that registers a superclass
ATOM WINAPI SuperCls_RegisterClassEx (
   PWNDCLASSEX pwc,              // lpfnWndClass member is base class WndProc.
   WNDPROC pfnWndProcSuperCls,   // Address of superclass WndProc function
   int cbClsAdditional,          // # of class extra bytes for superclass
   int cbWndAdditional);         // # of window extra bytes for superclass


// Function to retrieve the WndProc address of the base class
WNDPROC WINAPI SuperCls_GetWndProcBaseCls (HWND hwnd);


// Functions to manipulate a superclass's class extra bytes without affecting
// the base class's class extra bytes
WORD  WINAPI SuperCls_SetClassWord (HWND hwnd, int nIndex, WORD wNewWord);
WORD  WINAPI SuperCls_GetClassWord (HWND hwnd, int nIndex);
DWORD WINAPI SuperCls_SetClassLong (HWND hwnd, int nIndex, DWORD dwNewLong);
DWORD WINAPI SuperCls_GetClassLong (HWND hwnd, int nIndex);


// Functions to manipulate a superclass's window extra bytes without affecting
// the base class's window extra bytes.
WORD  WINAPI SuperCls_SetWindowWord (HWND hwnd, int nIndex, WORD wNewWord);
WORD  WINAPI SuperCls_GetWindowWord (HWND hwnd, int nIndex);
DWORD WINAPI SuperCls_SetWindowLong (HWND hwnd, int nIndex, DWORD dwNewLong);
DWORD WINAPI SuperCls_GetWindowLong (HWND hwnd, int nIndex);


/////////////////////////////// End of File ///////////////////////////////
```

358

Listing 5.11 *Arcade.RC*

Pong1.ICO

Pong2.ICO

Pong3.ICO

Pong4.ICO

Pong5.ICO

Pong6.ICO

Tetris1.ICO

Tetris2.ICO

```
//Microsoft Visual C++-generated resource script
//
#include "resource.h"

#define APSTUDIO_READONLY_SYMBOLS
/////////////////////////////////////////////////////////////////////////////
//
// Generated from the TEXTINCLUDE 2 resource
//
#include "afxres.h"


/////////////////////////////////////////////////////////////////////////////
#undef APSTUDIO_READONLY_SYMBOLS


#ifdef APSTUDIO_INVOKED
/////////////////////////////////////////////////////////////////////////////
//
// TEXTINCLUDE
//

1 TEXTINCLUDE DISCARDABLE
BEGIN
    "resource.h\0"
END

2 TEXTINCLUDE DISCARDABLE
BEGIN
    "#include ""afxres.h""\r\n"
    "\0"
END

3 TEXTINCLUDE DISCARDABLE
BEGIN
    "\r\n"
    "\0"
END


/////////////////////////////////////////////////////////////////////////////
#endif    // APSTUDIO_INVOKED


/////////////////////////////////////////////////////////////////////////////
//
// Dialog
//

IDD_ARCADE DIALOG DISCARDABLE  -32768, 5, 176, 64
STYLE WS_MINIMIZEBOX | WS_VISIBLE | WS_CAPTION | WS_SYSMENU
CAPTION "Arcade"
FONT 8, "MS Sans Serif"
BEGIN
    CTEXT           "Please select the game that you would like to play:",
```

Tetris3.ICO

Tetris4.ICO

Tetris5.ICO

Tetris6.ICO

Tetris7.ICO

```
                              IDC_STATIC,4,4,168,12
            CONTROL           "Pong",IDC_PONG,"AniBtn",WS_TABSTOP | 0x40,41,24,26,26
            CONTROL           "Tetris",IDC_TETRIS,"AniBtn",WS_TABSTOP | 0x40,109,24,26,
                              26
END


/////////////////////////////////////////////////////////////////////////////
//
// Icon
//

IDI_ARCADE              ICON        DISCARDABLE     "Arcade.ico"
IDI_PONG1               ICON        DISCARDABLE     "Pong1.ico"
IDI_PONG2               ICON        DISCARDABLE     "Pong2.ico"
IDI_PONG3               ICON        DISCARDABLE     "Pong3.ico"
IDI_PONG4               ICON        DISCARDABLE     "Pong4.ico"
IDI_PONG5               ICON        DISCARDABLE     "Pong5.ico"
IDI_PONG6               ICON        DISCARDABLE     "Pong6.ico"
IDI_TETRIS1             ICON        DISCARDABLE     "Tetris1.ico"
IDI_TETRIS2             ICON        DISCARDABLE     "Tetris2.ico"
IDI_TETRIS3             ICON        DISCARDABLE     "Tetris3.ico"
IDI_TETRIS4             ICON        DISCARDABLE     "Tetris4.ico"
IDI_TETRIS5             ICON        DISCARDABLE     "Tetris5.ico"
IDI_TETRIS6             ICON        DISCARDABLE     "Tetris6.ico"
IDI_TETRIS7             ICON        DISCARDABLE     "Tetris7.ico"

#ifndef APSTUDIO_INVOKED
/////////////////////////////////////////////////////////////////////////////
//
// Generated from the TEXTINCLUDE 3 resource
//


/////////////////////////////////////////////////////////////////////////////
#endif    // not APSTUDIO_INVOKED
```

Listing 5.12 *Resource.H*

```
//{{NO_DEPENDENCIES}}
// Microsoft Visual C++-generated include file
// Used by Arcade.rc
//
#define IDD_ARCADE                   105
#define IDI_ARCADE                   106
#define IDI_PONG1                    110
#define IDI_PONG2                    111
#define IDI_PONG3                    112
#define IDI_PONG4                    113
#define IDI_PONG5                    114
#define IDI_PONG6                    115
```

```
#define IDI_TETRIS1                    130
#define IDI_TETRIS2                    131
#define IDI_TETRIS3                    132
#define IDI_TETRIS4                    133
#define IDI_TETRIS5                    134
#define IDI_TETRIS6                    135
#define IDI_TETRIS7                    136
#define IDC_PONG                       1010
#define IDC_TETRIS                     1011

// Next default values for new objects
//
#ifdef APSTUDIO_INVOKED
#ifndef APSTUDIO_READONLY_SYMBOLS
#define _APS_NEXT_RESOURCE_VALUE       140
#define _APS_NEXT_COMMAND_VALUE        40001
#define _APS_NEXT_CONTROL_VALUE        1011
#define _APS_NEXT_SYMED_VALUE          140
#endif
#endif
```

CHAPTER SIX

Hooks

I consider hooks to be one of the most powerful features of Windows. They give an application the ability to trap events that are about to occur, either with respect to an individual thread or throughout the entire Windows system. In fact, not only can an application be notified when a particular event is about to happen, but also, for most hooks, the application can tell Windows to stop the event from being processed further.

Local and Remote Hooks

There are two broad categories of hooks: *local hooks* and *remote hooks*. Local hooks trap events that are destined for a thread running in the process that sets the hook. Remote hooks trap events destined for threads running in other processes. Local hooks can be installed on only a single thread at a time. But there are two varieties of remote hooks: *thread-specific* and *system-wide*. Thread-specific remote hooks trap events destined for a specific thread running in another process. System-wide hooks trap all events destined for all threads running in all processes on the entire system.

Installing a local hook is remarkably easy and has little impact on the system, but remote hooks have some notable downsides:

■ **System-wide remote hooks affect system performance.** System-wide hooks are called for every relevant event that occurs, regardless of what thread is destined to receive the event. Naturally, thread-specific hooks have some impact on the system, but the impact of a system-wide hook is far greater. As a result, system-wide hooks should be installed only when truly necessary and should remain installed for as little time as possible.

■ **System-wide hooks can affect the stability of other applications.** Naturally, if you write a hook that has a bug in it, you can crash your process. However, if your hook is installed on a system-wide basis, you can actually crash other processes! In a protected 32-bit environment, you would think that this sort of thing would simply not be possible; processes are not supposed to be able to affect one another. But system-wide hooks are one way that you can circumvent this protection, by executing code that you have written in the context of someone else's process. Because of this, you should take particular care when writing system-wide hooks.

■ **Remote hooks must be located in a dynamic-link library.** All remote hook procedures must reside in a dynamic-link library. The reason for this is that the code for the hook procedure must be injected by the operating system into the address space(s) of the other process(es). The system can do this only if the hook code is in a DLL, and, unfortunately, there is overhead in creating a whole dynamic-link library just for one small hook function.[1]

The injection of a DLL occurs just before the system calls the hook filter function—it does not occur at the time you call SetWindowsHookEx. However, calling UnhookWindowsHookEx causes the system to free the DLL as soon as you call UnhookWindowsHookEx but only after all threads have finished executing code in the filter function.[2]

---

[1]Even if you *could* place your hook procedure in an existing DLL, it would be much better to create a separate DLL for it. The reason for this is that, in the case of a system-wide hook, the entire DLL containing the hook procedure (and not just the hook procedure itself) is injected into all other processes on the system. So, the smaller your hook DLL is, the better.

[2]For more information about injecting DLLs with hooks, see Chapter 16, "Breaking Through Process Boundary Walls," of *Advanced Windows*.

Installing Hooks

Windows has 14 different types of hooks that you can install, each of which can be local or remote (with the exception of journal record and playback hooks, which are a special case—they are system-wide local hooks in that they are never injected into any other process' address space and therefore journal hook filter functions do not need to be placed in a DLL). But the methods used for installing and removing all hooks, whether local or remote, are identical. Later in this chapter, we will discuss the details of each hook and when to use each one.

An application installs a hook by calling SetWindowsHookEx:

```
HHOOK SetWindowsHookEx(int idHook, HOOKPROC hkprc,
    HINSTANCE hmod, DWORD dwThreadID);
```

When this function is called, Windows allocates a block of memory containing an internal data structure describing the newly installed hook. All these data structures are linked to form a linked list with each new node (data structure) being placed at the front of the list. After the node has been added, SetWindowsHookEx returns a handle to it. This value must be saved by the application and is used whenever the application needs to refer to the hook. We will see examples of this later.

The first parameter to SetWindowsHookEx, idHook, specifies the type of hook the application wishes to install. This must be one of the values listed in Table 6.1.

Table 6.1 *The fourteen types of Windows hooks.*

Hook identifier	Circumstances under which Windows calls the hook procedure
1. WH_CALLWNDPROC	Every time SendMessage sends a message to a window.
2. WH_CALLWNDPROCRET	Every time SendMessage returns after sending a message to a window.
3. WH_GETMESSAGE	Every time GetMessage or PeekMessage retrieves a message from the hooked thread's queue.

continued...

Hook identifier	Circumstances under which Windows calls the hook procedure
4. WH_KEYBOARD	Every time GetMessage or PeekMessage retrieves a WM_KEY-DOWN or WM_KEYUP message from the hooked thread's queue.
5. WH_MOUSE	Every time GetMessage or PeekMessage retrieves a mouse message from the hooked thread's queue.
6. WH_HARDWARE	Every time GetMessage or PeekMessage retrieves a hardware message from the hooked thread's queue that is not related to the keyboard or the mouse.
7. WH_MSGFILTER	Every time a dialog box, menu, or scrollbar created by the hooked thread is about to process a posted message.
8. WH_SYSMSGFILTER	Every time a dialog box, menu, or scrollbar created by any thread is about to process a posted message.
9. WH_JOURNALRECORD	Every time a message is retrieved from the system's hardware input queue.
10. WH_JOURNALPLAYBACK	Every time an event is requested from the system's hardware input queue.
11. WH_SHELL	Whenever a top-level, unowned window is created, activated, or destroyed; when the Taskbar needs to redraw a button; when the system needs the minimized rectangle of an application displayed on the Taskbar; when the current keyboard layout changes; and when the user presses Ctrl+Esc to invoke a Task Manager–like application.
12. WH_CBT	Every time a window is activated, created, destroyed, minimized, maximized, moved, or sized. Also, before completing a system command, before removing a mouse or keyboard event from the system's hardware input queue, before setting the input focus, and upon retrieving a WM_QUEUE-SYNC message.

Hook identifier	Circumstances under which Windows calls the hook procedure
13. WH_FOREGROUNDIDLE	When the foreground thread calls GetMessage and no message is available; this means that the thread is about to go to sleep.
14. WH_DEBUG	Every time any hook filter function is about to be called.

The second parameter, hkprc, is the address of the filter function that should process messages for the specified hook. If you are installing a remote hook, hkprc must reside in a DLL.

The third parameter, hmod, is the module handle of the DLL where hkprc resides (if you are installing a remote hook). If you are installing a local hook, hmod should be NULL. Notice that the prototype for SetWindowsHookEx declares hmod as an HINSTANCE rather than an HMODULE. Although this certainly looks sloppy, it is not a problem under Win32 because there is no distinction between HINSTANCEs and HMODULEs. They are one and the same.

The last parameter, dwThreadID, identifies the thread for which you want the hook installed. This parameter determines whether your hook is local or remote. If you specify a thread running in your application's process, your hook is local; otherwise, it is remote. To install a hook on the current thread, you can pass in the return value of GetCurrentThreadId. To install a system-wide hook, you simply pass in 0 (which is not a valid thread identifier) for dwThreadID. This procedure has the effect of hooking all threads in the system. And to install a hook on a thread associated with a specific window, you can pass in the return value of GetWindowThreadProcessId:

```
DWORD GetWindowThreadProcessId(HWND hwnd, LPDWORD lpdwProcessId);
```

When you pass a window handle to this function, it returns the ID of the thread that created the specified window. You can also pass the address of a DWORD that the function will set to the ID of the process that owns the thread. Usually, we are not interested in the process ID and can simply pass NULL for the lpdwProcessId parameter. Here is an example of how to set a hook on a thread that created a particular window:

```
DWORD dwThreadID = GetWindowThreadProcessId(hwnd, NULL);
SetWindowsHookEx(WH_KEYBOARD, hkprc, hmod, dwThreadID);
```

Most of the different hook types can be installed as either local or remote hooks. But there are two exceptions to this rule. First, WH_JOURNALRECORD and WH_JOURNALPLAYBACK are system-wide hooks that are not required to be in a DLL (they are local system-wide hooks). Second, a WH_SYSMSGFILTER hook does exactly the same thing as a WH_MSGFILTER hook with a dwProcessID of zero (i.e., it is always a system-wide hook). When installing a WH_JOURNALRECORD, WH_JOURNALPLAYBACK, or WH_SYSMSGFILTER hook, you must specify a dwThreadID of zero, or the hook will not be installed.

Whenever an event that is associated with the type of hook you have installed occurs, Windows calls the filter function that was specified to SetWindowsHookEx. The filter function must have the following prototype, regardless of the type of hook that has been installed:

```
LRESULT WINAPI FilterFunc (int nCode, WPARAM wParam, LPARAM lParam);
```

The name of the function, FilterFunc, is a place holder for your own function's name. The first parameter, nCode, specifies the hook code. The domain of values for this parameter depend on the type of hook that was installed. The values of the wParam and lParam parameters, as well as the LRESULT value returned from the function, all depend on the type of hook installed and the hook code passed in the nCode parameter.

A hook filter function's structure is similar to that of a window procedure. That is, the nCode parameter, much like a message, identifies the type of action that is to be performed by the filter function. The meanings of the wParam and lParam parameters depend on the type of action specified in nCode. We will examine the specific values of nCode, and the associated values of wParam and lParam for each nCode, later in this chapter.

The following code fragment shows a possible skeleton for a WH_KEYBOARD hook:

```
// The "g_hhook" global variable will be set to the return value from
// the call to the SetWindowsHookEx function.
static HHOOK g_hhook = NULL;
   .
   .
   .
LRESULT WINAPI Example_KybdHook (int nCode, WPARAM wParam, LPARAM lParam) {

   LRESULT lResult = CallNextHookEx(g_hhook, nCode, wParam, lParam);

   switch (nCode) {

      case HC_ACTION:

         // Do HC_ACTION processing...
         break;

      case HC_NOREMOVE:

         // Do HC_NOREMOVE processing...
         break;
   }
   return(lResult);
}
```

Uninstalling a Hook

When an application no longer needs a hook, it can be removed by calling UnhookWindowsHookEx:

```
BOOL UnhookWindowsHookEx(HHOOK hhook);
```

The hhook parameter specifies the handle of the hook that you wish to remove. This handle was originally returned from the call to SetWindowsHookEx when the hook was first installed. The return value from UnhookWindowsHookEx indicates whether the filter function has been successfully removed from the chain. If so, a nonzero value is returned.

Windows does not require that hook filter functions be removed in the reverse of the order in which they were installed. Whenever a hook is removed, Windows destroys the block of memory identifying the node and updates the links in the list.

If a thread installs a hook and then terminates before uninstalling the hook, the system automatically uninstalls the hook.

Hook Chains

A filter-function chain is formed when many applications install hooks of a particular type. When a particular event occurs, Windows calls the most recently installed filter function for that hook. For example, if Application A installs a system-wide WH_KEYBOARD hook, Windows calls this filter function whenever a keyboard message is retrieved by any thread. If Application B also installs a system-wide WH_KEYBOARD hook, Windows no longer calls the filter function installed by Application A. It calls only the one installed by Application B. It is the responsibility of each filter function to make sure that any previously installed filter functions are called!

The SetWindowsHookEx function returns the handle of a newly installed hook filter function. Any code that installs a new filter function must save this handle (usually in a global variable):

```
static HHOOK g_hhook = NULL;
   .
   .
   .
g_hhook = SetWindowsHookEx(WH_KEYBOARD, Example_KybdHook, hinst, NULL);
   .
   .
   .
```

If an error occurs, SetWindowsHookEx returns NULL.

If you want the remaining filter functions in the hook chain to be called, you must make a call to CallNextHookEx in your filter function (as you might have noticed in the preceding Example_KybdHook code fragment)[3]:

```
LRESULT CallNextHookEx(HHOOK hhook, int nCode, WPARAM wParam, LPARAM lParam);
```

---

[3]You may have noticed that many sources (including the SDK documentation) give the following out-of-date advice about CallNextHookEx: "If nCode is less than zero, the hook procedure must pass the message to the CallNextHookEx function without further processing and should return the value returned by CallNextHookEx." This information is not true now and has not been true since the days of Windows 3.0 (when the old SetWindowsHook function was still in use)! You can safely ignore this advice, as I have done in the Example_KybdHook code fragment in this chapter, and in all the applications included with this book that install hooks.

This function calls the next filter function in the chain and passes it the same nCode, wParam, and lParam parameters as it receives. Before the next filter function terminates, it is also expected to call CallNextHookEx, passing it the hook handle that was saved (probably in a global variable) when it was installed. CallNextHookEx uses the hook handle passed in the first parameter to traverse its linked list and determine which filter function to call next. If CallNextHookEx determines that there are no more filter functions to call, it simply returns 0 back to the calling filter function; otherwise, the return value is whatever the next filter function returned.

There are some rare cases where you might not want any remaining filter functions to be called. In this case, you would simply omit your call to CallNextHookEx in your filter function. By not putting in the call to CallNextHookEx, the remaining functions are not executed, and you may specify your own return value for the hook. Unfortunately, there is a catch to this. Another thread could install a hook after you. This new hook's filter function would then be called before yours. It might even have the same thing in mind as you do; so it might not call your filter function! This problem has no general-purpose solution. Unhooking your hook and rehooking it would make your filter function first in the hook chain, but there is no guarantee that someone else isn't trying to do the same thing. In short, hooks are a cooperative mechanism, and as such, there are no guarantees.

The Fourteen Types of Windows Hooks

The meanings of the parameters passed to your filter function will vary depending on the type of hook that is installed. Also, each hook type is best suited to solving a certain class of problems. Each of the fourteen types of windows hooks, listed in Table 6.1, is described in detail in this section.

1. WH_CALLWNDPROC
2. WH_CALLWNDPROCRET
3. WH_GETMESSAGE

One of the most useful utilities for debugging Windows programs is the Spy++ application supplied with Visual C++. This application allows you to monitor messages sent to a particular window (or to all windows in the system). By using the WH_CALLWNDPROC and WH_CALLWNDPROCRET hooks, a Spy++-like application can intercept all messages sent to a window, and all return values from those messages, and display that information in its own client area.[4] Spy++ also intercepts all posted messages that are retrieved via GetMessage or PeekMessage from the message queue belonging to the thread that created the window being spied upon. Spy++ does this by installing a WH_GETMESSAGE hook.

When a thread calls SendMessage, Windows checks to see whether a WH_CALLWNDPROC hook filter function has been installed on this thread. If one has, Windows calls the most recently installed WH_CALLWNDPROC filter function in the chain. The thread that called SendMessage is the same thread that executes the code in the filter function. The following table summarizes the parameters expected by the filter function and the return value expected by Windows.

nCode	wParam	lParam	lResult
HC_ACTION	The message is being sent by the current thread if wParam is nonzero	Points to a CWPSTRUCT structure	Not used, return zero

The HC_ACTION hook code notifies the filter function that a message has been sent to a window. The lParam parameter points to a CWPSTRUCT structure that has the following prototype in **WinUser.H**:

---

[4]The current version of Spy++ doesn't actually install a WH_CALLWND-PROCRET hook because this hook is not supported under Windows NT 3.5 or Windows NT 3.51. This hook was added to the Win32 API for applications like Spy++ and will be used by future versions of Spy++.

```
typedef struct tagCWPSTRUCT {
    LPARAM  lParam;
    WPARAM  wParam;
    UINT    message;
    HWND    hwnd;
} CWPSTRUCT, *PCWPSTRUCT, NEAR *NPCWPSTRUCT, FAR *LPCWPSTRUCT;
```

Because messages are sent so frequently in Windows, installation of a WH_CALLWNDPROC hook is likely to have a significant impact on performance. For this reason, WH_CALLWNDPROC hooks are usually used only for debugging purposes.

One important note about WH_CALLWNDPROC is in order. The filter function for a WH_CALLWNDPROC hook is called when the hooked thread calls the SendMessage function—not when the window procedure is called to process a sent message! This is counterintuitive. If you were writing a Spy++-like application, you would naturally think to install a WH_GETMESSAGE hook so that you would see messages posted to the window being spied upon. And, you would also naturally think that you should install a WH_CALLWNDPROC hook on the thread that created the window in order to see all the messages sent to the window. However, if you do this, you will see only messages that are sent to the window by its creating thread. If any other threads send messages to the window, your filter function will not see these messages. In order to see all the messages sent to a particular window, you must install a system-wide WH_CALLWNDPROC hook and monitor the hwnd member of CWPSTRUCT. This is also true for the WH_CALLWNDPROCRET hook as well.

In 16-bit Windows, a WH_CALLWNDPROC filter function was able to modify the members of the CWPSTRUCT structure. The window procedure would then receive these modified values instead of the original parameters that were passed to it. Win32 no longer allows this to happen. In Win32, even if a filter function modifies the structure's members, the window procedure still receives the values originally sent to it.

When a call to SendMessage returns, Windows calls the most recently installed filter function in the chain of WH_CALLWNDPROCRET filters. The thread that called SendMessage is the same thread that executes the code in the filter function. The following table summarizes the parameters expected by the filter function and the return value expected by Windows.

nCode	wParam	lParam	lResult
HC_ACTION	The message is being sent by the current thread if *wParam* is nonzero; otherwise, this message was sent to this window by another thread	Points to a CWPRETSTRUCT structure	Not used, return zero

The HC_ACTION hook code notifies the filter function that a return value is about to be returned to a caller of SendMessage. The lParam parameter points to a CWPRETSTRUCT structure that has the following prototype in **WinUser.H**:

```
typedef struct tagCWPRETSTRUCT {
    LRESULT lResult;
    LPARAM  lParam;
    WPARAM  wParam;
    UINT    message;
    HWND    hwnd;
} CWPRETSTRUCT, *PCWPRETSTRUCT, NEAR *NPCWPRETSTRUCT, FAR *LPCWPRETSTRUCT;
```

The return value from SendMessage is in the lResult member of this structure. Like a WH_CALLWNDPROC filter function, a WH_CALLWNDPROCRET filter function cannot successfully modify the members of the CWPRETSTRUCT structure. Even if a filter function modifies the structure's lResult member, the thread that called SendMessage will still receive the value that was returned by the window procedure.

To intercept messages retrieved from a thread's queue (by calls to the GetMessage and PeekMessage functions), you must install a WH_GETMESSAGE hook. The thread that calls GetMessage or PeekMessage is the same thread that executes the code in the filter function. The following table summarizes the parameters expected by the filter function and the return value expected by Windows.

nCode	wParam	lParam	lResult
HC_ACTION	NULL	Points to an MSG structure	Not used; return zero

The HC_ACTION hook code notifies the filter function that the message was retrieved from the hooked thread's queue. When the filter function receives this notification, the call to GetMessage has not yet returned, and therefore DispatchMessage has not yet been called. The hooked thread's message loop may do some processing and filter out certain messages causing them never to be processed by a window procedure. A Spy++-like application cannot determine whether a given message is ever processed by a window procedure.

The lParam parameter points to a MSG structure that has the following prototype in **WinUser.H**:

```
typedef struct tagMSG {
    HWND      hwnd;
    UINT      message;
    WPARAM    wParam;
    LPARAM    lParam;
    DWORD     time;
    POINT     pt;
} MSG, *PMSG, NEAR *NPMSG, FAR *LPMSG;
```

Unlike the WH_CALLWNDPROC and WH_CALLWNDPROCRET filter functions, a WH_GETMESSAGE filter function can modify the members of its MSG structure. If a WH_GETMESSAGE filter function does this, the MSG structure returned to the caller of GetMessage/PeekMessage will reflect the changes made by the filter function.

4. WH_KEYBOARD

5. WH_MOUSE

6. WH_HARDWARE

The WH_KEYBOARD, WH_MOUSE, and WH_HARDWARE hooks are used to intercept hardware input events. Figure 6.1 shows the course of hardware input events as they pass though the system and the various hardware-input-related hook filter functions.

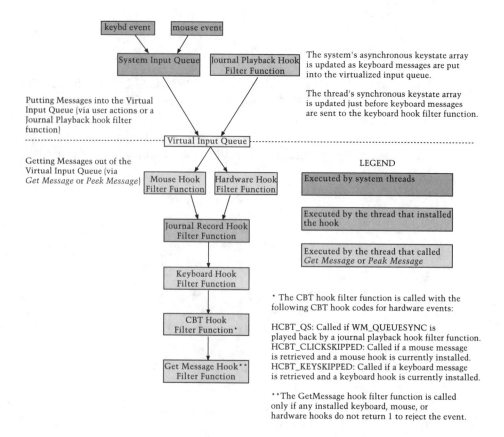

Figure 6.1 *Hardware input message filtering.*

When a thread's call to GetMessage or PeekMessage is about to extract a hardware input message, the system calls the appropriate type of hook for the message. The thread that called GetMessage or PeekMessage is the same thread that executes the code in the filter function. All three hardware input hooks have roughly the same form, except that the meanings of wParam and lParam vary based on the type of input message.

The following table summarizes the parameters expected by the WH_KEYBOARD filter function and the return value expected by Windows.

nCode	wParam	lParam	lResult
HC_ACTION or HC NOREMOVE	Specifies the virtual key code of the key code of the key.	Same value as the lParam parameter of a WM_KEYDOWN message (next page)	Zero if message should be processed; one if the message should be discarded

The following table summarizes the parameters expected by the WH_MOUSE filter function and the return value expected by Windows.

nCode	wParam	lParam	lResult
HC_ACTION or HC_NOREMOVE	Specifies the mouse message	Points to a MOUSEHOOKSTRUCT structure	Zero if message should be processed; one if the message should be discarded

The following table summarizes the parameters expected by the WH_HARDWARE filter function and the return value expected by Windows.

nCode	wParam	lParam	lResult
HC_ACTION or HC_NOREMOVE	Not used, NULL	Points to a HARDWAREHOOKSTRUCT structure	Zero if message should be processed; one if the message should be discarded

If an event is retrieved via the PeekMessage function with the PM_NOREMOVE flag, the hardware input filter function receives a hook code of HC_NOREMOVE. If the message is actually being removed from the thread's queue, the HC_ACTION hook code is received instead.

The WH_KEYBOARD hook is used by an application when it wants to examine keystrokes. For example, a macro recorder might use this hook. Such a utility might let a user define a hot key, which would activate a prerecorded sequence of events. While running, it would use a keyboard hook to watch keyboard messages for the hot key. By installing the keyboard hook as a system-wide hook, it could watch all keystrokes even when other applications became active.

For WH_KEYBOARD filter functions, the wParam parameter identifies the virtual-key code of the pressed or released key, and the lParam parameter contains additional information about the keystroke event.

Bits in lParam	Description
0 through 15	Repeat count (number of times the keystroke is repeated as a result of the user holding down the key)
16 through 23	Scan code of key
24	This bit is on if the key is extended—extended keys are function keys or keys on the numeric keypad
25 through 26	Not used
27 through 28	Used internally by Windows
29	This bit is on if the Alt key was held down while the key was pressed
30	This bit is on if the key was down before the message was sent
31	This bit is on if the key is being released, off if it is being pressed

Windows does not allow a WH_KEYBOARD filter function to change the values in the wParam or lParam parameters before allowing the thread to process the message. If you want to write a hook filter function that converts all occurrences of one keystroke to another, you have to use the WH_GETMESSAGE hook, because this hook allows its filter functions to modify messages.

The WH_MOUSE hook is used by an application when it wants to examine mouse movements and button clicks, even when it does not have mouse capture. For example, let's say that some company is producing a product to help end users learn how to work with Windows. When the user loads the application, it installs a mouse hook and pops up a little help window on the screen. Now, whenever the mouse is moved over a screen element (such as a system menu, minimize box, scrollbar, caption, or desktop window), the mouse hook function can determine which screen element the cursor is over and display some help text in its little window. This application does not interfere in any way with the normal processing of the mouse in any other application.

For a WH_MOUSE filter function, the wParam parameter identifies the mouse message (WM_MOUSEMOVE, WM_LBUTTON-DOWN, WM_RBUTTONUP, and so on), and the lParam parameter is a pointer to a MOUSEHOOKSTRUCT that looks like:

```
typedef struct tagMOUSEHOOKSTRUCT {
    POINT    pt;
    HWND     hwnd;
    UINT     wHitTestCode;
    DWORD    dwExtraInfo;
} MOUSEHOOKSTRUCT, FAR *LPMOUSEHOOKSTRUCT, *PMOUSEHOOKSTRUCT;
```

The pt member contains the coordinates of the mouse cursor in screen coordinates. The hwnd member identifies the handle of the window that is about to receive the mouse message. The wHitTestCode member contains a hit test code identifying which screen element the mouse is over.[5]

The last member in this structure, dwExtraInfo, specifies extra information associated with the mouse event. This information can be set by using the mouse_event function and is normally retrieved in a window procedure by calling the GetMessageExtraInfo function.

An application uses the WH_HARDWARE hook when it wants to examine hardware events other than keyboard and mouse events. This hook exists mostly for applications that run under Windows with the pen extensions.

The lParam parameter of a WH_HARDWARE filter function is a pointer to a HARDWAREHOOKSTRUCT structure that looks like this:

```
typedef struct tagHARDWAREHOOKSTRUCT {
    HWND      hwnd;
    UINT      message;
    WPARAM    wParam;
    LPARAM    lParam;
} HARDWAREHOOKSTRUCT, FAR *LPHARDWAREHOOKSTRUCT, *PHARDWAREHOOKSTRUCT;
```

---

[5]Hit test codes (HT*) are enumerated in the **WinUser.H** header file. For more information about hit test codes, refer to the SDK documentation of the WM_NCHITTEST message.

7. WH_MSGFILTER

8. WH_SYSMSGFILTER

Some system components have their own internal modal message loops. For example, dialog boxes, menus, and scrollbars all do their own message retrieval. Because these message loops are not accessible to us, Windows provides a pair of message filter hooks (WH_MSGFILTER and WH_SYSMSGFILTER) whose purpose is to give us this access. Whenever a message is about to be processed by a system component, which retrieves its own messages, Windows calls the most recently installed WH_SYSMSGFILTER filter function. If the return value from the filter function is zero, the system calls the most recently installed WH_MSGFILTER filter function. If the WH_SYSMSGFILTER filter function returns a nonzero value, no WH_MSGFILTER filter functions are called.

There is one additional difference between a WH_MSGFILTER hook and a WH_SYSMSGFILTER hook. If you attempt to install a WH_SYSMSGFILTER with a nonzero thread ID, the hook will not be installed, because WH_SYSMSGFILTER hooks can only be installed on a system-wide basis. This means that they are always remote hooks and must therefore reside in a DLL.

The following table summarizes the parameters expected by both the WH_SYSMSGFILTER and WH_MSGFILTER filter functions and the return value expected by Windows.

nCode	wParam	lParam	lResult
MSGF_DIALOGBOX MSGF_MESSAGEBOX MSGF_MENU MSGF_MOVE MSGF_SIZE MSGF_SCROLLBAR MSGF_NEXTWINDOW MSGF_MAINLOOP	NULL	Points to a MSG structure	Zero if message should be processed; one if the message should be discarded

The lParam parameter for both the WH_SYSMSGFILTER and WH_MSGFILTER filter functions points to a MSG structure identifying the message to be processed. A filter function may alter any of the members of this structure before returning.

In the past, MSGF_NEXTWINDOW was sent to message filter hooks when the user pressed Alt+Tab or Alt+Esc to switch windows. Because Windows has transitioned to an asynchronous model of input handling, the MSGF_NEXTWINDOW hook code is no longer sent. It is included in the preceding table because the Win32 documentation has not yet removed it. You will never receive a MSGF_NEXTWINDOW hook code.

The last entry in the preceding table, MSGF_MAINLOOP, is a value you can use to tap into the WH_MSGFILTER hook from your application's message loop (Usually implemented inside your WinMain function). You do this by calling the CallMsgFilter function like this:

```
MSG msg;
while (GetMessage(&msg, NULL, 0, 0)) {
   if (!CallMsgFilter(&msg, MSGF_MAINLOOP)) {
      TranslateMessage(&msg);
      DispatchMessage(&msg);
   }
}
```

The first parameter to CallMsgFilter is the address of a MSG structure containing the information about the message about to be processed. This address will be passed to any installed message filter functions in the lParam parameter. The second parameter, MSGF_MAINLOOP, is the value that is passed to each message filter function in the nCode parameter.

Sometimes, you may create modal message loops in your own code in addition to a normal message loop as shown in the preceding code. In these loops, you may also want to notify any installed message filter functions. The **WinUser.H** header file defines a MSGF_USER symbol with a value of 4096. This value is the base value for any MSGF_* identifiers that you wish to define yourself. Unfortunately, if multiple applications define their own MSGF_* identifiers using this base, the values would conflict and a system-wide message filter function would have no idea what type of message loop was processing messages. The Win32 API needs another function that is the logical equivalent of RegisterWindowMessage that allows an application to register message filter codes. Because this function does not exist, WH_SYSMSGFILTER filter functions should never attempt to switch on a user-defined hook code sent with CallMsgFilter. Also, if you are going to use CallMsgFilter, it is not advisable to install a WH_SYSMSGFILTER hook. You should instead use a WH_MSGFILTER hook so that you are assured of receiving only hook codes that you know about.

The DlgDyn application in Chapter 3 uses an unusual technique to provide keyboard navigation for a modeless dialog box. Normally a modeless dialog box requires a message loop where you call IsDialogMessage. The IsDialogMessage function translates keyboard messages into dialog box activities (such as tabbing to the next control). Unfortunately, Windows makes it difficult to create modeless dialog boxes that have a modal dialog box as an owner because there is no accessible message loop. The modal dialog box's message loop is hardwired down inside the DialogBox function. However, using message filter hooks, it is possible to solve this problem. The following code (from **DlgDyn.C**) shows how the DlgDyn application in Chapter 3 solved this problem:

```c
// This message filter hook function exists to enable the keyboard interface
// for the modeless dialog box.
LRESULT WINAPI DlgDyn_MsgFilterProc (int nCode, WPARAM wParam, LPARAM lParam) {

    // This variable prevents infinite recursion caused by the call to
    // IsDialogMessage below (IsDialogMessage calls any installed message
    // filter hooks as its first order of business).
    static BOOL fRecurse = FALSE;
    LRESULT lResult;

    // If we are called recursively due to IsDialogMessage, we simply return.
    if (fRecurse) {

        // Returning FALSE tells the system that we want it to do its normal
        // processing for this message, (i.e., let IsDialogMessage do its stuff).
        // NOTE: We are not calling CallNextHookEx because we don't want the
        // same message to go through the same hook chain twice (although this
        // hook function will see it twice).
        return(FALSE);
    }

    // Here we unhook our hook and then re-hook ourselves to guarantee that our
    // hook procedure is at the front of the hook chain. This is necessary
    // because any hook procedure before us in the hook chain would see each
    // message twice. By installing ourselves at the front of the chain we get
    // the message first the second time it goes through the hook chain and
    // can simply stop the message from continuing through the hook chain when
    // we are recursing because of IsDialogMessage.
    adgVERIFY(UnhookWindowsHookEx(g_hhookMsgFilter));
    g_hhookMsgFilter = SetWindowsHookEx(WH_MSGFILTER, DlgDyn_MsgFilterProc,
        NULL, GetCurrentThreadId());
    adgASSERT(g_hhookMsgFilter != NULL);
```

```
    // Call any other hooks in the chain.  lResult is TRUE if the next hook
    // in the chain doesn't want any additional processing for the message.
    lResult = CallNextHookEx(g_hhookMsgFilter, nCode, wParam, lParam);

    // If the next hook in the chain wants to allow additional processing
    if (!lResult) {

        // Call IsDialogMessage, setting the static variable fRecurse to TRUE
        // to avoid infinite recursion.  If IsDialogMessage returns TRUE, the
        // message was processed and we DO NOT want normal processing for this
        // message.
        fRecurse = TRUE;
        lResult = IsDialogMessage(g_hwndModeless, (PMSG) lParam);
        fRecurse = FALSE;
    }
    return(lResult);
}
```

By installing a WH_MSGFILTER hook on DlgDyn's primary thread, we can intercept all the messages that are normally seen only by DialogBox. Then we can simply call IsDialogMessage, passing in the handle of the modeless dialog box (saved in the global variable g_hwndModeless), and the keyboard interface will come alive. Unfortunately, there is one further level of complication. The first order of business for IsDialogMessage is to call any installed WH_MSGFILTER filter functions; and this means us! Because this call would lead to infinite recursion, we set a static Boolean flag (fRecurse) inside the filter function before we call IsDialogMessage. We check this flag at the top of the message filter function. If the flag is set, our filter function was entered recursively because we called IsDialogMessage, so we simply return. A precautionary step was taken in implementing DlgDyn_MsgFilterProc: before calling IsDialogMessage, we unhook ourselves from the hook chain and then immediately re-hook ourselves, effectively jumping to the top of the hook chain. By doing this, we ensure that no other hook functions see our recursive entry into DlgDyn_MsgFilterProc (because this might be unexpected to them).

9. WH_JOURNALRECORD
10. WH_JOURNALPLAYBACK

Perhaps the most commonly used hooks are WH_JOURNAL-
RECORD and WH_JOURNALPLAYBACK. These hooks can be
used to add macro recording facilities to an application. But the
WH_JOURNALPLAYBACK hook can also be used to play back
event messages that you construct in memory. The SKDemo application in Chapter 8 uses this technique to force-feed keystrokes to
other applications.

Recall that both WH_JOURNALRECORD and WH_JOUR-
NALPLAYBACK are local, system-wide hooks and therefore are not
required to be in a DLL. Normally, when a system-wide hook is
installed, the thread that processes the message is the same thread
that executes the filter-function code. However, this is not true for
journal hooks. A journal hook's filter-function code is executed
only by the thread that installed the journal hook itself. This is the
reason why journal hook filter functions are not required to be in a
DLL.

When a thread (any thread) in the system requests a hardware
input message, the system wakes the thread that installed the journal playback hook and has this thread execute its filter function.
Likewise, when any thread in the system retrieves a hardware input
message from its virtualized input queue, the system first wakes
the thread that installed the journal record hook and has this thread
execute its filter function. When the journal-hook-installing thread
has completed processing the filter function, the system allows the
thread retrieving the message to continue its processing.

The reason why the system's architecture for these hooks is
like this is because these hooks deal with the low-level interception
of hardware input events. A journal playback hook really simulates
a user sitting in front of a computer entering hardware events.
Because the user is able to enter hardware events only one at a
time, the playing back of these events must also be done one at a
time. In order to ensure this serialization of input, the events must
be retrieved by a single thread—the thread that installed the journal
playback hook. The same holds true for recording: the processing of

hardware input events must be kept serialized so that the hook knows the exact order in which these events occurred.

If the system did not force journal hooks to work this way, then multiple threads would be executing the journal hook filter functions simultaneously—the filter functions would not be able to know the order in which the user generated the various hardware input events. For example, a low-priority thread that just started to process a keystroke message might be pre-empted by a higher-priority thread attempting to process a mouse click generated by the user after the key was pressed. If multiple threads executed journal hook filter functions, the higher-priority thread might call its journal record filter function first even though the mouse message was generated after the keystroke message.

There is a very bad potential downside to this architecture. Serializing all calls to journal hook filter functions forces the system to allow only one thread at a time to process hardware input events. This could potentially hang the input processing of the entire system. For example, imagine that Notepad and WordPad are both running and that Notepad is active. Now, the user presses the A key, followed by Alt+Tab, followed by the B key. Let's also imagine that Notepad enters an infinite loop when its thread receives the A key.

Here is what happens when a journal hook is not installed. Notepad receives the A key and enters its infinite loop. However, when the user presses Alt+Tab, the system's thread intervenes and makes WordPad active. The B key now goes to WordPad's thread. Note that the user is still able to use any applications that are running—it's just that Notepad's thread is hung and only Notepad cannot be used.

Now, let's review the same scenario but, this time, let's pretend that a journal hook is installed. Again, Notepad's thread will receive the A key and enter its infinite loop. Now, the user presses Alt+Tab, but the journal hook cannot process the key because Notepad's thread has not completed its processing of the A key. So, the Alt+Tab is forever queued in the system's input queue and the user's B key is queued up right behind the Alt+Tab key. If Notepad's thread remains in its loop, the system's input processing is effectively disabled.

Obviously, this is a serious issue, and Microsoft did something about it. When a journal hook is installed, the system looks specifically for the Ctrl+Esc key sequence. If the user hits this sequence, the system automatically uninstalls any installed journal hooks and posts a WM_CANCELJOURNAL message to the queues of the threads that installed these journal hooks. For more information about WM_CANCELJOURNAL and the serialization of input see the Echo, Capture, and SKDemo applications.

The following table summarizes the parameters expected by the filter function of a WH_JOURNALRECORD hook and the return value that is expected by Windows.

nCode	wParam	lParam	lResult
HC_ACTION	NULL	Points to an EVENTMSG structure	Not used, return zero
HC_SYSMODALON	NULL	NULL	Not used, return zero
HC_SYSMODALOFF	NULL	NULL	Not used, return zero

When the hook code to a WH_JOURNALRECORD hook filter function is HC_ACTION, the lParam parameter points to an EVENTMSG structure[6]:

```
typedef struct tagEVENTMSG {
    UINT    message;
    UINT    paramL;
    UINT    paramH;
    DWORD   time;
    HWND    hwnd;
} EVENTMSG, *PEVENTMSGMSG, NEAR *NPEVENTMSGMSG, FAR *LPEVENTMSGMSG;

typedef struct tagEVENTMSG *PEVENTMSG, NEAR *NPEVENTMSG, FAR *LPEVENTMSG;
```

For macro recording to be implemented in an application, a WH_JOURNALRECORD filter function should append each EVENTMSG structure received to a block of memory. This technique is demonstrated by the Echo application presented later in this chapter.

---

[6]I can offer no explanation for the various *MSGMSG definitions that are defined in **WinUser.H**. These definitions are clearly the ramblings of a madperson. You can use either, but the EVENTMSG definitions are preferred.

The HC_SYSMODALON and HC_SYSMODALOFF hook codes are used to notify a WH_JOURNALRECORD filter function that a system-modal message box has appeared or is being removed, respectively. If a Win32 application calls MessageBox using the MB_SYSTEMMODAL flag, both Windows 95 and Windows NT make the message box have the WS_EX_TOPMOST style but the message box is not system modal—you can easily switch to any other 16-bit or Win32 application. However, Windows 95 and Windows NT handle system-modal message boxes created by 16-bit applications in very different ways. Under Windows 95, a 16-bit application's system-modal message box is actually system-modal and stops all other applications (both 16-bit and Win32) from executing. Under Windows NT, a 16-bit application's system-modal message box prevents only other 16-bit applications in the same address space from executing. However, it does not affect any Win32 applications and it does not affect any 16-bit Windows applications that are running in a different address space.

For the reasons just described, a WH_JOURNALRECORD hook never receives the HC_SYSMODALON or HC_SYSMODALOFF hook codes except when a 16-bit application running under Windows 95 displays a system-modal message box. As more and more applications are ported to Win32, system-modal message boxes become less and less of a problem. Still, you should be prepared for this case. Your filter function should watch for the HC_SYSMODALON hook code and stop appending EVENTMSG structures to the memory block of recorded events. Then it should turn recording off and notify the user that a system-modal message box appeared. The Echo application in this chapter shows how to implement this logic.

Given a list of EVENTMSG structures (or equivalent event information), you can use WH_JOURNALPLAYBACK to play back the events in your list. When a WH_JOURNALPLAYBACK hook is installed, Windows ignores all mouse, keyboard, and pen input from the user and instead retrieves hardware events by calling the WH_JOURNALPLAYBACK filter function. While a playback hook is installed, the mouse will not affect the position of the mouse cursor on the screen. The following table summarizes the parameters expected by the filter function and the return values expected by Windows.

nCode	wParam	lParam	lResult
HC_GETNEXT	NULL	Points to an EVENTMSG structure	Number of milliseconds that the system should wait before processing the message
HC_SKIP	NULL	NULL	Not used; return zero
HC_SYSMODALON	NULL	NULL	Not used; return zero
HC_SYSMODALOFF	NULL	NULL	Not used; return zero

HC_SYSMODALON and HC_SYSMODALOFF serve the same purpose in a journal playback filter as they do in a journal record filter.

When the playback filter function receives an HC_GETNEXT hook code, the EVENTMSG information for the current event should be copied into the EVENTMSG structure pointed to by the lParam parameter. HC_GETNEXT is really a misnomer of sorts; it would be more appropriately named "HC_GETCURRENT", because it doesn't get the next event in your event list, it gets the current one.

The HC_SKIP hook code notifies the WH_JOURNALPLAY-BACK filter function that Windows is done processing the current event and that the filter function should prepare the next one (probably by simply incrementing a pointer into an array of EVENTMSG structures). So, a filter function should continue to return the current event in the event list every time Windows sends the HC_GETNEXT hook code. But then, when Windows sends the HC_SKIP hook code, the filter function should move the current pointer to the next event in the list. When the filter function receives the HC_SKIP hook code and determines that all the saved events have been played, the filter function can call the UnhookWindowsHookEx function to remove itself from the chain. A WH_JOURNALPLAYBACK filter function should not unhook itself during the processing of an HC_GETNEXT hook code.

When the filter function returns from processing HC_GET-NEXT, the time member of the EVENTMSG structure (pointed to by the lParam parameter) must contain the system time when the message should occur. To accomplish this, I recommend updating the time member of all the saved events immediately after the WH_JOURNALRECORD hook's filter function is removed. The time member in each EVENTMSG structure should reflect the number of milliseconds that have elapsed since recording started. The following code fragment shows how to calculate this:

```
PEVENTMSG pEventMsg;
int nEvents;
    .
    .
    .
while (nEvents >= 1)
   pEvent[--nEvents].time -= pEvent[0].time;
    .
    .
    .
```

The pEventMsg variable points to an array of saved EVENTMSG structures, and the nEvents variable contains the number of events that have been recorded.

When the WH_JOURNALPLAYBACK hook is installed, the application should save the current system time:

```
HHOOK g_hhook;
DWORD g_dwPlaybackStartTime;
    .
    .
    .
g_hhook = SetWindowsHookEx(WH_JOURNALPLAYBACK,
    (HOOKPROC) JrnlPlayBackHook, GetModuleHandle(NULL), 0);
g_dwPlaybackStartTime = GetTickCount();
    .
    .
    .
```

Then, when the HC_GETNEXT hook code is passed to the filter function, the function can copy the current EVENTMSG to the location pointed to by the lParam parameter and then change the time member to the proper playback time:

```
*((PEVENTMSG) lParam) = *pMySavedEvent;
 ((PEVENTMSG) lParam)->time += g_dwPlaybackStartTime;
```

The return value from the filter function indicates the number of milliseconds Windows should wait before playing back the event. If the playback time has passed, the function should return zero. The following code fragment shows how to calculate this value.

```
LRESULT lResult;
  .
  .
  .
switch (nCode) {

   case HC_GETNEXT:

      // Copy current event to the EVENTMSG structure pointed to by lParam.
      *((PEVENTMSG) lParam) = pEventMsg[wCurrentEvent];

      // Update time member in returned structure to desired system
      // playback time.
      ((PEVENTMSG) lParam)->time += g_dwPlaybackStartTime;

      // Return milliseconds Windows should wait before processing the event.
      lResult = ((LPEVENTMSG) lParam)->time - GetTickCount();
      if (lResult < 0)
         lResult = 0;
      break;
      .
      .
      .
}
return(lResult);
```

If you would like to have the recorded hardware input events played back at full speed instead of recorded speed, the filter function should change the time member in the copied structure to the current system time and return zero.

```
LRESULT lResult;
  .
  .
  .
switch (nCode) {

   case HC_GETNEXT:
      // Copy current event to the EVENTMSG structure pointed to by lParam.
      *((PEVENTMSG) lParam) = pEventMsg[wCurrentEvent];

      // Update time member in returned structure to desired system
      // playback time.
      ((PEVENTMSG) lParam)->time = GetTickCount();

      // Return milliseconds Windows should wait before processing the event.
      lResult = 0;
      break;
      .
      .
      .
}
return(lResult);
```

There are some issues to keep in mind when recording and playing back macros. Use of the mouse should be kept to a minimum. The EVENTMSG structures that WH_JOURNALRECORD receives contain the position of the mouse in screen coordinates. When a macro is played back, the windows on the screen may be in different locations or different sizes than when the macro was recorded. This may cause the mouse events to be sent to a window other than the original one. In addition, macros could be played back on a monitor having a different screen resolution from that of the monitor used when the events were recorded. Finally, incompatibilities could result when a macro recorded on one keyboard is played back on a machine connected to a keyboard with a different country setting.

There are some additional issues with respect to the journal record and playback hooks. These issues are discussed in the context of the Echo and Capture applications presented later in this chapter. The SKDemo application in Chapter 8 also discusses some of these issues.

11. WH_SHELL

The WH_SHELL hook is used by a shell application (such as the Windows 95 Taskbar) when it wants to be notified of changes in the appearance/location of applications. The following table summarizes the parameters expected by the WH_SHELL filter function and the return values expected by Windows.

nCode	wParam	lParam	lResult
HSHELL_WINDOWCREATED	Handle of window being created	NULL	Not used, return zero
HSHELL_WINDOWDESTROYED	Handle of window being destroyed	NULL	Not used, return zero
HSHELL_ACTIVATESHELLWINDOW	NULL	NULL	Not used, return zero
HSHELL_WINDOWACTIVATED	Handle of window being activated	TRUE if window is going to be full screen	Not used, return zero
HSHELL_GETMINRECT	Handle of window being minimized, maximized, or restored	Address of RECT structure to receive coordinates	Not used, return zero
HSHELL_REDRAW	Handle of window that is caption or icon	TRUE if window is flashing its caption	Not used, return zero
HSHELL_TASKMAN	NULL	NULL	Return TRUE to prevent the system from showing it's own task list
HSHELL_LANGUAGE	NULL	NULL	Not used, return zero

Whenever a top-level, unowned window is being created, the CreateWindowEx function calls the most recently installed WH_SHELL filter function and passes it a hook code of HSHELL_WINDOWCREATED. When a top-level, unowned window is being destroyed, the DestroyWindow function calls the WH_SHELL filter function with an HSHELL_WINDOWDE-STROYED hook code. In addition to these two fairly self-explanatory situations, there are three unusual special cases that also produce HSHELL_WINDOW* notification codes:

■ hiding a top-level, unowned window produces an HSHELL_WINDOWDESTROYED notification;

■ showing a top-level, unowned window produces an HSHELL_WINDOWCREATED notification;

■ changing the parent of a top-level window (either by calling SetParent or by setting the GWL_HWNDPARENT window long), produces an HSHELL_WINDOWDESTROYED notification followed by an HSHELL_WINDOWCREATED notification.

The handle to the window being created/destroyed is available in the wParam parameter, and you can send messages to the window if you like. The AppLog application presented later in this chapter installs a system-wide WH_SHELL hook and then uses the HSHELL_WINDOWCREATED and HSHELL_WINDOWDESTROYED hook notifications to keep track of any applications you start and shut down.

HSHELL_ACTIVATESHELLWINDOW is a leftover from 16-bit Windows. You will never receive this hook notify code.

The remaining shell hook codes are currently used only under Windows 95. Windows NT 3.51 does not support any of these hook codes. However, future versions of Windows NT will support them.

When a window is being minimized, maximized, or restored, the hook code HSHELL_GETMINRECT is passed to the most recently installed WH_SHELL filter function, indicating that the system needs the coordinates of the minimized rectangle for the window (for example, the rectangle of a button on the Taskbar). The wParam parameter contains the handle of the window, and the lParam parameter contains the address of a RECT structure to receive the coordinates. The system passes this minimum rectangle to the DrawAnimatedRects function in order to produce the zoom effect shown to the user when a window is minimized, maximized, or restored.

The HSHELL_WINDOWACTIVATED hook code indicates that activation has changed to a different top-level, unowned window. The wParam parameter contains the handle of the window. The

Windows 95 Taskbar watches for this notification so that it knows to depress the button that represents the currently active application.

When the icon or title of a window changes, the Windows 95 Taskbar needs to redraw the corresponding button. The hook code HSHELL_REDRAW notifies the shell application of such an event. The wParam parameter contains the handle of the window, which redrew its caption or changed its associated icon.

The HSHELL_TASKMAN notification code indicates that the user pressed Ctrl+Esc to invoke the Start menu or task manager (**TaskMan.EXE**). A shell application that provides a task list can return TRUE to prevent Windows 95 from displaying its task list.

The HSHELL_LANGUAGE hook code is used to indicate that a new keyboard layout has been loaded.[7] Windows 95 uses this hook to update the keyboard identifier, which is drawn on the Taskbar next to the clock. If you want to load a keyboard layout, but you don't want the HSHELL_LANGUAGE hook to be called, you can set the KLF_NOTELLSHELL flag in the fuFlags parameter of LoadKeyboardLayout. This can be useful if your application loads several keyboard layouts at a time because you can delay the processing of HSHELL_LANGUAGE by the shell until the last keyboard layout has been loaded. For more details about LoadKeyboardLayout, refer to the Win32 SDK documentation.

---

[7] You can add or change your keyboard layout via the Language tab of the Keyboard Properties dialog.

12. WH_CBT

The WH_CBT hook is used by an application that wishes to offer computer-based training (CBT) facilities to its users. When this hook is installed, Windows calls the associated filter function before activating, creating, destroying, minimizing, maximizing, moving, or sizing a window; before completing a system command; before removing a mouse or keyboard event from the thread's hardware input queue; before setting the input focus; and upon retrieving a WM_QUEUESYNC message. This hook is used so that an application can monitor a user's progress and can aid the user by performing certain tasks automatically.

For example, an application can give the user instructions on how to complete a certain process at the beginning of the session. Then later, the application can tell the user to execute that process. The CBT hook can be used to see if the user has executed the process successfully. In addition, many applications that offer CBT often focus on concepts new to the user but force the program to move more quickly through mundane tasks. For instance, a user might be learning how to format a document in a word processing application. There is no need for the application to force the user to enter a paragraph of text before demonstrating the formatting functions. In this case, a WH_CBT hook might install a WH_JOURNALPLAYBACK hook that will force keystrokes into the application creating the paragraph of text for the user. After all the keystrokes have been played, the WH_JOURNALPLAYBACK hook would be removed.

The following table summarizes the parameters expected by the WH_CBT filter function and the return values expected by Windows.

nCode	wParam	lParam	lResult
HCBT_ACTIVATE	Handle of window being activated	Points to a CBTACTIVATESTRUCT structure	Zero if window should be activated; one to prevent it
HCBT_CLICKSKIPPED	Identifies the mouse message removed from the queue	Points to a MOUSEHOOKSTRUCT structure	Not used; return zero
HCBT_CREATEWND	Handle of window being created	Points to a CBT_CREATEWND structure	Zero if window should be created; one to prevent it
HCBT_DESTROYWND	Handle of window being destroyed	NULL	Zero if window should be destroyed; one to prevent it
HCBT_KEYSKIPPED	Identifies the virtual-key code removed from the queue	Specifies the same information as sent in lParam to a window procedure when it receives a WM_KEYDOWN message	Not used; return zero
HCBT_MINMAX	Handle of window being minimized or maximized	LOWORD specifies a ShowWindow identifier (like SW_SHOW-MAXIMIZED)	Zero if window should be minimized or maximized; one to prevent it
HCBT_MOVESIZE	Handle of window being moved or sized	Points to a RECT structure	Zero if window should be moved or sized; one to prevent it
HCBT_QS	NULL	NULL	Not used; return zero
HCBT_SETFOCUS	Handle of window gaining input focus	Handle of window losing input focus	Zero if input focus should be changed; one to prevent it
HCBT_SYSCOMMAND	Specifies the system command selected by the user (SC_CLOSE, for instance)	Contains the same data as the lParam for a WM_SYSCOMMAND message	Zero if system command should be executed; one to prevent it

Whenever a new window is about to be activated, Windows calls the most recently installed WH_CBT filter function and passes it a value of HCBT_ACTIVATE. The wParam contains the handle of the window being activated, and the lParam parameter points to a CBTACTIVATESTRUCT structure:

```
typedef struct tagCBTACTIVATESTRUCT {
    BOOL    fMouse;
    HWND    hWndActive;
} CBTACTIVATESTRUCT, *LPCBTACTIVATESTRUCT;
```

The fMouse member is TRUE if the window is being activated as the result of a mouse click. The hWndActive member indicates the handle of the window that is currently active.

The HCBT_CLICKSKIPPED code is used by a CBT application when it wants to know when the user has clicked the mouse over a window so that the application can install a WH_JOURNALPLAY-BACK hook to force hardware events into the system's input queue. Windows calls the most recently installed WH_CBT filter function and passes it a hook code of HCBT_CLICKEDSKIPPED when a mouse-click message is removed from the queue and a mouse hook is installed. At this point, the WH_CBT filter function receiving the HCBT_CLICKSKIPPED code would install a WH_JOURNALPLAY-BACK hook to play back a sequence of events.

For example, a spreadsheet application might want to check if the user has clicked over a particular cell. It would do this by checking in its WH_MOUSE filter function if the mouse was over the desired cell. If it were, the filter function would return one, informing Windows that the message should not be processed by the application. At this point, Windows calls the WH_CBT filter function and passes it the HCBT_CLICKSKIPPED code so that the application can install a WH_JOURNALPLAYBACK hook to repeat a sequence of events like summing a row or column.

The wParam parameter for the HCBT_CLICKSKIPPED code identifies the mouse message that occurred, and the lParam parameter points to the same MOUSEHOOKSTRUCT structure that was sent to the WH_MOUSE hook filter functions. See the discussion of the WH_MOUSE hook earlier in this chapter for a description of this structure.

The HCBT_KEYSKIPPED code works in exactly the same way as HCBT_CLICKSKIPPED, except that HCBT_KEYSKIPPED relates to keyboard input messages rather than the mouse input messages.

Whenever a new window is about to be created, Windows calls the most recently installed WH_CBT filter function and passes it a hook code of HCBT_CREATEWND. The wParam contains the handle of the window created. At this point, Windows has actually created the window's data structure in memory but has not sent any messages to the window (such as WM_NCCREATE or WM_CRE-ATE). If the filter function returns one in response to this code, the window will be destroyed, and CreateWindowEx returns NULL to the thread attempting to create the window. If the filter function returns zero, the window is created, and the WM_NCCREATE and WM_CREATE messages are sent to it.

Although the window has not been sent the WM_NCCREATE and WM_CREATE messages by the time the filter function receives the HCBT_CREATEWND code, the filter function may send messages to the window. But beware that the window has not been fully initialized and that sending some messages can be problematic. Avoid doing this if at all possible.

When the HCBT_CREATEWND code is received by the filter function, the lParam parameter points to a CBT_CREATEWND structure:

```
typedef struct tagCBT_CREATEWNDA {
    struct tagCREATESTRUCTA *lpcs;
    HWND            hwndInsertAfter;
} CBT_CREATEWNDA, *LPCBT_CREATEWNDA;

typedef struct tagCBT_CREATEWNDW {
    struct tagCREATESTRUCTW *lpcs;
    HWND            hwndInsertAfter;
} CBT_CREATEWNDW, *LPCBT_CREATEWNDW;

#ifdef UNICODE
typedef CBT_CREATEWNDW CBT_CREATEWND;
typedef LPCBT_CREATEWNDW LPCBT_CREATEWND;
#else
typedef CBT_CREATEWNDA CBT_CREATEWND;
typedef LPCBT_CREATEWNDA LPCBT_CREATEWND;
#endif // UNICODE
```

The lpcs member is a pointer to a CREATESTRUCT structure containing all the parameters that were passed to CreateWindowEx when the thread attempted to create the window. The hwndInsertAfter member in the HCBT_CREATEWND structure indicates the handle of the window that this new window will be inserted after in the z-order. When the filter function receives the HCBT_CREATEWND notification, it can examine these values and modify them.

When a CBT application installs a journal playback hook, it needs to know when the playback of events has stopped. The WM_QUEUESYNC message can be used to provide this information. In your journal playback hook, when playback of

EVENTMSGs has completed, you can simply fill in the message member of the EVENTMSG structure with the value WM_QUEUE-SYNC and the paramL member of the same structure with the handle of the window, which should receive the WM_QUEUESYNC notification. Because WM_QUEUESYNC is special, Windows allows this message into the system input queue. The thread that created the window specified in paramL eventually pulls the WM_QUEUESYNC message out of its message queue. At this point, GetMessage or PeekMessage calls the most recently installed WH_CBT filter function, passing it a hook code of HCBT_QS. This indicates that playback of events with WH_JOURNALPLAYBACK has finished, and the CBT hook can remove the playback hook and continue with its business. The SKDemo application in Chapter 8 demonstrates use of the WM_QUEUESYNC message.

13. WH_FOREGROUNDIDLE

The WH_FOREGROUNDIDLE hook is called just before the thread that created the window in the foreground is about to be put to sleep. Suppose that WordPad is the active application. If WordPad's thread makes a call to GetMessage, and there are no messages in the queue to process, WordPad's thread can no longer do any useful work. So, the system puts the thread to sleep until a message shows up; but before putting the thread to sleep, the system calls the most recently installed WH_FOREGROUNDIDLE filter function.

The WH_FOREGROUNDIDLE hook was created for internal use by the system and is not likely to be useful to applications.[8] This hook is listed only for the sake of completeness. The following table summarizes the parameters expected by the WH_FORE-GROUNDIDLE filter function and the return values expected by Windows.

nCode	wParam	lParam	lResult
HC_ACTION	NULL	NULL	Not used, return zero

---

[8] If you spend enough time thinking about useful ways to take advantage of this hook, you're bound to consider an idea where you have a low-priority thread which waits for this hook notification. When the notification is received, the low-prioirty thread could raise its priority so that it gets its work done faster. This is *not* a good use of this hook. For one thing, there is no hook that tells you when a foreground thread is no longer idle so that you can lower the thread's prioity again. For another thing, the system will automatically schedule CPU time to the low-priority thread when the foreground thread becomes idle anyway. Also, raising a thread's priority does *not* make the thread run any faster—it simply prevents lower-priority threads from running. In addition, boosting your thread's priority could prevent the foreground thread from waking up again.

14. WH_DEBUG

The WH_DEBUG hook is used by an application when it wants to monitor installed hooks. The WH_DEBUG hook allows an application to install a filter function that is notified whenever any and all hook filter functions are called. This is usually used to help debug an application's use of hooks.

Remember that, when a new hook is installed, Windows calls that new hook's filter function before any of the already installed hooks. And this new filter function can call the next filter function in the chain, or it can break the chain by omitting the usual call to CallNextHookEx. If you install a hook and determine that your filter function is not being called, it may be that another hook was installed after yours and that hook is not calling CallNextHookEx. In this kind of situation, the WH_DEBUG hook can be helpful in determining which threads have installed hooks. Unless, of course, another application installs a WH_DEBUG hook after you install yours and the filter function for this new hook doesn't call CallNextHookEx. (Whoops, I guess Microsoft didn't think about this possibility!)

Whenever the system is about to call a hook filter function, it first calls the most recently installed WH_DEBUG filter function in the chain. The following table summarizes the parameters expected by the filter function and the return value expected by Windows.

nCode	wParam	lParam	lResult
HC_ACTION	Specifies the type of hook about to be called (one of WH_*)	Points to a DEBUGHOOKINFO structure	Zero if the hook about to be called should be executed; one to prevent it

Whenever a hook filter function (other than WH_DEBUG) is about to be called, Windows calls the most recently installed WH_DEBUG filter function and passes it a value of HC_ACTION. The wParam parameter identifies the type of hook about to be called. The lParam parameter points to a DEBUGHOOKINFO structure:

```
typedef struct tagDEBUGHOOKINFO {
    DWORD   idThread;
    DWORD   idThreadInstaller;
    LPARAM  lParam;
```

```
   WPARAM  wParam;
   int     code;
} DEBUGHOOKINFO, *PDEBUGHOOKINFO, NEAR *NPDEBUGHOOKINFO, FAR* LPDEBUGHOOKINFO;
```

The idThread member identifies the thread that is about to execute the filter function. The idThreadInstaller member identifies the thread that installed the hook identified by the wParam parameter.

The remaining members in the structure, lParam, wParam, and code, are the parameters that are to be passed to the filter function about to be called. You may inspect these values, but any modifications you make will be discarded.

As with all hooks, to allow the next WH_DEBUG hook filter function in the chain to be called, CallNextHookEx must be called from the WH_DEBUG filter function passing it the same parameters that were passed to the first filter function. Do not call CallNextHookEx and pass it the members in the DEBUGHOOKINFO structure.

The KeyCount Application

The KeyCount application (**KeyCount.EXE**), shown in Listings 6.1–6.7 (Starting on page 412), demonstrates how to use a system-wide keyboard hook to count keystrokes. When you invoke the application, the main application window appears, as shown in Figure 6.2.

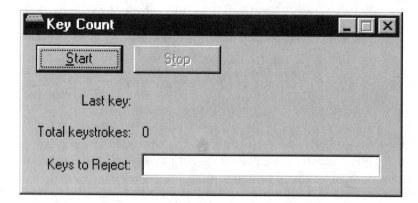

Figure 6.2 *The KeyCount application.*

KeyCount has two buttons: Start and Stop. Pressing the Start button installs a system-wide keyboard hook and shows you information about each key as it is pressed/released as well as the total number of keystrokes that have occurred since the Start button was pressed. In addition, KeyCount has an Edit control. KeyCount's keyboard hook returns one (rejecting the event) for each character listed in the Edit control, which has the effect of completely disabling these keys throughout the entire system. Pressing Stop removes the keyboard hook.

Tables 6.2 and 6.3 describe the files used to create this application and its associated DLL. (Because the KeyCount application installs a system-wide WH_KEYBOARD hook, a DLL is required.)

Table 6.2 *Files used to build the KeyCount application.*

File	Description
KeyCount.C	Contains WinMain and main window's dialog box and message cracker functions
KeyCount.MSG	MsgCrack input file used to create **KeyCount.H** (See Appendix B for details.)
KeyCount.H	Contains message cracker macros for the UM_KEYEVENT notification message
KeyCount.RC	Contains the dialog box template for the main application window and its icons
Resource.H	Contains IDs for all resources in the RC file
KeyCount.ICO	Contains the icon for the main window
KeyCount.MAK	Visual C++ project makefile for the application

Table 6.3 *Files used to build the KybdHk DLL.*

File	Description
KybdHk.C	Contains the implementation of the system-wide keyboard hook used to trap keystrokes as well as the KeyboardHook API functions to install and remove the hook.
KybdHk.H	Contains function prototypes for the KeyboardHook API functions used to install and remove the system-wide keyboard hook. Any source file that uses the KeyboardHook API must include this file.
KybdHk.MAK	Visual C++ project makefile for the keyboard hook DLL.

The **KybdHk.DLL** exports two functions:

```
KYBDHKLIBAPI BOOL WINAPI KeyboardHook_Start (HWND hwndPost,
   UINT uMsgNotify, HWND hwndEdit);
KYBDHKLIBAPI BOOL WINAPI KeyboardHook_Stop ();
```

KeyboardHook_Start takes three parameters. The first parameter, hwndPost, is the window that should be notified each time a keyboard event occurs. The second parameter, uMsgNotify, is the notification message that should be posted to hwndPost. The final parameter, hwndEdit, is the handle of an edit control that contains a list of characters for which the corresponding keyboard events should be rejected.

When you press the Start button, the KeyCount application's KeyCount_OnCommand function simply calls KeyboardHook_Start:

```
void KeyCount_OnCommand (HWND hwnd, int id, HWND hwndCtl, UINT codeNotify) {

   HWND hwndEdit;

   switch (id) {
      .
      .
      .
      case IDC_START:
         hwndEdit = GetDlgItem(hwnd, IDC_EDIT);
         if (KeyboardHook_Start(hwnd, UM_KEYEVENT, hwndEdit)) {
            SetDlgItemText(hwnd, IDC_LASTKEY, __TEXT(""));
            SetDlgItemInt(hwnd, IDC_KEYCOUNT, 0, FALSE);
            SETKEYCOUNT(hwnd, 0);
            EnableWindow(GetDlgItem(hwnd, IDC_START), FALSE);
            EnableWindow(GetDlgItem(hwnd, IDC_STOP),  TRUE);
            SetFocus(GetDlgItem(hwnd, IDC_STOP));
         } else {
            adgMB(__TEXT("Unable to start keyboard hook"));
         }
         break;

      case IDC_STOP:
         if (!KeyboardHook_Stop())
            adgMB(__TEXT("Unable to stop keyboard hook"));
         EnableWindow(GetDlgItem(hwnd, IDC_START), TRUE);
         EnableWindow(GetDlgItem(hwnd, IDC_STOP),  FALSE);
         SetFocus(GetDlgItem(hwnd, IDC_START));
         break;
   }
}
```

The notification message UM_KEYEVENT is defined as (WM_APP + 0). I didn't define a message using WM_USER as my base because the KeyCount application uses the system's dialog box class instead of a class that I register myself. Microsoft guarantees us that none of the system classes will use any values between WM_APP (0x00008000) and 0x0000BFFF. Therefore, WM_APP is the proper choice for defining our own UM_KEYEVENT message.

When you press the Stop button, KeyCount's KeyCount_On-Command function calls KeyboardHook_Stop.

When our keyboard filter function receives a keyboard notification, it posts a UM_KEYEVENT notification to KeyCount's main window. KeyCount's dialog box procedure handles this message in the KeyCount_OnKeyEvent function:

```
#define GETKEYCOUNT(hwnd)       ((UINT) GetWindowLong(hwnd, GWL_USERDATA))
#define SETKEYCOUNT(hwnd, c) SetWindowLong(hwnd, GWL_USERDATA, (UINT) c)
.
.
.
void KeyCount_OnKeyEvent (HWND hwnd, UINT vk, LPARAM lParam) {

   BOOL fDown = ((HIWORD(lParam) & KF_UP) == 0);
   TCHAR sz[128];
   UINT uKeyCount = GETKEYCOUNT(hwnd);
   TCHAR c = (TCHAR) LOWORD(MapVirtualKey(vk, 2));

   if (fDown)
      uKeyCount++;
   SetDlgItemInt(hwnd, IDC_KEYCOUNT, uKeyCount, FALSE);
   wsprintf(sz, __TEXT("char=%c, virtual key=%d <%s>"),
      IsCharAlphaNumeric(c) ? c : __TEXT('?'), vk,
      fDown ? __TEXT("pressed") : __TEXT("released"));
   SetDlgItemText(hwnd, IDC_LASTKEY, sz);

   SETKEYCOUNT(hwnd, uKeyCount);
}
```

KeyCount_OnKeyEvent retrieves the current keystroke count from GWL_USERDATA with the macro GETKEYCOUNT. If lParam does not have the KF_UP bit turned on, the key is pressed, and the keystroke count is incremented. Then the Total Keystrokes and Last Key fields are updated and KeyCount updates the keystroke count in GWL_USERDATA with the macro SETKEYCOUNT.

Now, let's turn our attention to how the hook is installed. KeyboardHook_Start saves the three parameters passed to it in global variables and then calls SetWindowsHookEx:

```
BOOL WINAPI KeyboardHook_Start (HWND hwndPost,
   UINT uMsgNotify, HWND hwndEdit) {

   HHOOK hhook;

   // Return FALSE if hook has already been installed.
   if (g_hhook != NULL)
      return(FALSE);

   adgASSERT(IsWindow(hwndPost));

   g_hwndPost   = hwndPost;
   g_uMsgNotify = uMsgNotify;
   g_hwndEdit   = hwndEdit;

   // Give up the remainder of our thread's time slice.
   // This gives us a better chance of getting all the way through the call
   // to SetWindowsHookEx and the variable assignment to g_hhook in one shot.
   // If we are preempted after the hook is set, but before the variable is
   // updated, it is possible for another thread to enter our hook filter
   // function before the hook handle is valid.  Under Windows NT this is not
   // a problem.  Under Windows 95, not having a valid hook handle will cause
   // CallNextHookEx to fail.  If there is some reason that it is critical
   // that your application succeed in calling the next filter function in
   // the chain, the only robust way to write this code is to use something
   // like the SWMRG (single-writer, multiple-reader guard) object developed
   // in Advanced Windows (Microsoft Press).
   Sleep(0);

   // Set our keyboard hook.
   hhook = SetWindowsHookEx(WH_KEYBOARD,
      KeyboardHook_HookProc, g_hinstDll, 0);

   // Ensure that g_hhook is always valid (even if we are preempted whilst
   // in the middle of writing to it) by updating the variable atomically.
   InterlockedExchange((PLONG) &g_hhook, (LONG) hhook);

   return(g_hhook != NULL);
}
```

Because we are installing a system-wide hook, dwThreadID is zero and the hmod parameter is the instance handle of **KybdHk.DLL**, which was passed to DllMain. Now, you probably noticed the call to Sleep before SetWindowsHookEx was called and the InterlockedExchange call afterward. These lines of code are to (partially) work around a potential problem with thread synchronization under Windows 95.

406

Under Windows NT, the HHOOK handle passed to CallNextHookEx is completely ignored. No matter what you pass in, Windows NT calls the next hook in the chain—Windows NT can do this because it maintains the chain and it knows which filter function it just called. Unfortunately, Windows 95 doesn't keep track of which filter function it just called and requires that this hook handle be valid. This may not seem like a big deal, but consider this possibility: Thread A sets a system-wide WH_KEYBOARD hook with SetWindowsHookEx. Thread A is then preempted after the hook has been set, but before the hook handle has been stored in the shared g_hhook variable. The hook handle variable is still uninitialized. Now, thread B retrieves a keystroke message. The hook filter function is called in the context of thread B, but the HHOOK variable is still NULL, so the call to CallNextHookEx fails to call the next hook filter function. This breakage in the hook chain can cause problems with other hooks that are already installed.

This problem can be completely solved only through the use of a thread synchronization object like the SWMRG (Single-Writer, Multiple-Reader Guard) object developed in *Advanced Windows*[9] (the "readers" are the threads that have had hooks installed on them, and the "writer" is the thread which called SetWindowsHookEx). However, we can greatly increase our chances of executing the SetWindowsHookEx function and the variable assignment, uninterrupted, by calling Sleep passing a value of zero (milliseconds) to give up the rest of our thread's time slice. When the thread is later reawakened, it will have a better chance of making it through the instructions that cause the thread synchronization problem. Naturally, this sort of "technique" is highly unreliable and depends on all sorts of things that are out of your control (such as thread priorities). But, I decided to add the call to Sleep because it certainly can't hurt, and the full solution to this problem with a SWMRG object is beyond the scope of this book.

---

[9]See Chapter 9, "Thread Synchronization," of *Advanced Windows* (Microsoft Press, 1995).

The call to InterlockedExchange in KeyboardHook_Start ensures that the hook handle in the shared section is updated atomically. InterlockedExchange guarantees that we cannot be preempted whilst in the middle of updating the hook handle. If we did get preempted at this unlucky time, the value in our shared variable would be corrupt.

The KeyboardHook_HookProc filter function that KeyboardHook_Start installs looks roughly like this:

```
static LRESULT WINAPI KeyboardHook_HookProc (int nCode,
   WPARAM wParam, LPARAM lParam) {

   if (nCode == HC_ACTION) {

      // Notify application's window that this thread received a keystroke.
      PostMessage(g_hwndPost, g_uMsgNotify, wParam, lParam);
      .
      .
      .
   }
   return(CallNextHookEx(g_hhook, nCode, wParam, lParam));
}
```

On an HC_ACTION code, the hook procedure receives notification of a keyboard event. We notify the KeyCount application (since it called KeyboardHook_Start) of the event by posting the notify message, g_uMsgNotify, to the notification window, g_hwndPost.

KeyboardHook_Start sets a system-wide keyboard hook. This means that when a keyboard event is retrieved by a thread in another process, the hook's filter function must be called. But the DLL containing the filter function is not loaded into the process's address space. So, the system makes the filter function available by internally calling LoadLibrary in order to inject the DLL into the process's address space. Once the DLL is injected, the system allows the thread to execute the filter function's code.

Now, an interesting problem arises: If some other application like Notepad were active, KeyboardHook_HookProc would be called in the context of Notepad's process. This is all fine, except that the instance of our DLL, which was injected into Notepad's process space will have its own separate g_hwndPost and g_uMsgNotify global variables. And unfortunately, these variables will have different values from the values we set in KeyboardHook_Start. In fact,

408

they will still be initialized as they were when the DLL was loaded into Notepad's address space (they would be NULL and WM_NULL, respectively). This problem is easily solved by putting these variables into a shared section:

```
// Calling SetWindowsHookEx with a thread ID of zero will cause this DLL to be
// injected into other processes. Therefore, we must declare a shared data
// section so that all mappings of our DLL (in all processes) share the same
// set of global variables.

#pragma comment(lib, "kernel32 " "-section:Shared,rws")
#pragma data_seg("Shared")

HHOOK g_hhook      = NULL;      // Hook handle for system-wide keyboard hook
HWND  g_hwndPost   = NULL;      // Window to notify of keyboard events
UINT  g_uMsgNotify = WM_NULL;   // Notification message to post to g_hwndPost
HWND  g_hwndEdit   = NULL;      // Characters to reject with hook

#pragma data_seg()
```

Now, when Windows maps our DLL into another process, these variables will be mapped to the same area of physical storage (although they might easily have different virtual addresses if the DLL was forced to load at a different base address). Because our variables are mapped to the same physical storage, they will always have the same values across all processes.[10]

The remainder of KeyboardHook_HookProc deals with rejecting the characters specified in the Edit control passed to KeyboardHook_Start (and saved in the global shared variable g_hwndEdit):

```
static LRESULT WINAPI KeyboardHook_HookProc (int nCode,
   WPARAM wParam, LPARAM lParam) {

   LRESULT lResult = CallNextHookEx(g_hhook, nCode, wParam, lParam);

   if (nCode == HC_ACTION) {

      TCHAR ac[2];
      BYTE bKeyState[256];
      UINT uScanCodeAndShiftState = HIWORD(lParam) & (0x00FF | KF_UP);
```

---

[10]For a lot more information about sharing data and how to use shared sections, see Chapter 11, "Dynamic Link Libraries," of *Advanced Windows* (Microsoft Press, 1995).

```
        // Notify application's window that this thread received a keystroke.
        PostMessage(g_hwndPost, g_uMsgNotify, wParam, lParam);

        // Translate keystroke to ANSI or Unicode and reject it if it's one
        // of the characters in g_hwndEdit.
        GetKeyboardState(bKeyState);
#ifdef UNICODE
        if (ToUnicode(wParam, uScanCodeAndShiftState,
            bKeyState, ac, 1, 0) == 1) {
#else
        if (ToAscii(wParam, uScanCodeAndShiftState,
            bKeyState, (PWORD) ac, 0) == 1) {
#endif
        TCHAR sz[256];
        FORWARD_WM_GETTEXT(g_hwndEdit, adgARRAY_SIZE(sz), sz, SendMessage);
        if (_tcschr(sz, ac[0])) {

            // Reject the key event.
            lResult = 1;
        }
    }
    }
    }
    return(lResult);
}
```

Before we can compare our keyboard event with the contents of the Edit control, we must first call the ToUnicode or ToAscii function[11] to translate the virtual-key code in wParam, and the scan code and shift state in lParam, to a character value. Then we call SendMessage to get the contents of the Edit control with a WM_GETTEXT message. If the key event corresponds to any of the characters in the Edit control, we return 1 to stop further processing of the event.

It would seem that I have finished explaining KeyCount at this point. But that innocent looking SendMessage call has a lot of reasoning behind it!

For one thing, why didn't I simply call GetWindowText? GetWindowText and sending a WM_GETTEXT message don't work the same way. GetWindowText doesn't send a WM_GETTEXT message. Instead, it calls DefWindowProc directly to get the window text. And, unfortunately, Edit controls are special—they override WM_GETTEXT and retrieve their contents from an internal buffer. Because DefWindowProc doesn't know about this, it just retrieves the window text, which is always empty. So we are forced to send a WM_GETTEXT message to retrieve the window text.

---

[11] For more information about ToAscii and ToUnicode, refer to Chapter 8.

Even though this difference in behaviors seems rather odd, the reasoning behind it is quite interesting. When you are switching between windows with Alt+Tab, the system needs to get the caption of each window so that it can display it as you cycle through the windows. Unfortunately, if one of the threads that created one of the windows is hung, the system is unable to get the caption text for the window by sending it a WM_GETTEXT message. SendMessage suspends, waiting for the hung thread to wake up and respond to the sent message. But that thread would never wake up, so the system would be unable to get the caption. Simply using GetWindowText circumvents this problem because DefWindowProc can always get the caption of a window regardless of the state of the thread that created the window.

There is actually another, more subtle reason for using SendMessage here. This has to do with thread synchronization. Because inter-thread *SendMessages* are sent through a thread's message queue, there is an implicit serialization of threads as a result. No matter how many threads attempt to access the window text of our edit control, *only one* thread will be able to access its contents at a time. To see why this is important, imagine that we architected KeyCount so that the KeyCount application passed a buffer to a function in the KybdHk DLL called KeyHook_SetRejectCharacters. Each time the Edit control changed, the new contents are passed to this function, which simply copies the new data into a global buffer in the shared section of the KybdHk DLL. All processes instantly see this new data. But there is a big problem with this! Because access to the buffer is not controlled, KeyHook_SetRejectCharacters might be preempted whilst in the middle of changing the data. At this point in time the global buffer in the shared section contains corrupt data that other threads are free to access! The result would probably not be catastrophic in the case of a trivial application like KeyCount, but the consequences to a real-world application might be grave indeed. In fact, a real-world application would want to use a synchronization object such as a SWMRG, as developed in *Advanced Windows*, because serializing access to data with SendMessage can potentially suspend other threads that might otherwise be doing useful work.

Listing 6.1 *KeyCount.C*

```
/*************************************************************************
Module name: KeyCount.c
Written by: Jonathan Locke
Notices: Copyright (c) 1995 Jeffrey Richter
Purpose: Keyboard hooks demonstration application
*************************************************************************/


#include "..\Win95ADG.h"          /* See Appendix A for details */
#include <windows.h>
#include <windowsx.h>
#pragma warning(disable: 4001)     /* Single line comment */
#include <tchar.h>
#include "KybdHk.h"
#include "KeyCount.h"
#include "Resource.h"
#pragma warning(disable: 4001)     /* Single line comment */


//////////////////////////////////////////////////////////////////////


// Force a link with the import library for KybdHk.dll
#pragma comment(lib, adgLIBBUILDTYPE adgLIBCPUTYPE "\\" "KybdHk")


//////////////////////////////////////////////////////////////////////


#define GETKEYCOUNT(hwnd)     ((UINT) GetWindowLong(hwnd, GWL_USERDATA))
#define SETKEYCOUNT(hwnd, c) SetWindowLong(hwnd, GWL_USERDATA, (UINT) c)


//////////////////////////////////////////////////////////////////////


BOOL KeyCount_OnInitDialog (HWND hwnd, HWND hwndFocus, LPARAM lParam) {

   adgSETDLGICONS(hwnd, IDI_KEYCOUNT, IDI_KEYCOUNT);

   // Make the keycount dialog topmost so that it is easy to watch keys in
   // applications that take up most or all of the screen.
   SetWindowPos(hwnd, HWND_TOPMOST, 0, 0, 0, 0, SWP_NOMOVE | SWP_NOSIZE);

   EnableWindow(GetDlgItem(hwnd, IDC_START), TRUE);
   EnableWindow(GetDlgItem(hwnd, IDC_STOP),  FALSE);

   // Reset keystroke count.
   SETKEYCOUNT(hwnd, 0);

   return(TRUE);                   // Accept default focus window.
}
```

```
/////////////////////////////////////////////////////////////////////////////

void KeyCount_OnKeyEvent (HWND hwnd, UINT vk, LPARAM lParam) {

   BOOL fDown = ((HIWORD(lParam) & KF_UP) == 0);
   TCHAR sz[128];
   UINT uKeyCount = GETKEYCOUNT(hwnd);
   TCHAR c = (TCHAR) LOWORD(MapVirtualKey(vk, 2));

   if (fDown)
      uKeyCount++;
   SetDlgItemInt(hwnd, IDC_KEYCOUNT, uKeyCount, FALSE);
   wsprintf(sz, __TEXT("char=%c, virtual key=%d <%s>"),
      IsCharAlphaNumeric(c) ? c : __TEXT('?'), vk,
      fDown ? __TEXT("pressed") : __TEXT("released"));
   SetDlgItemText(hwnd, IDC_LASTKEY, sz);

   SETKEYCOUNT(hwnd, uKeyCount);
}


/////////////////////////////////////////////////////////////////////////////

void KeyCount_OnCommand (HWND hwnd, int id, HWND hwndCtl, UINT codeNotify) {

   HWND hwndEdit;

   switch (id) {

      case IDCANCEL:                    // Allows dialog box to close.

         // Unhook keyboard hook before exiting.
         if (!KeyboardHook_Stop())
            adgMB(__TEXT("Unable to stop keyboard hook"));
         EndDialog(hwnd, id);
         break;

      case IDC_START:
         hwndEdit = GetDlgItem(hwnd, IDC_EDIT);
         if (KeyboardHook_Start(hwnd, UM_KEYEVENT, hwndEdit)) {
            SetDlgItemText(hwnd, IDC_LASTKEY, __TEXT(""));
            SetDlgItemInt(hwnd, IDC_KEYCOUNT, 0, FALSE);
            SETKEYCOUNT(hwnd, 0);
            EnableWindow(GetDlgItem(hwnd, IDC_START), FALSE);
            EnableWindow(GetDlgItem(hwnd, IDC_STOP),  TRUE);
            SetFocus(GetDlgItem(hwnd, IDC_STOP));
         } else {
            adgMB(__TEXT("Unable to start keyboard hook"));
         }
         break;

      case IDC_STOP:
         if (!KeyboardHook_Stop())
```

413

```
        adgMB(__TEXT("Unable to stop keyboard hook"));
      EnableWindow(GetDlgItem(hwnd, IDC_START), TRUE);
      EnableWindow(GetDlgItem(hwnd, IDC_STOP),  FALSE);
      SetFocus(GetDlgItem(hwnd, IDC_START));
      break;
   }
}


//////////////////////////////////////////////////////////////////////


BOOL WINAPI KeyCount_DlgProc (HWND hwnd, UINT uMsg,
   WPARAM wParam, LPARAM lParam) {

   switch (uMsg) {

      // Standard Windows messages
      adgHANDLE_DLGMSG(hwnd, WM_INITDIALOG, KeyCount_OnInitDialog);
      adgHANDLE_DLGMSG(hwnd, WM_COMMAND,    KeyCount_OnCommand);

      // Keyboard hook notification message
      adgHANDLE_DLGMSG(hwnd, UM_KEYEVENT,   KeyCount_OnKeyEvent);
   }

   return(FALSE);                    // We didn't process the message.
}


//////////////////////////////////////////////////////////////////////


int WINAPI WinMain (HINSTANCE hinstExe, HINSTANCE hinstPrev,
   LPSTR lpszCmdLine, int nCmdShow) {

   adgWARNIFUNICODEUNDERWIN95();
   adgVERIFY(-1 != DialogBox(hinstExe, MAKEINTRESOURCE(IDD_KEYCOUNT),
      NULL, KeyCount_DlgProc));

   return(0);
}


///////////////////////////////// End of File //////////////////////////////////
```

Listing 6.2 *KeyCount.MSG*

```
// Module name: KeyCount.msg
// Written by: Jonathan Locke
// Notices: Copyright (c) 1995 Jeffrey Richter
// Purpose: 'MsgCrack' input file for KeyCount application.
```

414

```
MessageBase WM_APP
MessageClass KeyCount

Message UM_KEYEVENT KeyEvent \
- Notification message posted by keyboard hook routine (in KybdHk.dll)\
 when a keyboard event occurs.
wParam UINT vk - Virtual keycode
lParam LPARAM lParam - Keystroke flags
 .
```

Listing 6.3 *KeyCount.H*

```
/*************************************************************************
Module name: KeyCount.h
Written by: Jonathan Locke
Notices: Copyright (c) 1995 Jeffrey Richter
Purpose: Message cracker for UM_KEYEVENT notification message.
*************************************************************************/

///////////////////////////////// Messages /////////////////////////////////


//{{adgMSGCRACK_MESSAGES

// Purpose: Notification message posted by keyboard hook routine (in
//          KybdHk.dll) when a keyboard event occurs.
// wParam:  UINT vk - Virtual keycode
// lParam:  LPARAM lParam - Keystroke flags
// Returns: void
#define UM_KEYEVENT              (WM_APP + 0)

//}}adgMSGCRACK_MESSAGES


///////////////////////////////// Message APIs /////////////////////////////////


//{{adgMSGCRACK_APIS

#define KeyCount_KeyEvent(hwnd, vk, lParam) \
  ((void)SendMessage((hwnd), UM_KEYEVENT, (WPARAM)(DWORD)(vk),
(LPARAM)(DWORD)(lParam)))

//}}adgMSGCRACK_APIS


///////////////////////////////// Message Crackers /////////////////////////////////


//{{adgMSGCRACK_CRACKERS

// void Cls_OnKeyEvent (HWND hwnd, UINT vk, LPARAM lParam)
```

415

```
#define HANDLE_UM_KEYEVENT(hwnd, wParam, lParam, fn) \
    ((fn)((hwnd), (UINT)(wParam), (LPARAM)(lParam)), 0)
#define FORWARD_UM_KEYEVENT(hwnd, vk, lParam, fn) \
    (void)((fn)((hwnd), UM_KEYEVENT, (WPARAM)(DWORD)(vk), (LPARAM)(DWORD)(lParam)))


//}}adgMSGCRACK_CRACKERS



////////////////////////////////// End of File //////////////////////////////////
```

Listing 6.4 *KeyCount.RC*

```
//Microsoft Visual C++ generated resource script.
//
#include "resource.h"

#define APSTUDIO_READONLY_SYMBOLS
/////////////////////////////////////////////////////////////////////////////
//
// Generated from the TEXTINCLUDE 2 resource.
//
#define APSTUDIO_HIDDEN_SYMBOLS
#include "windows.h"
#undef APSTUDIO_HIDDEN_SYMBOLS


/////////////////////////////////////////////////////////////////////////////
#undef APSTUDIO_READONLY_SYMBOLS


/////////////////////////////////////////////////////////////////////////////
//
// Icon
//

IDI_KEYCOUNT            ICON    DISCARDABLE    "KEYCOUNT.ICO"

/////////////////////////////////////////////////////////////////////////////
//
// Dialog
//

IDD_KEYCOUNT DIALOG DISCARDABLE  -32768, 5, 214, 79
STYLE WS_MINIMIZEBOX | WS_VISIBLE | WS_CAPTION | WS_SYSMENU
CAPTION "Key Count"
FONT 8, "MS Sans Serif"
BEGIN
    PUSHBUTTON      "&Start",IDC_START,7,4,50,14
    PUSHBUTTON      "S&top",IDC_STOP,63,4,50,14
    LTEXT           "",IDC_LASTKEY,68,28,138,9
    LTEXT           "0",IDC_KEYCOUNT,68,44,37,9
    RTEXT           "Last key:",IDC_STATIC,4,28,58,9
    RTEXT           "Total keystrokes:",IDC_STATIC,4,44,58,9
    RTEXT           "Keys to Reject:",IDC_STATIC,6,61,56,9
```

```
      EDITTEXT        IDC_EDIT,68,59,136,12,ES_AUTOHSCROLL
END


#ifdef APSTUDIO_INVOKED
/////////////////////////////////////////////////////////////////////////
//
// TEXTINCLUDE
//

1 TEXTINCLUDE DISCARDABLE
BEGIN
    "resource.h\0"
END

2 TEXTINCLUDE DISCARDABLE
BEGIN
    "#define APSTUDIO_HIDDEN_SYMBOLS\r\n"
    "#include ""windows.h""\r\n"
    "#undef APSTUDIO_HIDDEN_SYMBOLS\r\n"
    "\0"
END

3 TEXTINCLUDE DISCARDABLE
BEGIN
    "\r\n"
    "\0"
END

/////////////////////////////////////////////////////////////////////////
#endif    // APSTUDIO_INVOKED


#ifndef APSTUDIO_INVOKED
/////////////////////////////////////////////////////////////////////////
//
// Generated from the TEXTINCLUDE 3 resource.
//


/////////////////////////////////////////////////////////////////////////
#endif    // not APSTUDIO_INVOKED
```

Listing 6.5 *Resource.H*

```
//{{NO_DEPENDENCIES}}
// Microsoft Visual C++ generated include file.
// Used by KeyCount.rc
//
#define IDI_KEYCOUNT            101
#define IDC_START              1000
#define IDC_STOP               1001
#define IDC_KEYCOUNT           1002
#define IDC_LASTKEY            1003
```

```
#define IDD_KEYCOUNT                    1004
#define IDC_EDIT                        1005
#define IDC_STATIC                      -1

// Next default values for new objects
//
#ifdef APSTUDIO_INVOKED
#ifndef APSTUDIO_READONLY_SYMBOLS
#define _APS_NO_MFC                     1
#define _APS_NEXT_RESOURCE_VALUE        102
#define _APS_NEXT_COMMAND_VALUE         40001
#define _APS_NEXT_CONTROL_VALUE         1006
#define _APS_NEXT_SYMED_VALUE           101
#endif
#endif
```

Listing 6.6 *KybdHk.C*

```
/************************************************************************
Module name: KybdHk.c
Written by: Jonathan Locke
Notices: Copyright (c) 1995 Jeffrey Richter
Purpose: Dll which sets a system keyboard hook.
************************************************************************/


#include "..\Win95ADG.h"            /* See Appendix A for details */
#include <windows.h>
#include <windowsx.h>
#include <tchar.h>
#pragma warning(disable: 4001)      /* Single line comment */


// We must define KYBDHKLIBAPI as 'dllexport' before including KybdHk.h.
// KybdHk.h will see that we have already defined KYBDHKLIBAPI and
// will not (re)define it as 'dllimport'.
#define KYBDHKLIBAPI __declspec(dllexport)
#include "KybdHk.h"


///////////////////////////////////////////////////////////////////////


HINSTANCE g_hinstDll = NULL;        // KybdHk.dll's instance handle


///////////////////////////////////////////////////////////////////////


// Calling SetWindowsHookEx with a thread Id of zero will cause this DLL to be
// injected into other processes. Therefore, we must declare a shared data
```

418

```
// section so that all mappings of our DLL (in all processes) share the same
// set of global variables.

#pragma comment(lib, "kernel32 " "-section:Shared,rws")
#pragma data_seg("Shared")


HHOOK g_hhook       = NULL;       // Hook handle for system-wide keyboard hook
HWND  g_hwndPost    = NULL;       // Window to notify of keyboard events
UINT  g_uMsgNotify  = WM_NULL;    // Notification message to post to g_hwndPost
HWND  g_hwndEdit    = NULL;       // Characters to reject with hook

#pragma data_seg()


///////////////////////////////////////////////////////////////////////////////


static LRESULT WINAPI KeyboardHook_HookProc (int nCode,
   WPARAM wParam, LPARAM lParam) {

   LRESULT lResult = CallNextHookEx(g_hhook, nCode, wParam, lParam);

   if (nCode == HC_ACTION) {

      TCHAR ac[2];
      BYTE bKeyState[256];
      UINT uScanCodeAndShiftState = HIWORD(lParam) & (0x00FF | KF_UP);

      // Notify application's window that this thread received a keystroke
      PostMessage(g_hwndPost, g_uMsgNotify, wParam, lParam);

      // Translate keystroke to ANSI or Unicode and reject it if it's one
      // of the characters in g_hwndEdit.
      GetKeyboardState(bKeyState);
#ifdef UNICODE
      if (ToUnicode(wParam, uScanCodeAndShiftState,
         bKeyState, ac, 1, 0) == 1) {
#else
      if (ToAscii(wParam, uScanCodeAndShiftState,
         bKeyState, (PWORD) ac, 0) == 1) {
#endif
      TCHAR sz[256];
      FORWARD_WM_GETTEXT(g_hwndEdit, adgARRAY_SIZE(sz), sz, SendMessage);
      if (_tcschr(sz, ac[0])) {

            // Reject the key event.
            lResult = 1;
         }
      }
   }
   return(lResult);
}


///////////////////////////////////////////////////////////////////////////////
```

419

```
BOOL WINAPI KeyboardHook_Start (HWND hwndPost,
   UINT uMsgNotify, HWND hwndEdit) {

   HHOOK hhook;

   // Return FALSE if hook has already been installed.
   if (g_hhook != NULL)
      return(FALSE);

   adgASSERT(IsWindow(hwndPost));

   g_hwndPost   = hwndPost;
   g_uMsgNotify = uMsgNotify;
   g_hwndEdit   = hwndEdit;

   // Give up the remainder of our thread's timeslice.
   // This gives us a better chance of getting all the way through the call
   // to SetWindowsHookEx and the variable assignment to g_hhook in one shot.
   // If we are preempted after the hook is set, but before the variable is
   // updated, it is possible for another thread to enter our hook filter
   // function before the hook handle is valid.  Under Windows NT this is not
   // a problem.  Under Windows 95, not having a valid hook handle will cause
   // CallNextHookEx to fail.  If there is some reason that it is critical
   // that your application succeed in calling the next filter function in
   // the chain, the only robust way to write this code is to use something
   // like the SWMRG (single-writer, multiple-reader guard) object developed
   // in Advanced Windows (Microsoft Press).
   Sleep(0);

   // Set our keyboard hook.
   hhook = SetWindowsHookEx(WH_KEYBOARD,
      KeyboardHook_HookProc, g_hinstDll, 0);

   // Ensure that g_hhook is always valid (even if we are preempted whilst
   // in the middle of writing to it) by updating the variable atomically.
   InterlockedExchange((PLONG) &g_hhook, (LONG) hhook);

   return(g_hhook != NULL);
}


///////////////////////////////////////////////////////////////////////////


BOOL WINAPI KeyboardHook_Stop () {

   BOOL fOK = TRUE;

   // Only uninstall the hook if it was successfully installed.
   if (g_hhook != NULL) {
      fOK = UnhookWindowsHookEx(g_hhook);
      g_hhook = NULL;
   }
   return(fOK);
}
```

420

```
///////////////////////////////////////////////////////////////////////


BOOL WINAPI DllMain (HINSTANCE hinstDll, DWORD fdwReason, LPVOID lpvReserved) {

   switch (fdwReason) {

      case DLL_PROCESS_ATTACH:
         g_hinstDll = hinstDll;
         break;
   }
   return(TRUE);
}


/////////////////////////////////// End of File ///////////////////////////////////
```

Listing 6.7 *KybdHk.H*

```
/***************************************************************************
Module name: KybdHk.h
Written by: Jonathan Locke
Notices: Copyright (c) 1995 Jeffrey Richter
Purpose: Keyboard hooks dll function declarations
***************************************************************************/


#ifndef KYBDHKLIBAPI
#define KYBDHKLIBAPI    __declspec(dllimport)
#endif


///////////////////////////////////////////////////////////////////////


KYBDHKLIBAPI BOOL WINAPI KeyboardHook_Start (HWND hwndPost,
   UINT uMsgNotify, HWND hwndEdit);
KYBDHKLIBAPI BOOL WINAPI KeyboardHook_Stop ();


/////////////////////////////////// End of File ///////////////////////////////////
```

The AppLog Application

The AppLog application (**AppLog.EXE**), shown in Listings 6.8–6.12 (starting on page 425), demonstrates how to use a shell hook to monitor the creation and shutdown of application windows. When you invoke AppLog, the main application window shown in Figure 6.3 appears.

421

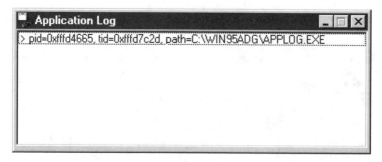

Figure 6.3 *The AppLog application.*

AppLog is a very simple application, containing just one control: a listbox. Each time an application starts up or shuts down, the process ID, thread ID, and path of that application is added to AppLog's listbox. After running Notepad and then MSPaint, AppLog will look like Figure 6.4.

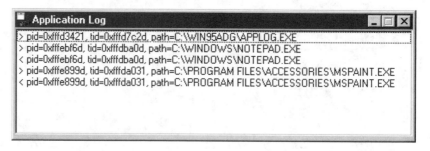

Figure 6.4 *The AppLog application after running Notepad and MSPaint.*

Tables 6.4 and 6.5 describe the files used to create this application and its associated DLL. (Because the AppLog application installs a system-wide WH_SHELL hook, a DLL is required.)

Table 6.4 Files used to build the AppLog application.

File	Description
AppLog.C	Contains WinMain and main window's dialog box and message cracker functions
AppLog.RC	Contains the dialog-box template for the main application window and its icons

File	Description
Resource.H	Contains IDs for all resources in the RC file
AppLog.ICO	Contains the icon for the main window
AppLog.MAK	Visual C++ project makefile for the application

Table 6.5 *Files used to build the ShellHk DLL.*

File	Description
ShellHk.C	Contains the implementation of the shell hook used to trap the creation/destruction of top-level windows by applications starting up and shutting down.
ShellHk.H	Contains function prototypes for the ShellHook API functions used to install and remove the shell hook. Any source file that uses the ShellHook API must include this file.
ShellHk.MAK	Visual C++ project makefile for the shell hook DLL.

The ShellHk.DLL exports two functions:

```
SHELLHKLIBAPI BOOL WINAPI ShellHook_Start (HWND hwndListBox);
SHELLHKLIBAPI BOOL WINAPI ShellHook_Stop ();
```

When the AppLog application starts up, it calls ShellHook_Start with the handle of a listbox placed in its client area. ShellHook_Start sets a system-wide shell hook whose sole purpose is to place entries in this listbox:

```
BOOL WINAPI ShellHook_Start (HWND hwndListBox) {

   HHOOK hhook = NULL;

   // Return FALSE if hook has already been installed.
   if (g_hhook != NULL)
      return(FALSE);

   adgASSERT(IsWindow(hwndListBox));
   g_hwndListBox = hwndListBox;


   // Give up the remainder of our thread's time slice.
   // This gives us a better chance of getting all the way through the call
   // to SetWindowsHookEx and the variable assignment to g_hhook in one shot.
```

```
// If we are preempted after the hook is set, but before the variable is
// updated, it is possible for another thread to enter our hook filter
// function before the hook handle is valid.  Under Windows NT this is not
// a problem.  Under Windows 95, not having a valid hook handle will cause
// CallNextHookEx to fail.  If there is some reason that it is critical
// that your application succeed in calling the next filter function in
// the chain, the only robust way to write this code is to use something
// like the SWMRG (single-writer, multiple-reader guard) object developed
// in Advanced Windows (Microsoft Press).
Sleep(0);

// Set our keyboard hook.
hhook = SetWindowsHookEx(WH_SHELL, ShellHook_HookProc, g_hinstDll, 0);

// Ensure that g_hhook is always valid (even if we are preempted whilst
// in the middle of writing to it) by updating the variable atomically.
InterlockedExchange((PLONG) &g_hhook, (LONG) hhook);

return(g_hhook != NULL);
}
```

The dwThreadID parameter passed to SetWindowsHookEx is zero, indicating that the hook should be system-wide, and the hmod parameter is the instance handle of the ShellHk DLL, which was saved in the global variable g_hinstDll by DllMain. Because ShellHk is a remote hook just like KeyCount's KybdHk, the same considerations arise with respect to shared variables and thread synchronization that were mentioned in the description of the preceding KeyCount application.

When the hook procedure, ShellHook_HookProc, receives an HSHELL_WINDOWCREATED notification or an HSHELL_WINDOWDESTROYED notification, it adds an entry to the listbox, describing the application window that was created or destroyed:

```
static LRESULT WINAPI ShellHook_HookProc (int nCode,
   WPARAM wParam, LPARAM lParam) {

   TCHAR sz[128], szPath[128];
   DWORD dwProcessID;
   HWND hwnd = (HWND) wParam;
   DWORD dwThreadID = GetWindowThreadProcessId(hwnd, &dwProcessID);
   LRESULT lResult = CallNextHookEx(g_hhook, nCode, wParam, lParam);

   switch (nCode) {

     case HSHELL_WINDOWCREATED:
     case HSHELL_WINDOWDESTROYED:

        // GetModuleFileName is being called in the context of the process in
        // which this DLL has been injected.
```

```
        if (!GetModuleFileName(NULL, szPath, adgARRAY_SIZE(szPath)))
            _tcscpy(szPath, __TEXT("<unknown>"));

        wsprintf(sz, __TEXT("%c pid=0x%08x, tid=0x%08x, path=%s"),
            (nCode == HSHELL_WINDOWCREATED ? __TEXT('>') : __TEXT('<')),
            dwProcessID, dwThreadID, szPath);

        ListBox_AddString(g_hwndListBox, sz);
        break;
    }

    return(lResult);
}
```

ShellHook_HookProc calls GetWindowThreadProcessID to get the thread and process identifiers associated with the window being created/destroyed. Then it calls GetModuleFileName with an HMODULE of NULL to get the complete path name of the executable image associated with the window. Normally you would expect "GetModuleFileName(NULL, ...)" to return the path name of the current process, **AppLog.EXE**. But don't forget, **ShellHk.DLL** has been injected into a remote process. Because GetModuleFilename is being called in the context of this remote process, it will return the path name to the executable image associated with that remote process rather than the path name to **AppLog.EXE**.

Listing 6.8 *AppLog.C*

```
/***************************************************************************
Module name: AppLog.c
Written by: Jonathan Locke
Notices: Copyright (c) 1995 Jeffrey Richter
Purpose: Shell hooks demonstration application
***************************************************************************/


#include "..\Win95ADG.h"            /* See Appendix A for details */
#include <windows.h>
#include <windowsx.h>
#pragma warning(disable: 4001)     /* Single line comment */
#include <tchar.h>
#include "ShellHk.h"
#include "Resource.h"


//////////////////////////////////////////////////////////////////////////


// Force a link with the import library for ShellHk.dll
#pragma comment(lib, adgLIBBUILDTYPE adgLIBCPUTYPE "\\" "ShellHk")
```

425

```
/////////////////////////////////////////////////////////////////////////


BOOL AppLog_OnInitDialog (HWND hwnd, HWND hwndFocus, LPARAM lParam) {

   adgSETDLGICONS(hwnd, IDI_APPLOG, IDI_APPLOG);
   if (!ShellHook_Start(GetDlgItem(hwnd, IDC_APPLOG))) {
      adgMB(__TEXT("Unable to start shell hook"));
      EndDialog(hwnd, IDCANCEL);
   }
   return(TRUE);                    // Accept default focus window.
}


/////////////////////////////////////////////////////////////////////////


void AppLog_OnSize (HWND hwnd, UINT state, int cx, int cy) {

   // When the user resizes the main window, we must resize the listbox child.
   SetWindowPos(GetDlgItem(hwnd, IDC_APPLOG), NULL,
      0, 0, cx, cy, SWP_NOZORDER);
}


/////////////////////////////////////////////////////////////////////////


void AppLog_OnCommand (HWND hwnd, int id, HWND hwndCtl, UINT codeNotify) {

   switch (id) {
      case IDCANCEL:               // Allows dialog box to close

         // Unhook shell hook before exiting.
         if (!ShellHook_Stop())
            adgMB(__TEXT("Unable to stop shell hook"));
         EndDialog(hwnd, id);
         break;
   }
}


/////////////////////////////////////////////////////////////////////////


BOOL WINAPI AppLog_DlgProc (HWND hwnd, UINT uMsg,
   WPARAM wParam, LPARAM lParam) {

   switch (uMsg) {

      // Standard Windows messages
      adgHANDLE_DLGMSG(hwnd, WM_INITDIALOG, AppLog_OnInitDialog);
```

```
      adgHANDLE_DLGMSG(hwnd, WM_COMMAND,    AppLog_OnCommand);
      adgHANDLE_DLGMSG(hwnd, WM_SIZE,       AppLog_OnSize);
   }
   return(FALSE);                 // We didn't process the message.
}


///////////////////////////////////////////////////////////////////////////


int WINAPI WinMain (HINSTANCE hinstExe, HINSTANCE hinstPrev,
   LPSTR lpszCmdLine, int nCmdShow) {

   adgWARNIFUNICODEUNDERWIN95();
   adgVERIFY(-1 != DialogBox(hinstExe, MAKEINTRESOURCE(IDD_APPLOG),
      NULL, AppLog_DlgProc));

   return(0);
}


///////////////////////////////// End of File //////////////////////////////
```

Listing 6.9 *AppLog.RC*

```
//Microsoft Visual C++ generated resource script.
//
#include "resource.h"

#define APSTUDIO_READONLY_SYMBOLS
///////////////////////////////////////////////////////////////////////////
//
// Generated from the TEXTINCLUDE 2 resource.
//
#define APSTUDIO_HIDDEN_SYMBOLS
#include "windows.h"
#undef APSTUDIO_HIDDEN_SYMBOLS


///////////////////////////////////////////////////////////////////////////
#undef APSTUDIO_READONLY_SYMBOLS


///////////////////////////////////////////////////////////////////////////
//
// Icon
//

IDI_APPLOG            ICON   DISCARDABLE    "APPLOG.ICO"

///////////////////////////////////////////////////////////////////////////
//
```

427

```
// Dialog
//

IDD_APPLOG DIALOG DISCARDABLE  0x8000, 5, 252, 76
STYLE WS_MINIMIZEBOX | WS_VISIBLE | WS_CAPTION | WS_SYSMENU | WS_THICKFRAME
CAPTION "Application Log"
FONT 8, "MS Sans Serif"
BEGIN
    LISTBOX             IDC_APPLOG,4,4,243,68,NOT LBS_NOTIFY | WS_VSCROLL |
                        WS_TABSTOP
END


#ifdef APSTUDIO_INVOKED
/////////////////////////////////////////////////////////////////////////////
//
// TEXTINCLUDE
//

1 TEXTINCLUDE DISCARDABLE
BEGIN
    "resource.h\0"
END

2 TEXTINCLUDE DISCARDABLE
BEGIN
    "#define APSTUDIO_HIDDEN_SYMBOLS\r\n"
    "#include ""windows.h""\r\n"
    "#undef APSTUDIO_HIDDEN_SYMBOLS\r\n"
    "\0"
END

3 TEXTINCLUDE DISCARDABLE
BEGIN
    "\r\n"
    "\0"
END

/////////////////////////////////////////////////////////////////////////////
#endif    // APSTUDIO_INVOKED


#ifndef APSTUDIO_INVOKED
/////////////////////////////////////////////////////////////////////////////
//
// Generated from the TEXTINCLUDE 3 resource.
//


/////////////////////////////////////////////////////////////////////////////
#endif    // not APSTUDIO_INVOKED
```

Listing 6.10 *Resource.H*

```
//{{NO_DEPENDENCIES}}
// Microsoft Visual C++ generated include file.
// Used by AppLog.RC
//
#define IDD_APPLOG                      101
#define IDC_APPLOG                      1000
#define IDI_APPLOG                      1001


// Next default values for new objects
//
#ifdef APSTUDIO_INVOKED
#ifndef APSTUDIO_READONLY_SYMBOLS
#define _APS_NO_MFC                     1
#define _APS_NEXT_RESOURCE_VALUE        102
#define _APS_NEXT_COMMAND_VALUE         40001
#define _APS_NEXT_CONTROL_VALUE         1002
#define _APS_NEXT_SYMED_VALUE           101
#endif
#endif
```

Listing 6.11 *ShellHk.C*

```
/*****************************************************************************
Module name: ShellHk.c
Written by: Jonathan Locke
Notices: Copyright (c) 1995 Jeffrey Richter
Purpose: Dll which sets a system shell hook.
*****************************************************************************/


#include "..\Win95ADG.h"          /* See Appendix A for details */
#include <windows.h>
#include <windowsx.h>
#pragma warning(disable: 4001)     /* Single line comment */
#include <tchar.h>
#pragma warning(disable: 4001)     /* Single line comment */


// We must define SHELLHKLIBAPI as 'dllexport' before including ShellHk.h.
// ShellHk.h will see that we have already defined SHELLHKLIBAPI and
// will not (re)define it as 'dllimport'.
#define SHELLHKLIBAPI __declspec(dllexport)
#include "ShellHk.h"
```

```
//////////////////////////////////////////////////////////////////////////


HINSTANCE g_hinstDll = NULL;        // ShellHk.dll's instance handle


//////////////////////////////////////////////////////////////////////////


// Calling SetWindowsHookEx with a thread id of zero will cause this DLL to be
// injected into other processes. Therefore, we must declare a shared data
// section so that all mappings of our DLL (in all processes) share the same
// set of global variables.

#pragma comment(lib, "kernel32 " "-section:Shared,rws")
#pragma data_seg("Shared")

HHOOK g_hhook       = NULL;    // Hook handle for systemwide shell hook
HWND  g_hwndListBox = NULL;    // Listbox in which to insert log strings

#pragma data_seg()


//////////////////////////////////////////////////////////////////////////

static LRESULT WINAPI ShellHook_HookProc (int nCode,
   WPARAM wParam, LPARAM lParam) {

   TCHAR sz[128], szPath[128];
   DWORD dwProcessID;
   HWND hwnd = (HWND) wParam;
   DWORD dwThreadID = GetWindowThreadProcessId(hwnd, &dwProcessID);
   LRESULT lResult = CallNextHookEx(g_hhook, nCode, wParam, lParam);

   switch (nCode) {

      case HSHELL_WINDOWCREATED:
      case HSHELL_WINDOWDESTROYED:

         // GetModuleFileName is being called in the context of the process in
         // which this Dll has been injected.
         if (!GetModuleFileName(NULL, szPath, adgARRAY_SIZE(szPath)))
            _tcscpy(szPath, __TEXT("<unknown>"));

         wsprintf(sz, __TEXT("%c pid=0x%08x, tid=0x%08x, path=%s"),
            (nCode == HSHELL_WINDOWCREATED ? __TEXT('>') : __TEXT('<')),
            dwProcessID, dwThreadID, szPath);

         ListBox_AddString(g_hwndListBox, sz);
         break;
   }

   return(lResult);
}
```

```
///////////////////////////////////////////////////////////////////////////

BOOL WINAPI ShellHook_Start (HWND hwndListBox) {

   HHOOK hhook = NULL;

   // Return FALSE if hook has already been installed.
   if (g_hhook != NULL)
      return(FALSE);

   adgASSERT(IsWindow(hwndListBox));
   g_hwndListBox = hwndListBox;

   // Give up the remainder of our thread's timeslice.
   // This gives us a better chance of getting all the way through the call
   // to SetWindowsHookEx and the variable assignment to g_hhook in one shot.
   // If we are preempted after the hook is set, but before the variable is
   // updated, it is possible for another thread to enter our hook filter
   // function before the hook handle is valid.  Under Windows NT this is not
   // a problem.  Under Windows 95, not having a valid hook handle will cause
   // CallNextHookEx to fail.  If there is some reason that it is critical
   // that your application succeed in calling the next filter function in
   // the chain, the only robust way to write this code is to use something
   // like the SWMRG (single-writer, multiple-reader guard) object developed
   // in Advanced Windows (Microsoft Press).
   Sleep(0);

   // Set our keyboard hook.
   hhook = SetWindowsHookEx(WH_SHELL, ShellHook_HookProc, g_hinstDll, 0);

   // Ensure that g_hhook is always valid (even if we are preempted whilst
   // in the middle of writing to it) by updating the variable atomically.
   InterlockedExchange((PLONG) &g_hhook, (LONG) hhook);

   return(g_hhook != NULL);
}


///////////////////////////////////////////////////////////////////////////

BOOL WINAPI ShellHook_Stop () {

   BOOL fOK = TRUE;

   // Only uninstall the hook if it was successfully installed.
   if (g_hhook != NULL) {
      fOK = UnhookWindowsHookEx(g_hhook);
      g_hhook = NULL;
   }
   return(fOK);
}


///////////////////////////////////////////////////////////////////////////
```

```
BOOL WINAPI DllMain (HINSTANCE hinstDll, DWORD fdwReason, LPVOID lpvReserved) {

    switch (fdwReason) {

        case DLL_PROCESS_ATTACH:
            g_hinstDll = hinstDll;
            break;
    }
    return(TRUE);
}


//////////////////////////////// End of File ////////////////////////////////////
```

Listing 6.12 *ShellHk.H*

```
/****************************************************************************
Module name: ShellHk.h
Written by: Jonathan Locke
Notices: Copyright (c) 1995 Jeffrey Richter
Purpose: Shell hooks dll function declarations
****************************************************************************/


// SHELLHKLIBAPI is defined as dllexport in the implementation file
// (shellhk.c). Thus, when this is included by shellhk.c, functions will be
// exported instead of imported.
#ifndef SHELLHKLIBAPI
#define SHELLHKLIBAPI    __declspec(dllimport)
#endif


///////////////////////////////////////////////////////////////////////////


SHELLHKLIBAPI BOOL WINAPI ShellHook_Start (HWND hwndListBox);
SHELLHKLIBAPI BOOL WINAPI ShellHook_Stop ();


//////////////////////////////// End of File ////////////////////////////////////
```

The Echo Application (a Macro Recorder)

The Echo application (**Echo.EXE**), shown in Listings 6.13–6.19 (starting on page 438), demonstrates how to use journal record and playback hooks to create a macro recorder that records and plays

432

back hardware input events. When you invoke Echo, the main application window shown in Figure 6.5 appears.

Figure 6.5 *The Echo application.*

Like most recorders, Echo has three buttons: Record, Play, and Stop. Initially, the Play and Stop buttons are disabled. Once you press the Record button to begin recording events, the Stop button will become enabled, allowing you to stop recording. When you press Stop, the Stop button will become disabled and the Play and Record buttons will both be enabled. Pressing Play at this point will play back the hardware events (mouse, keyboard, and pen) that you recorded.

Table 6.6 describes the files used to create this application.

Table 6.6 *The files used to build the Echo application.*

File	Description
Echo.C	Contains WinMain and main window's dialog box and message cracker functions.
Echo.MSG	MsgCrack input file used to create **Echo.H** (See Appendix B for details).
Echo.H	Contains message cracker macros for the UM_STOP notification message.
Record.C	Contains the implementation of the recorder. You can use this file in your own applications or modify it to suit your needs.
Record.H	Contains enumerations for error codes and recorder modes, as well as function prototypes for the recorder API functions. Any source file that uses the recorder API must include this file.
Echo.RC	Contains the dialog-box template for the main application window and its icons.
Resource.H	Contains IDs for all resources in the RC file.
Echo.ICO	Contains the icon for the main window.
Echo.MAK	Visual C++ project makefile.

The Echo application is composed of two primary pieces: the Echo application code, which creates Echo's main window and maintains the user interface, and the recorder code, which contains the guts of the macro recorder. Because the recorder code has a nice clean API that isn't dependent on the implementation details of the application code, you can easily use the recorder in your own applications.

The Echo Application Code

When Echo creates its main window, it initializes the macro recorder by calling Recorder_Init. Then it calls a function, Echo_UpdateButtons, to enable or disable the Play, Record, and Stop buttons appropriately. The current state of the recorder determines which buttons are enabled. The state of the recorder is obtained by calling the Recorder_GetMode function, which returns one of the following values:

```
typedef enum {
    RECMODE_STOPPED,      // Recorder is stopped
    RECMODE_RECORDING,    // Recorder is recording events
    RECMODE_PLAYING       // Recorder is playing back events
} RECMODE;
```

The Echo_UpdateButtons function is called throughout the code whenever the recorder's mode changes and the buttons need to be enabled or disabled.

When the user presses one of Echo's buttons, the corresponding recorder function is called:

```
// Returns: RECERR_OK, RECERR_CANTHOOK, RECERR_ACTIVE or RECERR_NOMEMORY
RECERR WINAPI Recorder_Record (HWND hwndNotify, UINT uMsgNotify);

// Returns: RECERR_OK, RECERR_CANTHOOK, RECERR_ACTIVE or RECERR_NOEVENTS
RECERR WINAPI Recorder_Play (HEVENTLIST h, HWND hwndNotify, UINT uMsgNotify);

// Returns: RECERR_OK or RECERR_INACTIVE
RECERR WINAPI Recorder_Stop (void);
```

When you press the Record button, Echo calls Recorder_Record with its own window handle and the notification message UM_STOP. The recorder module proceeds to record hardware events until it is stopped (either by the user or because an error occurred). When the recorder stops, it sends the UM_STOP notification message that was specified to Recorder_Record to the Echo main window. Echo's handler for the UM_STOP notification looks like this:

434

```
void Echo_OnStop (HWND hwnd, HEVENTLIST h, RECERR e) {

   // Echo_OnStop can be called when either recording or playing stops. If the
   // HEVENTLIST parameter is non-NULL, Echo_OnStop was called because
   // recording stopped, which means we need to save the HEVENTLIST for future
   // playback.
   if (h != NULL)
      SETEVENTLIST(hwnd, h);
   Echo_UpdateButtons(hwnd);
   Recorder_DisplayError(e);
}
```

If the HEVENTLIST[12] parameter h is NULL, Echo_OnStop was called because playing stopped. Otherwise, it was called because recording stopped, and h is a handle to an event list that can be played back with the Recorder_Play function when the user hits the Play button. If the UM_STOP notification was sent because an error forced the recorder to stop, the third parameter contains one of the following error codes:

```
typedef enum {
   RECERR_OK,         // Operation was successful
   RECERR_CANTHOOK,   // Hook cannot be installed
   RECERR_ACTIVE,     // Attempt to record/play while already recording/playing
   RECERR_INACTIVE,   // Attempt to stop recording while NOT recording
   RECERR_NOMEMORY,   // When attempting to start recording or during recording
   RECERR_NOEVENTS,   // Attempt playback with no events in memory block
   RECERR_SYSMODAL,   // System modal dialog box canceled recording
   RECERR_USERCANCEL  // User canceled with Ctrl+Esc
} RECERR;
```

Echo uses the function Recorder_DisplayError to display an error message description. If no error occurred, Recorder_DisplayError does nothing.

There is only one small complication. When the user presses Ctrl+Esc, the system automatically unhooks any journal record and playback hooks and posts WM_CANCELJOURNAL messages to the queues of any threads that have installed either of these hooks. The recorder needs to get this message so it can notify Echo that recording has stopped (and so the recorder can reset its hook handle to NULL).

---

[12]HEVENTLIST is a handle declared by the recorder in **Recorder.H** to abstract the idea of an event list. If the recorder wants to change the implementation of an event list in the future, it will be able to do so without breaking any applications that are using the recorder.

435

Unfortunately, WM_CANCELJOURNAL messages are not posted to Echo's main window. They are instead posted directly to Echo's message queue with a NULL window handle. There are two reasonable ways to retrieve such a message. The first approach is to trap the message when it is retrieved from Echo's message queue by installing either a WH_GETMESSAGE or a WH_(SYS)MSGFILTER hook. The second approach is to modify Echo to have its own message loop so that we can intercept the message when Echo retrieves it with GetMessage. I chose the latter approach. To make things easy, the recorder provides a function, Recorder_IsRecorderCanceled, which looks for the WM_CANCELJOURNAL message:

```
BOOL WINAPI Recorder_IsRecorderCanceled (PMSG pmsg);
```

The Recorder_IsRecorderCanceled function checks for WM_CANCELJOURNAL messages in the same way that the IsDialogMessage function checks for keystroke messages. Echo calls the Recorder_IsRecorderCanceled function inside its main message loop. If Recorder_IsRecorderCanceled detects a WM_CANCELJOURNAL message, it resets the recorder's hook handle to NULL and notifies Echo that recording/playback has stopped with the recorder error RECERR_USERCANCEL.

When Echo exits, it frees any existing event list by calling the function Recorder_Free:

```
void WINAPI Recorder_Free (HEVENTLIST h);
```

The Recorder Code

In the recorder implementation, a global variable holds the complete state of the recorder at any given time. This global variable, g_RecorderData, is a structure declared as follows:

```
typedef struct {
    HHOOK     hhookJournal;      // Journal hook handle
    RECMODE   RecMode;           // Recorder's operating mode
    HWND      hwndNotify;        // Window to notify
    UINT      uMsgNotify;        // Notification message to send
    RECERR    RecErr;            // Error that halted recording
    PRECSTAT  pRecStat;          // Recorded data
} RECORDERDATA;
```

The hhookJournal member holds the hook handle of the current journal record/playback hook. If there is no hook currently installed, hhookJournal is NULL. The current recorder mode (one of REC-MODE_*) is kept in the RecMode member. The hwndNotify and uMsgNotify members specify a target window and a notification message to send when recording/playback stops. RecErr is used to hold any error that may have halted recording. And most importantly, the pRecStat member points to a list of recorded events. This list is comprised of a RECTSTAT header structure followed by a list of EVENTMSG structures (defined in **WinUser.H**). The RECSTAT structure holds statistical data about the recorded/played events:

```
// Statistical information that appears at start of EVENTMSG list.
typedef struct {
    int nNumEvents;             // Number of recorded events
    int nNumEventsPlayed;       // Number of events played back
    DWORD dwStartTime;          // Time when playback started
} RECSTAT, *PRECSTAT;
```

When the recorder is asked to record, it sets a WH_JOURNALRECORD hook. The filter function for this hook, Recorder_JournalRecordProc, watches for HC_ACTION hook codes and records each accompanying EVENTMSG structure by appending it to the list of events stored in g_RecorderData.pRecStat. If the recorder runs out of memory for the event list, it stops recording with the error code RECERR_NOMEMORY. If Recorder_JournalRecordProc receives an HC_SYSMODALON hook code,[13] it sets a static variable, fPause, to TRUE. As long as this variable is TRUE, the Recorder_JournalRecordProc function ignores all HC_ACTION hook codes. Once the system-modal message box is removed, an HC_SYSMODALOFF hook code is sent to the filter function and the recorder is stopped with the error RECERR_SYSMODAL.

Whenever the recorder stops, it uninstalls any currently installed journal record/playback hook with UnhookWindowsHookEx. Then, if it was recording, it adjusts the times of the recorded EVENTMSG structures, by giving each a relative timestamp (subtracting the time at which recording began). The relative timestamp ensures that playback of events proceeds at the same speed at which events were originally recorded. Finally, Recorder_Stop sends the notification message g_RecorderData.uMsgNotify to the notification

---

[13]You will never receive an HC_SYSMODAL* message from a 32-bit application. Only 16-bit applications running under Windows 95 generate this hook code.

window g_RecorderData.hwndNotify. If it was recording that stopped, the wParam of this notification message is the current event list, g_RecorderData.pRecStat, cast as an HEVENTLIST handle. If it was playing that stopped, wParam is NULL. The lParam parameter specifies the value stored in g_RecorderData.RecErr. This error code represents the reason why recording/playback stopped. If it is RECERR_OK, no error occurred.

When the recorder is asked to play back an HEVENTLIST, it installs a journal playback hook. If the hook code passed to Recorder_JournalPlaybackProc is HC_GETNEXT, the filter function returns the current EVENTMSG from the list. If the hook code is HC_SKIP, the recorder skips to the next EVENTMSG in the list, stopping playback if there are no more events left.

Listing 6.13 *Echo.C*

```
/***************************************************************************
Module name: Echo.c
Written by: Jeffrey Richter and Jonathan Locke
Notices: Copyright (c) 1995 Jeffrey Richter
Purpose: A simple macro recorder application which demonstrates the use of
         journal record and playback hooks.
***************************************************************************/


#include "..\Win95ADG.h"          /* See Appendix A for details */
#include <windows.h>
#include <windowsx.h>
#pragma warning(disable: 4001)     /* Single line comment */
#include "Resource.h"
#include "Echo.h"
#include "Record.h"
#pragma warning(disable: 4001)     /* Single line comment */


///////////////////////////////////////////////////////////////////////////


#define GETEVENTLIST(hwnd)    ((HEVENTLIST) GetWindowLong(hwnd, GWL_USERDATA))
#define SETEVENTLIST(hwnd, h) SetWindowLong(hwnd, GWL_USERDATA, (LONG) (h))


///////////////////////////////////////////////////////////////////////////


void Echo_UpdateButtons (HWND hwnd) {

   RECMODE RecMode = Recorder_GetMode();
```

```
    // The RECORD button should be enabled if the recorder is stopped.
    BOOL fRec = (RecMode == RECMODE_STOPPED);

    // The PLAY button should be enabled if the recorder is stopped and there
    // are some events to be played back.
    BOOL fPlay = (RecMode == RECMODE_STOPPED) && (GETEVENTLIST(hwnd) != NULL);

    // The STOP button should be enabled if the recorder is not stopped.
    BOOL fStop = (RecMode != RECMODE_STOPPED);

    HWND hwndRec  = GetDlgItem(hwnd, IDC_RECORD);
    HWND hwndPlay = GetDlgItem(hwnd, IDC_PLAY);
    HWND hwndStop = GetDlgItem(hwnd, IDC_STOP);
    HWND hwndFocus;

    EnableWindow(hwndRec,  fRec);
    EnableWindow(hwndPlay, fPlay);
    EnableWindow(hwndStop, fStop);

    hwndFocus = (fPlay ? hwndPlay : (fStop ? hwndStop : hwndRec));

    SendMessage(hwnd, DM_SETDEFID, (fPlay ? IDC_PLAY :
       (fStop ? IDC_STOP : IDC_RECORD)), 0);

    SetFocus(hwndFocus);
}


/////////////////////////////////////////////////////////////////////////////


BOOL Echo_OnInitDialog (HWND hwnd, HWND hwndFocus, LPARAM lParam) {

    adgSETDLGICONS(hwnd, IDI_ECHO, IDI_ECHO);
    SETEVENTLIST(hwnd, NULL);
    Recorder_Init();
    Echo_UpdateButtons(hwnd);
    return(TRUE);                          // Accept default focus window.
}


/////////////////////////////////////////////////////////////////////////////


void Echo_OnStop (HWND hwnd, HEVENTLIST h, RECERR e) {

    // Echo_OnStop can be called when either recording or playing stops. If the
    // HEVENTLIST parameter is non-NULL, Echo_OnStop was called because
    // recording stopped, which means we need to save the HEVENTLIST for future
    // playback.
    if (h != NULL)
       SETEVENTLIST(hwnd, h);
    Echo_UpdateButtons(hwnd);
    Recorder_DisplayError(e);
}
```

```
////////////////////////////////////////////////////////////////////////

void Echo_OnCommand (HWND hwnd, int id, HWND hwndCtl, UINT codeNotify) {

   RECERR e = RECERR_OK;

   switch (id) {

      case IDCANCEL:                  // Allows dialog box to close.

         Recorder_Free(GETEVENTLIST(hwnd));

         // Terminate the application when user closes with system menu.
         PostQuitMessage(0);
         break;

      case IDC_RECORD:

         // If a macro was already recorded, free it.
         if (GETEVENTLIST(hwnd) != NULL) {
            Recorder_Free(GETEVENTLIST(hwnd));
            SETEVENTLIST(hwnd, NULL);
         }

         // Recorder sends UM_STOP notification to hwnd when recording stops.
         e = Recorder_Record(hwnd, UM_STOP);
         Echo_UpdateButtons(hwnd);
         Recorder_DisplayError(e);
         break;

      case IDC_PLAY:

         // Recorder sends UM_STOP notification to hwnd when playing stops.
         e = Recorder_Play(GETEVENTLIST(hwnd), hwnd, UM_STOP);
         Echo_UpdateButtons(hwnd);
         Recorder_DisplayError(e);
         break;

      case IDC_STOP:
         e = Recorder_Stop();
         Echo_UpdateButtons(hwnd);
         Recorder_DisplayError(e);
         break;
   }
}


////////////////////////////////////////////////////////////////////////


BOOL WINAPI Echo_DlgProc (HWND hwnd, UINT uMsg,
   WPARAM wParam, LPARAM lParam) {

   switch (uMsg) {
```

```
      // Standard Windows messages
      adgHANDLE_DLGMSG(hwnd, WM_INITDIALOG, Echo_OnInitDialog);
      adgHANDLE_DLGMSG(hwnd, WM_COMMAND,    Echo_OnCommand);

      // Stop notification message sent by Recorder_Stop
      adgHANDLE_DLGMSG(hwnd, UM_STOP,       Echo_OnStop);
   }

   return(FALSE);                    // We didn't process the message.
}


//////////////////////////////////////////////////////////////////////////


int WINAPI WinMain (HINSTANCE hinstExe, HINSTANCE hinstPrev,
   LPSTR lpszCmdLine, int nCmdShow) {

   MSG msg;
   HWND hwnd;

   adgWARNIFUNICODEUNDERWIN95();

   // Create a modeless dialog box instead of a modal dialog box because we
   // need to have more control over the message loop processing.
   hwnd = CreateDialog(hinstExe, MAKEINTRESOURCE(IDD_ECHO), NULL,
      Echo_DlgProc);
   adgASSERT(IsWindow(hwnd));

   // Continue to loop until a WM_QUIT message comes out of the queue.
   while (GetMessage(&msg, NULL, 0, 0)) {

      // A user can force local input state processing back on by pressing
      // Ctrl+Esc. When this happens, the operating system unhooks the journal
      // record/playback hook we have installed and notifies our thread by
      // posting it a WM_CANCELJOURNAL message. The function
      // Recorder_IsRecorderCanceled checks to see if the current message is a
      // WM_CANCELJOURNAL message, and if so, resets the recorder's hook
      // handle and stops recording with an error code of RECERR_USERCANCEL.
      Recorder_IsRecorderCanceled (&msg);

      // Call IsDialogMessage so that the keyboard can be used to control
      // focus in the dialog box.
      if (!IsDialogMessage(hwnd, &msg)) {
         TranslateMessage(&msg);
         DispatchMessage(&msg);
      }
   }

   // The application is terminating; destroy the modeless dialog box.
   DestroyWindow(hwnd);
   return(0);
}


/////////////////////////////////// End of File //////////////////////////////
```

Listing 6.14 *Echo.MSG*

```
// Module name: Echo.msg
// Written by: Jonathan Locke
// Notices: Copyright (c) 1995 Jeffrey Richter
// Purpose: 'MsgCrack' input file for Echo application.

MessageBase WM_APP
MessageClass Echo

Message UM_STOP Stop \
 - User-defined notification message sent by Recorder_Stop (see Record.c)\
 when recording or playing stops.
wParam HEVENTLIST h - Event list handle if it was recording that stopped.\
 If it was playing that stopped, h will be NULL.
lParam RECERR e - Recorder error code.  In the event of failure, this error\
 code indicates why playing/recording stopped.
 .
```

Listing 6.15 *Echo.H*

```
/******************************************************************************
Module name: Echo.h
Written by: Jonathan Locke
Notices: Copyright (c) 1995 Jeffrey Richter
Purpose: Message cracker for UM_STOP notification message.
******************************************************************************/

/////////////////////////////// Messages ///////////////////////////////////


//{{adgMSGCRACK_MESSAGES

// Purpose: User-defined notification message sent by Recorder_Stop (see
//          Record.c) when recording or playing stops.
// wParam:  HEVENTLIST h - Event list handle if it was recording that stopped.
//          If it was playing that stopped, h will be NULL.
// lParam:  RECERR e - Recorder error code. In the event of failure, this error
//          code indicates why playing/recording stopped.
// Returns: void
#define UM_STOP                 (WM_APP + 0)

//}}adgMSGCRACK_MESSAGES


/////////////////////////////// Message APIs ////////////////////////////////


//{{adgMSGCRACK_APIS
```

442

```
#define Echo_Stop(hwnd, h, e) \
   ((void)SendMessage((hwnd), UM_STOP, (WPARAM)(DWORD)(h), (LPARAM)(DWORD)(e)))

//}}adgMSGCRACK_APIS


/////////////////////////////// Message Crackers ///////////////////////////////


//{{adgMSGCRACK_CRACKERS

// void Cls_OnStop (HWND hwnd, HEVENTLIST h, RECERR e)
#define HANDLE_UM_STOP(hwnd, wParam, lParam, fn) \
   ((fn)((hwnd), (HEVENTLIST)(wParam), (RECERR)(lParam)), 0)
#define FORWARD_UM_STOP(hwnd, h, e, fn) \
   (void)((fn)((hwnd), UM_STOP, (WPARAM)(DWORD)(h), (LPARAM)(DWORD)(e)))

//}}adgMSGCRACK_CRACKERS


/////////////////////////////// End of File ///////////////////////////////
```

Listing 6.16 *Record.C*

```
/****************************************************************************
Module name: Record.c
Written by: Jeffrey Richter and Jonathan Locke
Notices: Copyright (c) 1993 Jeffrey Richter
Purpose: Macro recorder implementation.
****************************************************************************/


#include "..\Win95ADG.h"         /* See Appendix A for details */
#include <windows.h>
#pragma warning(disable: 4001)   /* Single line comment */
#include "Record.h"
#pragma warning(disable: 4001)   /* Single line comment */


///////////////////////////////////////////////////////////////////////////


// Statistical information that appears at start of EVENTMSG list.
typedef struct {
   int nNumEvents;              // Number of recorded events
   int nNumEventsPlayed;        // Number of events played back
   DWORD dwStartTime;           // Time when playback started
} RECSTAT, *PRECSTAT;
```

443

```
//////////////////////////////////////////////////////////////////////////////

typedef struct {
   HHOOK      hhookJournal;      // Journal hook handle
   RECMODE    RecMode;           // Recorder's operating mode
   HWND       hwndNotify;        // Window to notify
   UINT       uMsgNotify;        // Notification message to send
   RECERR     RecErr;            // Error which halted recording
   PRECSTAT   pRecStat;          // Recorded data
} RECORDERDATA;


//////////////////////////////////////////////////////////////////////////////


static RECORDERDATA g_RecorderData;


//////////////////////////////////////////////////////////////////////////////


void WINAPI Recorder_Init () {

   adgINITSTRUCT(g_RecorderData, FALSE);

   g_RecorderData.uMsgNotify = WM_NULL;
   g_RecorderData.RecMode = RECMODE_STOPPED;
   g_RecorderData.RecErr = RECERR_OK;
}


//////////////////////////////////////////////////////////////////////////////


static LRESULT WINAPI Recorder_JournalRecordProc (int nCode,
   WPARAM wParam, LPARAM lParam) {

   static BOOL fPause = FALSE;
   PRECSTAT pRecStat;
   PEVENTMSG pEvent;
   int nNumEvents;
   LRESULT lResult = CallNextHookEx(g_RecorderData.hhookJournal,
      nCode, wParam, lParam);

   switch (nCode) {

      case HC_ACTION:

         // If system-modal dialog box is up, don't record event.
         if (fPause)
            break;

         // Determine number of events in the memory block now.
         nNumEvents = g_RecorderData.pRecStat->nNumEvents + 1;
```

444

```
            // Increase size of the memory block to hold new event.
            pRecStat = realloc(g_RecorderData.pRecStat,
                sizeof(RECSTAT) + nNumEvents * sizeof(EVENTMSG));
            if (pRecStat == NULL) {

                // Insufficient memory; stop recording.
                g_RecorderData.RecErr = RECERR_NOMEMORY;
                Recorder_Stop();
                break;
            }
            g_RecorderData.pRecStat = pRecStat;

            // Append the new event to the end of the memory block.
            pEvent = (PEVENTMSG) &g_RecorderData.pRecStat[1];
            pEvent[g_RecorderData.pRecStat->nNumEvents] = *((PEVENTMSG) lParam);
            g_RecorderData.pRecStat->nNumEvents++;
            break;

    case HC_SYSMODALON:

            // Stop recording while system-modal dialog box is up.
            fPause = TRUE;
            break;

    case HC_SYSMODALOFF:

            // The system-modal dialog box is gone, stop recording and notify the
            // user that recording has stopped.
            fPause = FALSE;
            g_RecorderData.RecErr = RECERR_SYSMODAL;
            Recorder_Stop();
            break;
    }

    return(lResult);
}


//////////////////////////////////////////////////////////////////////////////


static LRESULT WINAPI Recorder_JournalPlaybackProc (int nCode,
    WPARAM wParam, LPARAM lParam) {

    PEVENTMSG pEvent;
    LRESULT lResult = CallNextHookEx(g_RecorderData.hhookJournal,
        nCode, wParam, lParam);

    switch (nCode) {

    case HC_SKIP:

            // Prepare to return the next event the next time the hook code is
            // HC_GETNEXT. If all events have been played, stop playing.
            if (++g_RecorderData.pRecStat->nNumEventsPlayed ==
```

```
                        g_RecorderData.pRecStat->nNumEvents)
                Recorder_Stop();
            break;

        case HC_GETNEXT:

            // Copy current event to the EVENTMSG structure pointed to by lParam.
            pEvent = (PEVENTMSG) &g_RecorderData.pRecStat[1];
            *((PEVENTMSG) lParam) =
                pEvent[g_RecorderData.pRecStat->nNumEventsPlayed];

            // Adjust 'time' by adding time that playback started.
            ((PEVENTMSG) lParam)->time += g_RecorderData.pRecStat->dwStartTime;

            // Return the number of milliseconds Windows should wait before
            // processing the event.
            lResult = ((PEVENTMSG) lParam)->time - GetTickCount();

            // If the event occurred in the past, have Windows process it now.
            if (lResult < 0)
                lResult = 0;
            break;

        case HC_SYSMODALOFF:

            // When the system-modal dialog box is removed, stop playing the
            // events and notify the application.
            g_RecorderData.RecErr = RECERR_SYSMODAL;
            Recorder_Stop();
            break;
    }

    return(lResult);
}


////////////////////////////////////////////////////////////////////////////


void WINAPI Recorder_DisplayError (RECERR e) {

    LPCTSTR pMessage = NULL;

    switch (e) {

        case RECERR_ACTIVE:
            pMessage = __TEXT("Recorder already recording/playing.");
            break;

        case RECERR_INACTIVE:
            pMessage = __TEXT("Recorder already stopped.");
            break;

        case RECERR_NOMEMORY:
            pMessage = __TEXT("Insufficient memory.");
            break;
```

446

```
      case RECERR_NOEVENTS:
        pMessage = __TEXT("No events to playback.");
        break;

      case RECERR_USERCANCEL:
        pMessage = __TEXT("Recorder canceled by user.");
        break;

      case RECERR_CANTHOOK:
        pMessage = __TEXT("Unable to set hook.");
        break;

      case RECERR_SYSMODAL:
        pMessage = __TEXT("Recorder canceled by system modal dialog.");
        break;

   }

   if (pMessage != NULL)
      adgMB(pMessage);
}


///////////////////////////////////////////////////////////////////////////


RECMODE WINAPI Recorder_GetMode (void) {

   return(g_RecorderData.RecMode);
}


///////////////////////////////////////////////////////////////////////////


void WINAPI Recorder_Free (HEVENTLIST h) {

   free((void*) h);
}


///////////////////////////////////////////////////////////////////////////


// Returns: RECERR_OK, RECERR_ACTIVE, RECERR_NOMEMORY or RECERR_USERCANCEL
RECERR WINAPI Recorder_Record (HWND hwndNotify, UINT uMsgNotify) {

   if ((g_RecorderData.RecMode == RECMODE_RECORDING) ||
       (g_RecorderData.RecMode == RECMODE_PLAYING))
      return(RECERR_ACTIVE);

   // Allocate and intialize the memory block to hold the statistical data.
   g_RecorderData.pRecStat = (PRECSTAT) malloc(sizeof(RECSTAT));
   if (g_RecorderData.pRecStat == NULL)
      return(RECERR_NOMEMORY);
   g_RecorderData.pRecStat->nNumEvents =
```

447

```
   g_RecorderData.pRecStat->nNumEventsPlayed = 0;

   // Save information so it can be used by Recorder_Stop.
   g_RecorderData.hwndNotify = hwndNotify;
   g_RecorderData.uMsgNotify = uMsgNotify;

   // Start record hook, reset error and signal that we are recording.
   // Turn on the event recording.
   g_RecorderData.hhookJournal = SetWindowsHookEx(WH_JOURNALRECORD,
      Recorder_JournalRecordProc, GetModuleHandle(NULL), 0);
   if (g_RecorderData.hhookJournal == NULL) {
      free(g_RecorderData.pRecStat);
      return(RECERR_CANTHOOK);
   }

   g_RecorderData.RecErr = RECERR_OK;
   g_RecorderData.RecMode = RECMODE_RECORDING;
   return(RECERR_OK);
}


/////////////////////////////////////////////////////////////////////////////


// Returns: RECERR_OK or RECERR_INACTIVE
RECERR WINAPI Recorder_Stop (void) {

   HEVENTLIST hEventList;

   switch (g_RecorderData.RecMode) {

      case RECMODE_STOPPED:
         return(RECERR_INACTIVE);

      case RECMODE_RECORDING:
         hEventList = (HEVENTLIST) g_RecorderData.pRecStat;
         break;

      case RECMODE_PLAYING:
         hEventList = NULL;
         break;
   }

   // Stop playback or recording of events.
   if (g_RecorderData.hhookJournal != NULL) {

      // If Recorder_Stop is called from Recorder_IsRecorderCanceled (as a
      // result of a WM_CANCELJOURNAL message), our hook has already been
      // unhooked by Windows and the hook handle will be NULL.
      UnhookWindowsHookEx(g_RecorderData.hhookJournal);
      g_RecorderData.hhookJournal = NULL;
   }
```

```
   if (g_RecorderData.RecMode == RECMODE_RECORDING) {

      // Recording stopped - modify all 'time' members in the EVENTMSG structs,
      // making each time relative to when recording started.
      PEVENTMSG pEvent = (PEVENTMSG) &g_RecorderData.pRecStat[1];
      int nNumEvents = g_RecorderData.pRecStat->nNumEvents;
      while (nNumEvents >= 1)
         pEvent[--nNumEvents].time -= pEvent[0].time;
   }
   g_RecorderData.pRecStat = NULL;

   // Signal ourselves and the notification window that we have stopped.
   g_RecorderData.RecMode = RECMODE_STOPPED;
   SendMessage(g_RecorderData.hwndNotify, g_RecorderData.uMsgNotify,
      (WPARAM) hEventList, (LPARAM) g_RecorderData.RecErr);

   return(RECERR_OK);
}


///////////////////////////////////////////////////////////////////////////


// Returns: RECERR_OK, RECERR_ACTIVE or RECERR_NOEVENTS
RECERR WINAPI Recorder_Play (HEVENTLIST h, HWND hwndNotify, UINT uMsgNotify) {

   if ((g_RecorderData.RecMode == RECMODE_RECORDING) ||
       (g_RecorderData.RecMode == RECMODE_PLAYING))
      return(RECERR_ACTIVE);

   if (((PRECSTAT) h)->nNumEvents == 0)
      return(RECERR_NOEVENTS);

   // Set new event list.
   g_RecorderData.pRecStat = (PRECSTAT) h;

   // Save notification information so it can be used by Recorder_Stop.
   g_RecorderData.hwndNotify = hwndNotify;
   g_RecorderData.uMsgNotify = uMsgNotify;

   // Initialize statistical data and save playback start time
   g_RecorderData.pRecStat->nNumEventsPlayed = 0;
   g_RecorderData.pRecStat->dwStartTime = GetTickCount();

   // Start playback hook, reset error and signal that we are playing.
   g_RecorderData.hhookJournal = SetWindowsHookEx(WH_JOURNALPLAYBACK,
      Recorder_JournalPlaybackProc, GetModuleHandle(NULL), 0);

   if (g_RecorderData.hhookJournal == NULL)
      return(RECERR_CANTHOOK);

   g_RecorderData.RecErr = RECERR_OK;
   g_RecorderData.RecMode = RECMODE_PLAYING;
   return(RECERR_OK);
}
```

449

```
//////////////////////////////////////////////////////////////////////////////

BOOL WINAPI Recorder_IsRecorderCanceled (PMSG pmsg) {

    BOOL fCanceled = (pmsg->message == WM_CANCELJOURNAL);
    if (fCanceled) {

        // The system unhooked our hook.
        g_RecorderData.hhookJournal = NULL;

        // Stop recording.
        g_RecorderData.RecErr = RECERR_USERCANCEL;
        Recorder_Stop();
    }
    return(fCanceled);
}


/////////////////////////////// End of File //////////////////////////////////
```

Listing 6.17 *Record.H*

```
/****************************************************************************
Module name: Record.h
Written by: Jeffrey Richter and Jonathan Locke
Notices: Copyright (c) 1995 Jeffrey Richter
Purpose: Macro recorder programmer's interface.
****************************************************************************/


typedef enum {
    RECERR_OK,          // Operation was successful.
    RECERR_CANTHOOK,    // Hook cannot be installed.
    RECERR_ACTIVE,      // Attempt to record/play while already recording/playing.
    RECERR_INACTIVE,    // Attempt to stop recording while NOT recording.
    RECERR_NOMEMORY,    // When attempting to start recording or during recording.
    RECERR_NOEVENTS,    // Attempt playback with no events in memory block.
    RECERR_SYSMODAL,    // System modal dialog canceled recording.
    RECERR_USERCANCEL   // User canceled with Ctrl+Esc.
} RECERR;


//////////////////////////////////////////////////////////////////////////////


typedef enum {
    RECMODE_STOPPED,        // Recorder is stopped
    RECMODE_RECORDING,      // Recorder is recording events
    RECMODE_PLAYING         // Recorder is playing back events
} RECMODE;
```

450

```
///////////////////////////////////////////////////////////////////////////


DECLARE_HANDLE(HEVENTLIST);


///////////////////////////////////////////////////////////////////////////


void WINAPI Recorder_Init ();
void WINAPI Recorder_Free (HEVENTLIST h);
void WINAPI Recorder_DisplayError (RECERR e);
RECMODE WINAPI Recorder_GetMode (void);
BOOL WINAPI Recorder_IsRecorderCanceled (PMSG pmsg);

// Returns: RECERR_OK, RECERR_CANTHOOK, RECERR_ACTIVE or RECERR_NOMEMORY
RECERR WINAPI Recorder_Record (HWND hwndNotify, UINT uMsgNotify);

// Returns: RECERR_OK, RECERR_CANTHOOK, RECERR_ACTIVE or RECERR_NOEVENTS
RECERR WINAPI Recorder_Play (HEVENTLIST h, HWND hwndNotify, UINT uMsgNotify);

// Returns: RECERR_OK or RECERR_INACTIVE
RECERR WINAPI Recorder_Stop (void);


//////////////////////////// End of File ////////////////////////////
```

Listing 6.18 *Echo.RC*

```
//Microsoft Visual C++ generated resource script.
//
#include "resource.h"

#define APSTUDIO_READONLY_SYMBOLS
///////////////////////////////////////////////////////////////////////////
//
// Generated from the TEXTINCLUDE 2 resource.
//
#include "windows.h"


///////////////////////////////////////////////////////////////////////////
#undef APSTUDIO_READONLY_SYMBOLS


///////////////////////////////////////////////////////////////////////////
//
// Dialog
//

IDD_ECHO DIALOG DISCARDABLE  -32768, 5, 180, 24
STYLE WS_MINIMIZEBOX | WS_VISIBLE | WS_CAPTION | WS_SYSMENU
CAPTION "Echo"
```

451

```
FONT 8, "MS Sans Serif"
BEGIN
    PUSHBUTTON       "&Record",IDC_RECORD,8,5,49,14
    PUSHBUTTON       "&Play",IDC_PLAY,65,5,49,14
    PUSHBUTTON       "&Stop",IDC_STOP,122,5,49,14
END


/////////////////////////////////////////////////////////////////////////
//
// Icon
//

IDI_ECHO                ICON    DISCARDABLE     "echo.ico"

#ifdef APSTUDIO_INVOKED
/////////////////////////////////////////////////////////////////////////
//
// TEXTINCLUDE
//

1 TEXTINCLUDE DISCARDABLE
BEGIN
    "resource.h\0"
END

2 TEXTINCLUDE DISCARDABLE
BEGIN
    "#include ""windows.h""\r\n"
    "\0"
END

3 TEXTINCLUDE DISCARDABLE
BEGIN
    "\r\n"
    "\0"
END

/////////////////////////////////////////////////////////////////////////
#endif    // APSTUDIO_INVOKED


#ifndef APSTUDIO_INVOKED
/////////////////////////////////////////////////////////////////////////
//
// Generated from the TEXTINCLUDE 3 resource.
//


/////////////////////////////////////////////////////////////////////////
#endif    // not APSTUDIO_INVOKED
```

452

Listing 6.19 *Resource.H*

```
//{{NO_DEPENDENCIES}}
// Microsoft Visual C++ generated include file.
// Used by echo.rc
//
#define IDD_ECHO                        101
#define IDI_ECHO                        102
#define IDC_RECORD                      1000
#define IDC_PLAY                        1001
#define IDC_STOP                        1002

// Next default values for new objects
//
#ifdef APSTUDIO_INVOKED
#ifndef APSTUDIO_READONLY_SYMBOLS
#define _APS_NEXT_RESOURCE_VALUE        103
#define _APS_NEXT_COMMAND_VALUE         40001
#define _APS_NEXT_CONTROL_VALUE         1001
#define _APS_NEXT_SYMED_VALUE           101
#endif
#endif
```

The Capture Application

The Capture application (**Capture.EXE**), shown in Listings 6.20–6.22 (starting on page 458), demonstrates how a journal record hook affects mouse capture. When you invoke the application, the main application window shown in Figure 6.6 appears.

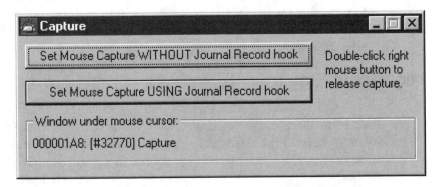

Figure 6.6 *The Capture application.*

Capture has two rather self-explanatory buttons: Set Mouse Capture WITHOUT Journal Record Hook and Set Mouse Capture USING Journal Record Hook. When you press one of these buttons, Capture captures the mouse. Then on each WM_MOUSEMOVE message, it updates the window handle, window class, and window text displayed inside the Window Under Mouse Cursor groupbox. Double-clicking the right mouse button on the dialog box's client area causes Capture to release the mouse capture.

Table 6.7 describes the files used to create this application.

Table 6.7 *The files used to build the Capture application.*

File	Description
Capture.C	Contains WinMain and main window's dialog box and message cracker functions
Capture.RC	Contains the dialog-box template for the main application window and its icons
Resource.H	Contains IDs for all resources in the RC file
Capture.ICO	Contains the icon for the main window
Capture.MAK	Visual C++ project makefile for the application

The Capture application is not so much about using journal record hooks per se, but rather about a particular side-effect of using journal record hooks. In fact, Capture's filter function, Capture_Journal-RecordProc, does nothing except call the next filter function with CallNextHookEx.

Local Input States

In an effort to make Windows 95 and Windows NT more robust than 16-bit Windows, Microsoft added local input state processing to these new 32-bit operating systems. Stated simply, local input state processing means that each thread (not process; but thread) thinks that it is the only thread in the system that gets keyboard or mouse messages. The local input state model is good because threads are isolated from one another, which prevents a given thread from affecting other threads.

For example, imagine the following scenario taking place in a 16-bit Windows environment. A task calls SetCapture and tells the system to direct all mouse messages to the message queue of the task that created the window that has the mouse capture. No matter what the user does with the mouse, all mouse messages are directed to this window. Now, let's say that there is a bug in this task that causes it to enter an infinite loop when the user clicks a mouse button. Under 16-bit Windows, the infinite loop means that mouse capture will never be released and the user will be unable to use the mouse any further. A robust operating system should not allow this to happen!

Local input state processing prevents a thread from doing this. For mouse capture, both Windows 95 and Windows NT work like this. When the user clicks the mouse, the thread calls SetCapture, and the system performs mouse capture on a system-wide basis. That is, mouse capture works just like it did under 16-bit Windows. However, when the mouse button is released (even if ReleaseCapture is not called), the system changes the way mouse capture is performed so that it is now on a thread-local basis. In other words, mouse messages are directed to the mouse capture window only when the mouse cursor is over a window created by the same thread as the mouse capture window. If the mouse cursor is over a window created by any other thread, the operating system routes the mouse messages as normal—as if no window had mouse capture.

For most applications, this change in Windows 95 and Windows NT will not be a problem. More specifically, any application that keeps to itself and does not try to do things to windows created by other threads should not have any problems when ported to Win32. Applications that manipulate other windows by sending, posting, or intercepting keystrokes or mouse events are likely to run into porting problems.

Let's look at an example of just such an application. Microsoft's Spy utility, which ships with Visual C++ 1.5, is such a utility. The 16-bit **Spy.EXE** application, allows the user to select a target window by selecting the Window.Window... menu option. This menu option causes a dialog box to be displayed, and Spy calls SetCapture to direct all mouse input to this dialog box. The user can now move the mouse on the screen while Spy updates its dialog box to show information pertaining to the window under the mouse cursor. When the user clicks the mouse button, Spy's dialog box gets the WM_LBUTTONDOWN message (regardless of where the mouse is on the screen) and starts watching window messages for the selected window.

If you look at the Win32 Spy++ application that ships with Visual C++ 2.x, you will see that it uses a different technique to allow a user to select a window. First, you must select the Spy.Find Window... menu item. This displays the dialog box shown in Figure 6.7. But Spy++ does not call SetCapture when the dialog box is invoked.

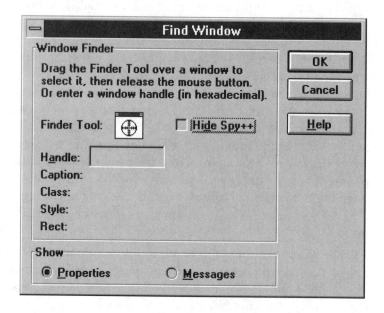

Figure 6.7 *The Spy++ Find Window dialog box.*

Instead, this dialog box has a tool called the Finder tool. To select a window on the screen, the user must position the mouse over the Finder tool, click, and then drag the Finder tool over the desired window. When the user clicks the mouse over the Finder tool, Spy++ calls SetCapture. While the mouse button is down, mouse capture is performed on a system-wide basis. This means that the user can move the mouse anywhere on the screen and all mouse messages are directed to the window whose handle was passed to SetCapture. However, when the user releases the mouse button, mouse capture is performed on a thread-local basis. This means that the system will direct all mouse messages to the window whose handle was passed to SetCapture only if the mouse is over a window created by the same thread. If the mouse is moved over a window created by a different thread, the system acts as though mouse capture is not set at all and simply directs the mouse messages to the window that would normally get them. Spy++ actually calls ReleaseCapture when the mouse button is released, so mouse capture is turned off completely for Spy++'s thread—it is not performed on a thread-local basis.

Because of the new local input state processing, Spy++ was forced to use a different technique than 16-bit Spy.

Journal Record Hooks and Local Input State Processing

There is an alternative solution to the problem with Spy++. This second solution is to turn off the operating system's local input state processing temporarily by installing a journal record hook. This is not something that should be done lightly, however, because without local input state processing, the Win32 environment behaves just like the 16-bit Windows environment. In other words, it is now possible for one thread to affect other threads and potentially hang all running processes!

In Windows 95 and Windows NT, local input state processing interferes with journal hooks. So, in order to maintain backward compatibility, installing either of these hooks causes the system to turn off local input state processing. When the journal record/playback hook is uninstalled, the system reverts to normal local input state processing again. But as long as local input state processing is turned off, all the threads share a common notion of mouse capture. This means that mouse capture is performed on a system-wide basis while a journal hook is installed.

The Capture application demonstrates this technique. When you click on the Set Mouse Capture WITHOUT Journal Record Hook button, the application simply calls SetCapture passing in the window handle of the dialog box. Then on each WM_MOUSE-MOVE message, Capture updates the information displayed inside the Window Under Mouse Cursor groupbox. Note that when you move the mouse over a window created by a thread other than the thread that created the dialog box, the text inside the groupbox does not change. This is local input state processing at work. If instead you click on the Set Mouse Capture USING Journal Record Hook button, you will notice that when you move the mouse, the text inside the groupbox changes. But, more importantly, this text changes no matter where the mouse cursor is on the screen; mouse capture is performed on a system-wide basis because Capture installed a journal hook.

Listing 6.20 *Capture.C*

```
/***********************************************************************
Module name: Capture.c
Written by: Jeffrey Richter and Jonathan Locke
Notices: Copyright (c) 1995 Jeffrey Richter
Purpose: Demonstrates how to disable the local input state processing.
***********************************************************************/


#include "..\Win95ADG.h"          /* See Appendix A for details */
#include <windows.h>
#include <windowsx.h>
#pragma warning(disable: 4001)    /* Single line comment */
#include <tchar.h>
#include <stdio.h>
#include "Resource.h"


///////////////////////////////////////////////////////////////////////


// Global hook handle for journal record hook (NULL when the not installed).
static HHOOK g_hhookJournalRecord = NULL;


///////////////////////////////////////////////////////////////////////


void Capture_CalcWndText (HWND hwnd, LPTSTR szBuf, int nLen) {

   TCHAR szClass[256], szCaption[256], szBufT[256];

   if (hwnd == NULL) {
     _tcscpy(szBuf, __TEXT("(no window)"));
     return;
   }
```

```
  if (!IsWindow(hwnd)) {
    _tcscpy(szBuf, __TEXT("(invalid window)"));
    return;
  }

  GetClassName(hwnd, szClass, adgARRAY_SIZE(szClass));
  GetWindowText(hwnd, szCaption, adgARRAY_SIZE(szCaption));

  _stprintf(szBufT, __TEXT("%08X: [%s] %s"), hwnd, szClass,
    (*szCaption == 0) ? __TEXT("(no caption)") : szCaption);
  _tcsncpy(szBuf, szBufT, nLen - 1);
  szBuf[nLen - 1] = 0;              // Terminate string
}


///////////////////////////////////////////////////////////////////////////


static LRESULT WINAPI Capture_JournalRecordProc (int nCode,
  WPARAM wParam, LPARAM lParam) {

  // This journal record function doesn't need to do anything so we just pass
  // the hook notification on to any other installed journal record hooks.
  return(CallNextHookEx(g_hhookJournalRecord, nCode, wParam, lParam));
}


///////////////////////////////////////////////////////////////////////////


BOOL Capture_OnInitDialog (HWND hwnd, HWND hwndFocus, LPARAM lParam) {

  adgSETDLGICONS(hwnd, IDI_CAPTURE, IDI_CAPTURE);
  return(TRUE);                     // Accept default focus window.
}


///////////////////////////////////////////////////////////////////////////


void Capture_OnCommand (HWND hwnd, int id, HWND hwndCtl, UINT codeNotify) {

  switch (id) {

    case IDCANCEL:

      // Terminate the application when the user selects
      // Close from the system menu.
      PostQuitMessage(0);
      break;

    case IDC_CAPTUREWITHOUTJRHOOK:

      // Set capture and change the mouse cursor shape. Note that the mouse
      // cursor shape is an up arrow ONLY when the cursor is over the
      // dialog box. Mouse cursor shape is also part of the local input
```

```
            // state processing.
            SetCapture(hwnd);
            SetCursor(LoadCursor(NULL, IDC_UPARROW));
            break;

         case IDC_CAPTUREUSINGJRHOOK:

            // Install a journal hook to turn off local input state processing,
            // set capture and change the mouse cursor shape. Note that the mouse
            // cursor shape is always an up arrow regardless of where the mouse
            // cursor is on the screen.
            g_hhookJournalRecord = SetWindowsHookEx(WH_JOURNALRECORD,
               Capture_JournalRecordProc, GetModuleHandle(NULL), 0);
            adgASSERT(g_hhookJournalRecord);
            SetCapture(hwnd);
            SetCursor(LoadCursor(NULL, IDC_UPARROW));
            break;
      }
   }


///////////////////////////////////////////////////////////////////////////////


int Capture_OnRButtonDown (HWND hwnd, BOOL fDoubleClick,
   int x, int y, UINT keyFlags) {

   if (fDoubleClick) {

      // The user double-clicked the right mouse button.
      ReleaseCapture();
      if (g_hhookJournalRecord != NULL) {

         // If a journal hook is installed, we must turn local input state
         // processing back on.
         UnhookWindowsHookEx(g_hhookJournalRecord);
         g_hhookJournalRecord = NULL;
      }
   }
   return(0);
}


///////////////////////////////////////////////////////////////////////////////


void Capture_OnMouseMove (HWND hwnd, int x, int y, UINT keyFlags) {

   TCHAR szBuf[128];
   POINT pt;

   // As the mouse moves, update the text in the box.

   // Get the position of the mouse cursor in screen coordinates. We can't use
   // the x & y parameters because they are in client-window coordinates.
```

```
    GetCursorPos(&pt);

    Capture_CalcWndText(WindowFromPoint(pt), szBuf, adgARRAY_SIZE(szBuf));
    SetDlgItemText(hwnd, IDC_WNDUNDERMOUSE, szBuf);
}


///////////////////////////////////////////////////////////////////////////


BOOL WINAPI Capture_DlgProc (HWND hwnd, UINT uMsg,
    WPARAM wParam, LPARAM lParam) {

    switch (uMsg) {

        // Standard Windows messages
        adgHANDLE_DLGMSG(hwnd, WM_INITDIALOG,     Capture_OnInitDialog);
        adgHANDLE_DLGMSG(hwnd, WM_COMMAND,        Capture_OnCommand);
        adgHANDLE_DLGMSG(hwnd, WM_MOUSEMOVE,      Capture_OnMouseMove);
        adgHANDLE_DLGMSG(hwnd, WM_RBUTTONDBLCLK,  Capture_OnRButtonDown);
    }
    return(FALSE);
}


///////////////////////////////////////////////////////////////////////////


int WINAPI WinMain (HINSTANCE hinstExe, HINSTANCE hinstPrev,
    LPSTR lpszCmdLine, int nCmdShow) {

    MSG msg;
    HWND hwnd;

    adgWARNIFUNICODEUNDERWIN95();

    // Create a modeless dialog box instead of a modal dialog box because we
    // need to have more control over the message loop processing.
    hwnd = CreateDialog(hinstExe, MAKEINTRESOURCE(IDD_CAPTURE), NULL,
        Capture_DlgProc);
    adgASSERT(IsWindow(hwnd));

    // Continue to loop until a WM_QUIT message comes out of the queue.
    while (GetMessage(&msg, NULL, 0, 0)) {

        if (msg.message == WM_CANCELJOURNAL) {

            // A user can force local input state processing back on by pressing
            // Ctrl+Esc. When this happens, the operating system notifies the
            // thread by posting a WM_CANCELJOURNAL message in the thread's
            // message queue. We can look for this here and notify the user that
            // local input state processing is back on.

            adgMB(__TEXT("System-wide mouse capture has been canceled"));
        } else {
```

461

```
        // Call IsDialogMessage so that the keyboard can be used to control
        // focus in the dialog box.
        if (!IsDialogMessage(hwnd, &msg)) {
            TranslateMessage(&msg);
            DispatchMessage(&msg);
        }
    }
}

    // The application is terminating; destroy the modeless dialog box.
    DestroyWindow(hwnd);
    return(0);
}


///////////////////////////////// End of File /////////////////////////////////
```

Listing 6.21 *Capture.RC*

```
////Microsoft Visual C++ generated resource script.
//
#include "Resource.h"

#define APSTUDIO_READONLY_SYMBOLS
/////////////////////////////////////////////////////////////////////////////
//
// Generated from the TEXTINCLUDE 2 resource.
//
#include "windows.h"


/////////////////////////////////////////////////////////////////////////////
#undef APSTUDIO_READONLY_SYMBOLS


/////////////////////////////////////////////////////////////////////////////
//
// Dialog
//


IDD_CAPTURE DIALOG DISCARDABLE  -32768, 5, 260, 80
STYLE WS_MINIMIZEBOX | WS_POPUP | WS_VISIBLE | WS_CAPTION | WS_SYSMENU
CAPTION "Capture"
FONT 8, "MS Sans Serif"
BEGIN
    DEFPUSHBUTTON   "Set Mouse Capture WITHOUT Journal Record hook",
                    IDC_CAPTUREWITHOUTJRHOOK,4,4,184,14
    DEFPUSHBUTTON   "Set Mouse Capture USING Journal Record hook",
```

```
                    IDC_CAPTUREUSINGJRHOOK,4,25,184,14
    LTEXT           "Double-click right mouse button to release capture.",-1,
                    196,8,60,27
    GROUPBOX        "Window under mouse cursor:",-1,4,44,252,28
    LTEXT           "HWND: [class] caption",IDC_WNDUNDERMOUSE,8,57,240,8
END


#ifdef APSTUDIO_INVOKED
/////////////////////////////////////////////////////////////////////////////
//
// TEXTINCLUDE
//

1 TEXTINCLUDE DISCARDABLE
BEGIN
    "Resource.h\0"
END

2 TEXTINCLUDE DISCARDABLE
BEGIN
    "#include ""windows.h""\r\n"
    "\0"
END

3 TEXTINCLUDE DISCARDABLE
BEGIN
    "\r\n"
    "\0"
END

/////////////////////////////////////////////////////////////////////////////
#endif    // APSTUDIO_INVOKED


/////////////////////////////////////////////////////////////////////////////
//
// Icon
//

IDI_CAPTURE             ICON    DISCARDABLE     "Capture.ico"

#ifndef APSTUDIO_INVOKED
/////////////////////////////////////////////////////////////////////////////
//
// Generated from the TEXTINCLUDE 3 resource.
//


/////////////////////////////////////////////////////////////////////////////
#endif    // not APSTUDIO_INVOKED
```

Listing 6.22 *Resource.H*

```
//{{NO_DEPENDENCIES}}
// Microsoft Visual C++ generated include file.
// Used by Capture.rc
//
#define IDD_CAPTURE                  102
#define IDC_WNDUNDERMOUSE            104
#define IDI_CAPTURE                  104
#define IDC_CAPTUREWITHOUTJRHOOK     1001
#define IDC_CAPTUREUSINGJRHOOK       1002

// Next default values for new objects
//
#ifdef APSTUDIO_INVOKED
#ifndef APSTUDIO_READONLY_SYMBOLS
#define _APS_NEXT_RESOURCE_VALUE     105
#define _APS_NEXT_COMMAND_VALUE      40001
#define _APS_NEXT_CONTROL_VALUE      1003
#define _APS_NEXT_SYMED_VALUE        101
#endif
#endif
```

CHAPTER SEVEN

Dragging and Dropping Files

With each new version of Windows, Microsoft takes a few more steps toward reaching its "Information at your Fingertips" objective. This objective allows computer users to concentrate more on getting their work done than on understanding and mastering the tools being used to complete that task. Certainly, one of the primary technologies created to help reach this objective is the concept of Object Linking and Embedding (OLE). This technology allows a user to select the host application that is best designed for the presentation of the data (for example, word processing, spreadsheet, or slide presentations). Once the host application has been decided, OLE allows the user to insert information into the host document in various forms by using other applications. For example, a user creating a document in a word processor can easily insert into the document a chart created by a spreadsheet program. When the user needs to edit or change this chart, the application best suited to process the work (in this case, the spreadsheet) is automatically invoked. The user can then change the data and the new chart is replaced in the document. This technology lets someone use whatever tools he or she is most comfortable with to get a job done, and OLE helps by seamlessly (almost) integrating these operations into the host application.

It is more natural for a user to concentrate on data instead of the programs required to process data. In addition to OLE, Windows offers another facility that allows users to think in this way. This technology is called drag-and-drop. Probably the easiest way to get the feel for drag-and-drop is by using the Windows 95 Explorer. Many end users have not had an easy time understanding the MS-DOS file system with its directory structures and hierarchies. The Explorer was designed to let users manipulate files more productively and efficiently.

Without a doubt, one of the features that makes the Explorer so easy to use is its drag-and-drop capabilities. Drag-and-drop simplifies several common tasks. First, you can copy and move files from one directory to another. Wherever the mouse is when its button is released is where the file will be moved or copied. The Explorer assumes that you are copying a file if you position the mouse cursor over a target directory on a drive other than the source file's drive. It assumes that the file is to be moved if the mouse is positioned over a directory present on the same drive as the selected file.

Using the Explorer, you can also open documents by dragging the desired document file and dropping it on top of an executable file. For example, if you drag the **Flock.BMP** file and drop it on top of the **PBrush.EXE** applications, the Explorer constructs the following command line and then executes it:

```
C:\WINDOWS\PBRUSH.EXE C:\WINDOWS\FLOCK.BMP
```

So far, in this discussion, we have dragged files from the Explorer to the Explorer. It is also possible to select files in the Explorer and to drag them outside the Explorer's window, dropping the files onto a running application's window. When you drop files from the Explorer onto a running application, the application opens the file that was dropped onto it. For example, if Notepad is running and I drag the **Setup.INF** file from the Explorer and drop it on top of Notepad, Notepad opens the file and its caption changes from "Untitled-Notepad" to "SETUP.INF-Notepad" to show that the file is the one currently being edited.

As you can see, this method of opening a file is extremely intuitive for a user. The user concentrates on the data and not the tool that is required to process it. If there is a printer icon on the desktop, the user can easily drop the file on top of it, causing the file to be printed instead of edited. If there were a spelling-checker application available, the user could just drop the file on top of the spelling

466

checker to have the document proofed for misspellings. This is the way users think—they are working on something and wish to perform different tasks on it. Normally, they do not want to load an editor (like Notepad) and edit several different files in succession.

Becoming a Dropfile Target

Modifying your application so that it is a dropfile target is extremely easy. To become a dropfile target, your application must first tell other applications, like the Explorer, that it can process file names dropped into it. This is done by specifying the extended window style WS_EX_ACCEPTFILES. This style requires that you create your application's window using the CreateWindowEx function instead of the more common CreateWindow function:

```
hwnd = CreateWindowEx(WS_EX_ACCEPTFILES, "ClassName", "Caption",
    WS_OVERLAPPED, CW_USEDEFAULT, CW_USEDEFAULT, CW_USEDEFAULT,
    CW_USEDEFAULT, NULL, NULL, hInstance, 0);
```

Alternatively, you could create the window and then call the DragAcceptFiles function:

```
void DragAcceptFiles(HWND hwnd, BOOL fAccept);
```

This function simply turns the WS_EX_ACCEPTFILES style for the specified window on or off, based on the value of the fAccept parameter. If fAccept is TRUE, the bit is turned on. It is possible for an application to turn this style on or off periodically while it is running. When the user is dragging a file name, the Explorer examines this style bit for the window that is directly under the mouse cursor. If the window does not have the WS_EX_ACCEPTFILES style on, the mouse cursor appears as it does in Figure 7.1. The cursor reminds the user that the file name cannot be dropped at the current location. If, on the other hand, the Explorer sees that the WS_EX_ACCEPTFILES style is on, it changes the cursor to look like Figure 7.2.

The Explorer also allows the user to select and drag several files at once. This feature is useful to open several source-code files by dropping them on Visual C++'s window, for example. Visual C++ knows how to process several file names dropped onto it at once and simply opens all of the files in its editor's windows.

Figure 7.1 *Cursor shape indicates that files cannot be dropped.*

Figure 7.2 *Cursor shape indicates that files can be dropped.*

Sometimes, it is necessary for a drag-and-drop target application to call the DragAcceptFiles function periodically. If an application's thread is printing a file, it should call DragAcceptFiles and pass FALSE as the fAccept parameter so that the user cannot drop any file names into the application before printing is complete. Once the document completes printing, the application calls DragAcceptFiles again with fAccept set as TRUE so that file names can again be dropped.

How It Works

When the user drags one or more file names and releases the mouse button, the Explorer allocates a block of memory and fills it with the list of file names that the user selected. Actually, each file's full path name is inserted into the block instead of just the file's name. The Explorer then posts a WM_DROPFILES message to the window that was under the mouse cursor when the user released the mouse button. The wParam parameter of this message indicates the handle[1] to this block of memory containing the selected file's path names. The lParam parameter for this message is not used.

---

[1]Although the GlobalAlloc and LocalAlloc functions exist in the Win32 API, they should be avoided in favor of the new HeapAlloc function. Unfortunately, there are some aspects of 16-bit Windows that are tied to the 16-bit memory allocation functions. Microsoft decided to leave some Win32 functions dependent on the older 16-bit functions. We see this here with respect to dragging and dropping files. The Explorer internally allocates its memory using GlobalAlloc instead of the new HeapAlloc function. We then receive the handle to this allocated memory in WM_DROP-FILES's wParam parameter.

Once this message has been received, the application calls the DragQueryFile function to process the memory block:

```
UINT DragQueryFile(HDROP hdrop, UINT uFileNum, LPTSTR lpszFile,
   UINT uMaxFileSize);
```

The hdrop parameter indicates the memory handle containing the list of path names that have been dropped into the window. (This handle was passed as the wParam parameter for the WM_DROP-FILES message.) The uFileNum parameter indicates which path name should be retrieved from the memory block. This value can be between zero and the number of path names dropped minus one. If the value is –1, DragQueryFile returns the total number of path names contained in the memory block.

When DragQueryFile is used to request an individual path name, the lpszFile parameter specifies the location of a buffer where the indicated path name should be copied. The uMaxFileSize parameter is the maximum number of characters that can be copied into this buffer. After copying the path name, DragQueryFile returns the number of characters actually copied into the buffer.

It is possible to determine the length of an individual entry's path name by specifying NULL as the lpszFile parameter to this function. When you do this, DragQueryFile returns the length of the specified path name.

The following code fragment from a dropfile target's window procedure demonstrates how all the dropped path names could be added to a listbox control:

```
void SomeCls_OnDropFiles (HWND hwnd, HDROP hdrop) {

   // The HWND of the listbox is in g_hwndLB

   // Get the number of pathnames that have been dropped.
   UINT uNumFiles = DragQueryFile(hdrop, -1, NULL, 0);
   UINT uNumChars;
   LPCTSTR pszPathname;

   // Add each pathname to the list box.
   while (uNumFiles--) {

      // Get the number of characters required by the file's pathname.
      uNumChars = DragQueryFile(hdrop, uNumFiles, NULL, 0);
```

```
       // Allocate memory to contain the pathname.
       pszPathname = malloc(sizeof(TCHAR) * (uNumChars + 1));

       // If not enough memory, skip this one.
       if (pszPathname != NULL) {
          // Copy the pathname into the buffer and add to the listbox.
          DragQueryFile(hdrop, uNumFiles, pszPathname, uNumChars);
          ListBox_AddString(g_hwndLB, pszPathname);
          free(pszPathname);
       }
   }

   // Free the memory block containing the dropped-file information.
   DragFinish(hdrop);
}
```

After the WM_DROPFILES message has been processed, the memory block containing all the path names must be freed via a call to DragFinish. If you do not call DragFinish, the memory block will not be freed until your process terminates.

In addition to the list of path names contained in the memory block, the Explorer also adds other information that may be useful to the dropfile target application. This information can be obtained by calling the DragQueryPoint function:

```
BOOL DragQueryPoint(HDROP hdrop, LPPOINT lpPoint)
```

As always, the hdrop parameter identifies the memory block while the lpPoint parameter is the address of a POINT data structure. DragQueryPoint copies the coordinates of the mouse cursor when the files were dropped into the lpPoint buffer. The x- and y-values in the POINT structure are relative to the client area of the window receiving the WM_DROPFILES message. The DragQueryPoint function also returns TRUE if the mouse cursor were in the client area of the window or FALSE if it were outside the client area. Of course, DragQueryPoint must be called before calling DragFinish.

An application can use this information to determine how to process the dropped path names. For example, WordPad opens a file if it is dropped on its non-client area (such as its title bar) and inserts the file as a link into the current document if it is dropped in WordPad's client area.

Sometimes, it does not make sense for an application to have more than one path name dropped into it. To use WordPad again as an example, when multiple files are dropped onto WordPad's non-client area, WordPad opens only one of the files and ignores the other entries in the memory block. When multiple files are dropped onto WordPad's client area, WordPad inserts all the files as shortcuts into the current document. Whether your application uses the dropped path names or not, the block of memory must still be freed by calling DragFinish.

The Touch Application

The Touch application (**Touch.EXE**), shown in Listings 7.1-7.3, (starting on page 474) demonstrates how to create a dropfile target application. When you invoke the application, the dialog box shown in Figure 7.3 appears:

Figure 7.3 *The Touch application.*

To use Touch, you select one or more files using the Explorer and then drag and drop them over Touch's window. Touch updates the date and time stamps of the dropped files so that they reflect the system's current time. The three checkboxes tell Touch which date and time stamps you wish to update. By default, Touch updates only each file's last-modified time leaving the file's creation time and last-access time alone. If you want Touch to update the other times as well, just select or deselect the checkboxes you desire before dropping files onto Touch's window.

Table 7.1 describes the files used to create this application.

Table 7.1 *Files used to build the Touch application.*

File	Description
Touch.C	Contains WinMain and the main window's dialog box and message cracker functions.
Touch.RC	Contains dialog-box template for main application window and its icons.

continued...

File	Description
Resource.H	Contains ID for all resources in the RC file.
Touch.ICO	Contains the icon for the main window.
Touch.MAK	Visual C++ project makefile.

When Touch's dialog box initializes, its Touch_OnInitDialog function is responsible for setting the initial state of the checkboxes. In addition, the DragAcceptFiles function is also called so that the dialog box's WS_EX_ACCEPTFILES flag is turned on. This is required so that the Explorer knows that files can be dropped on top of Touch's window.

The only thing of interest is how Touch responds to the WM_DROPFILES messages. When this message is received, the Touch_On-DropFiles function is called.

```
void Touch_OnDropFiles (HWND hwnd, HDROP hdrop) {

   HANDLE hfile;
   SYSTEMTIME st;
   FILETIME ft;

   // Get the number of files that have been dropped on us.
   int nNumFiles = DragQueryFile(hdrop, 0xFFFFFFFF, NULL, 0);
   PBYTE p = GlobalLock(hdrop);

   TCHAR szBadFiles[10240] =
      __TEXT("The following file(s) could not be opened:\n");
   BOOL fAnyBadFiles = FALSE;

   // Get the current system time and convert it to a file time.
   GetSystemTime(&st);
   SystemTimeToFileTime(&st, &ft);

   while (nNumFiles--) {

      TCHAR szFilename[_MAX_PATH];

      // Get the path of a single file that has been dropped on us.
      DragQueryFile(hdrop, nNumFiles, szFilename, adgARRAY_SIZE(szFilename));

      // Attempt to open the file so that we can alter its timestamp.
      // NOTE: On Windows NT, FILE_FLAG_BACKUP_SEMANTICS allows
      // directories to be opened.  Windows 95 will not open directories.
      hfile = CreateFile(szFilename, GENERIC_WRITE,
         FILE_SHARE_READ | FILE_SHARE_WRITE, NULL, OPEN_EXISTING,
         FILE_FLAG_SEQUENTIAL_SCAN | FILE_FLAG_BACKUP_SEMANTICS, NULL);
```

```
      if (hfile != INVALID_HANDLE_VALUE) {

        // If the file opened successfully, change the specified file times.
        adgVERIFY(SetFileTime(hfile,
          IsDlgButtonChecked(hwnd, IDC_UPDATECREATETIME)     ? &ft : NULL,
          IsDlgButtonChecked(hwnd, IDC_UPDATELASTACCESSTIME) ? &ft : NULL,
          IsDlgButtonChecked(hwnd, IDC_UPDATEMODIFIEDTIME)   ? &ft : NULL));
        CloseHandle(hfile);
      } else {

        if (0 == (GetFileAttributes(szFilename) & FILE_ATTRIBUTE_DIRECTORY)) {

        // We couldn't open the file so we'll append the file name to the
        // list of bad files.  We will not consider opening a directory
        // to be a problem.
          lstrcat(szBadFiles, szFilename);
          lstrcat(szBadFiles, __TEXT("\n"));
          fAnyBadFiles = TRUE;
        }
      }
   }

   if (fAnyBadFiles) {

     // If there were any files appended to the szBadFiles string, display
     // the error message box.
     adgMB(szBadFiles);
   }

   // We must free the memory containing the structure of dropped files.
   DragFinish(hdrop);
}
```

This function first determines the number of files that have been dropped and then obtains the system's current time. Then, the function enters a loop that cycles through all the dropped files. For each iteration, DragQueryFile is called to get the file's full pathname. Finally, the file is opened, and SetFileTime is called to change the file's date and timestamp based on the state of the three checkboxes.

Note that it is possible to drag and drop directories from the Explorer as well as files. When Touch attempts to open a directory when it is running on Windows NT, CreateFile successfully opens the file because the FILE_FLAG_BACKUP_SEMANTICS flag is specified. However, Windows 95 ignores the FILE_FLAG_BACKUP_SEMANTICS flag and fails to open the directory returning a handle value of INVALID_HANDLE_VALUE.

For any files that Touch has a problem opening, the file's full path name is added to a bad-files-list. However, I do not consider the failure to open a directory to be an error; therefore, directories are not added to the bad-files-list. Touch determines if a path name identifies a directory by calling the GetFileAttributes function and ANDing the result with the FILE_ATTRIBUTE_DIRECTORY flag.

Finally, just before Touch_OnDropFiles returns, it calls Drag Finish so that the memory block is properly destroyed. Remember that failing to do this results in a memory leak in your process's address space.

Touch.ICO

Listing 7.1 *Touch.C*

```
/*****************************************************************************
Module name: Touch.c
Written by: Jeffrey Richter
Notices: Copyright (c) 1995 Jeffrey Richter
Purpose: Demonstrates using a dialog box for an application's main window
*****************************************************************************/


#include "..\Win95ADG.h"            /* See Appendix B for details */
#include <windows.h>
#include <windowsx.h>
#pragma warning(disable: 4001)      /* Single-line comment */
#include <tchar.h>
#include "resource.h"



///////////////////////////////////////////////////////////////////////////


BOOL Touch_OnInitDialog (HWND hwnd, HWND hwndFocus, LPARAM lParam) {

   // Default to setting the file's last modified time only.
   CheckDlgButton(hwnd, IDC_UPDATECREATETIME,     BST_UNCHECKED);
   CheckDlgButton(hwnd, IDC_UPDATELASTACCESSTIME, BST_UNCHECKED);
   CheckDlgButton(hwnd, IDC_UPDATEMODIFIEDTIME,   BST_CHECKED);


   adgSETDLGICONS(hwnd, IDI_TOUCH, IDI_TOUCH);

   // Notify dropfile source applications that our window accepts dropped files.
   DragAcceptFiles(hwnd, TRUE);

   return(TRUE);                              // Accepts default focus window.
}



///////////////////////////////////////////////////////////////////////////
```

```
void Touch_OnDropFiles (HWND hwnd, HDROP hdrop) {

    HANDLE hfile;
    SYSTEMTIME st;
    FILETIME ft;

    // Get the number of files that have been dropped on us.
    int nNumFiles = DragQueryFile(hdrop, 0xFFFFFFFF, NULL, 0);
    PBYTE p = GlobalLock(hdrop);

    TCHAR szBadFiles[10240] =
        __TEXT("The following file(s) could not be opened:\n");
    BOOL fAnyBadFiles = FALSE;

    // Get the current system time and convert it to a file time.
    GetSystemTime(&st);
    SystemTimeToFileTime(&st, &ft);

    while (nNumFiles--) {

        TCHAR szFilename[_MAX_PATH];

        // Get the path of a single file that has been dropped on us.
        DragQueryFile(hdrop, nNumFiles, szFilename, adgARRAY_SIZE(szFilename));

        // Attempt to open the file so that we can alter its timestamp.
        // NOTE: On Windows NT, FILE_FLAG_BACKUP_SEMANTICS allows
        // directories to be opened.  Windows 95 will not open directories.
        hfile = CreateFile(szFilename, GENERIC_WRITE,
            FILE_SHARE_READ | FILE_SHARE_WRITE, NULL, OPEN_EXISTING,
            FILE_FLAG_SEQUENTIAL_SCAN | FILE_FLAG_BACKUP_SEMANTICS, NULL);

        if (hfile != INVALID_HANDLE_VALUE) {

            // If the file opened successfully, change the specified file times.
            adgVERIFY(SetFileTime(hfile,
                IsDlgButtonChecked(hwnd, IDC_UPDATECREATETIME)     ? &ft : NULL,
                IsDlgButtonChecked(hwnd, IDC_UPDATELASTACCESSTIME) ? &ft : NULL,
                IsDlgButtonChecked(hwnd, IDC_UPDATEMODIFIEDTIME)   ? &ft : NULL));
            CloseHandle(hfile);
        } else {

            if (0 == (GetFileAttributes(szFilename) & FILE_ATTRIBUTE_DIRECTORY)) {

            // We couldn't open the file, so we'll append the file name to the
            // list of bad files.  We will not consider opening a directory
            // to be a problem.
                lstrcat(szBadFiles, szFilename);
                lstrcat(szBadFiles, __TEXT("\n"));
                fAnyBadFiles = TRUE;
            }
        }
    }

    if (fAnyBadFiles) {
```

475

```
            // If there were any files appended to the szBadFiles string, display
            // the error message box.
            adgMB(szBadFiles);
        }

        // We must free the memory containing the structure of dropped files.
        DragFinish(hdrop);
}


//////////////////////////////////////////////////////////////////////////////


void Touch_OnCommand (HWND hwnd, int id, HWND hwndCtl, UINT codeNotify) {

    switch (id) {
        case IDCANCEL:                    // Allows dialog box to close
            EndDialog(hwnd, id);
            break;
    }
}


//////////////////////////////////////////////////////////////////////////////


BOOL WINAPI Touch_DlgProc (HWND hwnd, UINT uMsg,
    WPARAM wParam, LPARAM lParam) {

    switch (uMsg) {

        // Standard Window's messages
        adgHANDLE_DLGMSG(hwnd, WM_INITDIALOG,    Touch_OnInitDialog);
        adgHANDLE_DLGMSG(hwnd, WM_COMMAND,       Touch_OnCommand);
        adgHANDLE_DLGMSG(hwnd, WM_DROPFILES,     Touch_OnDropFiles);
    }
    return(FALSE);                        // We didn't process the message.
}


//////////////////////////////////////////////////////////////////////////////


int WINAPI WinMain (HINSTANCE hinstExe, HINSTANCE hinstPrev,
    LPSTR lpszCmdLine, int nCmdShow) {

    adgWARNIFUNICODEUNDERWIN95();
    adgVERIFY(-1 != DialogBox(hinstExe, MAKEINTRESOURCE(IDD_TOUCH),
        NULL, Touch_DlgProc));

    return(0);
}


///////////////////////////// End of File //////////////////////////////
```

Listing 7.2 *Touch.RC*

```
//Microsoft Visual C++-generated resource script
//
#include "resource.h"

#define APSTUDIO_READONLY_SYMBOLS
/////////////////////////////////////////////////////////////////////////////
//
// Generated from the TEXTINCLUDE 2 resource
//
#include "afxres.h"


/////////////////////////////////////////////////////////////////////////////
#undef APSTUDIO_READONLY_SYMBOLS


#ifdef APSTUDIO_INVOKED
/////////////////////////////////////////////////////////////////////////////
//
// TEXTINCLUDE
//

1 TEXTINCLUDE DISCARDABLE
BEGIN
    "resource.h\0"
END

2 TEXTINCLUDE DISCARDABLE
BEGIN
    "#include ""afxres.h""\r\n"
    "\0"
END

3 TEXTINCLUDE DISCARDABLE
BEGIN
    "\r\n"
    "\0"
END


/////////////////////////////////////////////////////////////////////////////
#endif    // APSTUDIO_INVOKED


/////////////////////////////////////////////////////////////////////////////
//
// Dialog
//

IDD_TOUCH DIALOG DISCARDABLE  -32768, 5, 100, 48
STYLE WS_MINIMIZEBOX | WS_VISIBLE | WS_CAPTION | WS_SYSMENU
CAPTION "Touch"
FONT 8, "MS Sans Serif"
```

```
BEGIN
    CONTROL         "Update &creation time",IDC_UPDATECREATETIME,"Button",
                    BS_AUTOCHECKBOX | WS_TABSTOP,4,4,79,10
    CONTROL         "Update &last-access time",IDC_UPDATELASTACCESSTIME,
                    "Button",BS_AUTOCHECKBOX | WS_TABSTOP,4,18,89,10
    CONTROL         "Update &modified time",IDC_UPDATEMODIFIEDTIME,"Button",
                    BS_AUTOCHECKBOX | WS_TABSTOP,4,32,80,10
END


/////////////////////////////////////////////////////////////////////////////
//
// Icon
//


IDI_TOUCH               ICON    DISCARDABLE     "Touch.ico"

#ifndef APSTUDIO_INVOKED
/////////////////////////////////////////////////////////////////////////////
//
// Generated from the TEXTINCLUDE 3 resource
//


/////////////////////////////////////////////////////////////////////////////
#endif    // not APSTUDIO_INVOKED
```

Listing 7.3 *Resource.H*

```
//{{NO_DEPENDENCIES}}
// Microsoft Visual C++-generated include file
// Used by Touch.rc
//
#define IDD_TOUCH                       103
#define IDI_TOUCH                       104
#define IDC_UPDATECREATETIME            1000
#define IDC_UPDATELASTACCESSTIME        1001
#define IDC_UPDATEMODIFIEDTIME          1002
#define IDC_SYSTEMTIME                  1003

// Next default values for new objects
//
#ifdef APSTUDIO_INVOKED
#ifndef APSTUDIO_READONLY_SYMBOLS
#define _APS_NEXT_RESOURCE_VALUE        106
#define _APS_NEXT_COMMAND_VALUE         40001
#define _APS_NEXT_CONTROL_VALUE         1006
#define _APS_NEXT_SYMED_VALUE           101
#endif
#endif
```

Becoming a Dropfile Source Application

You may have noticed that, up to now, the only way that applications can have files dropped on them is when the user initiates the drag-and-drop sequence from the Explorer. The reason for this is that the Windows Explorer is the only dropfile source application that comes with Windows. However, you can create other dropfile source applications by using the DROPFILES structure defined in the **ShlObj.h** header file:

```
typedef struct _DROPFILES {
    DWORD pFiles;  // Offset to the file list
    POINT pt;      // Position of mouse cursor (client coordinates)
    BOOL fNC;      // Was mouse in the window's non-client area?
    BOOL fWide;    // TRUE if file contains WIDE characters, FALSE otherwise
} DROPFILES, * LPDROPFILES;
```

This is the structure that the Explorer creates when the user drops files into a window. After allocating a memory block large enough to hold this structure, the pFiles member is initialized to the number of bytes in the structure; this is where the list of pathnames will begin.

The pt member is set to the x- and y-coordinates of the mouse when it was released (these coordinates are relative to the client area of the window under the mouse cursor). The fNC member is set to TRUE if the mouse is in the windows non-client area when the button is released. Following this structure in the memory block is the full path name for each of the file names (and directories) selected in the Explorer. These path names can be in either ANSI or Unicode characters; the fWide member of the DROPFILES structure indicates which. Each path name is terminated with a zero character and an extra zero character after the last path name indicates the end of the entire list.

To implement a dropfile source application, your application must create a memory block containing the structure described previously. I have written two functions to help you do this. The first function, DFSrc_Create, allocates a block of memory large enough to contain the DROPFILES structure and initializes its four data members. The functions returns the handle to this memory block or NULL if an error occurs.

```
HDROP WINAPI DFSrc_Create (PPOINT ppt, BOOL fNC, BOOL fWide) {

   HDROP hdrop;
   LPDROPFILES pDropFiles;

   // Allocate dynamic memory for the DFSRC data structure and for the extra
   // zero character identifying that there are no path names in the block yet.
   hdrop = GlobalAlloc(GMEM_MOVEABLE | GMEM_ZEROINIT,
      sizeof(DROPFILES) + (fWide ? sizeof(WCHAR) : sizeof(char)));

   // If successful, lock block and initialize the data members.
   if (hdrop != NULL) {
      pDropFiles = (LPDROPFILES) GlobalLock(hdrop);
      pDropFiles->pFiles = sizeof(*pDropFiles);
      pDropFiles->pt = *ppt;
      pDropFiles->fNC = fNC;
      pDropFiles->fWide = fWide;
      GlobalUnlock(hdrop);
   }

   return(hdrop);
}
```

The second function, DFSrc_AppendPathname, can be called repeatedly to append new path names to the memory block.

```
HDROP WINAPI DFSrc_AppendPathname (HDROP hdrop, PVOID pvPathname) {

   LPDROPFILES pDropFiles = (LPDROPFILES) GlobalLock(hdrop);

   // Point to first path name in list.
   PSTR  szPathA = (PSTR) pDropFiles + pDropFiles->pFiles;
   PWSTR szPathW = (PWSTR) szPathA;
   int nOffsetOfNewPathname, nPathSize;

   if (pDropFiles->fWide) {

      // Search for a path name where first character is a zero character
      while (*szPathW) {   // While the first character is nonzero.
         while (*szPathW)  // Find end of current path.
            szPathW++;
         szPathW++;        // Skip over the zero character.
      }

      // Get the offset from the beginning of the block
      // where the new path name should go.
      nOffsetOfNewPathname = ((PBYTE) szPathW - (PBYTE) pDropFiles);

      // Get the number of bytes needed for the new path name,
      // it's terminating zero character, and the zero-length
      // path name that marks the end of the list of path names.
      nPathSize = sizeof(WCHAR) * (wcslen(pvPathname) + 2);
   } else {
```

```
      // Search for a path name where first character is a zero character.
      while (*szPathA) {   // While the first character is nonzero
         while (*szPathA)  // Find end of current path.
            szPathA++;
         szPathA++;        // Skip over the zero character.
      }

      // Get the offset from the beginning of the block
      // where the new path name should go.
      nOffsetOfNewPathname = ((PBYTE) szPathA - (PBYTE) pDropFiles);

      // Get the number of bytes needed for the new path name,
      // it's terminating zero character, and the zero-length
      // path name that marks the end of the list of path names
      nPathSize = sizeof(char) * (strlen(pvPathname) + 2);
   }

   GlobalUnlock(hdrop);

   // Increase block size to accommodate new path name.
   hdrop = GlobalReAlloc(hdrop, nPathSize + nOffsetOfNewPathname,
      GMEM_MOVEABLE | GMEM_ZEROINIT);

   // If successful, append the path name to the end of the block.
   if (hdrop != NULL) {
      pDropFiles = (LPDROPFILES) GlobalLock(hdrop);

   if (pDropFiles->fWide)
      wcscpy((PWSTR) ((PSTR) pDropFiles + nOffsetOfNewPathname), pvPathname);
   else
      strcpy((PSTR) ((PSTR) pDropFiles + nOffsetOfNewPathname), pvPathname);

      GlobalUnlock(hdrop);
   }

   return(hdrop);                  // Returns the new handle to the block.
}
```

The first parameter to this function is the handle to the memory block created by a call to DFSrc_Create or a previous call to DFSrc_Append-Pathname. DFSrc_AppendPathname then locks the block and counts the number of bytes that are currently being used in it. The block is then enlarged by calling GlobalReAlloc so that it is large enough to contain all the block's current data plus the new path name being appended. If this is successful, the new path name is copied onto the end of the block, and the new memory handle is returned.

After all the path names are appended to the block with DFSrc_AppendPathname, the window under the mouse cursor can process the dropped path names. This is done by having the dropfile source application post a WM_DROPFILES message to the dropfile target, passing the memory handle returned from DFSrc_Append-Pathname as the wParam parameter. It is better to use PostMessage instead of SendMessage here so that the source application's thread is not suspended waiting for the target application's thread to process the dropped files.

If you are a savvy Win32 programmer, you should see an immediate problem with this technique: each process has its own, private address space. While it is possible for one process (say the Explorer) to allocate and initialize a block of memory and then pass the handle (via a window message) to another process, the receiving process will not be able to use the handle successfully. The memory block allocated in one process's address space cannot be accessed by another process. So how did Microsoft get the Explorer's drag-and-drop to work in Windows at all?

The PostMessage function checks explicitly for the WM_DROP-FILES message. When it sees that this message is being posted, it allocates a block of memory in the context of the process receiving the WM_DROPFILES message and copies the contents of the calling process's block into the newly allocated block. PostMessage then calls GlobalFree in the context of the calling process to free the original memory block. PostMessage next changes wParam for the message to the value of the memory allocated in the target process's address space. When the target window procedure receives the WM_DROPFILES message, wParam identifies a block of memory allocated in the target process's address space. DragQueryPoint, DragQueryFile, and DragFinish have no trouble manipulating this memory block.

Dropfile Source Application

The DFSrc demo application (**DFSrcDm.EXE**), shown in Listings 7.4-7.8, (starting on page 490) demonstrates how to create a dropfile source application. When you invoke the application, the dialog box shown in Figure 7.4 appears.

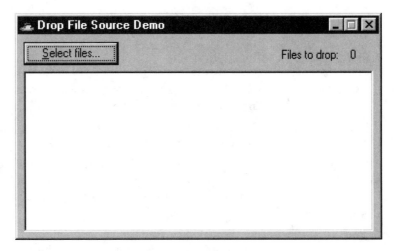

Figure 7.4 *The DFSrc application*

Initially the application has no files that it can drop. However, if you select the Select Files button, the common File Open dialog box appears and allows you to select one or more files. When you close the File Open dialog box, the list of files you have chosen are shown in the main dialog box's listbox. Note that the each file's full path name is shown. To drop these files onto another application, simply click and hold the mouse on any other part of the main dialog box's client area. The mouse cursor changes, and you may drop the mouse over another application's window. While you are moving the mouse, DFSrcDem checks the windows under the cursor to see if the WS_EX_ACCEPTFILES window style bit is turned on. If the bit is on, DFSrcDem changes the mouse cursor shape to an arrow; if the bit is off, the cursor is changed to the No cursor.

When you release the mouse over a window that has the WS_EX_ACCEPTFILES bit on, DFSrcDem creates the memory block containing the DROPFILES information and posts the WM_DROPFILES message to the target window. The target application performs whatever action it usually performs when files are dropped on top of it.

Table 7.2 describes the files used to create this application.

Table 7.2 *Files used to build the DFSrcDem application.*

File	Description
DFSrcDem.C	Contains WinMain and the main window's dialog box and message cracker functions.
DFSrcDem.RC	Contains dialog-box template for main application window and its icons.
DFSrc.C	Contains a library of functions that make it much easier for you to create a dropfiles source application. You can use this file in your own applications
DFSrc.H	Contains prototypes for the functions contained in the **DFSrc.C** file. Any source file that uses the library of functions in **DFSrc.C** must include this file.
Resource.H	Contains ID for all resources in the RC file.
DFSrcDem.ICO	Contains the icon for the main window.
DFSrcDem.MAK	Visual C++ project makefile.

When you select the Select Files button, the DFSrcDem_On-Command function is called. This function initializes an OPENFILE-NAME structure and then calls the GetOpenFileName function. If the user presses the OK button, GetOpenFileName returns TRUE, and the listbox is updated to reflect all the selected files. If the user selects a single file, the buffer contains the file's full path name. For example, if the user selects only Notepad, the buffer looks like:

```
"C:\\Windows\\NOTEPAD.EXE\0"[2]
```

However, when the user selects multiple files with GetOpen-FileName, the lpstrFile buffer contains the zero-terminated path, followed by a zero-terminated file name for each file selected. At the end of the buffer is an extra zero character that marks the end of all the files. For example, if the user selects Notepad, PBrush, and Calc from the **C:\Windows** directory, the buffer looks like:

---

[2]Note that there is not another "\0" here at the end of the buffer.

484

```
"C:\\Windows\0NOTEPAD.EXE\0PBRUSH.EXE\0CALC.EXE\0\0"3
```

Because of the different formats possible inside lpstrFile buffer, I have created some functions that help parse this information. These functions are all implemented in the **DFSrc.C** file and can be taken and used in your own projects. I'll describe the functions briefly, but I encourage you to examine the source code file for more details.

The MultiStrUtil_FindStr function returns the address to a string in a buffer that contains a set of zero-terminated strings.

```
LPCTSTR WINAPI MultiStrUtil_FindStr (LPCTSTR szStrAll, int nIndex, PINT pnMax);
```

The szStrAll parameter points to the multistring buffer, and the nIndex parameter identifies the string that you are interested in. MultiStrUtil_FindStr's return value is the address of the desired string or NULL if the index is too big. This function also returns the number of strings in the full buffer if you pass the address of an integer as the last parameter (and pass –1 for the nIndex parameter).

The FileOpenUtil_AreMultipleFilesSelected function accepts the pointer to an OPENFILENAME structure that was initialized by an earlier call to the GetOpenFileName function. FileOpenUtil_ AreMultipleFilesSelected returns TRUE if the lpstrFile buffer contains multiple files or FALSE if only a single file was selected.

```
BOOL WINAPI FileOpenUtil_AreMultipleFilesSelected (OPENFILENAME *pofn);
```

The FileOpenUtil_GetNumFiles function accepts the pointer to an OPENFILENAME structure that was initialized by an earlier call to the GetOpenFileName function. FileOpenUtil_GetNumFiles returns the number of files that are contained in the lpstrFile buffer.

```
int WINAPI FileOpenUtil_GetNumFiles (OPENFILENAME *pofn);
```

---

[3]The buffer formats described reflect the format of the buffer when the OFN_EXPLORER flag is specified. Windows NT 3.51 ignores the OFN_ EXPLORER flag and uses the older format where file names are separated by spaces. So that DFSrcDem works correctly on Windows NT 3.51, I have added code that changes the older space-delimited buffer to the new zero-character-delimited buffer.

The FileOpenUtil_GetFile function accepts the pointer to an OPENFILENAME structure, an index, and a pointer to another buffer. The function fills the szPathname buffer with the full path name of the file at the specified index.

```
int WINAPI FileOpenUtil_GetFile (OPENFILENAME *pofn, int nIndex,
   LPTSTR szPathname);
```

DFSrcDem spreads all its drag-and-drop handing over three window messages: WM_LBUTTONDOWN, WM_MOUSEMOVE, and WM_LBUTTONUP. Let's begin by looking at the DFSrcDem_OnLButton-Down function.

```
void DFSrcDemo_OnLButtonDown (HWND hwnd, BOOL fDoubleClick,
   int nIndex, int y, UINT keyFlags) {

   // Make sure that there are some files to be dropped.
   if (ListBox_GetCount(GetDlgItem(hwnd, IDC_PATHNAMELIST)) == 0) {

      adgMB(__TEXT("No files to drop."));
      return;
   }

   // Initiate the drag-and-drop sequence.
   SetCapture(hwnd);
}
```

This function simply checks to see if there are path names in the listbox to drop; if so, it sets mouse capture to initiate the user's drag-and-drop sequence. The WM_MOUSEMOVE and WM_LBUTTON-UP messages perform the remainder of this sequence.

As the user moves the mouse, DFSrcDemo_OnMouseMove is called, and its only responsibility is to change the mouse cursor shape so that the user has a visual indication as to whether files can be dropped or not.

```
void DFSrcDemo_OnMouseMove (HWND hwnd, int x, int y, UINT keyFlags) {

   // If we don't have capture, the user didn't initiate the drag-and-drop
   // sequence — we have nothing to do here.
   if (GetCapture() != hwnd)
     return;

   // Get cursor position and window under the cursor.
   SetCursor(IsWindow(DFSrc_OkToDrop(NULL)) ?
      LoadCursor(GetWindowInstance(hwnd), MAKEINTRESOURCE(IDC_DROPOK)) :
      LoadCursor(NULL, IDC_NO));
}
```

The real work for determining whether files can be dropped or not is contained in the DFSrc_OkToDrop function. This function is contained in the **DFSrc.C** library.

```
// Macro to ease source code readability.
#define IsAcceptingFiles(hwnd) \
   ((GetWindowExStyle((hwnd)) & WS_EX_ACCEPTFILES) != 0)


///////////////////////////////////////////////////////////////////////////


HWND WINAPI DFSrc_OkToDrop (PPOINT ppt) {

   POINT ptMousePos;
   HWND hwndTarget;

   if (ppt == NULL) {

      // If the caller passes NULL, assume that they want the mouse position
      // at the time of the last-retrieved window message.
      ptMousePos.x = LOWORD(GetMessagePos());
      ptMousePos.y = HIWORD(GetMessagePos());
   }

   hwndTarget = WindowFromPoint(ptMousePos);

   // See if the target window or any of its parent windows are prepared to
   // accept dropped files.
   while (IsWindow(hwndTarget) && !IsAcceptingFiles(hwndTarget))
      hwndTarget = GetParent(hwndTarget);

   // If it's OK to drop files, return the HWND of the target window or NULL
   // if we do not have a target window accepting files.
   return((IsWindow(hwndTarget) && IsAcceptingFiles(hwndTarget))
      ? hwndTarget : NULL);
}
```

Each time DFSrc_OkToDrop is called, the location of the mouse is acquired. Then, the window under the mouse is checked to see if it has the WS_EX_ACCEPTFILES style bit turned on. If the style is off, the window's parent window is checked. If none of the windows in the hierarchy have the WS_EX_ACCEPTFILES style, a window handle of NULL is returned to the caller. However, if a valid target window is found, its handle is returned. The DFSrcDem_OnMouseMove function uses this return value to decide which shape the mouse cursor should be.

When the mouse button is released, the DFSrcDem_OnLButtonUp function is called.

```
void DFSrcDemo_OnLButtonUp (HWND hwnd, int x, int y, UINT keyFlags) {

    HWND hwndTarget, hwndLB = GetDlgItem(hwnd, IDC_PATHNAMELIST);
    RECT rc;
    POINT ptMousePos;
    int nIndex, nNumFiles = ListBox_GetCount(hwndLB);
    HDROP hdrop, hdropT;
    TCHAR szPathName[_MAX_PATH];

    // If we don't have capture, the user didn't initiate the drag-and-drop
    // sequence — we have nothing to do here.
    if (GetCapture() != hwnd)
        return;

    // End the drag-and-drop sequence.
    ReleaseCapture();

    // Get the HWND of the target window.
    hwndTarget = DFSrc_OkToDrop(NULL);

    if (!IsWindow(hwndTarget)) {

        // If the target window is invalid, we have nothing else to do.
        return;
    }

    // Get the client rectangle of the target window and convert the mouse
    // position to the target's client coordinates so that we can tell if
    // the mouse is in the target's client area when we call DFSrc_Create.
    GetClientRect(hwndTarget, &rc);
    ScreenToClient(hwndTarget, &ptMousePos);

    // Create dropfile memory block and initialize it.
#ifdef UNICODE
    hdrop = DFSrc_Create(&ptMousePos, !PtInRect(&rc, ptMousePos), TRUE);
#else
    hdrop = DFSrc_Create(&ptMousePos, !PtInRect(&rc, ptMousePos), FALSE);
#endif

    if (hdrop == NULL) {
        adgMB(__TEXT("Insufficient memory to drop file(s)."));
        return;
    }

    // Append each path name to the dropfile memory block.
    for (nIndex = 0; nIndex < nNumFiles; nIndex++) {

        ListBox_GetText(hwndLB, nIndex, szPathName);
        hdropT = DFSrc_AppendPathname(hdrop, szPathName);

        if (hdropT == NULL) {
            adgMB(__TEXT("Insufficient memory to drop file(s)."));
            hdrop = GlobalFree(hdrop);
            break;  // Terminates the 'for' loop.
        } else {
            hdrop = hdropT;
```

```
        }
    }

    if (hdrop != NULL) {

        // All path names appended successfully; post the message to the
        // dropfile target window.
        FORWARD_WM_DROPFILES(hwndTarget, hdrop, PostMessage);

        // Update the window's caption to reflect the number of selected files
        // available for dropping.
        SetDlgItemInt(hwnd, IDC_NUMFILES, 0, FALSE);
        ListBox_ResetContent(hwndLB);

        // NOTE: We should not call GlobalFree passing in hdrop.  The system
        // will free it for us after it creates a copy of it in the target
        // process's address space.  The target process is responsible for
        // freeing it's copy of the hdrop by calling DragFinish.
    }
}
```

This function calls ReleaseCapture to end the user's drag-and-drop
sequence. It then calls DFSrc_OkToDrop to determine if the user
has released the mouse over a valid drop target window. If the user
releases the mouse button over a valid drop target window,
DFSrc_Create is called passing it the mouse position (converted to
the target window's client coordinates), a Boolean value indicating
whether the mouse is in the window's client area, and another
Boolean value indicating whether we intend to add Unicode path
names or ANSI path names to the data buffer. This last parameter is
decided based on whether UNICODE is defined when the source
code module is compiled.

If DFSrc_Create returns a non-NULL handle, DFSrcDem_On-
LButtonUp then iterates through a loop that retrieves each path
name from the listbox and appends it to the data buffer. After all
the path names have been appended, the WM_DROPFILES message
(with the handle to the DROPFILES memory block as the wParam
parameter) can be posted (not sent) to the target window.

```
FORWARD_WM_DROPFILES(hwndTarget, hdrop, PostMessage);
```

The DFSrcDem application then resets itself by erasing the contents of its listbox. Note that the application does not free the
memory block; PostMessage frees the source process's memory
block, and the target frees its memory block by calling DragFinish.

489

Listing 7.4 *DFSrcDem.C*

DFSrcDem.ICO

```
/*****************************************************************************
Module name: DFSrcDem.c
Written by: Jeffrey Richter
Notices: Copyright (c) 1995 Jeffrey Richter
Purpose: Demonstrates how to create a dropfile source application
*****************************************************************************/


#include "..\Win95ADG.h"          /* See Appendix B for details. */
#include <windows.h>
#include <windowsx.h>
#pragma warning(disable: 4001)     /* Single-line comment */
#include "DFSrc.h"
#include "Resource.h"


///////////////////////////////////////////////////////////////////////////


BOOL DFSrcDemo_OnInitDialog (HWND hwnd, HWND hwndFocus, LPARAM lParam) {

   adgSETDLGICONS(hwnd, IDI_DFSRCDEMO, IDI_DFSRCDEMO);
   ListBox_SetHorizontalExtent(GetDlgItem(hwnd, IDC_PATHNAMELIST),
     _MAX_PATH * LOWORD(GetDialogBaseUnits()));

   return(TRUE);                   // Accepts default focus window.
}


///////////////////////////////////////////////////////////////////////////


void DFSrcDemo_OnCommand (HWND hwnd, int id,
   HWND hwndCtl, UINT codeNotify) {

   TCHAR szAllFileNames[1024]  = { 0 }, szPathname[_MAX_PATH];
   OPENFILENAME ofn;
   int nNumFiles, nIndex;
   HWND hwndLB = GetDlgItem(hwnd, IDC_PATHNAMELIST);
   LPTSTR szT;

   switch (id) {
      case IDCANCEL:              // Allows dialog box to close.
         EndDialog(hwnd, id);
         break;

      case IDC_SELECTFILES:      // "File Select!" menu item

         // Initialize structure for calling the "Open File" common dialog box.
         adgINITSTRUCT(ofn, TRUE);
         ofn.hwndOwner = hwnd;
         ofn.lpstrFilter = __TEXT("All files\0*.*\0");
```

490

```
            ofn.Flags = OFN_ALLOWMULTISELECT |
                OFN_FILEMUSTEXIST | OFN_HIDEREADONLY | OFN_EXPLORER;

            // Set up the buffer to receive the selected file(s).
            szAllFileNames[0] = 0;
            ofn.lpstrFile = szAllFileNames;
            ofn.nMaxFile = adgARRAY_SIZE(szAllFileNames);

            ListBox_ResetContent(hwndLB);
            if (GetOpenFileName(&ofn)) {

#ifndef WINDOWSNT_COMPATIBILITY

                // Windows NT 3.51 ignores the OFN_EXPLORER flag. This means that
                // the files in the returned buffer are space delimited instead of
                // zero-character delimited (like Windows 95). So, the following
                // 'if' block converts the space delimiters to zero-character
                // delimiters. When Windows NT supports OFN_EXPLORER, this 'if'
                // block should be removed.

                if (ofn.lpstrFile[ofn.nFileOffset - 1] == __TEXT(' ')) {

                    // If the buffer is space delmited, convert all space
                    // characters to zero characters.
                    for (szT = ofn.lpstrFile; *szT != 0; szT++)
                        if (*szT == __TEXT(' '))
                            *szT = 0;
                    // Extra terminate zero character to mark end of all strings
                    *szT = 0;
                }
#endif

                nNumFiles = FileOpenUtil_GetNumFiles(&ofn);
                for (nIndex = 0; nIndex < nNumFiles; nIndex++) {

                    // Get the full path name to append.
                    FileOpenUtil_GetFile(&ofn, nIndex, szPathname);
                    ListBox_AddString(hwndLB, szPathname);
                }
            } else {
                nNumFiles = 0;
            }

            // Update the "Files to Drop" static window to reflect the number
            // of selected files available for dropping.
            SetDlgItemInt(hwnd, IDC_NUMFILES, nNumFiles, FALSE);
            break;
    }
}


///////////////////////////////////////////////////////////////////////////////


void DFSrcDemo_OnLButtonDown (HWND hwnd, BOOL fDoubleClick,
```

```
      int nIndex, int y, UINT keyFlags) {

      // Make sure that there are some files to be dropped.
      if (ListBox_GetCount(GetDlgItem(hwnd, IDC_PATHNAMELIST)) == 0) {
        adgMB(__TEXT("No files to drop."));
        return;
      }

      // Initiate the drag-and-drop sequence.
      SetCapture(hwnd);
    }


    ///////////////////////////////////////////////////////////////////////////


    void DFSrcDemo_OnMouseMove (HWND hwnd, int x, int y, UINT keyFlags) {

      // If we don't have capture, the user didn't initiate the drag-and-drop
      // sequence -- we have nothing to do here.
      if (GetCapture() != hwnd)
        return;

      // Get cursor position and window under the cursor.
      SetCursor(IsWindow(DFSrc_OkToDrop(NULL)) ?
        LoadCursor(GetWindowInstance(hwnd), MAKEINTRESOURCE(IDC_DROPOK)) :
        LoadCursor(NULL, IDC_NO));
    }


    ///////////////////////////////////////////////////////////////////////////


    void DFSrcDemo_OnLButtonUp (HWND hwnd, int x, int y, UINT keyFlags) {

      HWND hwndTarget, hwndLB = GetDlgItem(hwnd, IDC_PATHNAMELIST);
      RECT rc;
      POINT ptMousePos;
      int nIndex, nNumFiles = ListBox_GetCount(hwndLB);
      HDROP hdrop, hdropT;
      TCHAR szPathName[_MAX_PATH];

      // If we don't have capture, the user didn't initiate the drag-and-drop
      // sequence -- we have nothing to do here.
      if (GetCapture() != hwnd)
        return;

      // End the drag-and-drop sequence.
      ReleaseCapture();

      // Get the HWND of the target window.
      hwndTarget = DFSrc_OkToDrop(NULL);

      if (!IsWindow(hwndTarget)) {

        // If the target window is invalid, we have nothing else to do.
```

492

```
        return;
    }

    // Get the client rectangle of the target window and convert the mouse
    // position to the target's client coordinates so that we can tell if
    // the mouse is in the target's client area when we call DFSrc_Create.
    GetClientRect(hwndTarget, &rc);
    ScreenToClient(hwndTarget, &ptMousePos);

    // Create dropfile memory block and initialize it.
#ifdef UNICODE
    hdrop = DFSrc_Create(&ptMousePos, !PtInRect(&rc, ptMousePos), TRUE);
#else
    hdrop = DFSrc_Create(&ptMousePos, !PtInRect(&rc, ptMousePos), FALSE);
#endif

    if (hdrop == NULL) {
        adgMB(__TEXT("Insufficient memory to drop file(s)."));
        return;
    }

    // Append each path name to the dropfile memory block.
    for (nIndex = 0; nIndex < nNumFiles; nIndex++) {

        ListBox_GetText(hwndLB, nIndex, szPathName);
        hdropT = DFSrc_AppendPathname(hdrop, szPathName);

        if (hdropT == NULL) {
            adgMB(__TEXT("Insufficient memory to drop file(s)."));
            hdrop = GlobalFree(hdrop);
            break;                       // Terminates the 'for' loop.
        } else {
            hdrop = hdropT;
        }
    }

    if (hdrop != NULL) {

        // All path names appended successfully, post the message to the
        // dropfile target window.
        FORWARD_WM_DROPFILES(hwndTarget, hdrop, PostMessage);

        // Update the window's caption to reflect the number of selected files
        // available for dropping.
        SetDlgItemInt(hwnd, IDC_NUMFILES, 0, FALSE);
        ListBox_ResetContent(hwndLB);

        // NOTE: We should not call GlobalFree passing in hdrop.  The system
        // will free it for us after it creates a copy of it in the target
        // process's address space.  The target process is responsible for
        // freeing it's copy of the hdrop by calling DragFinish.
    }
}
```

///

```
BOOL WINAPI DFSrcDemo_Proc (HWND hwnd, UINT uMsg,
   WPARAM wParam, LPARAM lParam) {

   switch (uMsg) {
      adgHANDLE_DLGMSG(hwnd, WM_INITDIALOG,   DFSrcDemo_OnInitDialog);
      adgHANDLE_DLGMSG(hwnd, WM_COMMAND,      DFSrcDemo_OnCommand);
      adgHANDLE_DLGMSG(hwnd, WM_LBUTTONDOWN,  DFSrcDemo_OnLButtonDown);
      adgHANDLE_DLGMSG(hwnd, WM_MOUSEMOVE,    DFSrcDemo_OnMouseMove);
      adgHANDLE_DLGMSG(hwnd, WM_LBUTTONUP,    DFSrcDemo_OnLButtonUp);
   }

   return(FALSE);                // We didn't process the message.
}


//////////////////////////////////////////////////////////////////////////////


int WINAPI WinMain (HINSTANCE hinstExe,
   HINSTANCE hinstPrev, LPSTR lpszCmdLine, int nCmdShow) {

   adgWARNIFUNICODEUNDERWIN95();
   adgVERIFY(-1 != DialogBox(hinstExe, MAKEINTRESOURCE(IDD_DFSRCDEMO),
      NULL, DFSrcDemo_Proc));

   return(0);
}


////////////////////////////// End of File //////////////////////////////////
```

Listing 7.5 *DFSrc.C*

```
/*****************************************************************************
Module name: DFSrc.c
Written by: Jeffrey Richter
Notices: Copyright (c) 1995 Jeffrey Richter
Purpose: Drop file source library functions.
*****************************************************************************/


#include "..\Win95ADG.h"        /* See Appendix B for details. */
#include <windows.h>
#include <windowsx.h>
#pragma warning(disable: 4001)   /* Single-line comment */
#include <ShlObj.h>              /* For DROPFILES structure */
#include <tchar.h>
#include <limits.h>
#include "DFSrc.h"


//////////////////////////////////////////////////////////////////////////////
```

494

```
// Macro to ease source code readability
#define IsAcceptingFiles(hwnd) \
   ((GetWindowExStyle((hwnd)) & WS_EX_ACCEPTFILES) != 0)


/////////////////////////////////////////////////////////////////////////////


HWND WINAPI DFSrc_OkToDrop (PPOINT ppt) {

   POINT ptMousePos;
   HWND hwndTarget;

   if (ppt == NULL) {

      // The caller passes NULL. Assume that they want the mouse position
      // at the time of the last retrieved window message.
      ptMousePos.x = LOWORD(GetMessagePos());
      ptMousePos.y = HIWORD(GetMessagePos());
   }

   hwndTarget = WindowFromPoint(ptMousePos);

   // See if the target window or any of its parent windows are prepared to
   // accept dropped files.
   while (IsWindow(hwndTarget) && !IsAcceptingFiles(hwndTarget))
      hwndTarget = GetParent(hwndTarget);

   // If it's OK to drop files, return the HWND of the target window or NULL
   // if we do not have a target window accepting files.
   // the WS_EX_ACCEPTFILES style.
   return((IsWindow(hwndTarget) && IsAcceptingFiles(hwndTarget))
     ? hwndTarget : NULL);
}


/////////////////////////////////////////////////////////////////////////////


HDROP WINAPI DFSrc_Create (PPOINT ppt, BOOL fNC, BOOL fWide) {

   HDROP hdrop;
   LPDROPFILES pDropFiles;

   // Allocate dynamic memory for the DFSRC data structure and for the extra
   // zero character identifying that there are no path names in the block yet.
   hdrop = GlobalAlloc(GMEM_MOVEABLE | GMEM_ZEROINIT,
      sizeof(DROPFILES) + (fWide ? sizeof(WCHAR) : sizeof(char)));

   // If successful, lock block and initialize the data members.
   if (hdrop != NULL) {
      pDropFiles = (LPDROPFILES) GlobalLock(hdrop);
      pDropFiles->pFiles = sizeof(*pDropFiles);
      pDropFiles->pt = *ppt;
      pDropFiles->fNC = fNC;
```

```
      pDropFiles->fWide = fWide;
      GlobalUnlock(hdrop);
   }

   return(hdrop);
}


////////////////////////////////////////////////////////////////////////////


HDROP WINAPI DFSrc_AppendPathname (HDROP hdrop, PVOID pvPathname) {

   LPDROPFILES pDropFiles = (LPDROPFILES) GlobalLock(hdrop);

   // Point to first path name in list.
   PSTR  szPathA = (PSTR) pDropFiles + pDropFiles->pFiles;
   PWSTR szPathW = (PWSTR) szPathA;
   int nOffsetOfNewPathname, nPathSize;

   if (pDropFiles->fWide) {

      // Search for a path name where first character is a zero character.
      while (*szPathW) {           // While the first character is nonzero
         while (*szPathW)          // Find end of current path.
            szPathW++;
         szPathW++;                // Skip over the zero character.
      }

      // Get the offset from the beginning of the block
      // where the new path name should go.
      nOffsetOfNewPathname = ((PBYTE) szPathW - (PBYTE) pDropFiles);

      // Get the number of bytes needed for the new path name,
      // it's terminating zero character, and the zero-length
      // path name that marks the end of the list of path names.
      nPathSize = sizeof(WCHAR) * (wcslen(pvPathname) + 2);
   } else {

      // Search for a pathname where first character is a zero character.
      while (*szPathA) {           // While the first character is nonzero
         while (*szPathA)          // Find end of current path.
            szPathA++;
         szPathA++;                // Skip over the zero character.
      }

      // Get the offset from the beginning of the block
      // where the new path name should go.
      nOffsetOfNewPathname = ((PBYTE) szPathA - (PBYTE) pDropFiles);

      // Get the number of bytes needed for the new path name,
      // it's terminating zero character, and the zero-length
      // path name that marks the end of the list of path names.
      nPathSize = sizeof(char) * (strlen(pvPathname) + 2);
```

```
    }

    GlobalUnlock(hdrop);

    // Increase block size to accommodate new path name.
    hdrop = GlobalReAlloc(hdrop, nPathSize + nOffsetOfNewPathname,
      GMEM_MOVEABLE | GMEM_ZEROINIT);

    // If successful, append the path name to the end of the block.
    if (hdrop != NULL) {
      pDropFiles = (LPDROPFILES) GlobalLock(hdrop);

    if (pDropFiles->fWide)
      wcscpy((PWSTR) ((PSTR) pDropFiles + nOffsetOfNewPathname), pvPathname);
    else
      strcpy((PSTR)  ((PSTR) pDropFiles + nOffsetOfNewPathname), pvPathname);

      GlobalUnlock(hdrop);
    }

    return(hdrop);                     // Returns the new handle to the block.
}


///////////////////////////////////////////////////////////////////////////////


LPCTSTR WINAPI MultiStrUtil_FindStr (LPCTSTR szStrAll, int nIndex,
  PINT pnMax) {

  int nNumStrs = 0;
  LPCTSTR szStrSingle = szStrAll;

  if (nIndex == -1)
    nIndex = INT_MAX;

  // Find the nIndex'th string.
  // If the next string contains no characters, we have reached the end.
  while ((*szStrSingle != 0) && (nNumStrs < nIndex)) {

    // Find the end of a string.
    szStrSingle = _tcschr(szStrSingle, 0) + 1;
      nNumStrs++;
  }

  if (pnMax != NULL)
    *pnMax = nNumStrs;

  // If there are fewer strings than requested, return NULL.
  return((nNumStrs < nIndex) ? NULL : szStrSingle);
}

///////////////////////////////////////////////////////////////////////////////
```

```
BOOL WINAPI FileOpenUtil_AreMultipleFilesSelected (OPENFILENAME *pofn) {

   // The offset of the file name is beyond the length of the
   // first string. The first string contains only a path instead
   // of a path and a file name.
   return(_tcslen(pofn->lpstrFile) < pofn->nFileOffset);
}


///////////////////////////////////////////////////////////////////////////


int WINAPI FileOpenUtil_GetNumFiles (OPENFILENAME *pofn) {

   int nNumFiles = 1;
   if (FileOpenUtil_AreMultipleFilesSelected(pofn)) {
      (void) MultiStrUtil_FindStr(pofn->lpstrFile, -1, &nNumFiles);

      // Because the first string is a path, there is one less file than
strings.
      nNumFiles--;
   }
   return(nNumFiles);
}


///////////////////////////////////////////////////////////////////////////


int WINAPI FileOpenUtil_GetFile (OPENFILENAME *pofn,
   int nIndex, LPTSTR szPathname) {

   _tcscpy(szPathname, MultiStrUtil_FindStr(pofn->lpstrFile, 0, NULL));
   if (FileOpenUtil_AreMultipleFilesSelected(pofn)) {
      _tcscat(szPathname, __TEXT("\\"));
      _tcscat(szPathname, MultiStrUtil_FindStr(pofn->lpstrFile,
         nIndex + 1, NULL));
   }
   return(_tcslen(szPathname));   // Returns length of string.
}


/////////////////////////////// End of File ////////////////////////////////
```

Listing 7.6 *DFSrc.H*

```
/****************************************************************************
Module name: DFSrc.h
Written by: Jeffrey Richter
Notices: Copyright (c) 1995 Jeffrey Richter
Purpose: Drop file source library functions
```

498

```
************************************************************************/


HWND  WINAPI DFSrc_OkToDrop (PPOINT ppt);
HDROP WINAPI DFSrc_Create (PPOINT ppt, BOOL fNC, BOOL fWide);
HDROP WINAPI DFSrc_AppendPathname (HDROP hdrop, PVOID pvPathname);



//////////////////////////////////////////////////////////////////////


LPCTSTR WINAPI MultiStrUtil_FindStr (LPCTSTR szStrAll, int nIndex,
   PINT pnMax);

BOOL    WINAPI FileOpenUtil_AreMultipleFilesSelected (OPENFILENAME *pofn);

int     WINAPI FileOpenUtil_GetNumFiles (OPENFILENAME *pofn);

int     WINAPI FileOpenUtil_GetFile (OPENFILENAME *pofn, int nIndex,
   LPTSTR szPathname);


///////////////////////////// End of File /////////////////////////////
```

Listing 7.7 *DFSrcDem.RC*

DropOk.CUR

```
//Microsoft Visual C++ generated resource script.
//
#include "resource.h"

#define APSTUDIO_READONLY_SYMBOLS
/////////////////////////////////////////////////////////////////////////
//
// Generated from the TEXTINCLUDE 2 resource.
//
#define APSTUDIO_HIDDEN_SYMBOLS
#include "windows.h"
#undef APSTUDIO_HIDDEN_SYMBOLS


/////////////////////////////////////////////////////////////////////////
#undef APSTUDIO_READONLY_SYMBOLS


/////////////////////////////////////////////////////////////////////////
//
// Icon
//

IDI_DFSRCDEMO          ICON    DISCARDABLE     "DFSrcDem.ico"
```

499

```
//////////////////////////////////////////////////////////////////////////
//
// Cursor
//

IDC_DROPOK              CURSOR  DISCARDABLE     "DropOK.cur"

//////////////////////////////////////////////////////////////////////////
//
// Dialog
//

IDD_DFSRCDEMO DIALOG DISCARDABLE  -32768, 5, 175, 103
STYLE WS_MINIMIZEBOX | WS_VISIBLE | WS_CAPTION | WS_SYSMENU
CAPTION "Drop File Source Demo"
FONT 8, "MS Sans Serif"
BEGIN
    DEFPUSHBUTTON   "&Select files...",IDC_SELECTFILES,4,4,65,14
    LTEXT           "Files to drop:",IDC_STATIC,108,8,44,8
    LTEXT           "0",IDC_NUMFILES,156,8,16,8
    LISTBOX         IDC_PATHNAMELIST,4,22,168,78,NOT LBS_NOTIFY |
                    LBS_NOINTEGRALHEIGHT | WS_VSCROLL | WS_HSCROLL |
                    WS_TABSTOP
END


#ifdef APSTUDIO_INVOKED
//////////////////////////////////////////////////////////////////////////
//
// TEXTINCLUDE
//

1 TEXTINCLUDE DISCARDABLE
BEGIN
    "resource.h\0"
END

2 TEXTINCLUDE DISCARDABLE
BEGIN
    "#define APSTUDIO_HIDDEN_SYMBOLS\r\n"
    "#include ""windows.h""\r\n"
    "#undef APSTUDIO_HIDDEN_SYMBOLS\r\n"
    "\0"
END

3 TEXTINCLUDE DISCARDABLE
BEGIN
    "\r\n"
    "\0"
END

//////////////////////////////////////////////////////////////////////////
#endif   // APSTUDIO_INVOKED
```

```
#ifndef APSTUDIO_INVOKED
/////////////////////////////////////////////////////////////////////////////
//
// Generated from the TEXTINCLUDE 3 resource.
//


/////////////////////////////////////////////////////////////////////////////
#endif    // not APSTUDIO_INVOKED
```

Listing 7.8 *Resource.H*

```
//{{NO_DEPENDENCIES}}
// Microsoft Visual C++-generated include file
// Used by DFSrcDem.rc
//
#define IDC_DROPMANY              102
#define IDC_DROPONE               103
#define IDC_DROPOK                103
#define IDI_DFSRCDEMO             104
#define IDD_DFSRCDEMO             105
#define IDC_NUMFILES              1001
#define IDC_SELECTFILES           1002
#define IDC_PATHNAMELIST          1003
#define IDC_STATIC                -1

// Next default values for new objects
//
#ifdef APSTUDIO_INVOKED
#ifndef APSTUDIO_READONLY_SYMBOLS
#define _APS_NO_MFC               1
#define _APS_NEXT_RESOURCE_VALUE  106
#define _APS_NEXT_COMMAND_VALUE   40001
#define _APS_NEXT_CONTROL_VALUE   1004
#define _APS_NEXT_SYMED_VALUE     101
#endif
#endif
```

Other Uses for Drag-and-Drop

The drag-and-drop metaphor can be extended to allow users to work more efficiently with the applications you develop. For example, look at how Word for Windows and Visual C++ have changed the way people use text editors by allowing users to select a region of text so that it can be dragged and dropped into a new location in users' documents. Similarly, Excel allows users to select a range of cells in spreadsheets so that they can be moved or copied to other locations. Adding this type of capability is fairly easy given the data structure and functions discussed previously. In addition, all the dragging and dropping takes place inside one application; you do not need to rely on a standard protocol to which other applications must adhere. Because of this, the code could be implemented so as not to break in future versions of Windows. A rough outline of actions to take include:

- Creating your own user-defined message, something like UM_DROPTEXT, instead of WM_DROPFILES.

- Creating your own DFSrc_Create function that has the same parameters as my DFSrc_Create function with any additional information. For example, to move text, you might include a starting address in the file for the text that is to be moved and the number of characters. For a spreadsheet, you might specify a range of cells.

- Processing the WM_LBUTTONDOWN, WM_MOUSEMOVE, and WM_LBUTTONUP messages in any way that is particular to your situation. For example, you could change the cursor to your own desired shape as the user passes over different regions of your application's window.

- Once you receive your own user-defined message indicating that the data have been dropped, performing whatever actions you desire and freeing the memory block.

CHAPTER EIGHT

Processing Keystrokes

In this chapter, we take a close look at how Windows processes keystrokes. At first glance, it would seem that this procedure is simple, but Windows was primarily designed to work well with a mouse, and much of the keyboard support in Windows was added as an afterthought. Unfortunately, the developers of Microsoft Windows were not able to hide a number of ugly keyboard hacks from Windows software developers, like us.

The Keyboard and Scan Codes

Let's begin our discussion by examining the PC keyboard. The keyboard is actually a complex device that contains its very own microprocessor. It has features such as auto-repeat; indicator lights for Caps Lock, Num Lock, and Scroll Lock; function keys; Shift, Alt, and Ctrl keys that modify the next key to be pressed; and duplicate keys that perform the same action. Also, keyboard layouts vary from country to country. In the United States alone, there are 81-key keyboards, 101-key keyboards, QWERTY-style keyboards, and Dvorak keyboards.

Considering all the different types of keyboards and that Windows is device-independent by design, it's apparent that much work had to be done to implement keyboard support.

When you press a key on the keyboard, the microprocessor in the keyboard detects the physical key that has been pressed and generates a hardware interrupt that is handled by the installed keyboard device driver. When generating the hardware interrupt, the keyboard passes a scan code to the system's interrupt service routine. A scan code is an 8-bit binary number that identifies the physical key on the keyboard. The high bit (bit 7) of the scan code is cleared if the key is being pressed and is set if the key is being released.

When manufacturers design keyboards, they determine the scan code value that will be generated by each physical key on the keyboard. For example, a manufacturer might assign the value 0x04 to the 3 key. This means that whenever a user presses the 3 key, the keyboard generates an interrupt and passes a scan code value of 0x04 to the keyboard device driver. Because a scan code identifies only a physical key, the keyboard offers no indication of whether the user attempted to enter a 3 or a pound sign (#).

Scan code values are closely tied to the keyboard hardware, and different keyboards require different device drivers. Fortunately, most keyboard manufacturers do standardize somewhat, and keyboard device drivers tend to be language-specific rather than manufacturer-specific. In other words, you'll need one keyboard driver for a Portuguese keyboard and a different driver for an English keyboard, but you probably won't need a different driver for different English keyboards.

Keyboard Drivers and Virtual-Key Codes

Windows has attempted to abstract all hardware devices for developers. This means that Win32 application writers shouldn't need to worry about scan codes, and we shouldn't ever have to write code that is specific to a particular keyboard. In order to abstract all keyboard devices, Microsoft had to come up with a standard coding method that identifies all keys on a keyboard. This coding method is documented and is what Win32 developers should use. The codes are called virtual-key codes. You can find the virtual-key code table in the Win32 Programmer's Reference and in the **WinUser.H** header file. It is the job of the Windows' keyboard device driver to convert the keyboard's scan code values into virtual-key code values.

Unfortunately, many of the virtual-key codes defined in **WinUser.H** have names that are not obvious. For example, the Alt key is identified by VK_MENU (since pressing and releasing the Alt key activates an application's menu) and the Page Up and Page Down keys are defined as VK_PRIOR and VK_NEXT, respectively. Also, some virtual-key codes do not represent physical keys on a keyboard at all. The virtual-key values VK_LBUTTON and VK_RBUTTON represent whether the left or right mouse button is down. (To add to the confusion, these virtual-key codes really mean the physical left and right mouse button whether or not the user has told Windows to logically swap the mouse buttons.)

From Driver to System Input Queue

After the keyboard driver has converted a keyboard scan code to a virtual-key code, the driver must append the keystroke event to the system's input queue. Both Windows 95 and Windows NT have a single-system input queue that holds keyboard, mouse, and pen messages. A keyboard device driver appends keystroke messages to this queue by calling the keybd_event function (contained in **User32.DLL**):

```
VOID keybd_event(BYTE bVirtualKey, BYTE bScanCode,
   DWORD dwFlags, DWORD dwExtraInfo);
```

bVirtualKey identifies a virtual-key code (determined by the keyboard device driver), bScanCode is the hardware scan code (delivered by the keyboard), dwFlags is a combination of flags as shown in Table 8.1.

Table 8.1 *Flags that can be passed to keybd_event's dwFlags parameter.*

Flag Identifier	Meaning
KEYEVENTF_EXTENDEDKEY	If specified, the scan code is preceded by a prefix byte having the value 0xE0 (224).
KEYEVENTF_KEYUP	If specified, the key is being released. If not specified, the key is being depressed.

The dwExtraInfo parameter specifies some additional device-specific data. These data are rarely used, and zero is usually passed to keybd_event. After a hardware message is retrieved by GetMessage or PeekMessage, a thread can get the value of this extra data by calling the GetMessageExtraInfo function:

```
LONG GetMessageExtraInfo(VOID);
```

Likewise, the mouse driver appends messages to the system's input queue by calling mouse_event:

```
VOID mouse_event(
    DWORD  dwFlags,        // Flags specifying various motion/click variants
    DWORD  dx,             // Horizontal mouse position or position change
    DWORD  dy,             // Vertical mouse position or position change
    DWORD  cButtons,       // Unused, reserved for future use, set to zero
    DWORD  dwExtraInfo     // 32 bits of application-defined information
    );
```

If you want to force a set of keystrokes into the system, the keybd_event function offers a good way of doing this. The Win32 documentation also states that you can copy the contents of the screen or the active window to the Clipboard by simulating the user pressing the Print Screen key as follows:

```
// Capture the full screen to the Clipboard.
keybd_event(VK_SNAPSHOT, 0, 0, 0);   // bScanCode = 0

// Capture the active window to the Clipboard.
keybd_event(VK_SNAPSHOT, 1, 0, 0);   // bScanCode = 1
```

The Key State Arrays

There is a thread, internal to the system, called the Raw Input Thread (RIT). The RIT is sleeping most of the time, waiting for a message to appear in the system's input queue. When keybd_event appends a message, the RIT wakes up, examines the message, updates the system's asynchronous key state array, and appends the proper keystroke message to the thread owning the window that currently has the input focus.

The system's asynchronous key state array is an internal array consisting of 256 entries—one entry for each virtual-key code. As keystroke messages are removed from the system's input queue, the RIT sets or clears bits in the array so that the array always reflects the current state of the keyboard—which keys are down and which keys are up.

A thread can call the GetAsyncKeyState function to determine the current, real-time state of a key on the keyboard:

```
SHORT GetAsyncKeyState(int nVirtKey);
```

This function accepts only one parameter, a virtual-key code, and returns a short integer. If the high-bit of the returned integer is set, the physical key identified by the virtual-key code is currently depressed. If the high-bit is cleared, the physical key is up. The low bit of the return value indicates whether the state of the key has changed since an earlier call to GetAsyncKeyState: 1 if it has changed and 0 if not. There is one important thing to note about the GetAsyncKeyState function. If the calling thread does not own the window that currently has focus, GetAsyncKeyState always returns zero. Microsoft made this adjustment to prevent one thread from seeing which keystroke messages are being processed by another thread's windows.

After the RIT has finished updating the system's asynchronous input queue, the RIT dispatches the keystroke message to a window. The RIT does this by first determining which thread created the window that currently has focus. Then, the RIT appends the keystroke message to this thread's virtualized input queue. Each and every thread has its own virtualized input queue. This queue is just like the system's input queue except that it contains only hardware messages that are destined for a window created by the thread.

In addition to the virtualized input queue, each thread also has its very own synchronous key state array. When a thread calls GetMessage or PeekMessage, these functions check to see if a keystroke message is being removed from the thread's virtualized input queue. If a keystroke message is being removed, these functions update the thread's synchronous key state array before returning the message.

The thread's synchronous key state array, therefore, represents the status of all the keys on the keyboard at the time the most recent message was removed from the thread's virtualized input queue. A thread can access its synchronous key state array using the GetKeyState function:

```
SHORT GetKeyState(int nVirtKey);
```

Like the GetAsyncKeyState function, this function also takes a virtual-key code as its only parameter and also returns a short integer. In fact, the high bit of the integer indicates whether or not the button is down just like the GetAsyncKeyState function. For GetKeyState, however, the low bit of the return value indicates whether or not the key is toggled. This bit is only meaningful when examining the Caps Lock (VK_CAPITAL), Scroll Lock (VK_SCROLL), or Num Lock (VK_NUMLOCK) keys.

Remember that the thread's synchronous key state array indicates the status of keys as the keyboard messages are removed from the thread's virtual input queue. This means that you can tell the state of all the keys on the keyboard at the time a message is processed. In other words, if the user pounds on the keyboard's keys while you are processing a message, your thread's synchronous key state array is not affected.

Here is an example of why you might want to use the GetKeyState function. Say that you have a window procedure that receives a WM_COMMAND message when the user selects a menu item. However, if the Shift key is down when you receive the WM_COM-MAND message, you might want to perform a different action. To pull this off, write your code as follows:

```
void Cls_OnCommand (HWND hwnd, int id, HWND hwndCtl, UINT codeNotify) {

    switch (id) {
        case IDM_MENUITEM:
            if (GetKeyState(VK_SHIFT) & 0x8000) {
                // The Shift key is down.
            } else {
                // The Shift key is up.
            }
            break;
        .
        .
        .
}
```

If I were to use GetAsyncKeyState in the preceding code, the code might not work right. In this case, it is possible that the thread will begin processing the WM_COMMAND message but, before the thread calls GetAsyncKeyState, the user might release the Shift key. GetAsyncKeyState returns the current state of the keyboard and not the state when the last message was retrieved. In the preceding sample code, the wrong code will potentially be executed.

Now that you know when to use GetKeyState, I'll demonstrate a good use for GetAsyncKeyState. Let's say that when the user presses the mouse button, you want to enter a loop that iterates until the mouse button is released.

```
void Cls_OnLButtonDown (HWND hwnd, BOOL fDoubleClick,
   int x, int y, UINT keyFlags) {

   // Determine which mouse button to really check
   int vkMouseBtn = GetSystemMetrics(SM_SWAPBUTTON) ?
      VK_RBUTTON : VK_LBUTTON;

   while (GetAsyncKeyState(vkMouseBtn) & 0x8000) {
      // Do loop processing.
   }
}
```

The WM_LBUTTONDOWN message occurs whenever the primary mouse button is clicked. Usually, this is the left mouse button, but if the user has swapped the mouse buttons via the Mouse Properties dialog box, the message will occur when the right mouse button is clicked instead. As I mentioned, passing a value of VK_LBUTTON to GetAsyncKeyState or GetKeyState checks the state of the physical left mouse button whether or not the user has swapped mouse buttons via the Mouse Properties dialog box. When the preceding routine calls GetAsyncKeyState, it must first determine which mouse button really should be checked. It does this by calling GetSystemMetrics and passing the SM_SWAPBUTTON identifier. GetSystemMetrics returns TRUE if the user had swapped mouse buttons or FALSE if not. This lets vkMouseBtn be set correctly to either VK_LBUTTON or VK_RBUTTON.

After vkMouseBtn is set, the code calls GetAsyncKeyState repeatedly to check whether the user has released the primary mouse button. If I instead call GetKeyState here, my thread will be stuck in an infinite loop! The call to GetKeyState will keep returning whether or not the mouse button was down when the WM_LBUTTONDOWN message was dispatched. Because the primary mouse button is always down when a WM_LBUTTONDOWN message is processed, GetKeyState will always return with the high bit set.

Now, let's look at two more functions that a thread can call to manipulate its synchronous key state array. The first function is called GetKeyboardState:

```
BOOL GetKeyboardState(PBYTE pbKeyState);
```

This function accepts as its only parameter a pointer to an array of 256 bytes. After the call, this array contains a copy of the thread's current synchronous key state array. Like the GetKeyState function, the high bit of each byte in the array indicates whether the key was down at the time the last message was retrieved from the thread's queue, and the low bit indicates whether a toggle key was toggled or not. A thread can use GetKeyboardState to reference the state of several keys. To examine the state of a virtual key, all you need to do is use the virtual-key code as an index into this array. For example, to check if the Spacebar is down, you would do the following:

```
BYTE pbKeyState[256];
BOOL fSpaceIsDown;
GetKeyboardState(pbKeyState);
fSpaceIsDown = (pbKeyState[VK_SPACE] & 0x80) != 0;
```

When a message is being processed, a thread can take a snapshot of the keyboard using GetKeyboardState, save this information in a global or static array, and reference this snapshot of the keyboard while processing future messages. This type of keyboard snapshot is not used frequently, and more often than not, GetKeyboardState is used in conjunction with the SetKeyboardState function:

```
BOOL SetKeyboardState(PBYTE pbKeyState);
```

SetKeyboardState allows a thread to change its synchronous key state array. Its only parameter is the address to a 256-byte array containing the desired state of each virtual key. The following code shows how a thread can make itself think that the Spacebar is down:

```
BYTE pbKeyState[256];
GetKeyboardState(&pbKeyState);
pbKeyState[VK_SPACE] |= 0x80;
SetKeyboardState(&pbKeyState);
```

To change the state of a single key like this, you must call GetKeyboardState first. This call fills the byte array with the current state of all the keys. It is necessary because SetKeyboardState changes all the virtual key entries at once—there is no way to change individual keys.

SetKeyboardState changes the state of all the virtual keys; however, if you change the state of the Caps Lock, Num Lock, or Scroll Lock toggle keys, the LED lights on the user's keyboard will not turn on or off. If you want to toggle the state of one of these keys and affect its associated LED light, you need to use the GetKeyState, keybd_event, and MapVirtualKey (discussed shortly) functions:

```
void ToggleLockKey (BYTE bVirtKey, BOOL fLocked) {

   // NOTE: bVirtKey must be VK_CAPITAL, VK_NUMLOCK, or VK_SCROLL.

   // Get the current state of the toggle key.
   BOOL fKeyLocked = GetKeyState(bVirtKey) & 1;
   if (fKeyLocked == fLocked) {

      // The key is in the requested state; do nothing.
   } else {

      // The key is not in the requested state,
      // toggle it by pressing and releasing the key.
      keybd_event(bVirtKey, MapVirtualKey(bVirtKey, 0), 0, 0);
      keybd_event(bVirtKey, MapVirtualKey(bVirtKey, 0), KEYEVENTF_KEYUP, 0);
   }
}
```

For the bVirtKey parameter, you pass the virtual-key code (VK_CAPITAL for Caps Lock, VK_NUMLOCK for Num Lock, or VK_SCROLL for Scroll Lock) that identifies the toggle key that you wish to ensure is on or off. The fLocked parameter indicates what state you want the key to be in. The function first calls GetKeyboardState to get the current state of the desired key. If bit 0 is on, the key is currently toggled. If the state matches the state requested by the fLocked parameter, nothing is done. However, if the state does not match, keybd_event is called twice: once to simulate pressing the key and a second time to simulate releasing the key. This action, of course, toggles the state of the key.

The Keystroke Messages

As every Win32 developer knows, a thread retrieves WM_(SYS)KEYDOWN and WM_(SYS)KEYUP messages from its virtual input queue by calling GetMessage or PeekMessage. Once the message is retrieved, the application usually calls DispatchMessage to have the message processed by the window with the keyboard input focus. When the window procedure receives WM_(SYS)KEYDOWN or WM_(SYS)KEYUP, the wParam parameter contains the virtual-key code, and the lParam parameter contains a series of flag bits as shown in Table 8.2.

Table 8.2 *Description of flag bits in WM_(SYS)KEY* message's lParam parameter.*

Bits	Meaning
0–15	Specifies the repeat count. The value is the number of times the keystroke is repeated because the user is holding down the key.
16–23	Specifies the scan code. The value depends on the original equipment manufacturer (OEM).
24	Specifies whether the key is an extended key, such as a function key or a key on the numeric keypad. The value is 1 if it is an extended key; otherwise, it is 0.
25–26	Not used.
27–28	Used internally by Windows.
29	Specifies the context code. The value is 1 if the Alt key is held down while the key is pressed; otherwise, the value is 0.
30	Specifies the previous key state. The value is 1 if the key is down before the message is sent, or it is 0 if the key is up.
31	Specifies the key-transition state. The value is 1 if the key is being released, or it is 0 if the key is being pressed.

To make working with the high word of the lParam parameter easier, the **WinUser.H** header files contain a number of identifiers as shown in Table 8.3.

Table 8.3 *Identifiers used with keyboard message's flags.*

Identifier	Value
KF_EXTENDED	0x0100
KF_DLGMODE	0x0800
KF_MENUMODE	0x1000
KF_ALTDOWN	0x2000
KF_REPEAT	0x4000
KF_UP	0x8000

When you use these identifiers, make sure that you are always ANDing them with the HIWORD of the lParam as follows:

```
void Cls_OnKey (HWND hwnd, UINT vk, BOOL fDown, int cRepeat, UINT flags) {

    BOOL fIsExtendedKey;

    // The following line of code is correct.
    fIsExtendedKey = HIWORD(lParam) & KF_EXTENDED;

    // The following line of code is incorrect.
    fIsExtendedKey = lParam & KF_EXTENDED;
    .
    .
    .
}
```

Because the preceding identifiers are defined in **WinUser.H**, Microsoft has half-heartedly documented the two internal bits, bits 27 and 28. These bits are associated with the KF_DLGMODE and KF_MENUMODE identifiers, respectively. My experiments have shown that these bits tell Windows what mode it is in as keystrokes are being processed. For example, if a menu is pulled down, the KF_MENUMODE bit will be set to 1.

Because all these key up/down messages give only the virtual-key code in the wParam, it is difficult for an application to work with keystrokes. Suppose that you were writing a window procedure for a window that behaves like an edit control. If you added characters to a buffer every time you received a WM_KEYDOWN message, you would have to check the status of the Shift, Ctrl, Alt, Caps Lock, and Num Lock keys to convert the virtual-key code to an actual character. If the user pressed the A key, the WM_KEYDOWN message will have a VK_A in the wParam parameter. The application doesn't know at this point if the user wants an uppercase *A*, lowercase *a*, or maybe a Ctrl+A. Because this is a very difficult way for window procedures to deal with keys, a call to the TranslateMessage function is necessary.

TranslateMessage is usually called in a thread's message loop after the call to GetMessage or PeekMessage and before the call to DispatchMessage. TranslateMessage examines the type of message that was just retrieved; if the message is not keyboard-related, the function simply returns FALSE. If the message is keyboard-related, Translate-Message examines the thread's synchronous key state array and converts the virtual-key code to a character. It then places a WM_CHAR message (where the wParam parameter contains the translated character) in the thread's message queue (not the thread's virtualized input queue). This guarantees that the WM_CHAR message will be retrieved the next time the thread calls GetMessage or PeekMessage.

So, a window procedure should process the WM_CHAR message when looking for characters instead of processing the WM_KEY-DOWN message. For an edit-like window class, the window procedure inserts the WM_CHAR's character from wParam into its buffer. However, there are many other keys such as the scroll keys (Left Arrow, Right Arrow, Up Arrow, Down Arrow, Page Up, Page Down, and so on) that do not translate into characters because Translate-Message does not generate WM_CHAR messages for these virtual-key codes. In order to process these keys, a window procedure must examine the virtual-key code associated with each WM_KEYDOWN message. For this reason, window procedures that interact heavily with the keyboard require that both the WM_KEYDOWN and WM_CHAR messages be processed.

Internally, TranslateMessage uses the ToAscii[1] function to convert a virtual-key code to a character.[2]

```
int ToAscii(UINT uVirtKey, UINT uScanCode, PBYTE pbKeyState,
    PWORD pwTransKey, UINT fuState);
```

As you can see, the first two parameters are the virtual-key code (wParam) and the scan code (bits 16–23 of lParam) for the keyboard message. The third parameter, pbKeyState, is the address of a 256-byte array containing the state of the keyboard that should be used when this function attempts the conversion. TranslateMessage passes the address of the thread's synchronous key state array for this parameter. The fourth parameter, pwTransKey, is a pointer to a WORD that will receive the translated character or characters. If more than one character is generated, the first is usually a diacritical mark like an accent or

---

[1]ToAscii converts a virtual-key code to its character equivalent (if one exists). The resulting character may or may not be an ASCII character.

[2]There is also a ToUnicode function that works identically to the ToAscii function except that it translates the virtual-key code into a Unicode character. Unfortunately, Windows 95 does not fully implement this function; it is fully implemented on Windows NT.

umlaut, which causes TranslateMessage to place WM_(SYS)DEAD-CHAR messages in the thread's message queue.[3] Any additional characters are placed in the message queue as WM_(SYS)CHAR messages. The last parameter, fuState, must be a 1 if a menu is active or a 0 otherwise. Table 8.4 shows the possible return values from ToAscii.

Table 8.4 *Value that ToAscii can return.*

Value	Meaning
Negative	The key is a dead key.
0	The specified virtual key has no translation for the current state of the keyboard.
1	One character was copied to the buffer.
2	Two characters were copied to the buffer. This is usually an accent and a dead key character, when the dead key cannot be translated otherwise.

As you can see, a lot of conversions take place in Windows. Most of these conversions occur within various Win32 functions while your window procedure just waits to receive the appropriate message. If you want to do some manual conversions, there are some additional functions that you will find helpful.

The VkKeyScan function accepts a character as its only parameter and returns the equivalent virtual-key code and shift state.

```
short VkKeyScan(TCHAR uChar);
```

---

[3]Some characters are not completely formed until the user presses two keys on the keyboard. For example, a user generates the umlaut-O character (Ö) by first pressing the key for an umlaut (double-dot) and then pressing the O key. When the user presses the first key, the system generates a WM_DEADCHAR message. Then, when the user presses the O key, the system generates a WM_CHAR message where the wParam parameter indicates the full umlaut-O character. Because the WM_CHAR message contains the full character, most window procedures ignore the WM_DEADCHAR message. However, a text editor application might offer feedback to the user by processing the WM_DEADCHAR message in order to display an umlaut on the screen without moving the caret position.

If this function is unable to translate the specified character, the function returns –1; otherwise, the low byte contains the virtual-key code, and the high byte contains the shift state flags. Table 8.5 shows the possible shift state bit flags.

Table 8.5 *Shift state flags returned by VkKeyScan.*

Value	Meaning
1	The Shift key is required.
2	The Ctrl key is required.
4	The Alt key is required.

Another function, MapVirtualKey, can be used for several different types of conversions:

```
UINT MapVirtualKey(UINT uKeyCode, UINT fuMapType);
```

The type of conversion that this function performs is determined by the second parameter, fuMapType, which can be any value shown in the Table 8.6.

Table 8.6 *Methods of calling the MapVirtualKey function.*

fuMapType	uKeyCode	Return value
0	Virtual-key code	Scan code
1	Scan code	Virtual-key code
2	Virtual-key code	Unshifted character
3	Scan code	Virtual-key code*

*Passing an fuMapType of 3 and an fuMapType of 1 is almost identical. The difference is that a fuMapType of 3 causes MapVirtualKey to attempt to distinguish between left- and right-shift keys while a fuMapType of 1 does not.

The System Key Difference

So far I have conveniently avoided mentioning the differences between system keys and normal keys. Actually, there is no difference at all as far as the preceding discussion goes. As far as Windows is concerned, a system key/character is a key/character that is generated while an Alt key is depressed. Well, it is almost this simple. You see, if the Ctrl key is down in addition to the Alt key, the key/character is not considered to be a system key. The sequence of keystrokes shown in Table 8.7 gives some example of what constitutes a system key.

Table 8.7 *Key sequences and WM_SYSKEY* messages.*

Entry	Pressed/Released	Key	Message generated
1	Pressed	Alt	WM_SYSKEYDOWN
2	Released	Alt	WM_SYSKEYUP
3	Pressed	Alt	WM_SYSKEYDOWN
4	Pressed	Ctrl	WM_KEYDOWN
5	Pressed	A	WM_KEYDOWN
6	Released	A	WM_KEYUP
7	Released	Ctrl	WM_KEYUP
8	Pressed	A	WM_SYSKEYDOWN
9	Released	A	WM_SYSKEYUP
10	Pressed	A	WM_SYSKEYDOWN
11	Pressed	Ctrl	WM_KEYDOWN
12	Released	A	WM_KEYUP
13	Released	Ctrl	WM_KEYUP
14	Released	Alt	WM_KEYUP

Entries 1 and 2 in Table 8.7 show what happens when the Alt key is pressed and released. In this case, Windows generates system key messages where the wParam parameter contains VK_MENU.

In entries 3–5, notice that pressing the Alt key generates a WM_SYSKEYDOWN but, as soon as the Ctrl key is pressed, Windows generates WM_KEYDOWN messages (even though the Alt key is not released).

Entries 6 and 7 simply show the result of releasing the A and Ctrl keys—nothing too spectacular here. In entries 8 and 9, the A key is pressed and released, causing system key messages to appear.

Now let's look at entries 10–13. The important thing to note in these entries is that key messages are not necessarily symmetric. In other words, just because Windows sends a WM_SYSKEYDOWN doesn't mean that you'll get a matching WM_SYSKEYUP in the future.

Entry 14 is rather curious. At this point, no other keys are down except for the Alt key, yet when it is released, Windows generates a WM_KEYUP message instead of a WM_SYSKEYUP message. This entry also contradicts what happened in Entry 2 of Table 8.7. Windows is definitely doing something strange here! The secret is, if any other keyboard event occurs before the release of the Alt key, Windows generates a WM_KEYUP message when the Alt key is released instead of the expected WM_SYSKEYUP message.

Simulating Keystrokes to Other Application Windows

Many applications want to be able to force keystrokes into other application's windows. For example, many years ago I purchased a thesaurus program for Windows. This application was designed to work seamlessly with any word processor. When the application is invoked, it installs a keyboard hook (see Chapter 6 for more information about hooks). To find a synonym, all I have to do is highlight a word in my text, and press Ctrl+Alt+T. The thesaurus program's keyboard hook watches for this key sequence and simulates pressing an Alt+E, C sequence of keystrokes to the application having the focus (the word processor). This sequence of keys causes the word processor to open its Edit menu and select the Copy menu option.

When this sequence completes, the thesaurus program brings itself to the foreground and looks up the word on the Clipboard. At this point, I can choose a synonym and press a button marked Replace. The thesaurus program now copies the new word to the Clipboard, reactivates the word processor, and simulates an Alt+E, P key sequence. This action simulates the Edit Paste option in the word processor, causing the old word (which is still highlighted) to be replaced.

Another use for simulating keystrokes might be to create a script for application testing. One traditional method of application testing requires that people pound away at the keys all day trying to make the program crash. It's best to perform regression testing to make sure that the programmers haven't broken something that was once working correctly. Regression testing usually involves retyping the same thing over and over again during the development cycle of the application. Keystroke simulation can both reduce the effort and make it more accurate.

Another use for keystroke simulation could be a phrase library. A phrase library is a kind of macro playback facility. Say that you're writing an application where you want to enable the user to play back a sequence of keystrokes. For example, I might want to redefine the tilde (~) key so that every time I press it, the following key sequence is generated: Ctrl+Esc, R, Calc, Enter. This sequence causes the Taskbar's Start menu to pop open (Ctrl+Esc), selects the Run menu option (R), and executes the Calc application (Calc, Enter).

Why Sending or Posting Keyboard Messages Is a Bad Idea

When I first set out to write this application, I immediately thought of simulating keystrokes by posting WM_CHAR messages. First, you would retrieve the handle to the window to which you want to start simulating keystrokes. Depending on the application, you might already know the handle, or you might call FindWindow or possibly WindowFromPoint—it doesn't matter what method you use. Then, you would post this window a WM_CHAR message using PostMessage. Of course, the wParam and lParam parameters would have to be prepared correctly for the key you wish to simulate.

Right off the bat there are problems. What if you want to send Alt+F to open the application's File menu? There is no way of sending an Alt key using a WM_CHAR message because Alt is not a character. The solution to this problem is to post WM_SYSKEYDOWN messages to the window instead of WM_CHAR messages. But, if you post WM_KEYDOWN messages, you must also post WM_KEYUP messages. This requires that the program be a little smarter and do more work. So, posting the Alt+F sequence becomes something like this:

```
PostMessage(hwnd, WM_SYSKEYDOWN, VK_MENU, ...);
PostMessage(hwnd, WM_SYSKEYDOWN, VK_F, ...);
```

519

```
PostMessage(hwnd, WM_SYSKEYUP,   VK_F, ...);
PostMessage(hwnd, WM_KEYUP,      VK_MENU, ...);
```

Note the use of WM_SYSKEYDOWN/UP. You might wonder why PostMessage is used instead of SendMessage. The reason is that posted messages are retrieved from the thread's message queue by a call to GetMessage. If a thread is interested in characters instead of processing virtual-key codes, the thread calls TranslateMessage after GetMessage returns. If SendMessage is used instead of PostMessage, the messages go directly to the window procedure and TranslateMessage never gets called.

Here are a couple of more problems. The first problem with PostMessage is that synchronization can't be handled correctly. Say that you simulate a Tab character to a control in a dialog box, causing the keyboard focus to change to another child control window. In this case, the next call to PostMessage should use a different window handle as its first parameter. You might think you could correct this problem by calling GetFocus before each call to PostMessage and using the return value as the window handle to post the next keyboard message to.

But this solution won't work because PostMessage doesn't cause the keystroke message to be sent and processed immediately. The messages can be processed only when control is yielded, so you must yield control to other applications between posting each individual message. Calling SendMessage would be useful if not for the fact that TranslateMessage won't get called. The PostMessage technique also doesn't work well because the GetFocus function returns only the handle of a window created by the calling thread. If a window created by another thread has focus, GetFocus always returns NULL. You can fix this problem by attaching the two threads' local input states together using the AttachThreadInput function:

```
BOOL AttachThreadInput(DWORD idAttach, DWORD idAttachTo, BOOL fAttach);
```

Another problem with PostMessage and SendMessage is that neither of these functions places a keystroke message in the thread's virtualized input queue. As mentioned, when a thread removes a message from the thread's virtualized input queue, Windows updates the thread's synchronous key state array. Now, if a window procedure is processing a posted (or sent) keystroke message and calls GetKeyState, it will get back the wrong information. If the window procedure uses this information to determine the action it should take while processing the keystroke message, it'll execute the wrong operation.

As you can see, there is no good way to simulate keystrokes using either PostMessage or SendMessage. The only time that either of these methods works is if you are intimately familiar with the behavior of the window you are simulating keystrokes to. I decided to find a different method.

What About Calling keybd_event?

Having discarded the idea of using PostMessage or SendMessage, I was led to the idea of calling the keybd_event function to simulate keystrokes. Actually I implemented a function that used keybd_event and it worked well! Using keybd_event, we don't have to determine which keys are system keys and which keys are regular keys. Also, the system determines how to set up the keystroke message's lParam parameters bit flags, and the system's asynchronous key state array and each thread's synchronous key state array are updated correctly!

Alas, there are two problems with using the keybd_event function that really bothered me. First, if a long sequence of keys is fed into the system's input queue, it is possible for the user to type keys on the keyboard, and these keys would be interspersed into the simulated-key stream. The behavior of the window receiving the keystroke messages is unpredictable.

The second thing that I didn't like about using keybd_event was that there was no way to tell when all the simulated keystrokes had been processed. For example, the thesaurus application that I talked about in the beginning of this section forces an Alt+E, C sequence to tell the word processor to copy the highlighted word to the Clipboard. After the key sequence executes, the thesaurus application knows that the data is on the Clipboard and that it can open the Clipboard and retrieve the selected word. If the thesaurus application forced the keystrokes using keybd_event, it would not know when those keystrokes were processed, and, therefore, it could not be certain when it should open the Clipboard and retrieve its contents.

Given the shortcomings of using keybd_event, I was forced to find an alternate approach.

Using Ye Olde Journal Playback Hook

Finally, I settled on using a journal playback hook to simulate keystrokes. Chapter 6 discusses the journal playback hook in great detail, so I will not go into a lot of detail here. Installing a journal playback hook causes the system to disable all keyboard and mouse hardware input. In fact, the mouse cursor's location is frozen on the screen and only moves if the playback hook plays back a mouse move message or if the journal playback hook is uninstalled.

When the journal playback hook is installed, the system calls the hook's filter function in order to get the next hardware event to be dispatched to the various windows in the system. In order to simulate keystrokes, my journal playback filter function manufactures WM_(SYS)KEYDOWN/UP messages each time it is called. After all the keys in the desired sequence are played back, the hook is uninstalled.

The two problems mentioned in the previous section are solved when using a journal playback hook. First, because a journal playback hook disables the hardware input, the problem of the user interspersing hardware messages with the simulated key sequence is solved. Second, because installing a journal playback hook causes the system to attach the virtualized input queues of all threads in the system together, the hook filter function is called after each keystroke message is completely processed. This means that we can easily determine the point in which a whole sequence of keystrokes has been processed.

It is obvious that using a journal playback hook is the best technique to use for simulating keystrokes. It guarantees that both the asynchronous and synchronous key state arrays are updated correctly and that synchronization of window focus is maintained. The bad news is that the journal playback solution requires a lot of coding. The good news is that I have done it all for you!

The SKDemo Application

The SKDemo application (**SKDemo.EXE**), shown in Listings 8.1-8.5 (starting on page 525) demonstrates how to force keystrokes into other applications. When you invoke the application, the dialog box in Figure 8.1 appears.

The Windows combobox at the top contains the list of top-level windows in the system. You can refresh the contents of this combobox at any time by pressing the Refresh button. The Key String combobox contains a set of predefined test strings that you can send to various windows. In addition, you can edit the text in this combobox to create your own test strings.

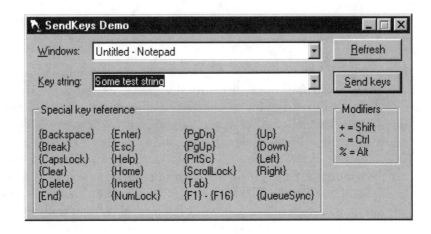

Figure 8.1 *The Send Keys demo.*

When you press the Send Keys button the following code, contained in **SKDemo.C**, executes:

```
void SKDemo_OnCommand (HWND hwnd, int id, HWND hwndCtl, UINT codeNotify) {

    TCHAR szBuf[MAXKEYSTRBUFFERSIZE];
    SKERR SKErr;
    HWND hwndCB, hwndT;
    int nIndex;

    switch (id) {
        .
        .
        .
        case IDC_SENDKEYS:
            hwndCB = GetDlgItem(hwnd, IDC_WINDOWS);
            nIndex = ComboBox_GetCurSel(hwndCB);
            hwndT = (HWND) ComboBox_GetItemData(hwndCB, nIndex);
            if (!IsWindow(hwndT)) {
                adgMB(__TEXT("Window no longer exists."));
            } else {
```

```
            Edit_GetText(GetDlgItem(hwnd, IDC_KEYSTRING),
               szBuf, adgARRAY_SIZE(szBuf));
            if ((SKErr = SendKeys(hwnd, szBuf)) != SKERR_NOERROR) {
               adgMB(g_szSKErrors[SKErr]);
            } else
               SetForegroundWindow(hwndT);
         }
         break;
         .
         .
         .
      }
   }
```

First, the handle to the window selected in the Windows combobox is retrieved and tested to ensure that it still exists. Then, the string of keys in the Key String combobox is retrieved and the SendKeys function is called passing the handle of the SKDemo window and the string of keys. If SendKeys returns anything but SKERR_NO-ERROR, an error occurred, and the user is notified with a message box indicating the type of error. If SendKeys parsed the string successfully, then the playback hook has also been installed, and the hook will start playing back the string of keys when our thread returns back to its message loop.

Just before completing the processing of the WM_COMMAND message, the preceding code calls SetForegroundWindow to activate the desired window. It is important that the SetForegroundWindow be called after the hook is installed. The reason for this is that activating a window of another thread is an asynchronous event. If we were to call SetForegroundWindow before installing the hook, we would not be guaranteed that the desired window is actually ready to receive keystrokes when the playback hook gets called. However, after the hook is installed, all the thread's virtualized input queues and local input state variables are shared. If we call SetForegroundWindow at this time, we know that the desired window is in the foreground by the time the function returns.

While keys are being played back, the user can cancel the journal playback hook by pressing Ctrl+Esc. If the user does this, the system notifies SKDemo by posting a WM_CANCELJOURNAL message to the thread's message queue. When SKDemo's message loop receives this message, it displays the dialog box shown in Figure 8.2. Table 8.8 describes the files used to create this application.

Figure 8.2 *Cancelling the journal playback hook.*

Table 8.8 *Files used to build the SKDemo application.*

File	Description
SKDemo.C	Contains WinMain and the main window's dialog box and message cracker functions.
SendKeys.C	Contains a library of functions that make it much easier to play back keystrokes. You can use this file in your own applications.
SendKeys.H	Contains prototypes for the functions contained in the **SendKeys.C** file. Any source file that uses the library of functions in **SendKeys.C** must include this file.
SKDemo.RC	Contains dialog-box template for main application window and its icons.
Resource.H	Contains ID for all resources in the RC file.
SKDemo.ICO	Contains the icon for the main window.
SKDemo.mak	Visual C++ project makefile.

Listing 8.1 *SKDemo.C*

SKDemo.ICO

```
/******************************************************************************
Module name: SKDemo.c
Written by: Jeffrey Richter
Notices: Copyright (c) 1995 Jeffrey Richter
Purpose: Demonstrates using a dialog box for an application's main window
******************************************************************************/


#include "..\Win95ADG.h"        /* See Appendix A for details. */
#include <windows.h>
#include <windowsx.h>
#pragma warning(disable: 4001)   /* Single-line comment */
```

```
#include "SendKeys.h"
#include "resource.h"


/////////////////////////////////////////////////////////////////////////


#define MAXKEYSTRBUFFERSIZE    1024


/////////////////////////////////////////////////////////////////////////


BOOL SKDemo_OnInitDialog (HWND hwnd, HWND hwndFocus, LPARAM lParam) {

   int x;
   HWND hwndCB;
   TCHAR *szKeyStrings[] = {
      __TEXT("Some test string"),
      __TEXT("%fonsetup.txt{Enter}"),
      __TEXT("^{ESC}"),
      __TEXT("Notify when playback complete{QueueSync}"),
      __TEXT("{F1}"),
      __TEXT("!@#$&*<>?:"),
      __TEXT("z{Left}{Del}ABCD"),
      __TEXT("xyz{Home}+{End}{Del}ABCD"),
      __TEXT("{CAPSLOCK}abc{CAPSLOCK}abc"),
      __TEXT("%"),
      __TEXT("%+{TAB}"),
      __TEXT("{{}Braces{}}"),
      __TEXT("%F"),
      __TEXT("{x 10}"),
      __TEXT("{H 20}"),
      __TEXT("{LeFt 5}"),
      __TEXT("{%}{+}+{^}{D}"),
      __TEXT("Error test: Missing close brace{ENTER"),
      __TEXT("Error test: Invalid key {BOBO}"),
      __TEXT("Error test: Missing close parenthesis+(jeff"),
      __TEXT("Error test: Invalid count {z z}"),
      __TEXT("Error test: String too long{J 3000}")
   };

   // Load the key strings combobox with a set of default string.
   hwndCB = GetDlgItem(hwnd, IDC_KEYSTRING);
   ComboBox_LimitText(hwndCB, MAXKEYSTRBUFFERSIZE);
   for (x = 0; x < adgARRAY_SIZE(szKeyStrings); x++)
      ComboBox_AddString(hwndCB, szKeyStrings[x]);
   ComboBox_SetCurSel(hwndCB, 0);

   // Force the initial loading of the window caption combobox.
   FORWARD_WM_COMMAND(hwnd, IDC_WNDREFRESH,
      GetDlgItem(hwnd, IDC_WNDREFRESH), BN_CLICKED, PostMessage);

   adgSETDLGICONS(hwnd, IDI_SKDEMO, IDI_SKDEMO);
   return(TRUE);                     // Accepts default focus window.
```

```
}

///////////////////////////////////////////////////////////////////////////

static const TCHAR *g_szSKErrors[] = {
   __TEXT("No error"),
   __TEXT("Missing close brace"),
   __TEXT("Invalid key"),
   __TEXT("Missing close parenthesis"),
   __TEXT("Invalid count"),
   __TEXT("String too long"),
   __TEXT("Can't install hook")
};

///////////////////////////////////////////////////////////////////////////

void SKDemo_OnCommand (HWND hwnd, int id, HWND hwndCtl, UINT codeNotify) {

   TCHAR szBuf[MAXKEYSTRBUFFERSIZE];
   SKERR SKErr;
   HWND hwndCB, hwndT;
   int nIndex;

   switch (id) {
      case IDC_WNDREFRESH:
         hwndCB = GetDlgItem(hwnd, IDC_WINDOWS);
         ComboBox_ResetContent(hwndCB);

         for (hwndT = GetFirstChild(GetDesktopWindow());
               IsWindow(hwndT); hwndT = GetNextSibling(hwndT)) {

            if (IsWindowVisible(hwndT)) {
               GetWindowText(hwndT, szBuf, adgARRAY_SIZE(szBuf));
               if (szBuf[0] != 0) {
                  nIndex = ComboBox_AddString(hwndCB, szBuf);
                  ComboBox_SetItemData(hwndCB, nIndex, hwndT);
               }
            }
         }
         ComboBox_SetCurSel(hwndCB, 0);
         break;

      case IDC_SENDKEYS:
         hwndCB = GetDlgItem(hwnd, IDC_WINDOWS);
         nIndex = ComboBox_GetCurSel(hwndCB);
         hwndT = (HWND) ComboBox_GetItemData(hwndCB, nIndex);
         if (!IsWindow(hwndT)) {
            adgMB(__TEXT("Window no longer exists."));
         } else {
            Edit_GetText(GetDlgItem(hwnd, IDC_KEYSTRING),
               szBuf, adgARRAY_SIZE(szBuf));
```

527

```
            if ((SKErr = SendKeys(hwnd, szBuf)) != SKERR_NOERROR) {
                adgMB(g_szSKErrors[SKErr]);
            } else
                SetForegroundWindow(hwndT);
        }
        break;

    case IDCANCEL:                  // Allows dialog box to close.
        PostQuitMessage(0);
        break;
    }
}


/////////////////////////////////////////////////////////////////////////////


void SKDemo_OnQueueSync (HWND hwnd) {

    adgMB(__TEXT("Got WM_QUEUESYNC message!"));
}


/////////////////////////////////////////////////////////////////////////////


BOOL WINAPI SKDemo_DlgProc (HWND hwnd, UINT uMsg,
    WPARAM wParam, LPARAM lParam) {

    switch (uMsg) {

        // Standard Window's messages
        adgHANDLE_DLGMSG(hwnd, WM_INITDIALOG, SKDemo_OnInitDialog);
        adgHANDLE_DLGMSG(hwnd, WM_COMMAND,    SKDemo_OnCommand);
        adgHANDLE_DLGMSG(hwnd, WM_QUEUESYNC,  SKDemo_OnQueueSync);
    }
    return(FALSE);                  // We didn't process the message.
}


/////////////////////////////////////////////////////////////////////////////


int WINAPI WinMain (HINSTANCE hinstExe, HINSTANCE hinstPrev,
    LPSTR lpszCmdLine, int nCmdShow) {

    MSG msg;
    HWND hwnd;

    adgWARNIFUNICODEUNDERWIN95();

    // Create a modeless dialog box instead of a modal dialog box because we
    // need to have more control over the message loop processing.
    hwnd = CreateDialog(hinstExe, MAKEINTRESOURCE(IDD_SKDEMO), NULL,
        SKDemo_DlgProc);
    adgASSERT(IsWindow(hwnd));
```

```
   // Continue to loop until a WM_QUIT message comes out of the queue.
   while (GetMessage(&msg, NULL, 0, 0)) {

      // A user can cancel a journal playback hook by pressing Ctrl+Esc. When
      // this happens, the operating system unhooks the journal playback hook
      // we have installed and notifies our thread by posting it a
      // WM_CANCELJOURNAL message.
      if (msg.message == WM_CANCELJOURNAL)
         adgMB(__TEXT("Sendkeys canceled by user"));

      // Call IsDialogMessage so that the keyboard can be used to control
      // focus in the dialog box.
      if (!IsDialogMessage(hwnd, &msg)) {
         TranslateMessage(&msg);
         DispatchMessage(&msg);
      }
   }

   // The application is terminating; destroy the modeless dialog box.
   DestroyWindow(hwnd);
   return(0);
}


//////////////////////////////// End of File //////////////////////////////////
```

Listing 8.2 *SendKeys.C*

```
/******************************************************************************
Module name: SendKeys.c
Written by: Jeffrey Richter
Notices: Copyright (c) 1995 Jeffrey Richter
Purpose: Functions to simulate keystrokes to Windows applications
******************************************************************************/


#include "..\Win95ADG.h"        /* See Appendix A for details. */
#include <windows.h>
#include <windowsx.h>
#pragma warning(disable: 4001)   /* Single-line comment */
#include <tchar.h>
#include <stdio.h>
#include "SendKeys.h"


//////////////////////////////////////////////////////////////////////////////


static struct {
   SHORT   asVirtKeys[1024];      // Virtual-key codes for playback
```

```
    int     nVirtKeyNum;            // Index into asVirtKeys
    int     nMaxVirtKeys;           // Max entries in asVirtKeys
    LPCTSTR pszKeys;                // Pointer to next character in input string
    BOOL    fNoTokensRetrievedYet;  // Flag that indicates playback beginning
    HHOOK   hhook;                  // Hook handle of playback hook
    HWND    hwndQueueSyncTarget;    // Window to receive WM_QUEUESYNC messages
} g_SKD = { { 0 }, 0, 0, NULL, TRUE, NULL, NULL };


//////////////////////////////////////////////////////////////////////////////


// We are creating a virtual key that represents the playback of a
// WM_QUEUESYNC message. We chose -1 as the value for this virtual key because
// Windows virtual keys range from 0 to 255.
#define VK_QUEUESYNC ((SHORT) -1)


// The table of special key codes
typedef struct {
    SHORT sVirtKey;
    LPCTSTR szKeyName;
} SPECIALKEY;


static const SPECIALKEY g_SpecialKeys[] = {
    { VK_QUEUESYNC, __TEXT("QUEUESYNC")  },
    { VK_CAPITAL,   __TEXT("CAPSLOCK")   },
    { VK_NUMLOCK,   __TEXT("NUMLOCK")    },
    { VK_SCROLL,    __TEXT("SCROLLOCK")  },
    { VK_ESCAPE,    __TEXT("ESCAPE")     },
    { VK_ESCAPE,    __TEXT("ESC")        },
    { VK_RETURN,    __TEXT("ENTER")      },
    { VK_HELP,      __TEXT("HELP")       },
    { VK_SNAPSHOT,  __TEXT("PRTSC")      },
    { VK_TAB,       __TEXT("TAB")        },
    { VK_CONTROL,   __TEXT("BREAK")      },
    { VK_CLEAR,     __TEXT("CLEAR")      },
    { VK_BACK,      __TEXT("BACKSPACE")  },
    { VK_BACK,      __TEXT("BS")         },
    { VK_BACK,      __TEXT("BKSP")       },
    { VK_DELETE,    __TEXT("DELETE")     },
    { VK_DELETE,    __TEXT("DEL")        },
    { VK_INSERT,    __TEXT("INSERT")     },
    { VK_LEFT,      __TEXT("LEFT")       },
    { VK_RIGHT,     __TEXT("RIGHT")      },
    { VK_UP,        __TEXT("UP")         },
    { VK_DOWN,      __TEXT("DOWN")       },
    { VK_PRIOR,     __TEXT("PGUP")       },
    { VK_NEXT,      __TEXT("PGDN")       },
    { VK_HOME,      __TEXT("HOME")       },
    { VK_END,       __TEXT("END")        },
    { VK_F1,        __TEXT("F1")         },
    { VK_F2,        __TEXT("F2")         },
    { VK_F3,        __TEXT("F3")         },
    { VK_F4,        __TEXT("F4")         },
```

```
{ VK_F5,        __TEXT("F5")        },
{ VK_F6,        __TEXT("F6")        },
{ VK_F7,        __TEXT("F7")        },
{ VK_F8,        __TEXT("F8")        },
{ VK_F9,        __TEXT("F9")        },
{ VK_F10,       __TEXT("F10")       },
{ VK_F11,       __TEXT("F11")       },
{ VK_F12,       __TEXT("F12")       },
{ VK_F13,       __TEXT("F13")       },
{ VK_F14,       __TEXT("F14")       },
{ VK_F15,       __TEXT("F15")       },
{ VK_F16,       __TEXT("F16")       },
{ 0,            NULL                }
};


///////////////////////////////////////////////////////////////////////////


// Convert a special key string to its equivalent virtual-key code.
static SHORT SendKeys_SpecialKeyToVirtKey (LPCTSTR pszSpecialKey) {

   const SPECIALKEY* psk = g_SpecialKeys;
   SHORT sVirtKey;                  // Assumes that pszSpecialKey not found.

   // Scan the array and compare each of the possible strings.
   while (((sVirtKey = psk->sVirtKey) != 0) &&
          (_tcsicmp(pszSpecialKey, psk->szKeyName) != 0))
      psk++;

   if ((sVirtKey == 0) && (_tcslen(pszSpecialKey) == 1)) {

      // The special key was not found in the list.
      // If the special key is a single character, convert that character to
      // its virtual-key code equivalent.
      // Note 1: This must come after the preceding loop so that special single
      //         characters are checked first (i.e.-"~" (tilde)).
      // Note 2: This check is necessary for other special single characters
      //         (i.e.-"+^%{}()).
      sVirtKey = VkKeyScan(*pszSpecialKey);
   }

   return(sVirtKey);
}


///////////////////////////////////////////////////////////////////////////


#define APPENDVIRTKEY(sVirtKey) \
   {                                                                        \
      if (g_SKD.nMaxVirtKeys == adgARRAY_SIZE(g_SKD.asVirtKeys)) { \
         SKErr = SKERR_STRINGTOOLONG;                                       \
         break;                                                            \
      } else                                                               \
```

```
                g_SKD.asVirtKeys[g_SKD.nMaxVirtKeys++] = sVirtKey;          \
    }


// Function to preprocess the next token in the input string.
static SKERR SendKeys_PreprocessKeys (void) {

    TCHAR cChar;                  // Current character being processed
    TCHAR szSpecialKey[16];       // Buffer big enough for a special key name
    LPCTSTR pEndOfToken;          // Pointer to end of current token
    SHORT sVirtKey = 0;           // Virtual key equivalent of token
    int nCount = 1;               // Number of times to play back virtual key
    SKERR SKErr = SKERR_NOERROR;  // Current error state

    // Get the next character from the input string.
    switch (cChar = *g_SKD.pszKeys++) {

        case 0:                   // Reached the end of the input string
            g_SKD.pszKeys--;      // Point back to the zero-byte
            break;

        case __TEXT('('):         // Beginning of subgroup

            // While not at the end of the input string and not at a close paren
            while ((*g_SKD.pszKeys != 0) && (*g_SKD.pszKeys != __TEXT(')'))) {

                // Add the next character to the array.
                SKErr = SendKeys_PreprocessKeys();
                if (SKErr != SKERR_NOERROR)
                    break;
            }

            // If terminating because of end of string and not because of right
            // paren, there is an error.
            if (*g_SKD.pszKeys == 0)
                SKErr = SKERR_MISSINGCLOSEPAREN;
            else
                g_SKD.pszKeys++;        // Skips past the close paren.
            break;

        case __TEXT('~'):         // Presses the Enter key.
            APPENDVIRTKEY(VK_RETURN); // Presses the Enter key.
            break;

        case __TEXT('+'):         // Presses the Shift key.
        case __TEXT('^'):         // Presses the Control key.
        case __TEXT('%'):         // Presses the Alt key.

            cChar = (TCHAR) ((cChar == __TEXT('+')) ? VK_SHIFT :
                        ((cChar == __TEXT('^')) ? VK_CONTROL : VK_MENU));
            APPENDVIRTKEY(cChar);     // Presses the Shift/Control/Alt keys.

            // Call preprocess keys recursively to get the keys to which we
            // are applying the modifiers here.
            if ((SKErr = SendKeys_PreprocessKeys()) != SKERR_NOERROR)
```

```
         break;

      APPENDVIRTKEY(cChar);              // Releases the Shift/Control/Alt keys.
      break;

   case __TEXT('{'):            // Beginning of special key text
      if (*g_SKD.pszKeys == __TEXT('}')) {

         // The special character is a close brace.
         sVirtKey = VkKeyScan(__TEXT('}'));

         // Point past the virtual key.
         pEndOfToken = ++g_SKD.pszKeys;
      }

      // Locate the end of the first token in the braced expression.
      // This is either:
      //    1. The end of string,
      //    2. a special word/symbol followed by a close brace, or
      //    3. a special word/symbol followed by a space and a number.
      pEndOfToken = _tcspbrk(g_SKD.pszKeys, __TEXT(" }"));

      if (pEndOfToken == NULL) {
         SKErr = SKERR_MISSINGCLOSEBRACE;
         break;
      }

      if (sVirtKey == 0) {

         // The key must not be the close brace. We must determine the
         // virtual key corresponding to this special key.
         int nNumChars = pEndOfToken - g_SKD.pszKeys;
         _tcsncpy(szSpecialKey, g_SKD.pszKeys, nNumChars);
         szSpecialKey[nNumChars] = 0; // Force string termination
         sVirtKey = SendKeys_SpecialKeyToVirtKey(szSpecialKey);
         if (sVirtKey == 0) {
            SKErr = SKERR_INVALIDKEY;
            break;
         }
      }

      // Calculate the repeat count for this special character.
      if (*pEndOfToken == __TEXT(' ')) {
         if ((_stscanf(++pEndOfToken, __TEXT("%d"), &nCount) == 0) ||
            (nCount == 0)) {

            SKErr = SKERR_INVALIDCOUNT;
            break;
         }
      }

      // Point to char after the closing brace so that parsing may continue.
      g_SKD.pszKeys = _tcschr(pEndOfToken, __TEXT('}'));
      if (g_SKD.pszKeys == NULL) {
         SKErr = SKERR_MISSINGCLOSEBRACE;
```

```
                    break;
            }
            g_SKD.pszKeys++;         // Skip over the close brace

        if (sVirtKey == VK_QUEUESYNC) {

            // Add special VK_QUEUESYNC virtual key that will cause a
            // WM_QUEUESYNC message to be played back to the
            // hwndQueueSyncTarget window.
            APPENDVIRTKEY(VK_QUEUESYNC);
            break;
        }

        // Add this special key to the virtual-key list by falling through
        // to the following default case.

    default:                         // Just a normal character
        if (cChar != __TEXT('{')) {

            // We didn't fall through from the preceding case.
            sVirtKey = VkKeyScan(cChar);
        }

        if (HIBYTE(sVirtKey) & 1)
            APPENDVIRTKEY(VK_SHIFT); // Presses the Shift key.

        while (nCount--)
            APPENDVIRTKEY(LOBYTE(sVirtKey));

        if (HIBYTE(sVirtKey) & 1)
            APPENDVIRTKEY(VK_SHIFT); // Releases the Shift key.
        break;
    }
    return(SKErr);
}


//////////////////////////////////////////////////////////////////////////////


SKERR WINAPI SendKeys_InitPreprocessKeys (LPCTSTR pszPassedKeys) {

    SKERR SKErr;

    // Clear out the array and the index into the array.
    g_SKD.nMaxVirtKeys = g_SKD.nVirtKeyNum = 0;

    // Use an internal variable for input string parsing.
    g_SKD.pszKeys = pszPassedKeys;

    // While there are more more characters in the string to be parsed, call
    // the preprocessor to evaluate the next token.
    while (*g_SKD.pszKeys != 0)
        if ((SKErr = SendKeys_PreprocessKeys()) != SKERR_NOERROR)
            break;
```

```
      return(SKErr);
}


////////////////////////////////////////////////////////////////////////////


// This function returns the next key event from the array.
// It returns True if a token was retrieved from the list and
// False if there were no more tokens to retrieve.
// This function is also used to initialize playback.  This is done by
// calling it and passing zero in the psVirtKey parameter.
static BOOL SendKeys_GetToken (SHORT *psVirtKey,
   BOOL *pfPressDown, BOOL *pfSysKey) {

   static SHORT sVirtKey = 0;
   static BOOL fKeyIsDown = FALSE;
   static BOOL fKeyPressWhileAltDown = FALSE;
   static BOOL fShiftDown = FALSE, fControlDown = FALSE, fAltDown = FALSE;

   if (psVirtKey == NULL) {

      // Prime the token engine.
      sVirtKey = 0;
      fKeyIsDown = FALSE;

      // Ensure that none of the shift state keys are down.
      fShiftDown = fControlDown = fAltDown = FALSE;

      // Start playback from the first (0th) entry in the array.
      g_SKD.nVirtKeyNum = 0;
      return(TRUE);
   }

   // Make sure that the key is not a shift state key.
   if ((sVirtKey != VK_SHIFT) && (sVirtKey != VK_CONTROL) &&
      (sVirtKey != VK_MENU)) {

      // If we last played back a key and said that it was down, we now have
      // to play back the same key and say that it is up.
      if (sVirtKey != 0 && fKeyIsDown) {
         *psVirtKey = sVirtKey;    // Same key as last time.
         sVirtKey = 0;             // Next time in, use a new key.
         *pfPressDown = FALSE;     // Release the key.
         *pfSysKey = fAltDown && !fControlDown; // Is it a SYS key?
         fKeyPressWhileAltDown = TRUE;
         return(TRUE);
      }
   }

   // Have all the key events in the array been played back?
   if (g_SKD.nVirtKeyNum == g_SKD.nMaxVirtKeys)
      return(FALSE);               // No more tokens to playback.

   // Do special processing if we are playing back a shift state key.
```

535

```
        switch (*psVirtKey = sVirtKey = g_SKD.asVirtKeys[g_SKD.nVirtKeyNum++]) {

            case VK_SHIFT:

                // Toggle the state of the Shift key.
                *pfPressDown = (fShiftDown = !fShiftDown);
                break;

            case VK_CONTROL:

                // Toggle the state of the Ctrl key.
                *pfPressDown = (fControlDown = !fControlDown);
                break;

            case VK_MENU:

                // Toggle the state of the Alt key.
                *pfPressDown = (fAltDown = !fAltDown);

                // If the Alt key is going down, reset this flag.
                if (fAltDown)
                    fKeyPressWhileAltDown = FALSE;
                break;

            case VK_QUEUESYNC:

                // To prevent playing back a VK_QUEUESYNC keydown and keyup, we
                // pretend that a key is played back by setting sVirtKey to zero.
                sVirtKey = 0;
                break;

            default:

                // For any other key, make the event a keydown.
                *pfPressDown = fKeyIsDown = fKeyPressWhileAltDown = TRUE;
                break;
        }

        // Do some special checking to determine if the key is a SYS key or not.
        if ((sVirtKey == VK_MENU) && (!fAltDown))
            *pfSysKey = !fKeyPressWhileAltDown && !fControlDown;
        else
            *pfSysKey = fAltDown && !fControlDown;

        return(TRUE);
}


//////////////////////////////////////////////////////////////////////////////////


// This is the journal playback hook callback function. Every time it is
// called, Windows requests the next keyboard event to be played back.
// This function determines what the next event is by calling
// SendKeys_GetToken, fills an EVENTMSG structure with the correct information
// about the keyboard event and playback time, and returns to let Windows
```

```
// process it. After all events have been played back, the function uninstalls
// itself and sets the g_SKD's hhook member to NULL.
LRESULT WINAPI SendKeys_JrnlPlayBackHook (int nCode,
   WPARAM wParam, LPARAM lParam) {

   PEVENTMSG pEvent;
   static SHORT sVirtKey = 0;
   static BOOL fKeyDown = FALSE;
   static BOOL fSysKey = FALSE;

   if (g_SKD.fNoTokensRetrievedYet) {

      // If no tokens have ever been retrieved from the list, we must force
      // ourselves to get the first one in case Windows sends us a HC_GETNEXT
      // notification BEFORE an HC_SKIP notification.
      SendKeys_GetToken(&sVirtKey, &fKeyDown, &fSysKey);
      g_SKD.fNoTokensRetrievedYet = FALSE;
   }

   switch (nCode) {

   case HC_SKIP:

      // Prepare to return the next event the next time the hook code is
      // HC_GETNEXT. If all events have been played, stop playing.
      if (!SendKeys_GetToken(&sVirtKey, &fKeyDown, &fSysKey)) {

         // There were no more tokens left to get.
         UnhookWindowsHookEx(g_SKD.hhook);
         g_SKD.hhook = NULL;

      }
      break;

   case HC_GETNEXT:

      // Copy current event to the EVENTMSG structure pointed to by lParam.
      pEvent = (PEVENTMSG) lParam;
      pEvent->time = GetTickCount();
      if (sVirtKey == VK_QUEUESYNC) {
         pEvent->message = WM_QUEUESYNC;
         pEvent->paramL = (UINT) g_SKD.hwndQueueSyncTarget;
         pEvent->paramH = 0;
      } else {
         if (!fSysKey)
            pEvent->message = fKeyDown ? WM_KEYDOWN : WM_KEYUP;
         else
            pEvent->message = fKeyDown ? WM_SYSKEYDOWN : WM_SYSKEYUP;

         // Scan code and virtual key.
         pEvent->paramL = sVirtKey;

         // Scan code; bit 15 is extended key.
         pEvent->paramH = MapVirtualKey(sVirtKey, 0);
      }
      break;
   }
```

537

```
     // Number of milliseconds Windows should wait before processing the event.
     return(0);
}


//////////////////////////////////////////////////////////////////////////////////


SKERR WINAPI SendKeys (HWND hwndQueueSyncTarget, LPCTSTR pszKeys) {

   BYTE abKeyState[256];
   SKERR SKErr = SendKeys_InitPreprocessKeys(pszKeys);
   if (SKErr != SKERR_NOERROR)
      return(SKErr);

   SendKeys_GetToken(NULL, NULL, NULL); // Primes the token pump.
   g_SKD.fNoTokensRetrievedYet = TRUE;
   g_SKD.hwndQueueSyncTarget = hwndQueueSyncTarget;

   // Install the journal playback hook.
   g_SKD.hhook = SetWindowsHookEx(WH_JOURNALPLAYBACK,
      SendKeys_JrnlPlayBackHook, GetModuleHandle(NULL), 0);
   if (g_SKD.hhook == NULL)
      return(SKERR_CANTINSTALLHOOK);

   GetKeyboardState(abKeyState);       // Gets the current state of the keyboard.
   abKeyState[VK_CONTROL] &= 0x7f;     // Forces the Ctrl key off.
   abKeyState[VK_MENU]    &= 0x7f;     // Forces the Alt key off.
   abKeyState[VK_SHIFT]   &= 0x7f;     // Forces the Shift key off.
   abKeyState[VK_CAPITAL] &= 0x7e;     // Forces the Caps Lock key off.
   abKeyState[VK_NUMLOCK] &= 0x7e;     // Forces the Num Lock key off.
   SetKeyboardState(abKeyState);       // Sets the new state of the keyboard.

   return(SKERR_NOERROR);
}


////////////////////////////////// End of File //////////////////////////////////
```

Listing 8.3 *SendKeys.H*

```
/*****************************************************************************
Module name: SendKeys.h
Written by: Jeffrey Richter
Notices: Copyright (c) 1995 Jeffrey Richter
Purpose: Functions to simulate keystrokes to Windows applications
*****************************************************************************/


typedef enum {
   SKERR_NOERROR,
```

```
    SKERR_MISSINGCLOSEBRACE,
    SKERR_INVALIDKEY,
    SKERR_MISSINGCLOSEPAREN,
    SKERR_INVALIDCOUNT,
    SKERR_STRINGTOOLONG,
    SKERR_CANTINSTALLHOOK
} SKERR;


//////////////////////////////////////////////////////////////////////////


SKERR WINAPI SendKeys (HWND hwndQueueSyncTarget, LPCTSTR szKeys);


/////////////////////////////// End of File ///////////////////////////////
```

Listing 8.4 *SKDemo.RC*

```
//Microsoft Visual C++-generated resource script
//
#include "resource.h"

#define APSTUDIO_READONLY_SYMBOLS
/////////////////////////////////////////////////////////////////////////////
//
// Generated from the TEXTINCLUDE 2 resource
//
#include "afxres.h"

/////////////////////////////////////////////////////////////////////////////
#undef APSTUDIO_READONLY_SYMBOLS


#ifdef APSTUDIO_INVOKED
/////////////////////////////////////////////////////////////////////////////
//
// TEXTINCLUDE
//

1 TEXTINCLUDE DISCARDABLE
BEGIN
    "resource.h\0"
END

2 TEXTINCLUDE DISCARDABLE
BEGIN
    "#include ""afxres.h""\r\n"
    "\0"
END

3 TEXTINCLUDE DISCARDABLE
BEGIN
    "\r\n"
    "\0"
END
```

539

```
//////////////////////////////////////////////////////////////////////////////
#endif    // APSTUDIO_INVOKED


//////////////////////////////////////////////////////////////////////////////
//
// Dialog
//

IDD_SKDEMO DIALOG DISCARDABLE  -32768, 5, 280, 119
STYLE WS_MINIMIZEBOX | WS_VISIBLE | WS_CAPTION | WS_SYSMENU
CAPTION "SendKeys Demo"
FONT 8, "MS Sans Serif"
BEGIN
    CONTROL         "&Windows:",IDC_STATIC,"Static",SS_SIMPLE | WS_GROUP,8,6,
                    40,8
    COMBOBOX        IDC_WINDOWS,48,4,168,120,CBS_DROPDOWNLIST | CBS_SORT |
                    WS_VSCROLL | WS_TABSTOP
    PUSHBUTTON      "&Refresh",IDC_WNDREFRESH,224,3,50,14
    CONTROL         "&Key string:",IDC_STATIC,"Static",SS_SIMPLE | WS_GROUP,
                    8,26,40,8
    COMBOBOX        IDC_KEYSTRING,48,24,168,120,CBS_DROPDOWN |
                    CBS_AUTOHSCROLL | WS_VSCROLL | WS_TABSTOP
    DEFPUSHBUTTON   "&Send keys",IDC_SENDKEYS,224,24,50,14
    GROUPBOX        "Special key reference",IDC_STATIC,4,44,212,72
    LTEXT           "{Backspace}\n{Break}\n{CapsLock}\n{Clear}\n{Delete}\n[End}",
                    IDC_STATIC,8,60,44,48
    LTEXT           "{Enter}\n{Esc}\n{Help}\n{Home}\n{Insert}\n{NumLock}",
                    IDC_STATIC,61,60,44,48
    LTEXT           "{PgDn}\n{PgUp}\n{PrtSc}\n{ScrollLock}\n{Tab}\n{F1} - {F16}",
                    IDC_STATIC,114,60,44,48
    LTEXT           "{Up}\n{Down}\n{Left}\n{Right}\n\n{QueueSync}",
                    IDC_STATIC,167,60,44,48
    GROUPBOX        "Modifiers",IDC_STATIC,224,44,48,40
    LTEXT           "+ = Shift\n^ = Ctrl\n% = Alt",IDC_STATIC,228,56,40,24
END


//////////////////////////////////////////////////////////////////////////////
//
// Icon
//

IDI_SKDEMO              ICON    DISCARDABLE     "SKDemo.ico"

#ifndef APSTUDIO_INVOKED
//////////////////////////////////////////////////////////////////////////////
//
// Generated from the TEXTINCLUDE 3 resource.
//


//////////////////////////////////////////////////////////////////////////////
#endif    // not APSTUDIO_INVOKED
```

Listing 8.5 *Resource.H*

```
//{{NO_DEPENDENCIES}}
// Microsoft Visual C++-generated include file
// Used by SKDemo.rc
//
#define IDC_TIME                    100
#define IDD_CLOCK                   101
#define IDI_ICON1                   102
#define IDI_CLOCK                   102
#define IDD_SKDEMO                  103
#define IDI_SKDEMO                  104
#define IDC_WINDOWS                 1000
#define IDC_KEYSTRING               1001
#define IDC_SENDKEYS                1002
#define IDC_WNDREFRESH              1003
#define IDC_STATIC                  -1

// Next default values for new objects
//
#ifdef APSTUDIO_INVOKED
#ifndef APSTUDIO_READONLY_SYMBOLS
#define _APS_NEXT_RESOURCE_VALUE    105
#define _APS_NEXT_COMMAND_VALUE     40001
#define _APS_NEXT_CONTROL_VALUE     1000
#define _APS_NEXT_SYMED_VALUE       101
#endif
#endif
```

The SendKeys Function

SendKeys is a very popular function that's implemented in Basic, the Visual Basic programming system, the Microsoft Excel macro language, and the Word for Windows WordBasic language. The SendKeys syntax seems to be slightly different in each implementation. In keeping with tradition, my version of SendKeys also has a slightly different syntax (most similar to the version for Visual Basic) as described shortly.

When SendKeys is called, the first thing it does is preprocess the string of characters passed to it by calling the SendKeys_InitPreprocessKeys function. This function converts the string of characters to an array of virtual-key codes. The array is stored in the global g_SKD structure's asVirtKeys array; the nMaxVirtKeys member maintains the maximum number of elements in this array. When this array is played back, the nVirtKeyNum member contains the index into the array of the next virtual-key code to be played back. When nVirtKeyNum is (nMaxVirtKeys – 1), the entire array has been played back.

When SendKeys_InitPreprocessKeys is called, it initializes the nMaxVirtKeys and nVirtKeyNum member variables to zero and sets the pointer member, pszKeys, to point to the string of characters. Now, SendKeys_InitPreprocessKeys enters into a *while* loop calling the SendKeys_PreprocessKeys function until all of the tokens have been parsed from the string. If an error occurs along the way, SendKeys_PreprocessKeys halts and returns an error value.

For example, imagine that the user has passed SendKeys a long string. Because the asVirtKeys array is of a fixed length, SendKeys returns SKERR_STRINGTOOLONG. If all went successfully, SendKeys_PreprocessKeys returns SKERR_NOERROR and SendKeys installs the journal playback hook to play back the keys. I will discuss how this works later. For now, let's take a closer look at how the SendKeys_PreprocessKeys function fills the asVirtKeys array.

Every time SendKeys_PreprocessKeys is called, it attempts to determine what the next token is in the string. There are several possibilities here.

The Character Is a Zero-Byte

If the first character of the next token is a zero-byte, SendKeys_PreprocessKeys assumes that it has reached the end of the string and returns SKERR_NOERROR.

The Character Is a Parenthesis

If SendKeys_PreprocessKeys determines that the next character is an open parenthesis, it simply calls itself recursively until the end of the string is reached or until a close parenthesis is found. I'll explain why this is necessary shortly.

The Character Is a Tilde (~)

A tilde is just a shorthand way of expressing the Enter special key {Enter}, so a VK_RETURN is appended to the array.

The Character Is a Modifier

The next tokens that SendKeys_PreprocessKeys looks for are any of the special token modifiers +, ^, or %. If SendKeys_PreprocessKeys finds any of them, it appends a VK_SHIFT, VK_CONTROL, or VK_MENU code, respectively, to the array and calls itself recursively. During the recursive level, SendKeys_PreprocessKeys appends the next token to the asVirtKeys array and returns. When SendKeys_PreprocessKeys returns from the recursive level, a second VK_SHIFT, VK_CONTROL, or VK_MENU code is appended to asVirtKeys—the same code that was appended before the recursive call is appended again.

The Character Is an Open Brace

If the next token starts with an open brace, SendKeys_Preprocess-Keys must check for several different cases:

- The first case is "{}}". This allows you to specify a close brace key in the character stream.

- The next case is some string representing a special key (for example, "{BACKSPACE}").

- The third case is a key (possibly a special key) followed by a space and a number. For example, "{Right 10}" means that the Right Arrow key should be simulated ten times.

SendKeys_PreprocessKeys checks to see if the string represents a special key by calling the SendKeys_SpecialKeyToVirtKey function. This function accepts a zero-terminated string as its only parameter and returns a SHORT integer representing the virtual-key code of the special key. If the key string is compared with each entry in the entire g_SpecialKeys table without finding a match, SendKeys_SpecialKeyToVirtKey checks if the key string is 1 byte long. If it is, the virtual-key code of the single character is returned. Otherwise, zero is returned indicating that the key string could not be translated into a virtual-key code.

If the virtual-key code for the special key is found, SendKeys_PreprocessKeys checks to see if a repeat count has been specified before the close brace. Finally, the virtual-key code is appended to the end of the asVirtKeys array. The virtual-key code is actually appended the number of times indicated by the count. If a count is not specified, the key is appended only once. Also, just before every code is appended to asVirtKeys, SendKeys_PreprocessKeys checks the high byte of the virtual-key code to see if its low bit is set. If this bit is set, it indicates that the shift state was lost when converting the character to its virtual-key code equivalent.

543

For example, if the string contained *s*, this would generate a virtual-key code of VK_S. If the string was *S*, this also generates a virtual-key code of VK_S. When the VkKeyScan function returns, it returns a 2-byte word. The low byte contains the virtual-key code and the high byte contains shift state flags. Bit 0 of this high byte will be set when VkKeyScan converts the capital S. This indicates that the Shift key is necessary to convert the virtual-key code back to ANSI. Because the asVirtKeys array stores only virtual-key codes, not shift states, SendKeys_PreprocessKeys must append an entry of VK_SHIFT into the array.

This is done for the playback part of SendKeys. Up to now, I have been appending single virtual-key codes to the array for any character. For example, if the string contained a *J*, a single VK_J goes into the asVirtKeys array. During playback, two events must be generated for this one key code, keydown and then keyup. But you can't do this for shift-state keys. If you handle Shift keys the same way, the string +j would generate keystrokes like this:

```
shift keydown
shift keyup
j keydown
j keyup
```

This would end up sending a lowercase *j* to the system instead of the desired uppercase *J*. You need to send the following sequence instead:

```
shift keydown
j keydown
j keyup
shift keyup
```

During playback, the asVirtKeys array is traversed one character at a time. If the virtual-key code in the array is not a shift-state key, the journal playback hook will return a keydown event for the character the first time it is called and a keyup event for the same character the next time it is called.

If the journal playback hook sees that the next character to be played back is a shift-state key, it returns a keydown event for the shift-state key and sets a flag to remind itself that the key has been pressed but has not yet been released. As more virtual-key codes are requested from the hook, the hook checks to see if it is about to return a shift-state key. If it is, it checks its flag to see if the key is already down, and if so, the hook function returns a keyup event for the Shift key and resets its flag.

For example, say that you have a string consisting of "^%(AB)". When this string is preprocessed, the asVirtKeys array is filled as shown in Table 8.9. For every other character parsed by SendKeys_ PreprocessKeys, the character is converted to its virtual-key code equivalent and appended to the asVirtKeys array.

Table 8.9 *Contents of the asVirtKeys Array*

Index	Virtual-Key Code	Comments
0	VK_CONTROL	VK_CONTROL appended and pre-processor calls itself recursively (1 level deep).
1	VK_MENU	VK_MENU appended and preprocessor calls itself recursively again (2 levels deep). The parser then sees the open parenthesis and calls itself recursively (3 levels deep). Nothing is appended to the array for the open parenthesis.
2	VK_A	VK_A appended.
3	VK_B	VK_B appended.
4	VK_MENU	Preprocessor sees the closing parenthesis and returns (2 levels deep). Preprocessor returns again, having processed the token after the % (1 level deep). Upon return, the preprocessor appends another VK_MENU.
5	VK_CONTROL	Preprocessor returns, having processed the token after the ^ (0 levels deep). Upon return, the preprocessor appends another VK_CONTROL.

Now it's time to discuss how this array of key codes gets played back into the system. When the SendKeys function gets control back from SendKeys_InitPreprocessKeys, it calls the SendKeys_GetToken function, telling it that playback is about to begin and that it should initialize itself. SendKeys_GetToken sets its internal flags to indicate that no keys have been pressed so far and that playback is going to start from the zeroeth entry in the asVirtKeys array.

Next, SendKeys installs a journal playback hook and saves the handle to this hook in the hhook member variable. After the hook is installed, SendKeys calls GetKeyboardState, turns off the bits that represent the Ctrl, Alt, Shift, Caps Lock, and Num Lock keys, and then calls SetKeyboardState so that the thread's synchronous key state array reflects these values. This precaution is necessary because the user might be holding down the Shift key, and this would affect the case of the characters as they are played back.

Earlier in this chapter, I mentioned that you should call the keybd_event function when you want to toggle the state of the various toggle keys. However, in SendKeys, I can do it by calling SetKeyboardState because the local input state variables of all the threads in the system are attached because there is a journal playback hook installed. This means that all the threads see the same key state information.[4]

SendKeys now returns to its caller with the journal playback hook still installed. At the time when SendKeys returns, none of the keystrokes have yet to be played back. The calling thread must process a message loop in order for the playback hook to be called periodically to play back keystrokes. If you want to know when all the keystrokes have been played back and processed, you should add a {QueueSync} special key to the end of your key string. When the playback hook sees the {QueueSync} key, it causes a WM_QUEUE-SYNC message to be posted to your window. The window procedure can look for this message and know when all the keystrokes have been processed. SKDemo's main window displays the message box in Figure 8.3 when it receives a WM_QUEUESYNC message.

After the hook has been installed, Windows calls the hook function every time a hardware event is required. The hook function calls SendKeys_GetToken to retrieve information about the next event. For each call, SendKeys_GetToken determines the virtual-key code for the next event, whether the event is a keydown or a keyup event and whether

---

[4]For more information about threads and their local input states, see the Capture application presented in Chapter 6 and the "Windows Messages and Asynchronous Input" chapter in my *Advanced Windows* book.

the key is a system key or not. When SendKeys_GetToken returns, it indicates whether it returned a real event or whether the entire array has been played back and there are no more tokens left to process.

Figure 8.3 *SKDemo received a WM_QUEUESYNC message.*

When the hook function sees that SendKeys_GetToken has indicated that no more tokens exist, it uninstalls the hook and sets the hhook member back to NULL. If SendKeys_GetToken did return information for an event, the hook function prepares the EVENTMSG structure with the appropriate WM_(SYS)KEYUP/DOWN or WM_QUEUE-SYNC message and returns this event back to Windows.

SendKeys

The SendKeys function sends one or more keystrokes to the active window as if they were typed from the keyboard.

```
SKERR WINAPI SendKeys (HWND hwndQueueSyncTarget, LPCTSTR pszKeys);
```

Parameters

- hwndQueueSyncTarget - identifies a window that will receive a WM_QUEUESYNC message every time the {QueueSync} special key is played back. If this value is NULL, the WM_QUEUE-SYNC message can be processed in the thread's message loop.

- pszKeys - specifies a string of text representing the list of keystrokes to be simulated.

Return Value

This function returns an enumerated type indicated the result of calling the function. It can be one of the values shown in Table 8.10.

Table 8.10 *Possible SendKeys return values.*

Value	Meaning
SKERR_NOERROR	Function executed successfully.
SKERR_MISSINGCLOSEBRACE	An open brace has no matching close brace.
SKERR_INVALIDKEY	A special key was used that is not recognized.
SKERR_MISSINGCLOSEPAREN	An open parenthesis has no matching close parenthesis.
SKERR_INVALIDCOUNT	An invalid count was specified.
SKERR_STRINGTOOLONG	The string passed is too long to process.
SKERR_CANTINSTALLHOOK	The journal playback hook could not be installed.

Each key is represented by one or more characters. To specify a single keyboard character, use the character itself. For example, to represent the letter *a*, pszKeys should point to a buffer that looks like this: "a". If you want to represent more than one character, append each additional character to the one before. To represent the letters *a*, *b*, and *c*, pszText should point to a buffer that looks like this: "abc". The plus (+), caret (^), and percent sign (%) have special meanings. To specify one of these special characters, enter the character inside braces. For example, to specify the plus sign, use "{+}". To send a "{" character or a "}" character, use "{{}" or "{}}", respectively. To specify characters that are not displayed when you press a key (such as Enter or Tab) and other keys that represent actions rather than characters, use the codes shown in Table 8.11.

In addition to the special key codes shown in Table 8.11, there is also a {QueueSync} key code. When a {QueueSync} key is played back, rather than sending WM_(SYS)KEY* messages, SendKeys sends a WM_QUEUESYNC message to the window identified by the hwndQueueSyncTarget parameter. Because the SendKeys function returns immediately, before playing back any of the keys, an application can look for the WM_QUEUESYNC message inside a window procedure to determine when all the keys have been played. For example, the following line calls SendKeys, and the hwndMain window receives a WM_

QUEUESYNC message after all keys have been played back. When the WM_QUEUESYNC message is received, you are guaranteed that all the keystrokes preceding the {QueueSync} token have been played back and processed.

```
SKERR SKErr = SendKeys(hwndMain, "Some string{QueueSync}");
```

Table 8.11 *Special key codes recognized by SendKeys.*

Key	Code	Key	Code	Key	Code
Backspace	{Backspace} or {Bs}or {Bksp}}	Help	{Help}	Tab	{Tab}
Break	{Break}	Home	{Home}	F1 to F16	{F1} to {F16}
Caps Lock	{CapsLock}	Insert	{Insert}	Up Arrow	{Up}
Clear	{Clear}	Num Lock	{NumLock}	Down Arrow	{Down}
Delete	{Delete} or {Del}	Page Down	{PgDn}	Left Arrow	{Left}
End	{End}	Page Up	{PgUp}	Right Arrow	{Right}
Enter	{Enter} or ~	Print Screen	{PrtSc}		
Esc	{Escape} or {Esc}	Scroll Lock	{ScrollLock}		

To specify keys combined with any combination of Shift, Ctrl, and Alt, precede the regular key code with one or more of the codes shown in Table 8.12. To specify that Shift, Ctrl, and/or Alt should be held down while several keys are pressed, enclose the keys in parentheses. For example, to hold down the Shift key while pressing E then C, use "+(EC)". To hold down Shift while pressing E, followed by C without the Shift key, use "+EC". To specify repeating keys, use the form {key number} where there is always a space between key and number. For example, "{left 42}" means press the Left Arrow key 42 times; "{× 10}" means press the character × 10 times.

Table 8.12 *Modifier codes recognized by SendKeys.*

Key	Code
Shift	+
Ctrl	^
Alt	%

CHAPTER NINE

Version Control

From a Win32 developer's point of view, the bulk of Windows is composed of three main dynamic-link libraries: **User32.DLL**, **GDI32.DLL**, and **Kernel32.DLL**. These DLLs are responsible for managing Windows' user interface, graphical device interface, and memory management, respectively. With each new version of Windows, Microsoft adds new features (such as sound and video support, OLE, shell support, and remote procedure calls). Instead of implementing the code that encompasses each of these additional features into User32, GDI32, or Kernel32, Microsoft creates additional DLLs to handle each of these tasks. For example, the shell support is contained in the **Shell32.DLL** library, and some of the OLE support is split between the two **OLECli32.DLL** and **OLESvr32.DLL** libraries.

If you are writing a Win32 application using Visual C++ 2.0, you might also be linking with **MSVCRT20.DLL**. This DLL contains all the C-Runtime library routines like sprintf and memset. However, if you are using Visual C++ 2.1, you may also be linking with a file called **MSVCRT20.DLL**. This file is not the same file that ships with Visual C++ 2.0 even though it has the exact same name. The Visual C++ group allows any applications developed with Visual C++ to redistribute this DLL royalty free. This seems to be a benefit, but there some potential problems.

Let's look at a typical scenario. A user goes to a computer store and purchases a new shrink-wrapped copy of the "Solve All Your Problems with the Click of a Mouse" (SAYPWTCOAM) program. This program was compiled and linked using Visual C++ 2.1 and redistributes the **MSVCRT20.DLL** file; this file is copied to the user's hard disk automatically when the user installs the program.

Now, 6 months later, the same user goes back to the computer store and purchases a copy of the "Why Should I Lend You Mine When You've Broken Yours Already" (WSILYMWYBYA) program. This program was compiled and linked using Visual C++ 2.0. It also ships with a file called **MSVCRT20.DLL** but this file is older than the Visual C++ 2.1 file already installed on the user's hard drive. What should happen when the user installs the just-purchased program?

If the WSILYMWYBYA program installs its older version on top of the existing version, the SAYPWTCOAM program may not work in the future. And, if the user doesn't attempt to run the SAYPWT-COAM program for another 3 months, he or she might have no idea why the program no longer executes properly. Microsoft goes to great measures to assure you that the **MSVCRT20.DLL** file that comes with Visual C++ 2.1 is a complete superset of the one that ships with Visual C++ 2.0. This means that always installing the more recent version of the file should never adversely affect programs that are linked to the older version.

Here is another potential problem. Often, the language-dependent parts of an application are contained in DLLs. However, a vendor might give all the DLLs the same name, say **Res.DLL**. This means that there is an **Res.DLL** file for English resources, another **Res.DLL** for German resources, and so on. Then, upon installation, the Setup program detects which language the user prefers and copies the proper language version of **Res.DLL** to the user's hard disk. This architecture can wreak havoc on end users because different programs may install different versions of these files, overwriting the previously installed language DLL. So, all of a sudden, when a user in Germany uses a program they haven't used in 4 months, all the dialog boxes and menus appear in English instead of in German as they did before.

The answer to all these problems and many others lies in the VERSIONINFO resource. This resource is placed in each of your executable's or DLL's resource files (RC), just like any other icon, cursor, dialog box, or string table resource.

There are several reasons why you should include a version resource in all your binary files. First, it can offer additional information to an application, like what language files the user has installed and what computer an application, DLL, or driver was designed for. Second, the information can be used for diagnostic purposes. If a user is having trouble getting an application to work, it may well be that some of the executables and DLLs are not synchronized. For example, if an application requires that version 3.0 of a particular DLL be used, the application can read the version control resource information from the DLL and determine if the program is able to execute correctly before the user gets too involved with the application. If your application doesn't explicitly check the version information in a required DLL, the user could run a utility program like VerShow (shown later in this chapter) to check the version information and report this to your technical support people.

Finally, you can build the contents of an About box by using the information in the file's version control resource. I highly recommend this. This way you simply update version information in your resource file rather than manually updating the version control resource as well as the template for the About dialog box.

Here is a sample of what a version resource looks like.

```
//////////////////////////////////////////////////////////////////////
// Version stamp for this DLL

#include "winver.h"

#ifdef _DEBUG

// Version Info for MFC30[U]D.DLL
VS_VERSION_INFO     VERSIONINFO
  FILEVERSION       3,1,0,0
  PRODUCTVERSION    2,1,0,0
  FILEFLAGSMASK     VS_FFI_FILEFLAGSMASK
#ifndef RELEASE
  FILEFLAGS         VS_FF_DEBUG|VS_FF_PRERELEASE
#else
  FILEFLAGS         VS_FF_DEBUG
#endif
  FILEOS            VOS_NT_WINDOWS32
  FILETYPE          VFT_DLL
  FILESUBTYPE       0   // not used
BEGIN
   BLOCK "StringFileInfo"
   BEGIN
      BLOCK "040904E4" // Lang=US English, CharSet=Windows Multilual
      BEGIN
         VALUE "CompanyName",     "Microsoft Corporation\0"
         VALUE "FileDescription", "MFCDLL Shared Library - Debug Version\0"
         VALUE "FileVersion",     "3.1.000\0"
```

```
              VALUE "InternalName",    "MFCDLLD\0"
              VALUE "LegalCopyright",  "Copyright (C) Microsoft Corp. 1993-1994\0"
              VALUE "LegalTrademarks", "\0"
              VALUE "OriginalFilename","MFC30D.DLL\0"
              VALUE "ProductName",     "Microsoft (R) Visual C++\0"
              VALUE "ProductVersion",  "2.1.000\0"
          END
      END
      BLOCK "VarFileInfo"
      BEGIN
          VALUE "Translation", 0x409, 1252
              // English language (0x409) and the Windows ANSI codepage (1252)
      END
  END

#else // RETAIL

// Version Info for MFC30[U].DLL
VS_VERSION_INFO      VERSIONINFO
  FILEVERSION        3,1,0,0
  PRODUCTVERSION     2,1,0,0
  FILEFLAGSMASK      VS_FFI_FILEFLAGSMASK
#ifndef RELEASE
  FILEFLAGS          VS_FF_PRERELEASE
#else
  FILEFLAGS          0 // Final version
#endif
  FILEOS           VOS_NT_WINDOWS32
  FILETYPE         VFT_DLL
  FILESUBTYPE      0   // Not used
BEGIN
  BLOCK "StringFileInfo"
  BEGIN
      BLOCK "040904E4" // Lang=US English, CharSet=Windows Multilual
      BEGIN
          VALUE "CompanyName",     "Microsoft Corporation\0"
          VALUE "FileDescription", "MFCDLL Shared Library - Retail Version\0"
          VALUE "FileVersion",     "3.1.000\0"
          VALUE "InternalName",    "MFCDLL\0"
          VALUE "LegalCopyright",  "Copyright (C) Microsoft Corp. 1993-1994\0"
          VALUE "LegalTrademarks", "\0"
          VALUE "OriginalFilename","MFC30.DLL\0"
          VALUE "ProductName",     "Microsoft (R) Visual C++\0"
          VALUE "ProductVersion",  "2.1.000"
      END
  END
  BLOCK "VarFileInfo"
  BEGIN
      VALUE "Translation", 0x409, 1252
          // English language (0x409) and the Windows ANSI codepage (1252)
  END
END

#endif
```

This version resource is from the Microsoft Foundation Class (MFC) Library's **MFCDLL.RC** file that ships with Visual C++ 2.1. You'll notice that the file **WinVer.H** is included at the top. This file is very important because it contains several identifiers that are used within the VERSIONINFO block. The first part of the resource (from FILEVERSION to FILESUBTYPE) contains fixed-length binary information. Table 9.1 describes the meaning of these fields.

Table 9.1 *VERSIONINFO resource fields.*

Field	Description
FILEVERSION	Specifies the file's version number. It consists of four 16-bit integers. If you specify less than four, the resource compiler pads the remaining integers with zeroes. For example, you could state a version as "3,51,0,61" to represent version 3.51.0.61.
PRODUCTVERSION	Specifies the product's version for which this file is distributed. It consists of four 16-bit integers just like the FILEVERSION field.
FILEFLAGSMASK	Specifies which bits in the FILEFLAGS field are valid. This value should always be VS_FFI_FILEFLAGSMASK (defined in WinVer.H to have a value of 0x0000003FL).
FILEFLAGS	A set of flags (from **WinVer.H**) that are ORed together. The list of possible flags follows: VS_FF_DEBUG VS_FF_INFOINFERRED VS_FF_PATCHED VS_FF_PRERELEASEV S_FF_PRIVATEBUILD VS_FF_SPECIALBUILD
FILEOS	Specifies the operating system for which the file was designed. The list of possible identifiers from **WinVer.H** follows: VOS_DOS_WINDOWS16 VOS_DOS_WINDOWS32 VOS_OS216_PM16 VOS_OS232_PM32 VOS_NT_WINDOWS32

continued...

555

Field	Description
FILETYPE	Specifies the type of file. The list of possible identifiers from **WinVer.H** follows: VFT_UNKNOWN VFT_APP VFT_DLL VFT_DRV VFT_FONT VFT_VXD VFT_STATIC_LIB
FILESUBTYPE	Specifies the subtype of the file. If the file type is not VFT_DRV, VFT_FONT, or VFT_VXD, this field should be set to VFT2_UNKNOWN. If the file type is VFT_DRV, this field must be one of the following identifiers: VFT2_UNKNOWN VFT2_DRV_PRINTER VFT2_DRV_KEYBOARD VFT2_DRV_LANGAUGE VFT2_DRV_DISPLAY VFT2_DRV_MOUSE VFT2_DRV_NETWORK VFT2_DRV_SYSTEM VFT2_DRV_INSTALLABLE VFT2_DRV_SOUND VFT2_DRV_ COMM VFT2_DRV_INPUTMETHOD If the file type is VFT_FONT, this field must be one of the following identifiers: VFT2_UNKNOWN VFT2_FONT_RASTER VFT2_FONT_VECTOR VFT2_FONT_TRUETYPE. If the file type is VFT_VXD, this field must be the virtual-device identifier included in the virtual-device control block.

Following the fixed-length portion of the VERSIONINFO resource is the variable-length portion. This section is divided into two subsections, VarFileInfo and StringFileInfo.

The VarFileInfo section describes the variable information part of the resource. Currently, there is only one type of variable information, "Translation." This section describes which languages are supported by the file. Following the string "Translation," is a sequence of number pairs. In the VERSIONINFO resource shown previously, the first number in the pair, 0x0409, indicates the language Id for which a StringFileInfo section exists. A language Id is a combination of a primary language Id and a sub-language Id. Table 9.2 shows the primary language Ids and the sub-language Ids defined in the **WinNT.H** header file.

Table 9.2 *Primary language and sub-language identifiers.*

Primary language Id	Primary language	Sub-language Id	Sub-language
0x02	LANG_BULGARIAN	0x01	SUBLANG_CHINESE_TRADITIONAL
0x04	LANG_CHINESE	0x02	SUBLANG_CHINESE_SIMPLIFIED
0x1a	LANG_CROATIAN	0x03	SUBLANG_CHINESE_HONGKONG
0x05	LANG_CZECH	0x04	SUBLANG_CHINESE_SINGAPORE
0x06	LANG_DANISH	0x01	SUBLANG_DUTCH
0x13	LANG_DUTCH	0x02	SUBLANG_DUTCH_BELGIAN
0x09	LANG_ENGLISH	0x01	SUBLANG_ENGLISH_US
0x0b	LANG_FINNISH	0x02	SUBLANG_ENGLISH_UK
0x0c	LANG_FRENCH	0x03	SUBLANG_ENGLISH_AUS
0x07	LANG_GERMAN	0x04	SUBLANG_ENGLISH_CAN
0x08	LANG_GREEK	0x05	SUBLANG_ENGLISH_NZ
0x0e	LANG_HUNGARIAN	0x06	SUBLANG_ENGLISH_EIRE
0x0f	LANG_ICELANDIC	0x01	SUBLANG_FRENCH
0x10	LANG_ITALIAN	0x02	SUBLANG_FRENCH_BELGIAN
0x11	LANG_JAPANESE	0x03	SUBLANG_FRENCH_CANADIAN
0x12	LANG_KOREAN	0x04	SUBLANG_FRENCH_SWISS
0x14	LANG_NORWEGIAN	0x01	SUBLANG_GERMAN

continued...

Primary language Id	Primary language	Sub-language Id	Sub-language
0x15	LANG_POLISH	0x02	SUBLANG_GERMAN_SWISS
0x16	LANG_PORTUGUESE	0x03	SUBLANG_GERMAN_AUSTRIAN
0x18	LANG_ROMANIAN	0x01	SUBLANG_ITALIAN
0x19	LANG_RUSSIAN	0x02	SUBLANG_ITALIAN_SWISS
0x1b	LANG_SLOVAK	0x01	SUBLANG_NORWEGIAN_BOKMAL
0x24	LANG_SLOVENIAN	0x02	SUBLANG_NORWEGIAN_NYNORSK
0x0a	LANG_SPANISH	0x02	SUBLANG_PORTUGUESE
0x1d	LANG_SWEDISH	0x01	SUBLANG_PORTUGUESE_BRAZILIAN
0x1f	LANG_TURKISH	0x01	SUBLANG_SPANISH
		0x02	SUBLANG_SPANISH_MEXICAN
		0x03	SUBLANG_SPANISH_MODERN

You can construct a language Id using the MAKELANGID macro:

```
#define MAKELANGID(p, s) (((( WORD)(s)) << 10) | (WORD)(p))
```

For example, the language Id for U.S. English is constructed as follows:

```
LANGID langidUSEnglish = MAKELANGID(LANG_ENGLISH, SUBLANG_ENGLISH_US);
```

After the preceding line executes, the variable langidUSEnglish contains the value 0x0409[1].

The second number in the pair, 1252, indicates the character set for which the StringFileInfo section exists. For Win32 binary files you should always use the Unicode code page (1200) because the resource compiler always outputs resource strings in Unicode. Table 9.3 shows the list of character sets that are currently recognized by Windows.

---

[1]Notice that the MAKELANGID macro shifts the sub-language Id by 10 bits, not by 8 bits.

Table 9.3 *Character sets recognized by Windows.*

Code Page	Description
0	7-bit ASCII
932	Windows, Japan (Shift - JIS X-0208)
949	Windows, Korea (Shift - KSC 5601)
950	Windows, Taiwan (GB5)
1200	Unicode
1250	Windows, Latin-2 (Eastern European)
1251	Windows, Cyrillic
1252	Windows, Multilingual (ANSI)
1253	Windows, Greek
1254	Windows, Turkish
1255	Windows, Hebrew
1256	Windows, Arabic

If you wanted to include additional string information for other languages and/or character sets, you would just add another pair to the "Translation" field in the resource. For example, to add the Greek language and Greek character set, the line would look like this:

```
VALUE "Translation", 0x0409, 1252, 0x0408, 1253
```

Notice that the string "Translation" appears only once in the VarFileInfo subsection and that language and character-set information is always added in pairs.

Following the VarFileInfo subsection is the StringFileInfo subsection. This section consists of zero-terminated strings that offer more detailed version information about the file. The StringFileInfo subsection can be divided into multiple blocks, one for each language and character set specified in the VarFileInfo section. Referring to the VERSIONINFO resource shown earlier, there is only one block, identified by the string "040904E4." The first four characters of this string ("0409") come from the hexadecimal value for the language (0x0409 is U.S. English). The last four characters

("04E4") come from the hexadecimal value for the character set. In this case, the character Id 1252 decimal is 04E4 in hexadecimal, representing the Windows Multilingual (ANSI) character set.

Within this block is the string information for the file. To keep this section as flexible as possible, Microsoft chose to identify each of the possible fields with a string name. This is the name that appears immediately to the right of the VALUE keyword. Currently, there are 12 recognized fields. Table 9.4 lists them.

Table 9.4 *String field names that can appear in a StringFileInfo section.*

String name	Required	Description
"Comments"	N	Additional information for diagnostic purposes.
"CompanyName"	Y	Company that produced the file.
"FileDescription"	Y	File description to be presented to users.
"FileVersion"	Y	Version number for the file.
"InternalName"	Y	Internal name for the file.
"LegalCopyright"	N	Copyright notices for the file.
"LegalTrademarks"	N	Any trademarks that apply to the file.
"OriginalFilename"	Y	Original name of the file in case user renames it.
"PrivateBuild"	*	Explanation of what makes this build private.
"ProductName"	Y	Name of product for which file is distributed.
"ProductVersion"	Y	Version of product for which file is distributed.
"SpecialBuild"	*	Explanation of what makes this build special.

When creating a string block, it is not necessary to use all the string fields shown in Table 9.4. The Required column indicates whether that string field must appear or not. Two of the entries, "PrivateBuild" and

"SpecialBuild", are required if their respective bits have been turned on in the FILEFLAGS field contained in the fixed-length section. The order in which any of these strings appear, as well as the case of each string, is not significant.

When creating the string block, it is important that you explicitly place a zero byte at the end of each string, for example:

```
VALUE "ProductName", "Microsoft (R) Visual C++\0"
```

Notice the "\0" after the last plus sign (+). You must do this yourself because, unlike the C compiler that places a zero byte automatically at the end of every string, the resource compiler does not do this. However, if you use Visual C++ to edit your version resource, Visual C++ automatically appends the extra zero character.

When this VERSIONINFO resource is compiled by the resource compiler, the resource compiler concatenates all the information into a large block of memory. You can use various functions contained in the **Version.DLL** library to read this version information into memory and parse it.

First, to load the version resource into memory, you must call the GetFileVersionInfoSize function:

```
DWORD GetFileVersionInfoSize(LPTSTR lpszFile, LPDWORD lpdwHandle);
```

The first parameter is the path name of the file that is expected to contain a VERSIONINFO resource. The second parameter is a pointer to a double-word variable that always receives a zero[2]. This function returns the number of bytes required to hold the file's resource information. If the file couldn't be found or does not contain any resource information, GetFileVersionInfoSize returns 0.

Once you have the size required to hold the resource information, you can allocate a block of memory large enough to hold the data and then call GetFileVersionInfo:

---

[2]The 16-bit Windows versions of these functions return a handle to the version resource. Win32 no longer needs this information, but Microsoft decided not to change the prototype of this function when porting it to Win32. You can pass NULL for this parameter.

```
BOOL GetFileVersionInfo(LPTSTR lpszFile, DWORD dwHandle,
  DWORD cbBuf, LPVOID lpvData);
```

This function actually loads the VERSIONINFO resource into the memory block that you previously allocated. The first parameter is again the path name of the file from which you wish to retrieve the version information. The second parameter is ignored. The third parameter specifies the size of the buffer that is available to hold the version information. It should be at least the size returned by the previous call to GetFileVersionInfoSize, or GetFileVersionInfo will truncate the information. The last parameter is the memory address of the block that is to be filled with the version information. If the data are loaded successfully, GetFileVersionInfo returns TRUE; otherwise, FALSE is returned.

Once the version information is contained in our memory block, you can use the VerQueryValue function to retrieve the various pieces of information it contains. VerQueryValue has the following prototype:

```
BOOL VerQueryValue(const LPVOID pBlock, LPTSTR lpSubBlock,
  LPVOID *lplpBuffer, PUINT puLen);
```

The first parameter is the memory address to the block containing the version information. This is the same address that was passed as the last parameter to GetFileVersionInfo. The second parameter, lpSubBlock, is a pointer to a zero-terminated string that represents the information that you are requesting. This will be discussed in more detail shortly. The third parameter is a pointer to a void pointer. When VerQueryValue is called, it searches through the memory block for the information that you request. If it successfully locates that information, VerQueryValue fills the void pointer with the address of the located information within the memory block. You can then use this address to access the data requested. The last parameter, puLen, is a pointer to an unsigned integer that VerQueryValue fills with the length of the data value that it found. For example, if you asked VerQueryValue to locate the "CompanyName" information and the string stored there was "ABC," VerQueryValue would fill the integer that puLen pointed to with the number four (three letters plus a zero character).

VerQueryValue returns nonzero if it found the requested information. Otherwise, it returns zero, indicating that the requested information did not exist or that the contents of the memory block was invalid.

Now, let's come back to the second parameter, lpSubBlock. The string that's passed can have one of three forms. The first form is a string that contains nothing but a backslash (\). For example, if you call VerQueryValue like this:

```
PVOID pvVerInfo;
VS_FIXEDFILEINFO *pvsffi;
UINT uLen;
.
.
.
// Get the size of the version information.
uLen = GetFileVersionInfoSize(szPathname, NULL);

// Allocate a buffer to hold it.
pvVerInfo = malloc(uLen);

// Read the version information into the buffer.
GetFileVersionInfo(szPathname, NULL, uLen, pvVerInfo);

// Find the memory address where the fixed portion begins.
VerQueryValue(lpVerInfo, "\\", &pvsffi, &uLen);
```

VerQueryInfo locates the fixed-length portion of the version resource information and fills the pvsffi pointer with the address of where that information is in the memory block. The data is in the form of a VS_FIXEDFILEINFO structure (defined in **WinVer.H**).

```
typedef struct _VS_FIXEDFILEINFO {  // vsffi
    DWORD dwSignature;          // e.g., VS_FFI_SIGNATURE = 0xFEEF04BD
    DWORD dwStrucVersion;       // e.g., VS_FFI_STRUCVERSION = 0x00010000
    DWORD dwFileVersionMS;      // e.g., 0x00020000 = "2.0"
    DWORD dwFileVersionLS;      // e.g., same as dwFileVersionMS
    DWORD dwProductVersionMS;   // e.g., same as dwFileVersionMS
    DWORD dwProductVersionLS;   // e.g., same as dwFileVersionMS
    DWORD dwFileFlagsMask;      // e.g., VS_FFI_FILEFLAGSMASK = 0x0000003F
    DWORD dwFileFlags;          // e.g., VS_FF_DEBUG | VS_FF_PRERELEASE
    DWORD dwFileOS;             // e.g., VOS_DOS_WINDOWS32 (Windows 95)
    DWORD dwFileType;           // e.g., VFT_DRIVER
    DWORD dwFileSubtype;        // e.g., VFT2_DRV_KEYBOARD
    DWORD dwFileDateMS;         // e.g., 0
    DWORD dwFileDateLS;         // e.g., 0
} VS_FIXEDFILEINFO;
```

The first two members of this structure, dwSignature and dwStruc-Version, are set by the resource compiler when the resource is compiled. They are used so that the version control functions know that they are working on a data block that contains version information. So that the functions themselves can support future versions of this structure, they also check the dwStrucVersion member. The last two members in this structure, dwFileDateMS and dwFileDateLS, are also set by the resource compiler. The current version of the resource compiler always sets these members to zero. All the remaining members in the structure have a one-to-one correspondence with the fields in the VERSIONINFO resource.

Once VerQueryValue has filled in the pvsffi variable with the address of this structure, you can reference any structure member to obtain various pieces of information about the file. If you wanted to determine if the file contained debugging information, for example, you could do this:

```
BOOL fHasDebugInfo = (pvsffi->dwFileFlags & VS_FF_DEBUG);
```

The second form of calling VerQueryValue is when the lpSubBlock parameter points to a string that contains "\VarFileInfo\Translation." For example, if you call VerQueryValue like this:

```
PDWORD pdwTranslationInfo;
UINT uLen, uCharSetID;
LANGID langid;
.
.
.
VerQueryValue(pvVerInfo, "\\VarFileInfo\\Translation",
    (PVOID *) &pdwTranslationInfo, &uLen);

langid = LOWORD(*pdwTranslationInfo);
uCharSetId = HIWORD(*pdwTranslationInfo);
```

VerQueryValue locates the Translation subsection within the VarFileInfo section of the version information resource and returns a pointer to it in the pdwTranslationInfo variable. When VerQueryValue returns, pdwTranslationInfo points to the list of language/character-set pairs. The low word of each pair contains the language Id and the high word contains the character set Id. The uLen variable is filled with the number of bytes in the Translation section when VerQueryValue returns. Dividing this value by 4 gives you the number of translation pairs in the version resource.

If you want to display the language information to the user as a string, you can use the VerLanguageName function:

```
DWORD VerLanguageName(DWORD idLang, LPTSTR lpszLang, DWORD cbLang);
```

This function accepts as its first parameter a language Id as retrieved from the Translation section in a version resource. It then fills a string buffer pointed to by the lpszLang parameter with a zero-terminated string that identifies the language. The last parameter is the maximum length of the buffer. If a language Id value of 0x0814 is passed as the idLang parameter, for example, the lpszLang buffer will be filled with "Norwegian-Nynorsk." If a language Id is passed to this function that is not recognized, VerLanguageName will fill the buffer with the string "Language-Neutral." It is important to note that this function returns the length of the string copied into the buffer. In the case of an unknown language Id, the function returns the length of the "Language-Neutral" string and does not indicate an error.

The last form of calling VerQueryValue is when the lpSubBlock parameter points to a string that contains "\StringFileInfo\Lang-CharSet\StringName." This form requests that VerQueryValue locate a language-specific string from a block in the StringFileInfo section of the version resource. The Lang-CharSet part is a concatenation of a language and character-set identifier pair found in the translation table by a previous call to VerQueryValue. The Lang-CharSet part must be specified as a hexadecimal string. The last part of the string, StringName, identifies one of the predefined strings shown in Table 9.4. For example, if you call VerQueryValue like this:

```
PDWORD pdwTranslationInfo;
UINT uLen;
char szStringFileInfo[50];
LPCSTR szCompanyName;
.
.
.
VerQueryValue(pvVerInfo, "\\VarFileInfo\\Translation",
    (PVOID *) &pdwTranslationInfo, &uLen);

wsprintf(szStringFileInfo, "\\StringFileInfo\\%04x%04x\\CompanyName",
    LOWORD(*pdwTranslationInfo), HIWORD(*pdwTranslationInfo));
```

```
VerQueryValue(pvVerInfo, szStringFileInfo,
    (PVOID *) &szCompanyName, &uLen);
```

VerQueryInfo locates the "CompanyName" string within the language block identified by the first translation pair and returns a pointer to it in the szCompanyName variable.

The VerShow Application

The VerShow application (**VerShow.EXE**) shown in Listings 9.1-9.3 (starting on page 570) demonstrates how to extract the version resource information contained inside a file. When you invoke the application, the main application window shown in Figure 9.1 appears:

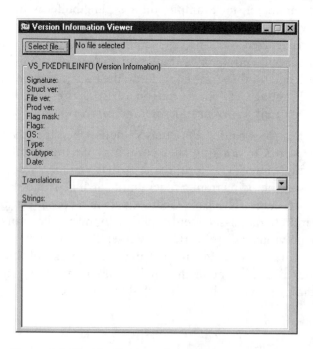

Figure 9.1 *The VerShow application.*

In order to view the version resource information contained inside a file, you must press the Select File button. This causes the File Open dialog box to appear, allowing you to select the file for which you want to see version control information. To make selecting files easier, the Files of Type combobox is filled only with the types of files that may contain version control information: executables,

DLLs, device drivers, fonts, virtual device drivers, and static-link libraries.

After selecting a file, VerShow updates its display information with the file's version resource information. If you tell VerShow to view the **VerShow.EXE** file itself, the information shown in Figure 9.2 is displayed.

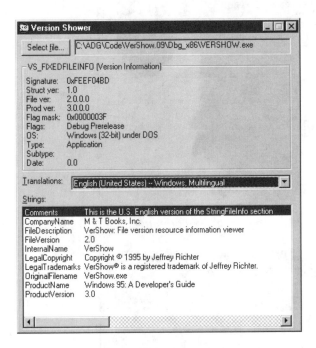

Figure 9.2 *VerShow's file resource information.*

The Translations combobox lists all language translations in which the version resource information is available. The VerShow application contains the same version information in three different languages. If you select German, VerShow's Strings listbox changes to reflect the German version of the version information's String FileInfo section, as shown in Figure 9.3.

Unfortunately, most companies do not put version resources inside their files. This practice is a mistake because it makes it much less likely that these files can be identified. If you ask VerShow to examine a file that does not contain any version resources, VerShow updates its display to look like Figure 9.4.

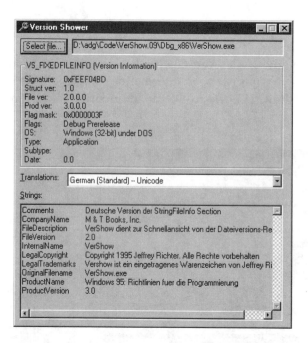

Figure 9.3 *The German resource information.*

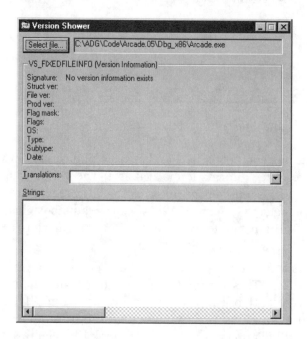

Figure 9.4 *A file with no resource information.*

The Windows 95 shell also supports version resource information to some degree. If you ask the shell to view the properties of a file that contains a version resource, the properties dialog box will have a Version tab. For example, Figure 9.5 was captured while viewing the properties for the VerShow.EXE file.

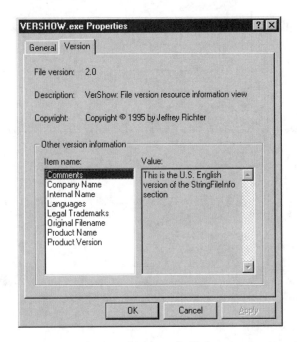

Figure 9.5 *The Windows 95 shell showing version information.*

Unfortunately, this property page shows only the English language version of the version resource's StringFileInfo section. It offers no way to see the strings in any other language.

Table 9.5 describes the files used to create this application.

Table 9.5 *Files used to build the VerShow application.*

File	Description
VerShow.C	Contains WinMain and main window's dialog box and message cracker functions.
VerShow.RC	Contains dialog-box template for main application window and its icons.

continued...

File	Description
Resource.H	Contains IDs for all resources in the RC file.
VerShow.ICO	Contains the icon for the main window.
VerShow.MAK	Visual C++ project makefile.

VerShow.ICO

Listing 9.1 *VerShow.C*

```
/****************************************************************************
Module name: VerShow.c
Written by: Jeffrey Richter
Notices: Copyright (c) 1995 Jeffrey Richter
Purpose: Version resource shower
****************************************************************************/


#include "..\Win95ADG.h"          /* See Appendix A for details. */
#include <windows.h>
#include <windowsx.h>
#pragma warning(disable: 4001)     /* Single-line comment */
#include <tchar.h>
#include "resource.h"


///////////////////////////////////////////////////////////////////////////


// The Version functions require the Version.lib library.  Because
// VC++ 2.x doesn't link with Version.lib by default, I must force it.
#pragma comment(lib, "Version.lib")


///////////////////////////////////////////////////////////////////////////


#define  VERBUFSIZE  2048


///////////////////////////////////////////////////////////////////////////


typedef struct {
   DWORD dwID;
   LPTSTR szName;
} VALUELIST;


const VALUELIST g_vlFileType[] = {
   { VFT_APP,          __TEXT("Application")          },
   { VFT_DLL,          __TEXT("Dynamic-link library") },
   { VFT_DRV,          __TEXT("Device driver")        },
```

```
   { VFT_FONT,          __TEXT("Font")               },
   { VFT_VXD,           __TEXT("Virtual device")     },
   { VFT_STATIC_LIB,    __TEXT("Static library")     },
   { 0,                 NULL                         }
};

const VALUELIST g_vlFileOSAppType[] = {
   { VOS__WINDOWS16,    __TEXT("Windows (16-bit)")   },
   { VOS__PM16,         __TEXT("PM (16-bit)")        },
   { VOS__PM32,         __TEXT("PM (32-bit)")        },
   { VOS__WINDOWS32,    __TEXT("Windows (32-bit)")   },
   { 0,                 NULL                         }
};

const VALUELIST g_vlFileOSPlatform[] = {
   { VOS_DOS,       __TEXT("DOS")          },
   { VOS_OS216,     __TEXT("OS/2 (16-bit)") },
   { VOS_OS232,     __TEXT("OS/2 (32-bit)") },
   { VOS_NT,        __TEXT("Windows NT")   },
   { 0,             NULL                   }
};

const VALUELIST g_vlDriverSubType[] = {
   { VFT2_DRV_PRINTER,      __TEXT("Printer")        },
   { VFT2_DRV_KEYBOARD,     __TEXT("Keyboard")       },
   { VFT2_DRV_LANGUAGE,     __TEXT("Language")       },
   { VFT2_DRV_DISPLAY,      __TEXT("Display")        },
   { VFT2_DRV_MOUSE,        __TEXT("Mouse")          },
   { VFT2_DRV_NETWORK,      __TEXT("Network")        },
   { VFT2_DRV_SYSTEM,       __TEXT("System")         },
   { VFT2_DRV_INSTALLABLE,  __TEXT("Installable")    },
   { VFT2_DRV_SOUND,        __TEXT("Sound")          },
   { VFT2_DRV_COMM,         __TEXT("Comm")           },
   { VFT2_DRV_INPUTMETHOD,  __TEXT("Input method")   },
   { 0,                     NULL                     }
};

const VALUELIST g_vlFontSubType[] = {
   { VFT2_FONT_RASTER,      __TEXT("Raster")     },
   { VFT2_FONT_VECTOR,      __TEXT("Vector")     },
   { VFT2_FONT_TRUETYPE,    __TEXT("TrueType")   },
   { 0,                     NULL                 }
};


/////////////////////////////////////////////////////////////////////////////


// This function appends the text names of the styles to a string buffer. It
// is used for the class styles, window styles, and extended window styles.
LPCTSTR VerShow_FindValueString (const VALUELIST Values[], DWORD dwValue) {

   int nValueIndex;

   for (nValueIndex = 0; Values[nValueIndex].szName != NULL; nValueIndex++) {
```

```
    if (Values[nValueIndex].dwID == dwValue) {

        // If we found the value, return the address of the string.
        return(Values[nValueIndex].szName);
    }
  }
  return(__TEXT("Unknown"));     // We didn't find the value.
}


//////////////////////////////////////////////////////////////////////////////


void VerShow_ConstructFixedStr (LPTSTR szBuf, PVOID pVerInfo) {

  VS_FIXEDFILEINFO *pvsffi;
  UINT uLen;
  TCHAR szFlags[1024], szVxdID[20];
  LPCTSTR szSubType = __TEXT("");
  DWORD dwTemp;

  if (pVerInfo == NULL) {
    lstrcpy(szBuf, __TEXT("No version information exists"));
    return;
  }

  // Get the address to the VS_FIXEDFILEINFO structure data.
  VerQueryValue(pVerInfo, __TEXT("\\"), (PVOID *) &pvsffi, &uLen);

  // Create the file flag string.
  szFlags[0] = 0;
  dwTemp = pvsffi->dwFileFlags;
  if (dwTemp & VS_FF_DEBUG)        lstrcat(szFlags, __TEXT("Debug "));
  if (dwTemp & VS_FF_PRERELEASE)   lstrcat(szFlags, __TEXT("Prerelease "));
  if (dwTemp & VS_FF_PATCHED)      lstrcat(szFlags, __TEXT("Patched "));
  if (dwTemp & VS_FF_PRIVATEBUILD) lstrcat(szFlags, __TEXT("PrivateBuild "));
  if (dwTemp & VS_FF_INFOINFERRED) lstrcat(szFlags, __TEXT("InfoInferred "));
  if (dwTemp & VS_FF_SPECIALBUILD) lstrcat(szFlags, __TEXT("SpecialBuild "));

  // Determine the file subtype.
  switch (pvsffi->dwFileType) {
    case VFT_DRV:
      szSubType = VerShow_FindValueString(g_vlDriverSubType,
        pvsffi->dwFileSubtype);
      break;

    case VFT_FONT:
      szSubType = VerShow_FindValueString(g_vlFontSubType,
        pvsffi->dwFileSubtype);
      break;

    case VFT_VXD:
      wsprintf(szVxdID, __TEXT("%ld"), pvsffi->dwFileSubtype);
      szSubType = szVxdID;
      break;
```

```
      case VFT_APP: case VFT_DLL: case VFT_STATIC_LIB: default:
         szSubType = __TEXT("");
         break;
   }

   wsprintf(szBuf,
      __TEXT("0x%08lX\n")          // Signature
      __TEXT("%d.%d\n")            // Structure version
      __TEXT("%d.%d.%d.%d\n")      // File version
      __TEXT("%d.%d.%d.%d\n")      // Product version
      __TEXT("0x%08lX\n")          // File flags mask
      __TEXT("%s\n")               // File flags
      __TEXT("%s under %s\n")      // File OS
      __TEXT("%s\n")               // File type
      __TEXT("%s\n")               // File subtype
      __TEXT("%d.%d"),             // File date converted to something

      pvsffi->dwSignature,
      HIWORD(pvsffi->dwStrucVersion),      LOWORD(pvsffi->dwStrucVersion),

      HIWORD(pvsffi->dwFileVersionMS),     LOWORD(pvsffi->dwFileVersionMS),
      HIWORD(pvsffi->dwFileVersionLS),     LOWORD(pvsffi->dwFileVersionLS),

      HIWORD(pvsffi->dwProductVersionMS), LOWORD(pvsffi->dwProductVersionMS),
      HIWORD(pvsffi->dwProductVersionLS), LOWORD(pvsffi->dwProductVersionLS),
      pvsffi->dwFileFlagsMask,             szFlags,

      VerShow_FindValueString(g_vlFileOSAppType,
         pvsffi->dwFileOS & 0x0000FFFF),
      VerShow_FindValueString(g_vlFileOSPlatform,
         pvsffi->dwFileOS & 0xFFFF0000),
      VerShow_FindValueString(g_vlFileType, (UINT) pvsffi->dwFileType),
      szSubType,
      pvsffi->dwFileDateMS,                pvsffi->dwFileDateLS);
}


///////////////////////////////////////////////////////////////////////////


void VerShow_ConstructVariableStr (LPTSTR szBuf, PVOID pVerInfo,
   UINT uTranslationNum) {

   TCHAR szFieldPath[200];
   LPCTSTR szData, const *szField;
   DWORD *pdwTranslation;
   UINT uLen;
   static const LPCTSTR g_szFields[] = {
      __TEXT("Comments"),
      __TEXT("CompanyName"),
      __TEXT("FileDescription"),
      __TEXT("FileVersion"),
      __TEXT("InternalName"),
      __TEXT("LegalCopyright"),
```

573

```
        __TEXT("LegalTrademarks"),
        __TEXT("OriginalFilename"),
        __TEXT("PrivateBuild"),
        __TEXT("ProductName"),
        __TEXT("ProductVersion"),
        __TEXT("SpecialBuild"),
        NULL
    };

    if (pVerInfo == NULL) {
        lstrcpy(szBuf, __TEXT("No version information exists"));
        return;
    }

    szBuf[0] = 0;  // Clears the contents of the string

    VerQueryValue(pVerInfo, __TEXT("\\VarFileInfo\\Translation"),
        (PVOID *) &pdwTranslation, &uLen);
    pdwTranslation += uTranslationNum;

    for (szField = &g_szFields[0]; *szField != NULL; szField++) {
        wsprintf(szFieldPath, __TEXT("\\StringFileInfo\\%04x%04x\\%s"),
            LOWORD(*pdwTranslation), HIWORD(*pdwTranslation), *szField);

        // NOTE: The cast to (LPTSTR) is necessary because
        //       the following VerQueryValue is prototyped incorrectly in
WINVER.h.
        if (VerQueryValue(pVerInfo, (LPTSTR) szFieldPath,
            (PVOID *) &szData, &uLen) && (uLen > 0)) {

            wsprintf(_tcschr(szBuf, 0), __TEXT("%s\t%s\r\n"), *szField, szData);
        }
    }
}


//////////////////////////////////////////////////////////////////////////


void VerShow_InitFileVerInfo (HWND hwnd, LPCTSTR pszPathname) {

    DWORD dwVerSize, *pdwTranslation;
    PVOID pVerInfo;
    UINT uLen, x;
    TCHAR szBuf[VERBUFSIZE];

    // If the user was already viewing a file's resource data, clean up.
    pVerInfo = (PVOID) GetWindowLong(hwnd, GWL_USERDATA);
    if (pVerInfo != NULL) {
        free(pVerInfo);
        SetWindowLong(hwnd, GWL_USERDATA, (LONG) (pVerInfo = NULL));
    }

    SetDlgItemText(hwnd, IDC_PATHNAME, pszPathname);
    if (pszPathname == NULL) {
```

```
      // If a NULL path name is passed, we should just clean up.
      return;
   }


   // Calculate the size of the version control resource information.
   // NOTE: The cast to the following (LPTSTR) is necessary because
   //       GetFileVersionInfoSize is prototyped incorrectly in WINVER.h.
   dwVerSize = GetFileVersionInfoSize((LPTSTR) pszPathname, NULL);
   if (dwVerSize > 0) {

      // Allocate a memory block large enough to hold the version information.
      if ((pVerInfo = malloc(dwVerSize)) != NULL) {

         // Load the version information into memory.
         // NOTE: The cast to the following (LPTSTR) is necessary because
         //       GetFileVersionInfo is prototyped incorrectly in WINVER.h.
         GetFileVersionInfo((LPTSTR) pszPathname, 0, dwVerSize, pVerInfo);
         SetWindowLong(hwnd, GWL_USERDATA, (LONG) pVerInfo);
      } else {
         adgMB(__TEXT("Insufficient memory."));
      }
   }


   // Update the VS_FIXEDFILEINFO information.
   VerShow_ConstructFixedStr(szBuf, pVerInfo);
   SetDlgItemText(hwnd, IDC_FIXEDFILEINFODATA, szBuf);

   // Update the Translations combobox.
   ComboBox_ResetContent(GetDlgItem(hwnd, IDC_TRANSLATIONS));
   if (pVerInfo != NULL) {
      VerQueryValue(pVerInfo, __TEXT("\\VarFileInfo\\Translation"),
         (PVOID *) &pdwTranslation, &uLen);
      for (x = 0; x < uLen; x += 4, pdwTranslation++) {
         // Get the string name for the language number.
         VerLanguageName(LOWORD(*pdwTranslation), szBuf, adgARRAY_SIZE(szBuf));
         lstrcat(szBuf, __TEXT(" -- "));
         // Get the string name for the code page number.
         LoadString(GetWindowInstance(hwnd), HIWORD(*pdwTranslation),
            _tcschr(szBuf, 0),
            (UINT) (adgARRAY_SIZE(szBuf) - (_tcschr(szBuf, 0) - szBuf)));
         // Add the string to the combobox.
         ComboBox_AddString(GetDlgItem(hwnd, IDC_TRANSLATIONS), szBuf);
      }
      // Select the first translation entry as the default.
      ComboBox_SetCurSel(GetDlgItem(hwnd, IDC_TRANSLATIONS), 0);
   }

   // Update the string information for the default translation.
   VerShow_ConstructVariableStr(szBuf, pVerInfo, 0);
   SetDlgItemText(hwnd, IDC_STRINGS, szBuf);
}
```

//

```
BOOL VerShow_OnInitDialog (HWND hwnd, HWND hwndFocus, LPARAM lParam) {

  adgSETDLGICONS(hwnd, IDI_VERSHOW, IDI_VERSHOW);
  return(TRUE);                    // Accepts default focus window.
}



////////////////////////////////////////////////////////////////////////////


void VerShow_OnCommand (HWND hwnd, int id, HWND hwndCtl, UINT codeNotify) {
  OPENFILENAME ofn;
  TCHAR szPathname[128], szBuf[VERBUFSIZE];

  switch (id) {

    case IDCANCEL:                 // Allows dialog box to close
      VerShow_InitFileVerInfo(hwnd, NULL);
      EndDialog(hwnd, 0);
      break;

    case IDC_SELECTFILE:
      adgINITSTRUCT(ofn, TRUE);
      ofn.hwndOwner = hwnd;
      ofn.lpstrFilter =
        __TEXT("Executables (*.exe)\0*.EXE\0")
        __TEXT("DLLs (*.dll)\0*.DLL\0")
        __TEXT("Device drivers (*.drv)\0*.DRV\0")
        __TEXT("Fonts (*.fon)\0*.FON\0")
        __TEXT("Virtual devices (*.386)\0*.386\0")
        __TEXT("Static libraries (*.lib)\0*.LIB\0")
        __TEXT("All files (*.*)\0*.*\0");
      ofn.lpstrFile = szPathname; ofn.lpstrFile[0] = 0;
      ofn.nMaxFile = adgARRAY_SIZE(szPathname);
      ofn.Flags = OFN_HIDEREADONLY | OFN_FILEMUSTEXIST | OFN_EXPLORER;
      if (GetOpenFileName(&ofn)) {
        VerShow_InitFileVerInfo(hwnd, ofn.lpstrFile);
      }
      break;

    case IDC_TRANSLATIONS:
      if (codeNotify == CBN_SELCHANGE) {

        // Update the string information for the selected translation.
        VerShow_ConstructVariableStr(szBuf,
          (PVOID) GetWindowLong(hwnd, GWL_USERDATA),
          ComboBox_GetCurSel(hwndCtl));
        SetDlgItemText(hwnd, IDC_STRINGS, szBuf);
      }
      break;
  }
}


////////////////////////////////////////////////////////////////////////////
```

```
BOOL WINAPI VerShow_DlgProc (HWND hwnd, UINT uMsg,
   WPARAM wParam, LPARAM lParam) {

   switch (uMsg) {

      // Standard Windows messages
      adgHANDLE_DLGMSG(hwnd, WM_INITDIALOG, VerShow_OnInitDialog);
      adgHANDLE_DLGMSG(hwnd, WM_COMMAND,    VerShow_OnCommand);
   }
   return(FALSE);
}


///////////////////////////////////////////////////////////////////////////


int WINAPI WinMain (HINSTANCE hinstExe, HINSTANCE hinstPrev,
   LPSTR lpszCmdLine, int nCmdShow) {

   adgWARNIFUNICODEUNDERWIN95();
   adgVERIFY(-1 != DialogBox(hinstExe,
      MAKEINTRESOURCE(IDD_VERSHOW), NULL, VerShow_DlgProc));

   return(0);
}


///////////////////////////// End of File /////////////////////////////////
```

Listing 9.2 *VerShow.RC*

```
// Microsoft Visual C++-generated resource script
//
#include "resource.h"

#define APSTUDIO_READONLY_SYMBOLS
///////////////////////////////////////////////////////////////////////////
//
// Generated from the TEXTINCLUDE 2 resource
//
#define APSTUDIO_HIDDEN_SYMBOLS
#include "windows.h"
#undef APSTUDIO_HIDDEN_SYMBOLS
#include "ver.h"
#include "vershow.h"


///////////////////////////////////////////////////////////////////////////
#undef APSTUDIO_READONLY_SYMBOLS


///////////////////////////////////////////////////////////////////////////
```

```
//
// Icon
//

IDI_VERSHOW           ICON    DISCARDABLE    "VerShow.ico"

/////////////////////////////////////////////////////////////////////////////
//
// Version
//

VS_VERSION_INFO VERSIONINFO
 FILEVERSION 2,0,0,0
 PRODUCTVERSION 3,0,0,0
 FILEFLAGSMASK 0x3fL
#ifdef _DEBUG
 FILEFLAGS 0x3L
#else
 FILEFLAGS 0x2L
#endif
 FILEOS 0x10004L
 FILETYPE 0x1L
 FILESUBTYPE 0x0L
BEGIN
    BLOCK "StringFileInfo"
    BEGIN
        BLOCK "040704e4"
        BEGIN
            VALUE "Comments", "This is the German version of the StringFileInfo
section\0"
            VALUE "CompanyName", "M & T Books, Inc.\0"
            VALUE "FileDescription", "VerShow dient zur Schnellansicht von
Datei-Versions und -Ressourceninformation\0"
            VALUE "FileVersion", "2.0\0"
            VALUE "InternalName", "VerShow\0"
            VALUE "LegalCopyright", "Copyright 1995 Jeffrey Richter. Alle
Rechte vorbehalten\0"
            VALUE "LegalTrademarks", "Vershow ist ein eingetragenes
Warenzeichen von Jeffrey Richter\0"
            VALUE "OriginalFilename", "VerShow.exe\0"
            VALUE "ProductName", "Windows 95: Richtlinien fuer die
Programmierung\0"
            VALUE "ProductVersion", "3.0\0"
        END
        BLOCK "040904e4"
        BEGIN
            VALUE "Comments", "This is the U.S. English version of the
StringFileInfo section\0"
            VALUE "CompanyName", "M & T Books, Inc.\0"
            VALUE "FileDescription", "VerShow: File version resource information
viewer\0"
            VALUE "FileVersion", "2.0\0"
            VALUE "InternalName", "VerShow\0"
            VALUE "LegalCopyright", "Copyright \251 1995 by Jeffrey Richter\0"
            VALUE "LegalTrademarks", "VerShow\256 is a registered trademark
```

```
of Jeffrey Richter.\0"
            VALUE "OriginalFilename", "VerShow.exe\0"
            VALUE "ProductName", "Windows 95: A Developer's Guide\0"
            VALUE "ProductVersion", "3.0\0"
        END
        BLOCK "040c04e4"
        BEGIN
            VALUE "CompanyName", "M & T Books, Inc.\0"
            VALUE "FileDescription", "\0"
            VALUE "FileVersion", "2.0\0"
            VALUE "InternalName", "VerShow\0"
            VALUE "LegalCopyright", "Copyright \251 1995\0"
            VALUE "OriginalFilename", "VerShow.exe\0"
            VALUE "ProductName", "\0"
            VALUE "ProductVersion", "3.0\0"
        END
    END
    BLOCK "VarFileInfo"
    BEGIN
        VALUE "Translation", 0x407, 1252, 0x409, 1252, 0x40c, 1252
    END
END


/////////////////////////////////////////////////////////////////////////////
//
// Dialog
//

IDD_VERSHOW DIALOG DISCARDABLE  -32768, 5, 275, 261
STYLE WS_MINIMIZEBOX | WS_VISIBLE | WS_CAPTION | WS_SYSMENU
CAPTION "Version Shower"
FONT 6, "Helv"
BEGIN
    PUSHBUTTON      "Select &file...",IDC_SELECTFILE,4,4,48,14
    CONTROL         "(Please select a file)",IDC_PATHNAME,"Static",
                    SS_LEFTNOWORDWRAP | SS_NOPREFIX | WS_BORDER | WS_GROUP,
                    56,4,212,14
    GROUPBOX        "VS_FIXEDFILEINFO (Version Information)",IDC_STATIC,4,24,
                    264,96
    LTEXT           "Signature:\nStruct ver:\nFile ver:\nProd ver:\nFlag
mask:\nFlags:\nOS:\nType:\nSubtype:\nDate:",
                    IDC_FIXEDFILEINFOFIELDS,8,36,40,80,SS_NOPREFIX
    LTEXT           "",IDC_FIXEDFILEINFODATA,48,36,216,80,SS_NOPREFIX
    LTEXT           "&Translations:",IDC_STATIC,4,124,44,8
    COMBOBOX        IDC_TRANSLATIONS,52,124,216,80,CBS_DROPDOWNLIST |
                    WS_VSCROLL | WS_GROUP | WS_TABSTOP
    LTEXT           "&Strings:",IDC_STATIC,4,140,32,10
    EDITTEXT        IDC_STRINGS,4,152,264,104,ES_MULTILINE | ES_AUTOHSCROLL |
                    ES_READONLY | WS_VSCROLL | WS_HSCROLL
END


#ifdef APSTUDIO_INVOKED
```

579

```
//////////////////////////////////////////////////////////////////////////
//
// TEXTINCLUDE
//

1 TEXTINCLUDE DISCARDABLE
BEGIN
    "resource.h\0"
END

2 TEXTINCLUDE DISCARDABLE
BEGIN
    "#define APSTUDIO_HIDDEN_SYMBOLS\r\n"
    "#include ""windows.h""\r\n"
    "#undef APSTUDIO_HIDDEN_SYMBOLS\r\n"
    "#include ""ver.h""\r\n"
    "#include ""vershow.h""\r\n"
    "\0"
END

3 TEXTINCLUDE DISCARDABLE
BEGIN
    "\r\n"
    "\0"
END

//////////////////////////////////////////////////////////////////////////
#endif    // APSTUDIO_INVOKED


//////////////////////////////////////////////////////////////////////////
//
// String Table
//

STRINGTABLE DISCARDABLE
BEGIN
    0                   "7-bit ASCII"
END

STRINGTABLE DISCARDABLE
BEGIN
    932                 "Windows, Japan (Shift - JIS X-0208)"
END

STRINGTABLE DISCARDABLE
BEGIN
    949                 "Windows, Korea (Shift - KSC 5601)"
    950                 "Windows, Taiwan (GB5)"
END

STRINGTABLE DISCARDABLE
BEGIN
    1200                "Unicode"
```

```
END

STRINGTABLE DISCARDABLE
BEGIN
    1250                    "Windows, Latin-2 (Eastern Europe)"
    1251                    "Windows, Cyrillic"
    1252                    "Windows, Multilingual"
    1253                    "Windows, Greek"
    1254                    "Windows, Turkish"
    1255                    "Windows, Hebrew"
    1256                    "Windows, Arabic"
END


#ifndef APSTUDIO_INVOKED
/////////////////////////////////////////////////////////////////////////////
//
// Generated from the TEXTINCLUDE 3 resource
//


/////////////////////////////////////////////////////////////////////////////
#endif    // not APSTUDIO_INVOKED
```

Listing 9.3 *Resource.H*

```
//{{NO_DEPENDENCIES}}
// Microsoft Visual C++-generated include file
// Used by VerShow.rc
//
#define IDD_VERSHOW                 101
#define IDI_VERSHOW                 102
#define IDC_PATHNAME                1000
#define IDC_FIXEDFILEINFOFIELDS     1001
#define IDC_FIXEDFILEINFODATA       1002
#define IDC_TRANSLATIONS            1003
#define IDC_STRINGS                 1004
#define IDC_SELECTFILE              1005
#define IDC_STATIC                  65535

// Next default values for new objects
//
#ifdef APSTUDIO_INVOKED
#ifndef APSTUDIO_READONLY_SYMBOLS
#define _APS_NO_MFC                 1
#define _APS_NEXT_RESOURCE_VALUE    103
#define _APS_NEXT_COMMAND_VALUE     40001
#define _APS_NEXT_CONTROL_VALUE     1007
#define _APS_NEXT_SYMED_VALUE       101
#endif
#endif
```

When you press the Select File button, the VerShow_OnCommand function initializes an OPENFILENAME structure and calls GetOpenFileName, which allows you to select a file. After you've selected a file, VerShow_OnCommand updates all the dialog box's controls with the version information by calling:

```
PVOID VerShow_InitFileVerInfo (HWND hwnd, LPCTSTR pszPathname);
```

This function first checks to see if there is already a memory block containing the version information for the previously selected file. If so, it frees the block:

```
// If the user was already viewing a file's resource data, clean up.
pVerInfo = (PVOID) GetWindowLong(hwnd, GWL_USERDATA);
if (pVerInfo != NULL) {
   free(pVerInfo);
   SetWindowLong(hwnd, GWL_USERDATA, (LONG) (pVerInfo = NULL));
}
```

Notice that the address to the selected file's version information is saved in the dialog box's GWL_USERDATA window bytes. After freeing this block, VerShow_InitFileVerInfo concentrates on the newly selected file.

First, it places the file's path name in the static window at the top of the dialog box. Then, it allocates a block of memory and reads the new file's version information into it:

```
// Calculate the size of the version control resource information.
// NOTE: The cast to (LPTSTR) is necessary because
//       GetFileVersionInfoSize is prototyped incorrectly in WINVER.h.
dwVerSize = GetFileVersionInfoSize((LPTSTR) pszPathname, NULL);
if (dwVerSize > 0) {

   // Allocate a memory block large enough to hold the version information.
   if ((pVerInfo = malloc(dwVerSize)) != NULL) {

      // Load the version information into memory.
      // NOTE: The cast to (LPTSTR) is necessary because
      //       GetFileVersionInfo is prototyped incorrectly in WINVER.h.
      GetFileVersionInfo((LPTSTR) pszPathname, 0, dwVerSize, pVerInfo);
      SetWindowLong(hwnd, GWL_USERDATA, (LONG) pVerInfo);
   } else {
      adgMB(__TEXT("Insufficient memory."));
   }
}
```

You can see that GetFileVersionInfoSize is called first in order to get the number of bytes required to hold the version information. Then, malloc is called to allocate this block. And finally, GetFileVersionInfo is used to read the data from the file into the block. After the version information is read into memory, the address of the block is saved in the dialog box's GWL_USERDATA window bytes.

Note that there are several small prototyping bugs with the version functions. Many of them are prototyped as expecting pointers to strings, when in fact, they should be prototyped as expecting pointers to constant strings. For this reason, I have had to put some additional casts in my code so that the compiler does not complain. Hopefully, Microsoft will fix these prototype errors in future versions of the Windows header files.

Now that the resource information is in memory, VerShow_ InitFileVerInfo can update the dialog box's controls. The VS_FIXED-FILEINFO information is updated first by placing a call to VerShow_ ConstructFixedStr, which parses the members of the VS_FIXEDFILE-INFO structure and fills a string buffer with the results. This buffer is then placed in a static control in the dialog box:

```
// Update the VS_FIXEDFILEINFO information.
VerShow_ConstructFixedStr(szBuf, pVerInfo);
SetDlgItemText(hwnd, IDC_FIXEDFILEINFODATA, szBuf);
```

Then, VerShow_InitFileVerInfo fills theTranslations combobox by calling VerQueryValue to determine how many bytes are in the Translation section. This function also returns the memory address of the Translation data. Next, a loop is created that iterates through each of the translation values. For each iteration, VerLanguageName is called to get the string name of the language. Then, LoadString is called to get the name of the code page from VerShow's own string table resource. Each constructed string is appended to the combobox. When the loop is all finished, the zeroeth entry in the combobox is selected as the default:

```
// Update the Translations combobox.
ComboBox_ResetContent(GetDlgItem(hwnd, IDC_TRANSLATIONS));
if (pVerInfo != NULL) {
```

```
VerQueryValue(pVerInfo, __TEXT("\\VarFileInfo\\Translation"),
    (PVOID *) &pdwTranslation, &uLen);
for (x = 0; x < uLen; x += 4, pdwTranslation++) {
    // Get the string name for the language number.
    VerLanguageName(LOWORD(*pdwTranslation), szBuf, adgARRAY_SIZE(szBuf));
    lstrcat(szBuf, __TEXT(" — "));
    // Get the string name for the code page number.
    LoadString(GetWindowInstance(hwnd), HIWORD(*pdwTranslation),
        _tcschr(szBuf, 0),
        (UINT) (adgARRAY_SIZE(szBuf) - (_tcschr(szBuf, 0) - szBuf)));
    // Add the string to the combobox.
    ComboBox_AddString(GetDlgItem(hwnd, IDC_TRANSLATIONS), szBuf);
}
// Select the first translation entry as the default.
ComboBox_SetCurSel(GetDlgItem(hwnd, IDC_TRANSLATIONS), 0);
}
```

Just before VerShow_InitFileVerInfo returns, it must fill the Strings read-only edit control with the string information from the file's version resource. This is done by calling VerShow_ConstructVariableStr, passing it the address of a string buffer that is to receive the parsed information, the address of the version information memory block, and the index into the combobox that identifies the language selected by the user. When VerShow_ConstructVariableStr returns, the string buffer is placed in the read-only edit control:

```
// Update the string information for the default translation.
VerShow_ConstructVariableStr(szBuf, pVerInfo, 0);
SetDlgItemText(hwnd, IDC_STRINGS, szBuf);
```

The Win95ADG.h Header File

All the applications in this book include the **Win95ADG.h** header file before including any other header file. The **Win95ADG.h** header file exists in order to make life a little easier. The file contains macros, linker directives, and other things that are common across all the applications. The names of all the macros in **Win95ADG.h** are prefixed with "adg" (A Developer's Guide) so that you can easily identify them when perusing the source code for the applications. To try out different build options, all you have to do is modify the **Win95ADG.h** file and rebuild.

The remainder of this appendix discusses each of the sections contained within the **Win95ADG.h** header file, giving a rationale and description of each.

Build Options

Warning Level 4

When I develop software, I always do my best to ensure that the code compiles both error and warning free. I also like to compile at the highest warning level possible. This way, the compiler is doing the most work for me and is examining even the most minute details of my code. For the Microsoft C/C++ compilers, this means that I built all the applications on the companion disc using warning level 4.

Unfortunately, Microsoft's Operating Systems group doesn't share my sentiments about warning level 4. As a result, when I set the applications to compile at warning level 4, there are many lines in the Windows header files that cause the compiler to generate warnings. Fortunately, these warnings do not represent problems in the code; most are generated by unconventional uses of the C language. These uses rely on compiler extensions that almost all vendors of PC-compatible compilers implement.

This section of the **Win95ADG.h** header file explicitly tells the compiler to ignore some common warnings using the #pragma warning directive.

Defining Versions

Almost all the applications in this book take advantage of features that have been added to Windows 95 and Windows NT 3.51[1]. In order to gain access to these new features, the WINVER macro must be defined prior to including **Windows.h**:

```
#define WINVER 0x0400
```

Without this definition, the compiler would complain every time we referenced the new WM_CAPTURECHANGED message, for example. In addition, we must also tell Windows that our application is Windows 4.0-aware so that the system will enable all the features that we rightfully deserve as a Windows 4.0 application.

```
// Force all EXEs/DLLs to be built for Windows 4.0. Comment out the following
// #pragma line to create samples that run under Windows NT 3.1 or Win32s.
// NOTE: Windows NT 3.5 and 3.51 run Win32 programs marked as 4.0.
#pragma comment(lib, "kernel32 " "-subsystem:Windows,4.0 ")
```

The preceding line tricks the compiler into emitting linker directives into the module's OBJ file. The linker then knows to mark the application as being Version 4.0-aware. I would use a more straightforward approach, but bugs in version 2.55 of Microsoft's linker prevent me[2].

STRICT Type Checking

All the applications are compiled taking advantage of the STRICT type-checking support available in the Windows header files. This support makes sure that I assign HWNDs to HWNDs and HDCs to HDCs, and so forth. With STRICT defined, the compiler issues a warning if, for example, I attempt to assign an HWND to an HDC.

---

[1]In some cases, even Windows NT 3.51 doesn't support some of these features yet.

[2]If you want to understand more about this, see Appendix B of *Advanced Windows*, Microsoft Press, 1995.

In order to turn STRICT type checking on, the compiler must have the STRICT macro defined prior to including the Windows header files. This is why all the source code files include **Win95ADG.h** before including **Windows.h**.

Unicode

All the applications are written so that they can be compiled as either ANSI or Unicode. By default, the applications compile using ANSI strings and characters, but by defining the UNICODE and _UNICODE macros, the applications compile using Unicode strings and characters. By defining the UNICODE macro in **Win95ADG.h**, it is easy for me to control how I want the applications to build. For more information on Unicode, see the "Unicode" chapter of *Advanced Windows*.

CPU Portability Macros

The CPU portability macros exist so that you can use the #pragma comment directive to force the linker to link with a DLL's import library automatically. For example, the KeyCount application links to the **KybdHk.dll**. Rather than putting the details of this in the MAK file, we put a linker directive right in the source code using the following line:

```
// Force a link with the import library for KybdHk.dll
#pragma comment(lib, adgLIBBUILDTYPE adgLIBCPUTYPE "\\" "KybdHk")
```

The adgLIBBUILDTYPE macro expands to either "Dbg_" or "Rel_" depending on whether you are building a debug or release version of the application. The adgLIBCPUTYPE macro expands to "x86," "MIPS," "Alpha," or "PPC" depending on your target CPU platform. This means that the #pragma line will expand to

```
#pragma comment(lib, "Dbg_x86\\KybdHk")
```

when you build a debug version of the KeyCount application for an Intel x86 machine.

Useful Macros

The adgARRAY_SIZE Macro

The adgARRAY_SIZE macro is a useful macro that I tend to use in almost all the programs I write. It simply returns the number of elements in an array. It does this by using the sizeof operator to first calculate the size of the entire array in bytes. It then divides this number by the number of bytes required for a single entry in the array. Here is the macro.

```
// This macro evaluates to the number of elements in an array.
#define adgARRAY_SIZE(Array) (sizeof(Array) / sizeof((Array)[0]))
```

The adgINRANGE Macro

The adgINRANGE macro evaluates to TRUE if a value is within a range. The end points of the range are included.

```
// This macro evaluates to TRUE if val is betwen lo and hi inclusive.
#define adgINRANGE(lo, val, hi) (((lo) <= (val)) && ((val) <= (hi)))
```

The adgASSERT and adgVERIFY Macros

To help find potential problems while developing the applications, we frequently sprinkled adgASSERT macros throughout the code. The adgASSERT macro is defined as follows:

```
// Put up a message box if an assertion fails in a debug build.
#ifdef _DEBUG
#define adgASSERT(x) if (!(x)) adgASSERTFAIL(__FILE__, __LINE__, #x)
#else
#define adgASSERT(x)
#endif
```

This macro tests if the expression identified by x is TRUE and, if not, displays a message box indicating the file, line, and the expression that failed. In release builds of the applications, this macro expands to nothing. The adgVERIFY macro is almost identical to the adgASSERT macro except that the expression is evaluated in release builds as well as debug builds. The macro is defined as follows:

```
// Assert in debug builds, but don't remove the code in retail builds.
#ifdef _DEBUG
#define adgVERIFY(x) adgASSERT(x)
#else
#define adgVERIFY(x) (x)
#endif
```

The adgHANDLE_DLGMSG Macro

When using message crackers with dialog boxes, you should not use the HANDLE_MSG macro from Microsoft's **WINDOWSX.H** header file (as I mistakenly did in *Advanced Windows*). The reason is because the HANDLE_MSG macro doesn't return TRUE or FALSE indicating whether a message was handled by the dialog-box procedure. The following adgHANDLE_DLGMSG macro below solves this problem:

```
// The normal HANDLE_MSG macro in WINDOWSX.H does not work properly for dialog
// boxes because DlgProc's return a BOOL instead of an LRESULT (like
// WndProcs). This adgHANDLE_DLGMSG macro corrects the problem.
#define adgHANDLE_DLGMSG(hwnd, message, fn)                              \
   case (message): return (SetDlgMsgResult(hwnd, uMsg,                  \
      HANDLE_##message((hwnd), (wParam), (lParam), (fn))))
```

Window Extra Byte Macros

The Window Extra Byte macros make it more convenient to store and retrieve data from window extra bytes. To use these macros to access extra bytes, the application must declare a data structure with a member for each of the elements to be stored. Each member should be a 2- or 4-byte entity. For example, a window class that needs to store a window handle and a DWORD value would declare a structure like this:

```
typedef struct {
   HWND hwndChild;
   DWORD dwLastEventTime;
} CLS_WNDEXTRABYTES;
```

When the application is initializing the WNDCLASSEX structure to pass to RegisterClassEx, the cbWndExtra member of this structure should be initialized as follows:

```
WNDCLASSEX wc;
adgINITSTRUCT(wc, TRUE);      // See below
wc.cbWndExtra = sizeof(CLS_WNDEXTRABYTES);
```

This guarantees that the proper number of extra bytes is always allocated. If you later add, delete, or change any of the members in the structure, the sizeof operator returns the proper length of the structure when the module is recompiled.

Storing information in the window instance's extra bytes is accomplished like this:

```
adgSETWINDOWLONG(hwnd, CLS_WNDEXTRABYTES, dwLastEventTime, GetTickCount());
```

The adgSETWINDOWLONG macro is defined as follows:

```
#define adgSETWINDOWLONG(hwnd, structure, member, value) \
    SetWindowLong(hwnd, adgMEMBEROFFSET(structure, member), (LONG) (value))
```

This macro calls the SetWindowLong function passing the offset of the structure's member as computed by the adgMEMBEROFFSET macro. A member's offset into the structure is the same as its offset into the window's extra bytes. Therefore, the offset is also automatically determined at compile time. If members of the structure change, recompiling the module automatically generates the correct offsets.

Values stored in the window's extra bytes are retrieved by the adgGETWINDOWLONG macro, defined as follows:

```
#define adgGETWINDOWLONG(hwnd, structure, member) \
    GetWindowLong(hwnd, adgMEMBEROFFSET(structure, member))
```

This macro is similar to adgSETWINDOWLONG except that it calls GetWindowLong and doesn't require an additional parameter specifying a new value.

The adgMB Macro

The adgMB macro simply puts up a message box. The caption is the full path name of the executable file for the calling process.

```
#define adgMB(s) {                                              \
    TCHAR szTMP[128];                                           \
    GetModuleFileName(NULL, szTMP, adgARRAY_SIZE(szTMP));       \
    MessageBox(GetActiveWindow(), s, szTMP, MB_OK);             \
    }
```

The adgINITSTRUCT Macro

The adgINITSRTUCT macro is by far my favorite of all the macros in **Win95ADG.h**. I love this macro! In Win32 programming, we frequently have to allocate a data structure, zero it, and initialize the first member of the structure to the size of the structure. I have seen many programmers either forget to do one or both of these things. The result is that their calls to Win32 functions fail for no apparent reason, or worse, coincidentally work—sometimes!

If you religiously use the adgINITSTRUCT macro, you will be ensured that the structure's members are always cleared to zero. You must explicitly state whether or not you want the first member to be initialized to the size of the structure. If you pass TRUE as the second parameter, the size will be automatically initialized—this way, you will never forget!

```
// Zero out a structure. If fInitSize is TRUE then initialize the first int to
// the size of the structure. Many structures like WNDCLASSEX and STARTUPINFO
// require that their first member be set to the size of the structure itself.
#define adgINITSTRUCT(structure, fInitSize)                          \
   (ZeroMemory(&(structure), sizeof(structure)),                     \
   fInitSize ? (*(int*) &(structure) = sizeof(structure)) : 0)
```

The adgSETDLGICONS Macro

Because most of the applications use a modal dialog box as their main window, we must manually change the dialog box's icon so that it is displayed correctly on the Taskbar, in the task switch window, and in the application's caption itself. The adgSETDLGICONS macro is always called when our dialog boxes receive a WM_INITDIALOG message so that the icons are set correctly. Here is the macro.

```
// The call to SetClassLong is for Windows NT.
// Sending the WM_SETICON messages is for Windows 95.
#define adgSETDLGICONS(hwnd, idiLarge, idiSmall)                       \
   SetClassLong(hwnd, GCL_HICON, (LONG)                               \
      LoadIcon(GetWindowInstance(hwnd), MAKEINTRESOURCE(idiLarge))),  \
   SendMessage(hwnd, WM_SETICON, TRUE,  (LPARAM)                      \
      LoadIcon(GetWindowInstance(hwnd), MAKEINTRESOURCE(idiLarge))),  \
   SendMessage(hwnd, WM_SETICON, FALSE, (LPARAM)                      \
      LoadIcon(GetWindowInstance(hwnd), MAKEINTRESOURCE(idiSmall)))
```

The adgWARNIFUNICODEUNDERWIN95 Macro

Windows 95 does not support Unicode as completely as Windows NT. In fact, applications that call Unicode functions will not run on Windows 95 at all! Unfortunately, Windows 95 does not give any notification whatsoever if an application compiled for Unicode is invoked. For the applications in this book, this means that the applications start and terminate with no indication that they ever attempted to execute. This drove us absolutely nuts! So, we created this adgWARNIFUNICODEUNDERWIN95 macro so that we would know when we attempted to run a Unicode-compiled application under Windows 95. Here is the macro.

```
#ifdef UNICODE

#define adgWARNIFUNICODEUNDERWIN95() {                                        \
    OSVERSIONINFOA VerInfo;                                                   \
    adgINITSTRUCT(VerInfo, TRUE);                                             \
    GetVersionExA(&VerInfo);                                                  \
    if ((VerInfo.dwPlatformId == VER_PLATFORM_WIN32_WINDOWS) &&              \
        (VerInfo.dwMajorVersion == 4) && (VerInfo.dwMinorVersion == 0))     \
      MessageBoxA(NULL, "Windows 95 doesn't support Unicode", NULL, MB_OK); \
    }

#else

#define adgWARNIFUNICODEUNDERWIN95()

#endif
```

This macro expands to nothing if UNICODE is not defined. Otherwise, it explicitly declares an ANSI version of an OSVER-SIONINFO structure and then calls the ANSI version of the GetVersionEx function. The macro then checks to see if the application is running on Windows 95, and, if so, the ANSI version of MessageBox is called to notify us that the applications won't work correctly. Note that this macro will cease to function properly if Windows 96 (or whatever they call it) does not have better Unicode support.

The WM_CAPTURECHANGED Message Cracker Macros

The HANDLE_WM_CAPTURECHANGED and FORWARD_WM_CAPTURECHANGED message crackers are defined because Microsoft did not add these message crackers to the **WindowsX.H** header file. These message cracker macros are defined as follows:

```
/* void Cls_OnCaptureChanged(HWND hwnd, HWND hwndNewCapture) */
#define HANDLE_WM_CAPTURECHANGED(hwnd, wParam, lParam, fn) \
    ((fn)((hwnd), (HWND)(lParam)), 0L)
#define FORWARD_WM_CAPTURECHANGED(hwnd, hwndNewCapture, fn) \
    (void)(fn)((hwnd), WM_CAPTURECHANGED, (WPARAM)(HWND)(hwndNewCapture), 0L)
```

Listing A.1 *Win95ADG.h*

```
/****************************************************************************
Module name: Win95ADG.h
Written by: Jeffrey Richter and Jonathan Locke
Notices: Copyright (c) 1995 Jeffrey Richter
Purpose: Common header file for "Windows 95: A Developer's Guide"
         Contains handy macros and definitions used throughout
         the sample applications
****************************************************************************/

/* Disable ridiculous warnings so that the code */
/* compiles cleanly using warning level 4.      */

/* nonstandard extension 'single line comment' was used */
#pragma warning(disable: 4001)

// nonstandard extension used : nameless struct/union
#pragma warning(disable: 4201)

// nonstandard extension used : bit field types other than int
#pragma warning(disable: 4214)

// Note: Creating precompiled header
#pragma warning(disable: 4699)

// unreferenced inline function has been removed
#pragma warning(disable: 4514)

// unreferenced formal parameter
#pragma warning(disable: 4100)

// indirection to slightly different base types
#pragma warning(disable: 4057)

// named type definition in parentheses
#pragma warning(disable: 4115)

// nonstandard extension used : benign typedef redefinition
#pragma warning(disable: 4209)


///////////////////////// Windows Version Build Option /////////////////////////


#define WINVER 0x0400


//////////////////////////// Application Build Option ////////////////////////////
```

```
// Force all EXEs/DLLs to be built for Windows 4.0. Comment out the following
// #pragma line to create samples that run under Windows NT 3.1 or Win32s.
// NOTE: Windows NT 3.5 and 3.51 run Win32 programs marked as 4.0.
#pragma comment(lib, "kernel32 " "-subsystem:Windows,4.0 ")


/////////////////////////// STRICK Build Option ///////////////////////////////


// Force all EXEs/DLLs to use STRICT type checking.
#define STRICT


/////////////////////////// Unicode Build Option //////////////////////////////


// Force all EXEs/DLLs to be compiled for Unicode.
// Uncomment the next line to compile using Unicode strings.
//#define UNICODE
#ifdef UNICODE
#define _UNICODE
#endif


/////////////////////////// CPU Portability Macros /////////////////////////////


// If no CPU platform was specified, default to the current platform.
#if !defined(_PPC_) && !defined(_ALPHA_) && !defined(_MIPS_) && !defined(_X86_)
    #if defined(_M_IX86)
        #define _X86_
    #endif
    #if defined(_M_MRX000)
        #define _MIPS_
    #endif
    #if defined(_M_ALPHA)
        #define _ALPHA_
    #endif
    #if defined(_M_PPC)
        #define _PPC_
    #endif
#endif

#if defined(_DEBUG)
    #define adgLIBBUILDTYPE "Dbg_"
#else
    #define adgLIBBUILDTYPE "Rel_"
#endif

#if defined(_X86_)
    #define adgLIBCPUTYPE "x86"
#elif defined(_MIPS_)
    #define adgLIBCPUTYPE "MIPS"
#elif defined(_ALPHA_)
    #define adgLIBCPUTYPE "Alph"
#elif defined(_PPC_)
```

```
     #define adgLIBCPUTYPE "PPC"
#else
     #error Win95ADG.h : Unknown CPU platform.
#endif


///////////////////////////// adgARRAY_SIZE Macro /////////////////////////////


// This macro evaluates to the number of elements in an array.
#define adgARRAY_SIZE(Array) (sizeof(Array) / sizeof((Array)[0]))


///////////////////////////// adgINRANGE Macro /////////////////////////////


// This macro evaluates to TRUE if val is betwen lo and hi inclusive.
#define adgINRANGE(lo, val, hi) (((lo) <= (val)) && ((val) <= (hi)))


///////////////////////////// Assert/Verify Macros /////////////////////////////


#define adgFAIL(szMSG) {                                                     \
     MessageBox(GetActiveWindow(), szMSG,                                    \
        __TEXT("Assertion Failed"), MB_OK | MB_ICONERROR);                   \
     DebugBreak();                                                           \
   }

// Put up an assertion failure message box
#define adgASSERTFAIL(file,line,expr) {                                      \
     TCHAR sz[128];                                                          \
     wsprintf(sz, __TEXT("File %hs, line %d : %hs"), file, line, expr);      \
     adgFAIL(sz);                                                            \
   }

// Put up a message box if an assertion fails in a debug build
#ifdef _DEBUG
#define adgASSERT(x) if (!(x)) adgASSERTFAIL(__FILE__, __LINE__, #x)
#else
#define adgASSERT(x)
#endif

// Assert in debug builds, but don't remove the code in retail builds
#ifdef _DEBUG
#define adgVERIFY(x) adgASSERT(x)
#else
#define adgVERIFY(x) (x)
#endif


///////////////////////////// adgHANDLE_DLGMSG Macro /////////////////////////////


// The normal HANDLE_MSG macro in WINDOWSX.H does not work properly for dialog
// boxes because DlgProc's return a BOOL instead of an LRESULT (like
```

595

```
// WndProcs). This adgHANDLE_DLGMSG macro corrects the problem.
#define adgHANDLE_DLGMSG(hwnd, message, fn)                           \
   case (message): return (SetDlgMsgResult(hwnd, uMsg,               \
      HANDLE_##message((hwnd), (wParam), (lParam), (fn))))


/////////////////////////// Window Extra Byte Macros ///////////////////////////


// Macros to compute the size and offset of structure members
#define adgMEMBEROFFSET(structure, member) (int) (&(((structure *)0)->member))

// Macros to compute offsets and get/set window values based on the layout of
// a structure
#define adgSETWINDOWWORD(hwnd, structure, member, value) \
   SetWindowWord(hwnd, adgMEMBEROFFSET(structure, member), (WORD) (value))
#define adgSETWINDOWLONG(hwnd, structure, member, value) \
   SetWindowLong(hwnd, adgMEMBEROFFSET(structure, member), (LONG) (value))
#define adgGETWINDOWWORD(hwnd, structure, member) \
   GetWindowWord(hwnd, adgMEMBEROFFSET(structure, member))
#define adgGETWINDOWLONG(hwnd, structure, member) \
   GetWindowLong(hwnd, adgMEMBEROFFSET(structure, member))


/////////////////////////// Quick MessageBox Macro ///////////////////////////


#define adgMB(s) {                                                    \
    TCHAR szTMP[128];                                                 \
    GetModuleFileName(NULL, szTMP, adgARRAY_SIZE(szTMP));             \
    MessageBox(GetActiveWindow(), s, szTMP, MB_OK);                   \
    }


/////////////////////////// Zero Variable Macro ///////////////////////////


// Zero out a structure. If fInitSize is TRUE then initialize the first int to
// the size of the structure. Many structures like WNDCLASSEX and STARTUPINFO
// require that their first member be set to the size of the structure itself.
#define adgINITSTRUCT(structure, fInitSize)                           \
   (ZeroMemory(&(structure), sizeof(structure)),                      \
   fInitSize ? (*(int*) &(structure) = sizeof(structure)) : 0)


/////////////////////////// Dialog Box Icon Setting Macro ///////////////////////////


// The call to SetClassLong is for Windows NT.
// Sending the WM_SETICON messages is for Windows 95.
#define adgSETDLGICONS(hwnd, idiLarge, idiSmall)                      \
   SetClassLong(hwnd, GCL_HICON, (LONG)                              \
      LoadIcon(GetWindowInstance(hwnd), MAKEINTRESOURCE(idiLarge))), \
   SendMessage(hwnd, WM_SETICON, TRUE, (LPARAM)                      \
      LoadIcon(GetWindowInstance(hwnd), MAKEINTRESOURCE(idiLarge))), \
```

```
    SendMessage(hwnd, WM_SETICON, FALSE, (LPARAM)                          \
        LoadIcon(GetWindowInstance(hwnd), MAKEINTRESOURCE(idiSmall)))


//////////////////////////// UNICODE Check Macro //////////////////////////////


#ifdef UNICODE

#define adgWARNIFUNICODEUNDERWIN95() {                                      \
    OSVERSIONINFOA VerInfo;                                                \
    adgINITSTRUCT(VerInfo, TRUE);                                          \
    GetVersionExA(&VerInfo);                                               \
    if ((VerInfo.dwPlatformId == VER_PLATFORM_WIN32_WINDOWS) &&            \
        (VerInfo.dwMajorVersion == 4) && (VerInfo.dwMinorVersion == 0))    \
        MessageBoxA(NULL, "Windows 95 doesn't support Unicode", NULL, MB_OK); \
    }

#else

#define adgWARNIFUNICODEUNDERWIN95()

#endif


////////////////// WM_CAPTURECHANGED Message Cracker Macros ///////////////////


// I have defined message cracker macros for the WM_CAPTURECHANGED message
// because Microsoft did not do this in the WINDOWSX.H header file.

/* void Cls_OnCaptureChanged(HWND hwnd, HWND hwndNewCapture) */
#define HANDLE_WM_CAPTURECHANGED(hwnd, wParam, lParam, fn) \
    ((fn)((hwnd), (HWND)(lParam)), 0L)
#define FORWARD_WM_CAPTURECHANGED(hwnd, hwndNewCapture, fn) \
    (void)(fn)((hwnd), WM_CAPTURECHANGED, (WPARAM)(HWND)(hwndNewCapture), 0L)


/////////////////////////////// End of File //////////////////////////////////
```

APPENDIX B

The MsgCrack Utility

Message cracker macros are very useful when writing Windows applications in C. Using them will make your code more readable and maintainable than using more ad-hoc methods such as the all-too-common "gigantic switch statement" method. Unfortunately, for messages that you define yourself, there are no preexisting message crackers. Anyone who has written message crackers by hand can tell you that it's a very time-consuming and error-prone process. The MsgCrack utility that comes with this book[1] makes it easy to create reliable message crackers.

MsgCrack takes two arguments: an input file (normally with the extension msg) and an output file (normally with the extension h). The statements in the input file define each message sufficiently that MsgCrack can create a message definition, a message API, and a pair of message cracker macros (one for HANDLE_?M_* and one for FORWARD_?M_*) for each message in the file.

---

[1]The **MsgCrack.bat** Perl script can be found in the **MsgCrack.0B** directory. You can experiment with the example MsgCrack input file (**MsgCrack.msg**) in the same directory. Other examples can be found in the application directories for various chapters in this book, including: **CustCntl.04**, **Arcade.05**, **Echo.06**, and **KeyCount.06**. For more information on Perl, please refer to the **ReadMe.txt** file in the **MsgCrack.0B** directory.

Although MsgCrack will create the output file if it doesn't exist, MsgCrack won't overwrite an already existing output file. Instead, it appends the following information:

```
///////////////////////////////// Messages /////////////////////////////////////

//{{adgMSGCRACK_MESSAGES

    <MsgCrack generated message definitions>

//}}adgMSGCRACK_MESSAGES


//////////////////////////////// Message APIs ////////////////////////////////////

//{{adgMSGCRACK_APIS

    <MsgCrack generated message APIs>

//}}adgMSGCRACK_APIS


/////////////////////////////// Message Crackers //////////////////////////////////

//{{adgMSGCRACK_CRACKERS

    <MsgCrack generated message crackers>

//}}adgMSGCRACK_CRACKERS
```

In subsequent invocations, MsgCrack will replace each of these tagged sections with new information, leaving the rest of your file intact. However, any changes you make between the section markers will be discarded.

A very simple MsgCrack input file might look like this:

```
MessageBase WM_USER
Message EM_SETBRUSH Example_SetBrush - Sets brush and returns old brush.
wParam HBRUSH hbrNew - New brush
Returns HBRUSH - Old brush
.
```

If you run this example through MsgCrack, you will get the following output:

```
///////////////////////////////// Messages /////////////////////////////////////


//{{adgMSGCRACK_MESSAGES
```

```
// Purpose: Sets brush and returns old brush.
// wParam:  HBRUSH hbrNew - New brush
// lParam:  N/A
// Returns: HBRUSH - Old brush
#define EM_SETBRUSH            (WM_USER + 0)


//}}adgMSGCRACK_MESSAGES


/////////////////////////////// Message APIs ////////////////////////////////


//{{adgMSGCRACK_APIS

#define Example_SetBrush(hwnd, hbrNew) \
   ((HBRUSH )SendMessage((hwnd), EM_SETBRUSH, (WPARAM)(DWORD)(hbrNew), 0))


//}}adgMSGCRACK_APIS


/////////////////////////////// Message Crackers ////////////////////////////////


//{{adgMSGCRACK_CRACKERS

// HBRUSH  Cls_OnExample_SetBrush (HWND hwnd, HBRUSH hbrNew)
#define HANDLE_EM_SETBRUSH(hwnd, wParam, lParam, fn) \
   (LRESULT)(fn)((hwnd), (HBRUSH)(wParam))
#define FORWARD_EM_SETBRUSH(hwnd, hbrNew, fn) \
   (HBRUSH )((fn)((hwnd), EM_SETBRUSH, (WPARAM)(DWORD)(hbrNew), 0))


//}}adgMSGCRACK_CRACKERS
```

Table B.1 contains a list of valid MsgCrack input file commands.

Table B.1 *Valid MsgCrack input file commands*

Statement	Arguments	Description
//	<Comment string>	Allows you to put comments in your input file.
MessageBase	<Identifier string>	Lets you define a base message from which to number each subsequent message. For example, WM_USER. You must have a MessageBase statement in your input file before you define any messages. Declaring a new MessageBase automatically resets the current MessageOffset to zero.

continued...

Statement	Arguments	Description
MessageOffset	<Ordinal offset value>	Defines an ordinal offset from Message-Base for numbering subsequent messages. You can define a new Message-Offset as frequently as you like in your input file.
Message	<MESSAGENAME> <Class_MessageName> - <Description>	Defines a message. MESSAGENAME should be something like UM_MYMES-SAGE. The Class_MessageName parameter is used to name the message API macro. The Description should describe what the message does; it is included in the message declaration.
wParam	<Type> <Name> - <Description>	Defines the meaning of the wParam parameter, for example, "UINT nBoxes - Number of boxes to lift."
lParam	<Type> <Name> - <Description>	Defines the meaning of the lParam parameter, for example, "HBRUSH hbrBack - New background brush."
Returns	<Type> - <Description>	Defines the type and meaning of the return value. Unlike the wParam and lParam statements, the Returns statement does not allow you to name the value (because it is not needed to generate any of the macros).
	None	This statement must terminate every message in the input file.

Each statement must be on a line by itself. Because comments are a statement, they too must be placed on a line by themselves. Lines that are too long can be continued on the next line by placing a backslash (\) character at the end of the line. The hyphens listed in the statements in Table B.1 are required. If your input file has an error in it, MsgCrack will exit, indicating the line in the input file where the error occurred.

INDEX

4-byte place holders, 39
4-byte value association with
    windows, 45, 106
16-bit values, 22, 25, 239

A

ABM_SETTIMER, 336
adgARRAY_SIZE macro, 587–588
adgASSERT macro, 588
adgGETWINDOWLONG macro, 243–244,
    590
adgHANDLE_DLGMSG macro, 116,
    588–589
adgINRANGE macro, 588
adgINSTRUCT macro, 590–591
adgLIBBUILDTYPE macro, 587
adgMB macro, 590
adgMEMBEROFFSET macro, 590
"adg" prefixes for macros, 585
adgSETDLGICONS macro, 591
adgSETWINDOWLONG macro, 239, 590
adgSETWINDOWWORD macro, 239

adgVERIFY macro, 588
adgWARNIFUNICODEUNDERWIN95
    macro, 591–592
adgWM_CAPTURECHANGED message
    cracker macros, 592
Advanced Windows, 308, 364, 407, 411
Alpha AXP machines, xx, xxii
Alpha.BIN directory, xxii
Alt+Tab key window switching
    hangups, 411
Alt key processing, 517, 518
animated button class, 329
ANSI, xxi, 168, 592
appearance style categories for windows, 42
applications
    avoiding potential DLL conflicts,
        551–553
    testing by simulating keystrokes,
        518–519
    See also drag-and-drop file handling; test-
        ing applications; Win32 applications
application-specific integer window
    messages, 48
applications presented in this book, xviii
    installing, xxii
    installing on unsupported CPU
        platforms, xxii, xxiii–xxiv
    source code on CD-ROM accompanying

this book, xxii
see also AppLog application
(AppLog.EXE); Arcade applica-
tion (Arcade.EXE); Capture appli-
cation (Capture.EXE); Clock
application (Clock.EXE);
CustCntl application
(CustCntl.EXE); DFSrc demo
application (DFSrcDm.EXE);
Dialog Expand application
(DlgXpnd.EXE); DlgSize applica-
tion (DlgSize.EXE); Dynamic
Dialog Box application
(DlgDyn.EXE); Echo application
(Echo.EXE); KeyCount applica-
tion (KeyCount.EXE); NoDigits
application (NoDigits.EXE);
SKDemo application
(SKDemo.EXE); Tabstop applica-
tion (TabStops.EXE); Touch
application (Touch.EXE);
VerShow application
(VerShow.EXE); Voyeur applica-
tion; Voyeur application
(Voyeur.EXE)
AppLog application (AppLog.EXE)
described, 421–422, 423–425
files, 422–423
listings,
AppLog.C, 425–427
AppLog.RC, 427–428
Resource.H, 429
ShellHk.C, 429–432
ShellHk.H, 432
Arcade application (Arcade.EXE)
AniBtn window class, 334–339
described, 329–330, 331–334
files, 330–331
listings,
AniBtn.C, 334, 346–350
AniBtn.H, 334, 350–352
AniBtn.MSG, 352–353
Arcade.C, 343–346
Arcade.RC, 359–360
Resource.H, 360–361
SuperCls.C, 334, 353–358
SuperCls.H, 334, 358
window superclassing library
(SuperCls.C file), 335, 339–343
arrays, macro for returning number of elements, 587–588
arrow keys for dialog box navigation, 110
associating additional data with subclassed windows, 314
atoms
accessing local tables, 20
adding class names, 19
creating, 49
obtaining, 19, 20
returning value of class, 21

B

bargraph controls
Bargraph.C listing, 284–295
Bargraph.H listing, 296–300
Bargraph.MSG listing, 295–296
choosing, 257–261
described, 225, 226, 247
designing, 247–251
implementing, 251–253
painting, 253–257
WM_GETDLGCODE, 261–266
See also custom controls
BeginDeferWindowPos function, 196
BeginPaint function, 241–242
BGM_GETBARS, 250
BGM_GETHEIGHT, 248
BGM_SETBARS, 250
BGM_SETHEIGHT, 248, 249
BGN_BARPAINT, 250–251
BM_SETCHECK, 47–48
BM_SETIMAGE, 338
"BM_" system global window class mes-
sage identifier prefix, 47
BS_AUTORADIOBUTTON, 262
BS_DEFPUSHBUTTON, 262
BS_GROUPBOX, 262
"BS_" system global window class style
prefix, 41, 228
BuildDynamicDlgBox function, 165–166

C

C++ language, xix, 2
message maps, 11
CAboutDlg::OnSize function, 13

CallNextHookEx function, 370–371, 401, 402, 407
Capture application (Capture.EXE)
   described, 453–454
   files, 454
   listings,
      Capture.C, 458–462
      Capture.RC, 462–463
      Resource.H, 464
   local input states, 454–457
   local input states and journal record hooks, 457–458
cbClsExtra member, 24
"CBS_" system global window class style prefix, 41
"CB_" system global window class message identifier prefix, 47
CBT (computer-based training), 395
CD-ROM accompanying this book
   Welcome application, xxiii
   Win32 port of Perl, xxi
   See also applications presented in this book
character set specification by users, 552, 558
child controls, 29
   parent notification, 228–232
child windows
   in dialog boxes, 93–94, 101–105, 120–123
   familiarity as prerequisite, xviii
   of Run dialog box, 95–96
Choose Profile dialog box, normal and expanded versions, 134
C language, xix, 2
class-defined integer window messages, 46–48
Class Wizard dialog box, 11–12
Clipboard, copying screen with Print Screen key simulation, 506
Clock application (Clock.EXE), 114
   described, 115–117
   files, 115
   listings,
      Clock.C, 117–118
      Clock.RC, 118–120
      Resource.H, 120
   WinMain function, 116–117
CloseHandle function, 35
colors, for legends, 235–236, 238, 242

ComCtl32.DLL, 27, 28
CommCtrl.H, 230, 231
comments, for custom control window messages, 228
communication style categories for windows, 42
compiling
   applications, xx–xxi
   dialog box template script, 97
controls. *See* custom controls
copyrights for applications presented in this book, xviii–xix
CPU portability macros, 587
CreateDialog function, 29, 101
CreateDialogIndirectParam function, 102–105, 108, 120–121, 162
CreateDialogParam function, 101–102
CreateWindowEx function, 28, 29, 30–33
   avoiding using, 114
   with custom controls, 227–228
C-Runtime code, 2–3
CS_GLOBALCLASS, 18, 28, 238
CS_HREDRAW, 238
CS_VREDRAW, 238
Ctrl key processing, 517
cursor. *See* mouse cursor
CustCntl application (CustCntl.EXE)
   described, 267
   files, 267–268
   implementing, 268–269
   listings,
      Bargraph.C, 284–295
      Bargraph.H, 296–300
      Bargraph.MSG, 295–296
      CustCntl.C, 269–275
      CustCntl.RC, 300–302
      Legend.C, 275–280
      Legend.H, 236, 281–284
      Legend.MSG, 281
      Resource.H, 302–303
custom controls
   caution on overdoing, 226–227
   CustCntl application (CustCntl.EXE), 267–303
   described, 225–226
   designing, 226–227
   header file contents, 227, 228
   implementing, 232–233
   parent notification, 228–229
   window messages, 228

window styles, 227–228
WM_COMMAND, 229
WM_NOTIFY, 229–232
See also bargraph controls; legends

D

data structure macro (for initialization and
    clearing to zero), 590
debugging
    hook use, 401–402
    with Spy++ application, 372
    See also testing applications
DEBUGHOOKINFO structure, 401–402
DEC Alpha AXP machines, xx, xxii
DefDlgProc, 105–108
#defined values, 227, 239
DefWindowProc, 7, 8, 54
DestroyWindow function, 53
DFSrc demo application (DFSrcDm.EXE)
    described, 482–483, 484–489
    files, 484
    listings,
        DFSrc.C, 494–499
        DFSrcDem.C, 490–494
        DFSrcDem.RC, 499–501
        DFSrc.H, 498–499
        Resource.H, 501
dialog box editor, 96
dialog boxes, 196–223
    acquiring and returning information,
        44–45
    adding navigation capability, 109–110
    creating child and parent, 93–94,
        101–105, 120–123
    designing appearance, 94–101
    dynamic technique, 162–187
    expanding/shrinking technique,
        133–146
    familiarity as prerequisite, xviii
    layout technique, 188–123
    as main window (Clock example),
        114–120
    modal, 111–114
    modalless technique, 146–162
    modeless, 109
    tab order, 120–123
    Tabstop application, 123–132
    window procedure for class, 105–109

as windows, 93–94
See also custom controls; Dialog
    Expand application
    (DlgXpnd.EXE); DlgSize applica-
    tion (DlgSize.EXE); Dynamic
    Dialog Box application
    (DlgDyn.EXE); modalless dialog
    box technique (DlgMdlls.EXE);
    Tabstop application
    (TabStops.EXE)
DialogBox function, 29, 111
    use in this book's applications, xix
DialogBoxIndirectParam function,
    113–114, 162
Dialog Box Manager, 94
DialogBoxParam function, 111–113
    and modalless dialog box technique,
    146
DIALOGEX dialog box template, 97
Dialog Expand application (DlgXpnd.EXE)
    described, 135
    designing dialog box, 136–137
    examples, 135
    ExpandBox function, 137–140
    files, 136
    listings,
        DlgXpnd.C, 140–141
        DlgXpnd.RC, 143–145
        ExpndBox.C, 142–143
        ExpndBox.H, 143
        Resource.H, 145–146
    message filter hooks, 382–383
directories
    drag-and-drop handling with Explorer,
        473–474
    on CD-ROM accompanying this book,
        xxii
DispatchMessage function, 50, 52, 511
DLGC_BUTTON, 262
DLGC_DEFPUSHBUTTON, 262
DLGC_HASSETSEL, 263
DLGC_RADIOBUTTON, 262
DLGC_STATIC, 263
DLGC_WANTALLKEYS, 265
DLGC_WANTARROWS, 264
DLGC_WANTCHARS, 266
DLGC_WANTMESSAGE, 264, 265
DLGC_WANTTAB, 264
DlgDyn.EXE. *See* Dynamic Dialog Box
    application (DlgDyn.EXE)

"Dlg" functions, 94
DLGITEMTEMPLATEEX structure, 97,
    99–101, 167–168, 169
DLGITEMTEMPLATE structure, 98
DlgMdlls.EXE. *See* modalless dialog box
    technique (DlgMdlls.EXE)
DlgSize application (DlgSize.EXE)
    described, 196, 198
    examples of resized dialog boxes,
      190–191
    files, 197
    listings,
      DlgSize.C, 199–201
      DlgSize.RC, 221–222
      Layout.C, 202–219
      Layout.H, 219–221
      Resource.H, 222–223
    other uses, 198–199
    See also layout dialog box technique
DLGTEMPLATEEX structure, 97, 98–99,
    167
DLGTEMPLATE structure, 98
DlgXpnd.EXE. *See* Dialog Expand applica-
    tion (DlgXpnd.EXE)
DllCreateAnExeWindow function, 26
DLL files, 2
    for applications on various platforms,
      xxii
    avoiding potential conflicts, 551–553
    registering window classes, 25–27
    for remote hooks, 364, 367
    with subclassed windows, 311–312
DM_REPOSITION, 139
"DM_" system global window class mes-
    sage identifier prefix, 47
DragAcceptFiles function, 468, 472
drag-and-drop file handling, 466
    DFSrc demo application
      (DFSrcDm.EXE), 482–501
    with Explorer, 466–467, 479
    modifying applications as dropfile
      sources, 479–482
    modifying applications as dropfile tar-
      gets, 467–471
    OLE as alternative, 465
    other uses for, 501–502
    Touch application (Touch.EXE),
      471–478
DragFinish function, 470, 471, 474
DragQueryFile function, 469, 473

DragQueryPoint function, 470
drivers for keyboards, 504, 505
DROPFILES structure, 479
DS_NOFAILCREATE, 104
DS_SETFONT, 166, 168
"DS_" system global window class style
    prefix, 41
DWL_MSGRESULT, 109
Dynamic Dialog Box application
    (DlgDyn.EXE)
    creating template, 166–168
    described, 114, 162–166
    examples, 163, 164
    files, 165
    listings,
      DlgDyn.C, 169–173, 382–383
      DlgDyn.RC, 186–187
      DlgTmplt.C, 177–183
      DlgTmplt.H, 183–185
      DynDlg.C, 173–176
      Resource.H, 187
    managing templates memory block,
      168–169
dynamic link libraries. *See* DLL files

E

Echo application (Echo.EXE)
    application code, 434–436
    described, 432–433, 434
    files, 433
    listings,
      Echo.C, 438–441
      Echo.H, 442–443
      Echo.MSG, 442
      Echo.RC, 451–452
      Record.C, 443–450
      Record.H, 450–451
      Resource.H, 453
    recorder code, 436–438
EM_GETLINE, 48
EM_SETSEL, 263
EM_SETTABSTOPS, 62
"EM_" system global window class mes-
    sage identifier prefix, 47
EndDeferWindowPos function, 196
EndDialog function, 113, 147
EndPaint function, 247
EnumPropsEx function, 44

EnumProps function, 44
error checking
    omitted for clarity, 102, 111
    recommendation for, xx
Escape key for dialog box dismissal, 109
"ES_" system global window class style
        prefix, 41
EVENTMSG structures, 386
event trapping with hooks. *See* hooks
EXE files, 2
    for applications on various platforms,
        xxii
    dialog box template structures, 101
    registering window classes, 25–27
    See also applications; applications pre-
        sented in this book
ExitProcess function, 3
ExitWindowsEx function, 55
ExpandBox function, 137–140
expanding/shrinking dialog box technique
    described, 133–134
    Dialog Expand application
        (DlgXpnd.EXE), 135–146
Explorer and drag-and-drop file handling,
        466–467, 479
extended window styles, 42
extensions (filename), .msg, 599
extra byte handling, 24, 43, 73, 239
    Window Extra Byte macros, 589–590
ExtTextOut function, 246

F

filename extensions. *See* extensions (file-
    name)
File Open dialog box, as modal, 111
files, drag-and-drop handling, 466
Find All Files dialog box, resizing dialog
        boxes, 189
focus
    getting for custom controls, 240, 261
    moving with tab key in dialog boxes,
        120–123
FONTINFOEX structure, 97, 99, 168
FONTINFO structure, 98
foreign language specification by users,
        552, 558
FORWARD_WM_CREATE macro., 337

G

GCL_CBCLSEXTRA, 22, 24, 73
GCL_CBWNDEXTRA, 22, 24, 73, 74
GCL_HBRBACKGROUND, 22, 24
GCL_HCURSOR, 22, 24
GCL_HICON, 22, 24
GCL_HICONSM, 22, 24
GCL_HINSTANCE, 22
GCL_HMODULE, 22, 24
GCL_MENUNAME, 22, 24
GCL_STYLE, 22, 24
GCL_WINDPROC, 22, 24
GCW_ATOM, 19, 22
GDI32.DLL, 551
GetAsyncKeyState function, 506–507,
        508–509
GetAtomName function, 20
GetClassByte function, 73
GetClassInfoEx function, 20–21, 73
GetClassLong function, 19, 21, 24, 73
GetClassName function, 35, 73
GetClassWord function, 19, 21, 24, 73
GetClipboardFormatName function, 20
GetCurrentThreadId function, 367
GetFileAttributes function, 474
GetFileVersionInfo function, 561–562, 583
GetFileVersionInfoSize function, 561, 583
GetFirstChild macro, 195
GetKeyboardState function, 509–510
GETKEYCOUNT macro, 405
GetKeyState function, 507–508, 509
GetMessageExtraInfo function, 505
GetMessage function, 50, 51, 52, 112, 372,
        377, 505, 507
GetMessagePos function, 67–68
GetModuleHandle function, 26
GetNextDlgItem function, 122–123
GetNextSibling macro, 195
GetOpenFileName function, 582
GetProp function, 44, 309–311
GetSystemMetrics function, 509
GetTextExtentPoint32 function, 245–246
GETTHISDATA macro, 252–253
GetWindowDC function, 72
GetWindowFont macro, 245
GetWindowLong, 35–36, 37, 39
GetWindowText function, 410
GetWindowTextLength function, 245
GetWindowThreadProcessId function, 34,

367–368
GetWindowWord, 35–36
GlobalAlloc function, 468
GlobalGetAtomName function, 20
GWL_EXSTYLE, 36
GWL_HINSTANCE, 36
GWL_HWNDPARENT, 36
GWL_ID, 36
GWL_STYLE, 36
GWL_USERDATA, 36, 39, 66, 138, 139,
    146, 147
  control classes, 233
  with subclassed windows, 309, 314
GWL_WNDPROC, 36

H

HANDLE_MSG macro, 11, 116, 588–589
handles of windows, 5–6
  role in changing class attributes, 22
  role in changing window attributes, 36
HC_ACTION, 372, 374–375, 377, 400, 401
HCBT_ACTIVATE, 396
HCBT_CLICKSKIPPED, 396
HCBT_CREATEWND, 396, 397, 398
HCBT_ hook codes, 396
HCBT_KEYSKIPPED, 396
HC_GETNEXT, 388, 389
HC_NOREMOVE, 377
HC_SKIP, 388
HC_SYSMODALOFF, 387, 388, 437
HC_SYSMODALON, 387, 388, 437
HeapAlloc function, 468
"h" files, 599
HINSTANCE, 22, 26, 27, 28
HMODULE, 22
hooks
  advantages for event trapping, 363
  AppLog application (AppLog.EXE),
    421–432
  Capture application (Capture.EXE),
    453–464
  disadvantages, 363–364
  Echo application (Echo.EXE), 432–453
  and hook chains, 370–371
  installing, 365–369
  KeyCount application (KeyCount.EXE),
    402–421
  for simulating keystrokes, 522

types, 365–367
uninstalling, 369
HSSHELL_ACTIVATESHELLWINDOW,
  393
HSSHELL_GETMINRECT, 393
"HSSHELL_" hook codes, 392
HSSHELL_LANGUAGE, 394
HSSHELL_TASKMAN, 394
HSSHELL_WINDOWACTIVATED, 393
HSSHELL_WINDOWCREATED, 392, 393
HSSHELL_WINDOWDESTROYED,
  392, 393

I

icons
  and intuitive file handling, 466–467
  macro for setting, 591
imagelist controls, 329
Info.c file, 46–47
Info.H header file, 46
InitCommonControls function, 27
initialization
  of data structures, 590
  of Win32 applications, 3
INSTALL.BAT file, xxiii–xxiv
installing applications presented in this
    book, xxii, xxiii
integer window messages
  application-specific, 48
  class-defined, 46–48
IsDialogMessage function, 110, 122

J

journal record hooks, 365, 384–387, 391,
    432–433
  See also playback hooks

K

Kernel32.DLL, 551
keybd_event function, 505, 506, 521–522
keyboard
  complexity of, 503–504
  drivers, 504, 505

support for dialog box navigation,
109–110
KeyCount application (KeyCount.EXE)
described, 402–403, 404–411
files, 403
link to KybdHk.dll, 587
listings,
KeyCount.C, 412–414
KeyCount.H, 415–416
KeyCount.MSG, 414–415
KeyCount.RC, 416–417
KybdHk.C, 418–421
KybdHk.H, 421
Resource.H, 417–418
"KEYEVENTF_" flags, 505
keystroke messages, 511–516
keystroke processing
application for counting strokes, 402
key state arrays, 506–511
phrase library application, 519–522
scan codes, 503–504
SendKeys function, 541–549
simulating to other application windows, 518–522
SKDemo application (SKDemo.EXE),
522–541
system keys, 516–518
testing applications, 518–519
thesaurus application, 518
virtual-key codes, 504–505
KF_ALTDOWN, 512
KF_DLGMODE, 512, 513
KF_EXTENDED, 512
KF_MENUMODE, 512, 513
KF_REPEAT, 512
KF_UP, 512

L

language file specification by users, 552,
558
languages for programming, xix
layout dialog box technique
advantages, 188–189
described, 190, 192–194
DlgSize application (DlgSize.EXE),
196–223
examples of resized dialog boxes,
190–191

implementation, 194–196
LB_DELETESTRING, 228
LB_ERR, 228
lBOTTOM macro, 192
"LBS_" system global window class style
prefix, 41, 228
"LB_" system global window class message identifier prefix, 47
lCHILD macro, 193
legends
creating, 236–240
described, 225, 226
designing, 233–236
Legend.C listing, 275–280
Legend.H listing, 236, 281–284
Legend.MSG listing, 281
painting, 241–247
special messages for custom controls,
240–241
See also custom controls
lGROUP macro, 193
lHCENTER macro, 194
lHEIGHT macro, 192
lHEIGHTOF macro, 192
LIB files, 2
lLEFT macro, 192
LM_GETBOXBRUSH, 235
lMOVE macro, 194
LoadLibrary function, 27
LocalAlloc function, 468
local hooks, 363
local input states, 454–457
and journal record hooks, 457–458
lParam, 7, 8, 10
lpszClassName member, 16, 20, 35
lpszMenuName member, 21
lRIGHT macro, 192
LS_BIGBOX, 234, 243
LS_BOXBORDER, 234, 243
lSTRETCH macro, 193
lTOP macro, 192
lVCENTER macro, 194
lWIDTH macro, 192
lWIDTHOF macro, 192

M

macros
dialog box message handling, 106–107

GetWindowFont, 245
for handling window and class extra
    bytes, 24
message box, 590
message crackers, xix, 9, 592
window subclassing, 308
window superclassing, 337
See also Win95ADG.H header file
MAKELANGID macro, 558
MapDialogRect function, 195–196
MapVirtualKey function, 511, 516
maximizing dialog boxes. *See* Dialog
    Expand application
    (DlgXpnd.EXE)
MB_SYSTEMMODAL, 387
"MDIS_" system global window class
    style prefix, 41
message box macro, 590
message crackers
    macros, xix, 9, 592
    MsgCrack.BAT utility, xxi, 599–602
    for processing window messages, 8
message loops, 50–52
message maps, 11–13
messages
    mouse, 455
    window. *See* window messages
MFC Class Wizard dialog box, 11–12
MFCDLL.RC, 555
MFC (Microsoft Foundation Class)
    Library, 11
MIPS.BIN directory, xxii
MIPS machines, xx, xxii
modal dialog boxes, 111–114
modalless dialog box technique
    (DlgMdlls.EXE)
    described, 146–148, 149–153
    examples, 148, 149
    files, 149
    listings,
        DlgMdlls.C, 153–155
        DlgMdlls.RC, 160–161
        MdllsDlg.C, 155–157
        Modalles.C, 157–159
        Modalles.H, 159–160
        Resource.H, 161–162
modeless dialog boxes, 109
module local window classes, 25–27
mouse capture and journal record hooks,
    453–454

mouse cursor
    changing shape example, 23–24
    changing shape for file dropping, 467,
        468
mouse_event function, 506
MsgCrack.BAT file, xxi, 599–602
.msg extensions, 599
"MSGF_" hook codes, 380
MSGF_MAINLOOP, 380
MSGF_NEXTWINDOW, 380
MSGF_USER, 381
MSVCRT20.DLL, 551

N

navigation capability for dialog boxes,
    109–110
NM_FIRST, 230
NMHDR structures, 230
NM_LAST, 230
NoDigits application (NoDigits.EXE)
    described, 314, 315–317
    files, 315
    listing,
        NoDigCls.C, 319–320
        NoDigits.C, 317–319
        NoDigits.RC, 321–322
        Resource.H, 322–323

O

OLECli32, DLL, 551
OLE (Object Linking and Embedding), 465
OLESvr32, DLL, 551
OnSize function, 12
OpenProcess function, 34
orientation style categories for windows,
    43
OSVERSIONINFO structure, 592

P

page swapping, 2
parent dialog boxes, 101–105
parent notification, 228–232
PeekMessage function, 372, 377, 505, 507

performance considerations
    for subclassed windows, 311
    for system-wide remote hooks,
        363–364
Perl (Practical Extraction and Report
        Language) script, xxi–xxii
    MsgCrack.bat, 599
phrase libraries and keystroke simulation,
    519–522
platforms for application testing, xx
playback hooks, 365, 387–390, 432–433,
    522
    See also journal record hooks
PostMessage function, 51, 482, 520–521
PostQuitMessage function, 53, 54
PostThreadMessage function, 48
primary threads, 2
Print Screen key simulation, 506
processes
    described, 3–4
    IDs for, 4
    termination, 50
process global window classes, 27–28
process IDs, 4
programming seminars, xxiii
properties of windows, 43–45
PtInRect function, 258

R

RC files, dialog box template, 96–97
RegisterClassEx function
    calling legends, 236
    described, 16–19
    not called in this book's applications,
        xix
    and subclassing windows, 305–306
    and suPERclassing windows, 339–342
RegisterWindowMessage function, 20, 49,
    313
remote hooks, thread-specific and
    system-wide, 363
RemoveProp function, 43
resource control. *See* DLL files; version
    control
Richter, Jeffrey, e-mail address, xx
RIT (Raw Input Thread), 506–507
Run dialog box, 94–96

S

"Save changes to document?" message, 56
"SBM_" system global window class mes-
    sage identifier prefix, 47
"SBS_" system global window class style
    prefix, 41
scan codes for keyboards, 503–504
sections of memory for window messages,
    45–46
seminars on Win32 programming, xxiii
SendDlgItemMessage function, 100–101
SendKeys function, 541–549
SendMessageCallback function, 51
SendMessage function, 51, 372, 520–521
SendMessageTimeout function, 51
SendNotifyMessage function, 51
SetBrushOrgEx function, 244
SetCapture function, 455
SetClassLong function, 21, 23, 24
SetClassWord function, 21, 23, 24
SetFileTime function, 473
SetKeyboardState function, 510–511
SETKEYCOUNT macro, 405
SetProp function, 43
SetWindowContextHelpId function, 104
SetWindowLong, 35–36, 37, 38, 39, 106
SetWindowpOS function, 64–66
SetWindowsHookEx function, 364, 365,
    369, 370, 406
SetWindowWord, 35–36, 38
Shell32.DLL, 551
ShlObj.h header file, 479
shutdown of system for Win32 applica-
    tions, 55–59
SKDemo application (SKDemo.EXE)
    described, 522–524
    files, 525
    listings,
        Resource.H, 541
        SendKeys.C, 529–538
        SendKeys.H, 538–539
        SKDemo.C, 525–529
        SKDemo.RC, 539–540
SM_SWAPBUTTON, 509
source code, on CD-ROM accompanying
    this book, xxii
Spy++ application, 372, 455–457
"SS_" system global window class style
    prefix, 41

"STM_" system global window class message identifier prefix, 47
STRICT identifier, xx
STRICT type checking, 586–587
structures, macro for initialization and clearing to zero, 590
STYLELIST structures, 75
styles for windows, 39–43
    for custom controls, 227–228
subclassed windows. *See* window subclassing
SubClassWindow macro, 308
superclassed windows. *See* window superclassing
swapping of pages, 2
switch statements, 9, 11
SWMRG (Single-Writer Multiple-Reader Guard), 407, 411
system-global string window messages, 49
system keys, 516–518
system shutdown for Win32 applications, 55–59
system-wide remote hooks, 363–364

T

Tab key for dialog box navigation, 109
tab order for dialog boxes, 120–123
Tabstop application (TabStops.EXE), 123
    adding tab stops, 124–127
    described, 123–124
    files, 124
    listing, 127–132
TB_ENABLEBUTTON, 48
templates for dialog boxes, 96–97
TerminateProcess function, 34–35, 57
testing applications
    by simulating keystrokes, 518–519
    with macros for value insertion, 588
Tetris game selection program. *See* Arcade application (Arcade.EXE)
thesaurus application for simulating keystrokes, 518
THISDATA structure, 251–252
threads
    described, 2
    identification, 33–35
    identifying for hooks, 367
    local input states, 454–457

message queues, 51–54
RIT (Raw Input Thread), 506–507
sleeping and waking, 51
synchronization, 411
termination, 3, 50, 54
See also hooks
thread-specific remote hooks, 363
ToAscii function, 410, 514–515
Touch application (Touch.EXE)
    described, 471, 472–474
    files, 471–472
    listings,
        Resource.H, 478
        Touch.C, 474–476
        Touch.RC, 477–478
ToUnicode function, 410, 514
TranslateMessage function, 513–515, 520
trapping events with hooks, 363

U

UM_DROPTEXT, 502
UnhookWindowsHookEx function, 364, 369
Unicode, xxi, 99, 168
    macro defined in Win95ADG.h header file, 587
UnregisterClass function, 29–30, 236
User32.DLL, 105, 551

V

values, macro for range testing, 588
variables, static/global, cautions on use, 227, 309
VerLanguageName function, 565
VerQueryValue function, 562–565
VerShow application (VerShow.EXE)
    described, 566–569, 582–584
    files, 569–570
    listings,
        Resource.H, 581
        VerShow.C, 570–577
        VerShow.RC, 577–581
version control
    advantages of version resource for, 552–553

language Id macro (MAKELANGID), 558

problem of DLL conflicts, 551–552

using version resources (VERSION-INFO resource), 559–566

VerShow application (VerShow.EXE), 566–584

version resource sample, 553–561

version definition (WINVER macro), 586

VERSIONINFO resource, 552–566

videos on CD-ROM accompanying this book, xxiii

virtual-key codes for keyboards, 504

Visual C++ language, xx

    avoiding potential DLL conflicts, 551–553

    drag-and-drop file handling, 467

    Spy++ application, 372, 455–457

    See also Win32 applications

VK_CAPITAL, 511

VkKeyScan function, 515–516

VK_LBUTTON, 505, 509

VK_LEFT, 264, 266

VK_MENU, 504

VK_NEXT, 504

VK_NUMLOCK, 511

VK_PRIOR, 504

VK_RBUTTON, 505

VK_RETURN, 266

VK_RIGHT, 264, 266

VK_SCROLL, 511

VK_SPACE, 266

Voyeur application (Voyeur.EXE)

    files, 61–62

    initialization, 62

    listings,

        Resource.H, 62, 91

        Voyeur.C, 59, 61, 76–83

        Voyeur.RC, 61, 90–91

        VoyHelp.C, 61, 83–90

    operations, 59–61

    overview of concepts, 59

    releasing mouse capture, 69–70

    starting window, 59–56

    window class setting, 73–75

    window frame drawing, 70–73

    window selection, 67–68

    window style settings, 75–76

    window viewing process, 62–66

W

warning level 4, 585–586

Welcome application, xxiii

WH_CALLWNDPROC, 365, 372–375

WH_CALLWNDPROCRET, 365, 372–375

WH_CBT, 366, 395–399

WH_DEBUG, 367, 401–402

WH_FOREGROUNDIDLE, 367, 400

WH_GETMESSAGE, 365, 372–375

WH_HARDWARE, 366, 376–379

WH_JOURNALPLAYBACK, 366, 368, 384–391, 395

WH_JOURNALRECORD, 366, 368, 384–391, 437

WH_KEYBOARD, 366, 368–369, 376–379

WH_MOUSE, 366, 376–379

WH_MSGFILTER, 366, 368, 380–383

WH_SHELL, 366, 392–394

WH_SYSMSGFILTER, 366, 368, 380–383

Win32 applications

    "Alloc" functions, 468

    keyboard device independence, 504

    language for, xix

    local input states, 454, 455

    Perl script, xxi–xxii

    process overview and skeletal example, 2–4, 49–54

    role of windows, 1, 4–5

    system shutdown, 55–59

    See also dialog boxes; Visual C++ language; window classes

Win95ADG.H header file, xxii, 585

    adgARRAY_SIZE macro, 587–588

    adgASSERT macro, 588

    adgGETWINDOWLONG macro, 243–244, 590

    adgHANDLE_DLGMSG macro, 116, 588–589

    adgINRANGE macro, 588

    adgINSTRUCT macro, 590–591

    adgMB macro, 590

    adgMEMBEROFFSET macro, 590

    adgSETDLGICONS macro, 591

    adgSETWINDOWLONG macro, 239, 590

    adgSETWINDOWWORD macro, 239

    adgVERIFY macro, 588

    adgWARNIFUNICODEUNDERWIN95 macro, 591–592

adgWM_CAPTURECHANGED mes-
  sage cracker macros, 592
CPU portability macros, 587
listing, 593–597
STRICT type checking, 586–587
Unicode, 587
use of warning level 4, 585–586
version definition (WINVER macro),
  586
Window Extra Byte macros, 589–590
window classes
  attributes, 20–24
  familiarity as prerequisite, xviii
  module local, 25–27
  naming with lpszClassName, 16
  process global, 27–28
  registering, 4–5, 16–19
  registration preparation, 13–16
  system global, 28–29
  unregistering, 29–30
  See also window procedures; window
    subclassing; window superclass-
    ing
Window Extra Byte macros, 589–590
window messages
  application-specific integer, 48
  class-defined integer, 46–48
  for custom controls, 228
  filter hooks for, 380
  identifiers and descriptions of standard,
    6, 22
  message crackers, xix, 8, 9, 592
  message maps, 11–13
  sections, 45–46
  for subclassed windows, 312–313
  system-global string, 49
  for system shutdown, 55–59
  window handling with, 6–7, 49–54
window procedures
  description and prototype, 5–8
  dialog box class, 105–109
  familiarity as prerequisite, xviii
  maintaining, 9–13
  prototype, 5
  RegisterClassEx function, 16–19
  responses to window messages, 8
  in subclassed windows, 306–307
  and window messages, 6–7
  See also hooks; window classes
Windows 95

application development prerequisites,
  xviii
non-support of Unicode, 591–592
windows
  aborting creation upon failure of initial-
    ization, 32–33
  attribute modification, 35–39
  creating instances, 30–35
  destruction and termination proce-
    dures, 55–59
  handles, 5–6
  process termination, 33–35
  properties, 43–45
  styles, 39–43
  thread identification, 33–35
  tracking age, 38–39
  understanding difference from applica-
    tions, 1, 4–5
  See also child windows; custom con-
    trols; dialog boxes; hooks;
    Voyeur application
Windows' Dialog Box Manager, 94
Windows.H
  class attribute identifiers, 22
  window attribute identifiers, 36
Windows NT, xxii
window subclassing
  associating additional data, 314
  compared to window superclassing,
    327–329
  creating, 306–311
  described, 305–306
  NoDigits application (NoDigits.EXE),
    314–323
  window messages for, 312–313
window superclassing
  adding class and extra bytes, 325–327
  adding new menus, 327
  Arcade application (Arcade.EXE),
    329–361
  compared to window subclassing,
    327–329
  creating, 323–325
  described, 305, 323
  library for, 339–343
WindowsX.H header file, xix, 9
  GetWindowFont macro, 245
  macro for dialog box message handling,
    106–107
  macro for window subclassing, 308

macros for window superclassing, 337
WinMain function, 3
WinUser.H header file, 6
    CreateDialog function, 101
    DialogBox function, 111
    dialog box template structures, 98
    keyboard message flags, 512, 513
    legend messages, 235
    MSGF_USER, 381
    MSG structures, 375
    NMHDR structures, 230
    virtual-key codes for keyboards, 504
    window class extended styles, 42–43
    WM_APP, 313
WinVer.H, 555, 563
WINVER macro, 586
WM_APP, 313
WM_CANCELJOURNAL, 386, 435–436
WM_CAPTURECHANGED, 69, 70, 260
WM_CHAR, 6, 8, 264, 265, 514, 519
WM_CLOSE, 6, 52, 57
WM_COMMAND, 228–229
WM_CREATE, 32, 108
WM_CTLCOLOR, 235–236
WM_CTLCOLOREDIT, 106
WM_DESTROY, 33, 53, 57
WM_DROPFILES, 468, 472–473, 482, 502
WM_ENABLE, 241
WM_ENDSESSION, 56–58
WM_ERASEBKGRND, 240
WM_GETDLGCODE, 240, 261–266
WM_GETFONT, 240, 241
WM_GETICON, 22
WM_GETMINMAXINFO, 31, 198
WM_GETTEXT, 74, 410–411
WM_KEYDOWN, 264, 265, 517, 519
WM_KEYUP, 264, 265, 517
WM_KILLFOCUS, 240, 261
WM_LBUTTONDOWN, 6, 257, 502, 509
WM_LBUTTONUP, 257, 258, 502
WM_MOUSEMOVE, 6, 8, 67, 259, 454,
        458, 502
WM_MOVE, 32
WM_NCCALCSIZE, 32
WM_NCCREATE, 31, 108
WM_NCDESTROY, 53, 57
WM_NCPAINT, 7
WM_NOTIFY, 228, 229–232, 251
WM_ONCAPTURECHANGED, 69
WM_PAINT, 6, 8, 240, 241

WM_PARENTNOTIFY, 62–63
WM_QUERYENDSESSION, 55–56
WM_QUEUESYNC, 395, 398–399
WM_QUIT, 52
WM_RBUTTONUP, 69
WM_SETCURSOR, 70
WM_SETFOCUS, 240, 261
WM_SETFONT, 104, 105, 240–241
WM_SETICON, 22
WM_SETTEXT, 109
WM_SHOWWINDOW, 152–153
WM_SIZE, 32, 62
    message cracker function for, 9–11
    message map function for, 11–13
WM_STYLECHANGED, 38
WM_STYLECHANGING, 37, 38
WM_(SYS)CHAR, 515
WM_SYSCOMMAND, 7
WM_(SYS)DEADCHAR, 515
WM_(SYS)KEYDOWN, 511–512, 514, 517,
        519
WM_(SYS)KEYUP, 511–512, 514, 517
WM_TIMER, 336
WM_USER+n, 228
WM_USER, 235
WNDCLASSEX structures
    data members, 14–16
    example, 13–14
    filling with previously registered
        classes, 20
    initializing for extra bytes, 589
    not initialized in this book's applica-
        tions, xix
    storing information on, 18, 19
    and subclassed windows, 305–306
    and superclassed windows, 325–327,
        336, 341
WNDEXTRABYTES structures, 239
WordPad
    dropfile processing, 470–471
    failure to update settings, 57–58
WordPad dialog box and saving unsaved
        data message, 56
wParam, 7, 8, 10
WS_BORDER, 40, 76, 228
WS_CAPTION, 40, 76
WS_CHILD, 40
WS_CLIPCHILDREN, 40
WS_CLIPSIBLINGS, 40
WS_DISABLED, 40

WS_DLGFRAME, 40, 76
WS_EX_ACCEPTFILES, 42, 467
WS_EX_APPWINDOW, 42
WS_EX_CLIENTEDGE, 42
WS_EX_CONTEXTHELP, 42
WS_EX_CONTROLPARENT, 42, 103,
         122, 126
WS_EX_DLGMODALFRAME, 42
WS_EX_LEFT, 43
WS_EX_LEFTSCROLLBAR, 43
WS_EX_LTRREADING, 43
WS_EX_MDICHILD, 42
WS_EX_NOPARENTNOTIFY, 42, 104
WS_EX_RIGHT, 43
WS_EX_RIGHTSCROLLBAR, 43
WS_EX_RTLREADING, 43
WS_EX_STATICEDGE, 42
WS_EX_TOOLWINDOW, 42
WS_EX_TOPMOST, 42, 64
WS_EX_TRANSPARENT, 42
WS_EX_WINDOWEDGE, 42
WS_GROUP, 40, 41
WS_HSCROLL, 40
WS_MAXIMIZE, 40
WS_MAXIMIZEBOX, 40, 41, 76
WS_MINIMIZE, 40
WS_MINIMIZEBOX, 40, 41, 76
WS_OVERLAPPED, 40, 55
WS_POPUP, 40, 228
WS_SYSMENU, 40
WS_TABSTOP, 40, 41, 122, 123
WS_THICKFRAME, 40, 189
WS_VISIBLE, 40, 228
WS_VSCROLL, 40

X

x86.BIN directory, xxii

ABOUT THE AUTHORS

Jeffrey Richter

Jeffrey Richter was born in Philadelphia, PA and graduated in 1987 from Drexel University with a bachelor's degree in computer science. Jeff has been writing books about Windows programming since 1990. He is also a contributing editor to Microsoft Systems Journal, has written several articles and currently authors the Win32 Q & A column.

Jeff regularly speaks at industry conferences including Software Development, WINDEV and COMDEX. Jeff spends most of his time giving on-site Windows NT and Windows 95 training seminars to many companies including AT&T, DEC, Intel, Microsoft, and Pitney Bowes. He can be reached on the Internet at v-jeffrr@microsoft.com.

Jeff lives in Bellevue, WA where he is a frequent consultant to Microsoft. His code appears in Visual C++, Office 95, and other applications produced by the Personal Operating Systems group. While watching The Simpsons, he likes to eat teriyaki chicken bowls from CostCo and top it off with Ben and Jerry's ice cream. He has a passion for classic rock and jazz fusion bands.

Jonathan Locke

Jonathan Locke was born in Stamford, CT and graduated in 1988 from The Evergreen State College with a B.S. in computer science. Jonathan has a wide range of computer-related interests, including alternative programming languages, parsers and compilers, operating systems and computer graphics. A commercial Windows software developer since 1989, Jonathan has been instrumental in the creation of numerous shipping Windows applications, and is a founding member of Sealevel Software, a consulting company based in Bellevue, WA. He can be reached on the Internet at JonL@SealevelSoftware.com.

Jonathan presently lives in the Ballard district of Seattle but all too frequently finds himself commuting to Redmond! When on the west side of Lake Washington, he can be found running, lifting weights, playing bass guitar and hanging out at The Still Life coffee house in 0Fremont. Like Jeff, Jonathan is also a major fan of The Simpsons— they seem to remind him of Evergreen.